JUDAICA
TEXTS & TRANSLATIONS

*

FIRST SERIES

NUMBER THREE

The Book of Tradition

Sefer ha-Qabbalah

The Book of Tradition

Sefer ha-Qabbalah

Abraham ibn Daud

Translated from Hebrew by

Gerson D. Cohen

The Jewish Publication Society
Philadelphia

JPS is a nonprofit educational association and the oldest and foremost publisher of Judaica in English in North America. The mission of JPS is to enhance Jewish culture by promoting the dissemination of religious and secular works, in the United States and abroad, to all individuals and institutions interested in past and contemporary Jewish life.

Copyright © 1967 by The Jewish Publication Society

First JPS paperback edition 2010

All rights reserved.

No part of this book may be reproduced or transmitted in any form or by any means, electronic or mechanical, including photocopy, recording, or any information storage or retrieval system, except for brief passages in connection with a critical review, without permission in writing from the publisher:

The Jewish Publication Society
2100 Arch Street, 2nd floor
Philadelphia, PA 19103
www.jewishpub.org

Manufactured in the United States of America

ISBN: 978-0-8276-0916-7

JPS books are available at discounts for bulk purchases for reading groups, special sales, and fundraising purchases. Custom editions, including personalized covers, can be created in larger quantities for special needs. For more information, please contact us at marketing@jewishpub.org or at this address: 2100 Arch Street, Philadelphia, PA 19103.

PREFACE

In 1952, the late Professor Alexander Marx, a teacher with whom I had come to enjoy a close personal and professional relationship, urged me to prepare a new critical edition of Abraham ibn Daud's *Sefer ha-Qabbalah*. In the course of my work on the book, I soon became convinced that this little treatise was an excellent introduction to major aspects of the social and cultural climate of Jewish and Gentile Spain during the "golden age" of medieval Hebrew literature. As the product of one who was very much involved in the religious and intellectual activities of his day, the book also reflected the tensions and alliances within the Jewish community of Spain, thus affording the modern reader a firsthand glimpse into some of the realities of society in medieval Granada, Lucena, Seville, Cordova and Toledo. Its author was keenly conscious that the curtain had been rung down on a glorious epoch in Jewish history, and he tried desperately to immortalize it in accordance with his tastes and considered opinions.

To attempt to recapture and to convey the overtones and undertones of a style of life and expression from which the modern student is separated by some eight centuries, it was necessary not only to translate the text but to explain it in detail. In the Brief Notes I have given those comments and references which I felt would be helpful to the understanding of the text as well as the classical sources of Ibn Daud's data. More technical and extended discussions, which, while illuminating the text, were not vital for a first reading, have been relegated to the Supplementary Notes following the translation. Since any discussion of the problems connected with *Sefer ha-Qabbalah* presupposes a thorough study of the book, I have placed the Analysis and Interpretation after the translation rather than in the Introduction.

For technical reasons the Hebrew text with its critical apparatus has been printed as a separate section. In the margins of the translation the beginning of each Hebrew page is indicated by a bracketed number. Since my commentary is focused on the translation, references to *Sefer ha-Qabbalah* are to the chapter and line of the translation; thus Prologue. 7 and IV.112 refer to the translation of the Prologue, line 7, and Chapter IV of the translation, line 112 respectively. References to the Hebrew text when they are made in the notes are to the page and line number.

In seeking to make this work readable, I have wherever possible avoided the use of diacritical marks that seem to me to obfuscate far more than they illuminate. In the transliteration of names I have usually rendered biblical names as they are generally spelled in English. Rabbinic names have generally been rendered as in the *Jewish Encyclopedia* or in the English translation of H. L. Strack's *Introduction to the Literature of the Talmud and Midrash*. In the case of modern authors and titles, I have tried to adhere to title pages even *ad absurdum*. Scholars writing in Hebrew occasionally transliterate their names in different forms. Where they have not transliterated their names I have adopted the simplest form of transliteration possible. Citations from the Bible have always been made according to the Jewish Publication Society translations of *The Torah* and *The Holy Scriptures*, except where I felt that Ibn Daud's use of the citation required a different translation.

G. D. C.

CONTENTS

PREFACE — VII
INTRODUCTION

    I. INTRODUCTION TO A CLASSIC — XIII
   II. ABRAHAM IBN DAUD'S UNIVERSE OF DISCOURSE — XVI
      The Andalusian Foundation, XVI. To Toledo, XXVI.
      The Defense of the Faith, XXVIII.
  III. *Sefer ha-Qabbalah* AND ITS HISTORICAL BACKGROUND — XLIII
      The Karaite Challenge, XLIII. Karaism in Spain, XLVI.
      Earlier Histories of Tradition, L. *Qabbalah*-Tradition, LVI.
      The Argument of *Sefer ha-Qabbalah*, LVII.

SEFER HA-QABBALAH

      [PROLOGUE] — 3
  [I.] [THE BIBLICAL PERIOD] — 5
  [II.] [THE SUCCESSION OF TEACHERS IN THE DAYS OF THE SECOND TEMPLE] — 16
 [III.] [THE SUCCESSION OF TANNAIM] — 26
 [IV.] THE SUCCESSION OF AMORAIM — 32
  [V.] THE SUCCESSION OF THE SABORAIM — 43
 [VI.] THE SUCCESSION OF GEONIM — 46
[VII.] [THE SUCCESSION OF THE RABBINATE] — 63
      [EPILOGUE] — 91

SUPPLEMENTARY NOTES — 106
ANALYSIS AND INTERPRETATION

    I. THE STRUCTURE OF *Sefer ha-Qabbalah* — 149
   II. IBN DAUD'S SOURCES — 159
      Torah and "Greek Wisdom," 159. The Problem, 163. A. Biblical Chronology, 165. B. The Period of the Second Temple, 169. C. The Talmudic Period (Tannaim and Amoraim), 172. D. Ibn Daud's Principal Source for the Talmudic and Gaonic Ages, 177.
  III. THE SYMMETRY OF HISTORY — 189
      The Meaning of Symmetry, 212.

CONTENTS

IV. THE FOUR EMPIRES AND JEWISH HISTORY 223
   A. The Chronology of the Gentile Nations, 223. B. The Prices of Miscalculation and Indiscretion, 240. C. Edom Rediscovered, 250.

V. THE TYPOLOGY OF THE RABBINATE 263
   A. The Noble Types of Andalus, 263. B. The Noblest of the Noble: the Courtier-Rabbi, 269. C. The Sources of Inspiration of Ibn Daud's Typology, 276. D. Ignoble Villains, 289. E. The Unnamed Addressees of *Sefer ha-Qabbalah*, 293. F. The Reasons for the Esoteric Form, 302.

APPENDIX: The Language of *Sefer ha-Qabbalah* 305
GLOSSARY OF BASIC TERMS USED BY IBN DAUD 310
TABLE OF BASIC CHRONOLOGY 311
ABBREVIATIONS 312
BIBLIOGRAPHY 313
INDEX OF PERSONS AND PLACES 332
INDEX OF PASSAGES 346
ACKNOWLEDGMENTS 347

INTRODUCTION

I. INTRODUCTION TO A CLASSIC

If the extent of its influence is any criterion for labelling a work a classic, Abraham ibn Daud's *Sefer ha-Qabbalah* qualifies eminently. For countless students, scholars and cultivated laymen of eight centuries, the work has been and remains a prime source of information for much of Jewish history from the days of Alexander the Great until the Almohade invasion of Spain in the middle of the twelfth century. This is true not only in orthodox circles, where the work occupies a position of authority, particularly with reference to those events of which it is the sole reporter. Even in more critical circles, the impact of the book is still discernible in many modern works. Until relatively recent times, it was almost the exclusive source of information on the history of Spanish Jewry. Even after new data on "the golden age" of Jewish literature in Spain began to come to light, Ibn Daud's account of the four captives and of the life of Samuel ibn Nagrela the Nagid held a place of authority akin almost to that of an eye-witness account. Moreover, virtually all modern handbooks of talmudic history—Graetz, Halevy, Weiss, Strack, Moore—have adhered to Ibn Daud's enumeration of the generations of tannaim and amoraim, thereby according his periodization of talmudic history a quasi-canonical status.

Modern scholars were in reality merely re-echoing what had long been established practice in Jewish historiography. In Jewish circles, Ibn Daud's history achieved much the same kind of influence that the works of Orosius and Isidore had in medieval Christian historiography. The evidence of his influence on all subsequent Jewish historical writing is easily discerned and indeed impressive. In form and content, Ibn Daud's work had a crucial influence on all later Jewish histories of tradition, which either began where Ibn Daud had left off or attempted to fill in the gaps in his account. His *Sefer ha-Qabbalah* was the most important single source for the historical writings of Menahem Meiri of Perpignan, Isaac Israeli of Toledo, Saadiah ibn Danan of Granada, Joseph b. Zaddik of Arevalo, and Abraham Zacuto.[1] Zacuto, in fact, virtually copied the greater portion of Ibn Daud's work and reproduced it in his own work on history,[2] and it was by way of his *Sefer Yuḥasin* that Ibn Daud's data and perio-

---

1 Cf. M. Steinschneider, *Die Geschichtsliteratur der Juden* (Frankfurt a.M., 1905), pp. 55f., 71 f., 88 f., 98 f.
2 Abraham Zacuto, *Liber Juchasin* ed. by H. Filipowski, (London, 1857); 2nd ed., with introduction by A.H. Freimann (Frankfurt a.M., 1925), pp. xiv, xvi, 198b f.

dization gained much of their authority in the eyes of later scholars. In 1510, at about the same time that Zacuto was completing his work, Abraham b. Solomon of Torrutiel composed a new *Sefer ha-Qabbalah*, which was to supplement Ibn Daud's work with data on the men from 1180 down to the beginning of the the sixteenth century. The scholars of that and the subsequent century, Solomon ibn Verga, Joseph ha-Kohen, Gedaliah ibn Yaḥya, David Gans, Joseph Sambari and David Conforte, drew upon Ibn Daud's work constantly, albeit not always with full acknowledgment.[3] Azariah de' Rossi, the father of Jewish scientific study of rabbinic literature, utilized his work freely and subjected his biblical chronology to a meticulous examination.[4] Indeed, Ibn Daud's authority was such as to gain for him recognition even among Karaite theologians, adherents of the very movement which he had set out to discredit and defeat.[5] His work also came to the attention of Christian students in abridgements and translations.[6]

Although the work was abridged, imitated and supplemented, it continued to hold its own as a popular and authoritative book. Nothing proves better the esteem in which it was held than the wholesale corruptions of, and tinkerings with, the text of this book on the part of copyists and glossators.[7] These pious readers sought quite ingenuously to correct and improve upon the state of a work which patently served a sacred function—the defense of the faith and the refutation of heresy. What could be more in keeping with the intent of the author than to correct "errors" in accordance with "authentic" tradition?

Obviously so eminent a work merits critical study on the basis of an accurate text, and it is such a new text that has served as the basis of our translation, commentary and analysis. This new edition has been prepared at a time when the copious sources on the Jews of Spain and the Mediterranean world, which are being increased almost daily, have largely displaced Ibn Daud's

3 Steinschneider, *op. cit.* pp. 101 f., 107 f.
4 Azariah de' Rossi, *Meor 'Enayyim*, ed. by D. Cassel (Vilna, 1864–66), pp. 150, 184, 199, 212, 126, 239, 292 f., 358 f. and "Maṣref la-Kesef," *ibid.*, pp. 10 f.
5 Cf. Z. Ankori, "Elijah Baschyahi: An Inquiry into his Traditions concerning the Beginnings of Karaism" [in Hebrew], *Tarbiz*, XXV (1955–56), 189 f. For a striking instance of outright lifting from *Sefer ha-Qabbalah* by the Karaite Caleb Afendopulo, cf. M. Steinschneider, *Catalogus Codicum Hebraeorum Bibliothecae Academiae Lugduno-Bataviae* (Leiden, 1858), pp. 383—394.
6 The first abridgement with Latin translation was published by Sebastian Muenster, *Kalendarium Hebraicum* (Basle, 1527), pp 26 f. A second and larger abridgement with a new translation was published by G. Genebrard, *Hebraeorum Breve Chronicon* (Paris, 1572). Two modern translations into German and Spanish are available: M. Katz, *Abraham ibn Dauds Sefer Hak-Kabbala* (Bern, 1907); J. Bages Torrida, tr., *Sefer Ha-Kabbalah* (*El Libro de la Tradicion*) (Granada, 1927).
7 Cf. our Hebrew introduction to the text of Ibn Daud's work.

chronicle as a source of Jewish history. As a source of information on the biblical, talmudic and gaonic periods, the work is virtually worthless. But now that it has been displaced as a source of historical information on earlier periods, the path is cleared for *Sefer ha-Qabbalah* to take its place as a primary source for the mind of Abraham ibn Daud and the issues that he and members of his class regarded as uppermost in the Jewish community of their day. Precisely in the measure that the work ceases to inform us about men and commmunities outside Ibn Daud's immediate experience, it begins to illuminate the world and mind of Ibn Daud himself. As such, it is one of the finest introductions we have to the Jewish community of twelfth-century Spain. It is in that spirit that we have studied the work and tried to elucidate it to the contemporary reader.

II. ABRAHAM IBN DAUD'S UNIVERSE OF DISCOURSE

The Andalusian Foundation

Abraham ibn Daud of Toledo revealed only one fact about his personal life, and that was his pride in having acquired his higher education under the tutorship of his maternal uncle, R. Baruk b. Isaac ibn Albalia.[1] However meager, this item conveys to us information that fixes the historical setting and the cultural context in which he was trained.

Ibn Albalia died early in September 1126, in Cordova, where he had functioned as rabbi, teacher and communal leader.[2] Since Ibn Daud's whole orientation was a Judeo-Arabic one, and his education was gained under one of the leading scholars of the day in the center of Judeo-Arabic culture, we may conclude with a fair measure of probability that he was born in one of the larger Jewish communities of Arabic Spain[3]—Andalus, the Jews and Arabs called it—such as Cordova, Lucena or Seville, no later than 1110.[4] Even if, as is unlikely, he arrived in Toledo long in advance of the mass flight of the Jews to the Christian north, he came there a mature man, whose personality had been indelibly stamped by the Arab south and the Ibn Albalia home in which he had been reared.

Although in retrospect the first four decades of the twelfth century appear as the beginning of the actual downfall of the Iberian-Arabic society that had reached its zenith in the tenth and eleventh centuries, from the point of view of a Jew, and for that matter of most Muslims, life in the early part of the twelfth century had at long last regained some of the stability and agreeableness that it

---

1 VII.443. All references otherwise unidentified are to chapter and line of our translation of *Sefer ha-Qabbalah*.
2 VII.444. Moses ibn Ezra, *Shiray ha-Ḥol*, 2 vols., ed. by H. Brody (Berlin-Jerusalem, 1935–1941), II, 175, introduction to no. 93. Cf. also *EJ*, II, 109; *EH*, III, 356; Ch. Schirmann, "The Life of Jehuda ha-Levi" [in Hebrew], *Tarbiz*, IX (1937–38), 49 f. Cf. also below, n. 12.
3 If I am not mistaken this suggestion was first made by Y. Baer and Z. Lichtenstein in *EH*, I, 196–197. That Ibn Daud was later identified as a Toletanian does not in any way indicate that he was born in Toledo; see the many examples collected by I. Twersky, *Rabad of Posquières* (Cambridge, 1962), p. 4 n. 14.
4 M. Steinschneider's objections to this date in *Die Hebraeischen Uebersetzungen des Mitelalters* (Berlin, 1893), p. 369 n. 2, are unfounded. If the later traditions that Ibn Daud died in 1181 are correct, it is not *likely* that he was born much before 1110.

was reputed to have had in the glorious days of the Cordovan caliphate and Amirid dictatorship.[5]

To be sure, by 1110 Andalus had been reduced to a number of districts rigidly controlled by Almoravide governors, who were in the service of Berber kings dwelling in Marrakesh in North Africa.[6] With the Almoravide take-over in Andalus after 1086, Jews who had formerly held posts in the royal service of the minor kingdoms (*los reinos de taifas*) were progressively removed from office. Ibn Albalia's father, Isaac, had been one of the first victims of the bloodless purge of Jewish civil servants in Seville in 1089 and had been compelled to remove to Granada, where he spent the last five years of his life.[7] One year later, in 1090, the Ibn Ezras of Granada suffered a far more traumatic downfall from their long-held positions of power and wealth and were compelled to flee to the Christian north.[8] Moreover, shortly after the turn of the century, the Jews of Lucena had to pay an enormous sum to the Almoravide leader to expiate their sin of tenacity to Judaism.[9] The old Jewish grandees were no longer lording it over Muslim underlings as they had done in times past.

However, the purge had struck only a very few, and was quickly forgotten as new Jewish names began to appear on the rosters of the Almoravide courts.[10] Most important of all, the specter of war had been largely removed following the banishment of the Abbasids of Seville and the reconquest for Islam of territories that had earlier fallen to the Christian invaders. The major part of An-

---

5   On the history and culture of Andalus, cf. *EI*, I[2], 486 ff.; R. Dozy, *Histoire des Musulmans d'Espagne*, new ed., 3 vols., ed. by E. Lévi-Provençal (Leiden, 1932). English tr. of the earlier, 3rd. ed. by G. Stokes under the title *Spanish Islam* (London, 1913); E. Lévi-Provençal, *Histoire de l'Espagne Musulmane*, 3 vols. (Paris, 1950–53); H. Pérès, *La Poésie Andalouse en Arabe Classique*, 2nd ed. (Paris, 1953); C. Sánchez-Albornoz, *La España Musulmana*, 2nd ed., 2 vols. (Buenos Aires, 1960). For brief but fine interpretations, cf. E. Lévi-Provençal, *La Civilisation Arabe en Espagne, Vue Générale*, 3rd ed. (Paris, 1961); A. Abel, "Spain: Internal Division," in G.E. von Grunebaum, ed., *Unity and Variety in Muslim Civilization* (Chicago, 1955), pp. 207–230. On the Jews of Andalus, cf. S.W. Baron, *A Social and Religious History of the Jews*, 2nd ed., 8 vols. and Index vol. (Philadelphia, 1952–60), III–VIII *passim* (henceforth this work is referred to as *SRH*); E. Ashtor, *Qorot ha-Yehudim bi-Sefarad ha-Muslimit*, 2 vols. (Jerusalem, 1960–66).
6   On the Almoravides, cf. *EI*, I, 318 f.; Dozy, *op.cit.*, III, 123 f. (English tr., pp. 694 f.); Sánchez-Albornoz, *op. cit.*, II, 161 f.
7   VII.332–333 and note there. Cf. also the passage in Sánchez-Albornoz, *op. cit.*, II, 177 f., reflecting the new normative spirit of intolerance to Jews and Christians.
8   H. Brody, "Moses ibn Ezra—Incidents in His Life," *JQR*, NS, XXIV (1933–34), 312 f.; Moses ibn Ezra, *Selected Poems*, ed. by H. Brody, tr. by S. Solis-Cohen, 2nd ed. (Philadelphia, 1945), p. xxvi.
9   Cf. Baron, *SRH*, III, 124 f.
10 Cf. Schirmann, "Life of Jehuda ha-Levi," pp. 51 f.

dalus, from Silves to Valencia, from Granada to Calatrava, had been preserved intact, pacified and integrated as it had not been for a century and more. True, echoes of *Reconquista* in the name of the Cross could be heard from Toledo. But the fall of Tudela and Saragossa in 1115 and 1118 to Alfonso el Batallador was far to the north, a long way off from the heart of Andalus and the centers of Jewry thriving within it. Even alarmists must have found reassurance in the reports of the dynastic wars and Portuguese defections that plagued the northern rulers. There was reason to hope that Christian might had on the whole been spent, and that, apart from sporadic forays and skirmishes, both camps would settle for the traditional stalemate that had kept Spain and Andalus sundered and different. It was a basically stable and confident Cordova in which Ibn Daud spent his formative years, in the company of men who loved their surroundings and made no secret of it.[11]

True, wars and upheavals had shorn Cordova of much of its uniqueness. Wealth and political talent, science and letters, philosophy and architecture were no longer confined to this former capital of the western caliphate. Seville and Granada, Malaga and Denia, Valencia and Saragossa and many others now had their fair share of philosopher-physicians, patrons and masters in the arts and sciences. But the "jewel of Andalus" never quite lost its magic hold on the imagination of those who had either survived the storms or were descended from families that cherished memories of the *pax Omayyada*. To the Brahmins of Cordova, both Jewish and Muslim, the seat of the Umayyads was still the hub of the Maghreb, its very soul.

Especially for the Jews the city never quite lost its central position as the home of many of the illustrious in wealth, learning and influence. Centrally situated on the Guadalquivir River, it remained a convenient meeting-ground for Sevil-

---

11 On the situation in Spain during the first three decades of the twelfth century, cf. R.B. Merriman, *The Rise of the Spanish Empire*, 4 vols. (New York, 1918-34), I, 69 f.; P. Aguado Bleye, *Manual de Historia de España*, 7th ed., 3 vols. (Madrid, 1954), I, 628 f.; *EI*, I², 495; Dozy, *op. cit.*, III, 148 f. (English tr., pp. 713 f.). Although Dozy obviously measured the period against the earlier days of glory and in the light of the "speedy" downfall of the Almoravide rule—and was followed by virtually all historians—the poems of Judah ha-Levi and of Moses ibn Ezra from this period are as good a testimony as any that while men may not have been living in paradise, they were certainly not suffering hell on earth. While these two poets speak of hard times which they experienced personally, they give no hint of turmoil or general collapse. Quite the contrary. Certainly, they do not corroborate Dozy's generalization that the situation of the Jews was "intolerable." That state of affaris was to come in 1148, and in some areas, as we learn from Judah ha-Levi, even earlier. However, even in the perspective of eight centuries, wherever possible we can and should appraise each decade invidually. From 1110 to 1126 was as long a time-span as from 1920 to 1936. Surely, it would be misleading to describe the mood of Europe, and of its Jews, in 1920 by what was happening in 1936.

lans, Lucenans, Granadans and those farther removed. While Lucena was distinguished by its almost totally Jewish population and by the academy made famous by Isaac ibn Giat, Isaac al-Fasi and Joseph ibn Megash, it was Cordova that the alumni of Lucena generally made the site of their meetings, which were frequent and enlivened by visitors from afar. Within this wide circle of men of means and taste, learning and influence, Albalia commanded a position of universal respect and, apparently, no little affection.[12]

Scion of an old and distinguished family, the life of Baruk ibn Albalia was typical of the rabbinic-courtier class of Andalus. He was born in Seville in the shadow of the royal palace, where his father, serving as court astrologer and as representative of the Jews, trained him in the ways expected of members of his class. Polished to perfection in the use of Arabic and in the writing of classical Hebrew, he was sent by his father from the latter's deathbed to Lucena to complete his rabbinical education under an erstwhile enemy of the family, R. Isaac al-Fasi. Under al-Fasi the younger Ibn Albalia studied only rabbinics, but he came to Lucena already imbued with his father's tradition that Torah alone did not complete a man. Only through a synthesis of dogmatic disciplines with "Greek wisdom" did a man become a gentleman, and a pious Jew an understanding one.[13]

What this "Greek wisdom" was we know principally from the Jewish philosophers of the following generations and from their Arabic models. Allowing for some minor variations in emphasis or substance, the curriculum for the attainment of such balanced wisdom had been established by the elite of Baghdad and transplanted to Cordova a hundred years earlier.[14] Physics, logic, mathe-

---

12 On the coterie of Jewish intellectuals, cf. VII.393 f., and esp. the superb studies of Schirmann, "Life of Jehuda ha-Levi," pp. 35 f. (ha-Levi's esteem for Ibn Albalia, pp. 50, 228) and "Poets Contemporary with Mose ibn Ezra and Jehuda Hallevi" [in Hebrew], *Studies of the Research Institute for Hebrew Poetry*, II (1936), IV (1938), VI (1945). For Moses ibn Ezra's praise of Ibn Albalia, cf. his *Shiray ha-Ḥol*, I, 92, no. 93. That Ibn Albalia himself wrote poetry was first noted by M. Zulay, "Bayn Kotlay ha-Makon le-Ḥeqer ha-Shirah ha-'Ibrit," *Alei Ayin: The Salman Schocken Jubilee Volume* (Jerusalem, 1948–52), p. 98.
13 VII.294–335, 422–444.
14 On the translation of Greek literature and the cultivation of "Greek" studies in Arabic garb, cf. the general surveys of R.A. Nicholson, *A Literary History of the Arabs* (Cambridge, 1956), chs. VI–IX; E. Gilson, *History of Christian Philosophy in the Middle Ages* (New York, 1955), pp. 181 f.; L. Gardet and M.-M. Anawati, *Introduction à la Théologie Musulmane* (Paris, 1948), esp. pp. 94 f. Brief but superb treatments are R. Klibansky, *The Continuity of the Platonic Tradition During the Middle Ages* (London, 1950); R. Walzer, "Arabic Transmission of Greek Thought to Medieval Europe," *Bulletin of the John Rylands Library*, XXIX (1945–46), 160 f.; idem, *Greek Into Arabic* (Oxford, 1962), esp. essays 1, 2, 14. For the introduction of these studies into Spain, cf. Lévi-

matics, astronomy, ethics, metaphysics and even rhetoric, all of them in Arabic translations of, and commentaries on, the classical philosophers, were to be harmoniously blended with Bible and Talmud, midrash and the codes, liturgy and dogma. Scrupulous adherence to the law of the rabbis was to be molded and adorned by courtly bearing and dignified speech. Cunning and wit and beauty in every expression were the indispensable limbs to the body of faith and observance they had inherited from the ancients.

Then, of course, there was the requirement of service to the community and generosity to the needy. Wealth was justified, for it freed a man from distractions and removed the temptation to cheapen his position. As a judge in the court of the autonomous Jewish communities, he was expected to demonstrate an irreproachable bearing, in which fairness and learning were clothed in studied humility and soft-spoken firmness. As a courtier, especially, his demeanor would have to be above criticism from every point of view—dedication and alertness, advice given and pitfalls avoided, intrigues shared and plots betrayed—for in this area men rarely, and Jews least of all, had the opportunity to repeat a mistake. But such was the fate of nobility, and the noble did not shirk his calling, least of all because only as a courtier did he have the opportunity to stand guard over and influence the fate of his people. Underneath the deep attachments to his home and countryside, there lurked forever the gnawing reality of his precarious political and economic position. Jewish power and Jewish influence in the highest echelons of state were vital to his safety, to the safety of his friends and of the Jews at large. Political unrest and bloodshed in any form were almost certain to consume more than a fair measure of Jewish lives and property. Confidence rested in strong government and rigid control of the populace by kings, whether Christian or Muslim, and in easy Jewish access to the ears of the monarch.

The Jewish courtier's relaxation was to be spent in the company of men of his class, men who like him were trained and dedicated to the cultivation of the arts and to guardianship over the community. It was not quite a closed club, but men were not admitted simply because they were Jews, or even Jews with money. The gifted poet (the indispensable trapping of an Andalusian court), a brilliant philosopher or accomplished scientist could gain admittance and patronage, provided he remembered to live by the rules, which were as unspoken but as real in Cordova as they have been in most high societies.[15]

Provençal, *Histoire*, III, 488 f. For the metamorphosis of Jewish literature and thought under the impact of Arabic studies, cf. Baron, *SRH*, vols. VI-VIII. See also next note.

15 While the history of Jewish *paideia* in Andalus has yet to be written, there are excellent treatments of various aspects of the subject. Extremely illuminating is H.A. Wolfson, "The Classification of Sciences in Medieval Jewish Philosophy," *Hebrew Union College*

INTRODUCTION   XXI

When, at about the age of twenty-six, Baruk came to Cordova to take up the post of rabbi and communal leader (his exact posts and station in relation to others are not clear), the way of Jewish gentlemen was already established. One did not boast of these achievements; they were assumed, prerequisite. They were memorialized and specified at momentous occasions—a wedding, a birth, a major victory, death. It is from such dedicatory poems that we know of the coterie and style of life identified with Ibn Albalia and his friends. Joseph ibn Megash, Joseph ibn Sahl, Joseph ibn Zaddik, Moses ibn Ezra, Judah ha-Levi, Oheb b. Meir ha-Nasi, Judah ibn Giat, Samuel ibn Moriel—these were the illustrious names who frequently met with R. Baruk ibn Albalia to relax and to discuss the major issues of the day. Were we to conjure up an imaginary soirée in Ibn Albalia's home, the talk might have been something like this:[16]

> A Jewish captive had to be ransomed;[17] a burdensome tax on the Jews had to be met;[18] a school was in straits;[19] a Jewish grandee had brought ridicule upon the Bible;[20] a Muslim fanatic was poisoning the air;[21] something had to be done about the brazen skepticism of youth as a consequence of the philosophy that was making headway.[22] What did you think of Ibn Ezra's book on

Jubilee Volume (Cincinnati, 1925), pp. 263 f.; cf. also M. Guedemann, *Das juedische Unterrichtswesen waehrend der spanisch-arabischen Periode* (Vienna, 1873); S. Assaf, *Meqorot le-Toledot ha-Ḥinuk be-Israel*, 4 vols. (Tel Aviv, 1925–1947), II, 8 f., where many of the relevant sources are collected. However, the best source for the way of life and the *Weltanschauung* of the courtier class remains the testaments and eulogies of the philosophers and poets themselves. Excellent examples are Samuel ibn Nagrela's instructions to his sons and his collections of wisdom known as *Ben Mishlay*; see Samuel ibn Nagrela, *Diwan:Kol Shiray R. Samuel ha-Nagid*, 3 vols., ed. by A.M. Habermann and S. Abramson (Tel Aviv, 1947–1953), I, 38, 39, 69, and all of vol. II. A classic summary is the testament of Judah ibn Tibbon to his son Samuel, in which Ibn Nagrela's life and wisdom are held up as models; *Hebrew Ethical Wills*, 2 vols., ed. and tr. by I. Abrahams (Philadelphia, 1926), I. 51 f., Cf. also J. Schirmann, "The Function of the Hebrew Poet in Medieval Spain," *Jewish Social Studies*, XVI (1954), 235 f.

16 The subjects for this imaginary *soirée* have been culled from contemporary documents.
17 S.D. Goitein, "Autographs of Yehuda Hallevi" [in Hebrew], *Tarbiz*, XXV (1955–56), 397 f.
18 Schirmann, "Life of Jehuda ha-Levi," pp. 45, 50, n. 54.
19 *Ibid.*, p. 53; S.D. Goitein, *Jewish Education in Muslim Countries* [in Hebrew] (Jerusalem, 1962), pp. 176 f. Note the activities of the ubiquitous Ḥalfon b. Nethanel.
20 Joseph b. Judah ibn Aknin, *Divulgatio Mysteriorum Luminumque Apparentia* [in Arabic], ed. and tr. into Hebrew by A.S. Halkin (Jerusalem, 1964), pp. 490–491.
21 Cf. the tract of 'Abd Allah, the last king of Granada, denouncing Joseph ibn Nagrela and reviving the anti-Jewish incitements of a half century earlier; E. Lévi-Provençal, "Les 'Mémoires' de 'Abd Allah, Dernier Roi Ziride de Grenade," *Al-Andalus*, III (1935), 233 f., IV (1936–39) 29 f.; Dozy, *Histoire*, III, 70 f. (English tr., pp. 651 f.). On Arabic polemics against the Jews and Judaism, cf. below, n. 45.
22 Note the series of philosophical apologiae for Judaism that emerged from the Cordova-

prosody?[23] A pity his brothers and he had such bad luck.[24] Did you hear how ha-Levi brought the house down when someone brought a woman into a philosophical gathering?[25] How much money have you put into R. Ḥalfon's business? Thank God for Ḥalfon; how else would we keep in contact with the Jews of Cairo with much greater efficiency than the regular mails?[26] Something has been happening of late to Judah ha-Levi—he seems to take awfully seriously the prayers for return to the Holy-Land. Do you think he is superstitious?[27] Of all the silly rumors, somebody said he was thinking of writing a book rejecting all philosophy, and, what is more, that he has been discussing his views with a Karaite physician of Toledo.[28] Those Karaites never do give up, do they? I thought that what Ibn Ferrizuel did to them had taught them a thing or two.[29] Which reminds me of a wonderful interpretation of a verse I heard from that young Abraham ibn Ezra of Tudela. Sharp tongue he has.[30] R. Baruk, that was a beautiful talk you gave at the academy this morning, trenchant and extensive, reminded me of your father's *Spice Peddler's Basket*....[31]

Such was the air Ibn Daud breathed and adored around 1125 when he was but a lad at the home of his uncle. If he was never mentioned in any of the documents that have come down to us from that circle, it is no accident. He was of the next generation, and apparently no prodigy in any of the fields they held dear. He listened and probably dreamed of what place he would have in the chain of this circle. What he actually did after his uncle died, or for that matter even before, we have no way of knowing. All we can say for certain is that his education and tastes, which were later reflected in his writings, were

---

Lucena circle in the twelfth century; works of Joseph ibn Zaddik, Moses ibn Ezra, Abraham ibn Ezra, Judah ha-Levi, Moses Maimonides, Abraham ibn Daud discussed in J. Guttmann, *Philosophies of Judaism*, tr. by D.W. Silverman (Philadelphia, 1964), pp. 110 f. For an actual report of Jewish skepticism, albeit of half a century earlier, cf. M. Perlmann, "Ibn Hazm on the Equivalence of Proofs," *JQR*, NS, XL (1949–50), 279 f.

23   Moses ibn Ezra, *Kitab al-Muḥadarat w'al-Mudhakarat*, tr. into Hebrew under the title *Shirat Israel* by B.Z. Halper (Leipzig, 1923–24); cf. M. Steinschneider, *Die Arabische Literature ćer Juden* (Frankfurt a.M., 1902), p. 150.
24   Cf. Brody, "Moses ibn Ezra—Incidents in His Life," pp. 309 f.
25   Ibn Aknin, *Divulgatio*, pp. 176 f.
26   S.D. Goitein, "The Biography of Rabbi Judah ha-Levi in the Light of the Cairo Geniza Documents," *PAAJR*, XXVIII (1959), 41 f.
27   Schirmann, "Life of Jehuda ha-Levi," p. 230, where ha-Levi's reports on what his friends have been saying are quoted.
28   Goitein, "Biography of Judah ha-Levi," pp. 46 f.
29   Epilogue. 57 f.; Y. Baer, *A History of the Jews in Christian Spain*, I (Philadephia, 1961) 50 f.
30   Cf. M. Friedlaender, *Ibn Ezra Literature, IV: Essays on the Writings of Abraham ibn Ezra* (London, s.a.), pp. 126 f.
31   VII.324 f., and cf. above, n. 12.

very much in keeping with the curriculum of the courtier circle we have briefly described.

However, no two men are exactly alike, and the broad outlines of Ibn Daud's own personality must be drawn from his own writings of a much later period. Quite obviously, his education did not stop with the death of his uncle. But the foundation had been laid; the rest was super-structure.

To begin with, Arabic was his mother tongue and remained to the end his most convenient tool of expression. Certainly the processes of reasoning and abstraction came most easily to him in Arabic, as they had to ha-Levi and Maimonides. When he did write in Hebrew, which obviously he mastered thoroughly, he would often slip into an Arabism or literal translation of an idiom or expression, as was common in his circle.[32] But however important, language was only the outer trapping.

Steeped in rabbinic lore from earliest childhood, he had acquired a thorough knowledge of Scripture, rabbinics, Jewish philosophy, Hebrew poetry and sacred history. Apart from copious citations from the Bible and Talmud, Ibn Daud sprinkled his books with quotations from Hebrew poets he had known and read.[33] He had clearly studied thoroughly and critically the philosophical works of Saadiah, Solomon ibn Gabirol and Judah ha-Levi.[34] On the other hand, he was also well versed in whatever Greek literature was available to him in Arabic translation. Besides apparently being familiar with a Christian translation of the Bible, as well as with the New Testament and Quran, he had read works of Plato, Aristotle, Hippocrates and Galen.[35] From Arabic sources, too, he doubtless drew his acquaintance with astrological notions, which he by no means rejected,[36] and his knowledge of ancient and medieval Gentile his-

---

32 Cf. below, pp. 305 f.
33 Cf., e.g., Abraham ibn Daud, *Ha-Emunah ha-Ramah*, ed. and tr. into German by S. Weil (Frankfort a.M., 1852), Hebrew text pp. 61, 69, 89, 91; cf. also S. Pinsker, "Toledot R. Abraham ibn Daud," *Ha-Mizpah*, III (1886), 7 n. 7; J. Guttmann, *Die Religionsphilosophie des Abraham ibn Daud aus Toledo* (Goettingen, 1879), p. 32.
34 *Emunah Ramah*, pp. 2 ff. Cf. D. Kaufmann, *Geschichte der Attributenlehre in juedischen Religionsphilosophie des Mittelalters von Saadja bis Maimuni* (Gotha, 1877), pp. 241 f.; W. Bacher, "Der Arabische Titel des religionsphilosophischen Werkes Abraham ibn Daud's," *ZDMG*, XLVI (1892), 541 f.
35 Guttmann, *Religionsphilosophie*, pp. 14 f.; F.S. Bodenheimer, "The Biology of Abraham ben David Halevi of Toledo," *Archives Internationales d'Histoire des Sciences*, IV (1951), 57, 61. Cf. also *Sefer ha-Qabbalah* II.97, III.69, 98–99, Epilogue.172; Abraham ibn Daud, *Zikron Dibray Romi* (cf. n. 80 for full reference), s.v. Commodus, Constantine.
36 *Emunah Ramah*, p. 86; M. Arfa, *Abraham ibn Daud and the Beginnings of Medieval Jewish Aristotelianism* (unpublished doctoral dissertaion, Columbia University, 1954), p. 135, n. 2; cf. also *Sefer ha-Qabbalah* VII. 331. On the importance of astrology in sophisticated circles in the twelfth century, cf. Moses Maimonides, *Epistle to Yemen*,

tory. Of the Arabic philosophers he mentioned by name only Alfarabi, whom, as his thinking indicates, he admired greatly.[37] Above all, although he never acknowledged the fact, he seems to have absorbed thoroughly the writings of Ibn Sina (Avicenna) and to have appropriated the Aristotelian thought which the great Arab philosopher had expounded in his commentaries.[38]

In other words, Ibn Daud, like many another Jew and Muslim of his day, had grown up in two cultural worlds simultaneously: the world of revelation and the schoolhouse of philosophy. Like many other medieval scholars, he assumed that both revelation and philosophy were equally valid sources of knowledge, which could and had to be reconciled and synthesized. Following the pattern legitimized by Saadiah, he learned to fashion a cohesive universe of discourse in which philosophy and religion stated the same truths, albeit in different vocabularies.[39] In line with the new intellectual milieu of twelfth-century Andalus, he rejected the philosophic eclecticism of Saadiah, the neo-Platonism of Ibn Gabirol, and the anti-philosophism of Judah ha-Levi. In their stead he adopted the new current of Aristotelianism, which, thanks to Ibn Bajjah and the scholars of Toledo, was then making its inroads into all three religious communities of his day.[40] Ibn Daud thus became "the first to attempt a systematic reconstruction of Judaism in the light of Aristotelianism."[41] As such, his philosophic work is a milestone in the history of Jewish theology, one which is all the more notable because of its affinity to the thought of Maimonides, the Jewish peripatetic *par excellence*.[42]

---

ed. by A.S. Halkin (New York, 1952), Hebrew introduction, pp. xxi–xxii; R. J. Lemay, *Abu Ma'shar and Latin Aristotelianism in the Twelfth Century* (Beirut, 1962), pp. xxii f.

[37] *Emunah Ramah*, p. 65. Cf. next note.

[38] Guttmann, *Religionsphilosophie*, p. 16; Arfa, *op. cit.*, pp. 119, 130 f. Cf. also below, to n. 57.

[39] Cf. H.A. Wolfson, *Religious Philosophy* (Cambridge, 1961), chapters I, IX; idem, *Philo*, 2 vols. (Cambridge, 1947), I, 194 f.; R. Walzer, "Arabic Transmission of Greek Thought," pp. 175 f. For graphic representations of this idea in Christian art, see Plates 1 and 2 at the end of Klibansky, *op. cit.*

[40] Cf. S. Munk, *Mélanges de Philosophie Juive et Arabe* (Paris, 1859), pp. 268 f.; Arfa, *op. cit.*, pp. 333 f.; M. Alonso, "Las Fuentes Literarias de Domingo Gundisalvo," *Al-Andalus*, XI (1946), 159 f. For the major philosophical influences on the Jewish intelligentsia of the twelfth century, cf. references above in n. 14; see esp. S. Pines' essay on Maimonides, which applies, *mutatis mutandis*, to the whole circle of philosophers of Spain, in Moses Maimonides, *The Guide of the Perplexed*, tr. by S. Pines (Chicago, 1963), pp. lvii f.

[41] Arfa, *op. cit.*, p. 111. On the traces of earlier Jewish Aristotelianism, cf. S. Pines, "A Tenth-Century Philosophical Correspondence," *PAAJR*, XXIV (1955), 103 f., 136.

[42] *Ibid.*, pp. 140 f.; Guttmann, *Philosophies of Judaism*, pp. 143 f.

In the last analysis, however, medieval Jewish philosophy, like its Christian counterpart, was often a form of religious apologetic, an attempt to validate traditional dogma by the very same philosophical systems which were undermining traditional faith and practice. The medieval Jewish philosopher, accordingly, set out to prove that the philosopher's categories, far from contradicting the tenets of revelation, were actually a handmaiden of religion, which supported Scripture and tradition when these were properly understood.[43] As a consequence, medieval Jewish thinkers often felt called upon to engage in open polemics with the sects and systems that attacked their orthodoxy and to reestablish the Jewish claim to possessing the one true faith and, most important, the correct pattern of conduct.[44] In the footsteps of his forebears, Saadiah and Ibn Nagrela, Ibn Daud later showed himself to be thoroughly familiar with anti-Jewish polemics and learned to defend vigorously his religious tradition against all attacks of sectarian-Jewish or Christian-Muslim origin,[45] or against those deriving from philosophic skepticism and the rejection of all religious knowledge.[46] His interests thus lay in the mastery of his tradition and in recapturing the philosophic truths he believed to have been revealed at Sinai, but which were often neglected by his brethren and left to Greeks and Arabs.[47]

Apart from these very general tendencies, his life and work are a blank to us until 1160 or 1161, when he composed his books. It is not hard to imagine what had happened in the interim, though how the changes in conditions affected Ibn Daud himself remains a considerable puzzle.

---

43 Guttmann, *ibid.*, pp. 3 f.; A.S. Halkin, "Judeo Arabic-Literature," *The Jews: Their History, Culture and Religion*, 2 vols., ed. by L. Finkelstein (New York, 1949), II, 788, 805; Wolfson, *Philo*, I, 155 f.; *idem, The Philosophy of the Church Fathers*, I (Cambridge, 1956), 97 f.; Gilson, *op. cit.*, pp. 3 f.; *idem, The Spirit of Medieval Philosophy* (New York, 1940), pp. 22 f., 36 f.

44 See the illuminating linguistic observations by Wolfson, "Classification of Sciences," pp. 310 f.

45 For this and what follows, cf. the excellent study by M. Schreiner, "Zur Geschichte der Polemik zwischen Juden und Muhammedanern," *ZDMG*, XLII (1888), 591 f., and esp. 628 f. Cf. also references given below, n. 70.

46 Cf. above, n. 22. On Saadiah's attempt at meeting the challenge of skepticism, and of which Ibn Daud took note, cf. A.J. Heschel, *The Quest for Certainty in Saadia's Philosophy* (New York, 1944).

47 On the dissemination of this notion in medieval philosophy, cf. Wolfson, *Philo*, I, 160 f. That Ibn Daud shared this view is clear from his habit of listing at the end of each section in his philosophical treatise those verses in Scripture which demonstrate the philosophical ideas he has just expounded; cf. esp. *Emunah Ramah*, p. 63 l. 9.

To Toledo

By the middle of the fourth decade of the century, the optimists of Andalus must have had second thoughts about the end of the turmoil on the Iberian peninsula. Alfonso VII had stabilized his domain, and the crusade against the Saracen was clearly on the march again. In one or two campaigns the Christians had reached uncomfortably close to Cordova and Seville, and they did not always distinguish between Israelite and Ishmaelite. The grip of the Almoravides was not as tight as in the past, particularly now that a certain Muhammad ibn Tumart had begun translating his theology into a military program that was recording one success after another.[48] It was a long and bitter revolution that Ibn Tumart's Almohades began around 1121, but by 1147 they had overrun all of the Maghreb and crossed the Straits of Gibraltar.[49] When the blow finally did come in the west and its Andalusian extremity, it struck like lightning in its force and effect. One Jewish community after another was wiped out, along with thousands of Christians and opposing Muslims.[50] Thousands of Jews went over to Islam, many of them secretly trying to continue practicing Judaism, in what was to become the first large-scale precursor of later Sefardi Marranism. From Fez to al-Mahdiyya, from Silves to Malaga, not a Jew could retain his identity, at least not openly and without disguise. Of those who survived and perhaps eluded the authorities—baffling many a contemporary and subsequent inquirer—the family of R. Maimon of Cordova was to achieve the greatest renown.[51] As far as the Jewish communities of the west were concerned, Andalus was no more, and the only glimmer of hope lay far to the east in Egypt or to the north of Calatrava in Christian Spain. Ibn Daud was one of the many Jews who found a new home in Toledo,[52] and it is with that city that his name was forever to be associated by subsequent generations of Jews.[53]

By 1140, Toledo had become, in the words of a renowed medievalist, the *"grande ville de la renaissance médiévale, point de jonction entre les cultures mus-*

---

48 On the deterioration of conditions in Spain, from the point of Jews, cf. Y. Baer, "The Political Situation of the Spanish Jews in the Age of Jehuda Halevi" [in Hebrew], *Zion*, I (1935–36), 6 f.; Schirmann, "Life of Jehuda ha-Levi," pp. 235 f.

49 Cf. A. Huici Miranda, *Historia Politica Del Imperio Almohade* (Tetuan, 1956); Sánchez-Albornoz, *op. cit.*, II, 202 f.

50 Cf. VII.453–455 and notes there.

51 Cf. D. Yellin and I. Abrahams, *Maimonides* (Philadelphia, 1903), pp. 24 f., 33 f. and notes, pp. 220 f.; Baron, *SRH*, III, 291.

52 VII.465; Epilogue.101 f.

53 Cf. above, n. 3.

ulmane et chrétienne."⁵⁴ Although firmly in the hands of the Christian *Emperador*, and supreme symbol of the *Reconquista* campaign,⁵⁵ it remained a border city in which the effects of centuries of Muslim overlordship, terminated but fifty-five years earlier, were still discernible from a number of perspectives. Encompassing within its jurisdiction four distinct and "autonomous" communities—Christians, Muslims, Jews and Karaites⁵⁶—it, more than any other city of the twelfth century, reflected a cosmopolitan atmosphere reminiscent of Baghdad and Cordova in the ninth and tenth centuries. However, in the present instance the process of cultural transmission had been reversed. Aristotle in Arabic and the compendia of Arabs were being translated into Latin under the patronage and encouragement of the archbishops of the city. From France, Italy and England scholars were attracted to the city, where with almost feverish haste works on astrology, physics and philosophy were being rendered into Latin, under the direction of Dominicus Gundisalvus, by John of Seville, Gerard of Cremona, Alfred of Sarashel, and an otherwise unidentified Jew called Avendauth.⁵⁷ The latter's claim to distinction lies in his having translated Avicenna's *De Anima* from Arabic into Spanish for Gundisalvus, who then translated the material into Latin.

Although the exact identity of Avendauth, or Avendahut Israelita, remains problematic, a number of circumstances about the one work which is definitely associated with his name combine to identify him with Abraham ibn Daud; and a number of scholars regard this suggestion, which originates with Mlle. d'Alverny, as established. Ibn Daud and Avendauth the Jew both showed great familiarity with the works of Avicenna and, of course, expertise in Arabic. That Ibn Daud, like his older contemporary, Judah ha-Levi,⁵⁸ should know Spanish, reflects his easier access to the vernacular rather than to Latin, which was, of course, gained usually only in the course of a Christian education. That an Aristotelian-Avicennist by such a similar sounding name should have

---

54   G. Théry, *Tolède, Grande Ville de la Renaissance Médiévale* (Oran, 1944). Despite considerable efforts, I have never been able to locate a copy of this book.
55   For the most comprehensive account until 1102, cf. R. Menendez Pidal, *La España del Cid*, 5th ed., 2 vols. (Madrid, 1956). For the subsequent events, cf. the references above, n. 11.
56   On the Jews of Toledo under Muslim rule, cf. Ashtor, *op. cit.*, pp. 211 f. On the Karaites there, cf. below, pp. XLVI f.
57   Cf. Lemay, *op. cit.*, pp. 9 f., where the earlier literature is cited and discussed. For somewhat more popular treatments, cf. Gilson, *History*, pp. 235 f.; R.R. Bolgar, *The Classical Heritage* (New York, 1964), pp. 172 f.—The whole discussion on Avenauth-Ibn Daud took on a new turn as a consequence of the study of M.T. d'Alverny, "Avendauth?" *Homenaje a Millas-Vallicrosa*, 2 vols. (Barcelona, 1954–56), I, 19–43.
58   Baron, *SRH*, VII, 192, 312, n. 74.

been living in Toledo just at about the time when Ibn Daud, even if he came there as late as 1148, would have begun to establish himself there makes the suggestion extremely attractive. Beyond that we cannot go, as yet. However, if Avendauth and Ibn Daud were indeed one and the same, we have a recurrence of a phenomenon long familiar to men of the Andalusian courtier class; namely, that it was principally through linguistic expertise in two languages and knowledge of special disciplines that a Jew could hope to gain entree into the civil—in this case, the ecclesiastical—service.[59] Certainly this identification, if correct, would help explain Ibn Daud's uncommon Jewish interest in the history of Rome and the beginnings of Christianity on the Iberian peninsula.

Whatever the reality of the case, by 1160 Ibn Daud had taken up his pen to write to and for the Jews.

The Defense of the Faith

Of the four books ascribed to Ibn Daud, only two have survived. He himself mentions an anti-Karaite exegetical treatise on the legal interpretation of Scripture,[60] while from a cryptic remark of a later author we learn of a "distinguished" book on astronomy which he composed.[61] Neither of these works is available even in quotation. Any estimate of Ibn Daud and his work must, therefore, be confined to the two of his works available to us: his philosophical treatise *al-'Aqida al-Rafi'a*, known only from the Hebrew translation *ha-Emunah ha-Ramah* (The Sublime Faith);[62] and his tri-partite historical treatise of which *Sefer ha-Qabbalah* is in reality but the first and best-known section.[63] The char-

---

59 VII.182 f.; Judah ibn Tibbon's testament in Abrahams, *Hebrew Ethical Wills*, I, 59; Pérès, *op. cit.*, pp. 23 f.

60 Epilogue. 136.

61 Isaac Israeli, *Liber Jesod Olam*, 2 vols., ed. by B. Goldberg and L. Rosenkranz (Berlin, 1846–48), II (Book IV, ch. 18), f. 35 end of col. b.

62 Cf. above, n. 33. On the Hebrew translation, cf. Steinschneider, *Hebraeischen Uebersetzungen*, pp. 369 f.; *idem, Arabische Literatur der Juden*, pp. 154 f.; Arfa, *op. cit.*, p. 1 n. 2.

63 II.84; Epilogue.164 f.; Abraham ibn Daud, *MBSh* (cf. below, n. 88 for full reference), end.—The name *Sefer ha-Qabbalah* was later used for all three parts; cf. J. Rosenthal, "From 'Sefer Alfonso'" [in Hebrew], *Studies and Essays in Honor of Abraham A. Neuman* (Leiden, 1962), p. 612 n. 5, where the reference should be to *MBSh*, f. 69a.— Writing almost three and a half centuries after Ibn Daud, Abraham Zacuto was the first, and for that matter the last, to cite Ibn Daud's work by the name of *Dorot 'Olam*, The Generations of the World; Abraham Zacuto, *Liber Juchasin*, 2nd ed., p. xiv, where references are listed. Since Zacuto also refers to the book by its more conventional title, *ibid.*, Elbogen conjectured that the new title given by Zacuto may have been an overall name for all three parts of the work, while *Sefer ha-Qabbalah* designated only the first

acteristic common to all of his surviving works is their theologico-polemical intent. His three historical essays, namely the history of rabbinic tradition, the excursus on the rulers of Rome, and his abridgment of the *Josippon*, as well as his philosophical treatise, are all concerned in one way or another with defending and validating orthodox Jewish dogma and practice.

According to Ibn Daud, *The Sublime Faith* was composed in response to an inquiry by one of his contemporaries on how it was possible to square the belief in the omnipotence of God with human freedom and responsibility.[64] But this declaration is quickly seen to be but the initial stimulus, or the literary apologia, for what turns into a systematic defense of revelation and Judaism. While recognizing the value of R. Saadiah's synthesis of faith and reason, Ibn Daud found it totally inadequate by the intellectual criteria of his own time and place. Solomon ibn Gabirol's *Fons Vitae* was worse than that. Having spoken of religion as a general phenomenon, as a truth accessible to any rational man, he had undermined the claim of the Jew to a unique possession, to an irreplaceable body of beliefs and conduct.[65] Accordingly, Ibn Daud lashed out at skeptics and, above all, at Gabirol, for a shallow philosophy that was untenable by any standard of measurement, least of all the Jewish.[66]

The work was thus basically an *apologia pro religione Judaica* and specifically singled out the two daughter religions of Judaism as targets of attack. Arguing for the impossibility of the abrogation of the Torah, Ibn Daud took special pains to confute the Christian and Muslim contention that the revelation to the Jews had been superseded by a new covenant. Though in theory, he admitted, the ritual sections—as apart from the historical and ethical, which are utterly incontestable—admit of abrogation, Scripture placed the stamp of eternity on them by such words as: "It is a law for all time throughout the generations, in all your settlements" (Lev. 3.17). Like many another Jew, he asserted that his coreligionists need not take seriously the Muslim charge that the Hebrew Scriptures had been falsified. The uninterrupted chain of Jewish generations who have transmitted a text on which all Jews unanimously agree constitutes empirical evidence that the charge is preposterous. The Muslim arguments that, on

division; I. Elbogen, "Abraham ibn Daud als Geschichtsschreiber," *Festschrift zum seibzigstem Geburtstag Jakob Guttmanns* (Leipzig, 1915), p. 187. While this suggestion is plausible, it is rather odd that no manuscript or medieval authority gives even the slightest hint of the name cited by Zacuto. It may well be that Zacuto found the title *Dorot 'Olam* in the manuscript he had before him—if, indeed, he did not supply it himself—where some pious scribe or copyist had inserted it on the basis of Gen. 9.12 or Deut. 32.7.

64 *Emunah Ramah*, p. 1.
65 *Ibid.*, p. 2.
66 For summaries and analyses, cf. works listed above, nn. 33-36, 42.

the one hand, the Hebrew Scriptures contain references offensive to the Deity, and that, on the other, Scripture foretold Muhammad's mission, were equally unfounded. An objective reading of the verses in question, he claimed, will demonstrate the ignorance of the proponents of the latter argument, while a rational analysis of the so-called offensive verses will show that they cannot be taken literally.[67] Significantly, too, he felt compelled to refute the claim that Judaism is committed by the scriptural promises of retribution in this world to a denial of immortality. The Torah's primary concern was with the masses of men, and it, therefore, addressed them in language they could easily comprehend. The careful student, however, would discern ample references to immortality and other-worldly reward.[68] Finally, he attacked the arch-heresy of Karaism by demonstratin g on philosophic grounds the validity of, and necessity for, rabbinic "oral" tradition.[69]

Little, if any, of this polemic against Islam is original. Much of it may have been inspired by the writings of Samuel ibn Nagrela, who, in turn, had evoked the violent diatribes of Ibn Ḥazm against Judaism.[70] Much more may have been taken from the written and unwritten corpus of polemical replies current in Jewish circles. In his defense of rabbinic doctrine, Ibn Daud clearly appropriated intellectual categories that had long since been recognized in philosophic

---

[67] *Emunah Ramah*, pp. 75–81, 91. Jewish apologetics harped on these themes repeatedly; cf. Halkin's introduction to Maimonides, *Epistle to Yemen*, pp. xv f., where the uniqueness of Ibn Daud's concession of even the theoretical possibility of the abrogation of certain commandments is noted. That Maimonides also felt that way has been argued by L.V. Berman, *Ibn Bajjah and Maimonides* (dissertation submitted to Hebrew University, Jerusalem, 1959), pp. 104 f.; cf. also L. Strauss' introductory essay to Maimonides, *Guide of the Perplexed*, pp. xxxv f.—On the Muslim proofs for the abrogation of the Torah, cf. the index to scriptural verses compiled by E. Strauss, "Darkay ha-Pulmus ha-Islami," *Sefer ha-Zikaron le-Bayt ha-Midrash la-Rabbanim be-Vienna* (Jerusalem, 1946), pp. 183 f. That Ibn Daud had the anti-Jewish polemics of Samuel ibn Abbas in mind, as contended by D. Kaufmann in *REJ*, X (1865), 251 f., has been refuted by Halkin, *loc cit.*, n. 120. On Jewish concern with Christian and Muslim exegesis, cf. M. Zucker, *Rav Saadya Gaon's Translation of the Torah* [in Hebrew] (New York, 1959), p. 6 n. 16*; B. Cohen, *Law and Tradition in Judaism* (New York, 1959), p. 198 n. 89. On Christian arguments against the Muslims on the very same grounds, cf. N. Daniel, *Islam and the West* (Edinburgh, 1960), pp. 47 f.

[68] *Emunah Ramah*, p. 39.

[69] *Ibid.*, pp. 84 f.

[70] Cf. I. Goldziher, "Proben muhammedanischer Polemik gegen des Talmud," *Jeschurun*, ed. by J. Kobak, VIII (1872–75), 81; E. Garcia Gomez, "Polemica Religiosa entre Ibn Hazm e Ibn Nagrela," *Al-Andalus*, IV (1936–39), 1 f.; M. Perlmann, "Eleventh-Century Authors on the Jews of Granada," *PAAJR*, XVIII (1949), 260 f.; J. Schirmann, "Samuel Hannagid, The Man, The Soldier, The Politician," *Jewish Social Studies*, XIII (1951), 110 f.

circles. Thus, in defense of the doctrine of freedom of the will, he invoked as proofs the evidence of "reason, Scripture and tradition."[71] In defending the conditions prerequisite to the attainment of prophecy, he appealed to "common consent" (what the Latins had called *consensus omnium*, and the Arabs, *ijmā'*), i.e., of the Jewish people, who all agree on the requirements.[72] Jewish ritual practice was validated by him on the ground that faithfully transmitted data and practices are as authentic and reliable as knowledge gained by sensory perception. Thus, in keeping with the thesis spelled out in *Sefer ha-Qabbalah*, he could look upon rabbinic tradition as unimpeachable, since it derived from an "uninterrupted tradition," a system of reports and beliefs handed down from master to disciple.[73]

It will be seen that the *Sefer ha-Qabbalah* was essentially nothing but a historical excursus, the detailed evidence for Ibn Daud's contention that Judaism is validated principally by its claim to being an uninterrupted tradition, and further supported by the general consensus of its adherents. For the evidence against tradition adduced from reason, his historical work would find no use; indeed, it rejected it outright.[74] That was because the tradition is primarily a system of practices which are not *grounded* in reason but in the revealed divine command.[75] Having previously established the validity of these categories as criteria of evidence, he could then proceed to document his views by the evidence from history. Theological problems could be totally ignored in *Sefer ha-Qabbalah*, for they had already been disposed of in his philosophical treatise.

Historians of philosophy have been unanimous in pointing out that considerable portions of Ibn Daud's philosophy remained crude and were beset with problems of which he had taken no account. To a certain extent this can be attributed to his position as the Aristotelian pioneer within Judaism; perhaps, too, to his personal shortcomings as a writer and philosopher. It also may well be that for him philosophy was not so much an intellectual challenge as an avowed tool for his polemical ends. A recent study of his philosophy points out that "wherever the contradiction between religious and philosophical opinion is so plain as to be inescapable, instead of attempting to bridge the difference, he simply plays safe by staying on the religious side of the abyss without pro-

---

71 *Emunah Ramah*, p. 97; cf. Saadiah Gaon, *The Book of Beliefs and Opinions*, tr. by S. Rosenblatt (New Haven, 1948), pp. 16 f.; Heschel, *op. cit.*, pp. 10 f., 44 f.

72 *Emunah Ramah*, p. 74. On *ijma'* and Ibn Daud's invocation of the argument, cf. below, pp. LX f.

73 *Emunah Ramah*, pp. 65, 75, 78. For Muslim parallels to this argument, cf. Schreiner, *op. cit.*, pp. 628, n. 2, 629, n. 1.

74 Epilogue.134. Of course, Ibn Daud would not hesitate to invoke reason when it supported his argument; cf. below, pp. LXI f.

75 *Emunah Ramah*, p. 4. Cf. Guttmann, *Religionsphilosophie*, pp. 163 f., 180 f.

ducing a rational justification for his action."[76] In other words, his philosophy shows an unconcealed predisposition in favor of religious tradition.

In the context of Ibn Daud's work as a whole, one of the most interesting aspects of the book consists in what is usually regarded as a relatively insignificant question, namely, the date of composition of this treatise. It is occasionally stated that *al-'Aqida al-Rafi'a* was composed in 1160, without regard to the implication of the author's own statement that it was written in 4921 A.M., or 1160–1161 C.E.,[77] the very same year in which he wrote *Sefer ha-Qabbalah*.[78] If both philosophy and history were written, or issued, approximately simultaneously, it may well be that each of them was only a part of a total and integrated scheme, which we may title "The Defense of Judaism through Reason and History."

In that very same year, then, Ibn Daud wrote his history of rabbinic tradition. To this he added a brief survey of Roman history and a long account of Jewish history during the days of the Second Temple. In the case of these three tracts, Ibn Daud openly confessed that he had been motivated by polemical-apologetic considerations. At first blush, the polemics appear to have been largely submerged in historical disquisitions that had little connection with his avowed aims. However, as we shall see, all three parts of his historical writing follow a consistent pattern and, by and large, stick to their subjects as Ibn Daud construed them.

In the course of his survey of rabbinic tradition, an analysis of which we shall postpone for later chapters, Ibn Daud inserted a tangential paragraph on the correct date of Jesus the Nazarene.[79] While establishing to his own satisfaction that the Christian date for Jesus was false, and derived from anti-Jewish motives, he added a special appendix to demonstrate in detail the total unreliability of the New Testament as a source of historical evidence.

The aim of this appendix, entitled *Zikron Dibray Romi*, "A History of Rome from the Time of its Foundation until the Rise of the Muslim Empire,"[80] was

---

76 Arfa, *op. cit.*, p. 3. Cf. also Wolfson, "Classification of Sciences," pp. 313 f.
77 Weil in *Emunah Ramah*, p. 78 n. 2; Munk, *op. cit.*, p. 268; Kaufmann, *Attributenlehre*, p. 243 n. 239. The oversight doubtless derives from Weil's mistaken calculation of Ibn Daud's date for the revelation at Sinai; cf. I.82.
78 V.9–10.
79 II.95 f.
80 References to this tract and to *Malkay Bayyit Sheni* (cf. below) are to the conveniently paginated edition in *Seder 'Olam Rabba we-Seder 'Olam Zuta u-Megillat Ta'anit we-Sefer ha-Qabbalah le-ha-Rabad* (Amsterdam, 1711). However, since this edition reproduced a censored text, all quotations and data were drawn from ed. princeps of Mantua, 1514. Unfortunately, only two MSS of this work were available to me, both of them of the inferior class described in the Hebrew introduction.

to show—in reality, merely to assert—that between the crucifixion of Jesus and the writing of the New Testament there existed a hiatus of three centuries according to the Christian reckoning and of four centuries according to the Jewish one! In other words, even if one could grant that from the time of the composition of the Gospels until the twelfth century, the Christians had faithfully guarded their Scripture against textual contamination, the claims of the New Testament would gain nothing thereby; for in no way can these books claim to represent the teachings of Jesus. The New Testament was nothing but a fabrication of Constantine. Moreover, this fact was known to Constantine's contemporary, Arius, who composed a refutation of the doctrines of the New Testament, while later emperors, like Constantius and Julian, actually rejected all Christian teaching and returned to their ancestral tradition of idolatry.[81]

Since Ibn Daud ascribed the Christain Scripture to Constantine, he apparently felt called upon to place this emperor in the exact setting of Roman history.[82] Futhermore, a knowledge of Roman history was essential to the Jew if he was to understand his people's history in the fateful days of the Second Temple. Thus, the book of *Josippon*, one of Ibn Daud's prime sources, had itself begun its account of early Jewish history with a description of Roman beginnings. However, since the account of Roman history in *Josippon* was fragmentary and largely a patchwork of Roman myths, Ibn Daud corrected the Jewish data at his disposal on the basis of what he considered new and superior sources, and surveyed in outline the history of Rome from Romulus and Remus until its "end."[83]

Quite apart from mere correlation of Jewish history with Roman, there was a deeper interest on the part of the medieval Jew in the growth of the Roman Empire and the spread of Christianity. According to *Josippon* and rabbinic tradition, the fourth beast or kingdom of Daniel's vision (Dan. 7) was Rome, and

81   ZDR, f. 49a, bottom. Cf. Maimonides, *Epistle to Yemen*, p. 14 and n. 15 there, from which it will be seen that Ibn Daud shared a theory held by many. For a somewhat similar line of argument by David al-Muqammiṣ against Christian ritual, cf. L. Nemoy, "Al-Qirqisani's Account of the Jewish Sects and Christianity," *HUCA*, VII (1930), 367. For Ibn Ḥazm's rejection of Christianity on similar grounds, cf. J.W. Sweetman, *Islam and Christian Theology*, 2 parts in 3 vols. (London, 1945-55), part II, vol. I, 231 f.
82   On this device as proof of possession of authentic data, cf. below, pp. L f. That *Josippon* itself may have been composed as a Jewish retort to the *testimonium Flavianum* has been suggested by H. Lewy, "Josephus the Physician: A Medieval Legend of the Destruction of Jerusalem," *Journal of the Warburg Institute*, I (1937), 227 n. 2.
83   On *Josippon* and his theory of history, cf. Y. Baer, "Sefer Yosifon ha-'Ibri," *Sefer Dinaburg* (Jerusalem, 1949), pp. 178 f.; D. Flusser, "The Author of the Book of Josiphon: His Personality and His Age" [in Hebrew], *Zion*, XVIII (1953), 109 f. I have also dealt with Josippon's feelings on Rome at length in a paper, "Esau as Symbol in Medieval Jewish Thought," to be published in vol. IV of the *Texts and Studies* of the Lown Institute at Brandeis University.

Jews eagerly followed its growth in anticipation of its final downfall.[84] Like *Josippon*, Ibn Daud thought it pertinent to define the limits of this world empire in terms of contemporary geography, and he therefore outlined the course of the conquest of Spain by the Goths and the subsequent Christianization of the country. In doing this, Ibn Daud supplemented his Hebrew source by material from Gentile historians. Moreover, whereas *Josippon* had ended his correlation of Jewish and Roman history with the destruction of the Temple, Ibn Daud continued it down to the Muslim conquest.[85]

Of all of Ibn Daud's works, this little excursus on the history of Rome from Romulus to Reccared is the only one which in any way betrayed the new setting in which he was working. From his account as it stands, one could not have gleaned that Muslims had ever so much as set foot on the Iberian peninsula. Spain and Andalus were treated as one, the climax of the work being the spread of Christianity to the peoples of Spain. There is just a chance that the work, apart from intending to "confute" Christian claims, was also intended to serve other immediate Jewish needs. In *Sefer ha-Qabbalah*, Ibn Daud had indicated that the Jews first came to Spain in the days of Titus and had been living there ever since. Indeed, he himself was a direct descendant of the first Jewish nobles to arrive in Merida at the invitation of the Roman governor.[86] Since Merida and the other cities listed in *Zikron Dibray Romi* as having been conquered by "Theodoric, king of the Suevi," had been or were still housing major Jewish communities, this historical tract could be used for special pleading on the part of the Jews. They could now cite the evidence for their contention that in no wise should they be treated as Muslims and, therefore, as interlopers on Spanish soil. If anything, they had been there from pre-Gothic days when the king of the land "was yet an idolator."[87]

As a second appendix to his history of tradition, Ibn Daud composed *Dibray Malkay Israel be-Bayyit Sheni*, a "History of the Kings of Israel during [the

---

84 *Josippon*, ed. by H. Hominer (Jerusalem, 1956), ch. 23, p. 90; Baer, "Sefer Yosifon," pp. 179 f.—On Ibn Daud's theory of the four empires, cf. below, pp. 235 f.
85 For a brief discussion of the geographic names and etymologies in this tract, cf. M. Schwabe, "Zikron Bayt Romi," *REJ*, XXXV (1897), 287 f.—While it may be contended that Ibn Daud stopped his account at the point that his source did, the fact remains that he had easy access to information on the later history of Spain. From our Analysis and Interpretation, ch. IV, it will be seen that Ibn Daud told only as much of the history of Rome as was necessary for his own purposes.
86 VII.294 f.
87 Such arguments from precedent go back to Josephus. For a somewhat later use of this type of argument by the Jews of Narbonne, cf. the gloss to *Sefer ha-Qabbalah* in A. Neubauer, *Medieval Jewish Chronicles*, 2 vols. Oxford, (1887–95), I, 82; H. Gross, "Meir b. Simon und seine Schrift Milchemeth Mizwa," *MGWJ*, XXX (1881), 298.

Days of] the Second Temple,"[88] which consists almost exclusively of an abridgement of the pertinent sections of *Josippon*.[89] As his sources, Ibn Daud mentions "the book of Joseph the priest the son of Gorion and other reliable works,"[90] doubtless meaning by the latter the text of *Midrash 'Eser Galuyot* (Midrash on the Ten Exiles), which he incorporated at the end of his account, as well as the few facts which he drew from rabbinic literature.[91]

In this work on the remote Jewish past, Ibn Daud openly proclaimed that his eye was on the future—the messianic restoration of the Jewish people. Twice in *Sefer ha-Qabbalah* he had indicated his intention of recounting the history of the second Jewish kingdom, "because it serves as a source of great consolation."[92] The simple evidence would "refute the Sadducees, who claim that all of the consolatory passages in the Bible were fulfilled for Israel in the days of the Second Temple."[93] Once again, at the outset of his treatment of the Second Temple period, he reaffirmed his conviction that the prophecies of redemption, especially the restitution of the Davidic dynasty, could not as yet have been fulfilled.[94]

The restoration of Jewish self-government under the Persians and the later establishment of a Jewish monarchy by the Maccabees constituted no challenge to this assertion, for those had been specifically foreseen and foretold by Zechariah. To prove this, he closed his work with a midrashic analysis of the symbols in Zech. 11.4–17, which he applied to the events of the Second Temple. Accord-

---

88 Cf. above, n. 80. The title of this tract, which strictly speaking is inaccurate, may have been inspired by the expression *malkay bayyit sheni* in *Josippon*, ch. 92, p. 377; *MBSh*, f. 76a.
89 The recension of *Josippon* utilized by Ibn Daud was essentially the longer one printed in Constantinople, 1510, and thereafter reprinted many times; cf. Flusser, *op. cit.*, pp. 110 n. 4, 114 n. 24; G.D. Cohen, "The Story of Hannah and her Seven Sons in Hebrew Literature" [in Hebrew], *Mordecai M. Kaplan Jubilee Volume*, 2 vols. (New York, 1953), Hebrew vol. pp. 181, 121. However, Flusser's later contention that Ibn Daud's *Josippon* already had the interpolation on the life of Alexander deriving from the *Historia de Preliis* is not demonstrable, as far as I can see; cf. D. Flusser, "An 'Alexander Geste' in a Parma MS" [in Hebrew], *Tarbiz*, XXVI (1956–57), 166. Cf. also below, p. 170.
90 *MBSh*, f. 50a; cf. also 70b.
91 *Ibid.*, f. 77b–79a; 50a–b, where the rabbinic data on the translation of the Septuagint are incorporated. However, Baer's contention in "Sefer Yosifon," pp. 183 f., that Ibn Daud wrote his abridgement as an orthodox corrective against *Josippon*, where the latter had adopted unorthodox views, is unfounded. Ibn Daud, it will be seen, followed *Josippon* almost slavishly, even against rabbinic tradition; cf. below, pp. 170 f.
92 II.85 f.
93 Epilogue.165 f.
94 *MBSh*, f. 50a.

ingly, the Jew need not lose hope that God had forsaken His people, for a true understanding of the biblical prophecies would indicate that the wondrous events of retribution and rejuvenation were yet to come.[95]

How crucial this question was to Ibn Daud is indicated by the fact that he also singled it out in his philosophic work—as proof that God had not yet given any indication that these prophecies had come to pass, and consequently that the Jews were now in a state of complete rejection.[96] The belief that the Jews would be collectively restored from exile to freedom and to their pristine glory was a cardinal dogma of rabbinic Judaism. On this point the centuries-long controversy between Jews and Christians hinged: had the Messiah already come, or had he not yet appeared? If he had come, then Jewish persistence in the rabbinic heritage was a self-torturing mockery. Medieval Jewish literature, accordingly, abounded with affirmations of faith in the messianic fulfillment and with speculation as to how and when it would come to pass.[97] However, Ibn Daud's singling out of the Sadducees as his devil's advocate enables us to define with a fair amount of certainty the ostensible target of his attack and refutation.

"Among the Karaites of Khorasan and Jibal," the Karaite Ya'qub al-Qirqisani reported, "there are some who assert that the promised Messiah had already come and passed away, also that the Temple which the Jews hope to build is the one built by Zerubbabel and that there is going to be no other."[98] In contending with these Karaites, Saadiah had adopted three lines of retort: first, he calculated on the basis of Scripture the time of the Messiah, showing that it had not yet arrived; secondly, after an exegetical examination of the texts in question, he concluded that they indicated a period far-off and not one close at hand to the biblical speakers; finally, he cited fifteen messianic prophecies that had not yet been fulfilled, thereby showing that whatever appeared to have been fulfilled could not really be explained as messianic *fulfillment*. It has been conjectured that in this polemic Saadiah had in mind principally the Karaite Salmon b. Yeruḥim, who in his commentary on the Psalms expressed the view that "the

---

95 *Ibid.*, f. 79a–b.—Abraham ibn Ezra also explained the section in Zech. as symbolic of events that occurred in the days of the Second Temple.
96 *Emunah Ramah*, p. 77.
97 Cf. J. Even-Shmuel, *Midreshay Geulah*, 2nd ed. (Jerusalem, 1954); Halkin's introduction to Maimonides, *Epistle to Yemen*, pp. xxvi f.; A.H. Silver, *A History of Messianic Speculation in Israel* (New York, 1927), esp. chs. II and III. (Silver's statement on p. 77 that Ibn Daud's philosophical treatise "makes no mention at all of the Messiah" requires qualification in the light of the reference in the previous note.) Cf. also A.L. Williams, *Adversus Judaeos* (Cambridge, 1935), *passim* and esp. pp. 211 f.
98 Nemoy, *op. cit.*, p. 395. Cf. also p. 365, where the Christians are cited as having the same point of view. A century after Ibn Daud, the same argument was invoked by Raymund Martini; Williams, *op. cit.*, p. 253.

end" had already come and gone.⁹⁹ Be that as it may, Ibn Daud apparently heard the argument revived by Karaites in his own milieu and felt required to refute them. Jewish messianic hopes in Spain had been high in the twelfth century, and the frustration which followed the appearance and disappearance of messianic pretenders must have stirred him to reply.¹⁰⁰ In defense of the faith, he adopted the third of Saadiah's methods by testing the facts of history against the scriptural promises. The events of the Second Commonwealth, he felt, left no room for doubt that the messianic age was yet to come.¹⁰¹ To clinch his argument, he appended an interpretation of the very passage in Zechariah which Karaite exegetes had interpreted as symbolizing the disputes between Rabbanites and Karaites.¹⁰² This midrash, which may go back to Ibn Daud's *Josippon* source,¹⁰³ merely reversed the Karaite interpretation of the symbols and equated "the destructive ones" with the priests of the Second Temple, who were the progenitors of the Samaritan-Sadduceean heresy.¹⁰⁴

However, once again, Ibn Daud's survey acutally took up more than the explicitly stated issue. Since the days of the Second Temple were notorious for the proliferation of Jewish sects and heresies,¹⁰⁵ Ibn Daud utilized the opportunity to substantiate his theory—which he shared with many of his contemporaries—that the Jewish sectarians of the twelfth century had an old and consistent past. In Ibn Daud's view, the origins of Karaism were to be sought in two Jewish schisms of Second Temple days. The first was the Samaritan here-

---

99 Cf. Saadiah, *op. cit.*, ch. 8, p. 312; H. Malter, *Saadia Gaon, His Life and Works* (Philadelphia, 1921), p. 239 n. 524; and esp. B.M. Lewin, "Pirqay Peraqim mi-Milḥamot R. Saadiah Gaon," *Ginze Kedem*, VI (1944), 3 f.
100 Cf. Halkin's introduction to Maimonides, *Epistle to Yemen*, p. xxx.
101 The view that the record of history is pregnant with consolation, i.e., can help sustain the Jews in times of stress, was also expressed, albeit somewhat differently, by Maimonides, *Iggeret ha-Shemad* and *Epistle to Yemen*, pp. 8 f. The bleak past foretold by the prophets can serve as assurance that their predictions of comfort will also be realized, *ibid.*, p. 78. For the talmudic roots of this idea, cf. *B. Mak.* 24a-b.
102 Cf. S. Poznanski, "Miscellen ueber Saadja," *MGWJ*, XXXIX (1895), 446 n. 1; S. Pinsker, *Lickute Kadmoniot* (Vienna, 1860), Appendix p. 42; R. Mahler, *Karaites* [in Yiddish] (New York, 1947), pp. 323, 374.
103 *Josippon*, ch. 97, pp. 405 f. The original authorship of this sermon is still uncertain, for its substance is credited to Ibn Daud by Kimhi in his commentary on Zech. 11.14, and Kimhi certainly knew *Josippon* in the longer version. I do not understand at all the reason for the statement of Silver, *op.cit.*, p. 215 that Ibn Daud's sermon is "not authentic."
104 Ḥobelim of Zech. 11.7. For this equation, cf. immediately below on Ibn Daud's theory of the origin of Karaism.
105 *ARN*, I, 5, p. 26 (ed. Schechter); *Yer.* Sanhed. 10.6, f. 29c. Although the proof-text of the latter passage indicates that the period of the First Temple was in the mind of R. Johanan, it could well be applied to the Second, as Ibn Daud knew from his *Josippon* source. Moreover, the Talmud was full of injunctions against ways of the sectarians.

sy instigated by Sanballat the Horonite and his friends, who in bitterness over their expulsion from the Temple in Jerusalem erected a rival temple on Mount Gerizim. "This," he had stated in *Sefer ha-Qabbalah*, "was the origin of heresy."[106] Unexpressed but assumed in this account is the talmudic description of the Samaritans (Cutheans) as a sect that denied the resurrection and was consequently to be equated with the sect of Zadok and Boethus.[107] The second schism occurred when the latter two, originally disciples of Antigonus of Soko, distorted their master's statement on divine retribution and denied the existence of a world to come. Proceeding on their theory, they founded the Sadduceean sect and repaired to Mount Gerizim, where they became the doctrinal leaders of the new sect.[108] Since Sadduceeism had been defined in rabbinic literature as a system acknowledging the validity of only the written Torah,[109] medieval Jews generally designated Karaites by "sectarian" (*Min*) and "Sadducee" almost interchangeably;[110] and Ibn Daud, though he was fully aware that Karaism was a much later phenomenon, did so with reference to the Sadducees.[111] However, his anachronistic use of terms was deliberate and intended to stress his theory that Anan "the Karaite" had merely revived an old heresy which had fallen into merited disrepute as early as the destruction of the Second Temple. Moreover,

106 II.40. (I have translated a bit more freely here than in the Translation itself.)
107 Sifre Num., par. 112, p. 122 (ed. Horovitz); *B.* Sanhed. 90b (and cf. R. N.N. Rabbinovicz, *Variae Lectiones*, IX, 249); Kutim 2.8 (ed. Higger, *Seven Minor Tractates*, p. 67). The Samaritans were known for this denial to the Muslims; cf. M. Asin Palacios, *Abenhazam de Cordoba y su Historia Critica de las Ideas Religiosas* (5 vols., Madrid, 1927–32), II, 211. Ibn Daud was careful to distinguish between the two heresies of the Samaritans and of Zadok and Boethus, but he claimed that they had merged; cf. *Josippon*, ch. 5, p. 33 and ch. 29, p. 112. Thus, his confusion of the Samaritans with the Sadducees, for which he was taken to task by S. Poznanski, "Anan et ses Ecrits," *REJ*, XLIV (1902), 169, n. 6, is deliberate.
108 II.44 f.
109 Cf. *Encyclopedia Talmudit*, VII, 1 f.
110 Cf. Poznanski, "Anan et ses Ecrits," pp. 170 f.; M. Sultanski, *Zeker Ṣaddiqim*, ed. by S. Poznanski (Warsaw, 1920), Introduction, p. 9; Ahimaaz b. Paltiel, *Megillat Ahimaaz*, ed. by B. Klar (Jerusalem, 1944), p. 49, 1.6 and notes *ad loc.*, p. 173. Early Karaites were quite willing to accept this identification, although, to be sure, they saw no pejorative overtones therein; cf. Nemoy, *op. cit.*, p. 326. For later Karaite rejection of this identification, cf. J. Mann, *Texts and Studies in Jewish History and Literature*, 2 vols. (Cincinnati and Philadelphia, 1931–35), II, 295, 302 f.— Ibn Daud never once refers to the Karaites by name, but always by the epithet of *min*, sectarian or heretic. This, too, was common Rabbanite practice; cf. Goitein, "Autographs of Yehuda Hallevi," p. 409.— On Karaite possession of "Sadduceean" literature, cf. H.H. Rowley, *The Zadokite Fragments and the Dead Sea Scrolls* (Oxford, 1952), pp. 22 f.; Z. Ankori, *Karaites in Byzantium* (New York, 1959), pp. 4, 20.
111 *MBSh*, f. 55b, 56a.

even Anan's base motives were not new to him. His personal bitterness and frustration merely duplicated the identical motives of Second Temple schismatics, whose only ground for rejection of rabbinic tradition was vindictive spite.[112]

The tracing of the roots of medieval sectarianism to the schisms and heresies of the Second Temple had additional implications, particularly in the context in which the origin of heresy was narrated. In the account of *Josippon*, the history of the Jews in the days of the Second Temple, especially after the death of Alexandra Salome, constituted one long and progressive series of incidents leading to the destruction of the Temple and the shattering of whatever vestiges of Jewish self-government had remained with the Jews after the Roman conquest under Pompey. Ibn Daud found this picture perfectly appropriate to his needs, for, in keeping with his source, he described the calamities that befell the Jews as consequences of the intemperate and irresponsible behavior of the Zealots. In revolting against Rome, as every Jew knew, these "lawless ones of Israel" had acted in defiance of the rabbinic sages,[113] and thus the calamities of Jewish history could all be traced to defiance of rabbinic discipline. Although Ibn Daud was careful to distinguish between heretics and "lawless ones," in medieval Hebrew usage the distinction was often overlooked, the term "lawless ones" being used for murderers, traitors and apostates.[114] However, Ibn Daud hinted that there was a historic connection between these "lawless ones" and the heretics, for it was only after the spirit of brotherly love within the Jewish people had been disrupted through Maccabean defection to the Sadduceean heresy that their dynasty fell and the Zealots came on the scene. In other words, one defiance of Rabbinism led to another. These Zealots turned out to be the deadliest enemy of the Jews, for it was they who drove the Romans to destroy the Temple, quite against the intentions of Vespasian and Titus.[115] There can be little doubt that Ibn Daud was attempting to some extent to counteract the Karaite contention that it was the Rabbanites who were to be identified as "the lawless ones of Israel" and that, accordingly, they were the ones to be held accountable for the destruction.[116] Ibn Daud's history of the Second Temple thus reaffirmed his thesis that rabbinic control and rabbinic discipline were the only safe course for the Jews to follow. But whatever his intention in this regard, foremost in

---

112 VI.43 f. Cf. also below, pp. 155 f.
113 Cf. *ARN*, I, 4, p. 22.
114 Cf. *Josippon*, ed. by J.F. Breithaupt (Gotha, 1707), Index, *s.v.* פריצים. Jews and Karaites interpreted Daniel's use of this term as a reference to Jesus and his disciples; Maimonides, *Epistle to Yemen*, p. 12 and Halkin's note 14 there. In *ARN*, I, 5, p. 26, the heretical schism of Zadok and Boethus is described as a פרצה.
115 I.207–208; *MBSh*, p. 57a, 72a, 79b.
116 Pinsker, *Lickute Kadmoniot*, Appendix p. 101.

his mind was the thesis with which he had begun his work, to wit, that the period of the Second Temple was hardly an age of messianic fulfillment.

To his history of the destruction, Ibn Daud added the text of the Midrash on the Ten Exiles. Since, according to this tract, the final exile of the Jews by Vespasian had brought them to Spain, the account was brought home to his contemporary reader. The work closed with the sermon on Zechariah and with an expression of the traditional hope that the messianic era would soon be at hand.

Even before proceeding to a more extended treatment of *Sefer ha-Qabbalah*, we have enough information at our disposal to ask what it was that motivated this four-fold defense of Jewish tradition. So much special pleading and polemical concern manifestly reflect some contemporary challenge. Although we shall be able to appreciate the full implications of his plan only after further examination, the immediate external stimulus is apparent from the time and place themselves in which his books were composed.

Scarcely a dozen years had passed since the exile from Andalus. Grief and despair were felt and expressed by many of the refugees, and especially by those who had not managed to escape to Aragon and Castile. In the very same year that Ibn Daud was issuing his messages of consolation and reaffirmation, R. Maimon the Judge, living in seclusion in the environs of Fez, was dispatching his Epistle of Consolation to his confrères who had been given the ultimate alternative—Islam or death.[117] Not long after, Moses, his son, would formulate another message of hope and comfort, showing the way to accommodation and persistence.[118]

On all sides, in Christian territory as well as Muslim, the memory and the grief were doubtless aggravated by the taunts of Muslims, Karaites and Christians. The events of the mid-century, in Andalus and in Germany, in the Holy Land and North Africa, must have seemed to many Jews to be visible proof that Jewry had been condemned to contempt and to suffering at the hands of God and man. Were these calamities that had befallen the Jews indeed not a recurrence of the calamities that had begun with the destruction of the Temple and of Jewish government, which the Christians had claimed had come as a consequence of and punishment for the crucifixion of Jesus?[119] Toledo was the

---

117 [Maimon b. Joseph] "The Letter of Consolation of Maimun b. Joseph," ed. and tr. by L.M. Simmons, *JQR*, II (1890), 62–101, [335–368]; idem, *Iggeret ha-Neḥamah*, tr. into Hebrew by B. Klar (Jerusalem, 1944–45).

118 Moses b. Maimon, "Iggeret ha-Shemad," *Ḥemdah Genuzah* (ed. by H. Edelmann, Koenigsberg, 1856), pp. 74 f.; a recent edition with commentary is available in *Rambam la-'Am*, XX (Jerusalem, 1959–60), 29 f.

119 II.105. For Arab taunts and humiliations, cf. M.S. Munk, *Notice sur Joseph Ben-Iehouda* (Paris, 1842), p. 45. A.S. Halkin, "Le-Toledot ha-Shemad Bimay ha-al-Muwaḥḥidin,"

center of the great Christian revival in Spain, and there can be little doubt that the vigorous Cluniac propaganda that was being disseminated there included also the rehearsal of this old Christian proof of the rejection of the Jews.[120] No, said Ibn Daud, the truth will yet be proved; the consolation is still to come. The Almighty, who had chastized, had also prepared the balm of healing by preparing the road in northern Spain and in southern France. It was the duty of the Jew to hold staunchly to his faith and to rebuild his new community in the image of old Cordova. Arabic and Hebrew could flourish in the north no less than in the south. The courtier and the rabbi, by no means new to Christian Spain, could again join hands to erect the edifice that had flourished for centuries in glorious Andalus. Judah ibn Ezra's power, money and loyalties—displayed lavishly and lovingly on behalf of the refugees from the south—could, in alliance with the Ibn Megashes, recapture the atmosphere of Ibn Albalia and al-Fasi. The poetry and the philosophy, the sciences and the Torah could display the same harmony on the shores of the Tagus as they had on the Guadalquivir.[121]

Strangely enough, of all of Ibn Daud's works, the least original one, his abridgement of *Josippon*, was the first to be translated into a European language and became the one best known to European Christian readers, although its author's name was soon forgotten.[122] In Hebrew literature, the work along with the history of Rome was largely neglected in favor of the longer and more "authoritative" *Josippon*. The history of Rome was of even lesser value than the abridgement of the *Josippon* to Jewish and Christian readers, who, if they were interested, had access to much better and more accurate sources. The only section which occasionally attracted special attention was the sermon on Zechariah, which was appended to a number of manuscripts of *Sefer ha-Qabbalah* and even to *Josippon*'s history.[123]

The Joshua Starr Memorial Volume (New York, 1953), pp. 106 f. Though the taunts of the Karaites are not on record, they can be seen from between the lines of *Sefer ha-Qabbalah* itself; cf. also below, p. XLV n. 6. For expressions of Jewish despondency and grief in Spain from the time of the second Crusade, cf. Schirmann, "Life of Jehuda ha-Levi," pp. 235 f.; Baer, "Political Situation of the Spanish Jews," p. 7.

120 For the history of this debate, with particular reference to Jewish government, cf. A. Poznanski, *Schiloh* (Leipzig, 1904); for Peter the Venerable, cf. pp. 349 f. The theme of Jewish suffering as proof of divine rejection had only shortly before been reiterated in Spain by the Jewish apostate Petrus Alfonsi; cf. G.D. Cohen, "The Story of the Four Captives," *PAAJR*, XXIX (1960–61), 79 f.

121 VII.465 f.; Epilogue.86 f.

122 Cf. Steinschneider, *Die Geschichtsliteratur der Juden*, pp. 47 f. for a partial list of translations and editions.

123 Cf. Hebrew introduction and above, n. 103.

His philosophical work suffered an even worse fate. Although translated into Hebrew twice, the book was almost completely ignored until the nineteenth century, having been displaced by the masterpiece of Moses Maimonides. Only with the rise of modern scholarship was it rediscovered and studied, but chiefly as the bridge from Saadiah and Gabirol to Maimonides and the Aristotelians of the thirteenth century.

By contrast, his *Sefer ha-Qabbalah*, if by no means a best seller, enjoyed a steady history of manuscript transmission and publication in print.[124] Since it covered the same ground that the Epistle of R. Sherira Gaon had and much more, told its story in a simple Hebrew style, and focused its sights exclusively on the history of rabbinic tradition, it largely displaced older and historically more reliable works and quickly became a classic source for medieval Jewish history. Ibn Daud's public, of course, largely disregarded his claim that this work was actually but one part of a trilogy. *Sefer ha-Qabbalah* contained not only the essential information that most interested the Jewish reading public; it also gave fullest expression to the *Weltanschauung* uniting Jews of purely rabbinic orientation with those whose studies had been exposed to the challenge of philosophy. Accordingly, it quickly began to circulate as a separate work, and has been read as such to the present day.

To the modern student, his data and narrative are most interesting for the point of view for which they were supposed to win adherents. We must now turn to a closer examination of the background of the work before us and the challenge that it sought to meet.

---

124 Cf. Hebrew introduction.

III. *SEFER HA-QABBALAH* AND ITS HISTORICAL BACKGROUND

As we have already indicated, Ibn Daud composed his *Sefer ha-Qabbalah* to prove from history that rabbinic tradition constituted the attested fulfillment of the revelation in Scripture. The proof afforded by the evidence of history was to him obvious and irrefutable. By providing a detailed enumeration of Jewish teachers from earliest times until the twelfth century, coupled with full chronological data and relevant historical background, Ibn Daud demonstrated that the Rabbanites possessed a complete and accurate record of the history of their non-scriptural tradition. Moreover, since this survey traced the roots of this tradition to the days of Moses and Joshua, the Karaite contention that rabbinic tradition was a late fabrication, an innovation totally lacking the attestation of antiquity of Scripture, was automatically invalidated. Conversely, since the Rabbanites of Andalus and Toledo could trace their genealogy, spiritual as well as familial, to the acknowledged leaders of Jewry and Judaism in ancient times, they represented the legitimate body of authority over the Jewish community and the authentic arbiters of its faith and practices.

Both in content as well as in method, Ibn Daud's treatise followed closely the plan of defense and attack long previously developed by religious apologists of Judaism, Christianity and Islam. To the learned reader the work contained no essential surprises. The Karaite diatribe and the Rabbanite counterattack had been expounded and rehearsed on both sides of the fence for several centuries. Indeed, even for "the students" to whom the work was ostensibly addressed, Ibn Daud could with confidence refer to Karaite attacks obliquely and cryptically, for they were well known in all Arabic-Jewish circles. If the work presents any enigma to the modern—for example, in its insistence on having proved an unchanged and unadulterated tradition merely by listing a string of authorities and their successors—it is precisely owing to the tacit assumptions underlying its patterns of thought and argument, which were an integral part of the intellectual milieu of his day and which are quite alien to ours.

The Karaite Challenge[1]

All shades of Karaite opinion maintained that rabbinic Judaism, with its laws, customs and dogmas, was a fabrication of the rabbis of the Talmud, which had

---

1 The following summary treats only the dogmatic side of the Karaite polemic against Rab-

no warrant or attestation in the divine revelation to Moses and the prophets who succeeded him. In the face of Scripture's explicit injunction against adding to, or subtracting from, any of its commandments (Deut. 4.2, 12.1), the rabbis had composed, and their disciples preserved, a vast corpus of rites and beliefs that were nothing but human invention. The following facts, the Karaites held, were proof of this contention: 1) Scripture itself gave no indication that any laws not recorded in it are to be enacted and fulfilled; in other words, the so-called "Oral Torah," the Mishna and its cognate literature, was merely human legislation, not of Mosaic or prophetic origin. 2) The rabbis of the Talmud often flatly contradicted the explicit provisions of Scripture by the type of practice which they ordained; e.g., though the Bible had expressly forbidden the use of fire in Jewish homes on the Sabbath,[2] the rabbis established that the day should be ushered in by the kindling of "Sabbath lights."[3] 3) The rabbis themselves betrayed the falsehood of their tradition by the countless and endless disputes among them on the correct application of the prescriptions of the Torah, and, what is more, by the flagrant differences in practice between them. If talmudic law was indeed of divine origin, why was it not as anonymous and as peremptory as the law of Moses; why, on virtually every point, did one find that the school of Hillel, for example, ordained one form of practice and the school of Shammai the very opposite? 4) The Rabbanite claim to be heir to the Mosaic-prophetic tradition was not attested by the common consensus of Jews, for while all Jews testified by their agreement on the divinity of Scripture to the validity of its commands, the same consensus of opinion did not obtain with regard to rabbinic law.

In arguing thus from Scripture and reason, the Karaites invoked the terms commonly employed in the religious discussions of the Muslim world; *bid'a* (innovation), *'ijma'* (consensus of opinion), *kufr* (unbelief), and *khilaf* (transgression, violation). The sum total of their polemic against rabbinic Judaism was an implied charge of blasphemy because of the latter's implication that God would ordain one thing and change His mind by commanding another.[4] Virtually every Jewish apologist in the Muslim world had to take up the cudgels

---

binism. For fuller treatment of this subject as well as analyses of the social elements underlying the conflict and with full references to the earlier literature, cf. L. Nemoy, *Karaite Anthology* (New Haven, 1952); Ankori, *Karaites in Byzantium*; Baron, *SRH*, V, 209 f. and Index vol., s.v. Karaites and Karaism.
2 Ex. 35.3.
3 Cf. Prologue.19–21.
4 On Jewish sensitivity to this charge, cf. above p. xxx, text to n. 67.

INTRODUCTION   XLV

against this formidable doctrinal attack,[5] since from Karaite circles the arguments against Rabbinism spread to Muslim and Christian polemicists, who, in turn, hurled them at the Jews.[6]

---

5   The literature of Rabbanite polemic against Karaism is enormous, reflecting the seriousness of the challenge. For the literature and arguments up until the time of Ibn Daud, cf. Ankori, *op. cit.*; Baron, *SRH*, V, 275 f.; H. Malter, S*aadia Gaon*, p. 260; S. Poznanski, "Jacob ben Ephraim, ein Antikaraeischer Polemiker des X. Jahrhunderts," *Gedenkbuch zur Erinnerung an David Kaufmann* (Breslau, 1900), pp. 167 f.; A. Freimann, "Meschullam b. Kalonymos' Polemik gegen die Karaeer," *Judaica: Festschrift zu Hermann Cohen's siebzigstem Geburtstage* (Berlin, 1912); A.S. Halkin, "A Fragment of Saadyah's Introduction to the Commentary on the Pentateuch" [in Hebrew], *Louis Ginzberg Jubilee Volume*, 2 vols. (New York, 1945), Hebrew vol., pp. 129 f.; Zucker, *op. cit.*, where references will be found also to his various papers in which much new material has been brought to light. Cf. also below, n. 18.
6   Cf. I. Goldziher, "Proben muhammedanischer Polemik, etc.," p. 102, n. 16; F. Baer, "Abner aus Burgos," *Korrespondenzblatt des Vereins zur Gruendung und Erhaltung einer Akademie fuer die Wissenschaft des Judentums* (1929), pp. 28–30 (and cf. S. Grayzel, *The Church and the Jews in the XIIIth Century* [Philadelphia, 1933], pp. 339–340). The striking similarity between Ibn Ḥazm's attacks on Jewish mystical tracts (cf. Asin Palacios, *Abenhazam de Cordoba*, II, 385–392) and those of the Karaites has been analyzed in detail by S. Lieberman, *Shkiin* (Jerusalem, 1938), pp. 11–18. Although the Muslims and Christians seized not so much on the doctrinal attack of Karaism on Rabbinism as on the former's abuse of rabbinic *aggadah*—angelology, mystical references to the deity, anthropomorphism, etc.—they did not entirely omit the attack on the foundations of Rabbinism. For a summary of the Muslim polemic, which although published a few years after *Sefer ha-Qabbalah* drew on the whole tradition of the Muslim attack on Rabbinism, see Samau'al-Maghribi, "Ifham al-Yahud," ed. and tr. by M. Perlmann, *PAAJR*, XXXII (1964).—In earlier studies, Perlmann questioned the Karaite origin of the early Muslim polemic against Judaism, arguing from the fact, which he demonstrated, that one of the more outspoken Muslim polemicists of the twelfth century, Ibn Qayyim, drew his anti-Jewish diatribe from Samau'al al-Maghribi; cf. M. Perlmann, "Ibn Qayyim and Samau'al al-Maghribi," *Journal of Jewish Bibliography*, III (1942), 71 f.; *idem*, "Eleventh Century Andalusian Authors on the Jews of Granada," pp. 278 f. However, I do not see that Perlmann's evidence really undermines the explanation accepted ever since Goldziher first attributed some of these arguments, specifically Ibn Ḥazm's diatribes against Rabbinism and rabbinic angelology, to Karaite parentage. In the first place, the Christians, whom Perlmann considers the real source of the non-Samau'alite arguments, would not have found angelology objectionable in principle. Moreover, Perlmann ignored the detailed analysis of the Karaite attacks against *aggadah* in Lieberman's study. Finally, the material published by Perlmann himself points to some Karaite influence on the Muslim polemicists, for they consistently invoked Karaite-style arguments against the reliability of rabbinic tradition, pointed to Karaism as evidence against rabbinic claims and, interestingly enough, always treated the Karaites a lot more gently than they did the Rabbanites; cf. Perlmann, "Eleventh Century Andalusian Authors," pp. 276 f.; Samau'al al-Maghribi, *op. cit.*, pp. 36 f., 56 f., 67 f.

Karaism in Spain

From its original home in Iraq, Karaism quickly spread to Syria and Palestine, Egypt, Byzantium and Spain.[7] Virtually nothing is known of how early the new sect struck root in Spanish soil. However, even the scanty evidence available makes it fairly clear that Ibn Daud's contention that the heresy was introduced into Spain by Abu'l-Taras in the eleventh century was not only strictly incorrect, but probably a deliberate simplification to fit a schematological—and, accordingly, all the more suspect—mould for explaining the dissemination of a way of life.[8] In reality, Karaism had had much older roots and a firmer base in Spain than Ibn Daud was willing to admit.

The Spanish Muslim encyclopedist and theologian Ibn Ḥazm (994–1064), in his review of the various Jewish sects, has this to say of the Karaites: "The Ananites are the adherents of Anan, descendant of David, of the tribe of Judah whom the Jews call Karaites and heretics. Their teaching forbids the transgression of the laws of the Torah and of what is enjoined in the books of the prophets, peace be on them. However, the doctrines of the rabbis, whom they regard as falsifiers, they reject outright. This sect inhabits Iraq, Egypt, and Syria. Within Spain they live in Toledo and Talavera."[9] Ibn Ḥazm, writing not later than 1064, thus spoke of this sect as a settled and recognizable community. This would be most unusual, if, as Ibn Daud would have us believe, the community was the exclusive product of Abu'l-Taras' activity not long before Ibn Daud's own day.

An interesting sidelight is shed on this conclusion by the report of R. Natronai Gaon (*ca.* 853-856) that he had learned about Anan's book of laws from Eleazar Alluf of Lucena.[10] If the Spanish rabbi had seen the Ananite work in his native land, Karaism must have spread to Spain by the middle of the ninth cen-

---

[7] Cf. S. Poznanski, "Reshit Hityashbut ha-Qaraim bi-Jerusalem," *Jerusalem*, ed. by A.M. Luncz, X (1913), 83 f.; J. Mann, *The Jews in Egypt and in Palestine Under the Fatimid Caliphs*, 2 vols (Oxford, 1920–22), index, s.v. Karaites; *idem, Texts and Studies*, esp. vol. II; Ankori, *op. cit.*, pp. 58 f.

[8] Epilogue. 47 f.—For an analysis of this story and a convincing rejection of its reliability, cf. Z. Ankori, "Elijah Bashyachi: An Inquiry into His Traditions," pp. 44 f., 63, 183 f.; *idem, Karaites in Byzantium*, pp. 34 f.

[9] Asin Palacios, *op. cit.*, II, 211; Perlmann, "Eleventh Century Andalusian Authors," p. 280.

[10] *Seder R. Amram Gaon*, 2 vols. (Warsaw, 1865), I, 38a; *Seder R. Amram ha-Shalem*, ed. by L. Frumkin, 2 vols. (Jerusalem, 1912), II, 207; B.M. Lewin, *Otzar ha-Geonim*, 13 vols. (Haifa-Jerusalem, 1928–43), III (Pesaḥim), 89 f. On Eleazar Alluf, cf. M. Margalioth, *Hilkhot Hannagid* (Jerusalem, 1962), pp. 4 f.

tury. Moreover, if there was any justice to the accusation of Dunash b. Labrat against his rival Menahem b. Saruq that the latter had been corrupted by Ananite ideas,[11] we would have a further confirmation of its presence in tenth-century Spain. Ibn Ḥazm's thorough familiarity with Karaite arguments against Rabbinism makes it probable that he had conversed with Karaites at first hand and had known them well.

Ibn Ḥazm's testimony is confirmed by his Jewish contemporary, Samuel ibn Nagrela (993–ca.1056). In a legal discussion concerning the ritual of reading the Torah, Ibn Nagrela took exception to a certain practice as being purely sectarian. "Now, there was never any sectarian practice among them [i.e., the Jews of Spain]," he claimed, "except in a number of villages near the land of Edom [i.e., Christian Spain]. These people are reported to have secret sectarian leanings, but they deny this. Our ancestors flogged some of them... who died as a consequence of the punishment."[12] Ibn Nagrela's statement thus confirms Ibn Ḥazm's report on the area of Karaite concentration in Spain. Furthermore, his admission that cryptic sectarians were known to his ancestors would place them back at least fifty years, i.e., as early as 1000 C.E. In the light of the evidence surveyed up to this point, it appears much more plausible to suggest that a community of long standing had by the end of the eleventh century mustered sufficient vigor and courage to come out of hiding.

At best, then, Ibn Daud's account can only help to explain the renascence of Karaism in Spain in the middle of the eleventh century. Until that time, apparently, Karaism had been totally inconsequential there, But around 1050, a Castilian Jew of Rabbanite upbringing, Abu'l-Taras, went to Jerusalem and was converted to Karaism by the renowned Karaite legalist, commentator and philosopher, Abu'l-Faraj Furqan ibn Asad (known in Hebrew as Yeshu'ah b. Judah).[13] From a recently discovered letter of 1053, we know that Abu'l-Taras was not the only Spanish "Rabbanite" to go to Palestine at that time and "convert" to Karaism. That at least two other "Rabbanites" from Toledo went there and openly adopted Karaism[14] suggests that the Karaite community of Spain had been compelled to go underground to some extent but that it had not by any means been eliminated.[15]

---

11 Cf. Dunash b. Labrat, *Teshubot*, ed. by H. Filipowski (London, 1855), p. 75; S.D. Luzzatto, *Bet ha-Oṣar*, 3 vols. (Lemberg, Przemysl, Cracow, 1847–49), I, 34b f.; Pinsker, *Lickute Kadmoniot*, Appendix, pp. 163 f.; Poznanski, "Anan et ses Ecrits," pp. 192 f.; Baron, *SRH*, VII, 21 f.
12 Judah b. Barzillai al-Barceloni, *Sefer ha-'Ittim*, ed. by J. Schorr (Cracow, 1903), p. 267.
13 Cf. n. 8.
14 S. Assaf, *Meqorot u-Meḥqarim be-Toledot Israel* (Jerusalem, 1946), pp. 106 f.
15 Ibn Nagrela himself conceded that the Karaites had recouped some of their strength in his own day; cf. Samuel ibn Nagrela, *Diwan* (ed. Habermann), I, part 1, p. 98.

The situation seems to have been reversed with Abu'l-Taras' return home. Armed with zeal and apparently with no little ability, he circulated one of his Palestinian master's works in Castile and won new adherents.[16] After his death, his followers elected his widow as their teacher (*Mu'allima*). They could no longer be overlooked. However, their growth was sharply checked around 1090 by Joseph ibn Ferrizuel Cidellus, physician to Alfonso VI, king of Castile, when the Jewish courtier expelled them from all but one of the cities of his country, and later on in 1147 by similar acts on the part of Judah ibn Ezra Almoxarif. Thanks to the activities of these two pious officials, Ibn Daud assures us, the Karaites were steadily decreasing in number.[17]

That this last statement was not altogether free of wishful thinking is indicated by the gradually increasing familiarity and concern of Rabbanite authors with Karaite doctrines and exegesis. Judah ibn Bal'am, Judah b. Barzillai, Moses ibn Ezra, Judah ha-Levi, Joseph ibn Zaddik and Abraham ibn Ezra[18] all cite Karaite practice and literature and occasionally mention conversations with Karaites themselves.[19] Clearly, Karaism had by then come out into the open, and its literature was available for study and criticism. Indeed, some exchange of information must have come through direct discussion, for the acerbity of official or public polemic did not always interfere with the maintaining of cordial relations between Rabbanites and Karaites, any more than it affected the normal relationships of Jews, Christians and Muslims.[20]

Despite Ibn Daud's assurances that the sect had been suppressed, a violent outbreak between Rabbanites and Kariates occurred some seventeen years after his writing in the northern city of Carrion where, it would seem, the Karaites had even been able to compel the Rabbanites to conform publicly to Karaite Sabbath prohibitions. In the dispute that ensued, the aid of the Karaite leader of Burgos was invoked, indicating that the sect was by no means restricted to one community. Once again the Karaites were suppressed by the strong-armed activities of Alfonso IX's royal physician, Joseph Alfacar. At the end of the

---

16 Cf. n. 8. For a list of Ibn Ezra's references to Abu'l-Faraj's Bible commentary, cf. Poznanski, "Reshit Hityashbut ha-Qaraim," p. 108 n. 1.

17 Epilogue.57 f., 119 f. Cf. also Baer, *History of the Jews in Christian Spain*, I, 51, 65, 77.

18 Cf. Poznanski, "Anan et ses Ecrits," *REJ*, XLV (1902), 193 f.; Judah b. Barzillai, *Commentar zum Sefer Jezira* [in Hebrew], ed. by S.J. Halberstamm (Berlin, 1885), p. 13 and cf. above, n. 12; Baer, "Abner aus Burgos," p. 30; S. Horovitz, "Der Mikrokosmos des Josef ibn Saddik," *Jahres-Bericht des Juedisch-Theologischen Seminars Fraenckel'scher Stiftung* (Breslau, 1903), pp. 44, 47, 72; M. Friedlaender, *op. cit.*, pp. 109 f., 116, 125 f., 145 n. 1; P.R. Weiss, "Ibn Ezra, the Karaites and the Halakah" [in Hebrew], *Melilah*, I, (1944), 35 f., II (1946), 121 f., III–IV (1950), 188 f.

19 Goitein, "Autographs of Yehuda Hallevi," p. 409.

20 Cf. Moses ibn Ezra's revealing personal anecdote in *Shirat Israel*, p. 56.

thirteenth century, however, Moses de Leon was still combatting the "Sadducees" in the northern parts of the country, although a century earlier Todros Abulafia had been credited with having uprooted them.[21]

In the light of all this evidence, it does not require too much theorizing to find the immediate stimulus for Ibn Daud's anti-sectarian polemic. Ibn Daud, it will be recalled, was now living in Toledo, and all reports confirm that it was in the vicinity of that city that the Karaites were concentrated. The sect may well have shown signs of recouping its strength and of making overtures to the ruling powers to grant them the same autonomous privileges accorded to the Rabbanite community. If that was the case, Ibn Daud, as spokesman of the Rabbanite community, seized the occasion to motivate his chronicle with a cause on which all Rabbanites would be in accord. As we shall soon see, Ibn Daud had other motives in mind as well, but these would gain a readier hearing if the cause of piety underlay everything else. Anti-Karaism, as Yitzhak Baer has noted, was one of the enduring policies of the Jewish courtier class of the north.[22] As a disciple and adherent of that class, Ibn Daud seized upon its program as the stimulus for, and framework of, his treatise.

How much direct contact Ibn Daud himself had with Karaites or their literature is difficult to say. In all, he mentioned six names: Anan, his son Saul, Qirqisani, Abu'l-Faraj, Abu'l-Taras and his wife.[23] Of Karaite literature, he claimed acquaintance only with one work of Abu'l-Faraj, namely his commentary on the Pentateuch.[24] His charge that Abu'l-Faraj was virtually unique among Karaites in having composed a book[25] either feigned or demonstrated a profound ignorance of the wealth of Karaite literature that was accessible to his Rabbanite Spanish contemporaries.[26] That Ibn Daud had been both irked and influenced by the encyclopedic scholar Qirqisani, perhaps by way of Abu'l-Faraj, is fairly clear from his diatribe against him. The conclusion forces itself on us that Ibn Daud deliberately chose to ignore any more exact information and based his judgment on what he saw of Abu'l-Faraj's work and on what he had heard of Abu'l-Taras' activity. Naturally he did not trouble himself about fine distinctions between Anan and his successors, who, as Karaites, had

---

21   I. Loeb, "Polémistes Chrétiens et Juifs en France et en Espagne," *REJ*, XVIII (1889) 60 f.; *idem*, "Notes sur l'Histoire des Juifs," *ibid.*, XIX (1890), 206 f.; Joseph b. Todros Abulafia, "Iggeret," ed. by S.J. Halberstamm, *Jeschurun*, ed. by J. Kobak, VIII (1872–75), Hebrew section, p. 41.
22   Cf. above, n. 17.
23   II.21–22, 146; VI.43 f.; Epilogue.16–17, 47 f.
24   Epilogue.130 f.
25   *Ibid.*, 124 f.
26   Cf. above, nn. 1, 18.

in many ways modified his teachings. To Ibn Daud they were all of a piece—heretics, Sadducees.²⁷

Earlier Histories of Tradition

In his lost exegetical work, Ibn Daud probably employed the time-honored Rabbanite method of refuting Karaite legal interpretations of Scripture by displaying the textual-philological unsoundness of their interpretations. One aspect of this Rabbanite argument was to demonstrate that Scripture itself implied the existence of an "oral" key to its text by speaking only in broad categories while omitting obviously essential details. Ibn Daud mentioned this argument in his chronicle in passing.²⁸ However, as his main weapon of defense of Rabbinism, he exploited a method that had been employed by his precursors but never so fully and exhaustively as in his own work. That method is the Muslim technique of "attestation," i.e., authenticating a tradition or practice (Arabic: *isnad al-ḥadith*) by scrutinizing the process of its transmission.²⁹

Since virtually all of Islam's extra-Quranic tradition was dependent on the veracity of the informants, the Muslim experts on *ḥadith* came to regard history, and above all biography, as a handmaiden of dogmatics and theology. Accordingly, they leaned heavily on biographical study as a method of verifying the corpus of Muslim traditions. "According to the Muslim view, a tradition can only be considered credible when its *isnad* offers an unbroken series of reliable authorities."³⁰ In connection with the *isnad*, Muslim scholars investigated each authority—when and where he flourished, who were his masters, disciples and friends—and classified them into various categories (*tabaqat*): friends of the prophet, friends of the friends, etc., and later by discipleship, profession and locale.³¹ "If a tradition can be traced through an unbroken chain of trustworthy authorities to a companion of the prophet, it is usually called *musnad* ("supported"). If it also contains special observations regarding all the authorities (e.g., if it is expressly mentioned that all the authorities swore an oath as they handed on the tradition, or that they all gave one another the

27 Cf. *ibid.* For the latest and most thorough examination of the stages in the development of Karaism, cf. Zucker, *op. cit.*, pp. 143 f.
28 I.92 f.
29 Cf. H.A.R. Gibb and J.N. Kramers, eds., *Shorter Encyclopedia of Islam* (Leiden, 1953), pp. 116 f., s.v. *Hadith*; J. Schacht, *The Origins of Muslim Jurisprudence* (Oxford, 1950), pp. 3 f. For an excellent early example of such a Muslim work on the principles of attestation, cf. Al-Ḥakim Abu 'Abdallah Muhammad b. 'Abdallah al-Naisaburi, *An Introduction to the Science of Tradition*, ed. and tr. by J. Robson (London, 1953).
30 Gibb and Kramers, *op. cit.* pp. 117.
31 Cf. F. Rosenthal, *A History of Muslim Historiography* (Leiden, 1952), pp. 34, 43 n. 1, 83, 331 f.

hand), the tradition is called *musalsal*...."³² The influence of these categories on Ibn Daud's work is apparent in almost every line of *Sefer ha-Qabbalah*, and their relation to earlier Jewish tradition calls for precise delimitation.

As J. Horovitz noticed, the *isnad* method of authenticating a tradition bears a distinct resemblance to the talmudic style in which laws and homiletical traditions are quoted by an authority in the name of one or more earlier teachers.³³ On occasion, a variant chain is offered in the Talmud for the very same statement, with no other intention than that of establishing who the earlier authorities were. However, although precision in the attribution of statements is validated in rabbinic literature on obvious ethical grounds,³⁴ there was a much older technical reason, which was paradoxically more closely related to later Muslim method than was the one of purely ethical considerations. For a practice to be ritually valid, it had to be supported by tradition; innovation was in Judaism, as in other religions, anathema. Hence, individual rabbis as well as whole schools in Judaism constantly gave their religious pedigree when the authenticity of their statements was in question.³⁵ The classic instance of this type of religious chain is the one in the opening chapter of the Ethics of the Fathers (*Abot*), which begins with Moses and proceeds to enumerate those who succeeded him as recipients of the Oral Law. Except in rare instances, however, no attempt was made by the rabbis to trace particular traditions back through their detailed chains of transmission. The usual practice was for an authority to report a statement in the name of one or more sources, and that was sufficient. Nor does any need seem to have been felt for drawing up a complete chronological or classificatory list of authorites. The first such detailed schemata to appear in Jewish literature date from Muslim times and appear to bear the influence of Muslim methodology.

It is of little import whether the highly developed Muslim method of footnoting derives from Jewish influence or represents an independent parallel development.³⁶ The fact remains that the Muslim method of full and detailed religious genealogy lent itself to Jewish appropriation without any feeling on the

---

32 Gibb and Kramers, *op. cit.*, p. 118; cf. also Schacht, *op. cit.*, pp. 11 f., 17.
33 J. Horovitz, "Alter und Ursrung des Isnad," *Der Islam*, VIII (1917), 47.
34 *M.* Abot 6.6. (= *Pereq Qinyan Torah*); *B.* Ber. 4b. (beg.).
35 For individuals, cf. *M.* Pe'ah 2.6; 'Eduyot 1.6, 5.7, 8.7; *B.* Ber. 27b, Yoma 66b. For schools, cf. L. Finkelstein, *Mabo le-Massektot Abot ve-Abot d'Rabbi Nathan* (New York, 1950), pp. 5 f. For the Greek origins of these supporting "chains," cf. E. Bickerman, "La Chaine de la Tradition Pharisienne," *Revue Biblique*, LIX (1952), 44 f.
36 Cf. Horovitz, *loc.cit.*; Rosenthal, *op. cit.*, p. 83.—Every civilization preserves, or fabricates, some genealogical attestation of the families and/or traditions which it seeks to legitimate; B. Malinowski, *Magic, Science and Religion and Other Essays* (New York, 1954), pp. 67 f. On the role of attestation in the polemic between Judaism, Christianity

part of Jews that they were taking over anything new. Did not the Talmud itself contain chronological chains and require the reporting of a statement in the name of its author?[37]

The two outstanding lists of the bearers of tradition from gaonic, i.e., Muslim, times are the *Seder Tannaim wa-Amoraim*[38] and the Epistle of R. Sherira Gaon.[39] Composed probably in the year 885, i.e., more than a century after the composition of the earliest works of Muslim *isnad*,[40] the *Seder Tannaim wa-Amoraim* is divided into two sections: the first contains lists of the authorities of tradition from Moses until the end of the saboraic period; the second enumerates a series of rules for the identification of anonymous or pseudonymous statements and, above all, the rules for deciding between conflicting views recorded in the Talmud. The first section, namely the list and chronology of authorities, is obviously ancillary to the second, with its rules for legal decision in which the chronological sequence of authorities plays an important role. Particularly significant is the fact that a number of these rules are not to be found in talmudic literature and obviously date from saboraic or early gaonic times. The coincidence of its publication with the period when the challenge of Karaism was first confessed by Rabbanite leaders makes it impossible to dismiss the work simply as a manifestation of talmudic systematization. An attempt at *isnad* is patent throughout in the effort not only to systematize but also to legitimize legal codification.[41]

Not long after this, the first explicit effort at demonstrating the authenticity of rabbinic tradition by tracing its chain of transmission was made by R. Saadiah Gaon. In the second part of his polemical *Sefer ha-Galuy*, he elucidated the chronology of the biblical period and of the following five centuries during which rabbinic tradition had been transmitted orally. This chronology, he stated in his introduction, will prove that the Mishna and Talmud were "*transmitted orally without interruption* until the time of their commitment to writing."[42]

---

and Islam in the Middle Ages, cf. the apposite remarks of Y. Kaufmann, *Golah we-Nekar*, 2 vols (Tel Aviv, 1929–32), I. 318 f. Cf. also below, n. 66.

37   For the various ancient traditions on the correct practice, cf. S. Lieberman, *Hayerushalmi Kiphshuto* (Jerusalem, 1934), pp. 20 f.

38   *Seder Tannaim we-Amoraim* ed, and tr. into German by K. Kahan (Frankfurt a.M., 1935) (henceforth referred to as *STW*).

39   Sherira Gaon, *Iggeret R. Schirera Gaon in franzoesicshen und spanischen Version*, ed. by B.M. Lewin (Haifa, 1921) (henceforth referred to as *ISG*).

40   Cf. L. Ginzberg, *Geonica*, 2 vols. (New York, 1909), I, 177; *STW*, p. xii; Horovitz, *op. cit.*, pp. 39 f.; Schacht, *op. cit.*, p. 37.

41   Cf. Poznanski's introduction to Sultanski, *op. cit.*, p. 28; Ginzberg, *op. cit.*, I, 111, 122 f.

42   A. Harkavy, *Zikron la-Rishonim*, 6 vols. (St. Petersburg and Berlin, 1879–1903), V, 152. 153 194, 268 f.; H. Malter, "Saadiah Studies," *JQR*, NS, III (1912–13), 491, 497. The

In other words, no one could bring the charge against Judaism that a hiatus of fifteen centuries existed between the supposed authorship of the Oral Law and its commitment to writing.⁴³ Saadiah, the arch-foe of Karaism, insisted (on one occasion, that of the calendar, even *ad absurdum*) on the antiquity of the tradition, and even claimed antiquity for such questionable texts as "The Scroll of the Hasmoneans."⁴⁴ In line with Muslim practice, he, too, invoked the general consensus of the Jews as sufficient proof of every authentic tradition.⁴⁵

In 986, a little over half a century after Saadiah's work, R. Sherira Gaon of Pumbeditha dispatched his famous Epistle to Jacob b. Nissim ibn Shahin of Qairawan in reply to the latter's question: "How was the Mishna compiled?"⁴⁶ Though the reason for this query is nowhere stated, B.M. Lewin adduced strong evidence in support of his explanation that here, too, the Karaite challenge played the decisive role.⁴⁷ Certainly the question was understood in that sense by Sherira, who proceeded to explain the method of the rabbinic legal literature (in Arabic terms: how we arrive at our *sunna*), and then to give a systematic chronological list of the bearers of tradition from the days of Hillel to his own time. That Jacob b. Nissim requested, and that Sherira wrote, an account of the Babylonian geonim down to the year of his writing is best explained by their desire to demonstrate the unbroken chain of tradition which the Rabbanites possessed. The accurate data which he could adduce about the lives of his forebears, his frank admission of the lack of chronological data where he did not have any, and his ability to classify each authority in relation to the other as master, disciple and colleague provided, as far as Rabbanites were concerned, overwhelming evidence of the authenticity of their claims (in Arabic terms: *ḥadith musalsal*).⁴⁸ That Sherira had accepted many of the categories employed in the intellectual circles of this milieu is shown by his attempt on another occasion to validate particular forms of rabbinic practice by invoking the "consensus of opinion" on how a rite should be practiced.⁴⁹

There can be little doubt that the Rabbanites seized eagerly on this type of "scientific" proof. In the eleventh century, Nissim b. Jacob of Qairawan, the

translation given in the text is Malter's. Cf. also S. Atlas and M. Perlmann, "Saadia on the Scroll of the Hasmoneans," *PAAJR*, XIV (1944), 6/7, line 14.
43 For the force of this argument, cf. above, pp. XXXII f.
44 Cf. Atlas and Perlmann, "Saadia on the Scroll of the Hasmoneans," pp. 1 f.
45 Cf. Malter, *Saadia Gaon*, pp. 171 f.
46 Cf. above, n. 39. For my translation, "compiled," cf. I. Elbogen, "Wie steht es um die zwei Rezensionen des Scherira-Briefes," *Festschrift zum 75-Jaehrigen Bestehen des Juedisch-Theologischen Seminars Fraenckel'scher Stiftung*, 2 vols. (Breslau, 1929), II, 63 f.
47 *ISG*, pp. vi f.
48 Cf. above, n. 32.
49 *ISG*, p. xiii.

son of the addressee of Sherira's Epistle, compiled a "Sequence of the Recipients of the Torah,"[50] and R. Samuel b. Hofni Gaon in his Arabic introduction to the Talmud also gave a history of the tradition.[51] In Andalus, a century later, Judah ha-Levi felt obligated to include in his philosophic defense of Judaism at least a brief excursus demonstrating the Rabbanite chain of tradition.[52] R. Nathan Ab ha-Yeshiba of Palestine prefaced his commentary to the Mishna with a similar survey,[53] while in North Africa Maimonides introduced his commentary not only with a brief history of the tradition but with several classifications of the tannaim, including chronological, geographical and occupational ones. Somewhat later, he prefaced his great code with a chain of transmitters extending from Moses to the last of the amoraim.[54]

This polemical device was not without its effect. The Karaite apologists also began to trace their history back to the earliest times so as to free themselves from the Rabbanite charge of *bid'a* (innovation). Significantly enough, Qirqisani prefaced his great code of Karaite law and practice with a history of Jewish sects providing the historical precedents for the Karaite schism, which he traced back to the defection of Jeroboam I![55]

In short, Ibn Daud had introduced nothing new when he used this genealo-

---

50 Cf. S. Poznanski, *Esquisse historique sur les Juifs de Kairouan* [in Hebrew] (Warsaw, 1909), p. 38. Cf. also below, pp. 174 f., 186 f.

51 E. Roth, "A Gaonic Fragment Concerning the Oral Chain of Tradition" [in Hebrew], *Tarbiz*, XXVI (1956–57), 410 f. and S. Abramson, "R. Samuel b. Hofni's Introduction to the Talmud" [in Hebrew], *ibid.*, pp. 421 f., where reference is made to the fragment published earlier by J.N. Epstein but wrongly ascribed by him to Nissim b. Jacob.

52 Judah ha-Levi, *Kitab al-Khazari*, tr. by H. Hirschfeld (New York, 1927), III.64 f. Note also the outline of the history of tradition in the thanksgiving poem of Samuel ibn Nagrela, *Diwan* (ed. Habermann), I., part 1, p. 96.

53 Cf. S. Assaf, *Tequfat ha-Geonim we-Sifrutah*, ed. by M. Margalioth (Jerusalem, 1955), pp. 296 f. Assaf did not note the interesting fact that R. Nathan transmitted the names of authorities by numbered generations, which he labelled "*al-tabaqa* 2, *al-tabaqa* 3, etc." Though I have not seen the edition of Sachs-Kafiḥ (listed by M.M. Kasher and J.B. Mandelbaum, *Sarei ha-Elef* [New York, 1959], p. 117), I did consult the unique MS of this work in the Library of The Jewish Theological Seminary of America.

54 Cf. Moses Maimonides, *Mishnah 'im Payrush R. Moses b. Maimon*, I, ed. and tr. into Hebrew by J. Kafiḥ (Jerusalem, 1963), Zera'im, pp. 49 f.; for his explicit use of the *tabaqat* genre of classification, cf. *ibid.*, pp. 52 ff.; *idem*, *Mishneh Torah*, introduction. Cf. also Schreiner, *op. cit.*, p. 629, n.; S.W. Baron, "The Historical Outlook of Maimonides," *PAAJR*, VI (1935), 75 f., 96 f.

55 Nemoy, "Al-Qirqisani's Account, etc.," pp. 322 f. For other Karaite efforts at tracing the history of their sect to ancient times, cf. Poznanski, "Anan et ses Ecrits," *REJ*, XLIV (1902), 162 f.; *idem*, introduction to Sultanski, *op. cit.*, pp. 5 f.; Mann, *Texts and Studies*, II, 128 f.; Z. Ankori, "Some Aspects of Karaite-Rabbanite Relations," *PAAJR*, XXIV (1955), 11 f.; XXV (1956), 161.

gical method to defend his tradition. In essence, he was merely bringing the record up to date and giving the Spanish rabbinical academies the role of standard-bearers now that the Babylonian academies were supposedly no longer in existence. Although over one third of his work is devoted to but two centuries of rabbinic activity in Spain, the first portions of his account were necessary prolegomena to his thesis that the rabbis of Spain were the legitimate heirs to Jewish authority and tradition.

Ibn Daud added several other features to his work, which were also characteristic devices of the Muslim historians. To the *tabaqat* method of verification of transmitters of *ḥadith*, the later Muslim historians had added a further refinement of classifying persons by *qarn* or generation. Employed especially in connection with biographies and local histories of tradition, the "generation" device was adopted as an added method of proving authoritative knowledge for the evaluation of a person as a link in the chain.[56] Since the science of *ḥadith* required the study of the biographies of the transmitters, Muslim historians further developed the genre of local histories to facilitate the classification of local traditions and their authorities.[57] Ibn Daud will be seen to have absorbed this Muslim method, which, in view of earlier Jewish precedent, was assimilable to his needs without fear of offending. Like the Muslim works from which he had learned, he carefully classified each authority by time and place, at the same time adding pertinent biographical material which would give his account added weight.

Ibn Daud's scheme of Jewish history is to divide the scholars of the past into generations and to place each authority in a *numbered* category with reference to his master-colleague-disciple associations. Thus, R. Johanan b. Zakkai represented the tenth generation after the men of the Great Assembly,[58] R. Judah the Prince the fourth generation of tannaim,[59] R. Ashi the sixth generation of the amoraim,[60] and so on for the thirty-eight generations from the Return under Zerubbabel until the days of R. Joseph ibn Megash.[61] In his survey of talmudic times, he listed within each generation all the scholars he could identify from talmudic literature, occasionally adding a detail or two about their personal lives. In the case of the biblical and early post-biblical periods, Ibn Daud certainly had ample Jewish precedent for the classification of authorities by num-

---

56 Rosenthal, *op. cit.*, pp. 75 f., 144.
57 *Ibid.*, pp. 39, 89, 144.
58 II.153, 169.
59 III.89–97.
60 IV.58.
61 Epilogue.12.

bered generations. The Talmud itself had applied it to the early biblical period,[62] while Saadiah, in *Sefer ha-Galuy*, traced "eleven generations" during which the Mishna had been compiled.[63] Ibn Daud, however, carried the scheme through the saboraic, gaonic and "rabbinical" periods to give added weight to his claim that Judaism could boast an unimpeachable chain.

Finally, Ibn Daud synchronized with his purely Jewish account those details of Gentile history which he found of especial interest and pertinence.[64] In this also he was apparently following the Muslim chroniclers, who placed special emphasis on external cultural and religious development, and who took particular pleasure in human-interest stories.[65] In short, Ibn Daud had absorbed the method of his Jewish and Muslim predecessors by enlisting history in the service of religious polemics and by modelling his chronicle after the patterns established by the accepted scientists of tradition for the verification of religious claims.

Qabbalah-Tradition

The extension of a time-honored talmudic principle in accordance with the criteria refined by the Arabic intelligentsia is further reflected in the key word of the work, *qabbalah*. The use of this noun as a synonym for tradition derives ultimately from talmudic usage in which the authority of a tradition or of rabbinic succession is often designated by the verb *qibbel* ("received").[66] However, in talmudic Hebrew the noun *qabbalah* has an entirely different technical con-

---

[62] *M.* Abot 5.1.
[63] Harkavy, *op. cit.*, p. 194. Cf. also above, nn. 53–54, from which it will be seen that this method became standard for the listing of classical authorities, the term *tabaqat* being employed in the sense of *qarn*.
[64] Cf. esp. IV.86 f.; V.30 f.; Epilogue.65 f.
[65] Rosenthal, *op. cit.*, p. 91.—Ibn Daud may also have wished to counter the Muslim charge that Jewish chronology "and the synchronization of Jewish events with the history of other peoples, about which information is contained in Jewish sources" were replete with error. This charge had been made by Abu Ma'shar al-Balki whose works on astrology had attained great renown in Toledo in Ibn Daud's day; F. Rosenthal, *The Technique and Approach of Muslim Scholarship* (= Analecta Orientalia, 24. Rome, 1947), p. 29, col. b. and n. 2 there. On the importance of accurate chronology as proof of authenticity, cf. also Wolfson, *Religious Philosophy*, pp. 237 f.
[66] Cf., e.g., *M.* Pe'ah 2.6, 'Eduyot 1.6, Abot 1.1 f.; W. Bacher, *Tradition und Tradenten* (Leipzig, 1914), pp. 1 f. For the same use of παρέλαβον in I Cor. 2.23, Galatians 1.12, cf. H. Strack and P. Billerbeck, *Kommentar zum Neuen Testament aus Talmud und Midrasch*, 3rd ed., 4 vols. and Indices (Munich, 1961), III, 444. On the centrality of *paradosis* or "handing over" in Christian thought, cf. R. Bultmann, *Theology of the New Testament*, 2 vols., tr. by K. Grobel (New York, 1951–55), II, 119 f.

notation.⁶⁷ The extension of the nominal form in gaonic times into a technical term designating oral rabbinic tradition reflects the need that was felt for a Hebrew term parallelling the Arabic *naql* and *khabar*, and thus betrays the same underlying influences as the literary genre which Ibn Daud employed.⁶⁸ Ibn Daud's insistence that the traditions he reported were absolutely true, and that the "chain" of succession which he described was one of sanctity untainted by interruption or hiatus,⁶⁹ has a familiar ring to students of Islam, in which *isnad saḥiḥ* and *isnad musalsal* ("verified" and "concatenated" attestations) have the same purpose and weight. Thus, in his very choice of terms as well as of concepts, Ibn Daud — and, of course, all others who used such terms — hoped to convince an audience that had absorbed the basic premises and vocabulary of Arabic scholarship.

The Argument of Sefer ha-Qabbalah

All this serves to explain merely the setting in which *Sefer ha-Qabbalah* was composed. What is vital to the understanding of the work is the often unexplained, or partially explained, meaning which Ibn Daud attached to seemingly innocuous terms and data. Lest there be any mistake about the full significance of his chronological survey, Ibn Daud provided his readers with an introductory and closing statement explaining the full import of a tradition that had been handed down fro m master to disciple generation after generation.⁷⁰

This work, he told his readers, would demonstrate that the teachings of the rabbis are all traceable back to the men of the Great Assembly, who took over the tradition from the prophets. Never did the talmudic authorities introduce any innovations into Judaism except in the express instance of legislation (*taqqanot*), which was made by unanimous consent for the safekeeping of the Law. The contention that the tradition contains no human fabrication is not refuted

---

67 In the Talmud, the term is used for teachings drived from the prophetic and hagiographic portions of Scripture; cf. Bacher, *loc. cit.*; A. Kohut, *Aruch Completum*, VII, 57b–58a; C.J. Kasowski, *Thesaurus Talmudis* IX, 59. The only possible exception known to me is *ARN*, II, 42, p. 117. Cf. also references in next note.
68 Cf. L. Ginzberg's note in I. Efros, *Philosophical Terms in the Moreh Nebukim* (New York, 1924), p. 142; Tur-Sinai's additions to Eliezer ben Iehuda, *Thesaurus Totius Hebraitatis*, XI, 5696b; cf. also N. Wieder, "Three Terms for 'Tradition'," *JQR*, NS, XLIX (1958-59), 108 f.— On qabbalah as *naql* or *khabar*, cf. Harkavy, *op. cit.*, p. 195; Halkin, "A Fragment of Saadyah's Introduction, etc.," pp. 140.17, 150.6.
69 Epilogue.14–15, 139.
70 On the "introduction" as a characteristic Muslim influence on Jewish treatises, cf. A.S. Halkin, "The Judeo-Islamic Age," *Great Ages and Ideas of the Jewish People*, ed. by L.W. Schwarz (New York, 1956), p. 224.

by the presence of disputes between the rabbinic authorities on the proper method of fulfilling the laws. This argument does not hold—and obviously derives solely from sectarian aims—for the rabbis can never be found to question these laws *in principle* (*sc.*, as the Karaites do), but differ only on details. This latter circumstance is, to be sure, a personal shortcoming of the disputants,[71] who should have been more attentive to the details of their masters' tradition, but can carry no weight against the tradition *per se*.

It does not require very attentive reading to perceive that Ibn Daud's work does not even begin to prove what the prologue and epilogue claim that it does. All Ibn Daud showed, at best, was that one man followed another in taking over rabbinic authority in an orderly and unbroken chain of succession. Nowhere did he attempt to demonstrate that each man subscribed to the principles or exegetical methods held by his predecessor or contemporaries. Ultimately, Ibn Daud seems to be arguing *ex silentio*. Since they never openly questioned fundamentals, obviously they accepted them! It is at this point that we must supply the associations and meanings that were so obvious to Ibn Daud and so alien to later patterns of thought.

To Ibn Daud, as to any orthodox Jew (or Muslim, for that matter), true succession was synonymous with faithful adherence to the master's teachings. An authentic disciple is a faithful transmitter: he is basically a witness to the tradition; he alters nothing, does not innovate, and certainly never disputes his master's teachings. This is an assumption that rests on talmudic law and on reports on sages, as well as on the Muslim definitions of a disciple of good character.[72] Hence, if the good character of the teachers and successors of each generation was attested, and if the chain of transmission could be traced without gaps back to the prophets, indeed to Moses himself, the antiquity and probity of the tradition were considered demonstrated.

It was not mere partisanship that prompted Ibn Daud to stress the piety, saintliness and highmindedness of the rabbis, and the baseness, egocentricity and niggardliness of the Karaites. The character of the men in question was in his mind the very essence of the argument, for the probity of a *hadith* depended ultimately on the probity of its bearers. The personal ambitions of the fathers of the Samaritan and Karaite heresies determined and infected whatever they

---

71 That this is the meaning popularly given to the phrase quoted in Prologue.18 is shown by Maimonides' vehement efforts to reinterpret it; cf. *Mishna* (ed. Kafih) Zera'im, p. 20.
72 Epilogue.13. That the tradition is transmitted through testimony is indicated by the key word of the tractate 'Eduyot: "so and so testified." Cf. also Maimonides, *Mishneh Torah*, Yesoday ha-Torah, 8.2; Bacher, *Tradition und Tradenten*, pp. 15 f. On the classical method of reporting a tradition, cf. *M.* Yeb. 15.2, Neg. 7.4. Abot 5.7; *B.* Yoma 66b. For the Muslim attitude, cf. G.E. von Grunebaum, *Medieval Islam*, 2nd ed. (Chicago, 1953), pp. 240 f.; cf. also above, n. 66.

preached and underlay the systems they established. Where the rabbis were transmitters, the fathers and doctors of other religions were fabricators. The one tradition was divine and revealed, the other(s) human and manufactured.

Given these assumptions, the body of the work takes on meaning. Each authority and his rightful successor were carefully dated. Relevant attendant circumstances were fully described, so that the reader might be convinced of a fully preserved and well-attested tradition with its claims and demands.

Nor was this a mere parochial record. The rabbis were as much in full possession of the history of falsehood and deviation as they were of truth and orthodoxy. Ibn Daud followed in the path of virtually all historians of doctrinal succession by weaving into his account of legitimate tradition the stories of dissidence, secession and outright imposture.[73] We are thus confronted with a tradition that is seemingly sure of itself and no less certain about other codes and doctrines. Samaritanism was the product of lust and of error compounded by arrogance;[74] Karaism the fruit of envy and hatred.[75] Christianity was the fabrication of would-be disciples of Jesus, who never knew their master.[76] Manichaeism was the doctrine of a twisted mind,[77] and, like the blasphemies of Ḥiwi, actually resulted in new scriptures.[78] Islam grew out of the pretensions of one who appeared late in history with no substance to validate his claims.[79]

However, all these asides on other religions and sects were obviously only parenthetical to his major target of attack, the Karaites. Against these he invoked not only the rabbinic proof of antiquity and unbroken line of succession—both of which the Karaites lacked—but two further lines of attack, which are rather surprising in the mouth of a medieval European Jew.

In the first place, the baselessness of the Karaite pretensions was demonstrated by the fact that the overwhelming majority of Jews have been Rabbanites and have held the Karaites in utter contempt. The Rabbanites were to be found everywhere, while the Karaites were clustered in a few remote and isolated settlements. Where they did live in the vicinity of Rabbanites, they were compelled to hold their peace. Indeed, it was only thanks to the adherence of the

---

73 Cf. III.40 f.; Epilogue 21 f., 47 f. and the following six notes. The history of error as part of the history of truth goes back to Lactantius and Eusebius. The classic Jewish example is, of course, Maimonides, *Mishneh Torah*, Hilkot 'Abodah Zarah, 1. On Arabic studies of comparative religion, cf. A. Mez, *The Renaissance of Islam*, tr. by Salahuddin Khuda Baksh and D.S. Margaliouth (Patna, 1937), pp. 209 f.
74 II.23 f., 44 f.
75 VI. 43 f.
76 Cf. II.95 f.; above, pp. xxxii f.
77 IV.147 f.
78 VI.173 f.
79 V.37 f.

Rabbanites to the requirements of their own law that the Karaites were not punished in full accord with their deserts.[80] (One marvels at how a Jew, who doubtless heard this line of attack against his people and tradition from Muslims and Christians, could turn about and employ it against his own adversaries.) Finally, the worth of Karaism was demonstrated by its fruits. Literarily and culturally sterile, Karaite leadership had demonstrated its unworthiness by the fact that it never represented Jewish interests and never brought any material benefit to the Jewish community at large.[81] By contrast, Rabbanite Judaism was as rich in poets as it was in scholars and linguists and, above all, endowed with courtiers and men of affairs, who have at all times brought strength and consolation to the house of Israel.[82]

We need not concern ourselves here with these preposterous arguments, which, to say the least, are factually unsupportable. The spread of Karaism, its strength and cultural flowering, are part of a record that is by now too well known to require repetition. What is of interest is the source of these arguments, which Ibn Daud invoked as the *coup de grâce* to his polemic.

Actually, this line of appeal derived from the same sources as the *isnad* method itself. The argument from cultural creativity (or sterility) and the appeal to the authority of persons who have benefitted the community was an appeal to the virtue of "philanthropy" which the true philosopher-king bears to his fellow men.[83] Judaism was thus shown to be a true philosophy, Karaism a selfish and partisan doctrine. Similarly, the argument from majority or the consensus of Jewish opinion derived from Arabic jurisprudence and philosophy where consensus (*ijma'*) was proof of the truth of a practice or doctrine.[84]

However, this last appeal requires a further word of explanation, for although Ibn Daud was not the first medieval Jew to invoke this line of reasoning,[85] he did make certain distinctions that merit elucidation.

Ibn Daud clearly distinguished between the consensus of the rabbis of the Talmud and that of the Jews of his own day. The consensus of talmudic times

---

80   Epilogue.21 f., 58 f.
81   *Ibid.*, 124 f.
82   *Ibid.*, 137 f.
83   Cf. L. Strauss,"Farabi's *Plato*," *Louis Ginzberg Jubilee Volume*, pp. 377 f. For the classical roots of this concept, cf. W. Jaeger, *Paideia*, 3 vols. (New York, 1945), III, 310 nn., 74–75. For the Jewish equivalents, cf. *Encyclopedia Talmudit*, I, 98 f., VI, 149 f., and the many rabbinic injunctions on consideration for the community (*ṣibbur*).
84   Cf. *EI*, II, 448; Schacht, *op. cit.*; von Grunebaum *op. cit.*, pp. 149 f. M.Z. Madina, *The Classical Doctrine of Consensus in Islam* (unpublished doctoral dissertation, University of Chicago, 1957). For the ancient antecedents of this principle, cf. Schacht, p. 83; Wolfson, *The Philosophy of the Church Fathers*, I, 104, 110 f. and esp. 495.
85   Cf. above, nn. 45, 49; Judah ha-Levi, *Kitab al-Khazari*, I.45 f., 86, 88, III.38 f.

was pictured in the classical Muslim terms of unanimity.[86] In arguing from unanimity, he merely turned against the Karaites the very same retort he had made to Muslim polemics against Judaism.[87] The rabbis, he maintained, were unanimous on all "root" or basic commandments; their differences of opinion were only on matters of detail and hence inconsequential.[88] Furthermore, he read the classical Muslim doctrine of unanimity into rabbinic legislation, although he would have been hard put to adduce evidence for his statement.[89] Like the Muslim jurists, too, he argued from the silence of the rabbis' contemporaries as evidence of their tacit consent.[90] To be sure, Ibn Daud did not make the fine distinction that the Muslim jurists had between the consent of the people as a whole and the consent of the scholars of each generation. It sufficed for him to invoke broad categories, which were generally accepted and over which he apparently felt there could be no argument.

The consensus of post-talmudic times, when sectarianism had been revived, was quite another matter. Here Ibn Daud shifted to the evidence of the geographic dissemination of Rabbinism. What he meant to say is that since the Rabbanites were spread all over the world, they were to be trusted, for it would have been impossible for all of them to agree on a lie.[91] The Karaite rupture of the consensus of the community was of no consequence, for the Karaites were an insignificant minority of innovators, who were disqualified from expressing any view in the face of the general consensus of opinion. Once again, Ibn Daud was but echoing the broad outlines of the highly developed Muslim theory of *ijma'*.[92]

Into this basic line of polemic, Ibn Daud injected a few flourishes that were, in reality, but extensions of his primary theme. To the evidence of history Ibn Daud added weight by appealing to the force of reason and of miracles. In reply to the Karaite contention that reason negated an oral revelation—if the written Law of the Lord is perfect, what need is there of a second one! —Ibn

---

86 Prologue.11; II.145 f. For the Muslim counterpart, cf. Schacht, *op. cit.*, pp. 42 f., 94; Madina, *op. cit.*, pp. 5, 12, 114 f.
87 Cf. above, pp. xxx.
88 Prologue. 15 f. For the Muslim counterparts of this reasoning, cf. Schacht, *op. cit.*, p. 106.
89 Cf. Prologue.11. The Muslim doctrine of consensus was predicated on the assumption that God would not permit all of His flock to fall into error. The Jews made no such assumption in classical times; cf. Lev. 4.13 and *M*. Hor. 1.4–5. Cf. also M. Zucker, "Fragments from Rav Saadya Gaon's Commentary to the Pentateuch" [in Hebrew], *Sura*, II (1955–56), 321, n. 28.
90 II.145 f. For the Muslim argument from silence (*ijma' sukuti*), cf. Schacht, *op. cit.*, pp. 44, 61 f.; Madina, *op. cit.*, pp. 134 f.
91 Epilogue.23 f. Cf. above, p. xxix.
92 Cf. Schacht, *op. cit.*, pp. 82, 259; Madina, *op. cit.*, pp. 55 f., 76.

Daud argued that the very generalized form of biblical commands required the assumption of details that were transmitted orally.[93] This was a point on which Saadiah and others had expatiated centuries earlier, and Ibn Daud acquitted himself by referring to it in passing.

In describing the meeting between Alexander the Great and Simeon the Righteous, Ibn Daud pointed up the "miracle" wrought for the Jews through the Rabbanite Simeon. Alexander retracted his decision to destroy Jerusalem and, instead, honored the city and its high priest.[94] Now, the proof from miracles goes back to the biblical writings and was invoked by Church Fathers and medieval philosophers.[95] But though Ibn Daud contrasted the miracle performed through Simeon with the impotence of Anan and Qirqisani, the Karaites, his real point seems to have been the recognition of Rabbanite authority by Gentile rulers. The acknowledgment of Rabbanite leadership by Alexander the Great, the Herodians,[96] the Romans,[97] Persians[98] and Muslims[99] as well as the Christian kings of Spain[100] gave "objective" support to his claim that Rabbinism had always been the recognized form of Jewish law and government. These instances also validated Ibn Daud's implied claim for the legitimacy of such authority on the part of the Jewish courtiers of his own day, whose glory lay in "accomplishing good for Israel."[101] Not the least important aspect of this last virtue, in Ibn Daud's opinion, was the consistent policy maintained by the Jewish courtiers in the north of persecuting the Karaites whenever opportunity offered itself.[102] They were but following in the footsteps of Ezra the Scribe, the early John Hyrcanus and R. Saadiah Gaon.[103]

In short, Ibn Daud's chronicle portrayed Jewish leadership of all ages as a chain composed of uniform links. Only the time, names and places of the links varied. Their tradition and way of life had never changed. Their loyalty to the legacies they had received were conclusive testimony to their honesty and authenticity and to the legitimacy of their claim to govern.

---

93 Cf. above, n. 28.
94 II.20 f.
95 Cf. *ibid.*, Supplementary Notes.
96 II.129 f., 146.
97 II.163; III.83 f.; *ZDR*.
98 IV.158.
99 V.40.
100 Epilogue. 89 f.
101 Cf. VII.234, 335, 422.
102 Epilogue.57 f., 63, 119 f.
103 II.27–28, 61–62; VI.152 f.

SEFER HA-QABBALAH

(THE BOOK OF TRADITION)

[PROLOGUE]

1] The purpose of this Book of Tradition is to provide students with the evidence that all the teachings of our rabbis of blessed memory, namely, the sages of the Mishna and the Talmud, have been transmitted: each great sage and righteous man having received them from a great sage and righteous man, each head of an academy and his school having received them from the head of an academy and his school, as far back as the men of the Great Assembly, who received them from the prophets, of blessed memory all. Never did the sages of the Talmud, and certainly not the sages of the Mishna, teach anything, however trivial, of their own invention, except for the enactments which were made by universal agreement in order to make a hedge about the Torah.

Now should anyone infected with heresy attempt to mislead you, saying: "It is because the rabbis differed on a number of issues that I doubt their words," you should retort bluntly and inform him that he is "a rebel against the decision of the court"; and that our rabbis of blessed memory never differed with respect to a commandment in principle, but only with respect to its details; for they had heard the principle from their teachers, but had not inquired as to its details, since they had not waited upon their masters sufficiently. As a case in point, they did not differ as to whether or not it is obligatory to light the Sabbath lamp; what they did dispute was "with what it may be

---

2 *Students*: See S.N.
4 *Transmitted*: Lit., received. In other words, the persons to whom statements are ascribed in the Talmud did not fabricate them; they merely reported ancient traditions.
6 *School*: See S.N.
7–8 Cf. Abot 1.1. Cf. also VI.48 f.; Epilogue.12 f.
8 *Never did etc.*: See S.N.
10 *Of their own invention*: Cf. also II.107. *Enactments*: Heb., *taqqanot*; cf. *JE*, XI, 669–676.
11 *Universal agreement*: See S.N. *A hedge about the Torah*: Cf. Abot 1.1; *ARN*, I, 2, p. 14 (*B*. Ber. 3b, beg.); R. Eleazar b. Jacob's report in *B*. Yeb. 90b.
12 *Heresy*: I.e., Karaism. *Mislead you*: Lit., whisper to you.
13 *Because the rabbis differed*: A difference of opinion indicates that at least one of the views does not represent authentic "tradition." See S.N.
14 *Rebel*: Sc., and is guilty of a capital offense; *M*. Sanhed. 11.1. See S.N.
16–17 *Principle... details*: See S.N.
18 *Had not waited etc.*: Cf. *Tos*. Hag. 2.9 (ed. Lieberman), p. 384 and parallels. For the technical meaning of "waiting upon scholars" see Alon, *Toledot*, I, 330 f.; J. Goldin, *The Living Talmud*, p. 232.
19–20 *Obligatory to light etc.*: Cf. *B*. Shab. 25b and see S.N.

lighted and with what it may not be lighted." Similarly, they did not differ as
[2] to whether we are required to recite || the *Shema'* evenings and mornings; what
they differed on was "from when may the *Shema'* be recited in the evenings"
and "from when may the *Shema'* be recited in the mornings." This holds
25 true for all of their discussions.

20-21 *M*. Shab. 2.1.
22 *Shema'*: See *JE*, XI, 266.
23-24 *M*. Ber. 1.1, 2. See S.N.

[I]

[THE BIBLICAL PERIOD]

From [the creation of] Adam until the Flood	1656 years
From the Flood until [the birth of] Abraham	292
From the birth of Abraham until his first departure from Haran	52
From his departure from Haran until the covenant between the pieces of flesh	18
He returned to Haran and remained there thus returning to the land of Cannan at age of 75.	5 years
From that time until the birth of Isaac	25
From that time until the birth of Jacob	60
[From that time] until Jacob went down to Egypt	130
[From that time] until the death of Jacob	17
[From that time] until the death of Joseph	53
From the death of Joseph until the emergence from Ephraim and Gilead of the false prophets who misled Israel and were killed	110
[From that time] until the Exodus	30

The Exodus occurred in Nisan of the year 2449.

---

2 Seder ʻOlam 1 (ed. Ratner) p. 1; Seder ʻOlam Zuta (ed. Neubauer), p. 68. The figure is derived from the chronological data of Gen. 5 and 7.6.

3 See the chronological data of Gen. 11.10–26.

4 See S.N.

5–6 Sc., for Abraham was seventy years old at the time of the covenant; cf. Seder ʻOlam 1 (ed. Ratner) p. 4 n. 22 (ed. Marx, German translation, p. 2 n. 4).

7–8 Cf. Gen. 12.4.

9 Cf. *ibid.* 21.5.   10 *Ibid.* 25.26.   11 *Ibid.* 47.9.   12 *Ibid.* 47.28.

13 Joseph was thirty-nine years old at the time he invited his father and brothers to join him in Egypt (cf. Gen. 41.46, 53; 45.6). Presumably, Jacob and his family came to Egypt the following year when Joseph was forty. Joseph died at the age of 110 (*ibid.* 50.26) thus surviving Jacob by fifty-three years.

14–15 Cf. Mekhilta de Rabbi Ishmael, *Beshallaḥ* 1 (ed. Lauterbauch), I, 172 f. and see S.N.

16 Sc., completing the 430 years from the time of the covenant between the flesh and 400 years from the birth of Isaac, which is the way rabbinic tradition harmonizes Gen. 15.13 with Ex. 12.40–41; cf. Mekhilta de-Rabbi Ishmael, *Pisḥa* 14 (ed. Lauterbach) I, 111–113; Kasher, *Torah Shelemah*, III, 655 nn. 141–142; XII, 52 nn. 601–603.

17 This date represents the sum of all the chronological data given above; see also S.N. For the month, see Ex. 12.2.

[From that time] until the building of the Temple	480 years

The Temple was built in the year 2929.

[From that time] until the destruction of the Temple	433 years

However, only 410 years were reckoned for it, since the kingship was not taken into account after the exile of Jehoiakim.

The following is a detailed enumeration:

In the desert	40
Joshua	28
The elders who outlived Joshua	17
Othniel	40
Ehud	80
the last one of which overlapped with Shamgar's	1
Deborah and Barak	40
Gideon	40
Abimelech	3
Tola	23
Jair	22
Jephthah	6
Ibzan	7
Elon	10
Abdon	8
Samson	20

18 I Ki. 6.1.
19 This figure is explained in the text immediately below.
21 *410 were reckoned to it*: Sc., in rabbinic tradition; *Tos.* Zeb. 13.6 (ed. Zuckermandel), p. 499; *B.* Yoma 9a; *Yer.* Meg. 1 (end), f. 72d; Wayyik. R. 21.9 (ed. Margulies), p. 487 and parallels. See S. N.
22 *Exile of Jehoiakim*: Cf. Dan. 1.1 and II Chr. 36.6. See also S.N.
24 Sc., of the 480 and 433 just given.
25 Num. 32.13; Josh. 5.6.
26 Seder 'Olam 12 (ed. Ratner), pp. 50 f. See S.N.
27 Cf. Josh. 24.31; Jud. 2.7. See S.N.
28 Jud. 3.11.
29 *Ibid.* 3.30.
30–31 *Ibid.* 3.31. In other words, Shamgar's reign overlapped with Ehud's and does not count as a separate datum in this table; Seder 'Olam 12 (ed. Ratner), p. 53.
32 Jud. 5.31.   33 *Ibid.* 8.28.   34 *Ibid.* 9.22.   35 *Ibid.* 10.2.
36 *Ibid.* 10.3.   37 *Ibid.* 12.7.   38 *Ibid.* 12.9.   39 *Ibid.* 12.11.
40 *Ibid.* 12.4.   41 *Ibid.* 15.20.

[THE BIBLICAL PERIOD]

	Eli	40
4]	Samuel	11
	Saul	2
45	David	40
	Solomon	40

The construction of the Temple was begun in the third year of his reign.

	Rehoboam	17
50	Abijah	3
	Asa	41
	Jehoshaphat	25
	Jehoram	8
	Ahaziah	1
55	Athaliah	6
	Joash	40
	Amaziah	29
	Uzziah	52
	Jotham	16
60	Ahaz	16
	Hezekiah	29
	Manasseh	55
	Amon	2
	Josiah	31
65	Jehoahaz	3 months
	Jehoiakim	11
	Jehoiachin	3 months
	Zedekiah	11

42 I Sam. 4.18.
43 Cf. Seder 'Olam 13 (ed. Ratner), p. 56; *B*. Zeb. 118b (and Rabbinovicz, *Variae Lectiones* XIV, 249 n. 40); *B*. Temur. 14b–15a; Midrash Samuel (ed. Buber), p. 83.
44 I Sam. 13.1 and see references in previous note.
45 II Sam. 5.4; I Ki. 2.11.
46 I Ki. 11.42.
47–48 Cf. I Ki. 6.1; II Chr. 3.2. Ibn Daud ostensibly diverges from Scripture in order to arrive at a total of 480 years from the Exodus to the construction of the Temple; see I.18, and S.N.

49 I Ki. 14.21.	50 *Ibid.* 15.2; see S.N.	51 I Ki. 15.10	52 *Ibid.* 22.42; see S.N.
53 II Ki. 8.17.	54 *Ibid.* 8.26.	55 *Ibid.* 11.3.	56 *Ibid.* 12.2.
57 *Ibid.* 14.2.	58 *Ibid.* 15.2.	59 *Ibid.* 15.33.	60 *Ibid.* 16.2.
61 *Ibid.* 18.2.	62 *Ibid.* 21.1.	63 *Ibid.* 21.19.	64 *Ibid.* 22.1.
65 *Ibid.* 23.31.	66 *Ibid.* 23.36.	67 *Ibid.* 24.8.	68 *Ibid.* 24.18.

This yields a total of 433 years from the end of the third year of Solomon's reign until the destruction of the Temple.

Jehoiachin, his son Shealtiel, his son Zerubbabel, his son Meshullam, his son Hananiah, his son Berechiah, his son Hasadiah, his son Isaiah, his son Obadiah, his son Shecaniah, his son Shemaiah, his son Neariah, his son Hezekiah — it is said that Hillel was the brother of Hezekiah son of Neariah — all these were princes of Israel in Babylonia.

Hillel left Babylonia and became the patriarch in Palestine 100 years before the destruction of the Second Temple. Rabban Gamaliel the Elder was his son, Rabban Simeon b. Gamaliel his son, Rabban Gamaliel his son, Rabban Simeon b. Gamaliel his son, Our Saintly Master his son, Rabban Gamaliel Beribbi his son, R. Judah the Prince his son.

[5] Moses our master, may he have peace, received the Torah at Sinai, that is, the Ten Commandments, in Sivan, || 2449, and the remainder of the commandments in the course of the forty days which he spent on the mountain ([i.e.] until the seventeenth of Tammuz, when he descended and broke the tablets) and during the remainder of the first year of the Exodus and the second year, until the ninth of Ab when the spies returned from spying out the land and they refused to go up. Then the decree was issued that our ancestors should not enter the Land. Henceforth, they did not receive any commandment at all.

69 *433*: See S.N.
70 *Until the destruction*: In the eleventh year of Zedekiah's reign; Jer. 39.2. — The total of 433 is arrived at by reckoning thirty-eight years of Solomon's reign to the Temple — since the year in which its construction was begun is reckoned as its first — and the reigns of Jehoahaz and Jehoiachin as equivalent to one year each. This is in accordance with the talmudic principle that a part of a year is reckoned as a whole one; *B*. R.H. 10b.
71–75 What follows is a list of twenty-one *nesiim* or princes of the Davidic house based on Seder 'Olam Zuta. See S.N.
74 *It is said etc.*: See S.N.
76 *100 years etc.*: *B*. Shab. 15a.
77–80 *Rabban Gamaliel etc.*: The following is a list of the Hillelide *nesiim* or partriarchs in Palestine; cf. *STW* (ed. Kahan), p. 3 par. 3. See S.N.
79 *Our Saintly Master*: R. Judah the Prince; cf. III. 78.   81 Abot 1.1.
82 *Sivan*: Ex. 19.1. See S.N. *2449*: See I.17. *The remainder of the commandments*: Ex. 24.12 (and *B*. Ber. 5a).
83 *Forty days*: Ex. 24.18.
84 Ex. 32.19; *M*. Ta'an. 4.6; Seder 'Olam 6 (ed. Ratner, p. 28 and n. 6; ed. Marx, p. 14, translation p. 23); Ginzberg, *Legends*, VI, 32 n. 188; 56 n. 286.
86–88 Num. 13–14; Dt. 1.26; *M*. Ta'an. 4.6; Seder 'Olam 8 (ed. Ratner, p. 37; ed. Marx, p. 18, translation p. 29 nn. 13, 16); Ginzberg, *Legends*, VI, 93 n. 510; 96 n. 532.
88 *Henceforth, they did not etc.*: See S.N.

Moses our master, may he have peace, passed away on Sabbath afternoon on the seventh of Adar, 2489.

Joshua, the son of Nun, may he have peace, received from him the written Torah as well as the oral Torah. Consider the fact that Moses our master, may he have peace, used to sit and judge all Israel from morning until evening. However, the written Torah does not contain one in a thousand of all the possible contingencies. After that he placed over them chiefs of thousands, hundreds, fifties, and tens. He said to them: "Hear out your fellow men and decide justly." Concerning himself he said: "Thus I instructed you at that time about the various things that you should do." This instruction is none other than the oral Torah. With reference to slaughtering and the laws pertaining to it, it is written: "As I have instructed you, you may eat." This indicates that in connection with slaughtering he was given commandments which are not recorded in the Torah. Now, it is inconceivable that he did not inform Joshua of these.

Joshua transmitted the Torah to the elders and passed on to eternal life in the year 2517. The elders who outlived Joshua transmitted it to the prophets, who transmitted it generation after generation until Haggai, Zechariah, ‖ and Malachi. The prophets transmitted it to the men of the Great Assembly. The latter were Zerubbabel, son of Shealtiel son of Jeconiah king of Judah, and those who came with Zerubbabel: Jeshua, Nehemiah, Seraiah, Reelaiah, Mordecai, Bilshan, Mispar, Bigvai, Rehum, Baanah. These were the leaders of the Great Assembly.

89 *Seder R. Amram* (ed. Frumkin), II, 101. See S.N.
90 *Seder 'Olam* 10 (ed. Ratner, pp. 41–42; ed. Marx, p. 20); *Tos*. Sota 11.7-9 (ed. Zuckermandel), p. 315; *B*. Kid. 38a. *2489*: See I. 17, 25.
91-92 Abot 1.1. See *JE*, IX, 423–426, s.v. "Oral Law," and S.N.
92 *Consider*: Sc., in proof of the contention that Moses transmitted an *oral* Torah as well as a written one.
92-93 *Moses... used to sit etc.*: Ex. 18.14.
95 *Possible contingencies*: See S.N. *He placed etc.*: Ex. 18.21, 25; and see S.N.
96 *Hear out*: Dt. 1.16.
97 *Thus*: Ibid. 1.18.
99 *None other than the oral Torah*: Sc., for nowhere does Scripture record the details of Moses' instructions. Obviously, therefore, they must have been given to them orally; see S.N.
100 Dt. 12.21. See S.N.
102 *It is inconceivable etc.*: Cf. Num. 27.22-23; see S.N.
104 Abot 1.1.
105 *2517*: See I.26. *The elders etc.*: *ARN*, I, 1, p. 2.
108 *Zerubbabel*: Ezra 3.2; I Chr. 3.17.
109 *Jeshua etc.*: Ezra 2.2; Neh. 7.7; see S.N.
111 See *JE*, XI, 640 f., s.v. "Synagogue, Great."

The First Temple was built in the year 2929 and remainded standing 427 years. It was destroyed after a seven-year war and remained in ruins for seventy years. However, in the forty-ninth year after its destruction, which
115 was the first year of the reign of Cyrus king of Persia, they began to rebuild it. Then Rehum the commander and Shimshai the scribe wrote a letter against them to Cyrus king of Persia, to which he replied: "Make ye now a decree to cause these men to cease, and that this city shall be not builded, until a decree shall be made by me." "And it ceased unto the second year of the reign
120 of Darius king of Persia."

Behold how trustworthy are the consolations of our God, blessed be His name, for the chronology of their exile corresponded to that of their redemption. Twenty-one years passed from the beginning of their exile until the destruction of the Temple and the cessation of the monarchy. Similarly, twenty-one years passed
125 from the time its rebuilding was begun until it was completed. This follows, since in the year which was partly the third and partly the fourth of Jehoiakim's reign, Nebuchadnezzar began his reign and went up against Jerusalem. The Lord gave Jehoiakim king of Judah into his hand, as well as Daniel, Hananiah, Mishael, and Azariah in the third year of Jehoiakim's reign. This was the
[7] 130 first year of the reign of Nebuchadnezzar || king of Babylon. Seven years later, Jehoiakim died and Jehoiachin began to reign. Then Nebuchadnezzar came up and carried away Jechoiachin king of Judah and ten thousand captives as well as seven thousand warriors, a total of seventeen thousand persons. How-

---

112 *2929*: See I.19 f. *427 years*: Sc., since the work of construction lasted seven years (I Ki. 6.38), and the last year of its construction overlapped with the first year of its operation; see above, I.69–70.
113 *Seven-year war*: See S.N.
114 *Seventy years*: Jer. 29.10; Zech. 1.12; Dan. 9.1; II Chr. 36.21. See also below, I.151 f. *Forty-ninth year*: See I.175 f.
115 *First year etc.*: Ezra 1.1–5; 3.2.
116 *Rehum etc.*: *Ibid.* 4.8.
117 *To Cyrus*: See S.N. *Make ye etc.*: Ezra 4.21.
119 *And it ceased*: *Ibid.* 4.24.
121 *The consolations* are the events of the restoration and are regarded by Ibn Daud as all the more wondrous in view of their symmetrical correspondance with the events leading up to the exile. See below, pp. 189 f.
123 *Twenty-one years passed*: Explained in detail, lines 126 f.
124 *Similarly, twenty-one etc.*: Explained in detail below, lines 210 f.
126–130 This chronology represents Ibn Daud's harmonization of Jer. 25.1 and Dan. 1.1 f. See S.N.
130 *Seven years later:* Sc., since Jehoiakim reigned eleven years; II Ki. 23.36 and cf. *ibid.* 24.12.
131–133 *Nebuchadnezzar came up etc.*: *Ibid.* 24.8–16.

ever, in the book of Jeremiah only three thousand and twenty-three are recorded, for Jeremiah merely recorded the heads of families. Similarly, he did not record Nebuchadnezzar's coming up against Jehoiakim when he took Daniel captive. Nebuchadnezzar came up again in the sixth year of Zedekiah's reign, which was the eighteenth year of Nebuchadnezzar's reign, and carried away eight hundred and twenty-two men of Israel. Again, in the twenty-third year of Nebuchadnezzar, he carried Zedekiah off and destroyed the Temple. Because of the fractional years between them, only twenty-one full years elapsed between the captivity of Daniel and the captivity of Zedekiah. Nebuchadnezzar continued to reign for twenty-two years, for he reigned for a total of forty-five years and died. Evil-merodach, his son, reigned for twenty-two years. "In the first year of his reign, he lifted up the head of Jehoiachin king of Judah." Evil-merodach died, and his son Belshazzar reigned for three years. His officers conspired against him and smote him, and he died in his banquet house. This is what Isaiah had prophecied: "They prepare the table, they light the lamps, they eat, they drink — 'Rise up, ye princes, anoint the shield.'" Thus was fulfilled for Nebuchadnezzar the prophecy: "And all the nations

134 Jer. 52.28. See S.N.
135 *He did not record etc.*: Cf. above to lines 126–130. According to Ibn Daud, therefore, the earliest events of Nebuchadnezzar's reign which Jeremiah recorded date from the second half of the former's first regnal year.
137–138 *Sixth year of Zedekiah... eighteenth year of Nebuchadnezzar:* This is a flagrant contradiction of the chronology of Jer. 32.1. For explanation, see below, lines 140–142.
138–139 *Eighteenth year etc.*: Jer. 52.29. Ibn Daud's "twenty-two" instead of the "thirty-two" of the Masoretic text is patently a *lapsus calami* either of Ibn Daud or of one of the parent MSS.
139 *In the twenty-third etc.*: Jer. 52.30. Note the contradiction of II Ki. 25.8 and cf. below.
140–142 *Because of the fractional years etc.*: In other words, Nebuchadnezzar's first and last regnal years overlapped with those of his predecessor and successor respectively, leaving an actual total of twenty-one for his own reign. See S.N.
143–144 *Forty-five years*: Cf. *B. Meg.* 11b, where the figure is derived from Jer. 52.30–31. *Evil-merodach*: See S.N.
144 *Twenty-two years*: This figure is derived by a process of elimination: since Babylon ruled for seventy years in all (Jer. 25.11–12; 29.10), and of these Nebuchadnezzar ruled for forty-five and Belshazzar for three (below, line 146), there remain twenty-two for Evil-merodach. See S.N.
145 Jer. 52.31. Note that the majority of MSS do not quote the verse exactly.
146 *Three years*: Dan. 8.1, and see S.N. *His officers conspired*: Dan. 5.30; Ginzberg, *Legends*, IV, 345; VI, 430 nn. 2, 4.
148–149 Isa. 21.5. Verses 2 and 9 "indicate" that the passage refers to Belshazzar's last carousals; cf. also Cant. R. to 3.4; *Oeuvres Complètes de Saadia*, III, 29 f., French trans. pp. 35 f.; Finkelstein, *Commentary of David Kimhi on Isaiah*, p. 120.
150 Jer. 27.7; for the fulfillment, see Dan. 5.30–6.1.

shall serve him, and his son, and his son's son." This includes forty-five years of Nebuchadnezzar, twenty-two of Evil-merodach, and three of Belshazzar, making a total of seventy years for the kingdom of Babylon.

Now inasmuch as the Jews were not redeemed "in the first year of Darius the son of Ahasuerus, of the seed of the Medes, who was made king over the realm of the Chaldeans," Daniel, may he have peace, was astonished; and thus Scripture says: "In the first year of his reign, I, Daniel, meditated in the books over the number of years, whereof the word of the Lord came ‖ to Jeremiah the prophet, that He would accomplish for the desolations of Jerusalem seventy years" down to "Seventy weeks are decreed upon thy people and upon thy holy city, to finish the transgression, and to make an end of sin, and to forgive iniquity, and bring in everlasting righteousness, and to seal vision and prophet, and to anoint the most holy place." He disclosed to him the length of the exile and the time of the redemption. "Seventy weeks" are 490 years: seventy during which the Temple remained in ruins, and the 420 years of the Second Temple until the invasion of Vespasian and Titus. "To finish the transgression, and to make an end of sin, and to forgive iniquity" refers to the rebuilding of the Temple. "And to bring in everlasting righteousness" refers to the return of the Jews to the good life in that they did not serve other gods, and did not marry foreign women, and did not despise the command-

---

151–152 See above, I.142 f.
153 *Seventy years*: Jer. 25.11–12; 29.10.
154 *In the first year etc.*: Dan. 9.1 (and cf. 5.30–6.1).
157 *Ibid.* 9.2.
160 *Down to*: The Hebrew word עד is used here as an ellipsis and indicates that the entire portion in Daniel is to be read in connection with Ibn Daud's next section; cf. II.136, "as far as." *Seventy weeks*: Dan. 9.24.
163 *He*: I.e., Gabriel (Dan. 9.21).
164 *Seventy weeks*: What follows is an interpretation of Dan. 9.24 f., which is taken to refer to the days of the Second Temple.
165 *420 years*: Seder 'Olam 28 (ed. Ratner), p. 130 and n. 49 there; *Tosef.* Zeb. 13.6 (ed. Zuckermandel), p. 499; *Yer.* Meg. 1 (end), f. 72d; *B.* Yoma 9a; *B.* A.Z. 9a.
166 *Until the invasion of Vespasian and Titus*: In other words, the 420 years do not include the period during which Vespasian and Titus were in Palestine; see below, I.190–193. Ibn Daud thus contradicts or reinterprets the official rabbinic figure on the length of the Second Temple period.
168 *The rebuilding of the Temple*: Sc., for the expiation of sin is the function of the Temple service; cf. Moore, *Judaism*, I, 497 f.
169–170 *Other gods*: Ginzberg, *Legends*, IV, 359; VI, 449 n. 57.
170 *Foreign women*: Ezra 10.17; Neh. 10.31. *Did not despise the commandments*: Ibn Daud may be referring obliquely to sectarian practice; cf. *B.* 'Erub. 21b and *B.* Sanhed. 99b, where the expression is used for "Epicureans."

[THE BIBLICAL PERIOD] 13

ments, and in that they established the practice of reading the Torah on Mondays and Thursdays and on the Sabbath. "And to seal vision and prophet" refers to the demise of Haggai, Zechariah and Malachi. "And to anoint the most holy place" refers to the building of the Temple, the Sanctuary, and the Holy of Holies. "Know therefore and discern, that from the going forth of the word to restore and to build Jerusalem unto one anointed, a prince, shall be seven weeks" refers to the fact that they began to build Jerusalem in the year following Daniel's prayer, which was the first year of Cyrus king of Persia, who was called "anointed," for so Scripture says: "Thus saith the Lord to His anointed, to Cyrus, whose right hand I have holden." The angel informed Daniel that "from the going forth of the word," that is, from the time that Jeremiah said this, meaning from the time of the captivity of Zedekiah, "unto one anointed, a prince," who was Cyrus, "shall be seven weeks," or forty-nine years; and that the reckoning is not from the captivity of Daniel but from that of Zedekiah. The following is a detailed enumeration of this calculation: Nebuchadnezzar after the destruction, 22; Evil-merodach, 22; Belshazzar, 3; Darius, 1; and the first year of Cyrus—|| totalling 49 years, which are "seven weeks." There remained another 21 years after they had begun to build it according to the grant of Cyrus king of Persia. Subtract from "seventy weeks" the "seven weeks," and there remain sixty-three weeks. Subtract from these

---

171 *Reading the Torah*: Cf. Mekhilta de R. Ishmael, *Vayassa'* 1 (ed. Lauterbach), II, 90, and see Finkelstein, *Ha-Pershim ve-Anshe Keneset ha-Gedolah*, p. 58.

173 *The demise of Haggai, Zechariah and Malachi*: Sc., when prophecy came to an end; cf. II.18; Seder 'Olam 30 (ed. Ratner), p. 140; *Tos.* Sota 13.2 (ed. Zuckermandel), p. 318; *B.* Sanhed. 11a.

174 *Refers to the building etc.*: Cf. Sifra, *Aḥaray Mot* 8.8 (ed. Weiss, f. 83b); *B.* Yoma, 61a. *Sanctuary*: See *M.* Middot 4.1. *Holy of Holies*: Lit., innermost [chamber].

175–176 Dan. 9.25. For the interpretation, cf. Saadia *apud* Ibn Ezra to Dan. 9.24.

178 *The year following Daniel's prayer*: See Dan. 9.1. This was the first year of Cyrus, since Darius the Mede reigned but one year; Seder 'Olam 28 (ed. Ratner), pp. 128 f.; *B.* Meg. 11b; Ginsberg, *Studies in Daniel*, pp. 19, 72 f.

179 *Thus saith*: Isa. 45.1.

182 See Jer. 29:10. *The captivity of Zedekiah*: See I.139–140.

184 *The reckoning*: Sc., of seventy years in Jer. 29.10. *The captivity of Daniel*: See above, I.126 f.

186 *Nebuchadnezzar... twenty-two*: Nebuchadnezzar destroyed Jerusalem in the twenty-third year of his reign and reigned forty-five in all; above, I.139. *Evil-merodach etc.*: See I.144–152.

187 *The first year of Cyrus*: See above, I.115.

188 *Another 21 years*: Sc., for the completion of the Temple and for the fulfillment of Jeremiah's prophecy of seventy years. For a detailed breakdown of these twenty-one years, see below, I.210 f.

weeks sixty-two weeks, which are the 420 years during which the kingdom endured, and there remains one week, which was spent in the war with Vespasian and Titus, his step-son, who was called his son. Concerning the 420 years of habitation, he says: "And for threescore and two weeks, it shall be built again, with broad place and moat." As for the phrase, "but in troublous times," it refers to the great tribulation with which the wall was built, as Scripture says: "So neither I, nor my brethren, nor my servants, nor the men of the guard that followed me, none of us put off our clothes, every one that went to the water had his weapon," and as further explained in the remainder of the section. Of the time following the 420 years, he says: "And after the threescore and two weeks shall an anointed one be cut off, and be no more"; this refers to King Agrippa and his son Monobaz whom Vespasian defeated and killed three and a half years before the destruction of the Temple. Now Vespasian and Titus came up and "made a firm covenant with many" in the final week; however, in the latter half of the week he broke his covenant and caused the sacrifice and the offering to cease, "and upon that wing of detestable things placed that which causeth appalment," because the lawless ones of Israel incited him. This is what is meant by "and the people of a prince that shall come shall destroy the city and sanctuary."

Now the redemption of Israel was as follows: Belshazzar was killed, and Darius the son of Ahasuerus, of the seed of the Medes, was made king over

191 *Sixty-two weeks*: See Dan. 9.25. *420 years*: This is the official rabbinic figure for the life span of the Second Temple; see above, I.164 and S.N.
192 *One week... in the war*: The wording is not precise, for it contradicts the statement below, I.203-204. What Ibn Daud seems to mean is that during the last week they were under the hegemony of Vespasian and Titus; cf. Saadia *apud* Ibn Ezra, *loc. cit.* However, Ibn Daud probably employed this phraseology deliberately in order to suggest a symmetry between the wars of destruction of both Temples; see above, I.112 f.
193 *His step-son*: See S.N.
194-195 Dan. 9.25. *But in troublous times*: Ibid.
197 Neh. 4.17.
199-200 *Remainder of the section*: Sc., of Neh.
200-201 Dan. 9.26.
202 Cf. *Josippon* 67, pp. 291 f.; Ibn Daud, *MBSh*, f. 72b, and see S.N.
204 *Made a firm covenant*: Dan. 9.27, and cf. Ibn Ezra to Dan. 9.24. See S.N.
206 *Upon that wing*: Dan. 9.27 (I have deviated slightly from the accepted translation to bring out Ibn Daud's use of the verse). Cf. note to line 204, and see S.N.
207 *The lawless ones*: I.e., the Zealots; see S.N.
209 *And the people*: Dan. 9.26.
210 See I.124, 146 f. What follows seems to be an interpretation of Dan. 10.13: "But the prince of the kingdom of Persia withstood me one and twenty days." Cf. *Emunah Ramah*, p. 68.
211 *Darius*: Dan. 6.1; 9.1.

[THE BIBLICAL PERIOD] 15

the kingdom of the Chaldeans; and he reigned one year and died. Cyrus reigned after him for 3 years. In the first year of his reign the Lord stirred up his spirit to build the Temple, and after that he ordered the construction halted. || He reigned 3 years, when the queen of the Scythians killed him, for he had killed her two sons, both of whom were emperors. After him Ahasuerus reigned 16 years and died. He was succeeded by his son to whom Esther had given birth, namely Darius, who is the very same as Artaxerxes. In the second year of his reign, the Temple was built. He was seven years old when he began to reign, and he reigned 32 years. Alexander of Macedon went up against him and smote him and killed him. This was in the thirtieth year after the rebuilding of the Temple. Thus, the Persian Empire was cut off, and the empire of Greece began.

213 *3 years*: Cf. Dan. 10.1, which gives the highest figure recorded in Scripture of the extent of Cyrus' reign. *In the first year*: Ezra 1.1 f.
215 *The construction halted*: Cf. ibid. 4.5 f. *The queen of the Scythians*: Cf. *Josippon* 3, p. 24, and see S.N.
217 *Ahasuerus reigned 22 years*: Ibn Daud probably arrived at this figure by elimination, for of the seventy years between the destruction and the final rebuilding of the Temple, only sixteen, or those of Ahasuerus, were not accounted for. Classical Jewish sources, Seder 'Olam 29 (ed. Ratner), p. 134 and *B*. Meg. 11b, credit him with but fourteen years. — The order of the Median-Persian rulers is derived in Jewish sources from Dan. 5.30–6.1 and Ezra 4.5–6; cf. Ginsberg, *Studies in Daniel*, p. 19.
218 *Darius*: Cf. Ginzberg, *Legends*, VI, 452 n. 5.
218–219 *The same as Artaxerxes*: B. R.H. 3b–4a; Ginzberg, *Legends*, VI, 432; Ginsberg, *Studies in Daniel*, p. 72 n. 53.
219 *In the second year of his reign*: Ezra 4.24.
220 *Seven years old*: Esther was taken to the royal palace in the seventh year of Ahasuerus' rule (Esther 2.16). Presumably, she was married the following year and gave birth in Ahasuerus' ninth year. Hence, her son might well not yet have reached his eighth birthday when Ahasuerus died. If we understand the twelve month period of preparation (Esther 2.12) to have *followed* the taking of Esther to the royal palace, the chronology becomes perfectly clear. *Thirty-two years*: Neh. 5.14; 13.6.
221 *Alexander*: *Josippon* 5 f., 9, pp. 30 f., 48.
223 *The Persian empire etc.*: See S.N.

[II]

[11] [THE SUCCESSION OF TEACHERS IN THE DAYS
OF THE SECOND TEMPLE]

The second generation of the men of the Great Assembly was [that of] Simeon the Righteous, known otherwise as Iddo b. Joshua b. Jehozadak the
5 high priest. In his days the Persian Empire was destroyed by Alexander king of Greece. After he had destroyed the kingdom of Persia, this Alexander came to Jerusalem, seeking to destroy Jerusalem and to exile it a second time, in the fortieth year of the Temple. Simeon the Righteous went out to greet the King; and when the latter saw him, he honored and revered him and per-
10 mitted him to make a request. Simeon the Righteous asked of him not to destroy the Temple and not to exile the city, and the King ordered that this be done. Now all of his princes and his attendants were astonished, for they knew that he had intended to destroy them and that he never went back on his word. However, he said to them: "The image of this man leads me to victory
15 in my war." The King extracted an agreement from Simeon the Righteous that every son born to him and the priests in that year would be named Alexander after him, and that the Jews would begin the dating of their documents

---

1 For the title which I have provided to this chapter, cf. IV.172.

3 *The second generation*: Cf. Abot 1.2. For the first generation, cf. above, I.107–111. See S.N.

4 *Simeon... known otherwise as Iddo*: Since rabbinic sources (see note to line 6–7) speak of Simeon the Righteous as the high priest who met Alexander the Great, while Ibn Daud's text of *Josippon* referred to him by the name of Iddo, Ibn Daud identified the two. See further in S.N.

5–51 The account of Alexander's encounter with Simeon the Righteous and of the Samaritan schism is taken from *Josippon* 5, pp. 30–33, and further amplified from the biblical and rabbinic sources listed below.

6–7 *Alexander came to Jerusalem*: Cf. B. Yoma 69a; scholion to Megillat Ta'anit (ed. Lichtenstein), pp. 339 f.

8 *Fortieth year*: This figure is attained by elimination: the Second Temple stood 420 years in all (I.165) and was destroyed in the year 380 of the Seleucid Era (cf. B. A.Z. 9a–10a and commentaries), which, according to *SHQ*, begins with Alexander's conquest of Jerusalem. Furthermore, the Seleucid Era began 1000 years after the Exodus, while the Second Temple was built 960 years after the Exodus; see I.18, 21, 112–113, and II.18.

17 *The dating of their documents*: This datum, lacking in *Josippon*, is based on the conception widely entertained in Judeo-Arabic circles that the Seleucid Era, known in Arabic as "the Alexandrian Era" (*ta'rikh Iskandri*), commemorated Alexander's conquests; see H.J. Bornstein, "Ta'arikay Israel," *Ha-Tequfa*, VIII (1921), 290 f.

[THE SUCCESSION OF TEACHERS IN THE DAYS OF THE SECOND TEMPLE] 17

from that year. This was the year 1000 after their exodus from Egypt. At
that time Ezra the priest, Haggai, Zechariah, and Malachi passed away, and
20 prophecy was removed from Israel. This great miracle was performed for them
through Simeon the Righteous. Nothing like it was performed for Anan or
for al-Qirqisani, the fathers of the heresy!

[2]   King Alexander came upon many Cutheans in the land of Israel [who had
been there] since the days of Sennacherib. Their leaders were Sanballat the
25 Horonite and some of the people of Israel. Some of the sons of Joshua son of
Jehozadak the high priest had contracted marriages with them, and Ezra
the priest and Nehemiah the Tirshatha had expelled them from the house of
the Lord. When King Alexander came to the land of Israel, Sanballat the
Horonite and the leaders of the Cutheans paid him homage and requested of
30 him that his sons-in-law the priests and all those who had married foreign
women and refused to divorce them be permitted to build another temple
on Mount Gerizim. The King commanded that this should be done, and they
built the temple. Then the people were divided in two: half of the people
followed Simeon the Righteous and his pupil Antigonus and their school in

18   *Year 1000*: *B*. A.Z. 10a; cf. also Bornstein, *op. cit.*, IX, 220 n. 1. Thus, according to Ibn Daud, the Seleucid Era began in 3449 A.M.; cf. I.17.
19   *Ezra*: That Ezra died at this time probably derives from the tradition which identifies Ezra with Malachi; *B*. Meg. 15b; Targum to Mal. 1.1. The repetition of Malachi's name in the following phrase is thus a redundancy that was permitted to remain because of the classical sources on which Ibn Daud drew and which normally referred to the cessation of prophecy with the death of "Haggai, Zechariah and Malachi."
19–20   Seder 'Olam 30 (ed. Ratner), p. 140; *B*. Yoma 9b and parallels. Although these sources do not specifically equate the end of prophecy with the beginning of the Seleucid Era, the equation can be read into Seder 'Olam, and the two events had indeed been equated in medieval sources long before Ibn Daud; Bornstein, *op. cit.*, VIII, 293; idem, *Maḥloqet R. Saadia Gaon u-Ben Meir*, p. 72 n. 1.; Mann, *Jews in Egypt*, I, 31; II, 36.
20–22   The "miracle" of the encounter of Simeon the Righteous with Alexander is invoked as a retort to the Karaites, who claimed that the age of Rabbinism could not boast of miracles such as those recorded in Scripture; cf. Salmon b. Yeruḥim, *Wars of the Lord* 37:55 f. See further in S.N. For a similar line of argument, cf. II.146 f.
21–22   *The heresy*: Karaism. On these "fathers of the heresy" cf. Introduction, pp. XLIX f.
23   *Cutheans*: the usual Jewish name for the Samaritans; cf. Josephus, *Antiq*. IX, 14, 3 § 288.
24   *Sennacherib*: Like Rashi (*ad* Ezra 4.1–2), Ibn Daud follows the interpretation of Midrash 'Eser Galuyot (*MBSh*, f. 77b–78a) in identifying the king referred to in II Ki. 17.24 with Sennacherib; for the origin of this identification, cf. *M*. Yad. 4.4; Ginzberg, *Legends*, VI, 361 n. 51.
24–27   Cf. Ezra 9.1 f., 10.18; Neh. 4.1 f., 6.1 f., 13.1 f., 13.28.
34   *Antigonus*' name is introduced here because of the association of his disciples with the Samaritan-Sadduceean heresy; II.43 f. *And their school*: Cf. Prologue.6.

35 accordance with what they had received from Ezra and the prophets; and the [other] half followed Sanballat and his sons-in-law. They offered burnt-offerings and peace-offerings outside the house of the Lord and enacted statutes and ordinances as they devised out of their own heart. In this temple Manasseh son of Joshua son of Jehozadak served as priest, and Zadok, with his colleague
40 Boethus, assumed leadership. This was the genesis of the heresy.

Antigonus of Soko received [the Torah] from Simeon the Righteous and his school. He represents the third generation. "He used to say: 'Be not like slaves that serve their master for the sake of compensation; be rather like slaves who serve their master with the thought of no compensation.'" Zadok
45 and Boethus questioned him concerning this, and he replied that he was not
[13] certain about compensation in this world, but only about the world to come. However, they repudiated his words, saying: "Never have we heard about the world to come." Though they had been his disciples, they broke with him and went to the temple of Mount Gerizim where they assumed leadership.
50 This temple stood among the Cutheans and the heretics for approximately 200 years.

In the 212th year after the building of the Second Temple, corresponding to the year 3621, Mattathias b. Johanan the high priest, called Hasmonean,

35 *From Ezra and the prophets*: Sc., since Ezra served as the head of the first generation of the Great Assembly, which took over from the prophets; cf. I.107–111, and S.N.
37 *Outside the house of the Lord*: Sc., in violation of the injunction in Dt. 12.5 f. *Enacted statutes etc.*: See S.N.
39–40 *Zadok with... Boethus*: See lines 44 f.
40 *Assumed leadership*: I.e., became heads of the Samaritan "academy" where the dissident law was expounded. For the expression, cf. III.70, VII.27, 30 and frequently in *SHQ*. See S.N. *The genesis of the heresy*. For its revival, cf. VI.43 f. On Ibn Daud's theory of the relationship of the Samaritan schism to Karaism, cf. above, pp. xxxvii f.
41 Abot 1.3.
42 *The third generation*: Cf. II.1.
42–44 *He used to say*: Abot 1.3, and see S.N.
44–48 For the nucleus of this account, cf. *ARN*, I, 5, p. 26 and see below, p. 174 n. 89.
48 *Though they had been etc.*: See S.N.
49 *Went to... Mount Gerizim*: That the Samaritan temple served as a refuge for heretics is affirmed by *Josippon* 5, p. 33; 29, p. 112. See S.N.
50–51 *Two hundred years*: *Josippon* 28, p. 108; *MBSh*, f. 54a. Inasmuch as, according to the chronological data given in the following lines, the Samaritan temple was destroyed no earlier than 203 years after its foundation, Ibn Daud qualified the statement with the word "approximately."
52 *In*: Lit., for in. the passage which follows summarizes the events culminating in the destruction of the Samaritan temple. *212th year etc.*: *MBSh*, f. 51b, and cf. Cohen *SFC*, p. 103 n. 146.; below, pp. 170 f.
53 *3621*: See S.N. *Mattathias... the high priest, called Hasmonean*: On these names see S.N.

[THE SUCCESSION OF TEACHERS IN THE DAYS OF THE SECOND TEMPLE] 19

rebelled against Antiochus king of Greece. He and his sons rose up against the viceroy of the king of Greece, [then] ruling over Jerusalem, and killed him and all his army. [The] Hasmonean ruled one year and died. After him, his son Judah, the mighty warrior, ruled 6 years and died. After him, his brother Jonathan son of [the] Hasmonean, ruled 6 years and died. After him, his brother Simeon ruled 18 years and died.

After him, Johanan son of Simeon son of [the] Hasmonean [ruled]; he is the one called Hyrcanus the first. He went up and destroyed the temple of the Cutheans and slew the heretics. Upon his safe return, he tendered a feast for the sages. One of the elder sages became merry and said: "Let the royal crown suffice you; leave the crown of priesthood to the seed of Aaron." (The King's mother had been a captive, having been taken captive on Mount Modiʻim; for the gentiles had besieged his father Simeon on the mountain; and when he fled, his women-folk were taken and subsequently came back to him. Because of this, it was || whispered that the King was a profaned priest.) Now when the King heard this, he became very angry and ordered all of the sages put to death. The King was then very old, and after having served as high-priest for forty years, he bacame a Sadducee.

King Johanan died, and Alexander his son ruled in his stead. He is the one

---

54–82 The account of the Maccabees derives from *Josippon* 20–33 and from the rabbinic sources listed in the following notes. For Ibn Daud's fuller treatment, cf. *MBSh*, f. 51a–54b. For the chronological data which follow, cf. also Ibn Daud's sermon on Zech. 11.4–17, *ibid*. f. 79a–b; *Josippon, loc. cit.* and 65, p. 239; Seder ʻOlam Zuta (ed. Neubauer), p. 74 and Zacuto, *op. cit.*, pp. 90 f. Ibn Daud's figures do not always correspond with these sources or even with those in his other work; cf. Cohen, *SFC*, p. 102.

57 *The mighty warrior*: See S.N.   62 *Tendered a feast*: See S.N.
63 *Became merry*: Sc., with drink; cf. Esther 1.10.
67–68 *Came back to him*: Sc., and after their return from captivity, John Hyrcanus' mother conceived.
68 *A profaned priest*: According to rabbinic law, the wife of a priest who has been taken into captivity may not cohabit with her husband (*M. Ket.* 2.5–6, 9). If she does, any child issuing from their union is classified as *ḥalal*, or profaned, and disqualified from officiating as a priest; cf. *JE*, VI, 164 s.v. "Ḥalalah;" Maimonides, *Mishneh Torah*, 'Issuray Bi'ah, ch. 18; *Encyclopedia Talmudit*, II, 295.
70 *Very old*: Since John's mother was taken captive at the time of the Antiochene persecutions, and John himself had already served as high-priest for forty years, John could well have been over seventy years old at the time.
71 *Forty years*: This figure may represent a variant in Ibn Daud's copies of *B. Ber.* 29a and *B. Yoma* 9a, both of which read "eighty" in the editions.
72 *In his stead*: Although in *MBSh* (f. 54b), Ibn Daud took account of the reign of Judah Aristobulus, he omitted all reference to him here. This may be a *lapsus calami*, but cf. II.84.

called King Jannaeus. He hated the sages. At that time it was the Jewish custom to rejoice on the Day-of-the-Willow-Tree, and people used to strike one another with willow branches. On one Day-of-the-Willow-Tree they did this, while King Alexander was standing beside the altar offering a sacrifice, and one of the disciples struck him on the forehead with a citron. He then lifted his right hand from the altar and said: "A sword!" [Then] he, too, put many sages to death violently, except for Simeon ben Shetaḥ, who was his wife's brother. However, Joshua ben Peraḥyah, Simeon's colleague, fled to Alexandria in Egypt, until Simeon ben Shetaḥ pleaded with the King for mercy in his behalf, and he permitted him to return.

Now we do not want to interrupt the sequence of the tradition with a history of the kings of the Second Temple. However, when we complete the sequence of the tradition, we shall give an account of all of them, as well as of the parable about them in the words of the prophets of blessed memory, for this is a source of great consolation.

Jose b. Joezer of Zeredah and Joseph b. Johanan of Jerusalem received [the Torah] from Antigonus of Soko. They and their school represent the fourth generation.

Judah b. Tabbai and Nittai the Arbelite received [the Torah] from them. They and their school represent the fifth generation.

[15] Joshua b. Peraḥyah and Simeon b. Shetaḥ received [the Torah] from them. They and their school represent the sixth generation.

The historical works of the Jews state that this Joshua b. Peraḥyah was the teacher of Jesus the Nazarene. If this is so, [it follows that] he lived in

---

73 *Called King Jannaeus*: Sc., in rabbinic literature; cf. talmudic dictionaries, s.v. ינאי. For the source of what follows, cf. *Josippon* 33, pp. 119–120; *MBSh*, f. 55a.

74 *Day-of-the-Willow-Tree*: I.e., the festival of Tabernacles; cf. Lev. 23.40, and talmudic dictionaries, s.v. ערבה. *Used to strike one another etc.*: This statement, taken from *Josippon*, derives from a misunderstanding of *M. Suk.* 4.4–5.

78 *A sword*: See S.N. *Violently*: See S.N.

79–80 *Simeon... his wife's brother*: B. Ber. 48a.

80–82 *B.* Sota 47a; *B.* Sanhed. 107b (in uncensored editions, e.g. *Der Babylonische Talmud* [ed. L. Goldschmidt], V, 324 f.; VII, 480 f.); and cf. also *B.* Kid. 66a.

85 *We shall give an account*: Viz., in Ibn Daud's work, *MBSh*.

86 *Parable*: Viz., Ibn Daud's sermon on Zechariah 11.4–17, *MBSh*, f. 50a, 79a–b. See S.N.

87 *Consolation*: Cf. Analysis and Interpretation, ch. III.

88–89 Abot. 1.4 and see S.N.

91 Cf. Abot 1.6 and see S.N.

93 Cf. Abot 1.8 and see S.N. to line 91.

95 *The historical works of the Jews etc.*: The reference is probably to the early versions of *Toledot Yeshu*; see *JE*, VII, 170 f. and S.N.

[THE SUCCESSION OF TEACHERS IN THE DAYS OF THE SECOND TEMPLE] 21

the time of King Jannaeus. However, the historical works of the Gentiles state that he was born in the days of Herod and crucified in the days of his son Archelaus. Now this is a significant difference of opinion, for there is a discrepancy between them of more than 110 years. The Gentile historians indicate their chronology in several different ways, [i.e.,] by saying that he was born in the year 312 of the Seleucid Era and crucified thirty-three years later; that he was born in the thirty-eighth year of the reign of Augustus king of Rome, in the days of Herod, and was crucified in the days of his son Archelaus. They argue this point so vehemently in order to prove that the Temple and kingdom of Israel endured for but a short while after his crucifixion. However, we have it as an authentic tradition from the Mishna and the Talmud, which did not distort anything, that R. Joshua b. Peraḥyah fled to Egypt in the days of Alexander, that is, Jannaeus, and with him fled Jesus the Nazarene. We also have it as an authentic tradition that he was born in the fourth year of the reign of King

97 *In the time of King Jannaeus*: *MBSh* (Mantua, 1513) censored in ed. Amsterdam f. 57b.
98 *Herod*: Cf. Matth. 2.1.   99 *Archelaus*: So also below, line 103. See S.N.
100 *Between them*: I.e., the Jewish and Gentile historians. *More than 110 years*: As noted by S. Krauss, *Das Leben Jesu*, p. 273 n. 4, this figure is incomprehensible, unless one assumes that Ibn Daud took the beginning of Jannaeus' reign and the end of Archelaus' as his terminal points. Even if Ibn Daud reckoned from his own date of the birth of Jesus until the Gentile date of the crucifixion, the figure would be in excess of 120 years, which indeed is the figure given in *ZDR*. However, in the figures given immediately below, lines 101–111, the discrepancy beween Jewish and Gentile historians seems to be one of eighty-six or eighty-nine years! On the gloss added in some of the MSS and editions, see S.N.
100–101 *Indicate their chronology in several different ways*: Lit., delimit (or define) their words with several distinguishing marks. See S.N.
102 *312 of the Seleucid Era*: I.e., the first year of the C.E. *Thirty-three years later*: Eusebius-Jerome, *Chronicon* (ed. Schoene), pp. 144–145, 148–149; (ed. Fotheringham), pp. 251, 256.
103 *Thirty-eighth year of... Augustus*: See IV.127.
105 *So vehemently*: Lit., so much.
105–106 *The Temple... endured etc.*: For this argument in Christian polemics, see e.g., Williams, *Adversus Judaeos*, pp. 50, 53 f., 57, 85, 100, 221, 225; Eusebius, *Eccles. Hist.*, II, v, 6, vi, 8, xxiii, 18, etc.; Orosius, *Apology*, VII.3 f. See also S.N.
107 *From the Mishna and Talmud*: This is not quite correct, for the Mishna has no information on the subject. Either Ibn Daud meant the sages of the Mishna—and Joshua b. Peraḥyah falls within this category — or the expression is a *lapsus calami* deriving from his habit of coupling Mishna and Talmud together (as in Prologue. 9.). For the talmudic source, see note to II. 80–82. Cf. Herford, *Christianity in Talmud and Midrash*, pp. 50 f. *Which did not distort*: Cf. Prologue. 8 f., and see S.N.
110 *An authentic tradition*: Viz., but not from the Talmud. I. Loeb, *Joseph Haccohen et les Chroniqueurs Juifs*, p. 89, suggests that the information derives from a recension of *Toledot Yeshu*.

Alexander, which was the year 263 after the building of the Second Temple, and the fifty-first year of the reign of the Hasmonean dynasty. In the year || [16] 299 after the building of the Temple, he was apprehended at the age of thirty-six in the third year of the reign of Aristobulus the son of Jannaeus.

115 Shemaiah and Abtalion received [the Torah] from them. They represent the seventh generation.

Hillel and Shammai received [the Torah] from them. They represent the eighth generation. Hillel went up from Babylonia at the age of forty, and studied for forty years and taught for forty years, the length of his life being 120 120 years. He was of the house of David of the seed of the royal line. He had eighty disciples of whom the greatest was Jonathan b. Uzziel and the least Rabban Johanan b. Zakkai. His colleague was Menahem, who died in Hillel's lifetime. They did not differ. After Menahem's post became vacant, Shammai took his place.

125 His son was Rabban Gamaliel the Elder, and his grandson was Rabban Simeon b. Gamaliel the first. These three functioned as patriarchs in the Temple for 100 years during the reign of the Herodian dynasty. For this was the practice in the [days of the] Second Temple: the king of the Hasmonean dynasty or of their slaves, the Herodian dynasty, ruled supreme in matters of war

112 *Fifty-first year of the... Hasmonean dynasty*: This figure cannot be squared with the chronological data given above, II.56–71. Apparently, Ibn Daud merely copied the source containing this "authentic tradition" without bothering to square its chronology with his own data.

113-114 *Thirty-six in the third year of... Aristobulus*: According to *MBSh*, f. 56a-b, Jannaeus reigned twenty-seven years and Alexandra Salome nine. Since Jesus was born in the fourth year of the former's reign, his thirty-sixth corresponded to Aristobulus' third. — On the point of Ibn Daud's argument, see S.N.

115 Abot 1.10. *From them*: Cf. S.N. to line 91.

117 Abot 1.12.

118-119 Sifre Deut. § 357 (ed. Finkelstein), p. 429.

120 *Of the house of David etc.*: See I.74; *B*. Shab. 56a; Ber. R. 98.8 (ed. Theodor-Albeck) p. 1259 and parallels; B.M. Lewin, *Otzar ha-Geonim*, VIII, Responsa, p. 188. *Eighty disciples etc.*: *ARN*, I, 14 (II, 28), p. 57 and parallels; *ISG* 8.13 f.

122 *Menahem*: M. Hag. 2.2. *Who died*: See S.N.

123 *They did not differ... Shammai*: Ibn Daud quotes *M*. Hag. 2.2 verbatim although the first half of the citation is irrelevant here.

125 *His son*: Viz., Hillel's son. *Rabban Gamaliel the Elder*: See also I.77.

126 *These three etc.*: Cf. *B*. Shab. 15a (bot.) and see S.N. *In the Temple*: Although the Talmud says that they functioned "in *the days* of the Temple" (בםני הבית), Ibn Daud insisted (correctly) that they officiated *in* the Temple (cf. *M*. Mid. 5.4) to emphasize the sacred authority of the Rabbanite patriarchs, who were the butt of Karaite attack. See also below.

129 *Their slaves, the Herodian dynasty*: Cf. *B*. B.B. 3b. *Ruled supreme etc.*: See S.N.

[THE SUCCESSION OF TEACHERS IN THE DAYS OF THE SECOND TEMPLE]

130 and in all affairs of state. However, all matters of law, statutes and ordinances were executed in accordance with the decision of the patriarch of the house of David and in accordance with the decision of the high priest and the Sanhedrin. Thus you find in the tractate of Sanhedrin: "It happened that Rabban Gamaliel the Elder was sitting on a step on the Temple hill, and Johanan the
135 well-known scribe was sitting before him with three cut sheets || in his hand.
7] He said to him: 'Take one sheet, etc.' as far as 'and take another sheet and write: "To our brethren of the Diaspora of Babylonia, and to our brethren of the Diaspora of Media, and to our brethren of the Diaspora of Greece, and to all the other Diasporas of Israel: May your peace be great. I hereby
140 inform you that the lambs are still too young and the doves still tender, and that the month of the barley crop has not yet arrived. It has, therefore, seemed fitting to me and to my colleagues to add one month to this year.' " Hence, we know that this Rabban Gamaliel was the head of the academy as well as patriarch, and that his actions were accepted throughout Palestine and through-
145 out the Diaspora of Israel. And neither the king nor anyone else in the world

---

131–132 *The decision of the patriarch... high priest and the Sanhedrin*: Whatever Ibn Daud's immediate source for this description of the religious arm in the days of the second Temple, ultimately the statement is derived from the decision-making powers enumerated in *M.* Shebu'ot 2.2: king, prophet, Urim we-Tummim (= high priest), Sanhedrin. Since the king mentioned there is one appointed by divine authority — which was not the case with the Hasmoneans and Herodians — and prophecy had ceased, the authorities remaining were high priest, the Sanhedrin and its two leaders, the head of the academy and patriarch. The latter two were doubtless regarded by Ibn Daud as having replaced prophet and king respectively.

133 *Tractate of Sanhedrin*: B. Sanhed. 11b (top), and cf. Rabbinovicz, *Variae Lectiones*, IX, 18.

134 *The Elder*: See S.N.

135 *Well-known*: Translation doubtful. *In his hand*: The reading is doubtful.

136 *As far as*: Hebrew, עד, serving as an ellipsis; see I.160. Ibn Daud omits the text of the first two epistles quoted in the Talmud, since it is the third, the one addressed to the Diaspora, which suffices to prove his point on the universal authority of the patriarch.

138 *And to our brethren of Greece*: These words are lacking in the Bab. Talmud but are found in *Yer.* Sanhed. 1.2, f. 18d.

143 *Head of the academy as well as patriarch*: Since Ibn Daud consistently distinguishes between these offices (see Cohen, *SFC*, pp. 107 f.), and inasmuch as Rabban Gamaliel dispatched these epistles without any co-signature, he manifestly combined in his own person two of the four offices of Jewish society (see note to line 131). See S.N.

144 *Accepted throughout Palestine*: The evidence is from the two epistles to the Galilee and the South alluded to in line 136. That his authority was accepted is indicated by the fact that no one demurred. Cf. also *Tosef.* Sanhed. 2.13 (ed. Zuckermandel), p. 418, line 4.

145 *Neither the king nor anyone else... demurred*: See S.N.

demurred. However, Qirqisani would not have been obeyed thus, and not [even] Anan! The Almighty, blessed be He, said: "You shall repair to the levitical priests, or the magistrate in charge at the time... Should a man act presumptuously and disregard the priest charged with serving the Lord your God, or the magistrate, that man shall die." Come and see whether this one was or was not a magistrate of Israel.

Hillel and his school represent the ninth generation.

Rabban Johanan b. Zakkai received [the Torah] from Hillel and Shammai. In his days Vespasian came up against Jerusalem. Now there lived in Jerusalem Abba Siqra, who was chief of the brigands as well as the son of Rabban Johanan ben Zakkai's sister. He went out secretly to King Vespasian and requested permission for Rabban Johanan b. Zakkai to come out to him. The King granted his request, and Rabban Johanan b. Zakkai went out to Vespasian. The King recognized || the greatness of his wisdom, and he honored and revered him at the very time when he was laying siege to Jerusalem. Then Nero king of Rome died, and the councillors of Rome voted to enthrone Vespasian. Accordingly, he departed for Rome and left his son Titus to besiege Jerusalem, and commanded him to render great homage to Rabban Johanan b. Zakkai. The Temple was destroyed in the year 3829. [At that time] Rabbi Ishmael b.

146–147 *Qirqisani... Anan*: Cf. II.21–22.   147–150 Deut. 17.9, 12. See S.N.

151 *A magistrate of Israel*: The exact implication of this title is obscure. The most likely explanation appears to me to be "a magistrate whose authority is acknowledged by all Israel." Thus, the anti-Karaitically oriented *Mishnah of R. Eliezer* (ed. Enelow), p. 123 line 2, proclaims that "whoever is vested with authority over Israel is [to be heeded] as Moses and Aaron were in their day." Cf. further, Zucker, "Tegubot li-Tenu'at Abaylay Zion etc.", p. 391. This explanation is in keeping with the taunt at Anan and Qirqisani, for they could claim no such universally acknowledged magistracy. For an alternative explanation see S.N., where the anti-Karaite polemic of this paragraph is also discussed.

152 *The ninth generation*: In line 118, Hillel and Shammai are said to represent the eighth generation. Ibn Daud thus distinguishes between the generation when Hillel and Shammai served together, and the subsequent generation when Hillel and his son and grandson served. That Hillel's leadership, in Ibn Daud's view, spanned two generations has been shown in *SFC*, pp. 107 f. Ibn Daud could not reckon Gamaliel the Elder and Simeon b. Gamaliel as a separate generation, for in his view Rabban Johanan b. Zakkai (see next line) took over directly from Hillel as head of the academy, while Rabban Simeon b. Gamaliel served as patriarch (see lines 165–166).

153 Abot 2.8. Ibn Daud departed from the chain listed in Abot 1.16, for he had placed Rabban Gamaliel in the ninth generation, and Rabban Simeon b. Gamaliel in the tenth.

154–163 B. Git. 56a–b, and see S.N.; *Josippon* 97, p. 404.

164 *3829*: The Second Temple was built in 3409 and remained standing 420 years; see note to II.8.

165 Elisha the high-priest and Rabban Simeon b. Gamaliel the Elder, who was then the patriarch, were killed. Titus also wished to put to death Rabban Gamaliel his son, but Rabban Johanan b. Zakkai pleaded with him, and he yielded.

Thus, there were ten generations from Zerubbabel and those who came
170 with him until Rabban Johanan b. Zakkai. He too lived 120 years: forty years he engaged in business; forty years he studied Torah and all wisdom known in his generation; and forty years he taught and judged Israel. After the destruction of the Temple, he went up to Jamnia and judged Israel from there, enacting new laws and making hedges about the Torah, up to the time when
175 he passed away in Jamnia.

164–166   *R. Ishmael b. Elisha etc.*: *MBSh*, f. 77b; *Josippon*, 97, p. 404; cf. *B.* Sota 48b; *ARN*, I, 38, p. 114 and parallels; *ISG* 74.9–12.
166–168   *Titus also wished etc.*: *MBSh* and *Josippon*, *loc. cit.*; cf. also *B.* Git. 56b.
169–170   Rabban Johana b. Zakkai represents the tenth generation; cf. note to line 152.
170   *He too*: Cf. II.118–119. *Lived 120 years etc.*: Sifre Deut. § 357 (ed. Finkelstein), p. 429; *B.* R.H. 31b.
171   *Torah and all wisdom*: Cf. *B.* Suk. 28a; *ARN*, II, 28, p. 59; *ISG* 9.3 f.
173   See note to lines 154–163. *Judged Israel:* Ibn Daud uses this expression to indicate that he now served only as head of a community, "the academy" having been destroyed; cf. VII. 356.
174   *New laws etc.*: Cf. Prologue. 10–11; for the statement here, cf. *M.* R.H. 4.1–4; *B.* R.H. 21b, 31b.
175   *In Jamnia*: I know of no source which indicates that he died in Jamnia, but cf. *ISG* 75.8–9 ("French" recension); cf. also *STW*, p. 5, line 5.

[III]

[THE SUCCESSION OF TANNAIM]

Rabban Gamaliel, the son of Rabban Simeon b. Gamaliel who was killed in the persecution, became head of the academy and patriarch after the passing away of Rabban Johanan b. Zakkai. His sister's husband was R. Eliezer b. Hyrcanus. His colleagues were: R. Joshua b. Hananiah, a great sage and president of the court (though he was but a smith [by occupation]); R. Jose the Galilean, a priest; R. Simeon b. Nethanel; R. Eleazar b. Arak; R. Johanan b. Nuri; R. Johanan b. Baroqa; Samuel ha-Qaton; R. Eleazar Ḥisma; R. Eleazar b. Azariah, a priest, tenth generation descendant of Ezra and a very wealthy man; R. Ḥalafta; and R. Jose b. Qisma. All these represent the first generation.

Rabban Gamaliel and R. Joshua had a falling out over testimony [on the appearance] of the new moon. Once witnesses came to Lydda and said: "We have seen it in the morning in the east and in the evening in the west." R. Joshua said: "They are false witnesses. How can people testify that a woman

---

1 For the title, cf. III.110.   2–4 *ISG* 75.9 f.
3 *Head of the academy and patriarch*: Cf. II.143.
4 *His sister's husband etc.*: *B.* Shab. 116a (end); *B.* B.M. 59b.
5–10 *His colleagues etc.*: Cf. the list, which differs in several details, in *ISG* 11.8 f. I have not noted the talmudic proofs for the contemporaneity of scholars in any generation, unless the name presents a problem from the point of view of chronology or identity. Otherwise, the information is readily available in standard handbooks and encyclopedias.
6 *President of the court*: *B.* B.K. 74b (end). *A smith*: *B.* Ber. 28a.
6–7 *R. Jose*: The identification of R. Jose ha-Kohen and R. Jose ha-Galilee seems to be Ibn Daud's. For a well-taken objection, cf. Zacuto, pp. 35b, 47a.
9 *B.* Ber. 27b (end); Yeb. 86b; *Yer.* Ma'as. Shen. 5.5, f. 56b–c.
12–20 For the original source of this story, cf. *M.* R.H. 2.8–9. Cf. also *ISG* 75.9 f.
13 *Lydda*: Ibn Daud or his source presumably thought that that was where official testimony on the new moon was received. On the possible source of this datum, as well as on the other variations from earlier versions of the story, cf. S.N.
15 *How can people testify etc.*: Although it is true that their testimony was first declared to be false, the metaphor was not used in connection with this incident, since it would indeed have been inappropriate. Ibn Daud or his source omitted the intermediate passage: "R. Johanan b. Nuri said: 'They are false witnesses!' However, when they came to Jamnia, Rabban Gamaliel accepted their testimony. On another occasion, two came and said: 'We saw the new moon at its appointed time, but on the following night it was not visible.' R. Dosa b. Horkinas said: 'They are false witnesses.! How can people testify that a woman has given birth when her belly is still swollen!' " See further in S.N.

has given birth when her belly is still swollen!" However, when they came to Jamnia, Rabban Gamaliel accepted them. Rabban Gamliel sent a message to R. Joshua: "I command you to appear before me with your staff and your money on the day which according to your reckoning is the Day of Atonement," and R. Joshua obeyed Rabban Gamaliel's command. Once again they were divided over whether the evening prayer is optional or obligatory. They differed again over whether a firstling whose lip was slit is to be treated as a blemished animal or not. In each of these cases Rabban Gamaliel forced his view on R. Joshua. The seventy elders, who were his colleagues, became so resentful || that they voted to remove Rabban Gamaliel as head of the academy. R. Eleazar b. Azariah was then appointed as head. Subsequently, the sages were reconciled to Rabban Gamaliel, and they reinstated him. However, R. Eleazar b. Azariah was not removed; but Rabban Gamaliel would lecture two weeks and R. Eleazar b. Azariah one week. When Rabban Gamaliel passed away during R. Joshua's lifetime, R. Joshua rose to repeal his decisions, and R. Johanan b. Nuri became enraged. Rabban Simeon b. Gamaliel was then appointed as patriarch. This was the first generation after the Destruction.

R. Akiba became head of the academy after Rabban Gamaliel. His colleagues were: Simeon b. Azzai; Simeon b. Zoma; Elisha *aher*; R. Tarfon; R. Ishmael; R. Judah b. Baba; R. Judah b. Tema, known as ben Dama; R. Ḥanina b. Teradion; R. Yeshebab the Scribe; R. Simai; and R. Ḥuspith the Interpreter. All these represent the second generation after the Destruction. In their days there lived in Babylonia R. Judah b. Bathyra, a colleague of Rabban Johanan b. Zakkai who outlived him for many years.

21   *B. Ber.* 27b.   22   *B. Bekorot* 36a. See S.N.   24–29   *B. Ber.* 27b–28a.
24   *The seventy elders, who were his colleagues*: Sc., since the Sanhedrin consisted of seventy-one members; *M. Sanhed.* 1.6.
25   *As head of the academy*: However, he was not removed from his position as patriarch; cf. II.143, and see S.N.
29–31   *When Rabban Gamaliel passed away etc.*: *Tosef.* Ta'an. 2.5 (ed. Lieberman), p. 330; *B. 'Erub.* 41a.
31   *R. Johanan b. Nuri became enraged*: And R. Joshua retracted his proposal. On Ibn Daud's purpose in recounting this series of incidents, see S.N.
32   *As patriarch*: Lit., as head with respect to the patriarchate; Cf. S.N. to II.40. Cf. also above, I.77–80; *ISG* 75.21. As the next line states, R. Akiba took over as head of the academy.
33   *R. Akiba*: As Zacuto, p. 37a, noted, no known earlier source makes this claim for R. Akiba, in the sense that Ibn Daud uses the term "head of the academy". See S.N. for a possible explanation.
34–36   See S.N.
35   *Known as ben Dama*: See S.N.
38–39   *ISG* 12.8. That he was a colleague of R. Johanan b. Zakkai is probably based on Ibn Daud's identification of this R. Judah with the Benay Bathyra of *B. R.H.* 29b.

40 In their days a certain man by the name of Koziba arose, claiming to be the Messiah of the seed of David. He revolted against Domitian king of Rome and slew his viceroy in Palestine. At that time Domitian king of Rome was only a youth and, therefore, could not withstand him. So this Koziba began to reign in Bethar in the fifty-second year after the destruction of the Temple.
45 He died while yet in power, and his son Rufus ||–which means redhaired–reigned
[21] after him. He too died, and his son Romulus reigned. Now there flocked to Koziba and his sons a great multitude of Israel, who returned from all their dwelling places. In the days of Romulus b. Rufus b. Koziba, Hadrian mobilized his forces, went up to Palestine and conquered Bethar on the ninth of Ab
50 in the year 73 of the destruction of the Temple. He slew Romulus and smote Israel a great blow such as had not been seen or heard even in the days of Nebuzaradan or in those of Titus.

R. Ḥanina b. Teradion was burned alive along with a scroll of the Torah, and R. Yeshebab the Scribe, R. Simai and R. Ḥuspith the Interpreter were
55 also slain. R. Judah b. Baba was slain too, since the king of Rome had decreed a persecution saying that whoever received ordination should be put to death, and whoever granted ordination should be put to death, and the city in which the ordination was performed should be destroyed. Accordingly, he went and stationed himself between two great cities, between Usha and Shefaram, and
60 ordained five elders: R. Meir, R. Judah, R. Jose, R. Simeon, and R. Eleazar b. Shammua. Then the enemy came upon him and speared him until his body was like a sieve. R. Eleazar b. Shammua was slain too. Prior to that, they

40–52 For a parallel account, see *ZDR*. On the facts and traditions behind this version of the Bar Kokba uprising, for which Ibn Daud's works are the earliest source, see Analysis, ch. IV That the uprising occurred in the days of R. Akiba's leadership follows from *Yer.* Ta'an. 4.8, f. 68b; Ekah R. to Lam. 2.2 (and in ed. Buber, p. 101); and from rabbinic traditions on the "Ten Martyrs." See S.N.
40 *Claiming to be the Messiah*: *B*. Sanhed. 93b.
43 *Could not withstand him*: For the style, cf. II Chr. 13.7.
44 *Fifty-second year etc.*: This is Ibn Daud's interpretation of the chronological datum on Bethar given in Seder 'Olam 30 (ed. Ratner), p. 146 and the sources listed above (to lines 40–52); Ekah R. to 4.18 (and in ed. Buber, p. 152). See S.N.
48 From the account in *ZDR* it is apparent that Ibn Daud meant Trajan, a confusion not unknown in ancient times; cf. Alon, *Toledot*, I, 249.
49 *Ninth of Ab*: *M*. Ta'an. 4.6.
50 *Year 73*: See S.N. to line 44.
52 *Nebuzaradan*: II Ki. 25.8 f. *Titus*: II.162 f.
53 *B*. A.Z. 18a.   54 See S.N.
55–62 *B*. Sanhed. 13b–14a; A.Z. 8b; *ISG* 14.
62 *R. Eleazar b. Shammua*: For an explanation of the appearance of this name in the medieval lists of the "Ten Martyrs," cf. L. Finkelstein, "The Ten Martyrs," in *Essays and Studies in Memory of Linda R. Miller* (New York, 1938), p. 50.

[THE SUCCESSION OF TANNAIM]

had combed the flesh of R. Akiba b. Joseph with combs of iron. All this happened to them in the war of Hadrian because of the provocation of Ben Koziba. Then there was fulfilled for them what had been written by Daniel: "And they that are wise among the people shall cause the many to understand; yet they shall stumble by the sword and by flame, by captivity and by spoil, many days."

In their days Ptolemy lived, and the book of the Almagest was written.

Rabban Simeon b. Gamaliel the second became head [of the academy] after the death of R. Akiba. His colleagues were: R. Meir, the outstanding one among them; R. Judah; R. Jose; R. Eleazar b. Shammua; R. Nathan; and R. Simeon b. Yoḥai. R. Meir and R. Nathan agreed to humiliate him publicly, since they were more learned than he. However, he learned of the plan, and thenceforth R. Meir and R. Nathan were not mentioned by name; R. Meir was referred to as "others" and R. Nathan as "some say." This represents the third generation after the Destruction.

[He was succeeded by] Our Saintly Master, that is, R. Judah — the patriarch and head of the academy — b. Rabban Simeon b. Gamaliel. "For the Lord saw the affliction of Israel, that it was very bitter," and He fulfilled for them

---

63 *B.* Ber. 61b. That his martyrdom occurred before those of the others is indicated by Semahot 8.9 (ed. Higger), p. 154 and the references cited there.

64 *Provocation of Ben Koziba*: Cf. I.207 f.

65–68 Dan. 11.33. That "the wise" are the scholars who perished in the days of the Hadrianic persecution was widely accepted in medieval exegesis; see S.N.

69 *Ptolemy*: Heb., Batlamiyus, the usual Arabic spelling. The inclusion of this datum in *SHQ* reflects the preponderant influence of Ptolemy in medieval science; cf. *EI* (new ed.), I, 1100 f. On the high station of the Almagest in Judeo-Arabic circles, cf. Steinschneider *Die Hebraeischen Uebersetzungen des Mittelalters*, pp. 519 f. and especially p. 520 n. 145 for references to Jewish authors who give a date for Ptolemy.

70 *Became head [of the academy]*: Cf. above, line 32; *B.* Hor. 13b; *ISG*, 14.21, 75.21.

71 *R. Meir, the outstanding etc.*: *B.* 'Erub. 13b, cited by *ISG* 28.13; cf. also *ibid.* 13.18, 15.1.

71–73 This list of contemporaries of R. Simeon b. Gamaliel II is identical with that of the five scholars ordained by R. Judah b. Baba (above, line 60 and cf. *ISG* 13.6 f.) with the addition of R. Nathan, on the basis of the incident that follows immediately.

73–76 *B.* Hor. 13b. See S.N.

77 *The third generation*: On this division of generations, which disagrees with that of *ISG* 17.19 f., 31.18, see below, pp. 205 f.

78–79 Cf. I.79; *STW* 2.6–7; *ISG* 16.21, 76.1.

78 *Our Saintly Master*: On the origin of this honorific, cf. *B.* Shab. 118b; *Yer.* Meg. 1.13, f. 72b; *JE*, VII, 333.

79 *For the Lord etc.*: II Ki. 14.26. Ibn Daud refers here to the Hadrianic persecutions (above, lines 40–67), and obviously has his eye on the following verse as embodied in the lifetime of R. Judah the Patriarch.

what had been written by Daniel: "Now when they shall stumble, they shall be helped with a little help." Hadrian died, and there reigned in Rome Antoninus son of Severus. He loved Our Saintly Master as himself, and it is said that Our Saintly Master converted him to Judaism secretly. The days of Our
85 Saintly Master were all happy ones for Israel, and he lived on for a long time. In his days Antoninus son of Severus died, and then Antipus ruled, and after the death of Antipus there ruled Commodus. All of them honored and revered Our Saintly Master throughout his life.

This R. Judah the Patriarch received [the Torah] from R. Eleazar b. Shammua
90 and from R. Jose. His colleagues were: R. Ishmael b. R. Jose; R. Simeon son of R. Johanan b. Baroqa; R. Eleazar b. R. Simeon b. Yoḥai; R. Eleazar
[23] and R. Simeon the sons of R. Judah; R. Joshua b. || Qarḥa; Symmachus; Pelimo; Ise b. Judah; R. Reuben Strobili; Hanan b. Phinehas; R. Pedath; R. Eleazar b. Perata; R. Jacob of Kefar Ḥittaya; and R. Phinehas b. Jair. He
95 composed the Mishna in the year 3949, which was the year 500 of the Seleucid Era and the year 120 of the destruction of the Temple. This represents the fourth generation after the Destruction.

In the days of Our Saintly Master the contents of the books of medicine were committed to writing, for Galen lived in his days. However, Hippocrates

---

81   Dan. 11.34. The "help" is in the respite from persecution enjoyed in the patriarchate of R. Judah. See S.N.
81–88   For Ibn Daud's parallel account, cf. *ZDR*.
83   *He loved Our Saintly Master*: Cf. *ISG* 21.14–15. *It is said etc.*: Cf. *Yer.* Meg. 1.13, f. 72b, and see S.N.
84   *Secretly*: Cf. *B*. A.Z. 10b on the clandestine visits of Antoninus to Rabbi. The secrecy is probably also indicated by the fact that Gentile historians of Rome had no knowledge of the fact.
86–87   *Antipus*: Cf. *ZDR*, where this name is again found as a synonym for "Antoninus the younger." Does it stem from an abridgment of Antoninus Pius (or, following the reading of MS ק, of Antoninus Verus)?
87   *Honored and revered*: See S.N.
89–90   *From R. Eleazar... and R. Jose*: Cf. *ISG* 16.12 f., which lists *R. Eleazar* and *R. Simeon* among others. On R. Judah as disciple of R. Jose, cf. *JE*, VII, 334.
90–94   *His colleagues etc.*: Cf. *ISG* 15.6–17.8 with which Ibn Daud's list differs as much as it agrees.
95   *Composed the Mishna*: *B*. Yeb. 64b. Cf. further Epstein, *Prolegomena ad Litteras Tannaiticas* [in Hebrew], p. 200. See S.N. *3949*: For the source of this date, cf. below, p. 211.
98–99   *The contents of the books of medicine etc.*: The wording is awkward and suggests that Galen committed to writing medical traditions of great antiquity. It may be that Ibn Daud had his eye on *M*. Pes. 4.9.
99   *Galen*: Cf. *ZDR*. On medieval Jewish interest in Galen, cf. Introduction, p. xxiii, and Steinschneider, *Hebraeischen Uebersetzungen*, pp. 650 f. *However, Hippocrates etc.*: The qualifying "however" derives from the common medieval association of Galen's name

100 the physician had written his books in the days of Mordecai and Esther, for he had been of that generation.

R. Hanina bar Hama became head of the academy after the demise of Our Saintly Master, for thus Our Saintly Master had enjoined. His colleagues were: Our Saintly Master's four sons, R. Hoshaiah, Rabbi Simeon, Rabban
105 Gamaliel, and R. Eleazar ha-Qappar; R. Hiyya; Bar Qappara; Levi; R. Efes; Samuel's father; and Rab, who was the son of R. Hiyya's brother as well as the son of his sister. Bar Qappara composed [the] Tosefta; R. Hiyya, R. Hoshaiah Beribbi, and R. Simeon Beribbi composed *baraitot* and *mekhilatot*. These were the last of the tannaim.
110   These then were the five generations of tannaim.

---

with Hippocrates in view of the former's commentaries to Hippocrates' works; cf. Walzer, *Galen on Jews and Christians*, pp. 8 f. On Jewish interest in Hippocrates, cf. Steinschneider, *loc. cit.*, pp. 657 f.; A.A. Altmann, "The Climatological Factor in Yehuda Hallevi's Theory of Prophecy" [in Hebrew], *Melilah* I (1944), 9–11, 13.

100 *In the days of Mordecai and Esther*: Arab historians, who were doubtless Ibn Daud's source for this dating, told of negotiations between Artaxerxes Longimanus and Hippocrates. While Mas'udi identified Artaxerxes as Artakhshast, others identified him by the later equivalent name of Ardashir, which Ibn Daud, in turn, regarded as synonymous with Ahasuerus; see IV.145, and *EI*, I, 784, s.v. Bukrat.

102 This contradicts the Talmud (cf. next note), which states that R. Hanina declined the post in favor of R. Efes, who served for two and a half years.

103 *For thus Our Saintly Master had enjoined*: B. Ket. 103b, cited by *ISG* 34.17. See S.N. The patriarchate was taken over by Rabban Gamaliel Beribbi; B. Ket. 103b and above, I.79–80.

104–105 *Our Saintly Master's four sons*: As Zacuto, p. 50b, noted, R. Judah had but two sons; but Ibn Daud credited him with four on the basis of his misunderstanding of the title "Beribbi," which each of these four is given in the Talmud and which Ibn Daud took to mean "the son of Rabbi [= Judah the Patriarch]." On the reading of the MSS see S.N.

106 *Rab*: The usual designation for R. Abba Arika in the Babylonian Talmud. *The son of R. Hiyya's brother etc.*: B. Sanhed. 5a (bot.). R. Hiyya's half-sister married R. Hiyya's half-brother with whom she had no blood ties whatever.

107 *Bar Qappara composed the Tosefta*: This statement, for which I can find no earlier source, is probably an interpretation of the talmudic reports on the "Mishna of Bar Qappara"; cf. e.g. *B. B.B.* 154b. See S.N.

108 On these men as compilers of *baraitot*, or non-mishnaic tannaitic traditions, cf. B. Cohen, *Mishna and Tosefta*, pp. 27 f.; Epstein, *Mabo le-Nusah ha-Mishna*, I, 25 f. By *mekhilatot*, Ibn Daud probably refers to all of the halakic or tannaitic *midrashim*; cf. Epstein, *Prolegomena ad Litteras Tannaiticas*, p. 546. I cannot locate any earlier tradition crediting these men with the compilation of halakic *midrashim*.

109 *The last of the tannaim*: STW, p. 9, end of par. 7; *ISG* 59.8 f.

[IV]

[24] THE SUCCESSION OF AMORAIM

The first generation was that of Rab and Samuel. At the end of Our Saintly Master's lifetime, in the year 3979, Rab went to Babylonia. There he found R. Shela; but since Rab was extremely humble, he refused to be appointed
5 head of the academy throughout R. Shela's lifetime until the latter passed away. Moreover, he refused to become the head in Nehardea where Samuel was living. Therefore, he went to Sura, which is Matha Meḥasia, and served as head there until he passed away in the year 4003. Then the members of his academy joined Samuel['s academy]. Samuel passed away in the year 4010.
10 He was quite accomplished in every aspect of Greek wisdom in addition to his Jewish learning. The following were their disciples: R. Judah, Rami bar Ḥama and R. Ḥama the sons of Ezekiel; R. Naḥman the Prince; Rabbah bar

  2 *The first generation*: *STW*, p. 9 par. 8; *ISG* 59.15–60.10. *Rab*: Cf. III.106. *At the end of Our Saintly Master's lifetime*: Though this is a reasonable inference on the part of Ibn Daud, I am not aware of any earlier source which indicates that Rab went to Babylonia at the *end* of Judah the Patriarch's lifetime.
  3 *3979 etc.*: *STW*, p. 4 line 1; *ISG* 78.5.
  4 *R. Shela*: Sc., in the position of head of the academy. *Since Rab was extremely humble*: Zacuto, p. 199a, thought that Ibn Daud drew this conclusion from *B.* Yoma 20b (cited in *ISG* 78.11–12), where it is reported that Rab served as R. Shela's *amora*.
  6–8 *Moreover, he refused etc.*: *ISG* 78.13–81.9.
  7 *Matha Meḥasia*: See S.N.
  8 *4003*: *STW*, p. 4 and *ISG* 81.9 concur in dating his death in 558 Sel. Era = 4007 A. M. See next note.
  9 *ISG* 81.10–82.5. Although the date of Samuel's death in *SHQ* disagrees with the one given in *STW*, p. 4 and *ISG* 82.5, Ibn Daud's date coincides with the relative chronology of these sources, which place Samuel's death seven years after that of Rab. On the origin of the discrepancy, see S.N. — In view of the fact that *SHQ* frequently differs with *ISG* on a date, but almost always coincides with it in terms of relative chronologies — i.e., in the number of years that elapsed between two events — wherever Ibn Daud's date corresponds only in relative terms to that of *ISG*, references to the latter are asterisked.
  10 *Greek wisdom*: I.e., astronomy and astrology; cf. VII.327, 331. Although *ISG* 81.19 makes reference to Samuel's expertness in the science of calendation (cf. *B.* Ber. 58b), Ibn Daud's wording suggests that he had in mind the *Baraita of Samuel*, a compendium of the astronomical rules of the Jewish calendar; cf. *JE*, II, 520. Ibn Daud may also have had in mind Samuel's renown as a physician; cf. *B.* B.M. 85b, 113b. See S.N.
  11–15 This list of disciples is independent of those in *STW*, p. 10 and *ISG* 60.10–11, 82.6–8.
  11–12 *R. Judah etc. the sons of Ezekiel*: The text of this line is highly suspect; see S.N.

Abbuha; R. Sheshet, who was blind; R. Anan; R. Mattena; R. Shimi bar Ashi; R. Ḥiyya bar Ashi; R. Isaac bar Ashayan; R. Ḥama bar Gurya; and
15 R. Kahana the first.

In their days the head of the academy in Palestine was R. Johanan, who received [the Torah] from R. Hoshaiah Beribbi. He lived for many years and indeed was head of the academy for eighty years. The following were his disciples: R. Ammi; R. Assi; R. Eleazar b. Pedat; R. Yannai; Ulla; Rabin;
20 R. Dimi; and R. Samuel bar Naḥmani.

25] The second generation was that of R. Judah and R. Huna. After the death of Samuel in 4010, R. Judah b. Ezekiel became head in Nehardea and R. Huna in Sura. Although R. Judah was superior to R. Huna in learning, inasmuch as R. Huna was related to the prince, the academy of Sura gained
25 the ascendancy. After R. Judah passed away, both academies came under the leadership of R. Huna. In his days, too, R. Johanan, head of the academy in Palestine, passed away, in 4039, and R. Ammi took over the headship of the academy there. R. Huna passed away in 4050, after having served as head of the academy for forty years. The following were their disciples: R.
30 Ḥisda; Rabbah bar Naḥmani; R. Joseph; R. Naḥman bar Isaac; R. Zeʻera; Rabbah bar R. Huna; and R. Hamnuna.

12 *R. Naḥman the Prince*: Cf. *B.* Ḥul. 124a, where he is called "the son-in law of the nasi." MS א and Zacuto, p. 199a, have corrected the text here accordingly. Whenever the term nasi is used in connection with a Babylonian, the reference is to the exilarch.
13 *Blind*: *B.* Ber. 58a. See S.N. *R. Shimi bar Ashi*: Actually, R. Shimi was of a later generation; cf. Hyman, *Toledoth Tannaim Ve'Amoraim*, p. 1114. Either Ibn Daud concluded that R. Shimi's association with R. Kahana (cf. sources listed by Hyman) were with R. Kahana I, or he associated him with R. Ḥiyya bar Ashi.
16 *STW*, p. 4. 9–10; *ISG* 81.12 f.   17 *From R. Hoshaiah*: *B.* ʻErub. 53a.
18 *Eighty years*: *ISG* 83.17; cf. also below, lines 26–27. See S.N.
19–20 This list is independent of *STW*, p. 10 par. 9, and *ISG* 60.16 f.
22 *In Nehardea*: As noted by Zacuto, p. 169b, this is incorrect, for R. Judah headed the academy of Pumbeditha; *ISG* 82.9. For an explanation of Ibn Daud's error, see S.N.
23–24 *ISG* 83.1–2, 84.6–7, 16–18.
25 *After R. Judah etc.*: This statement contradicts talmudic data, as noted by Zacuto, p. 146a, and the explicit statement of *ISG* 85.7–8, according to which R. Huna died before R. Judah. For a possible explanation of Ibn Daud's error, see S.N.
26–28 *R. Johanan... R. Ammi*: *ISG* 83.16, 84.4–5. Ibn Daud followed his source in disregarding the fact that the length of R. Johanan's term as head of the academy (see line 18), coupled with the date of his death, necessitated the conclusion that R. Johanan began his term as head of the academy in the lifetime of Judah the Patriarch and prior to the appointment of R. Ḥanina bar Ḥama (III.102)!
28–29 *R. Huna*: *ISG* 83.1*, 85.1* and cf. note to line 9.
29 *Their*: I.e., of R. Judah and R. Huna.
30–31 This list is apparently Ibn Daud's own compilation.

The third generation was that of R. Ḥisda, Rabbah and R. Joseph. R. Ḥisda was a disciple-colleague of R. Huna, and four years before the latter's death he established a school of his own. Later, when R. Huna passed away, R. Ḥisda took over as head of the academy for ten years until 4060. Then Rabbah bar Naḥmani was appointed and served as head of the academy for twenty-two years. Because of informers he was compelled to flee to the marshland, where he died in 4082. He was succeeded by R. Joseph for two years and a half; and he died in 4085. R. Joseph was called "Sinai" and Rabbah "an uprooter of mountains." Their disciples were: Abaye; Raba bar Joseph bar Ḥama bar Ezekiel; Rabina the first; R. Kahana the second; and many others, for Rabbah had twelve thousand disciples.

The fourth generation was that of Abaye and Raba. Abaye became head of the academy in the year of R. Joseph's death ‖ for fourteen years and passed away in 4099. After him Raba bar Joseph served as head in Meḥoza for another fourteen years and passed away in 4113.

The fifth generation was that of R. Naḥman bar Isaac, R. Papa, and R. Huna the son of R. Joshua. Following the death of Raba in 4113, R. Naḥman bar Isaac became head of the academy in Pumbeditha. Though [originally] a colleague of R. Ḥisda, he outlived him for a long time. After serving as head of the academy for four years, he died in 4117. At the outset of his term as head of the academy the academies split a second time. R. Papa became head

---

32 *ISG* 85.9–12.
33–34 *Ibid.* 84.17–20*. See S.N. to line 25.
35 *Ibid.* 85.9–11*.   36–38 *ISG* 86.6–10*.
37 *Twenty-two years*: See S.N. *Because of informers etc.*: *ISG* 87.1–11 citing *B*. B.M. 86a.
38–39 *ISG* 87.15–17*.
39–40 *Sinai... uprooter of mountains*: Metaphors for outstanding erudition and powers of dialectic reasoning, respectively. *ISG* 46.10, 85.19 f. citing *B*. Hor. 14a.
40–41 This list is apparently Ibn Daud's own compilation.
41 *Bar Ezekiel*: I do not know of any earlier source for this link in the genealogy; but cf. above, lines 11–12. The reading of MSS אפ "and Rami bar Ezekiel" represents an effort to correct the text in accordance with an attested genealogy.
42 *Twelve thousand disciples*: A free interpretation of *B*. B.M. 86a cited by *ISG* 87.13.
43–45 *ISG* 87.18* ("French" recension).   45 *Raba*: *Ibid.* 88.6.
46 *Ibid.* 89.5–6*.
48–49 *R. Naḥman bar Isaac*: *Ibid.* 89.10–11.
50 *A colleague of R. Ḥisda*: In other words, he was, properly speaking, a disciple of the second, and an authority of the third, generation.
51 *Four years*: *ISG* 89.11*.
52 *A second time*: The first occasion was in the days of Rab and Samuel (cf. above, lines 5 f.), but the breach had been healed when both academies returned to "R. Huna" (lines 25–26). After the healing of the breach, only one person served as head of the academy at any one time; *ISG* 89.7.

of the academy in Naresh, a city close by Sura, served for nineteen years in that office, and he died in 4132. After R. Naḥman bar Isaac passed away, R. Ḥama of Nehardea became head of the academy of Nehardea. He, too, died in 4132, after a term of fifteen years. As for R. Huna the son of R. Joshua, his name is not recorded among the heads of the academies.

The sixth generation was that of R. Ashi and the heads of the academies who lived in his days. From the days of Rabbi until R. Ashi, Torah and high office had not been combined in one person. During R. Papa's term, in 4127, R. Ashi became head of the academy of Sura for sixty years. In the fifth year of his office, R. Papa and R. Ḥama passed away. R. Zebid became head of the academy of Pumbeditha for eight years and died in 4140. He was succeeded by R. Dimi [who served] for three years and died in 4143. His successor was Rafram || bar Papa, who died in the same year. His sucessor was R. Kahana the second [who served] for twenty-eight years and died in 4171. His successor was R. Aḥa the son of Raba [who served] for two years and died in 4173. Thus, R. Papa as well as these six heads of academies all passed away within the lifetime of R. Ashi. R. Ashi passed away in 4187, which is equivalent to 738 of the Seleucid Era. He began to commit the Talmud to writing.

52–54 *R. Papa*: *Ibid.* 89.12–14*.
55 *Ibid.* 89.15–17 ("French" recension).
56 *4132, after a term of fifteen years*: I know of no source for this statement, which is repeated below, lines 61–62. *ISG* indicates that he served for twenty-one years.
57 *His name is not recorded etc.*: I.e., Ibn Daud cannot give the date and extent of his presidency. Although R. Huna b. Joshua's name is not mentioned by *ISG*, it is listed along side that of R. Papa in *STW*, p. 10. 13. On the significance of this datum as an index of Ibn Daud's use of sources, cf. below, p. 181.
58 *ISG* 90.14–15.
59–60 *Ibid.* 91.5–8 citing *B*. Git. 59a. *Rabbi*: I.e., Judah the Patriarch. *Torah and high office*: *ISG* explains that this combination was manifested by the submission of the exilarchs to his authority.
61 *R. Ashi*: *ISG* 93.15, 94.5. *ISG* says that he served "almost sixty years." *In the fifth year etc.*: Cf. above, line 56.
62–63 *R. Zebid*: *ISG* 89.17, 90.5*.
64 *Ibid.* 90.7–8*.
65 *Rafram bar Papa*: *Ibid.* 90.9, where the "French" recension gives no date for Rafram's death. Since Rafram's name was listed in his source without any extent of term, Ibn Daud concluded that he died in the same year as his predecessor.
65–66 *R. Kahana*: *Ibid.* 90.10, where Ibn Daud's source had read תשכ״ח for the תשב״ח of *ISG*.
67 *Ibid.* 90.12–13* combined with the explanation given in the previous note.
68 *Thus*: Lit., For. *These six*: Ḥama, Zebid, Dimi, Rafram, Kahana II, Aḥa.
70 *738 of the Seleucid Era*: *STW*, p. 5 n. 104; *ISG* 94.5–7 and variant 12 there. *He began to commit etc.*: This interpretation of *B*. B.M. 86a, cited by *STW*, pp. 8, 10, 32 and *ISG* 69.13–14, is most explicitly made by Nissim ibn Shahin, *Clavis Talmudica*, f. 3a. See S.N.

36   SEFER HA-QABBALAH

     The seventh generation was that of Meremar, Mar bar R. Ashi and their colleagues. After the death of R. Ashi, his seccessor as head of the academy of Sura was Meremar [who served] for five years and died in 4192. His successor was R. Idi bar Abin [who served] for twenty years and died in 4212.
75 His successor was R. Naḥman bar Huna [who served] for three years and died in 4215. Following these men, Mar bar R. Ashi succeeded to his father's post for thirteen years. Since those were good years, he was called R. Tabyomi. He died in 4228, which is equivalent to 779 of the Seleucid Era. His successor was Rabbah Tosefa'ah [who served] for six years and died in 4234. These
80 five men had been disciples of R. Ashi. Although some, like Meremar and R. Idi b. Abin, were [also] his colleagues, the others were disciples.

     In the year of Rabbah Tosefa'ah's death, the Persian Empire decreed
[28] frightful persecutions against the Jews. || [This was at the time] when the second calamity of the Persians was at hand. [This was "the second calamity"] for
85 the Persians had a monarchic government twice [in their history], and so too the Romans.

     The great city of Rome was built in the days of Hezekiah king of Judah by

72   *Colleagues*: See S.N.   73–75   *ISG* 94.8–13.
76–78   *STW*, p. 6; *ISG* 95.5–7.
77   *Tabyomi*: *Tab yomay* = happy (or, fortunate) of days. On the name in talmudic literature, cf. Kohut, *Aruch Completum*, IV, 7; *JE*, XI, 65. I cannot locate any earlier source for Ibn Daud's etymology. See S.N.
79   *ISG* 95.8–9 and variant 7 of "French" recension; 97.7–9 of "French" recension.
80   *Five men*: Meremar, Idi bar Abin, Naḥman bar Huna, Tabyomi, Rabbah Tosefa'ah. *Like Meremar etc.*: I cannot locate any source for this statement. See S.N.
82–83   See below, lines 160 f.; *ISG* 97.7–9.
83–84   *Second calamity... was at hand*: The first was when Alexander uprooted the Persian Empire; I.222, II.4. The second is described below, V.30 f. — For Ibn Daud's style, cf. Deut. 32.35.
85   *Had a monarchic government*: This odd translation of the Hebrew מלכו is demanded by the sense of the long excursus which follows; cf. below, p. 225 n. 11. For the significance of Ibn Daud's digression here, and especially of his symmetrical construction of history, see Analysis. ch. IV. *Had a monarchic government twice*: For the Arabic source of this conception, Ps.–Orosius, cf. G. Levi della Vida, "La Traduzione Araba della Storie di Orosio," *Al-Andalus*, XIX (1954), 286. The same conception of the first and second Persians is reflected in Ibn Khaldun, *The Muqaddimah* (trans. by F. Rosenthal), I, 57 f.; cf. also C. Issawi, *An Arab Philosophy of History* (London, 1950), p. 30, where the translation of the same passage reflects a bit more shaprly the notion Ibn Daud appropriated. For Ibn Daud's history of Persia, cf. below, lines 130 f. *And so too the Romans*: B. A.Z. 8b. For the symmetry of the history of east and west, cf. Isidore, *Etymologiae*, IX, 3.2–3 (ed. Lindsay).
87–90   *ZDR*.
87   *The great city of Rome*: For this expression, cf. *B*. Shab. 56b; Kohut, *Aruch Completum*, VII, 263 f. *In the days of Hezekiah*: Cf. Augustine, *City of God*, XVIII.22; Ps.–Orosius

two brothers, both of whom were great kings, the first one's name being Romulus and the second one's name being Remulus. Now Romulus plotted against his brother, killed him summarily and then ruled alone. He brought all of the west under Roman domination. After his death in Rome, the Romans paid him a great tribute by building a large round structure over his grave. Its diameter was approximately fifty cubits at the base, while its perimeter extended to 120 cubits; at the top it narrowed into a sort of cone. This structure, of great height, stands intact in Rome until this very day.

Similarly after the death of Romulus, the Romans enjoyed a state of tranquillity, and there was no one on earth who ruled over them until Nebuchadnezzar came and subdued them too, as it is written: "And all the nations shall serve him." However, in the days of his grandson Belshazzar, the Chaldean kingdom was destroyed, and the dominion passed over to Darius and then to Cyrus and, following that, to other kings. Finally, Alexander of Macedon, the emperor, rose up against them and destroyed the whole of the Persian Empire, as it is written: "He was moved with choler against him, and smote the ram, etc." Throughout this time the Romans were at first under the dominion of the Chaldeans, then of || the Persians, and finally of the Greeks.

---

in Levi della Vida, "La Traduzione Araba," p. 280 n. 1; *Josippon* 43, p. 145, where the statement was probably interpolated from *ZDR*.

89 *Remulus*: A common medieval variant for Remus; cf. A. Graf, *Roma nella Memoria e nelle Immaginazioni del Medio Evo* (Turin, 1923), p. 84 n. 5.

91 *The west*: Lit., the land of the Maghreb.

92 *A large round structure*: This is the renowned *meta Romuli*, on which cf. S.B. Platner and R. Ashby, *A Topographical Dictionary of Ancient Rome* (London, 1929), p. 340; Graf, *op. cit.*, pp. 84 f.

93–94 *Its diameter... 120 cubits*: For the style, cf. I Ki. 7.23; II Chr. 4.2. See S.N. — For a similar description by a Christian contemporary of Ibn Daud, cf. S. McN. Rushforth, "Magister Gregorius de Mirabilibus Urbis Romae: A New Description of Rome in the Twelfth Century," *Journal of Roman Studies*, IX (1919), 56 f., 58 (note by Sir T.L. Heath).

95 The *meta* remained largely intact until the end of the fifteenth century, and part of the monument remained standing even as late as 1518; cf. Platner and Ashby, *loc. cit.*; Rushforth, *loc. cit.*

98–99 Jer. 27.7. On Nebuchadnezzar and his successors as "cosmocrators," cf. Ginzberg, *Legends*, IV, 275 f.; VI, 368 n. 83. Cf. also *Josippon* 3, pp. 6 f.

99–103 Cf. above, I.146 f., 186 f., 210 f.

103 *He was moved etc.*: Dan. 8.7; cf. also verse 21, which indicates that this refers to Alexander.

105 *Chaldeans... Persians... Greeks*: I.e., the first three of the four world kingdoms described in Dan 7. See S.N.

[29] When the Hasmonean house gained the upper hand over Antiochus and his empire, the Romans also assembled and fought for their lives. Taking courage, they broke the yoke of the Greeks from their necks, subjected them and exacted tribute from them.

110 In the days of Jannaeus king of the Jews, the second period of Roman monarchy began. Their first king, Julius, was called Caesar, because when his mother had died he was still in her womb and her belly had to be cut open. He was a very great king, and he restored the monarchy to the Romans. For this reason his name was perpetuated in all of their kings, who were called 115 So-and-So Caesar. After his death, he was accorded an honor that was not granted to any other king in the world: an extremely high tower with iron spits inserted in its base which extended, branching out, to the top. Above them was a great casket of thick brass in which Julius was placed. This casket may be seen to this day.

120 He was succeeded by his brother's son, the emperor Augustus. It is said that he ruled over the whole world. In the fourth year of his reign he imposed a tribute of bronze on the whole world. Then he paved the Tiber River, on which Rome is situated, for twenty miles with very thick plates of bronze, although the river was very wide. To this day they continue to reckon according

---

106 Cf. above, II.52 f.

107-109 I do not know of any earlier source for this reconstruction of Roman history. Is Ibn Daud alluding here to the tribute exacted from Antiochus III after the battle of Magnesia (188 B.C.E.)?

110 *In the days of Jannaeus etc.*: In *MBSh*, f. 59a, Ibn Daud indicates that the second Roman monarchy under Caesar began in the days of Aristobulus and Hyrcanus II. For a suggested explanation of Ibn Daud's synchronization of the resurgence of Roman monarchy with the reign of Alexander Jannaeus, cf. below, pp. 229 f.

111-115 ZDR; *MBSh* f. 59a; *Josippon* 15, 42, pp. 65, 143; Isidore, *Etymologiae*, IX. 3, 12 cited by Ps.-Orosius in Levi della Vida, "La Traduzione Araba," p. 279 n. 1. See S.N.

116-119 This is the Vatican obelisk, which was known in medieval times as the tomb of Julius Caesar. The ball, or "casket," at its summit is now in the Museo dei Conservatori. Cf. Platner and Ashby, *op. cit.*, pp. 370 f.; Rushforth, *op. cit.*, p. 43; Graf, *op. cit.*, pp. 226 f., 230. Ibn Daud's description of the spits is not found in any of the medieval traditions known to me. See S.N.

120 *His brother's son*: This error probably stems from Ibn Daud's translation of his Arabic source (see next note), where Julius Caesar is called '*ammuhu*, which usually signifies "his paternal uncle," but is also used for "step-father"; cf. Dozy, *Supplément aux Dictionnaires Arabes*, s.v. 'Am.

121-129 For the Arabic source(s) underlying this account, cf. Levi della Vida, "La Traduzione Araba," pp. 271 f. and esp. 273 n. 3; *idem*, "The Bronze Era in 'Moslem' Spain," *JAOS*, LXIII (1943), 183 f.

121 *The fourth year of his reign*: I.e., 38 B.C.E. See line 127.

125 to the Bronze Era. The Romans possess many books in which his praises and
wisdom are recounted. They also || claim that there never was a king like him
in any nation in the world. In the thirty-eighth year of his reign Jesus the
Nazarene was born, for he ruled for fifty-two years over an empire that extended
over the whole world; so they say.

130   The same thing held true for the Persians. [Long] after their empire had
been destroyed in the days of Alexander, after the death of Antoninus, in the
days of R. Johanan, they assembled to fight for their lives and to remove
the yoke of the Romans from themselves. That was why, when Antoninus
died, Rabbi said: "The knot is broken." However, they did not attain great
135 power until after the death of Our Saintly Master in the days of R. Johanan.
The first of their kings was Ardashir son of Babek. He wrote to all groups

---

125   *The Bronze Era*: This is the Spanish *aera*, which exceeds chronology of the Christian era by 38, and by which events were regularly dated in Christian documents in Spain. See S.N.

127-128   In *ZDR* and *MBSh*, f. 69a, Ibn Daud follows the medieval chroniclers in crediting him with a reign of fifty-six years. Either Ibn Daud slipped here and wrote "of his reign" when he meant "of the Era" or, more likely, he meant "of his reign... over the whole world," which began with the tribute of bronze which he exacted from the whole world. Ibn Daud is thus not concerned with the extent of Augustus' reign as such, but with the length of this rule over all mankind. — In any event, the statement on Jesus contradicts the very thesis which Ibn Daud went to such length to deny, II.95 f. Clearly, Ibn Daud followed his Arabic source, which had the same datum at this point in the story; see note to lines 121–129. For the significance of Ibn Daud's reproduction of his source here, despite the apparent embarrassment it might cause him, see below, pp. 246 f.

129   *So they say*: Lit., as they say. See S.N.

130   *The same thing*: I.e., two periods of monarchic government; see above, to line 85.

131   *After the death of Antoniuns*: By the chronology of *ZDR*, this was in 3918 A.M.

131-132   *In the days of R. Johanan*: See note to line 134.

132-133   *To remove the yoke of the Romans*: See S.N.

134   *Rabbi*: See note to line 59-60. *The knot is broken*: B. A.Z. 10b. Ibn Daud interprets "the knot, or bond" as that of world dominion. This is a novel interpretation of which I can find no earlier instance. Cf. Krauss, *Antonius und Rabbi*, pp. 51 f. *They did not attain great power*: In other words, Rabbi's dictum had been a prophetic one, for the second Persian monarchy did not actually begin until somewhat later.

135   *After the death etc.*: According to Ps.–Orosius (see note to line 85), of which Ibn Daud's statement here reads almost like a verbatim translation, the second Persian monarchy began in the eleventh year of Commodus, which, according to Ibn Daud's data in *ZDR*, would correspond to the eighth year before Judah the Patriarch's death; cf. III.87 and *ZDR*. R. Johanan's activity began twenty years before and lasted sixty years after Judah's death; above, lines 18, 27.

136   *Ardashir*: See S.N. *He wrote*: I do not know any source for this account of Ardashir's communication to the Persians. See S.N.

of the Persians to inform them that for the past five hundred years they had been oppressed by the sword of Aristotle the sage, for Alexander had been his disciple. Accordingly, they took courage and made war against the Romans.
140 However, neither of them could defeat the other. Hence, the dominion was divided: Khuzistan, Iraq, Hamath, part of Greece, and all of Palestine as far as all of Arabia came under the Persians; while Rome, the Slav country, France, part of Greece, Egypt, Berber Africa, and Spain [remained] under the control of the Romans. Thus, for a second time, the Jews fell under the domination
145 of the Persians. At first, that is, in the days of Ardashir, who is Ahasuerus, they were friendly to the Jews, and so too in the days of King Shahpuhr.

137 *The past five hundred years etc.*: Since the Persian Empire was uprooted by Alexander in 3439 (cf. I.222), Ardashir's letter was written in 3939, forty years before the death of Judah the Patriarch. See S.N.

138 *Oppressed*: Lit., consumed. *The sword of Aristotle*: I am unable to determine whether this is merely figurative or based on some legend of an actual sword. See S.N. *Alexander had been his disciple*: For medieval traditions on Aristotle's relationship with Alexander cf. S. Carey, *The Medieval Alexander* (Cambridge, 1956), pp. 105 f.

140 *The dominion*: Sc., over the world. *Was divided*: What follows is a fanciful reconstruction of the conquests begun, according to Thaʻalibi, *Histoire* (ed. Zotenberg) p. 488, by Shahpuhr the son of Ardashir and settled by treaty with Constantine. Cf. also Tabari, *Chronique*, II, 2 f.

141 *Khuzistan*: Heb., Elam; cf. Benjamin of Tudela, *Itinerary* (trans. Adler), p. 51; Mann, *Texts and Studies*, II, 35 n. 66. Cf. also below, Epilogue. 25. *Iraq*: Heb., Shinar; cf. Mann, *loc. cit.*; Krauss, "Die Hebraeischen Bennenungen der Modern Voelker," *Jewish Studies in Memory of George A. Kohut*, p. 410 no. 85. *Hamath*: This is the same as the Arabic Ḥama and was identified with the country surrounding Antioch on the Orontes; cf. Wayyikra R. 5.3 (ed. Margulies), p. 105 and note there; Benjamin of Tudela, *op. cit.*, pp. 15, 31. It may be that Ibn Daud has reference to all of northern Syria. *Part of Greece*: I.e., the easternmost areas of Byzantium; cf. Krauss, "Die Hebraischen Bennenungen," p. 395 no. 30.

142 *Rome*: In all likelihood, Ibn Daud means *the land of Rum*, which is Byzantium; cf. Epilogue. 34. *Slav country*: Heb., Ashkenaz. Cf. Epilogue. 34, from which it will be seen that Ashkenaz is probably north of Byzantium. Hence, I have translated Ashkenaz as in Saadiah, *Oeuvres Complètes*, I, 17 to Gen. 10.3. *France*: Sc., in the Arabic sense of Ifranj; i.e., north of the Pyrenees from the Atlantic until the Slav country; cf. Lévi-Provençal, *La Péninsule Ibérique*, pp. 32 f.; Ibn Ezra, *Shirat Israel*, p. 62; Krauss, *loc. cit.*, p. 407 no. 73.

143 *Berber Africa*: Lit., [the land of the] Philistines; cf. VII.187, 193, 255; Epilogue. 73; cf. also Krauss, *loc. cit.*, p. 406 no. 67; and especially Harkavy, "Le-Toledot R. Samuel ha-Nagid," p. 47 n. 2.

144 *For a second time*: Cf. notes to lines 83-85, 99-103.

145 *Ardashir, who is Ahasuerus*: For this identification, cf. *Kitab at-Ta'rikh* in *MJC*, II, 108, line 9, where the biblical Ahasuerus is called Ardashir; cf. also above, note to III.100. See S.N.

145-146 I do not know any explicit source for this statement. Perhaps Ibn Daud inferred

THE SUCCESSION OF AMORAIM 41

In his days Mani came into the world, claiming that there are two gods in
[31] the universe. One || [of them] preserves and achieves all the good in the universe,
while the other destroys and does all the evil in the universe. He fabricated
150 a scripture for the Magians and amassed a great following. King Shahpuhr
slew him through his astuteness.

The Persians also had a king by the name of Hormizd, who died while his
wife was with child. The Persians then refused to enthrone anyone in place
of Hormizd. Instead, they attached a crown to his wife's belly, thereby enthron-
155 ing anyone to whom she might give birth, be it male or female. She gave
birth to a boy, and they declared him king on the day of his birth. He was
named Bahram after Mars, which was his star.

They had many other emperors who were friendly to the Jews, until the
Muslim Empire attained power and destroyed them from off the earth. Before
160 this, however, the Almighty, blessed be He, had turned their heart to hate
His people, so that the Persian king seized three Jewish notables: Amemar
bar Mar Yanqa bar Mar Zutra, the colleague of R. Ashi, R. Mesharshia,

---

this from *B. M.Q.* 26a and from the friendly relations between Shahpuhr and Samuel
implied by *B. Ber.* 56a and *Sanhed.* 98a.

147–151 For the medieval Arabic traditions on Mani and his system, cf. H.C. Puech, *Le Manichéisme: Son Fondateur, Sa Doctrine* (Paris, 1949). However, Ibn Daud's account of Mani's death cannot be traced to any of the traditions cited by Puech. See note to line 149–150. *Two gods*: For this formulation of Mani's doctrine, cf. Puech, pp. 74 f., 161 f.

149–150 *Fabricated a scripture*: See S.N. to 11.37. Cf. also Puech, pp. 66 f.

150–151 For a parallel account, cf. Abraham bar Ḥiyya, *Megillat ha-Megalleh*, pp. 138 f., where Shahpuhr VII is identified with Bahram, in whose reign Mani was executed, and where the king's strategem in trapping Mani is described. Ibn Daud probably drew from Abraham bar Ḥiyya or the latter's source.

152–157 This story is a variant of the one told by Agathias (IV.25) and Arabic chroniclers about Shahpuhr II; cf. W. Schickard, *Tarich h.e. Series Regum Persiae* (Tuebingen, 1628), p. 116, who first identified Ibn Daud's story with the other. Cf. further Tabari, *Geschichte* (trans. Noeldeke), pp. 51 f.,; Thaʻalibi, *op. cit.*, pp. 511 f.; Gibbon, *Decline and Fall of the Roman Empire*, ch. XVIII, n. 56; G. Rawlinson, *The Seventh Oriental Monarchy* (2 vols. New York, s.a.), I, 143. — The transference of the story from Shahpuhr to Bahram (cf. previous note for the reverse phenomenon) may derive from the importance of Bahram (= Mars) in Mazdean religion. However, there can be little doubt that the substitution of names had been made by Ibn Daud's source. See S.N.

159 Cf. V.30 f. Ibn Daud's style is deliberately calculated to give the impression that the downfall of the Persians came immediately after the persecutions he is about to describe; cf. also Ibn Verga, *Shebet Yehudah* (ed. Shohet-Baer), p. 21 and notes there, pp. 167–168. However, Ibn Daud himself obviously knew better.

160 *Had turned their heart etc.*: Cf. Ps. 105.25.

161–164 *ISG* 96.14 f. (Cf. also *STW* 4. 4–6). See S.N.

and the exilarch, whose name was Huna Mar, and put them to death. He also seized Jewish youths and compelled them to leave the fold, in Tebet, 4234.

165 In that same year Rabina became head of the academy for one year.

At the time that these men were heads of the academy in Sura, the following were heads of the academy in Pumbeditha: R. Gebihah of Be-Kethil became head of the academy in the year of R. Ashi's death for six years, and he died in 4193. His successor was Rafram [who served] for ten years and died in 170 4203. His successor was R. || Rehumi [who served] for thirteen years and died [32] in 4216. He was succeeded by R. Sama the son of Raba, who passed away in 4236.

Thus, there were seven generations of amoraim, five generations of tannaim, and nine generations of instruction in the Temple. In other words, from the 175 days of Zerubbabel and those who came up with him until the end of the days of Rabina and R. Sama son of Raba there were twenty-one generations in a period of 827 years.

---

164 *To leave the fold*: I.e., to commit apostasy. *4234*: The year of Rabbah Tosefa'ah's death; see line 82. See S.N.
165 This statement contradicts *STW* 6. 8; *ISG* 95.11; Nissim b. Jacob, *Clavis Talmudica*, f. 3b, all of which state that Rabina died in 4260. See S.N.
166 *These men*: I.e., the successors of R. Ashi; above, lines 71 f.
167–169 *R. Gebihah*: *ISG* 95.14–96.2. See S.N.
169 *Rafram*: *ISG* 96.3–4.
170 *R. Rehumi*: *Ibid.*, lines 5–7 of "French" recension. See S.N.
171 *R. Sama*: *ISG* 96.8, 97.10–11.
173 *Seven generations of amoraim*: Cf. above, line 71. *Five generations of tannaim*: Cf. III. 110.
174 *Nine generations of instruction etc.*: Although in II.169 and Epilogue. 2–3, Ibn Daud reckons ten generations to the second stage of Jewish history, he is careful to indicate here that he reckons only nine generations to the era after the cessation of prophecy; cf. II.19–20. On the other hand, Ibn Daud contradicts himself on the very next line by reckoning nine generations from Zerubbabel. For an explanation of this "slip," see below, pp. 205 f.
177 *827 years*: Zerubbabel came to Palestine in 3409; II.8.

[V]

THE SUCCESSION OF THE SABORAIM

The first generation was that of Rabbah Jose, who marks the beginning of the saboraic rabbis. He served as head of the academy after Rabina for thirty-eight years, until 4274. In the twenty-fourth year of his presidency, which was
5 the year 4260 and 811 of the Seleucid Era and 123 before the Muslim reckoning, the Talmud was sealed. Its composition had been begun in the days of R. Ashi, but it was sealed in the seventy-third year after his death. Thus, there were 311 years from the time of the writing of the Mishna until the sealing of the Talmud. From the time of the writing of the Mishna until this year,
10 that is, 4921, 972 years have passed. From the year of the sealing of the Talmud until this year 661 years have passed. Rabbah Jose died in 4274.

   2 *ISG* 97.12. *Rabbah Jose*: For this form of his name, cf. *ibid.* 70.2 (and Lewin's n. 1 there), 97.12 and variants; Ginzberg, *Geonica*, I, 4 n. 1.
   3 *After Rabina*: Although *ISG* indicates that Rabina survived Rabbah Jose's accession by twenty-four years, Ibn Daud was under the impression that Rabina had died sometime in 4235; cf. IV.165 and S.N. there. Now since Rabina was supposed to mark the end of the amoraic period and Rabbah Jose the beginning of the following period, Ibn Daud also inferred that Rabbah Jose succeeded to Rabina's post, although *ISG* makes no such claim. On Rabina as the end of the amoraic period, cf. sources listed in B.N.to IV.70.
   4 *Thirty-eight years, until 4274*: *ISG* 97.12 gives no chronological data for Rabbah Jose; see S.N.
   4–6 *STW* 6.9; *ISG* 97.12–13; Ibn Shahin, *Clavis Talmudica*, f. 3b.
   5–10 The multiple dates provided here indicate that 4260 is the real dividing point between the periods of the amoraim and saboraim. Thus, Rabbah Jose's presidency spanned portions of both eras.
   5 *123 before the Muslim reckoning*: Ibn Daud apparently dates the *hijra* from Tishri, 4383 [= September, 622]. Cf. *EI* s.v. Hijra. Other Jewish authors dated the *hijra* in Ab, 4382 [= July, 622]. Cf. Abraham bar Ḥiyya, *Sefer ha-'Ibbur*, p. 100; Joseph ibn Zaddik in *MJC*, I, 91.
   6 *Sealed*: The term for the completion of the Talmud is taken from Dan. 9.24 and implies that henceforth the talmudic canon, as it were, was closed, and nothing substantive was added to amoraic teaching. The geonim were well aware that the saboraim added sections in addition to revising it stylistically. However, they insisted that the Talmud had been "sealed" as prophecy had been in an earlier period. *Begun in the days of R. Ashi*: Cf. IV.70.
   8 *311 years from etc.*: The Mishna was written in 3949; III.95.
   10 *4921*: Sept. 1160–Sept. 1161.
   11 *4274*: See note to line 4.

The second generation of the saboraic rabbis was that of R. Aḥai bar Huna and his colleagues. R. Aḥai served as head of the academy for one year and died in 4275. He was succeeded by R. Samuel bar Raba [who served] for three years and died in 4278. He was succeeded by Rabina of Umṣa [who served] for one year and died in 4279. His successor was R. Teḥina [who served] for seven years and died in 4286. He was succeeded by R. Simona and R. ʿEna, the latter in Sura and the former in Pumbeditha. R. Simona lived until 4300. All these were of one generation.

[34] The second generation [also included] the disciples of R. Simona and R. ʿEna. However, their names were not recorded, inasmuch as the academies were closed for about fifty years after R. Simona's death, until 4349, because of the hostility of the Persian kings and their persecutions.

The third generation was that of R. Hanan of Ashiqiyya, who took over from the disciples of R. Simona and R. ʿEna. He was followed by R. Mari, R. Huna, R. Ḥanina, and R. Ḥinena respectively. All these were of one generation. R. Hanan of Ashiqiyya became head of the academy in 4349. He was followed by these four heads of the academy, whose terms of service, however, are not recorded.

The fourth generation was that of R. Isaac. In his days the Muslim Empire prevailed over the Persian Empire, and the Persian Empire was totally uprooted. ʿAli ibn Abi Talib, the king of the Arabs, came to Babylonia after the Arabs had been in control of the country for a number of years. (In the days of ʿUmar ibn al-Khattab, king of the Arabs, the Persian Empire had been up-

13–14 R. Aḥai: *ISG* 98.6–7*. See S.N.
14–15 R. Samuel bar Raba: *ISG* 98.11–13* ("French" recension). R. Samuel's predecessor is omitted by *SHQ*, but a year is added to the two which *ISG* credits to R. Samuel. — Unless the omission is germane to our text, we have not indicated names in *ISG* omitted in *SHQ*.
15–16 Rabina of Umṣa: *ISG* 98.13* (the three months of *ISG* becoming one year in *SHQ*).
16–17 R. Teḥina: *ISG* 99.1*.
17–18 R. Simona and R. ʿEna: Ibid. 99. 5–6.
19 *Until 4300*: This date is not recorded in *ISG* but is based on the statement of lines 21–23 that the academies were closed after his death for approximately fifty years. On Ibn Daud's use of "approximately" cf. Cohen, *SFC*. pp. 106 f.
20 *Also included*: See S.N.
21–23 *ISG* 99.10–100.1. However, *ISG* does not indicate the number of years that the academies remained closed.
24–25 *R. Hanan of Ashiqiyya, who took over etc.*: *ISG* 100.2, where, however, no mention is made of the disciples of R. Simona and R. ʿEna. Ibn Daud probably inserted a reference to these disciples, so that "the succession" would not be tainted by any interruption; cf. Epilogue. 14-15
24–29 *ISG* 100.1–14. See S.N.
30–31 *In his days etc.*: The exact date is given below, line 40.

35 rooted and the daughters of Yezdegerd taken into captivity. Then ʿUmar, king of the Arabs, gave Yezdegerd's daughter to R. Busatanai the exilarch. The latter converted her to Judaism and took her for a wife. Muhammad,
35] king of the Arabs, had begun to make his pretensions in 4374.) || Now when ʿAli ibn Abi Talib came to Babylonia, R. Isaac the head of the academy went
40 out to him, and this King ʿAli honored him and revered him in 4420.

The fifth generation was that of Mar Raba and Mar Huna, the latter in Sura and the former in Pumbeditha. They were succeeded by R. Sheshna, who was called Mesharshia bar Taḥlifa, and by R. Bussai. These four were of one generation. R. Mesharshia bar Taḥlifa passed away in 4449, and he was the
45 last of the saboraic rabbis. Thus, there were five generations of saboraic rabbis over a period of 187 years.

32-35 Cf. W. Muir–T. H. Weir, *The Caliphate* (Edinburgh, 1915), pp. 173 f., 253 f. C. Brockelmann, *History of the Islamic Peoples*, Eng. trans. (New York, 1944), pp. 55 f., 67.
32 *King of the Arabs*: I.e., the caliph, whose official title is Prince of the Faithful.
35 *The daughters of Yezedgerd*: Cf. Muir-Weir, *op. cit.*, p. 408 n. *Then 'Umar*: See S.N.
36-37 *R. Bustanai*: On this episode and its repercussions, cf. Baron, *SRH*, V, 8 f. See S.N.
38 *King of the Arabs*: See S.N. *4374*: I.e., 613-614 C.E. Cf. *STW*, p. 7 line 1 and variant 25. For Ibn Daud's synchronization with events in European history, cf. end of *ZDR*. See S.N.
39-40 *ISG* 101.1-7, where no date is given for the incident. For Ibn Daud's date, cf. below, p. 233. *ISG* speaks of ʿAli's entrance to Peroz-Shahpuhr, not Babylonia as a whole.
41-42 *ISG* 101.8-11.
42-43 *Ibid.* 102.1-5.
44 *R. Mesharshia*: *Ibid.* 102.8-9. Ibn Daud's source substituted Mesharshia for Bussai. *He was the last etc.*: On the termination of the saboraic period at this point, cf. below, p. 211.
46 *187 years*: This is an error in simple arithmetic, for counting from 4260, which is when the saboraic period really begins (see note to lines 5-10), the figure should be 189! Cf. below, pp. 198 f.

[VI]

THE SUCCESSION OF GEONIM

The first generation of the heads of the academy of Pumbeditha: R. Ḥinena of Nehar Peqod served as head of the academy for eight years until 4457. His successor was R. Hilai ha-Levi, who served as head of the academy for eighteen years and passed away in 4475.

The second generation: R. Jacob of Nehar Peqod served as head of the academy for eighteen years and passed away in 4493. His successor, R. Samuel — a descendant of Amemar, the colleague of R. Ashi — served as head [of the academy] for eighteen years and passed away in 4511. These were of Pumbeditha.

During the terms of these four heads of the academy, the following served as heads of the academy of Matha Meḥasia: R. Huna bar Joseph [began to serve] in 4449. His successor was R. Ḥiyya of Messena. The latter was succeeded by Mar Yanqa, who is the same as Raba bar Natronai and who became head [of the academy] in 4479. His successor was R. Judah Gaon. He was

---

1 *Geonim*: Although originally the title of Gaon was the prerogative of the head of the academy of Sura only, the distinction between the heads of Sura and Pumbeditha had long since been obliterated by Sherira, who applied the honorific even to amoraim, and, of course, to the heads of his own academy; cf. Ginzberg, *Geonica*, I, 46 f.; B.M. Lewin, *Mi-Tequfat ha-Geonim*: *R. Sherira Gaon* (Jaffa, 1917), pp. 9 f.

2 *Pumbeditha*: As is well known, in his account of the first three generations of geonim, Ibn Daud transposed the list of heads of Sura and Pumbeditha, recording the latter as heads of Sura and vice versa. For an explanation of this blunder, see below, p. 184. Ibn Daud's first two generations of Pumbeditha thus go back to *ISG* 106.1 f.

2-3 *R. Ḥinena*: *ISG* 106.4* (where Ibn Daud's source read 8 for the 5 of *ISG*; see B.N. to IV. 65-66; S.N. to V.4).

4-5 *R. Hilai*: *ISG* 106.5-6*.   6-7 *R. Jacob*: *Ibid*. 106.7-8*.

8-9 *Ibid*. 106.9-11*. For the translation "descendant", cf. Ginzberg, *Geonica*, I, 71 n. 2.

12 *Matha Meḥasia*: Sura; IV.7. See note to line 2 of this chapter.

12-33 *ISG* 102.8—103.13. Ibn Daud's occasional lack of chronological information reflects that of *ISG*.   12-13 *Began to serve*: See S.N.

13 *Messena*: For this translation of Mishan, cf. Mann, "The Responsa of the Babylonian Geonim as a Source of Jewish History," *JQR*, NS, VII (1917), 464.

14-15 *Mar Yanqa*: In *ISG* 102.15 he is identified with R. Natronai. The name Raba bar Natronai is obviously a product of some homoioteleuton on Ibn Daud's part, which resulted in making Rabia into the son of Natronai; cf. *ISG* 102.11-15. Ibn Daud's date coincides with that given by *ISG* for the accession of R. Natronai b. R. Nehemiah. Cf. Lewin's nn. 4-5 in *ISG* 102, and see also below, note to line 34.

succeeded by R. Joseph [who died] in 4499. He was succeeded by R. Samuel bar Mari [who died] in 4508. In the days of this R. Samuel there lived R. Simeon Qayyara, who, however, was not appointed gaon. He composed *Halakot Gedolot* in 1052 of the Seleucid Era, which is equivalent to 4501 or the third year of the term of R. Samuel bar Mari and the eighth year of the term of R. Samuel || the descendant of Amemar. He cited traditions "in the name of Kohen-Ṣedeq." However, we have no knowledge of a gaon of his days by the name of Kohen-Ṣedeq. It may, therefore, be that this Kohen-Ṣedeq, who had been his master, was a scholar who had not been appointed [gaon]. After R. Samuel bar Mari there was a great scholar [by the name of] R. Aḥa of Shabḥa, who composed his *She'eltot* on all the commandments specified in the Torah. This book, which has survived to this day, was examined and scrutinized by all who lived after him; we have heard that to this day not a single error has been detected in it. Nevertheless, this R. Aḥa was not appointed gaon because of the hostility of the exilarch of his generation

16 *Who died*: These words are technically incorrect, but Ibn Daud clearly understood this date and the one which follows it in that way, as may be seen from lines 19-20. Cf. also *Kitbay R. Abraham Epstein*, II, 283 n. 10. This misunderstanding of *ISG* by Ibn Daud or his source reflects the normal Arabic understanding of an unqualified date next to the name of a man in a work on the history of tradition; cf. Mez, *Renaissance of Islam*, pp. 190 f.

18-19 *R. Simeon Qayyara*: See S.N.

19 *Halakot Gedolot*: This work, the greatest of the gaonic legal compendia, has been published in two recensions; cf. *JE*, VII, 461 f.; *EJ*, VII, 848 f.; Baron, *SRH*, VI, 81 f., 364 n. 90.

21-22 *Traditions "in the name of Kohen-Ṣedeq"*: For a list of these traditions, cf. Epstein, "Ma'amar 'al Sefer Halakot Gedolot," in *Kitbay R. Abraham Epstein*, II, 405 f. Cf. also *ibid*. pp. 381 n. 6, 400 f.

22 *We have no knowledge etc.*: Sc., since Kohen-Ṣedeq was of the fifth generation of geonim; below, line 110. See S.N.

26 *She'eltot*: Lit., "Questions." This work consists of several sermons for each weekly portion of the reading of the Torah, each sermon being built around a halakic problem, which, in turn, serves as the focal point for a legal-moralistic discourse. Although the medieval schools had many more sermons available to them than those preserved in the printed editions, the evidence in no way confirms Ibn Daud's claim that the work treated all the commandments in the Torah. A critical edition of the sections on Genesis and Exodus has been published under the editorship of S.K. Mirsky, *Sheeltot*, 3 vols. (Jerusalem, 1959-1963). Mirsky's introduction to Genesis lists the earlier editions and critical treatments of the various problems connected with the work. Cf. also Baron, *SRH*, VI, 37 f.

27-29 *This book... was examined etc.*: See S.N.

29-32 *ISG* 103.8-13.

30 *The exilarch*: Solomon b. Ḥisdai; cf. Assaf, *Tequfat ha-Geonim*, pp. 33, 154; Baron, *SRH*, V, 15.

toward him. Instead, he appointed R. Aḥa's secretary, whose name was R. Natronai. Incensed at this, R. Aḥa went off from Babylonia to Palestine where he passed away. R. Natronai served as head [of the academy] for thirteen years until 4521. These eight heads of the academy in Matha Meḥasia served during the terms of the four heads of the academy of Pumbeditha.

The third generation of geonim in Pumbeditha: After the passing of R. Samuel in 4511, R. Mari ha-Kohen of Nehar Peqod served as head in Pumbeditha for eight years and passed away in 4519. He was succeeded by R. Ada [who served] for half a year and passed away in the very same year. He was succeeded by R. Jehudai [who served] for three years and a half and passed away in 4523. He composed *Halakot Pesuqot*, which he compiled from *Halakot Gedolot*. He was blind.

In his days there lived Anan and his son Saul, may the name of the wicked rot. Although this Anan was a descendant of the house of David and, at

---

31 *Secretary*: For this translation, cf. Ginzberg, *Geonica*, I, 16 n. 3. Assaf, *Tequfat ha-Geonim*, p. 154, understands the term in the sense of apprentice or outstanding student.

33-34 *R. Natronai*: *ISG* 103.7, 104.1*. See S.N.

34 *These eight*: Ibn Daud lists only seven: Huna b. Joseph, Ḥiyya of Messena, "Raba b. Natronai," Judah, Joseph, Samuel b. Mari, Natronai. The error obviously derives from the omission of a name which was listed in Ibn Daud's source, but which has been omitted in *SHQ*. In view of the fact that Ibn Daud had no knowledge of R. Natronai's successor, R. Abraham Kahana (*ISG* 103.14-15; cf. below, lines 63-64), it appears almost certain that the name recorded in *SHQ* as Raba bar Natronai was listed correctly in Ibn Daud's source as two different persons, Rabia and R. Natronai; cf. note to lines 14-15.

35 *The four*: See above, lines 1-9.

37-43 *ISG* 107.3-14* (and see note to line 2 of this chapter).

37 *R. Samuel in 4511*: Cf. above, lines 8-9.

38 *R. Ada*: In *ISG*, Aḥa. See S.N.

41 *Halakot Pesuqot*: Edited with an introduction by S. Sassoon (Jerusalem, 1950). Cf. also Baron, *SRH*, VI, 78 f. *Compiled from Halakot Gedolot*: Cf. above, line 19. Ibn Daud's remark is probably based on his own chronology for the date of composition of *Halakot Gedolot* and on his awareness of the great similarity of a number of passages in both works; cf. *Kitbay R. Abraham Epstein*, II, 381 f., 419; Sassoon, *Halakot Pesuqot*, Introduction, p. 22.

42 *He was blind*: See S.N.

43 *In his days*: *ISG* 107.14 and variant 15 of "French" recension; cf. also below, Epilogue. 16 f. *His son Saul*: Although not mentioned in *ISG*, his name is often coupled with that of Anan in medieval sources; cf. S. Poznanski, *Babylonishe Geonim im nachgaonaeischen Zeitalter*, pp. 127 f. *May the name of the wicked rot*: Prov. 10.7. See S.N.

44-50 For critical analyses of Ibn Daud's account, which probably goes back to some lost work of Saadiah, cf. L. Nemoy, "Anan ben David — A Reappraisal of the Historical Data," *Semitic Studies in Memory of Immanuel Loew* (Budapest, 1947), pp. 239 f.; idem, *Karaite Anthology* (New Haven, 1952), pp. 3 f.; and the critiques of Nemoy's evalua-

45 first, a scholar as well, || some blemish was detected in him, and he was, accord-
[38] ingly, not appointed gaon; nor was he vouchsafed divine assistance to become exilarch. Because of the sordid envy in his heart, he revolted and set out to seduce the Jews away from the tradition of the sages, which the latter had taken over from the prophets — [all of them] trustworthy witnesses reporting
50 in the name of trustworthy witnesses, as we have set forth in this book. Thus he became an elder who rebels against the decision of the court "in disregarding" the judges. He composed books, set up disciples, and fabricated "statutes that were not good, and ordinances whereby they should not live." Alas,

> tion of the Saadyanic account in Baron, *SRH*, V, 388; M. Zucker, "Against Whom Did Se'adya Gaon Write the Polemical Poem *Essa Meshali*" [in Hebrew], *Tarbiz*, XXVII (1957-58), 78 f.; idem, *Rav Saadya Gaon's Translation of the Torah*, pp. 143 f. However, it is quite improbable that Ibn Daud utilized any of the Saadyanic accounts that have been preserved or recently recovered, in view of the fact that Saadiah claimed that Anan's innovations were imitations of Muslim practice, an argument of which Ibn Daud would have made capital had he known it.
> 44 *Descendant of the house of David*: David the father of Anan was apparently the brother of Solomon b. Ḥisdai, the exilarch. Cf. the list of exilarchs in the *geniza* fragment published by Lewin in *ISG* 136; cf. also Mann, *Texts and Studies*, II, 129 f.; Assaf, *Tequfat ha-Geonim*, p. 33; Baron, *SRH*, VI, 200 f. That the exilarchs were of Davidic descent was taken for granted; cf. I.71 f., VI.218.
> 46 *Vouchsafed divine assistance*: See S.N. *To become exilarch*: That Anan sought to become "the head" is asserted by Saadiah in the fragment published by Zucker; see note to lines 44–50. Although the term "head" often denotes the position of exilarch, Ibn Daud may have taken it to include the headship of the academy and, accordingly, indicated why Anan was elected neither to the gaonate nor the exilarchate. See S. N. here and to II. 40.
> 47 *Because of the sordid envy*: The explanation of Karaism as emanating from personal bitterness, repeated below (Epilogue. 18 f.), was apparently first put forth by R. Natronai; cf. *Seder R. Amram Gaon*, ed. Warsaw, I, 38a; ed. Frumkin, II, 207; Lewin, *Otzar ha-Geonim*, II (Pesaḥim), 89 f. — On envy and personal frustration as the source of heresy, cf. above II.24 f. *He revolted*: Lit., he erupted. For the same expression, cf. Epilogue.61. See S.N.
> 48 *To seduce*: Cf. *M*. Sanhed. 7.10. The expression is used here in a popular and non-technical sense; cf. S.N. to Prologue. 14. *The tradition of the sages etc.*: Cf. Prologue. Epilogue. 12 f., 138 f.
> 51 *An elder who rebels etc.*: See Prologue. 14 and note there. *In disregarding etc.*: Dt. 17.12, the *locus classicus* for the law of the rebellious elder. Cf. also above, II.147 f.
> 52 *He composed books*: On Anan's writings, cf. Nemoy, *Karaite Anthology*, p. 395. See S.N. *Set up disciples*: Cf. Abot 1.1; see S.N. *Fabricated statutes*: Cf. Baron, *SRH*, VI, 481 n. 94 and S.N. to II.37. For a translation of selections from Anan's *Book of Precepts*, cf. Nemoy, *Karaite Anthology*, pp. 11 f. For an analysis of his legal tendencies, cf. the works of Zucker referred to in note to lines 44–50; Baron, *SRH*, V, 216 f., VII, 72 f., 110 f.
> 52–53 *Statutes etc.*: Ezek. 20.25. See S.N.
> 53 *Alas*: Lit., for. Ibn Daud now proceeds to explain why Anan had to do what he did *de novo*.

after the destruction of the Temple the heretics had dwindled until Anan came and gave them strength.

R. Jehudai was succeeded by R. Aḥunai [who served] for five years and passed away in 4528. He was succeeded by R. Mari ha-Levi bar R. Mesharshia [who served] for three years and a half and passed away in 4532. His successor was R. Bebai ha-Levi [who served] for ten years and a half and passed away in 4543, in the days of R. Manasseh b. Joseph head of the academy of Matha Meḥasia.

In the days of these geonim of Pumbeditha, the following served in Matha Meḥasia. R. Durai became head of the academy in 4521, the year of R. Natronai's death, served for six years and passed away in 4527. His successor was R. Ḥanina bar Mesharshia [who served] for four years and passed away in 4531. His successor was R. Malkiah [who served] for two years and passed away in 4533. He was succeeded by R. Ḥinenai bar R. Abraham [who served] until 4542, when he was deposed by the exilarch. He was succeeded by R. Huna ha-Levi bar R. Isaac, and the latter was succeeded by R. Manasseh b. Joseph [who served] until 4548.

---

54 *After the destruction etc.*: Ibn Daud thus indicates that in his view Anan's heresy is a continuation of the earlier Samaritan schism; cf. above pp. xxxvii f. *Had dwindled*: The style seems to be a deliberate play on *M. Sota* 9.15. See also S.N.

56 *R. Jehudai*: Lit., after him. *R. Aḥunai*: *ISG* 107.15–17 credits him with eight years, but cf. above, note to line 2–3.

57–61 *ISG* 108.1–8*.

60 *R. Manasseh*: Cf. below, line 69; see S.N.

61–63 *Matha Meḥasia*: See note to line 2.

63 *R. Durai*: *ISG* 103.16–104.2, where he is called R. Dudai; cf. variants to Hebrew text, 38.42. *The year of R. Natronai's death*: Above, lines 33–34.

64 *4527*: *ISG* 104.4 ("French" recension) gives that year as the date of accession of R. Dudai's successor. The dates of death of R. Ḥanina and R. Malkiah (immediately following) are similarly based on the date of accession of the succeeding gaon.

65 *R. Ḥanina*: *Ibid.* 104.3–6.

66 *R. Malkiah*: *Ibid.* 104.6–15, where his name is given as Malka.

67–68 *R. Ḥinenai*: *Ibid.* 104.18–105.2, where, however, 4542 is given as the date of accession. Ibn Daud thus transposes again the date of appointment to the date of termination or death; cf. above, note to line 16. The same error is repeated in the case of the following geonim.

69 *R. Huna*: *ISG* 105.3–5, where the date of appointment is given as 4546. *R. Manasseh*: *Ibid.* 105.7–8, and see note to lines 67–68.

The fourth generation of geonim of Pumbeditha: After R. Bebai ha-Levi, R. Isaiah ha-Levi bar Abba served as head of the academy for two years and passed away in 4556. His successor was R. Joseph bar R. Shela [who served] for nineteen years and passed away in 4575. His successor was R. Mordecai ha-Kohen [who served] for three years and passed away in 4578. His successor was R. Aḥunai [who served] for four years and passed away in 4582. He was succeeded by R. Joseph bar Judah [who served] for two years; he was a very saintly man, who enjoyed miraculous experiences. R. Judah, the grandfather of R. Sherira, who served as his scribe, testified that Elijah, may he be remembered for good, appeared in this R. Joseph's academy any number of times. His term lasted for two years, after which he died in 4584.

He was succeeded by R. Abraham bar R. Sherira [who served] for twelve years and passed away in 4596.

71–73 *After R. Bebai ha-Levi, R. Isaiah ha-Levi etc.*: Cf. above, line 59. R. Bebai in reality had been gaon of Sura, but Ibn Daud had erroneously transposed the list of geonim, as noted on line 2. However, beginning with R. Isaiah, R. Bebai's "successor", Ibn Daud's location of the geonim corresponds to that of *ISG*.

72–73 *R. Isaiah*: *ISG* 109.1–4. The chronological data on R. Isaiah, of course, imply a hiatus between the date of death of R. Bebai and that of R. Isaiah's accession; but this was inevitable, given the original confusion in Ibn Daud's lists. See S.N.

73–74 *R. Joseph*: The chronological data given here can in no wise be squared with that of *ISG* 109.5–6. However, if in the case of R. Joseph's successor Ibn Daud's source read קי״ח (cf. next note and above to lines 2–3), the extent of R. Joseph's term would be nine years, a figure which could easily have become corrupted to nineteen years.

74–75 *R. Mordecai*: This name is obviously a corruption of מר רב רבי of *ISG* 109.7, which became corrupted to רב מר רבי and then to רב מרדכי. The extent of R. Mordecai's term is explained by a reading in *ISG* 109.8 proposed in the previous note. — The date 4578, which I offer as the only possible emendation of the untenable readings of the MSS, is attested by Samuel ha-Nagid, MS Sassoon, p. 60, and Zacuto, p. 206.

76 *R. Aḥunai*: *ISG* 109.9–13*. The name in *ISG* is Ibumai or Ikumai, a name which is consistently transmitted by *SHQ* in a corrupted form; cf. lines 104 and 110, "Isomai."

77 *R. Joseph b. Judah*: *ISG* 109.12–13, where he is called Joseph b. Abba. On the extent of his term, cf. below, line 81.

78–80 This account is a free paraphrase of *ISG* 109.17–110.11; cf. variant 6 of "French" recension, which will explain Ibn Daud's use of "grandfather," rather than that of "great-great-grandfather." Sherira's grandfather as well as the latter's grandfather were both named Judah. For another error along the same lines, cf. below, note to line 208.

79 *Elijah, may he be remembered for good*: On this expression, cf. Lieberman, *Greek in Jewish Palestine*, p. 70 n. 23. See S.N.

81 *ISG* 110.11*.

82–83 *Ibid.* 110.13–15*. Although this sentence appears innocent enough and corresponds to that of *ISG*, it is one of the more baffling statements in *SHQ*. The most cursory examination of lines 84–85, 101, will demonstrate that Ibn Daud considered Abraham bar Sherira a gaon of Sura, which is why I have placed this item in a separate paragraph. On the other hand, the date of his death is reckoned from that of the death of Joseph

The fifth generation: R. Joseph bar R. Ḥiyya served as head of the academy of Pumbeditha for two years and passed away in 4586. His successor was R. Isaac bar R. Ḥiyya [who served] for seven years and passed away in 4593. His successor was R. Joseph Beribbi [who served] for two years and passed away in 4595. His successor was R. Paltoi [who served] for sixteen years and passed away in 4611. He was succeeded by R. Aḥai ha-Kohen [who served] for six months and passed away in 4611. After the demise of R. Aḥai, the members of the academy were divided [into two factions]. One faction sided with R. Menahem bar R. Joseph bar R. Ḥiyya whose appointment they favored, while the other party || sided with R. Mattithiah. This dispute continued for a year and a half, until R. Menahem's death. R. Mattithiah Beribbi served as head for ten years and passed away in 4621. He was succeeded by Rabbah bar Ammi [who served] for two years and a half and passed away in 4624. He was succeeded by R. Ṣemaḥ bar R. Paltoi [who served] for nineteen years and passed away in 4633. He was succeeded by R. Hai bar R. David [who served] for seven years and a half and passed away in 4641.

In the days of these geonim who served in Pumbeditha, [the following served] in Matha Meḥasia: After the aforementioned R. Abraham bar R. Sherira, R. Hilai bar R. Mari was appointed [and served] for nine years. He was suc-

b. "Judah", who was gaon in Pumbeditha. To compound the difficulty, the date given here for R. Abraham's death is clearly at variance with Ibn Daud's statement in lines 114–115 on the date of R. Amram's activity; see note there. Ibn Daud had clearly meant to list R. Abraham among the geonim of Sura, for reasons explained below, pp. 183 f., but had apparently failed to indicate that fact, while a later copyist, failing to see any indication of a new category here, added the date, which he arrived at by simple addition; see S.N.

84 *R. Joseph b. R. Ḥiyya*: *ISG* 110.15–16, 111.18–19; however, neither the date nor the extent of term agree with *ISG*. For the preceding gaon of Pumbeditha, according to *SHQ*, cf. lines 77 f.

86 *ISG* 112.1–2 (and variant 4 of "French" recension), 15* ("French" recension and variant 29 of "Spanish").   87 *R. Joseph Beribbi*: Ibid. 112.16–18*.

88–96 Ibid. 113*; however, according to *ISG*, R. Mattithiah's ten year term began *after* the death of R. Menahem (lines 94–95).

97–98 *R. Ṣemaḥ*: *ISG* 114.1–4 and variant 4 of "French" recension. *4633*: This is a flagrant error in simple arithmetic, and one which caused the copyists of MSS את and Zacuto to emend the 19 to 9. However, the error is attested by Samuel ha-Nagid, MS Sassoon, p. 61. Apparently, Ibn Daud overlooked the י of יט because of its proximity to the י in the name of Paltoi. For a mistake in the opposite direction, cf. below, line 105.

98–99 *R. Hai b. R. David*: *ISG* 114.5–7*. See S.N.

101–102 Cf. above, lines 82–83. According to *ISG* 108.5–10, 114.8 f., R. Hilai succeeded R. Bebai ha-Levi (above, line 59).

102 *R. Hilai*: *ISG* 114.8–10. The absence of dates in this sections reflects the situation in the parallel passage in *ISG*.

ceeded by R. Jacob bar R. Mordecai [who served] for eighteen years. His successor was R. Isomai bar R. Mordecai [who served] for eight years. He was succeeded by R. Isaac bar R. Jesse [who served] for twelve years. His successor was R. Hilai bar R. Hananiah [who served] for three years and a half. He was succeeded by R. Qimoi bar R. Ashi [who served] for three years and a half. He was succeeded by R. Moses ha-Kohen b. R. Jacob [who served] for ten years and a half. After his term no gaon was appointed for two years. Following that, R. Kohen-Ṣedeq Gaon bar R. Isomai Gaon was appointed [and he served] for ten years and a half. He was succeeded by R. Sar-Shalom bar R. Boaz [who served] for ten years. His successor was R. Natronai Gaon bar R. Hilai Gaon bar R. Mari [who served] for five years. He was succeeded by R. Amram bar Sheshna [who served] for eighteen years. He sent an order of the liturgy to Spain. This was in the days of || R. Hai bar R. David. He was

103 *R. Jacob*: *Ibid*. 114.11-12, where, however, the length of his term is said to be fourteen or nineteen years.
104 *Ibid*. 114.13-14, where Isomai's name is given as Ibumai or Ikumai; cf. above, note to line 76.
105 *Ibid*. 114.15-16, where the term is said to have lasted two years. The twelve of *SHQ* is the result of considering the second ʼ of the name of Jesse as part of the cipher; cf. note to lines 97-98. — On the "Isaac" of *SHQ* for "Zadok" of *ISG*, cf. *ISG* 114, variant 22 of "French" recension. See S.N.
106-114 *ISG* 114.16-115.16.
110 *Isomai*: Cf. note to line 104.
113 *Five years*: *ISG* 115, variants 10 and 13 of "French" and "Spanish" recensions respectively.
114-115 *An order of the liturgy*: On *Seder R. Amram*, cf. Baron, *SRH*, VII, 111 f., 274 f. *To Spain*: In *SHQ* and contemporary Hebrew texts, "Sefarad" usually denotes Muslim Spain, the Christian portion of the country generally being called the land of Edom; cf. Epilogue. 10; J.N. Epstein, "Seder R. Amram," *Ṣiyyunim*: *Qobeṣ le-Zikrono shel I. N. Simhoni* (Berlin, 1929), p. 122. However, Assaf, *Tequfat ha-Geonim*, pp. 180 f., has argued that the work was originally addressed to the Jewish community of Barcelona and from there despatched to the Jewish communities in the Muslim area.
115 *In the days of R. Hai b. R. David*: I.e., between 4633 and 4641; cf. lines 98-99. However, this statement contradicts the starting point of the chronology of this paragraph, which, according to the statement on lines 83 and 101, begins with the year 4596. According to the data presented hitherto, R. Amram's term could not possibly have begun before 4686, or more probably before 4690! This confirms our suggestion, made in the note to lines 82-83, that the date given for the death of R. Abraham b. Sherira is a later interpolation. Samuel ha-Nagid, MS Sassoon, p. 63, transmits our passage thus: "This was in the days of R. Hai bar R. David Kohen, 4636." However, this statement can no more be squared with the chronology given in *SHQ* than the other date. The only explanation that seems plausible is that Ibn Daud's *source* had concluded that R. Amram's term was partially synchronous with that of R. Hai b. David on the basis of his understanding of the division of sections in *ISG*. The latter begins its

[41] succeeded by R. Nahshon bar R. Zadok [who served] for eight years. He was succeeded by his maternal brother R. Ṣemaḥ bar R. Ḥayyim [who served] for seven years. His successor was R. Malkiah [who served] for one month and passed away. He was succeeded by R. Hilai bar R. Mishael [who served] for seven years. His successor was R. Jacob [who served] for thirteen years. After that, there was no scholar in Matha Meḥasia worthy of appointment. However, David b. Zakkai the Exilarch chose a certain weaver whose name was R. Yom-Tob and appointed him.

Subsequently, he sent word to Egypt and brought R. Saadiah al-Fayyumi from there. Accordingly, he became head of the academy in Matha Meḥasia [and served] for two years. After that, a great quarrel and dispute broke out between him and David b. Zakkai the Prince; for these exilarchs were not men of integrity, but [actually] used to purchase their authority from the kings like publicans. Once, David b. Zakkai

reckoning of the geonim of Pumbeditha with the accession of R. Isaiah ha-Levi in 1107 Sel. Era, i.e. 4556 A.M. (*ISG* 109.4) and concludes its enumeration of this series of geonim of Pumbeditha with the accession of R. Hai b. David ninety-four years later in 1201 Sel. Era, i.e. 4650 A.M. (*ISG* 114.5). Since Sherira then proceeded to enumer- the geonim of Sura, the first of this series being R. Hilai b. Mari, Ibn Daud's source assumed that R. Hilai's term began in the same year as that of R. Isaiah ha-Levi and concluded that R. Amram began his term in the very same year as R. Hai b. David, i.e. ninety-four years after the beginning of the "fourth generation." Ibn Daud incorporated the statement as he found it in his source without troubling to square it with the chronological details he had supplied.

116   *ISG* 116.1–2. On the name of R. Nahshon's father, see variants to Hebrew text and in *ISG*; cf. above, note to line 105.
117   *R. Ṣemaḥ*: *ISG* 116.3–5; see S.N.
118   *ISG* 116.6–9, where the name is rendered as Malka.
119   *R. Hilai b. R. Mishael*: This name is a product of homoioteleuton in *ISG* 116.13–16: R. Hilai b. Natronai and R. Shalom b. Mishael. The seven year term was that of the latter.   120   *R. Jacob*: *Ibid*. 116.19–20.
121   *No scholar ...worthy of appointment*: Lit., no scholar... or one worthy etc. Ibn Daud's wording suggests that his source combined the two statements of *ISG* 116.17–18 and 21 into one.
122–123   *R. Yom-Tob*: *Ibid*. 116.21–117.3, where he is credited with a term of four years. Although R. Yom-Tob's occupation is mentioned in *ISG*, Ibn Daud doubtless included it to convey the pejorative overtones intended by Sherira. For a parallel expression of contempt for an appointment of a weaver to high office, cf. Dozy, *Spanish Islam*, pp. 586 f.   124–127   *ISG* 117.11–22. See S.N.
126–127   *A great quarrel and dispute*: See S.N.
128–129   *These exilarchs were not men of integrity etc.*: Cf. below, lines 190 f.
129–143   This account of the dispute between Saadiah and David b. Zakkai is a variant of the story told by Nathan the Babylonian in *MJC*, II, 80 f. For modern studies of these accounts and analyses of their relationship, see S.N.

THE SUCCESSION OF GEONIM

130 was involved in a litigation in which he obtained a favorable judgment by improper means. He then sent it to R. Saadiah to countersign, but the latter refused. He then sent it a second time through his son Zakkai in order to coerce R. Saadiah into signing. The former said to him: "If you do not countersign, I will strike your head with a shoe." At once all of the members
135 of the academy became infuriated and, arising to a man, struck the son of the Prince considerably with their shoes. So, he went to his father in utter disgrace. His father then invoked the support of the government and that of a large faction of the community. R. Saadiah [found support] in another faction of the community, and they appointed Josiah b. Zakkai as exilarch in place
140 of his brother David. After that, David gained the upper hand with the help of the government and deposed his brother Josiah. He then sought to put R. Saadiah to death, and R. Saadiah went into hiding for approximately seven years. While in seclusion he composed all of his books. Now R. Saadiah
42] was of the nobility of [the tribe of] Judah, of the descendants of || Shelah the
145 son of Judah, and of the seed of R. Ḥanina b. Dosa. [Then] David b. Zakkai appointed R. Joseph bar R. Jacob bar R. Mordecai. Subsequently, however, David the Prince and R. Saadiah made peace; nevertheless, R. Joseph was not

---

131 *To countersign*: On the particular overtones of Saadiah's refusal to countersign, cf. A. Marx, "Rab Saadia Gaon," *Rab Saadia Gaon, Studies in His Honor*, ed. by L. Finkelstein (New York, 1944), p. 68; M. Auerbach, "Der Streit zwischen Saadja Gaon und dem Exilarchen David ben Sakkai," *Juedische Studien Joseph Wohlgemut... gewidmet* (Frankfurt a.M., 1928), p. 21.

132 *Zakkai*: According to Nathan the Babylonian the son's name was Judah. See S.N.

134 *I will strike your head with a shoe*: Nathan the Babylonian quotes the threat as "I shall strike you." For the expression in *SHQ*, cf. Midrash Ekah 1.1 par. 13, ed. Vilna f. 12a: טפח ליה על רישא בסנדליה. For variations on this stock expression of contempt, cf. *Aruch Completum*, IV, 61. See S.N.

137 *Invoked the support*: For the style, cf. I Sam. 30.6; Salmon b. Yeruḥim, *op. cit.*, p. 47 line 52.   138 *Large faction... another faction*: See S.N.

142-143 *Approximately seven years*: See S.N.

143 *While in seclusion he composed etc.*: This statement is incorrect, as has been noted repeatedly by modern scholars, beginning with Pinsker, *Lickute Kadmoniot*, Appendix p. 118. However, Ibn Daud may have based his statement on those works of Saadiah known to him, namely, *Sefer ha-Galuy* and the *Kitab al-Amanat* (Book of Beliefs and Opinions) both of which were composed during the Gaon's period of seclusion. Cf. Malter, *Saadia Gaon*, pp. 193, 269. Cf. below, line 158; see S.N.

144-145 Cf. Malter, *op. cit.*, p. 31.   145-149 Cf. *ISG* 118.1-12.

146 *Appointed*: Viz., as gaon. *Mordecai*: This is apparently a corruption of the name Natronai or Satia; cf. Harkavy, *Zikron la-Rishonim*, V, 228 n. 9; Lewin's note 1 in *ISG* 118; Auerbach, *op. cit.*, p. 6 n. 12a.

147-148 *R. Joseph was not removed etc.*: This erroneous conclusion seems to be based on

56   SEFER HA-QABBALAH

removed nor R. Saadiah reinstated to the gaonate. R. Joseph served as gaon for fourteen years. After that David b. Zakkai died. And after him R. Saadiah
150 passed away in 4702, when he was about fifty years of age, of black bile, after having composed any number of worthwhile books and having accomplished great good for Israel. He wrote refutations of the heretics and of those who denied the [authority of the] Torah. One of the latter was Ḥiwi al-Kalbi, who fabricated a scripture out of his own mind. R. Saadiah testified that he saw teachers of

the fact that R. Joseph was not deprived of the perquisites of office; cf. *ISG* 118.9; Nathan the Babylonian, *MJC*, II, 82; Malter, *op. cit.*, pp. 125 n. 271, 127. Cf. next note.

148–149   *R. Joseph served... fourteen years*: *ISG* 118.10 ("French" recension) states that it was Saadiah's term which lasted fourteen years. Ibn Daud's error may go back to a MS of *ISG* which read כלל שניה דמרב גאון ארבסר שני and which Ibn Daud (or his source) understood to refer to R. Joseph; cf. *ibid.*, variant 12 of "French" recension.

150   *4702*: *Ibid.* 118.11. *Fifty years of age*: This figure, on the basis of which Saadiah's millenium was celebrated in 1892, has now been rejected in the light of the statement of R. Dosa b. Saadiah that his father was just short of sixty at the time of his death; cf. J. Mann, "A Fihrist of Saadya's Works," *JQR*, NS, XI (1920–1921), 423 f.; Marx, "Rab Saadia Gaon," p. 57. As Mann observed, Ibn Daud's source probably contained a ס' which was not fully rounded and which Ibn Daud read as נ'. *Of black bile*: See S.N.

151   *Composed... worthwhile books*: On Saadiah's literary activity, cf. Malter, *op. cit.*, pp. 137 f.; Marx, "Rab Saadia Gaon," pp. 59 f., 66, 87, 93; Baron, *SRH*, Index vol. p. 132.

151–152   *Accomplished great good etc.*: This biblical expression (cf., e.g., Ex. 18.9; Jud. 8.35) is employed by Ibn Daud several times to denote communal leadership over and beyond pure scholarly activity; cf. line 157; VII.234, 335. See *S.N.* For the opposite, cf. Epilogue. 125. On this aspect of Saadiah's work, cf. S.W. Baron, "Saadia's Communal Activities," *American Academy for Jewish Research, Saadia Anniversary Volume* (New York, 1943), pp. 9–74.

152   *Heretics*: the Karaites; cf. Prologue. 12, II. 40, VI. 54. For Saadiah's works in this area, cf. note to line 151. *Those who denied etc.*: Ibn Daud thus clearly distinguishes between Karaites and skeptics who denied revelation. Cf. Zucker, "Against Whom did Se'adya Gaon Write etc.", p. 82.

153   *One of the latter:* As noted by Pinsker, *Lickute Kadmoniot*, p. 15, Ibn Daud's wording indicates that Ḥiwi was not the only skeptic of this kind known to Saadiah or Ibn Daud; for verification, cf. J. Mann, "An Early Theologico-Polemical Work," *HUCA*, XII–XIII (1937–1938), 411 f.; Zucker, *Rav Saadya Gaon's Translation of the Torah*, pp. 12 f., 17 f. *Ḥiwi al-Kalbi*: For the latest discussion on Ḥiwi, cf. Baron, *SRH*, VI, 299 f., 478 f. It is now generally assumed that al-Kalbi (the dog-like) is either an error or deliberate distortion of Ḥiwi's home, Balkh; cf. J. Rosenthal, "Ḥiwi al-Balkhi," *JQR*, NS, XXXVIII (1947–1948), 317–319. *Fabricated a Scripture*: Cf. S.N. to II.37.

154–156   Most modern authorities reject the implication of this statement that Ḥiwi actually composed an expurgated Bible; cf. Zucker, *Rav Saadya Gaon's Translation of the Torah*, p. 16 n. 39 and literature listed in previous note. Ibn Daud's report has been analyzed by S. Lieberman, *Yemenite Midrashim* [in Hebrew], (Jerusalem, 1940), pp. 26 f., who feels that Ibn Daud did not intend to accuse these elementary school teachers of deliberate heresy. On the basis of Yemenite texts, Lieberman

children giving instruction from it — both in the form of books and of tablets — to [their] pupils, until R. Saadiah succeeded in overcoming them. Now the rest of the acts of R. Saadiah and the goodness which he had shown unto Israel, behold, they are written in *Sefer ha-Galuy* and in the epistle which his son R. Dosa wrote to R. Ḥisdai the Nasi bar R. Isaac, may he rest in glory. After the passing of R. Saadiah the academy of Matha Meḥasia declined steadily, and R. Joseph finally emigrated to the city of al-Baṣra and died there.

The sixth generation [of geonim] in Pumbeditha: After R. Hai bar R. David, R. Qimoi bar R. Aḥunai became head [of the academy] in 4650 for eight years and a half; and he passed away in 4659. He was succeeded by R. Judah bar R. Samuel, the grandfather of R. Sherira, who passed away in

---

indicates that these instructors were Rabbanites who utilized expurgated Bibles in their classes. However, instead of explaining the text in accordance with rabbinic tradition, they interpreted it literally and thereby served as open prey for such critics as Ḥiwi. It was on this account that Saadiah exerted himself to stamp out their practice. — No special work by Saadiah addressed to school teachers is known, while his refutation of Ḥiwi is preserved only in part.

156–158 *Now the rest... behold etc.*: This biblical formula, characteristic of the style of the books of Kings and Chronicles (cf., e.g., I Ki. 11.41), is also employed by Saadiah in his polemic against Ben Meir; cf. H.J. Bornstein, *Maḥloqet* etc., pp. 64 f. Since Saadiah was renowned for his imitation of biblical style, it may well be that this sentence goes back to some Saadyanic work; cf. Harkavy, *Zikron la-Rishonim*, V. 136 f.

158 *Sefer ha-Galuy*: For references to the published fragments of this work, cf. Malter, *Saadia Gaon*, pp. 387 f.; S.M. Stern, "A New Fragment from the 'Sepher Ha-Galuy' of R. Saadyah Gaon" [in Hebrew], *Melilah*, V (1955), 133 f. On the name of the work, cf. Malter, p. 269; D. Yellin, "Ha-Shem ha-'Ibri le-Sefer ha-Galuy," *Studies in Jewish Bibliography... in Memory of A.S. Freidus* (New York, 1929), Hebrew section pp. 120 f.; Stern, p. 134.

159 *R. Dosa*: Cf. S. Poznanski, "R. Dosa be-R. Saadia Gaon," *ha-Goren*, VI (1905–1906), 41–61; Malter, *Saadia Gaon*, pp. 132 f. For a skeptical view of the implication that Ibn Daud saw this work, cf. Mann, *Texts and Studies*, I, 7 n. 9. *R. Ḥisadi*: Alias, Ibn Shaprut; cf. VII. 73. *May he rest in glory*: This slight variation on Isa. 11.10 is found frequently on Spanish Hebrew tombstones; cf. F. Cantera and J.M. Millas, *Las Inscripciones Hebraicas de España* (Madrid, 1956), p. 450 s.v. מנוחתו בכבוד. Cf. also S.N. to Epilogue. 57.

160–161 *ISG* 118.14-20.

161 *Emigrated*: For this usage of the Hebrew word "to flee" cf. VII. 82-83. The Hebrew is probably a translation of the Arabic هجر.

163–164 *ISG* 119.1-5 ("French" recension), where the father's name is rendered as Aḥi or Aḥai. — Ibn Daud glosses over the nine-year hiatus between the death of R. Hai (line 99) and the accession of his successor; Zacuto's reading of "eighteen years and a half" here represents an effort to heal the breach in the chronology.

165 *Ibid.* 119.7-10*.

4671. Although R. Mebasser ha-Kohen bar R. Qimoi Gaon was appointed as his successor, the prince, || David b. Zakkai, appointed R. Kohen-Ṣedeq bar R. Joseph. The academy then was split [into two factions]. However, when R. Mebasser ha-Kohen passed away, they all came under R. Kohen-Ṣedeq. The latter passed away in 4695. Then R. Hananiah, the father of R. Sherira, became head [of the academy] for five years and a half, and he passed away in 4701.

The seventh generation [of geonim]: After the passing of R. Hananiah, R. Aaron ha-Kohen b. Sarjada [became head of the academy]. He was a merchant and a wealthy man, who was appointed because of his affluence and not by virtue of any real worthiness of the post. He passed away in 4720. He was succeeded by R. Nehemiah [who served] for eight years.

He was succeeded by R. Sherira, who lived a very long life, in fact for about one hundred years. When he saw that his life was prolonged and that his son, R. Hai, was worthy of being head of the academy, he stepped down in favor of his son. The latter was R. Hai Gaon bar R. Sherira Gaon. He spread Torah abroad throughout Jewry more than all of the other geonim, and by his light walked those who sought the Torah from east and west. After living for ninety-nine years, he passed away on the eve of the last day of Passover

---

166–170 *Ibid.* 119.11–120.6.
166 *Mebasser*: I have adopted the Hebrew form of the name; Arabic: Mubashshir. *Was appointed*: Sc., by the members of the academy.
170–172 *R. Hananiah*: *ISG* 120.11–14*.
173–176 *Ibid.* 120.15–20, 121.5–6. On the name Sarjada, not found in *ISG*, cf. Malter, *Saadia Gaon*, p. 113 n. 240. See S.N.
176 *4720*: See S.N.
177 Cf. *ISG* 121.6–11. The length of R. Nehemiah's term is derived by subtracting the date of Ibn Sarjada's death from that of Sherira's accession; cf. line 201.
178 *Succeeded by Sherira*: *ISG* 121.12. *Who lived etc.*: On the dates of Sherira's life, cf. Mann, *Texts and Studies*, I, 109, where it is shown that Sherira died in Tishri, 1006 C.E.
180–181 *He stepped down etc.*: Cf. the gloss to *ISG* in Neubauer, *MJC*, I, 189 to n. 4; Mann, *Texts and Studies*, I, 109 n. 2.
181 *R. Hai Gaon b. R. Sherira Gaon*: The emphasis is not only on his renown but probably also to distinguish him from R. Hai b. David (above, line 98).
183 The line is a tapestry woven from biblical phrases: Isa. 60.3; Ex. 18.15b (cf. also Ezra 7.10 and Ps. 119.45), Mal. 1.11 (Ps. 113.3). Cf. also note to lines 185–186. For a similar evaluation of his influence by Samuel ibn Nagrela, cf. the latter's *Diwan* (ed. Sassoon), p. 12 lines 55 f. (= ed. Habermann. I, pt. 2, p. 132). On the extent of his influence, cf. Assaf, *Tequfat ha-Geonim*, pp. 198 f., 212. From Ibn Daud's remarks below, line 205, it would appear that Ibn Daud had in mind not only Hai's numerous responsa but also his books; cf. below, VII.268 f.; Baron, *SRH*, VI, 29 f., 70 f., 205 f., VII, 26 f.
184 *Ninety-nine years*: Cf. also Ibn Nagrela, *Diwan* (ed. Sassoon), p. 11 line 18 (ed. Haber-

185 in the year 1349 of the Seleucid Era, which is equivalent to 4798. Of the geonim before him there was none like him, and he was the last of the geonim. He was of the house of David, of the royal line, of the descendants of Zerubbabel the son of Shealtiel and of the princes and exilarchs who came after him. I have seen his seal affixed to documents which he issued, and a lion was
190 engraved in it just as there had been || on the pennant of the camp of Judah
14] and on the pennants of the kings of Judah. However, ever since the beginning of Muslim rule, the exilarchs did not exercise their authority fittingly. In fact, they used to buy their position with large sums of money, like publicans, and were worthless shepherds. Consequently, his ancestors did not wish to
195 become exilarchs, and they turned to the gaonate instead. He was [also] descended from Rabbah bar Abbuha. Some lawless Jews denounced R. She-

    mann, *loc cit.*, p. 129). *On the eve of the last day of Passover etc.*: From Ibn Nagrela's elegy in memory of R. Hai, it would seem that the day of his death was commemorated in the Jewish communities of Spain; cf. *Diwan* (ed. Sassoon), p. 11 line 16. See also S.N.

185–186 *Of the geonim before him etc.*: For the style, cf. II Ki. 23.25. — Since no gaon before him was his equal, and there was no gaon after him, this is tantamount to saying that Hai was among the geonim what Moses had been among prophets (cf. Dt. 34.10) and Josiah among kings; cf. note to line 202.

186 *He was the last of the geonim*: This statement is contradicted by Ibn Daud's own account below, lines 207 f., VII, 367 f. However, Ibn Daud is probably not referring here to R. Hai as the last person to hold the post or even *title* of Gaon but as the last of the gaonic *period*. Thus, although Hezekiah the Exilarch succeeded to the post of R. Hai, the former's term falls within the period of the rabbinate according to Ibn Daud's scheme; see S.N. and below, pp. 203 f.

187–188 *ISG* 60.11–15; "Sidray de-Shimusha Rabba we-Sidray Hekalot," *Bet ha-Midrash* (ed. Jellinek), VI, 109 (cited by Lewin, *Mi-Tequfat ha-Geonim: R. Sherira Gaon*, p. 24 n. 5); *Shiray Solomon b. Judah ibn Gabirol* (ed. Bialik–Ravnitzky), I, 89 line 17. *Of the descendants etc.*: Cf. above, I.71 f.; II.120. On the significance of the similarity of the style here to that of II. 120, cf. p. 202. *Princes and exilarchs*: The two are, of course, synonymous; cf. IV. 12. However, Ibn Daud distinguishes between the two here, probably in order to emphasize R. Hai's relationship to the Palestinian patriarchs of the Hillelide dynasty.

189 *His seal*: See S.N.

190 *The pennant of the camp of Judah*: Ginzberg, *Legends*, III, 234, 237, VI, 82 f. nn. 443, 447.

191 *Pennants of the kings of Judah*: I cannot locate any earlier reference to standards of the *kings* of Judah. This may be a retrojection on the analogy of medieval practice; cf. VII. 117 On the lions on Solomon's throne, cf. I Ki. 10.19–20.

191–195 *However, ever since etc.*: *ISG* 92.8 f. Cf. also above, lines 128–129.

193 *Like publicans*: On the Jewish attitude to these, cf. Alon, *Toledot*, I, 338 f.

194 *Worthless shepherds*: Zech. 11.17.

196 *Descended from Rabbah bar Abbuha*: *ISG* 60.15, 82.10–11. *Lawless Jews*: For the same expression, cf. I. 207. See S.N.

rira and R. Hai, and the king of Babylonia imprisoned them, confiscated all of their possessions and left them no source of support whatever. However, R. Sherira did manage to get some aid, although he was at the time approximately one hundred years old, and they were not deposed from the gaonate. R. Sherira became gaon in 4728 and R. Hai in 4758, their combined gaonate lasting seventy years: R. Sherira's for thirty and R. Hai's for forty. The latter's generation is the eighth generation of the gaonate.

In his days the head of the academy in Matha Mehasia was R. Samuel ha-Kohen b. Hofni, R. Hai's father in-law. He, too, composed many books. He passed away during R. Hai's term, four years before the death of R. Hai. However, the members of R. Hai's academy appointed Hezekiah the Exil-

197 *The king of Babylonia*: Probably, the Caliph al-Qadir; cf. Muir-Weir, *The Caliphate*, p. 579.
199 *Did manage to get some aid*: Lit., was suspended by one arm! See S.N.
200 *Approximately one hundred years old*: In other words, toward the very end of this life; cf. above, lines 178–179.
201 *4728*: ISG 121.12. *4758*: This date is incorrect and derives from Ibn Daud's schematology; cf. next note.
202 Although their combined gaonate lasted seventy years, Ibn Daud's division is more neat than accurate. Sherira's term as gaon lasted from 4728 to 4767 (= 968 – 1006 C.E.) and Hai's from 4764 to 4798 (= 1004–1038). However, during the last two years of Sherira's term, Hai served as (co-) gaon; Mann, *Texts and Studies*, I, 109. In other words, Sherira's term as gaon was longer than Hai's by any standard of measurement. Ibn Daud's crediting of forty years to Hai stems from his desire to picture R. Hai in terms reminiscent of heroes like Moses and Hillel; cf. nn. to lines, 183, 185–186, 187–188.
204–206 Cf. Mann, *Texts and Studies*, I, 145 f.
205 *Hai's father-in-law*: Cf. Samuel b. Hofni's letter in *ISG*, Appendix, p. xxix no. 6; Mann, *Texts and Studies*, I, 158. *He, too*: The allusion is probably to the prolific literary activity of Saadiah and Hai; cf. above, lines 151, 183. *Composed many books*: In a book-list from the Cairo Geniza, one entry reads: "Two booklets in which are enumerated the works of R. Samuel [b. Hofni]"; Assaf, "Ancient Book Lists" [in Hebrew], *Kirjath Sepher*, XVIII (1941–1942), 280 n. 8. Since, as Assaf indicates, a "booklet" generally consisted of ten leaves, R. Samuel's twenty-page bibliography must have indeed been enormous. On those of his works known, cf. Steinschneider, *Die Arabische Literatur der Juden*, pp. 108 f.; Assaf, *Tequfat ha-Geonim*, pp. 194 f.; cf. also Mann, *Texts and Studies*, I, 159; Baron, *SRH*, VI, 69 f.
206 *Four years before etc.*: I.e., 4794 (= 1033–34 C.E.). However, this date is incorrect, for Samuel b. Hofni died in 1013 and was succeeded by Dosa b. Saadiah, who died in 4794 (1033); Mann, "The Last Geonim of Sura," *JQR* NS, XI (1920–1921), 410 f. Mann suggests that the source of Ibn Daud's error is the gloss to *ISG* in *MJC*, I, 189 (end), where the name of *Israel b.* Samuel b. Hofni is omitted before the date of 1345 Seleucid Era [= 4794 A.M.]. Cf. also Ginzberg, *Geonica*, I, 13 n.
207 *However*: The style is cryptic, and a sentence must be understood to this effect: After the death of R. Hai, the academies would have been left without any gaon whatever, except for the fact that the members of the academy of R. Hai etc.

arch, the grandson of David b. Zakkai, to the see of R. Hai, of blessed memory. He served for a term of two years. Then informers denounced
210 him to the king, and the latter imprisoned him, put him in chains, tortured him grievously and left him no survivors. His two sons fled to Spain to R. Joseph ha-Levi the Nagid b. R. Samuel the Nagid, who had great affec-

207-208 *Hezekiah the Exilarch... to the see of R. Hai*: Cf. Judah b. Barzillai, *Sefer ha-Shetarot* (ed. Halberstamm), p. 87; Jerahmeel b. Solomon, in *MJC*, I, 178. Both these passages confirming Ibn Daud's account were first noted by Poznanski, "R. Dosa," p. 45 n. 11 and *idem*, *Babylonische Geonim im nachgaonaeischen Zeitalter*, pp. 1 f. See S.N.

208 *Grandson of David b. Zakkai*: In reality he was the grandson of David's grandson. However, Hezekiah's grandfather was also named Hezekiah, and the latter, too, had been an exilarch; A. Kamenetzky, "Deux Letres de l'Epoque du dernier Exilarque," *REJ*, LV (1908), 51; Mann, *Texts and Studies*, I, 183. For a similar error, cf. above, note to lines 78–79. See S.N.

209 *Two years*: This figure is historically untenable, since it can now be shown almost with certainty that Hezekiah the Exilarch was in office as late as 4815 (1055); cf. Poznanski, *Babylonische Geonim*, pp. 2 f.; Epstein's note *apud* Tyckoczynski, "Bustanai Rosh ha-Golah," pp. 155 n. 1, 156 n. 3; Samuel ibn Nagrela, *Diwan* (ed. Sassoon), p. 111 no. 143, dated 1055 (ed. Habermann, I, 139). Epstein also argued that the figure must be rejected on internal grounds: *SHQ* indicates that Hezekiah's sons fled in 4800 (1040) to Joseph the Nagid, because of the cordial relations which the latter maintained with Hezekiah. However, at that time Samuel ibn Nagrela was at the very height of his career. Mann, *Texts snd Studies*, I, 204 suggested emending the ב to כ, thus giving him a term of twenty years, which lasted until 1058. Though this is a most plausible suggestion (cf. above, note to line 176), I have not emended our text, inasmuch as there is no compelling evidence that Ibn Daud's original had a correct figure. The figure "two" may well have been Ibn Daud's error. Or, Ibn Daud may well have believed that the events described in the passage immediately following actually occurred in 1040 and that the sons fled to Joseph ha-Nagid, for it was with the latter that their names were associated in Spain. Interestingly enough the epitome of Samuel ha-Nagid, MS Sassoon, p. 64 reads (in lines 211-212 here): "His two sons fled to R. Samuel the Nagid in Granada, where he (!) remained (ויהיה שם) until the massacre." The omission of the name of Joseph may well be an error of the epitomist. On the other hand, the inclusion of this name in *SHQ* may be an early interpolation by a copyist who was misled by the reference to the massacre. If the latter is the case, Ibn Daud's statement would imply that in spite of the cliché used below about no survivors being left to Hezekiah, the latter somehow managed to regain his post. *Informers*: Cf. S.N. to line 196.

210 *The king*: Although, in view of the unstable conditions prevailing in Baghdad in this period, it is impossible to be certain of what is meant by the king, it may have been the Caliph al-Qaim (1031–1075); Muir-Weir, *op. cit.*, pp. 579 f.

211 *Left him no survivors*: Lit., left him not so much as a single male (English euphemism); I Sam. 25.22 etc. See S.N.

211-213 Cf. note to line 209, and reference to Ibn Nagrela's *Diwan* there, which corroborates Ibn Daud's statement on the affection of Ibn Nagrela for the Exilarch. See S.N.

[45] tion || for Hezekiah the Exilarch and head of the academy. They remained there with him until the time of the massacre in Granada, when the Nagid
215 was killed. One of the sons of Hezekiah then fled to the land of Saragossa where he married and had children. Afterwards, his descendants migrated to Christian Spain. One of them was R. Ḥiyya b. al-Daudi, who passed away in Castile in 4914. After him there did not remain in Spain a single person known to be of the house of David.
220 After Hezekiah the Exilarch and head of the academy, there were no more academies or geonim.

214 *The massacre in Granada*: VII.255 f.
215 *Saragossa* was then an independent kingdom ruled by the Banu Hud; cf. *El* IV, 157b. That it served as a haven for Jews fleeing from the Berbers is indicated below, VII.188.
216 *His descendants*: Cf. note to lines 8–9.
217 *Christian Spain*: Lit., the land of Edom. Cf. Epilogue. 70; above, note to lines 114–115; Krauss, "Die Hebraeischen Benennungen der Modernen Voelker," pp. 380 f. and especially 383 n. 13; *Ḥiyya al-Daudi*: See S.N.
218 *There did not remain in Spain etc..*: I cannot be certain whether in this instance Ibn Daud includes Christian Spain or denotes only what is generally meant by Sefarad, namely Muslim Spain; cf. previous note, and see S.N.
220–221 Recent research has demonstrated conclusively that this statement is untrue; see S.N. Moreover, Ibn Daud himself knew that his statement was not totally accurate; cf. VII. 367 f. Either Ibn Daud meant that the academies closed down completely for a *time*, or he allowed this error to creep into his text for other reasons. While Assaf, *Tequfat ha-Geonim*, p. 126, prefers the former solution, in *SFC* I have tried to show that the "error" was deliberate and tendentious; cf. also below, pp. 206, 264 f., 292 f.

[VII]

[THE SUCCESSION OF THE RABBINATE]

Prior to that, it was brought about by the Lord that the income of the academies which used to come from Spain, the land of the Maghreb, Ifriqiya, Egypt, and the Holy Land was discontinued. The following were the circumstances
5 that brought this about.

The commander of a fleet, whose name was Ibn Rumaḥiṣ, left Cordova, having been sent by the Muslim king of Spain, ʿAbd ar-Raḥman an-Nāṣir. This commander of a mighty fleet set out to capture the ships of the Christians and the towns that were close to the coast. They sailed as far as the coast of
10 Palestine and swung about to the Greek sea and the islands therein. [Here]

   1 *The Succession of the Rabbinate*: Although, in Ibn Daud's scheme, the first generation of the rabbinate begins with Samuel ibn Nagrela and R. Hananel (cf. below, lines 180 f., 287–288), a new chapter in his history actually begins at this point with the story of the four captives (lines 2–179), which serves to explain the transfer of rabbinic authority from Babylonia to the west; cf. Cohen, *SFC*, pp. 114 f.
   2 *Prior to that*: Sc., to the termination of the gaonate; cf. VI.186, 220. *Brought about by the Lord*: For the style, cf. I Ki. 12.15. *The income of the academies*: Viz., of Babylonia. On the maintenance of the academies by taxation and contributions from Jewish communities throughout the world, cf. below, lines 92 f.; Baron *SRH*, V, 18 f., 51 f.; Assaf, *Tequfat ha-Geonim*, pp. 66 f. See S.N.
   3 *Maghreb*: Lit., the west; which includes the central and further Maghreb, or the portion of northern Africa west of Ifriqiya; cf. *EI*, III, 108. See S.N. *Ifriqiya*: This name, an Arabization of the Latin "Africa," usually denotes the portion of northern Africa between Barqa and Bougie; cf. *EI*, II, 453. For a map of northern Africa reflecting the divisions in *SHQ*, cf. *Atlas of Islamic History*, ed. by H.W. Hazard, 3rd ed. (Princeton, 1954), p. 11.
   4 *The Holy Land*: Lit., the beautiful land; cf. Dan. 11.16, 41. See S.N.
   6 *The commander*: See S.N. *Ibn Rumaḥiṣ*: ʿAbd ar-Raḥman ibn Rumaḥiṣ, who served as admiral under ʿAbd ar-Raḥman III an-Nāṣir and under al-Ḥakam; cf. Cohen, *SFC*, p. 57.
   7 *ʿAbd Raḥman an-Nāṣir*: Reigned 912–961, proclaimed himself Caliph in 929; cf. *EI*, I (new ed.), 83 b.
   8 *To capture the ships etc.*: See S.N.
   9 *Close to the coast*: For this translation, cf. Kohut, *Aruch Completum*, VI, 114 a.
   9–10 *Coast of Palestine*: Lit., coast of the sea of Palestine. See next note.
  10 *The Greek sea*: I.e., the Mediterranean. This is a literal Hebrew translation of *Baḥr al-Rum*; cf. *EI*, I (new ed.), 934 f., where the Arabic divisions of the Mediterranean are described. Ibn Daud's conception of "the Greek sea and its islands" consistently mirrors that of the Arab geographers; cf. also Epilogue. 32 f.

they encountered a ship carrying four great scholars, who were travelling from the city of Bari to a city called Sefastin, and who were on their way to a Kallah convention. Ibn Rumaḥiṣ captured the ship and took the sages prisoner. One of them was R. Ḥushiel, the father of Rabbenu Hananel; another
15 was R. Moses, the father of R. Ḥanok, who was taken prisoner with his wife and his son, R. Ḥanok (who at the time was but a young lad); the third was R. Shemariah b. R. Elhanan. As for the fourth, I do not know his name. The commander wanted to violate R. Moses' wife, inasmush as she was ex-
[47] ceedingly beautiful. Thereupon, she cried out in Hebrew ‖ to her husband,
20 R. Moses, and asked him whether or not those who drown in the sea will be quickened at the time of the resurrection of the dead. He replied unto her: "The Lord said: I will bring them back from Bashan; I will bring them back from the depths of the sea." Having heard his reply, she cast herself into the sea and drowned.

25 These sages did not tell a soul about themselves or their wisdom. The commander sold R. Shemariah in Alexandria of Egypt; [R. Shemariah] proceeded to Fostat where he became head [of the academy]. Then he sold R. Ḥushiel on the coast of Ifriqiya. From there the latter proceeded to the city of Qairawan, which at that time was the mightiest of all Muslim cities in the land of the
30 Maghreb, where he became the head [of the academy] and where he begot his son Rabbenu Hananel.

11 *They encountered a ship etc.*: For an analysis of the following story, its sources and motives, cf. Cohen, *SFC*, pp. 70 f.
12 *Bari*: On the Jewish community there, cf. *Halachoth Kezuboth* (ed. Margulies), pp. 3 n. 14, 4, 10 n. 73; Baron, *SRH*, V, 56; VI, 119. *Sefastin*: No such place is known; for the various attempts at identification, cf. Cohen, *SFC*, p. 58 n. 8.
13 *Kallah convention*: A convocation conducted by the Babylonian academies twice a year for study and the collection of funds; cf. *JE*, VII, 423; Baron, *SRH*, Index vol., s.v. "*Kallah* assemblies." For the translation of this phrase, cf. Cohen, *SFC*, p. 58 n. 9.
14 *R. Ḥushiel*: Died ca. 1025; cf. V. Aptowitzer, "R. Chuschiel und Chananel," *Jahresbericht der Israelitisch-Theologischen Lehranstalt in Wien*, XXXVIII–XXXIX (1933).
15 *R. Moses... R. Ḥanok*: These two are the principal subjects of the story that follows.
17 *R. Shemariah b. R. Elhanan*: Died Dec. 31, 1011. For the latest summary of his activity, cf. S.D. Goitein, "Shemarya b. Elhanan," *Tarbiz*, XXXII (1962–63), 266 f. *I do not know his name*: See S.N.
20–24 For an earlier story of such a martyrdom, cf. *B. Git.* 57 b.
22 Ps. 68.23.
26 *Sold R. Shemariah*: Sc., to Jews, who ransomed him and set him free.
27 *Fostat*: Heb., *Miṣrayyim* (Egypt) = Arabic, *Miṣr* = Cairo, and in Jewish usage, Fostat. *Head [of the academy]*: Cf. II.40. See S.N.
29 *The mightiest of*: Lit., mightier than.
30 *Maghreb*: Although technically Qairawan was part of Ifriqiya rather than of the Maghreb, the distinction was often blurred; cf. note to line 3.

[THE SUCCESSION OF THE RABBINATE] 65

Then the commander arrived at Cordova where he sold R. Moses along with R. Ḥanok. He was redeemed by the people of Cordova, who were under the impression that he was a man of no education. Now there was in Cordova a synagogue that was called the College Synagogue, where a judge by the name of R. Nathan the Pious, who was a man of distinction, used to preside. However, the people of Spain were not thoroughly versed in the words of our rabbis, of blessed memory. Nevertheless, with the little knowledge they did possess, they conducted a school and interpreted [the traditions] more or less [accurately]. Once R. Nathan explained [the law requiring] "immersion [of the finger] for each sprinkling," which is found in the tractate Yoma, but he was unable to explain it correctly. Thereupon, R. Moses, who was seated in the corner like an attendant, arose before R. Nathan and said to him: "Rabbi, this would result in an excess of immersions!" When he and the students heard his words, they marvelled to each other and asked him to explain the law to them. This he did quite properly. Then each of them propounded to him || all the difficulties which they had, and he replied to them out of the abundance of his widom.

Outside the College there were litigants, who were not permitted to enter until the students had completed their lesson. On that day, R. Nathan the Judge walked out, and the litigants followed him. However, he said to them: "I am no longer judge. This man, who is garbed in rags and is a stranger,

33 *The people of Cordova*: See note to line 26 and S.N. here. On the Jewish community and quarter there, cf. Ashtor, *Qorot ha-Yehudim bi-Sefarad ha-Muslimit*, I, 191 f.
35 *College Synagogue*: Lit., the synagogue of the house of study. See S.N.
38–39 *The people of Spain etc.*: See S.N.
39 *Conducted a school*: See S.N.
39–40 *Interpreted [the traditions] more or less [accurately]*: Translation doubtful; cf. Cohen, *SFC*, p. 61 n. 22.
40–41 *Immersion [of the finger] etc.*: When sprinkling blood on the altar of gold on the Day of Atonement (cf. Lev. 16.18–19), the high-priest was to immerse his finger in the pan containing the blood for each of the seven sprinklings; cf. following notes.
41 *Yoma*: Tosef. Yoma 3.2 (ed. Lieberman), p. 240; cf. Lieberman's note there and especially his remarks in *Tosefta Ki-Fshutah*, IV, 778 f.; Cohen, *SFC*, p. 62 n. 22 a.
42–44 *But he was unable etc.*: R. Nathan apparently explained that the high-priest must immerse himself in the ritual bath after each sprinkling of blood. To this R. Moses objected that the law requires the high-priest to immerse himself but five times on the Day of Atonement (*M*. Yoma 3.3). But, according to R. Nathan's explanation, the number of immersions required of the high-priest would have exceeded five by far; Lieberman, *loc. cit.*
50 *Lesson*: On this word, cf. Cohen, *SFC*, p. 62 n. 24.
51 *Walked out*: Viz., without waiting, as was his custom, for the litigants to enter and present their cases.
52 *Stranger*: Lit., guest.

is my master, and I shall be his disciple from this day on. You ought to appoint him judge of the community of Cordova." And that is exactly what they did.

55 The community then assigned him a large stipend and honored him with costly garments and a carriage. [At that point] the commander wished to retract his sale. However, the King would not permit him to do so, for he was delighted by the fact that the Jews of his domain no longer had need of the people of Babylonia.

60 The report [of all this] spread throughout the land of Spain and the Maghreb, and students came to study under him. Morever, all questions which had formerly been addressed to the academies were now directed to him. This affair occurred in the days of R. Sherira, in about 4750, somewhat more or less.

R. Moses the Rabbi allied himself by marriage with the Ibn Falija family,
65 which was the greatest of the families of the community of Cordova, and took from them a wife for his son R. Ḥanok. [Subsequently,] the daughter of R. Ḥanok was married to one of the Ibn Falija family. Because of this, they are called by the surname Ibn Falija to this day.

R. Moses acquired numerous disciples, one of whom was R. Joseph b.
70 R. Isaac b. Shatnash ‖ surnamed Ibn Abitur. He interpreted the whole of the
[49] Talmud in Arabic for the Muslim King al-Ḥakam. Because of his prominence and his learning, he rejected R. Ḥanok the Rabbi, who had occupied his

53 *My master*: Sc., inasmuch as he taught R. Nathan the meaning of the law; cf. Abot 6.3; *B. B.M.* 33a (view of R. Jose).

55–56 *Stipend... costly garments*: See S.N.

58–59 *No longer had need of the people of Babylonia*: I.e., no longer needed to direct their legal problems to Babylonia and, consequently, contribute to their upkeep; see immediately below and cf. Cohen, *SFC*, pp. 114 f. On the expression "the people of Babylonia," cf. S.N. to line 33.

61–62 *All questions which had formerly etc.*: See S.N.

63 *R. Sherira*: Cf. above, VI.178–202. *4750*: 989–990 C.E. On the problems connected with, and significance of, this date, cf. Cohen, *SFC*, pp. 72, 95 f. and below, pp. 205 ff.

64 *R. Moses the Rabbi*: This way of referring to the rabbi of a community and more specifically to the head of an academy (cf. also below, lines 72 f.) is known from the Geniza and represents distinctly western usage; cf. S.D. Goitein, "New Sources Concerning the Nagids of Qayrawan and R. Nissim" [in Hebrew], *Zion*, XXVII (1961–62), 21; idem, "Shemarya b. Elhanan," pp. 267 f. See S.N. *Ibn Falija*: This family is otherwise unknown, except for a possible reference in the poetry of Isaac ibn Ḥalfon; cf. Cohen, *SFC*, pp. 63 n. 32, 118 n. 197; Itzhak ibn Khalfun, *Poems* (ed. A. Mirsky), p. 139.

67 *They*: I.e., the descendants of R. Moses and R. Ḥanok.

70 *Shatnash*: The exact spelling and pronunciation of this name are doubtful; cf. Cohen, *SFC*, p. 63 n. 35. *Ibn Abitur*: Died after 1012. On his life and work, cf. Schirmann, *Ha-Shirah ha-Ibrit bi-Sefarad u-bi-Provence*, I, 53 f., II, 677; Cohen, *SFC*, p. 72 n. 72.

71 *Al-Ḥakam*: Reigned 961–976; cf. *EI*, II, 223.

72 *R. Ḥanok the Rabbi*: Cf. note to line 64.

father's post. Accordingly, after the death of the great nasi, R. Ḥisdai b. R. Isaac, the community was divided by a bitter dispute. (In the days of R. Ḥisdai there was not a man in the world who could have disputed the authority of R. Ḥanok.) Every day there used to go out of Cordova to the city of al-Zahra seven hundred Jews in seven hundred carriages, each of them attired in royal garb and wearing the headdress of Muslim officials, all of them escorting the Rabbi. A second faction would escort Ibn Shatnash. Finally, the party of the Rabbi gained the upper hand, excommunicated Ibn Shatnash and banned him. [At that point] the King said to him: "If the Muslims were to reject me in the way the Jews have done to you, I would go into exile. Now you betake yourself into exile!"

Ibn Shatnash went from Spain to Pechina and encountered there R. Samuel ha-Kohen b. R. Josiah, a member of the community of Fez. The latter was mindful of the ban of the Rabbi, R. Ḥanok, and refused to converse with Ibn Shatnash. Thereupon, Ibn Shatnash angrily wrote him a long letter in Aramaic, in which he made a [grammatical] error. R. Samuel ha-Kohen replied to him, pointing out his error to him, but in a mild and tranquil tone. So Ibn Shatnash boarded a ship and went to the academy of Rabbenu Hai, being

73   *Nasi*: Prince. See S.N. *R. Ḥisdai*: Sc., Ibn Shaprut; died ca. 990. Cf. Baron, *SRH*, III, 155 f.; Ashtor, *Qorot ha-Yehudim bi-Sefarad ha-Muslimit*, I, 111 f.
76–79   The purpose of these excursions to al-Zahra was for each side to argue its case before the Caliph, who finally decided the issue in favor of R. Ḥanok. See S.N.
77   *Al-Zahra*: The royal city, some five miles west of Cordova, founded by ʿAbd ar-Raḥman III in November, 936; cf. *EI*, III, 92 f.; cf. also Cohen, *SFC*, p. 64 n. 40.
77–78   *Attired in royal garb etc.*: Cf. above, line 56.
78   *Headdress*: This word is translated by Ibn Janaḥ by the Arabic *qalansuwa*; Jonah ibn Janaḥ, *The Book of Hebrew Roots* (ed. A. Neubauer), p. 122. This was a high-pointed cap worn by Muslim officials, principally caliphs and *qadis*, in Abbasid times; but it went out of fashion in the East ca. 1000. See S.N.
80–81   *Excommunicated... and banned him*: Excommunication (*nidduy*) was a decree forbidding any association with a person, while banning (*ḥerem*) meant total exclusion from the community, coupled with public excoriation of the victim; cf. Assaf, *Ha-ʿOnashim Aḥaray Ḥatimat ha-Talmud*, pp. 31 f.; Mann, "The Responsa etc." *JQR* NS, X (1919), 348 f.
82   *Go into exile*: Lit., flee; cf. note to VI.161.
84   *From Spain to Pechina*: I.e., from Andalus to Pechina (Arabic: Bajjana). Technically, Ibn Daud's wording is anachronistic, for Pechina was incorporated into Andalus by ʿAbd ar-Raḥman III in 922. Until that time the city had been a semi-independent republic under the protection of the Umayyad rulers. However, since after the dissolution of the Umayyad kingdom, Bajjana was part of the independent kingdom of Almeria, Ibn Daud continued to think of the area as a separate state; cf. *EI*, I (new ed.), 864. *Pechina*: On the Jewish community there, cf. below, line 304. On the reading of some of the MSS, "the island" of Pechina, cf. Cohen, *SFC*, p. 65 n. 44.
89   *Pointing out his error*: See S.N.

[50] under the impression that Rabbenu || Hai would receive him and that the latter was an enemy of R. Ḥanok. [That impression] derived from the fact that the aforementioned four scholars had cut off the income of the academies, with the result that the academies were reduced to poverty. Nevertheless,
95 Rabbenu Hai let him know that he should not come, for if he should come he would observe the ban declared by the Rabbi. Accordingly, Ibn Shatnash went off to Damascus where he died.

Prior to that, however, the faction opposing the Rabbi, including those who supported Ibn Shatnash, had declined. Among these were two brothers,
100 merchants [and] manufacturers of silk, Jacob ibn Jau and his brother Joseph. They once happened to enter the courtyard of one of the king's eunuchs, who was in charge of the land of Takurunna, at a time when the Muslim elders of the territory under his charge had come to register a complaint against the officer he had appointed over them. They had also brought him a gift of
105 two thousand Ja'afariya gold peices. No sooner did they begin to speak than the minister issued an order to humiliate them, beat them with clubs, and have them hustled off to prison. Now, in the entrance to the palace there were a number of tortuous recesses into one of which the two thousand gold pieces fell. Although they protested vigorously, no one paid them any attention.
110 However, immediately [afterwards], Jacob ibn Jau and his brother Joseph entered [the palace], found the gold pieces and went off. Once they arrived home, they took counsel [on the matter], saying: "[Since] we have discovered this money in the royal palace, let us make a solemn agreement to return it there, coupled with gifts and offerings. Perhaps we shall be able in [that way] to

93 *Cut off the income of the academies etc.*: Cf. Mann, *Texts and Studies*, I, 111 f., 157. 187; Cohen, *SFC*, pp. 115 f.
96 *To Damascus*: See S.N.
98 *Prior to that*: Viz., to the death of Ibn Shatnash.
100 *Merchants and manufacturers of silk*: See S.N. *Ibn Jau*: For a summary of the known data on him, cf. Baron *SRH*, V, 44 f.; Cohen, *SFC*, p. 122. On the name Jau, cf. S.D. Goitein, "From the Mediterranean to India," *Speculum*, XXIX (1954), 191 n. 17.
102 *Takurunna*: Although most of the MSS read Tarragona, I have adopted the reading of MS ה, *Tkdna*, which may easily have been corrupted from the more appropriate Takurunna; cf. Cohen, *SFC*, p. 66 n. 47.
105 *Ja'afriya gold pieces*: These were gold dinars minted at Medinat al-Zahra by al-Ḥakam between 967/8 and 969/70; cf. Miles, *The Coinage of the Umayyads of Spain*, pp. 323 f.
106 *The minister*: Lit., the eunuch.
107 *Hustled off*: For the style, cf. Esth. 8.14.
113 *Let us make a solemn agreement*; Lit., come, let us swear.
114 *Gifts and offerings*: Viz., of funds and goods.

[THE SUCCESSION OF THE RABBINATE] 69

115 rid ourselves of the abuse of our enemies and gain the support of the King."
51] So they did just that, and they became successful in the silk business, making clothing of high quality and pennants that are placed at the tops of standards of such high quality as was not duplicated in all of Spain. They brought presents to King Hisham and to King al-Manṣur ibn Abi ʿAmir, his guardian, with
120 the result that King al-Manṣur became very fond of Jacob b. Jau. Accordingly, the former issued him a document placing him in charge of all the Jewish communities from Sijilmasa to the river Duero, which was the border of his realm. [The decree stated] that he was to adjudicate all their litigations, and that he was empowered to appoint over them whomsoever he wished and to exact
125 from them any tax or payment to which they might be subject. Furthermore, he placed at his disposal eighteen of his eunuchs clad in uniform, who conducted him in the carriage of a vicegerent. Then all the members of the community of Cordova assembled and signed an agreement [certifying] his position as nasi, which stated: "Rule thou over us, both thou, and thy son, and thy son's
130 son also." Upon taking office, he despatched a messenger to the Rabbi, R. Ḥanok, [threatening him] that, should he adjudicate [a litigation] between two people, he would cast him into the sea in a boat without oars.

Thereupon, all those who had opposed Ibn Shatnash switched to the latter['s side]. All [now] wrote letters to Ibn Shatnash [urging him] to return to Cordova
135 and [assuring him] that they would remove the Rabbi, R. Ḥanok, and appoint him as rabbi over them. To these he replied sternly, saying of the Rabbi: "I call upon heaven and earth as my witnesses that there is no one in all of Spain as worthy as he of presiding over the academy."

52] However, at the end of the first year of his rule as nasi, Ibn Jau was thrown
140 into prison by King al-Manṣur. The latter had been under the impression that Ibn Jau would produce great profits for him by taking money from Jews

115 *The abuse of our enemies*: On the tension between various Jewish families and factions in Cordova at that time, cf. Cohen, *SFC*, pp. 118 f.
117 *Pennants*: See S.N.
119 *Hisham*: Reigned 976–1009. *Al-Manṣur ibn Abi ʿAmir*: Officially the *ḥajib* or chamberlain of Hisham II, 977–991, he was actual ruler of the Umayyad domain and in 996 assumed royal titles: cf. *EI*, III, 254 f. *Guardian*: For the use of this word for *Ḥajib* or the governor over the affairs of state, cf. II Ki. 10.1 and Ibn Janaḥ, *The Book of Hebrew Roots*, p. 57 (Heb. trans., *Sefer Haschoraschim*, p. 38).
121 *Issued him a note*: Sc., of appointment; see S.N.
122 *Duero*: On the Hebrew spelling of this name, cf. Cohen, *SFC*, p. 67 n. 56.
126 *Clad in uniform etc.*: Cf. above, lines 56, 77–78.
127–128 *The community of Cordova*: I.e., the Jewish community.
129 *Rule thou etc.*: Jud. 8.22.
141 *Profits*: Lit., gifts.

in all the communities by fair means or foul and turn it over to him. Since [Ibn Jau] failed to do so, [al-Manṣur] threw him into prison, where he remained for about one year. Finally, on the day of a Muslim festival, King Hisham happened to pass by the prison on his way from the palace to his house of worship, while Ibn Jau was standing in the entrance to the prison directly in the view of King Hisham. When the latter saw him he asked his guardian al-Manṣur why he had done this to him. He replied: "Because he does not turn in any tribute from all his domain." Thereupon, King Hisham ordered that he be released and restored to his office. Although this was done, he did not regain quite the same [powers] which he had previously had.

Because of this situation and because Ibn Shatnash had sent a stern reply to the community of Cordova, the Rabbi was not removed following Ibn Jau's reinstatement in office. Finally, [Ibn Jau] died within the lifetime of the Rabbi. The Rabbi, saint that he was, was extremetly grieved at his death [as can be seen from the following]. [Ibn Jau] died on a Friday evening, and one of the Rabbi's in-laws of the Ibn Falija family came to him, believing that he would be bearing good tidings with the announcement of Jacob's death. However, the Rabbi burst into loud weeping. Ibn Falija said to him in amazement: "I came to bear you the good tidings of the death of your enemy, but you obviously love the man who hated you." The Rabbi replied to him: "I am distressed about the poor who ate regularly at his table. What are they to do tomorrow? If you support them, I shall not weep; as for myself, I am unable to give them support." [This last remark stemmed from the circumstance] that the Rabbi was not a man of means. Because of || his saintliness, he had refused to derive any profit from the honor of the Torah and consequently lived a life of austerity.

The Rabbi, R. Ḥanok, passed away in 4775, thirteen years before the demise of Rabbenu Hai, of blessed memory. Nevertheless, the communities

---

145–147 See S.N.
148–149 *Turn in any tribute*: For the style, cf. Isa. 18.7; Ps. 68.30. Cf. also Ibn Shaprut's letter to King Joseph of the Khazars; Kokovtzov, *Evreisko-Khazarskaya perepiska v X vieke*, p. 14, lines 5–6.
157 *In-laws of the Ibn Falija family*: Cf. above, lines 64 f. See S.N.
161 *Love the man etc.*: Cf. II Sam. 19.7.
161–163 Cf. Cohen, *SFC*, pp. 120 f., for an Arabic parallel to this story.
166 *Refused to derive any profit etc.*: This would imply that R. Ḥanok had refused the stipend which the community had awarded his father; cf. above, line 55. For this virtue, cf. Abot 4.5. See S.N.
186 *4775, thirteen years before etc.*: Since R. Hai died in 4798 (cf. VI.185), either the date of R. Ḥanok's death must be emended or the subsequent figure corrected to "twenty-three"; for the various conjectures, cf. Cohen, *SFC*, p. 69 n. 62 and below, pp. 201 f.

[THE SUCCESSION OF THE RABBINATE] 71

170 of west and east, did not resume the sending of gifts to the academies, inasmuch as these scholars raised many disciples, and [the knowledge of] the Talmud spread throughout the world.

Now the custom of the Rabbi, R. Ḥanok, of blessed memory, was as follows: Every year, on the last day of the Festival, he used to go up [to the pulpit]
175 to complete the reading of the Torah, accompanied by the outstanding men of the generation and the pillars of the congregation. In 4775 he went up in accordance with his custom, accompanied by the others. Since the pulpit was old, it broke and caved in. [In the accident] the Rabbi's neck was broken, and he died a few days later — after having raised up many disciples.

180 One of his outstanding disciples was R. Samuel ha-Levi the Nagid b. R. Joseph, surnamed Ibn Nagrela, of the community of Cordova. Besides being a great scholar and highly cultured person, R. Samuel was highly versed in

---

170 *The sending of gifts to the academies*: Cf. above, lines 2 f., 57 f., 93 f.
173 *Now the custom etc.*: Ibn Daud proceeds to recount the circumstances surrounding the death of R. Ḥanok.
174 *Festival*: I.e., of Tabernacles.
175 *To complete the reading of the Torah*: The annual completion of the cycle of the reading of the Torah on the last day of the Festival in Diaspora communities goes back to talmudic times and is the source of the name subsequently given to the day, *Simḥat Torah*; cf. B. Meg. 31a and *JE*, XI, 364 f.
176 *Pillars of the congregation*: Lit., eyes of the congregation, which is understood in Sifra, Ḥoba 4.6 (ed. Weiss), f. 19a (= B. Hor. 7b) to refer to the court, but which in medieval Hebrew was extended to mean distinguished men generally; cf. Ben Iehuda, *Thesaurus*, IX, 4439b (top); Pinsker, *Lickute Kadmoniot*, p. 126 (= David b. Abraham Alfasi, *Hebrew-Arabic Dictionary of the Bible* [ed. by S. Skoss, 2 vols. New Haven, 1936–45], II, 391).
177 *Pulpit*: Lit., ark.
179 *After having raised up many disciples*: Cf. Abot 1.1. Although this clause should more appropriately have been inserted above, line 169, Ibn Daud probably tacked the phrase on at this point in order to conclude his account of R. Ḥanok on a positive note; cf Tosef. Ber. 3.21 (ed. Lieberman), p. 17.
180 *One of his outstanding disciples*: See S.N. *R. Samuel ha-Levi ...ibn Nagrela*: For the many studies on his life and work, cf. the bibliography in Schirmann, *Ha-Shirah ha-Ibrit etc.*, II, 678. I have retained the spelling Nagrela demanded by the MSS, although the Arabic transcription of the name is Naghralla; cf. E. Lévi-Provençal, "Les 'Mémoires' de 'Abd Allah, Dernier Roi Ziride de Grenade," *Al-Andalus*, III (1935), 224 n. 23; S.M. Stern, "Life of Shmuel ha-Nagid" [in Hebrew], *Zion*, XV (1950), 135 n. 2. *Nagid:* See below, line 234.
181 *Cordova*: See S.N.
182 *Scholar*: Sc., in Jewish lore. *Cultured person*: Sc., in secular knowledge; cf. Dan. 1.4, from which the phrases describing Ibn Nagrela's virtues are appropriated.

Arabic literature and style and was, indeed, competent to serve in the king's palace. Nevertheless, he maintained himself in very modest circumstances as
185 a spice-merchant until the time when war broke out in Spain. With the termination of the rule of the house of Ibn Abi ʿAmir and the seizure of power by the Berber chiefs, the city of Cordova dwindled, and its inhabitants were compelled to flee. Some went off to Saragossa, where their descendants have remained down to the present, while others went to Toledo, where their
190 descendants have retained their identity down to the present.

[54] This R. Samuel, however, fled to Malaga, where he occupied a shop as a spice-merchant. Since his shop happened to adjoin the courtyard of Ibn al-ʿArif — who was the *Katib* of King Ḥabbus b. Maksan, the Berber king of Granada — the *Katib*'s maidservant would ask him to write letters for her to her master,
195 the Vizier Abu'l-Qasim ibn al-ʿArif. When the latter received the letters, he was astounded at the learning they reflected. Consequently, when, after a while, this Vizier, Ibn al-ʿArif, was given leave by his King Ḥabbus to return to his home in Malaga, he inquired among the people of his household: "Who wrote the letters which I received from you?" They replied: "A certain Jew

185–187 *War broke out in Spain etc.*: On the termination of Amirid rule in 1008 and the subsequent period of unrest (*fitna*), cf. Dozy, *Histoire*, II, 281 f. (Eng. trans., p. 538). Cordova finally fell to the Berbers on April 19, 1013; *ibid*, p. 305 (Eng. trans., p. 559).

187 *Berber chiefs*: Lit., the lords of the Philistines (Josh. 13.3); cf. above, IV. 143, note on "Berber Africa."

187–188 *Its inhabitants were compelled to flee*: Cf. Dozy, *op. cit.*, II, 306, 327 (Eng. trans., pp. 560 f., 579). For a parallel Jewish account, cf. Moses ibn Ezra, *Sefer Shirat Israel*, p. 65. Nevertheless, the Jewish community of Cordova did not cease to exist; cf. below, lines 309 f.

188 *Saragossa*: At the time of these uprisings, the governor of Saragossa defected and established an independent monarchy; cf. *EI*, IV, 157. On the Jewish quarter there, cf. Ashtor, *op. cit.*, pp. 218 f.

189 *Toledo*: On the Jewish quarter there, cf. *ibid.*, pp. 211 f.

190 *Retained their identity*: I.e., they are known as (descendants of) Cordovans.

191 *Malaga*: At the time of Ibn Nagrela's flight, Malaga remained in the hands of a pro-Umayyad governor, who threw in his lot with Ali ibn Ḥammud; cf. Dozy, *op. cit.*, II, 311 (Eng. trans., p. 564); *EI*, II, 253 f. Malaga and Granada were the two great centers of Berber control after the period of the *fitna*; cf. Pérès, *op. cit.*, p. 9.

192–205 For an analysis and Arabic parallel to the story of Ibn Nagrela's rise to power, cf. Stern, "Life of Shmuel ha-Nagid," pp. 135 f.

192 *Ibn al-ʿArif*: For his full name, cf. below, line 195.

193 *Ḥabbus b. Maksan*: Ruler of Granada, ca. 1026–1038; cf. Lévi-Provençal, "Les Mémoires," *Al-Andalus*, III (1935), 238 f. Although Ibn Daud refers to him as *King* Ḥabbus, his official title was *hajib* or chamberlain; *ibid.*, pp. 241, 244. None of the MSS of *SHQ* transcribe the names Maksan and Qasim (line 195) quite correctly.

196 *Learning they reflected*: Lit., his wisdom.

197 *Given leave*: For the style, cf. Neh. 13.6.

200 of the community of Cordova, who lives next door to your courtyard, used to do the writing for us." The *Katib* thereupon ordered that R. Samuel ha-Levi be brought to him at once, and he said to him: "It does not become you to spend your time in a shop. Henceforth you are to stay at my side." He thus became the scribe and counsellor of the counsellor to the King. Now the
205 counsel which he gave was as if one consulted the oracle of God, and thanks to his counsel King Ḥabbus achieved successes and became exceedingly great.

Subsequently, when the *Katib* Ibn al-ʿArif took ill and felt his death approaching, King Ḥabbus paid him a visit and said to him: "What am I going to do? Who will counsel me in the wars which encompass me on every side?"
210 He replied: "I never counselled you out of my own mind, but out of the mind of
[55] this Jew, my scribe. || Look after him well, and let him be a father and a priest to you. Do whatever he says, and God will help you."

Accordingly, after the death of the *Katib*, King Ḥabbus brought R. Samuel ha-Levi to his palace and made him *Katib* and counsellor. Thus, he entered
215 the King's palace in 4780.

Now the King had two sons, Badis the elder and Buluggin the younger. Although the Berber princes supported the election of the younger, Buluggin, as king, the people at large supported Badis. The Jews also took sides, with three of them, R. Joseph b. Megash, R. Isaac b. Leon and R. Nehemiah
220 surnamed Ishkafa, who were among the leading citizens of Granada, supporting Buluggin. R. Samuel ha-Levi, on the other hand, supported Badis. On the day of King Ḥabbus' death, the Berber princes and nobles formed a line to

---

204 *Scribe and counsellor of the counsellor*: In Arabic terms, he became *katib* and *vizie* to the Vizier.
204–205 *Now the counsel which he gave*: Cf. II Sam. 16.23. See S.N.
206 *Became exceedingly great etc.*: Cf. II Chr. 1.1; 17.12.
208–209 For the identical motif in the medieval versions of the Ahiqar story, which circulated in Arabic as well as in other languages, cf. *The Apocrypha and Pseudepigrapha of the Old Testament in English*, ed. by R.H. Charles (2 vols. Oxford, 1913), II, 727. Ibn Daud here alludes to Ibn Nagrela's activities as military commander as well as vizier; cf. H. Schirmann, "The Wars of Samuel Han-Nagid" [in Hebrew], *Zion*, I, 261 f., 357 f.; II, 185 f.; idem, "Samuel Hannagid, the Man, the Soldier, the Politician," *Jewish Social Studies*, XIII (1951), 99 f. Cf. also above, note to line 180.
211 *Look after him well*: Jer. 39.12. *Let him be etc.*: Jud. 17.10.
215 *4780*: This and other dates in Ibn Daud's account of Ibn Nagrela's rise to power have been seriously questioned by H. Schirmann, "Isaac ibn Halfon" [in Hebrew], *Tarbiz*, VII (1935–36), 300 f.; idem, "Samuel Hannagid, the Man, etc.," pp. 103 f.
217 *Although the Berber princes supported... Buluggin*: See S.N.
219 *R. Joseph b. Megash*: Cf. below, lines 396 f.
220 *Ishkafa*: On this name, cf. Baer, *History of the Jews in Christian Spain*, I, 386 n. 14 c.
222 *Formed a line*: Sc., to perform the ceremony of investiture and taking the oath of

proclaim his son Buluggin as king. Thereupon, Buluggin went and kissed the hand of his older brother Badis, thus acknowledging the latter as king. This happened in the year 4787. Buluggin's supporters turned livid with embarassment, but in spite of themselves they acknowledged Badis as king. Subsequently, his brother Buluggin regretted his earlier action and tried to lord it over his brother Badis. There was nothing, however trivial, that the King would do that Buluggin would not frustrate. When, after a while, his brother took ill, the King told the physician to withhold medications from his brother, [56] and the physician did just that. || Buluggin then died, and the kingdom was established in the hand of Badis. Thereupon, the three leading Jewish citizens mentioned above fled to the city of Seville.

Now R. Samuel was appointed as nagid in [4]787. He achieved great good for Israel in Spain, the Maghreb, Ifriqiya, Egypt, Sicily, indeed as far as the academy in Babylonia and the Holy City. He provided material benefits out of his own pocket for students of the Torah in all these countries. He also purchased many books — [copies] of the Holy Scriptures as well as of the Mishna and Talmud, which are also among the holy writings. Throughout Spain and the countries just mentioned, whoever wished to devote full time to the study of

allegiance (Arabic: *bay'a*); see next note. The Hebrew phrase itself is borrowed from tannaitic sources where it is used in various connections, but most notably in connection with the procession of condolence after burial; cf. *M*. Ber. 3.2.

223 *Kissed the hand etc.*: On this form of investiture and allegiance, cf. Ibn Khaldun, *Muqaddimah* (trans. Rosenthal), I, 428 f.; Mez, *op. cit.*, pp. 51, 89, 97, 137 f. See S.N.

225 *4787*: = 1026-7 C.E. This is incorrect, for Badis ascended the throne in 1038 (or in 1037, at the earliest); cf. Lévi-Provençal, "Les Mémoires," *Al-Andalus*, III, 245 n. 25.

227–229 On Buluggin's interference in the affairs of state, cf. Dozy, *Histoire*, III, 25, 28, 34 (Eng. trans., pp. 613 f.).

230 *The King told the physician etc.*: See S.N.

233 *Seville*: Sc., which since 1023 had been the capital of an independent kingdom and hostile to Badis; cf. *EI*, IV, 235 f., and below, lines 396 f.; Dozy, *Histoire*, III, 17, 50 f. (Eng. trans. pp. 605, 634 f.).

234 *Appointed as nagid*: Lit., ordained as nagid (= leader or prince of the Jewish community). On the origin and significance of this title, cf. S.D. Goitein, "The Title and Office of the Nagid, A Re-examination," *JQR* NS, LIII (1962-63), 93–119; idem, "New Sources Concerning the Nagids of Qayrawan and R. Nissim" [in Hebrew], *Zion*, XXVII (1962), 22 f.; idem, "Who Was the First Nagid" [in Hebrew], *ibid.*, p. 165; see also S.N. to line 73. *He achieved great good etc.* See note to VI.151–152.

236 *Holy City*: Jerusalem: cf. e.g., Isa. 52.1; Neh. 11.1. *He provided etc.*: On Ibn Nagrela's connections with scholars in these countries and his benefactions, cf. Margalioth, *Hilkhot Hannagid*, pp. 57 f.

238 *Purchased many books*: On the renown of his library, cf. *ibid.*, p. 46.

239–240 *Mishna and Talmud, which are also among etc.*: For the force of this anti-sectarian interjection, cf. Prologue.

[THE SUCCESSION OF THE RABBINATE] 75

the Torah found in him a patron. Moreover, he retained scribes who would make copies of the Mishna and Talmud, which he would present to students who were unable to purchase copies themselves, both in the academies of Spain as well as of the other countries we mentioned. These gifts were coupled
245 with annual contributions of olive oil for the synagogues of Jerusalem, which he would despatch from his own home. He spread Torah abroad and died at a ripe old age after having earned four crowns: the crown of Torah, the crown of power, the crown of a Levite, and towering over them all, by dint of good deeds in each of these domains, the crown of a good name. He passed
250 away in 4815.

His son, R. Joseph ha-Levi the Nagid, succeeded to his post. Of all the fine

241 *A patron*: See S.N.
245 *Contributions of olive oil*: On the emphasis on this virtue in Rabbanite circles in gaonic times, cf. M. Zucker, "Tegubot li-Tenuat Abaylay Zion ha-Qaraiyyim ba-Sifrut ha-Rabbanit," *Sefer ha-Yobel le-R. Ḥanok Albeck* (Jerusalem, 1963), p. 396; Mann, *Jews in Egypt*, I, 233; II, 292; Goitein, *Jewish Education in Muslim Countries*, p. 189. See S.N.
246 *He spread Torah abroad*: On Ibn Nagrela's renown as a talmudist, cf. Margalioth, *Hilkhot Hannagid*, pp. 52 f.
247 *Ripe old age*: Technically, the Hebrew expression would indicate that he died after having attained the age of seventy; cf. Abot 5.21. However, Moses Ibn Ezra, *Shirat Israel*, p. 67, indicates that he died at the age of sixty-three; cf. also Harkavy, "Le-Toledot R. Samuel ha-Nagid," pp. 36, 56 n. 3. Ibn Daud's phraseology is probably drawn from Ibn Nagrela's own musings on his "white hair", which both Ibn Nagrela as well as Ibn Daud used in a non-technical sense; cf. the passages from Ibn Nagrela's *Diwan* collected by Sassoon in the Introduction to his edition, pp. vii f. *Four crowns*: Cf. Abot 4.13. Although the Mishna specifically indicates that there are three crowns, the text was often understood to mean that the fourth virtue, that of a good name, is distinct from the other three; cf. the poem on the *four* crowns in Davidson, *Thesaurus*, I, nos. 7476-7; M. Zulay, "Le-Ḥeqer ha-Siddur we-ha-Minhagim," *Sefer Assaf* (Jerusalem, 1953), p. 310. *Crown of Torah*: Cf. line 246.
248 *Power*: Lit., greatness; cf. above, lines 214 f. *Levite*: Cf. above, line 180. On Ibn Nagrela's pride in his Levitic descent, cf. Schirmann, "Samuel Hannagid, the Man etc.," p. 100 n. 6. *Towering above them all etc.*: See S.N.
250 4815: Although this date is repeated below, line 316, the date of 4816 [= 1055/56] is now generally accepted as the correct one; cf. S. Assaf in *Tarbiz*, III (1931-32), 352; E. Lévi-Provençal, "Les Mémoires," *Al-Andalus*, III (1935), p. 249; Schirmann, "Samuel Hannagid, The Man, etc.," p. 126.
251 *R. Joseph ha-Levi*: Although his Hebrew name was Yehosef, I have rendered it in English as Joseph, Yosef and Yehosef being variants of the same name. For studies of his life and work, cf. the bibliography in Schirmann, *Ha-Shirah ha-Ibrit*, II, 680; cf. also F.B. Bargebuhr, "The Alhambra Palace of the Eleventh Century," *Journal of the Warburg and Courtauld Institutes*, XIX (1956), 192-258; A.M. Habermann, "Yehosef bar Samuel ha-Nagid," *Tesoro de los Judios Sefardies*, IV (1961), 44 f. *Succeeded*

qualities which his father possessed he lacked but one. Having been reared [57] in wealth and never || having had to bear a burden [of responsibility] in his youth, he lacked his father's humility. Indeed, he grew haughty — to his
255 destruction. The Berber princes became so jealous of him that he was killed on the Sabbath day, the ninth of Tebet [4]827, along with the community of Granada and all those who had come from distant lands to see his learning and power. He was mourned in every city and in every town. (Indeed, a fast had been decreed for the ninth of Tebet as far back as the days of our ancient
260 rabbis, who composed *Megillat Taʻanit*; but the reason had not been known. From this [incident] we see that they had pointed prophetically to this very day.) After his death, his books and treasures were scattered all over the world. So, too, the disciples he raised became the rabbis of Spain and the leaders of the following generation.

to his post: For the style, cf. Dan. 11.20, and note the appropriateness of the last half of the verse to Joseph's fate. The phrase is all the more apposite in view of its appearance in the biblical story of Joseph, Gen. 40.13; 41.13.

253 *Bear a burden of [responsibility]*: Cf. Lam. 3.27. Ibn Daud probably uses the phrase in the sense of the discipline of character that is acquired through privation; cf. above, line 184; I. Ratzabi, "The Translation of Lamentations by R. Saadya Gaon," *Tarbiz*, XIII (1941–42), 101 and Ibn Ezra to Lam. 3.27.

254 *Indeed, he grew haughty etc.*: II Chr. 26.16. Ibn Daud echoes the sentiments of the Muslim opponents of the Jewish courtier; cf. references in next note. For a more balanced view, cf. Schirmann, "Sammuel Hannagid, the Man, etc.," p. 119.

255 *The Berber princes etc.*: On the circumstances leading up to Joseph's death, cf. E. Lévi-Provençal, "Les Mémoires etc." *Al-Andalus*, III (1935), 249 f., 265 f. (French trans., pp. 283 f.); Dozy, *Histoire*, III, 70 f. (Eng. trans., pp. 650 f.); Baron, *SRH*, III, 307 n. 42; M. Perlmann, "Eleventh-Century Andalusian Authors on the Jews of Granada," *PAAJR*, XVIII (1948–49), 284 f.; cf. also S.M. Stern, "Two New Data About Hasdai b. Shaprut" [in Hebrew], *Zion*, XI (1945–46), 141–143.

256 *Sabbath day, the ninth of Tebet 4827*: Dec. 31, 1066 or Jan. 1, 1067; cf. Lévi-Provençal "Les Mémoires," *Al-Andalus*, III, 300. See S.N.

257 *And all those who had come etc.*: MSS אפק read: "All those who had come etc. *mourned him*." Although the reading is an attractive one, and certainly more appropriate stylistically, it is not confirmed by Zacuto, whose readings usually conform to this subdivision of MSS.

258 *He was mourned etc.*: No elegies commemorating the event have survived; but cf. Habermann, "Yehosef bar Samuel ha-Nagid," p. 50.

258–260 *A fast had been decreed etc.*: This parenthetical observation is almost a verbatim quotation from the medieval glosses to *Megillat Taʻanit*; cf. Neubauer, *MJC*, II, 24; M. Zulay, "Shibray Ṣelilim," *Sinai*, XXVIII (1950–51), 169 lines 46–47. On the source of this fast, cf. Lieberman, *Shkiin*, p. 10; cf. also M. Margalioth, "Moʻadim we-Ṣomoth be-Ereṣ Israel u-be-Babel bi-Tequfat ha-Geonim," *Aresheth*, (1943–44), pp. 215 f.; Zimmels, *Ashkenazim and Sephardim*, p. 160.

[THE SUCCESSION OF THE RABBINATE]

265 We turn now to recount the history of Ifriqiya. After the demise of R. Ḥushiel, the rabbinate in the city of Qairawan passed into the hands of his son and disciple R. Hananel and R. Nissim b. Jacob ibn Shahin, both of whom received [the tradition] from him. R. Nissim also received much from Rabbenu Hai, who held him in great affection and sent him letters in response to all of
270 his problems without exception. Indeed, it was through R. Nissim that R. Samuel ha-Nagid used to drink of the waters of Rabbenu Hai. R. Samuel helped R. Nissim considerably out of his own funds, inasmuch as the latter was not a man of means. Finally, they entered into a marriage alliance, with R. Nissim sending his daughter to become the wife of R. Joseph the Nagid.
275 Although a learned and pious woman, she did not appeal to him, inasmuch as she was a dwarf. When her husband the Nagid was killed, she fled to Lucena where she was maintained by the community quite honorably until the day of her death.

[58] R. Hananel became a very wealthy man owing to the fact that many merchants
280 in Qairawan showered him with capital. He had nine daughters [to whom] he left ten thousand gold pieces after his death. R. Nissim, too, had no son.

265–266 *The history of Ifriqiya*: For the "beginnings" of Jewish learning in Qairawan, cf. above, lines 27 f. Cf. also Hirschberg's introduction to Nissim b. Jacob ibn Shahin, *Ḥibbur Yafeh me-ha-Yeshu'ah*, pp. 9 f.; Baron, *SRH*, Index vol., s.v. Kairuwan. *The demise of R. Ḥushiel*: Cf. above, note to line 14.

266 *Passed into the hands of*: Lit., there were ordained.

267 *R. Hananel*: Cf. below, lines 279 f. *R. Nissim b. Jacob ibn Shahin*: Cf. Nissim b. Jacob, *op. cit.*, pp. 23 f. Although the MSS render the name in accordance with gaonic spelling as Ibn Shahun, I have transcribed it in accordance with the more accepted and no less attested form; on the name cf. *ibid.*, and cf. also Wayyikra Rabbah 5.2 (ed. Margulies), p. 102. *Both of whom received etc.*: For R. Nissim's acknowledgement of R. Ḥushiel as his master, cf. Nissim b. Jacob, *op. cit.*, p. 28.

268–269 *From R. Hai*: Cf. *ibid.*, pp. 30 f.

270 *Without exception*: Translation doubtful. See S.N. *It was through R. Nissim etc.*: See S.N.

271–272 *R. Samuel helped R. Nissim etc.*: For the close ties between them, cf. Margalioth, *Hilkhot Hannagid*, pp. 56, 62.

274 *Sending his daughter*: Sc., in the sense of marrying her off, as in Jud. 12.9; S. Abramson, "From the Works of R. Nissim Gaon" [in Hebrew], *Tarbiz*, XXVI (1956–57), 52 f., where Abramson also offers a plausible suggestion on the date of the event.

276 *The Nagid was killed*: Above, line 255. *Lucena*: On this town, the population of which was almost exclusively Jewish, cf. Schirmann, "Isaac b. Mar Saul ha-Meshorer mi-Lucena," *Sefer Assaf*, pp. 496 f.; Ashtor, *op. cit.*, pp. 202 f. Cf. also below, lines 336 f.

279 *R. Hananel*: Cf. above to line 14. *Many merchants etc.*: On the meritoriousness of supporting scholars in this way., cf B. Pes. 53b; cf. also S.N. to line 166.

281 *R. Nissim, too, had no son*: Actually, his son Jacob died at an early age; cf. Nissim b. Jacob, *op. cit.*, p. 33.

[Accordingly], with the demise of these two, talmudic learning came to an end in Ifriqiya except for a meager representation in al-Mahdiya through the leadership of the Banu Sogmar and in Qal'at Ḥammad through the leadership of Mar Solomon the Judge b. Formash. However, these men did not attain rabbinic posts, nor did they gain general recognition.

The generation of these three men, R. Hananel, R. Nissim and R. Samuel ha-Levi the Nagid, was the first generation of the rabbinate.

The mastery of the Talmud now rested [exclusively] in Spain, where there flourished five rabbis all of whom were named Isaac. Two of them were natives of Spain; a third came from a neighboring area; while the remaining two migrated from abroad.

The two Spaniards were R. Isaac b. R. Baruk and R. Isaac b. R. Judah.

R. Isaac b. R. Baruk b. R. Isaac b. R. Jacob b. R. Baruk b. Albalia of the the community of Cordova was a descendant of members of the community

282 [*Accordingly*]: Although Ibn Daud does not say this explicitly, the implication left by his juxtaposition of statements is that talmudic learning came to an end in Qairawan because these men had died without male heirs. For a more critical explanation, cf. Goitein, "New Sources Concerning the Nagids of Qayrawan," pp. 18 f., from which it will be seen that the Jewish community there suffered much the same fate as that of Cordova and for very similar reasons. Indeed, R. Nissim himself spent the last years of his life in al-Mahdiya, the port of Qairawan, where he and other Jews of his city found a haven. *With the demise of these two*: R. Nissim died early in the summer of 1062; *ibid.*, p. 17. R. Hananel died sometime between 1052/3 and 1067; S.D. Goitein, "A Colophon to R. Hai Gaon's Commentary to Hagigah" [in Hebrew], *Kirjath Sepher*, XXXI (1955–56), 368.

283 *Banu Sogmar*: For the known data on this family, cf. H.Z. Hirschberg, "The Bene Sogmar of al-Mahdiya" [in Hebrew], *Zion*, XXII (1957), 239 f.; Goitein, "New Sources etc.," pp. 17 f., 159.

284 *Qal'at Ḥammad*: The birthplace of R. Isaac al-Fasi and of his renowned student R. Ephraim; cf. below, line 380; Baron, *SRH*, VI, 368 n. 97. As far as I can determine, nothing further is known of the Jewish community there; cf. Baron, *ibid.*, n. 94.

286 *Recognition*: I.e., as authorities. Although there is no explicit evidence at hand which would prove that Ibn Daud's statement is highly tendentious, the fact that R. Isaac al-Fasi and his student R. Ephraim came from Qal'at Ḥammad to Spain as mature scholars and immediately received wide recognition is sufficient to arouse suspicion on the reliability of Ibn Daud's judgment; cf. below, lines 380 f.

291 *Natives of Spain*: I.e., Andalusians. *A third... from a neighboring area*: Cf. below, line 362. Ibn Daud rightly regards eleventh-century Denia as a separate kingdom; cf. *EI*, I, 938; Pérès, *op. cit.*, pp. 9 f. *The remaining two*: Cf. below, lines 371, 380.

of Merida [to which they had come under the following circumstances]. When Titus overpowered Jerusalem, his lieutenant in charge of Spain requested of him to send him some of the nobles of Jerusalem. Among the few whom he despatched there was a maker of curtains [for synagogue-arks] by the name
300 of Baruk, who was also skilled in silk-work. These people remained in Merida where they raised families, the [Jews of] Merida eventually increasing into a
59] sizable community. ‖ (R. Meir b. Vives informed me that he saw a circular letter of R. Saadiah Gaon, of blessed memory, with the following address: "To the community of Cordova, Elvira, Lucena, Pechina, Calsena, Seville,
305 the great city of Merida, and all the cities of Israel in its vicinity.") Owing to wars, Merida was destroyed, and the ancestors of this R. Isaac, the Rabbi, b. Albalia left home and settled in Cordova where they were counted among the leaders of the community.

This R. Isaac was born in Iyyar, 4795, and from childhood displayed a passion
310 for secular knowledge and Torah. Now there came to the city of Cordova a great scholar from France by the name of R. Paregoros, to whom this R.

---

296 *Merida*: Although the name is incorrectly spelled in the better class of MSS, I have permitted the poorer Hebrew orthography to remain, since the correct spelling in MSS ח may be the product of learned correction.

297 *When Titus overpowered Jerusalem etc.*: I know of no earlier source for this tale. Ultimately, it derives from the tradition that Vespasian exiled Jews to Spain at the time of the destruction of the Second Temple; cf. Seder ʿOlam Zuta, in Neubauer, *MJC*, II, 71 [= F. Lazarus, "Die Haeupter der Vertriebenen," *Jahrbuecher fuer Juedische Geschichte und Litteratur*, X (1890), 161 f.] Cf. also B. Klar, *Meḥqarim we-ʿIyyunim* (Jerusalem, 1954), p. 326 (citing Qirqisani, *Kitab al-Anwar*, II, 17, ed. Nemoy, I, 138). See S.N.

298 *The nobles of Jerusalem*: Cf. also below, Epilogue. 99 f.

301 *[The Jews of] Merida*: Cf. Ashtor, *op. cit.*, pp. 230 f.

302 *R. Meir b. Vives*: As far as I am aware, he is otherwise unknown.

303–305 For discussions of this letter in modern literature, cf. Harkavy, "Le-Toledot R. Samuel ha-Nagid," p. 41; *ISG*, p. 133 n. 2; Mann, *Texts and Studies*, I, 67; Baron, "Saadia's Communal Activities," p. 55 n. 103; idem, *SRH*, V, 16, 298 n. 13; Marx, "Rab Saadia Gaon," p. 91 n. 104.

304 *Pechina, Calsena*: Despite doubts by some modern scholars on the identity of these two names, the MSS evidence is unmistakeable. The variations in spelling of these names are easily explicable in the light of the Arabic forms of these names; cf. Lévi-Provençal, *La Péninsule Ibérique*, pp. 47, 195. On the communities there, cf. Ashtor, *op. cit.*, pp. 202, 207 f.

306 *Merida*: Viz., its Jewish community. Ibn Daud is probably alluding to the repeated uprisings and sieges which the city suffered in the ninth century; cf. *EI*, III, 463.

309 *This R. Isaac*: Above, line 294. *From childhood*: Lit., ever, always; I Ki. 1.6.

311 *From France*: See S.N. *Paregoros*: On a Paregoros of Narbonne (7th century), cf. Gross, *Gallia Judaica*, pp. 403 f. On the prevalence of this name, the Greek equivalent of Menahem, in talmudic times, cf. B. Mazar, *Beth Shearim*, I (Jerusalem, 1957), p. 137.

Isaac showed much kindness by providing for all his needs. Accordingly, he agreed to remain with him and instruct him. R. Samuel ha-Levi the Nagid was fond of R. Isaac ever since the latter's youth and would send him books
315 and [other] gifts urging him strongly to pursue his studies diligently. After R. Samuel ha-Levi the Nagid passed away in 4815, this R. Isaac composed a comprehensive work on the principles of the intercalation of the calendar for R. Samuel's son, R. Joseph ha-Levi the Nagid. The latter provided for him financially, and though R. Isaac [finally] moved to Granada to be at
320 his side, he actually divided his time between Cordova and Granada. Although he was in Granada on the day of the massacre, he was miraculously spared. Subsequently, having amassed a fortune, he acquired a huge library including
[60] many books || which had been the property of the Nagid and which had become scattered in many lands. He composed a great work which he entitled *The*
325 *Spice-Peddler's Basket*, in which he explained very many of the difficult legal sections of the Talmud. He passed away before he could complete it. He was [also] learned in Greek wisdom. He was but thirty-four years old when he achieved general recognition and was appointed as rabbi and nasi in 4829.

313 *He agreed etc.*: For the style, cf. Jud. 17.11. *And instruct him*: In the Hebrew, the subject changes in mid-sentence; hence, lit., and he [i.e., R. Isaac] took instruction from him. *R. Samuel... the Nagid was fond etc.*: Both men were descendants of families of Merida, and both were of the Jewish aristocracy of Cordova; Harkavy, "Le-Toledot R. Samuel ha-Nagid," p. 2.
314 *Would send him books*: Cf. above, lines 236 f.
316 *4815*: Cf. above, line 250.
317 *Comprehensive work etc.*: Lit., a compilation on the whole of "the secret of intercalation." On the reason for this name for the science of calendation, cf. Kohut, *Aruch Completum*, VI, 22; Kasher, *Torah Shelemah*, XIII, Introduction pp. 15 f. Kasher contends plausibly that by medieval times, the word "secret" had lost its original force and was used in the sense of "principles."
318–319 *Provided for him financially*: For the style, cf. Ezra 1.4 and S.N. to III.87. On Joseph ibn Nagrela's benefactions to scholars, cf. Moses ibn Ezra, *op. cit.*, p. 68.
321 *The day of the massacre*: Above, lines 255 f.
322 *Having amassed a fortune*: Lit., being a wealthy man; but cf. lines 318–319.
324 *Scattered in many lands*: Sc., because of the massacre; above, line 262.
325 *The Spice Peddler's Basket*: For the original meaning of this idiom, cf. *ARN*, I, 18 (ed. Schechter), p. 67 (Eng. trans., pp. 90 f.).
327 *Greek wisdom*: Cf. note to IV.10 and below, line 331 f. For a similar description of R. Isaac Albalia, cf. Moses ibn Ezra, *op. cit.*, p. 72. On the other hand, the term "Greek wisdom" may have a much wider connotation in this context than mere astronomy and astrology; cf. below, note to lines 350–352.
328 *Achieved general recognition*: Cf. note to line 286. *4829*: If, as the text seems to imply, Albalia's appointment was at least in part the result of royal favor, the date given here is short by one year; cf. below, p. 272 n. 55.

[THE SUCCESSION OF THE RABBINATE]

[This he attained] when the Muslim king known as al-Muʿtamid appointed
330 him as an official in his residence and palace, where he consulted him in the
science of astrology in which R. Isaac was learned in addition to his knowledge
of the Torah. He remained in office for approximately twenty years. He passed
away at the age of fifty-nine in the city of Granada in Nisan, 4854, after
having spread the knowledge of the Torah, raised disciples and accomp-
335 lished great good for Israel. He was our maternal grandfather.

R. Isaac b. R. Judah b. Giat, one of the leaders of the city of Lucena, also
displayed a passion for secular knowledge and Torah from childhood. The
two Nagids, R. Samuel and his son R. Joseph, honored him and provided
for him. When fate overtook R. Joseph the Nagid, the latter's son Azariah
340 fled to this R. Isaac the Rabbi. Remembering the kindnesses which Azariah's
elders had shown him, he in turn honored and provided for Azariah; indeed,
he even wanted to set him up as the head of the community of Lucena and
the other communities of Spain, despite the fact that Azariah was still but a
lad. However, "except the Lord build the house, they labour in vain that build
345 it," for R. Azariah ha-Levi [soon] passed away. So, R. Isaac b. R. Judah
was appointed as rabbi [and served in that capacity] until 4849. When he
fell seriously ill, his slaves brought him to Cordova for medical attention,
but he soon passed away there on a Sabbath. Accordingly, || his slaves removed
his body from Cordova, carried him all night and reached Lucena at dawn,

---

329 *Al-Muʿtamid*: Muḥammad (II) ibn ʿAbbad, ruler of Seville, !069–1091; conquered Cordova in 1070.
330 *Appointed him as an official*: For the style, cf. Gen. 45.8. *Consulted him etc.*: On al-Muʿtamid's passion for astrology, cf. Dozy, *Histoire*, III, 127, 149 (Eng. trans., pp. 697, 713).
332 *For approximately twenty years*: His retirement from service in the royal palace and transfer to Granada was probably connected with the restiveness of the masses, which was fanned by religious nationalism at the time of the Almoravide permeation of the peninsula; cf. Dozy, *Histoire*, III, 135 f. (Eng. trans., pp. 703 f.) and the references in note to line 255.
334–335 *Having spread etc.*: Cf. Abot 1.1, and note to VI.151–152.
336 *Giat*: This name has frequently been rendered in modern handbooks as Ghayyat. However, cf. Goitein's note in *Tarbiz*, XXIV (1954-55), 468, where the transliteration Ghiyath is proposed as the correct one.
338 *The two Nagids etc.*: On the close connection between them and Ibn Giat, cf. Shirmann, *Ha-Shirah ha-Ibrit*, I, 301; Margalioth, *Hilkhot Hannagid*, pp. 37 f., 67.
339–340 *Azariah fled*: Cf. above, line 276; Moses ibn Ezra, *op. cit.*, p. 68.
340 *The Rabbi*: Cf. note to line 64.
344 Ps. 121.1.
349 *Carried him all night etc.*: For the style, cf. II Sam. 3.2.

350 where they buried him with his fathers. In addition to his secular learning and his knowledge of the Torah, he was also a great poet and learned in Greek wisdom. He spread the knowledge of the Torah and raised many disciples.

One of his outstanding disciples was R. Joseph the Judge b. R. Jacob b. Sahl, a great scholar, a great poet and a pious man, who was appointed as
355 judge in the city of Cordova in Shebat, 4873, and who passed away in Nisan, 4884, after having judged Israel eleven years.

Among the disciples of R. Isaac b. R. Baruk was his son R. Baruk, whom we shall discuss [later], and R. Joseph b. R. Zadok b. Zaddik, a scholar the son of a scholar, a poet and pious man, who was appointed judge over Cordova
360 in Sivan, 4898, and who passed away in 4909, after having judged Israel for eleven years.

[The third of the Rabbis named Isaac] was a man [widely] designated as the colleague of R. Isaac b. R. Baruk and R. Isaac b. Judah. Indeed, he was called "al-Ḥaber" R. Isaac b. R. Moses, surnamed Ben Sakri of the community
365 of Denia. On occasion he is called "Rabbi" and on occasion "Ḥaber." How-

---

350–352 *Secular learning... Torah... Greek wisdom*: The enumeration of secular learning (lit., wisdom) and Greek wisdom as discrete categories alongside that of Torah may be intended to correspond to the three-fold division of philosophical sciences adopted by medieval Jewish philosophers, among them Ibn Daud: mathematics ("secular learning"; cf. Abot 3.18); physics ("Greek wisdom"), theology ("Torah"). The inclusion of "poet" in this list indicates that Ibn Giat was also accomplished in the propaedeutic or literary sciences. Cf. H. A. Wolfson, "The Classification of the Sciences in Mediaeval Jewish Philosophy," *Hebrew Union College Jubilee Volume* (Cincinnati, 1925), pp. 263 f., 279 f. Cf. also below, lines 442–443.

351 *Poet*: Cf. Moses ibn Ezra, *op. cit.*, p. 72; Schirmann, *Ha-Shirah ha-Ibrit*, II, 681. For his legal works, cf. M. M. Kasher, *Sarei ha-Elef* (New York, 1959), p. 430 (Index); Lewin, *Otzar ha-Geonim*, IX, 79 n. 2.

353 *One of his outstanding disciples*: See S. N. to line 180. Cf. also Moses ibn Ezra, *op. cit.*, pp. 74 f., who gives the date of his death as 4883. For a brief biography and bibliography, cf. Schirmann, *Ha-Shirah ha-Ibrit*, I, 358; II, 682.

356 *After having judged Israel*: Cf. Jud. 16.31. The expression indicates that Ibn Sahl was not the Rabbi, or head of the academy, but merely the judge of the community.

358 *We shall discuss*: Below, lines 423 f. *R. Joseph b. R. Zadok b. Zaddik* Cf. Schirmann, *Ha-Shirah ha-Ibrit*, I, 544 f.; II, 686. J. Guttmann, *Philosophies of Judaism*, trans. by D. Silverman (Philadelphia, 1964), pp. 114 f. On the name of his father, see S.N.

362 *[The third...] was a man etc.*: See S.N.

364 *Al-Ḥaber*: Lit., the Colleague. See S.N. *Ben Sakri*: Transliteration doubtful. M. Steinschneider, "Introduction to Arabic Literature of the Jews," *JQR*, XI (1899), 320, suggests as a possible rendering "Sukkari".

365 *Denia*: Cf. below, line 372. *On occasion etc.*: I.e., Ibn Daud is not certain as to which title he held officially, since he was not ordained by any of the aforementioned scholars.

[THE SUCCESSION OF THE RABBINATE] 83

ever, he was not a colleague of these men, nor did he attain any office in their days. He [finally] left Denia for the East, where he was appointed gaon and occupied the see of Rabbenu Hai, of blessed memory. Incidentally, we note that [by that time] all of Iraq had been left without a remnant of native talmudic scholarship.

2] The fourth was R. Isaac b. R. Reuben al-Bargeloni who came from Barcelona to the city of Denia. At that time Denia was fully settled and possessed mastery over the sea and contained a sacred community that was distinguished for its wealth and good deeds. Its inhabitants honored this R. Isaac and provided for him. He married into the family of Ibn Laktush, who were among the leaders of Denia, settled there and judged Israel until the day of his death. He was [also] a poet and composed *Azharot* as well as commentaries on some

367 *He finally left etc.*: For a discussion of this passage, cf. Poznanski, *Babylonische Geonim im nachgaonaeischen Zeitlater*, pp. 6 f., where the incident is dated ca. 1070. Cf. S.N. to line 372.
368 *Incidentally, we note etc.*: Not only is Ibn Daud's conclusion a *non sequitur*, but it is also incorrect and deliberately tendentious; cf. notes to VI.186, 220–221; VII.93. Cf. also next note.
369 *All of Iraq had been left etc.*: Lit., neither name nor remnant (Isa. 14.22) remained for talmudic learning in all of Shinar (cf. above, IV.140). Thus, Isaiah's prophecy was fulfilled in one way by the extinction of Babylonian scholarship, and Ibn Daud, accordingly, avoided using the name of Babylonia in this context.
371 *Al-Bargeloni*: The rarer Arabic form for the Barcelonian, pronounced al-Barjeluni; cf. *EI*, I (new ed.), 1054. This R. Isaac is one of the two characterized above, line 291, as having migrated to Spain from a foreign land, inasmuch as Barcelona was part of "the land of Edom" or Christian Spain; cf. the parallel account in J. Mann, "Glanures de la Gueniza," *REJ*, LXXIV (1924), 159; cf. above, note to VI.114–115, 217. On the Jewish community there, cf. Ashtor, *op. cit.*, pp. 222 f.; Baer, *History*, I, 24, 40 f. and *passim*; Baron, *SRH*, IV, 33 f.
372 *Denia was fully settled*: I.e., prior to the submission of the city to Almoravide or later Almohade control; cf. *EI*, I, 938. See S.N.
373 *Mastery over the sea*: Cf. *EI*, I, 616 s.v. Balearic Islands.
375 *Ibn Laktush*: On this prominent family, whose name was spelled in several ways (Laktush, Katush, Uktush, Ukhtuj), cf. S.D. Goitein, "R. Yehuda Hallevi in Spain in the Light of the Geniza Papers" [in Hebrew], *Tarbiz*, XXIV (1954–55), 139; idem, "Autographs of Yehuda Hallevi" [in Hebrew], *ibid.*, XXV (1955–56), 395 n. 7, 400 f.; idem, "The Biography of R. Judah ha-Levi in the Light of the Cairo Geniza Documents," *PAAJR*, XXVIII (1959), 43 f.
377 *Azharot*: Poems of legal context, generally, though not necessarily, for the festival of Shabuot; in the latter case, they contain poetic enumerations of the 613 commandments; Schirmann, *Ha-Shirah ha-Ibrit*, II, 702. For editions of R. Isaac's Azharot, cf. Kasher, *Sarei ha-Elef*, p. 290 no. 58; cf. also Davidson, *Thesaurus*, IV, 418.

chapters of the tractate of Ketubot and a commentary on the tractate of Erubin, all of which testify to his scholarship and acute mind.

380 By far the greatest of them all was R. Isaac b. R. Jacob b. al-Fasi of Qalʿat Ḥammad, a disciple of R. Nissim b. R. Jacob and of R. Hananel. When he was denounced in his native country by al-ʿAjab b. al-Khalfa and the latter's son Ḥayyim, he went into exile in 4848 and came to Spain, where R. Joseph the Nasi b. R. Meir b. Muhajir received him with honor
385 and provided for him. [At first] he went to the city of Cordova, where he re-remained for a while, and from there he went to the city of Lucena, where he remained until the day of his death. He passed away in Nisan, 4863 at about the age of ninety, after having raised many disciples and having gained world-wide recognition. He composed a code in the form of an abridged
390 Talmud. Ever since the days of R. Hai there has been no one who could match him in scholarship.

378 *Ketubot*: Cf. S.J.L. Rapoport, "Toledot R. Hai," *Toledot* (Warsaw, 1913), I, 182 n. 23; S. Assaf, "Ancient Book Lists" [in Hebrew], *Kirjath Sepher*, XVIII (1941–42), 281 to n. 15.

379 *Scholarship and acute mind*: For similar characterizations, cf. Moses ibn Ezra, *op. cit.* pp. 72 f.; al-Ḥarizi, *Taḥkemoni* (ed. Toporowsky), pp. 44 f. (=Schirmann, *Ha-Shirah ha-Ibrit*, II, 111 f.).

380 *By far the greatest*: This view is shared by Moses ibn Ezra, *op. cit.*, p. 73. *R. Isaac b. R. Jacob b. al-Fasi of Qalʿat Ḥammad*: For the latest discussion of his life and work, cf. Baron, *SRH*, VI, 84 f. Since there is no direct evidence that he ever spent any time in Fez, al-Fasi was probably his family name and Qalʿat Ḥammad his birthplace; cf. B. Benedikt, "Notes on the Biography of R. Isaac Alfasi" [in Hebrew], *Kirjath Sepher*, XXVI (1950–51), 119 f.

381 *A disciple of R. Nissim... and R. Hananel*: This statement has been seriously questioned by modern scholarship; cf. S.J.L. Rapoport, *op. cit.* II, 22, 32 (= "Toledot R. Hananel," nn. 11, 20); II, 95 (= "Toledot R. Nissim," n. 18); B. Benedikt's review in *Kirjath Sepher*, XXV (1949–50), 170; Hirschberg's introduction to Nissim b. Jacob ibn Shahin, *op. cit.*, p. 32. The statement, however, is in consonance with Ibn Daud's contention that the status of talmudic scholarship in Qalʿat Ḥammad was not very high; cf. above, lines 283 f. and note to line 286.

382–383 *Al-ʿAjab b. al-Khalfa and... Ḥayyim*: As far as I am aware, no futher information is available on this incident or on the persons involved.

384 *R. Joseph the Nasi b. R. Meir b. Muhajir*: The Ibn Muhajir family is well known as one of the noble Jewish families of Andalus; cf. J. Schirmann, "Poets Contemporary with Mose ibn Ezra and Yehuda Hallevi" [in Hebrew], *Studies of the Research Institute for Hebrew Poetry in Jerusalem*, VI (1945), p. 344, s.v. Ibn al-Muhajir. However, as Schirmann indicates, *ibid.*, p. 260 and IV (1938), 278, the name Shortmeqash in the MSS of *SHQ* may either be an alternate cognomen or an error. For another person named Shortmeqash, possibly R. Joseph's brother, cf. Epilogue. 153–154.

389 *An abridged Talmud*: On the age of this characterization, cf. Baron, *SRH*, VI, 368 n. 96.

390 *Ever since the days of R. Hai etc.*: Cf. VI.181 f.

These five constitute the second generation [of the rabbinate].

Among the outstanding disciples of R. Isaac b. R. Jacob were R. Joseph b. R. Meir ha-Levi and R. Baruk b. R. Isaac.

R. Joseph ha-Levi b. R. Meir ibn Megash was born in I Adar, 5837. His father, R. Meir, was a learned and influential man, while his grandfather was the very same who, as mentioned earlier, had fled from Granada because of King Badis and then entered the service of King Ibn 'Abbad. Ever since R. Joseph ha-Levi's youth, R. Isaac b. R. Baruk recognized in him a man of great scholarly talents. Accordingly, he urged R. Meir to provide R. Joseph with instruction day and night. [He did not hesitate to say this,] inasmuch as these two, R. Isaac b. R. Baruk and R. Meir ha-Levi ibn Megash, loved each other as their own souls. When R. Isaac b. al-Fasi came to Spain and settled in Lucena, R. Joseph ha-Levi travelled to him from Seville when he was about twelve years old, remained with him and studied under him day and night for about fourteen years. He became a discerning son to R. Isaac, who advanced him in his learning and conferred the degree of Rabbi upon him before he passed away. In his letter of [appointment] he stated that "even in the generation of Moses there had not been his equal. For with respect to the generation of Moses it is written: 'Pick men who are wise, discerning and recognized,' and it is written after that: 'So I took your tribal leaders, wise and recognized men,' but Scripture does not say that they were '*discerning* men.' However, he is both wise and discerning." After the demise || of R. Isaac,

---

392 *These five etc.*: Cf. above, line 290.
393 *R. Isaac b. R. Jacob*: I.e., al-Fasi.
394 *R. Baruk*: Below, lines 423 f.
397 *Mentioned earlier*: Above, lines 219, 232.
398 *Ibn 'Abbad*: 'Abbad b. Abu'l-Qasim Muhammad al-Mu'tadid, ruler of Seville, 1042–1069. In other words, the second Joseph ibn Megash was born in Seville; cf. below, line 404.
399 *Isaac b. Baruk*: On his position in Seville, cf. above, lines 329 f.
402–403 *Loved each other etc.*: I.e., as was the case with David and Jonathan; I Sam. 18.1,3.
406 *About fourteen years*: See S.N. *A discerning son*: As was the Joseph of yore; cf. Gen. 41.39. Needless to add, the many verses in the book of Proverbs about the "discerning" son who grasps wisdom and understanding also underlie the imagery employed here. Cf. also below, note to line 413. That he became a son to al-Fasi derives from the rabbinic statement that whoever teaches a person Torah becomes his father; *B.* Sanhed, 19b. Cf. also below, line 438 and Goitein, *Jewish Education*, p. 30 n. 13b.
408 *Letter [of appointment]*: Sc., as rabbi. See S.N.
408–412 *Even in the generation of Moses etc.*: *B.* Erub. 100b.
410 *Pick men etc.*: Deut. 1.13.
411 *So I took etc.*: Ibid. 1.15.
413 *Wise and discerning*: "Wise" is one who has absorbed knowledge; "discerning" is intelligent in his own right; Moses ibn Ezra, *op. cit.*, p. 35. On the scale of values reflected

R. Joseph ha-Levi occupied his see for thirty-eight years from Sivan, 4863, until Iyyar, 4901. Throughout these years the study of the Torah was his profession, and his renown extended from Spain to Egypt, indeed as far as Babylonia and all [other] countries. Over and beyond his great learning, his personal traits testified to the fact that he was of the seed of our master Moses, may he have peace, since he was the most humble of men. The Holy One, blessed be He, granted him broad understanding, a self-effacing disposition and a forgiving heart. May the Holy One, blessed be He, reward him for all the good which he accomplished for Israel.

R. Baruk b. R. Isaac b. Albalia was also born in I Adar, 4837, in the very same week as R. Joseph ibn Megash. He received the tradition from his father R. Isaac. Before his father, R. Isaac, passed away, the latter had a falling out with R. Isaac al-Fasi, as did R. Isaac b. R. Judah ibn Giat with R. Isaac al-Fasi. Now, when R. Isaac b. R. Baruk passed away, his son R. Baruk was about seventeen years old. He later told me that at the time of his father's demise, the latter summoned him and whispered into his ear — since he could no longer speak audibly — the following: "'Go to R. Isaac al-Fasi and tell him that I am about to leave this world and enter the next. I hereby forgive ‖ him for all the harsh things he said to me in writing and orally. I beseech him to

---

here, cf. L. Finkelstein's note to *Siphre Deut.*, par. 13 (ed. Finkelstein), p. 22. For similar adulation of Ibn Megash, cf. below, line 446 and Maimonides' Introduction to his commentary on the *Mishna* (ed. Kafih), I, 47.

415 *Iyyar, 4901*: Cf., however, S.D. Goitein, "The Last Phase of Rabbi Yehuda Hallevi's Life in the Light of the Geniza Papers" [in Hebrew], *Tarbiz*, XXIV (1954–55), 33, where a contemporary report is reproduced indicating that he died in Sivan of that year.

415–416 *The study of the Torah was his profession*: For this expression, cf. *B.* Ber. 16b; Shab. 11a.

416 *Renown*: Lit., the recognition of his authority.

418 *His personal traits testified etc.*: Cf. *B.* Bez. 32b; Ned. 20a. Cf. also Epilogue. 100.

419 *The most humble of men*: Like Moses; cf. Num. 12.3.

420 *Broad understanding*: For this translation of "broad heart", cf. *ISG* 29.15, and its opposite, *ibid.*, 62.17–63.1; Maimonides, *Epistle to Yemen* (ed. Halkin), p. 2 line 8. However, the phrase may signify generosity; cf. Judah ha-Levi, *Diwan* (ed. Brody) I, 126 line 55 (= ed. Zamora, I, 339); S. Abramson, "R. Judah ha-Levi's Letter on his Emigration to the Land of Israel" [in Hebrew], *Kirjath Sepher*, XXIX (1953–54), 138 n. 17.

425 *R. Isaac*: Above, lines 309 f.

425–426 *Falling out with R. Isaac al-Fasi*: The details of this dispute are unknown, but Graetz, *Geschichte*, VI, 77, advanced the plausible suggestion that his two opponents were hostile to the efforts of a foreign interloper to gain rabbinical authority over natives of Spain.

[THE SUCCESSION OF THE RABBINATE] 87

do the same. Stay with him, for I know that he will treat you very well and will teach you conscientiously.' So, after I buried my father and teacher, I went
435 to him in Lucena and transmitted the message that he had sent through me. At first, R. Isaac b. al-Fasi wept loud and long, but then turned to console me and comfort me, saying: 'Since your father, of blessed memory, has died, I shall be a father to you, and you shall be a son to me.' Accordingly, I remained in his home until I had studied the whole Talmud under him." After the death
440 of R. Isaac b. al-Fasi, of blessed memory, the renown of these two, R. Joseph ha-Levi and R. Baruk b. R. Isaac, extended throughout the land. In addition to his knowledge of the Torah and his secular learning, this R. Baruk was learned in Greek wisdom. He raised many disciples, of whom I am the least [in distinction]. He passed away at the end of Elul, 4886. He was survived by
445 R. Joseph ha-Levi, of blessed memory, for approximately fifteen years. As for the latter, he had no peer in his generation, which was the third generation [of the rabbinate].

After the demise of R. Joseph ha-Levi, of blessed memory, — whose generation was third of the Rabbinate — the world became desolate of academies
450 of learning. Although his son, R. Meir, and his nephew, R. Meir, were his disciples and received their authority from him, and, indeed, are great scholars — "before the impending calamity, the righteous had been taken away." After the demise of R. Joseph there were years of war, evil decrees and per-

433 *Stay with him etc.*: R. Isaac Albalia thus decided to commit his son's education to the same man to whom his friend R. Meir ibn Megash had committed his son's education; cf. above, lines 400 f.
438 *I shall be a father etc.*: Cf. above, line 406.
440 *The renown*: Cf. note to line 416.
442-443 *Torah... secular learning ...Greek wisdom*: Cf. above, note to lines 350-352.
443 *I am the least*: Ibn Daud was Baruk b. Albalia's nephew; cf. above, line 335. For this genre of modesty, cf. Maimonides, *Epistle to Yemen* (ed. Halkin), p. 2 line 16.
445 *Fifteen years*: Cf. above, line 415.
446 *No peer*: Cf. above, lines 408 f.
449-450 *The world became desolate*: For the style, cf. Ber. R. 26.6 (ed. Theodor-Albeck), p. 254; cf. also next note. *Academies of learning*: Probably a play on II Sam. 23.8. However, the whole remark may be an oblique reference to the sanctuaries mentioned in Lev. 26.31, which, according to classical interpretation, included houses of study; cf. Sifra, *Beḥuqotay*, 6.4 (ed. Weiss), f. 112a.
450 *His son R. Meir, and his nephew R. Meir*: On their activity, cf. below, lines 464 f.
451 *Authority*: Lit., tradition (*qabbalah*).
452 *Before the impending calamity etc.*: Isa. 57.1, and cf. *B. B. K.* 60a and Ibn Ezra to Isa. 57.1. The reference to R. Joseph with a verse on "the righteous" may be a subtle allusion to the frequent method of referring to the biblical Joseph as "the righteous"; cf. Ginzberg, *Legends*, V, 324 f.
453 *Years of war, evil decrees etc.*: The reference here is, of course, to the Almohade per-

secutions that overtook the Jews, who were compelled to wander from their homes, "such as were for death, to death; and such as were for the sword, to the sword; ‖ and such as were for the famine, to the famine; and such as were for captivity, to captivity." To Jeremiah's prophecy, there was now added "such as were [destined] to leave the faith." This happened in the wake of the sword of Ibn Tumart, which came into the world in [4]873, when he decreed apostasy on the Jews, saying: "Come, and let us cut them off from being a nation; that the name of Israel may be no more in remembrance." Thus, he wiped out every last "name and remnant" of them from all of his empire, from the city of Silves at the end of the world until the city of al-Mahdiya. Owing to this situation, R. Joseph's sons were unable to maintain academies and were [among] the first to flee to the city of Toledo. They have been making whatever effort they can to raise disciples, and the Holy One, blessed be He, has shown His approval of their deeds. They are the last of the talmudic scholars of the present age.

We have heard that in France there are great scholars and geonim and that

secutions, which, it is becoming increasingly clear, wreaked havoc in the Jewish communities of northern Africa and Andalus between 1145/46 and 1148. Cf. Hirschberg, "The Almohade Persecutions and the India Trade," pp. 134–53; Baron, *SRH*, III, 108, 124 f.; cf. also below, Epilogue. 73 f.

454 *Wander*: Lit., go forth in exile; for the style, cf. next note.

455 *Such as were etc.*: Jer. 15.2. The same verse is quoted by Ibn Aknin in his description of these events; cf. A.S. Halkin, "Le-Toledot ha-Shemad bi-May ha-al-Muwaḥiddin," *Joshua Starr Memorial Volume* (New York, 1953), p. 105 n. 41; cf. also the paraphrase in Hirschberg, "The Almohade Persecutions," p. 142/148, lines 14–15.

458 *Such as were destined to leave the faith*: On the apostasy required by the Almohades, and the literature which this form of persecution evoked, cf. Halkin, "Le-Toledot ha-Shemad," pp. 101 f.

459 *Ibn Tumart*: Muhammad ibn Tumart, the *mahdi*, and founder of the Almohade dynasty, ruled ca. 1121–ca. 1130. See S.N. *4873, when he decreed etc.*: The date is incorrect by any standard of measurement; however, see S.N.

460–461 *Come, and let us etc.*: Ps. 83.5.

462 *Name and remnant*: Isa. 14.22; cf. also Hirschberg, *loc cit.* in note to line 455.

463 *Silves*: In what is now Portugal; cf. *EI*, IV, 424. See S.N.

464 *Maintain academies*: Sc., in Lucena (cf. line 414), which was one of the first Andalusian communities to be destroyed; cf. S.N. to line 463.

465 *Were [among] the first to flee*: Cf. Am. 6.7. *Toledo*: Cf. Epilogue. 105 f.

466 *Effort... to raise disciples*: Cf. the plausible discussion on the activity of R. Meir ibn Megash in N. Wieder, "Judah ibn Shabbetai's Burnt Book" [in Hebrew], *Metsudah*, Dec., 1943, pp. 128 f.

467 *Has shown His approval*: This may well be an Arabism for "May the Holy One, blessed be He, show His approval." Cf. also variants.

469 *We have heard that in France*: See S.N. *Geonim*: On the use of this title in Narbonne,

[THE SUCCESSION OF THE RABBINATE] 89

470 each and every one of them is a rabbi who inherits the Torah appropriately, [i.e.,] with the intention of passing it on. Indeed, they have been bequeathing it in the spirit of the verse: "That I may cause those that love me to inherit substance, and that I may fill their treasuries." Each and every one of them served in his own area: the Rabbi-Gaon R. Moses b. R. Joseph, of blessed
475 memory, the Rabbi-Gaon R. Abraham b. R. Isaac, of blessed memory, and the Rabbi-Gaon R. Meir b. R. Joseph, of blessed memory, [who flourished] in Narbonne and who have caused the light of the Torah to shine on their students through [the study of] the Pentateuch, Scripture, Mishna, [Babylonian] Talmud and Palestinian [Talmud]. There is [also] one in the city of
480 Ramerupt by the name of R. Jacob. May the Holy One, blessed be He, protect

cf. B.Z. Benedict, "On the History of the Torah-Centre in Provence" [in Hebrew], *Tarbiz*, XXII (1950-51), 86; cf. also Poznanski, *Babylonische Geonim im nachgaonaeischen Zeitalter*, pp. 79, 104 f.

470 *Rabbi*: I.e., the head of an academy; cf. above, note to line 64. *Who inherits the Torah appropriately*: For the phrase, and my translation, cf. B. Hor. 11b; Maimonides, *Mishneh Torah*, Melakim 1.7.

472 *That I may cause etc.*: Prov. 8.21. Cf. also *ARN* I, 14 (ed. Schechter), p. 57 (Eng. trans. p. 74), where the verse is interpreted to mean that every aspect of the Torah has been transmitted, as is indeed stated below, lines 478-479.

474 *Served in his own area*: Exactly what Ibn Daud meant by this phrase is not clear to me. *R. Moses b. R. Joseph*: For a full study on this man, cf. B. Z. Benedict, "R. Moshe b. R. Joseph of Narbonne" [in Hebrew], *Tarbiz*, XIX (1947-48), 19-34. *Of blessed memory*: As Benedict indicates, ibid., p. 21, it is virtually certain that R. Moses died before 1165. However, if the "salutation for the dead" in the MSS of *SHQ* is not an addition of later copyists, the date of his death must be moved back to sometime before 1161.

475 *R. Abraham b. R. Isaac*: Cf. the introduction to Abraham b. Isaac, *Sefer ha-Eshkol*, 2 vols., ed. by S. and Ch. Albeck (Jerusalem, 1935-38), I, 3 f.; Benedict, "R. Moshe b. R. Joseph," pp. 20 f.; idem, "On the History of the Torah-Centre in Provence," pp. 103 f., 109; I. Twersky, *Rabad of Posquieres* (Cambridge, 1962), pp. 7 f. *Of blessed memory*: Albeck accepts the Meiri's testimony that he died in November 1158, while other scholars contend that this should be emended to 1178; cf. Gross, *Gallia Judaica*, p. 415; Abraham b. Isaac, *op. cit.*, I, 14 f.

476 *R. Meir b. R. Joseph*: Cf. *JE*, VIII, 436; Abraham b. Isaac, *op. cit.*, I, 8.

477 *Narbonne*: On the Jewish community there, cf. *JE*, IX, 169 f.; Benedict's studies listed in note to lines 469, 474; Twersky, *op. cit.*, pp. 19 f. For an effort to reconstruct the earlier history of the community, cf. A. Zuckerman, *The Jewish Patriarchate in Western Europe During the Carolingian Age* (Columbia University Ph.D. Dissertation, 1963).

478 *Pentateuch, Scripture, etc.*: By Scripture, of course, Ibn Daud means the prophetic books and Hagiographa. On the method of study in Provence, reflected in this enumeration, cf. Benedict, "On the History of the Torah-Centre etc.," pp. 92 f.

480 *R. Jacob*: b. Meir Tam; cf. V. Aptowitzer, *Introductio ad Sefer Rabiah* [in Hebrew] (Jerusalem, 1938), pp. 357 f.; Baron, *SRH*, Index vol, s.v. Tam, Jacob b. Meir; E. E.

and preserve their disciples and heirs and grant them the opportunity to study, teach and spread the knowledge of the Torah throughout Israel.

Urbach, *The Tosaphists* [in Hebrew] (Jerusalem, 1955), pp. 55 f.; S. Albeck, "Rabbenu Tam's Attitude to the Problems of his Time" [in Hebrew], *Zion*, XIX (1953–54), 104–41.

482 *Throughout Israel*: MSS פק add here: "So that their lips may move in their graves, thus fulfilling what is written: 'Move gently the lips of those that are asleep' " (Song of Songs 7.10). Cf. *B*. Yeb. 97a.

[EPILOGUE]

Thus there were ten generations from the prophets Haggai, Zechariah and Malachi until Rabban Johanan b. Zakkai, five generations of tannaim and seven generations of amoraim, giving a total of twenty-two generations until the end of the amoraic period. Then there were five generations of saboraic rabbis, eight generations of the gaonate and three generations of the rabbinate: the generation of R. Nissim, R. Hananel and R. Samuel the Nagid; the generation of the five rabbis named Isaac; and the generation of R. Joseph ha-Levi and R. Baruk b. R. Isaac. Thus, there were sixteen generations from the sealing of the Talmud until the demise of R. Joseph ha-Levi, of blessed memory. This gives a grand total of thirty-eight generations from Haggai, Zechariah and Malachi until R. Joseph ha-Levi, of blessed memory. All of them were trustworthy witnesses, who received [the tradition] on the testimony of trustworthy witnesses, and their sacred chain of tradition has never been broken.

Such is not the case with the heretics. The fact is that Anan the wicked and his son Saul, may the name of the wicked rot, were disciples of R. Jehudai, who broke with him and his tradition without any substantive ground whatever, but only out of the envy that overcame them. Hence, they cannot possibly

---

2–3 *Ten generations*: II.169.
3 *Five generations*: III.110.
4 *Seven generations*: IV.71, 173.
5 *Five generations*: V.41, 45.
6 *Eight generations*: VI.203. *Three generations*: VII.446, 449.
7 *The generation of R. Nissim etc.*: VII.180–288.
8 *The generation of the five etc.*: VII.290–392. *The generation of R. Joseph etc.*: VII.393–447.
10 *The sealing of the Talmud*: V.4–6.
12 *Trustworthy witnesses etc.*: Cf. Prologue. 4 f.; VI.48 f. See S.N.
14 *The sacred chain*: On the chain as a figure for a complete list of authorities transmitting a tradition, cf. *Yer.* Shab. 1.2 f. 3a. Cf. also the responsum of R. Ṣemaḥ Gaon in *Kitbay R. Abraham Epstein*, I, 40 par. 18.
16 *Such is not the case with the heretics*: For the same line of argument, cf. II.20 f., 145 f.
16–19 Cf. VI.43–55. The statement that Anan and Saul were disciples of R. Jehudai probably derives from Ibn Daud's view that Anan was a scholar. Since R. Jehudai was the master of the generation, Anan must have sat at his feet. For a different view, cf. S. Poznanski, "Anan et ses Ecrits," *REJ*, XLIV (1903), 167 n. 1.
18 *Who broke with him*: Cf. Poznanski, *ibid.*, XLV (1902), 67, for a possible specific example of such a direct break. However, the extent of Anan's divergence from gaonic tradition is reflected in his *Book of Precepts*; cf. note to VI. 52 *Without any substantive ground*:

20 say: "Thus have we received on the testimony of So-and-So [who received] from the prophets." Instead, they fabricate things out of their own hearts.

What is more, they are disqualified by the sheer meagerness of their number. You will note that Rabbanite communitites extend from the city of Sala at the extreme end of the Maghreb, as far as Tahert at the very beginning of the
25 Maghreb, to the end of Ifriqiya, Egypt, the Holy Land, Arabia, Iraq, Khuzistan, Fars, the land of Dedan, the land of the Girgashite — which is called Jurjan —
]68] Tabarestan and al-Daylam ‖ as far as the Volga. In the latter area there were a

E.g., precedent or consensus. Ibn Daud's argument doubtless alludes to the summons of Anan and later Karaites not to follow established practices; cf. Pinsker, *Lickute Kadmoniot*, Appendix pp. 33 f.

20 *Say*: Sc., as the Rabbanites can; cf. *M*. Peah 2.6.
21 *They fabricate*: For earlier Rabbanite claims along this line, cf. M. Zucker, "Le-Pitron Ba'yat Lamed-bet Middot," *PAAJR*, XXIII (1954), Hebrew section pp. 33 f.; Tobiah b. Eliezer, *Leqah Tob*, II (ed. Vilna), 38 f., 126. For Karaite citations of this charge, cf. Salmon b. Yeruḥim, *op. cit.*, 113.80 f.; Ankori, *Karaites in Byzantium*, pp. 223 f. Cf. also S.N. to line 12.
22 *Disqualified by the sheer meagerness etc.*: Although the phrase is taken from talmudic regulations on procedures of voting (cf. *B*. Sanhed. 10b), the argument is actually an application of the principle of consensus (*ijma'*). However, since consensus on Rabbanite tradition was not universal, its protagonists argued from majority. For earlier applications of this argument by Rabbanites, cf. Saadiah's argument against Ben Meir in Mann, "Varia," *Tarbiz*, V (1933–34), 275 lines 7–9; Qirqisani, *Kitab al-Anwar*, I, 1, p. 3 (Eng. trans., *HUCA*, VII, 320); Pinsker, *Lickute Kadmoniot*, Appendix p. 104. See also S.N.
23 *Rabbanite communities*: Lit., communities of Israel; cf. S.N. to II.149. *Sala*: Modern Salé, Morocco. On the existence of a Jewish community there, cf. the elegy referred to in S.N. to VII.463. Either Ibn Daud was unaware of the decimation of the community there, or at the time of his writing it had still managed to survive (cryptically ?).
24 *The extreme end of the Maghreb*: This is a literal translation of the Arabic description of this locale; cf. al-Himyari in Lévi-Provençal, *La Peninsule Ibérique*, text 18:10, French trans. p. 24 end of sect. 13. *Tahert, at the very beginning of the Maghreb*: Cf. note to VII.3. On Jews in Tahert, cf. S. Assaf, *Gaonic Responsa From Geniza MSS* [in Hebrew], (Jerusalem, 1928), p. 2.
25 *Ifriqiya*: Cf. above, VII.3. Ibn Daud's description moves from west to east. *Iraq, Khuzistan*: Cf. above, IV.141. On the provinces of Asia mentioned here, cf. the various articles in *EI* and G. Le Strange, *The Lands of the Eastern Caliphate* (Cambridge, 1905). The presence of Jewish communities in the Arab provinces of Asia was, of course, known to Ibn Daud on the basis of gaonic reports on the Jewish communities from Syria to India. The specific provinces listed are taken from the lists of the Arab geographers; cf. *ibid.*, and D.M. Dunlop, *The History of the Jewish Khazars* (Princeton, 1954), pp. 96, 210.
26 *Dedan*: Probably India; cf. Krauss, "Die Hebraeischen Bennenungen," p. 392.
27 *Al-Daylam*: None of the MSS spells the name correctly; but cf. also Benjamin of Tudela, *Itinerary* (ed. Adler), Hebrew text p. 36 (very end). *Volga*: Heb., Atil; cf. Dunlop, *op. cit.*, p. 91 n. 8. *In the latter area*: Ibn Daud's knowledge of the Khazars probably derived from the Khazar correpondence with Ḥisdai ibn Shaprut; see next note.

[EPILOGUE] 93

nation of Khazars who converted to Judaism, and their King Joseph sent a letter to R. Ḥisdai the Nasi b. R. Isaac b. Shaprut informing him that he and all of his people pursue Rabbanite usage scrupulously. (We have also seen some of their descendants in Toledo, scholars who informed us that their legal practice conforms to Rabbanite usage.) They are also found on all the islands of the Greek sea from the land of Venice (?) and Genoa (?) as far as Constantinople and Byzantium, as well as in all of the Slav country, Togarma, France, Apulia, Messena (?), Sicily, Lombardia as far as the River Rhone and Spain at the extreme end of the Maghreb. All of them, may the Lord restore them from their captivity, conform to the usage of the sages of the Mishna and the Talmud. The only exceptions are one city in the Maghreb, in the desert, by the name of Werejlan, a small number of them in Egypt and a small number in the Holy Land.

28–32 For a review of the whole subject, cf. Dunlop, *op. cit.*, pp. 89 f., and especially pp. 116 f.; Baron, *SRH*, III, 196 f.
30 *Pursue Rabbanite usage*: Whatever the merits of this claim, it was made by both Rabbanites and Karaites; cf. Judah ha-Levi, *Kitab al-Khazari*, Prologue; Ankori, *Karaites in Byzantium*, pp. 64 f., 70 f. For a critical appraisal, cf. Dunlop, *op. cit.*, pp. 92, 115, 195, 217, 221.
32 *They*: I.e., Rabbanite communities.
33 *Greek sea*: Cf. VII.10. *Land of Venice and Genoa*: For this interpretation of the Hebrew *Nbqry* and *Ggnt*, see S.N. See also next note here.
33–34 *Byzantium*: Lit., greater Rome. Ibn Daud's method of describing the dispersion of Jewish communities becomes clear from the map of Ibn Haukal, *Opus Geogpraphicum* (ed. Kramers), I between pp. 66 and 67. It will be seen there that the Italian boot, which is identified as Qaluria (= Calabria), is regarded as a penisula (= island) in the "Greek sea" of which the westernmost territory is the island (sic!) of Genoa and the easternmost portion the country of Venice. The easternmost peninsula of the "Greek" portion of the Mediterranean is that of Constantinople, which is part of the territory of al-Rum, i.e. the great Rome or Byzantium. *Slav country*: Cf. Saadia, *Oeuvres Complètes*, I, 17 trans. of Gen. 10.3. *Togarma*: Probably, the land of the Bulgars; cf. *ibid.* and Krauss, "Die hebraeischen Benennungen," p. 411. *France*: Cf. note to IV.142. Ibn Daud's enumeration of these three peoples probably derives from Gen. 10.3 with a metathesis of the second and third peoples in order to enable him to draw a full circle of the northern borders of the Greek sea.
35 *Messena*: This translation is most doubtful. See S.N. *Rhone*: See S.N.
37 *Conform to the usage... of the Mishna etc.*: Cf. *ISG* 30.12 f.
38 *One city in the Maghreb etc.*: The statement is an amplification of the argument from majority (above, line 22). Not only are the Karaites in the minority, but they are confined to small and isolated areas. For the same argument, cf. J. Mann, "An Early Theologico-Polemical Work," *HUCA*, XII–XIII (1937–38), 438, lines 10–12 and Mann's remarks, pp. 417 f.
39 *Werejlan*: On the renown of the Karaite community there, cf. H.Z. Hirschberg, "Qehillot Israel bi-Neot ha-Midbar shel Algeria," *Sinai, Sefer Yobel*, pp. 344 f.; Mann, *Texts and*

94   SEFER HA-QABBALAH

When the Jews used to celebrate the festival of Tabernacles on the Mount of Olives, they would encamp on the mountain in groups and greet each other warmly. The heretics would encamp before them like two little flocks of goats. Then the rabbis would take out a scroll of the Torah and pronounce a ban
45 on the heretics right to their faces, while the latter remained silent like dumb dogs.

[69]   Among those [heretics] living in the Holy Land there was *al-Sheikh* Abu'l-Faraj, may his bones be committed to hell. It happened that a certain fool from Castile, named Cid Abu'l-Taras, went over there and met the wicked
50 *al-Sheikh* Abu'l-Faraj, who seduced him into heresy. Under the guidance of

> *Studies*, II, 139. *A small number... in Egypt and... in the Holy Land*: This tendentious and incorrect picture has been totally refuted by modern scholarship. Not only were the Karaites not so insignificant a group in Palestine or Egypt during the eleventh century, but at times they overshadowed the Rabbanites in power and influence with the government. What is more, they were far more numerous and widespread than Ibn Daud knew or conceded. Cf. Baron, *SRH*, IV, 111 f.; V. 257 f.; Mann, *Jews in Egypt etc.*, I, 55 f., 134 f., 140 f., 176 f.; *idem, Texts and Studies*, II, 3 f. and index on Karaites in various lands; Ankori, *Karaites in Byzantium* and his very apposite observations on pp. 34 f. on this passage in *SHQ*.
>
> 41–46   On the annual pilgrimage after the Muslim conquest of Palestine to the Mount of Olives for the festival of Tabernacles and especially for the seventh day, "the day of the Hosannah," when the bans were pronounced, cf. Mann, *Jews in Egypt etc.*, I, 44 f., 164 f.; II, 189 f.; A. Yaari, "Hag ha-Sukkot bi-Jerusalem," *Sinai*, XXXVI (1955), 45 f.; Baron, *SRH*, III, 101; V, 279. See also note to lines 44–45. For the special emphasis on the celebration of this festival in Jerusalem, cf. Zech. 14.16, from which the messianic overtones of these gatherings becomes apparent.
>
> 43   *Like two little flocks etc.*: I Ki. 20.27. I.e., they bleat helplessly.
>
> 44–45   *The rabbis etc.*: The Karaites did not take this practice lying down and succeeded in having the practice forbidden in 1024; cf. Mann, *Jews in Egypt etc.*, I, 134 f., II, 62 f.; *idem, Texts and Studies*, I, 310 f. *Remained silent like dumb dogs*: For the style, cf. Isa. 56.10 and below, line 128. The same phrase was used by Karaites to depict the helplessness of the Rabbanites; cf. Wieder, *The Judean Scrolls and Karaism*, p. 203 n. 2.
>
> 47   *Al-Sheikh*: Arabic, for "the elder, the sage." See S.N. *Abu'l-Faraj*: His full name in Arabic was Abu' l-Faraj Furqan ibn Asad; in Hebrew, Yeshuah b. Judah; cf. S. Munk, *Notice sur Abou'l Walid Merwan ibn Djana'h* (Paris, 1851), p. 10 n. On his life and work, cf. Nemoy, *Karaite Anthology*, pp. 123 f., 396. Cf. also below, lines 130 f.
>
> 48   *Fool*: See S.N.
>
> 49   *Cid Abu 'l-Taras*: The spelling of his name is not certain, some of the better MSS rendering it as Abu'l-Atras. References to him in modern literature are always under the name recorded by the inferior class of MSS, Ibn al-Taras. The exact meaning of Cid or Sayyid is not clear. It may be an honorific for "the master" or "Nasi," or it may be a proper noun; cf. I. Goldziher, "Proben Muhammedanischer Polemik," *Jeschurun*, VIII (1872–75), 80 n. 12; M. Steinschneider, "An Introduction to the Arabic Literature of the Jews," *JQR*, XI (1899), 317 f.

[EPILOGUE] 95

the latter, Abu'l-Taras composed a work animated by seduction and perversion, which he introduced into Castile and [by means of which] he led many astray. When Abu'l-Taras passed on to hell, he was survived by his accursed wife, whom [his adherents] used to address as *al-Mu'allima* and on
55 whom they relied for authoritative tradition. They would ask each other what *Mu'allima's* usage was, and they would follow suit. [This went on] until the rise to power of the Nasi R. Joseph b. Ferrizuel, surnamed Cidellus, who suppressed them even beyond their former lowly state. He drove them out of all the strongholds of Castile except for one, which he granted them, since he
60 did not want to put them to death (inasmuch as capital punishment is not administered at the present time). However, after his death, the heretics erupted again until the reign of King Don Alfonso son of Raimund, king of kings, the *Emperador*. In his reign there rose nesiim who pursued the ways of their fathers and suppressed the heretics [again].
65   The following are the circumstances under which the heretics were suppressed

51 *Composed a work*: It is not clear whether Abu'l-Taras merely translated Abu'l-Faraj's work(s) into Hebrew or composed a new one reflecting his master's views. That at least some of the latter's compositions were available in Spain in the Arabic original is clear from the citations below, line 130 f. and Moses ibn Ezra, *Shirat Israel*, p. 173. For a full discussion of this passage in *SHQ* and its influence, cf. Z. Ankori, "Elijah Bashyachi" [in Hebrew], *Tarbiz*, XXV (1955-56), 44 f., 190 (on Jacob b. Simeon); idem, *Karaites in Byzantium*, index s.v. Yeshu'ah b. Yehudah. On Karaism in Spain, see above, pp. XLVI f.
54 *Al-Mu'allima*: Arabic feminine for "the teacher"; see S.N.
57 *R. Joseph b. Ferrizuel surnamed Cidellus*: On his activity, cf. Baer, *History of the Jews in Christian Spain*, I, 50 f., 68 f. See S.N.
58 *Suppressed them etc.*: On the war against the Karaites consistently conducted by the Jewish courtiers of Castile, cf. Baer, *History*, I, 65.
60 *Inasmuch as capital punishment is not etc..*: This statement is probably a quotation from some legal source; cf. Midrash Tannaim (ed. Hoffmann), p. 102, where the editor refers to Maimonides' *Mishneh Torah*, Sanhed. 14.11. Cf. also *ibid.*, Ḥobel u-Mazziq 8.10 and Maimonides' commentary to *M. Ḥul.* 1.2. See S.N.
61 *After his death*: Sometime after 1110; cf. reference to line 57. *The heretics erupted*: Lit., the envy (or filth) of the heretics erupted; cf. VI.47.
62 *Don Alfonso son of Raimund*: Alfonso VII. For Ibn Daud's dating of his reign, cf. below line 70. *King of kings*: Cf. Ezek. 26.7. The phrase is Ibn Daud's way of explaining the term *imperator*; cf. next note and see S.N.
63 *The Emperador*: On the use of this title by historians to refer to Alfonso VII, cf. Alfonso X el Sabio, *Primera Cronica General de España*, 2 vols., ed. by R. Menendez Pidal et al. (Madrid, 1955), II, 654a, and the editor's note on p. cxciii; cf. also R. Menendez Pidal, *El Imperio Hispanico y los Cinco Reinos* (Madrid, 1950), pp. 149 f., 172. On Alfonso's use of the title himself, cf. *ibid.*, p. 140, and P. Rassow, "Urkunden Kaiser Alfonso VII von Castilien 1126-1155," *Archiv fuer Urkundenforschung*, X (1928), 410; XI (1930), 66 f.
64 *Suppressed the heretics*: Cf. below, lines 119 f.
65 *The following are the circumstances etc.*: Ibn Daud provides the background for the

[70] in || Castile. This king, Don Alfonso son of Raimund, was a king of kings, and a righteous king. He prevailed over all the Ishmaelites living in Spain and compelled them to pay tribute. His kingdom grew mighty, "and the Lord gave him rest from all his enemies round about." Now the time that he reigned over
70 Edom was thirty-eight years. Inasmush as the kingdom grew strong under his hand, he succeeded in taking from the Ishmaelites Calatrava, which lies on the main road from the Ishmaelite to the Christian part of the country.

[At about that time] the rebels against the Berber kingdom had crossed the sea to Spain, after having wiped out every remnant of Jews from Tangiers to
75 al-Mahdiya. "Turn again thy hand as a grape-gatherer upon the shoots." They tried to do the same thing in all of the cities of the Ishmaelite kingdom in

---

circumstances leading to the suppression of Karaism. For this method of exposition, cf. II. 50–62 and note to II.51.

67 *Righteous king*: Cf. Ps. 110.4. The phrase is probably used to explain Alfonso's successful reign; cf. R. Moses Gikatilla *apud* Ibn Ezra *ad loc*. On the other hand, I cannot help but wonder whether Ibn Daud was not playing at the same time on the classical Christian interpretation of the phrase (Melchizedek). In any event, Ibn Daud's evaluation is hardly to be swallowed without a grain of salt; cf. Baer, *History*, I, 51 f. *He prevailed etc.*: Cf. A. Aguado Bleye, *Manual de Historia de España* (7th ed. 3 vols. Madrid, 1954), I, 636 f.

68–69 *And the Lord etc.*: II Sam. 7.1, quoted inexactly in the Hebrew.

70 *Edom*: Christian Spain; cf. VI.217. (I have retained the Hebrew form here in an effort to convey the biblical annalistic style which Ibn Daud imitates.) *Thirty-eight years*: Ibn Daud reckons from the point of view of a Toletanian, inasmuch as Alfonso entered the capital victoriously on Nov. 16, 1118; Menendez Pidal, *El Imperio Hispanico*, p. 140. (The figure "forty-eight" of *ed. pr.* may be a learned correction, reckoning Alfonso's accession from 1109; cf. P.E. Schramm, "Das Kastilische Koenigtum und Kaisertum waehrend der Reconquista," *Festschrift fuer Gerhard Ritter* (Tuebingen, 1950), pp. 97 f.) Although Alfonso VII died on August 21, 1157, Ibn Daud probably arrived at his figure of thirty-eight by reckoning from Jewish chronology: entrance into Toledo as *imperator* in 4879, death in 4917.

71 *Calatrava*: Fell to Alfonso VII in Jan., 1147.

72 *The main road*: For this translation cf. Ibn Janaḥ, *Book of Hebrew Roots*, p. 55 (Heb. trans., p. 37).

73 [*At about that time*]: Ca. 1148. *The rebels against the Berber kingdom*: I.e., the Almohades. For the same way of referring to the Almohades, cf. al-Ḥarizi, *op. cit.*, ch. 18 in Schirmann, *Ha-Shirah ha-Ibrit*, II, 142.220.

74 *After having wiped out etc.*: Cf. VII.453 f. *From Tangiers to al-Mahdiya*: Cf. VII.463.

75 *Turn again etc.*: Jer. 6.9. Ibn Daud represents the Almohade forces as speaking to themselves thus: Now that we have wiped out every remnant of the Jews in North Africa, let us now turn our hand to pluck the shoots, i.e., wipe out the remainder in Spain. For modern discussions of the event described herein, cf. Baer, *History*, I, 60 f.; Baron, *SRH*, IV, 31 f.

Spain, "'if it had not been the Lord who was for us,' let Israel now say." When the Jews had heard the report that the rebels were advancing upon them to drive them away from the Lord, God of Israel, those who feared the Lord's word fled for their lives, and "fathers" almost "failed to look back to their children for feebleness of hands." Some were taken captive by the Christians, to whom they willingly indentured themselves on condition that they be rescued from Muslim territory. Others fled on foot, naked and barefoot, their feet stumbling upon the mountains of twilight, with "the young children asking bread, and none to break it to them."

However, He who prepares the remedy before afflictions, exalted be His name, (as it is, indeed, written: "When I would heal Israel, then is the iniquity of Ephraim uncovered") anticipated [the calamity] by putting it into the heart of King Alfonso the *Emperador* to appoint ‖ our master and rabbi, R. Judah the Nasi b. Ezra, over Calatrava and to place all the royal provisions in his charge. The latter's forefathers had been among the leaders of Granada, holders of high office and men of influence in every generation [as far back as] the reign of Badis b. Ḥabbus, the king of the Berbers, and that of the latter's father, King Ḥabbus. There is a tradition current among the members of the community of Granada that they are descended from the inhabitants of Jerusalem, the holy city, from the tribes of Judah and Benjamin, not from [the inhabitants of] the villages

77 *If it had not been etc.*: Ps. 124.1. I.e., but for the Lord, the Almohades would have succeeded.
79 *To drive them away etc.*: Cf. Deut. 13.11, and above, VII.458.
79–80 *Those who feared etc.*: Cf. Ex. 9.20.
80 *"Fathers" almost "failed etc."*: Jer. 47.3.
83 *Fled on foot*: See S.N.
84 *Their feet stumbling etc.*: Almost a verbatim quotation of Jer. 13.16.
84–85 *The young children etc.*: Lam. 4.4.
86 *He who prepares the remedy etc.*: For the source of this expression, cf. *B. Meg.* 13b; for this particular form, cf. Ben Iehuda, *Thesaurus*, XII, 5752a n. 2. For the same thought, with the quotation of the verse which follows, by Ibn Aknin, cf. Halkin, "Le-Toledot ha-Shemad," p. 109.
87 *When I would heal etc.*: Hos. 7.1. I.e., only after the Lord had provided healing did He uncover the iniquity of Israel, i.e., permitted its sin to be requited through the travails of persecution.
89–90 *Judah the Nasi b. Ezra*: On his position cf. Baer, *History*, I, 77. See S.N.
91 *Leaders of Granada*: For the known history of the family, cf. Baer, *History*, I, 60 f.; Baron, *SRH*, IV, 31 f., 248; cf. also the bibliographies in Schirmann, *Ha-Shirah ha-Ibrit*, II, 683, 686 f. *Holders of high office*: Lit., heirs to royal authority; cf. Jud. 18.7, and Ibn Janaḥ, *Book of Hebrew Roots*, p. 542 (Heb. trans., p. 381).
92 *[Men] of influence*: Lit., [royal] authority; cf. Isa. 9.5, 6.
92–93 *Badis... and... Ḥabbus*: Cf. VII.193, 224 f.
93–97 *There is a tradition etc.*: For the identical tradition, and the same invidious distinction

or of the unwalled towns. However, this R. Judah the Nasi, his father and uncles, all four of whom were officers, R. Isaac, the first-born, and next to him R. Moses, the third R. Judah and the fourth R. Joseph, all of them are of royal blood
100 and descended of the nobility, as evidenced by their personal traits. Now when this great Nasi, R. Judah, was appointed over Calatrava, the city of refuge for the exiles, he supervised the passage of the refugees, released those bound in chains and let the oppressed go free by breaking their yoke and undoing their bonds. At his home and at his very table, where the refugees found rest, he
105 fed the hungry, provided drink for the thirsty and clothed the naked. Then, providing animals for all the feeble, he had them brought as far as Toledo in great dignity. [This he was able to do] by virtue of the awe and respect which he commanded among the Christians, who conveyed them. Although but a youth, he had already been exalted above the people, and lorded it over a
110 company of spearmen. Since he had no regard for silver, nor did he delight in gold, he did not keep for himself any of his share of the King's pay. All of his deeds were patterned after the son of Agrippa, who had said: "Whereas my

between the inhabitants of Jerusalem and the villagers, cf. Moses ibn Ezra, *Shirat Israel*, p. 62. The implication is that as descendants of the citizens of Jerusalem they were of the nobility and lineal descendants of those who built the Second Temple; cf. Ezra 1.5, as well as the rabbinic distinctions between urbanites and villagers in *B. Hag.* 13b and *Pesikta R.* 20 (ed. Friedmann), f. 95a. On the Jews of Andalus as members of the nobility of Jerusalem, cf. VII.296.

98 *The first-born etc.*: The style is patterned after II Sam. 3.3, where the sons of David are enumerated.

99 *R. Joseph*: Sc., the father of the Judah who was appointed by Alfonso VII.

99–100 *Of royal blood and descended etc.*: Cf. Dan. 1.3. See S.N. *As evidenced etc.*: See S.N.

102 *Released those bound in chains*: For this translation of Ps. 68.7, cf. Ibn Janaḥ, *Book of Hebrew Roots*, p. 334 (Heb. trans., p. 232); Ibn Ezra to Ps. 68.7; Ibn Gabirol *apud* Ben Iehuda, *Thesaurus*, V, 2309.

103 *Let the oppressed go free*: Isa. 58.6 and Ibn Ezra *ad loc*. *By breaking their yoke etc.*: Cf. Jer. 2.20; 5.5.

106 *Providing animals for all the feeble*: Cf. II Chr. 28.15.

108–109 *Although but a youth etc.*: Cf. Ps. 89.20 and Ibn Ezra's second interpretation there.

109–110 *Lorded it over a company of spearmen*: For this translation of Ps. 68.31 ("Rebuke the wild beast of the reeds"), cf. Ibn Ezra *ad loc*. Cf. also the similar praise of Joseph ibn Ferrizuel Cidellus by Judah ha-Levi, *Diwan* (ed. Brody), I, 158 line 19 (= ed. Zamora, I, 325). (For the addressee of that poem, cf. Baer, *History*, I, 392 n. 51.) Despite the opaqueness of the cliché, it is a reasonable conjecture that Ibn Daud here alludes to Judah ibn Ezra's influence with the Knights Templar at Calatrava; cf. A. Castro, *The Structure of Spanish History* (Princeton, 1954), pp. 208 f.

110 *He had no regard for silver, nor etc.*: Cf. Isa. 13.17.

112 *The son of Agrippa*: I.e., Monobaz; cf. I.202 and variants here. *Who said etc.*: *Tosef. Peah* 4.18 (ed. Lieberman), p. 60. *Below*: On earth. *Above*: In Heaven. On the diffusion of this motif, cf. Lieberman, *Tosefta Ki-Fshutah*, I, 191; H. Schwarzbaum,

father stored up his treasures below, I shall store up my treasures above."
2] Nevertheless, ‖ he conducted a huge business. Indeed, if he had performed but
115 these works of charity, his merit would have been more than enough, "for it was to save life that God had sent him ahead" of the refugees.

When all the nation had finished passing over [the border] by means of his help, the King sent for him and appointed him lord of all his household and ruler over all his possessions. He [then] requested of the King to forbid the
120 heretics to open their mouths throughout the land of Castile, and the King commanded that this be done. Accordingly, the heretics were suppressed and have not been able to raise their heads any longer. Indeed, they are dwindling steadily.

Moreover, there is a third characteristic [of the heretics] which you ought
125 to bear in mind. That is that they never did anything of benefit for Israel, nor produced a book demonstrating the cogency of the Torah or work of general

---

"International Folklore Motifs in Petrus Alphonsi's 'Disciplina Clericalis,'" *Sefarad* XXII (1962), 332 f.

114   *He conducted a huge business*: Cf. II Chr. 17.13.
114–115   *If he had performed etc.*: For the style, cf. C. J. Kasowski, *Thesaurus Talmudis*, VII, 232 f. דיינו, דיים, דיי. The genre is also employed in the related sense of gratitude, rather than that of merit, in the poem found in the *seder* ritual for Passover; cf. *The Passover Haggadah*, ed. and trans. by N. Glatzer (New York, 1953), pp. 42 f.
116   *For it was to save life etc.*: Gen. 45.5.
117   *When all the nation etc.*: Josh. 4.1.
118–119   *Appointed him lord etc.*: Cf. Gen. 44.8.
120   *To open their mouths*: I.e., to assert themselves; cf. Ezek. 29.21.
120–121   *And the King commanded etc.*: Est. 9.14.
121–122   *The heretics were suppressed etc.*: Cf. Jud. 8.28.
124   *A third characteristic*: The first two are a fabricated law unattested by any chain of transmission (above, lines 16 f.) and an inability to point to majority of number anywhere in the world (above, lines 22 f.)
125   *Never did anything of benefit for Israel*: Cf. note to VI. 151–152. On this virtue and the sin of its absence, cf. Ezek. 13.5; 22.30, and especially Ps. 106.23. On the curses invoked upon those who detach themselves from the community, especially in its hour of stress, cf. *B*. Ta'an. 11a. See S.N.
126   *A book demonstrating the cogency of the Torah*: Lit., a book adding strength to the Torah. For the force of the phrase, cf. talmudic dictionaries s.v. חזוק. For similar charges by earlier Rabbanites, cf. Zucker, "Against Whom Did Se'adya Gaon Write etc.," p. 70; Ankori, "Aspects of Karaite-Rabbanite Relations," *PAAJR*, XXV (1956), 176; idem, *Karaites in Byzantium*, pp. 358 f. It need hardly be added that Ibn Daud either did not know, or did not choose to recognize, the vast literary productivity of the Karaites toward this very end; cf., however, Ankori, *ibid.*, p. 359 n. 9. *General knowledge*: I.e., secular wisdom; cf. note to VII. 350–352.

knowledge or even a single poem, hymn or verse of consolation. "They are all dumb dogs who cannot even bark." If one of them finally did produce a book, he reviled, blasphemed and spoke insolently against Heaven. Witness the case of the boorish elder, al-Sheikh Abu'l-Faraj, whose work on the section "In the beginning," which opens with the words "In the beginning of darkness," speaks of God with terrible abominations, giving proof of his folly and ignorance. In [his commentary on] the section "These are the marches," he

127 *Poem, hymn or verse of consolation*: This triad probably is inspired by that of the "Kaddish," *shiratha, tushbeḥatha we-neḥematha*. Hence, the poem (*shirah*) probably refers to any hymn of praise whether intended for the liturgy or not. The hymn (*piyyut*) is probably a poem composed for incorporation into the service. The consolation (*neḥamah*) was probably a concluding hymn reaffirming faith in the messianic redemption. See S.N. — The accusation of Ibn Daud is only partially correct. Although some Karaites did compose liturgical poetry, the leading expositors of the sect denounced the Rabbanite form of the service and singled out for attack liturgical poems that were not scriptural; cf. Nemoy, "Al-Qirqisani's Account etc.," p. 332; Lewin, *Otzar ha-Geonim*, I, Responsa, p. 142; Poznanski, *Karaite Literary Opponents of Saadiah Gaon*, p. 10 n. 3; Mann, *Texts and Studies*, II, 51; Mahler, *Karaites*, pp. 376 f. See S.N.

127–128 *They are all etc.*: Isa. 56.10; cf. above, line 45.

130 *Boorish elder*: On this talmudic phrase, cf. Kohut, *Aruch Completum*, I, 318. Obviously Ibn Daud is playing on Abu'l-Faraj's title, *al-Sheikh* or *ha-zaken*; cf. above, note to line 47. However, he may also be playing on the way he was doubtless referred to by his Andalusian adherents, namely as *al-Sheikh al-Shammi* (= the Palestinian sage), which Ibn Daud converted to the phrase before us, *zaken ashmai*. The section "*In the beginning*": The first chapters of Genesis read in the synagogue as the first selection of the Torah in the cycle of weekly biblical readings; cf. *JE*, XII, 196.

131 *In the beginning of darkness*: The phrase is quoted verbatim in Arabic. Although the work by Abu'l-Faraj beginning with these words has not been identified, another philosophical commentary on the first sections of Genesis by him, *Bereshit Rabbah*, affords us some notion of what the first phrase meant; cf. Schreiner, *Studien ueber Jeschu'a ben Jehuda*, p. 89 n. 3, where a citation from the latter work indicates that Abu'l-Faraj took the word "in the beginning" to mean at the onset of the first evening, which is the beginning of created time. For another interpretation, cf. Pinsker, *Lickute Kadmoniot*, p. 217. In any event, Ibn Daud makes it quite clear that it was not only the first phrase of the work that outraged him. It was doubtless the general philosophical framework of Kalam, in accordance with which Abu'l-Faraj had interpreted the Torah, that provided the pretext for this virulent attack; cf. Schreiner, pp. 26 f. One need not, therefore, seek shocking heretical doctrines in Abu'l-Faraj's work. Ibn Daud, it will be recalled, had vented his wrath on a Rabbanite philosopher, Solomon ibn Gabirol, for a neo-Platonic approach that was no less distasteful to him; cf. Ibn Daud, *Emunah Ramah*, p. 3. *Au fond*, it was not Abu'l-Faraj's philosophy that elicited this outburst, but his Karaite halakah and above all his influence in Spain.

132 *Speaks of God with terrible abominations*: Probably a play on the phrase in Isa. 32.6. Cf. also Tobiah b. Eliezer, *Leqaḥ Tob*, I, to Ex. 20.2, p. 134.

132–133 *Folly and ignorance*: See S.N.

133 *The section*: Cf. note to line 130. *These are the marches*: Num. 33.36.

[EPILOGUE] 101

fabricated civil laws and laws of inheritance of his own invention without any evidence, authority or compelling reason, except for his statement: "Reason requires the following!" I composed a refutation of his work and exposed its folly to students.

[On the other side of the fence,] in the case of the rabbis, you can note the sacred chain [of transmission] which we have recounted. Besides those [listed herein], there were a || million saintly scholars [whose names we have not recorded], since we have listed only the heads of academies. Besides these, there were composers of works on the Holy Scriptures such as R. Judah b. R. David al-Fasi, of blessed memory, surnamed Ḥayyuj, who re-established the principles of the Hebrew language — these having been forgotten throughout

---

134 *Civil laws and laws of inheritance*: Abu'l-Faraj's commentary was thus on Num. 36. Since Ibn Daud distinguishes between two subjects of law in the work, it is probable that Abu'l-Faraj distinguished between women's rights in the inheritance of moveable property and land; cf. L. Ginzberg, *Genizah Studies*, II, 470.

135-136 *Reason requires the following*: Sc., legal interpretation of Scripture. In other words, Abu'l-Faraj was pitting his own reason against rabbinic interpretation in support of Karaite exegesis. Abu'l-Faraj's statement is quoted verbatim in Arabic. See S.N.

137 *To students*: Cf. Prologue. 2.

139 *Scared chain*: Cf. above, line 14.

140 *A million*: Lit., a thousand thousands. For the style, cf. Sifre Deut., par. 26 (ed. Finkelstein), pp. 38 f. *Saintly*: On this Arabic usage in Hebrew literature, cf. Nissim b. Jacob ibn Shahin, *Ḥibbur Yafeh etc.* (ed. Hirschberg), p. 3 n. 7.

143 *Ḥayyuj*: Cf. Baron, *SRH*, Index vol. s.v.

143-144 *Who re-established the principles etc.*: This statement is re-echoed frequently by medieval grammarians; cf. Munk, *Notice Sur Abou'l-Walid*, pp. 64 n. 2, 192 f., 196 f.; Harkavy, "Le-Toledot R. Samuel ha-Nagid," p. 43 n. 4. However, in listing only these three scholars as masters of the science of the Hebrew language, Ibn Daud clearly reflects his partisanship toward the school of Ibn Janaḥ and Moses Gikatilla, which is echoed in Ibn Tibbon's introduction to his translation of Ibn Janaḥ's *Kitab al-Luma'*; cf. Jonah ibn Janaḥ, *Sefer Hariqma* (ed. Wilensky) I, 3 f. It is inconceivable that Ibn Daud did not know of the other grammatical treatises listed by Ibn Tibbon there and by Abraham ibn Ezra in his introduction to *Sefer ha-Moznayyim*. However, Ibn Daud doubtless preferred to reckon some of those authors as poets rather than as grammarians, who to him were equivalent to exegetes.

144 *These having been forgotten etc.*: For the history and widespread repetition of this sentiment, cf. A. S. Halkin, "The Medieval Jewish Attitude Toward Hebrew," *Studies and Texts*, ed. by Alexander Altmann (Cambridge, 1963), I, 234 f. Ibn Daud's point in mentioning the recapture of the Hebrew language by Spanish Rabbanite exegetes and grammarians is to rebut the Karaite claim that their sectarian exegesis, in contrast with Rabbanite interpretation, was in keeping with Hebrew philology. Thus, Ibn Daud is reasserting the older Rabbanite claim to exclusive possession of the keys to the Hebrew language (*ahlu 'l-lughghat*) and consequently to the meaning of Scripture; cf. Nemoy, "Al-Qirqisani's Account etc.," pp. 319 f. See S.N.

145 the Diaspora — and R. Marenos b. Janaḥ, who supplemented the work begun by this R. Judah b. R. David. Besides these, there were R. Moses ha-Kohen b. Gikatilla and many other scholars, who composed for our benefit books, liturgies, poems, hymns in praise of our Creator, exalted be His name, and verses of consolation to fortify the hearts of Israel in the lands of their dis-
150 persion. In the days of R. Ḥisdai the Nasi the bards began to twitter, and in the days of R. Samuel the Nagid they burst into song. Among the men of the latter category were R. Solomon b. R. Judah b. Gabirol, a great scholar and poet; R. Isaac b. R. Judah b. Giat; R. Oheb the Nasi b. R. Meir the Nasi ibn Shortmeqash; R. Moses b. R. Jacob b. Ezra of the family of officials, a great
155 scholar learned in the Torah and in Greek wisdom, and a composer of poems and hymns — he renounced [the pleasures of] this world and looked forward

145   *R. Marenos b. Janaḥ*: His Hebrew name was Jonah. Cf. Baron, *SRH*, Index vol. s.v. Ibn Janah.
147   *Gikatilla*: Lived in the eleventh century. Cf. *ibid.*, s.v. Ibn Chiquitilla.
148–149   *Poems, hymns... and verses of consolation*: Cf. above, line 127 and note there. On the orthography of the Hebrew word for "Hymns of praise" (*tushbaḥot*), cf. S. Lieberman's note to Moses b. Maimon, *Hilkhoth Ha-Yerushalmi* (ed. Lieberman), pp. 23 n. 10, 76.
149   *To fortify the hearts etc.*: See S.N. to line 125.
150   *In the days of R. Ḥisdai the Nasi*: I.e., the second half of the tenth century; cf. VII.73 f. *The bards began to twitter*: I.e., Hebrew poetry began to emerge.
151   *The days of R. Samuel the Nagid*: The first half of the eleventh century; cf. VII.180 f. *They burst into song*: Cf. Ps. 68.34–35 and Ibn Ezra *ad loc.*; i.e., Hebrew poetry blossomed into full maturity. For this view of the history of Hebrew poetry, cf. also Moses ibn Ezra, *Shirat Israel*, pp. 63 f.; Al-Ḥarizi, *Taḥkemoni*, ch. 3 (ed. Toporowsky), p. 43 and especially ch. 18, p. 183, where the beginnings of Hebrew poetry in Spain are dated in the year 940 C.E. (For the latter text with commentary, cf. Schirmann, *Ha-Shirah ha-Ibrit*, II, 109 f., 134 f.). For modern appraisals of this conception, cf. Mann, *Texts and Studies*, I, 263 f.; A. Mirsky's Introduction to Itzhak ibn Khalfun, *Poems* (Jerusalem, 1961); Baron, *SRH*, VII, chs. XXXI–XXXII.
152   *R. Solomon b. R. Judah b. Gabirol*: 1021/22–ca. 1055. Cf. Schirmann, *Ha-Shirah ha-Ibrit*, I, 176 f.; II, 679 f.; Baron, *SRH*, Index vol. s.v. Ibn Gabirol; Guttmann, *Philosophies of Judaism*, pp. 89 f. Ibn Daud's praise here should be contrasted with his frontal attack on the poet in *Emunah Ramah*; cf. above, note to line 131.
153   *R. Isaac b. R. Judah b. Giat*: Cf. VII.336 f. *R. Oheb the Nasi b. R. Joseph the Nasi*: Lived in the eleventh century. Cf. Schirmann, *Ha-Shirah ha-Ibrit*, I, 327; II, 681. On his family name, cf. note to VII.384.
154   *R. Moses b. Jacob b. Ezra*: Ca. 1055–ca. 1138. Cf. Baron, *SRH*, Index vol. s.v. Ibn Ezra, Moses; Baer, *History*, I, 60 f.; Schirmann, *Ha-Shirah ha-Ibrit*, I, 362 f.; II, 683. *Of the family of officials*: Cf. above, lines 89 f.
155–156   *Poems and hymns*: Cf. the edition of Moses ibn Ezra, *Collected Liturgical Poems*, ed. by S. Bernstein (Tel-Aviv, 1957).
156   *He renounced the pleasures etc.*: For Moses ibn Ezra's own statement to that effect, cf. his *Shirat Israel*, pp. 85 f., 89. The same evaluation of Moses ibn Ezra is echoed by Judah ha-Levi; cf. Halper's introduction, *ibid.*, p. 13.

[EPILOGUE] 103

to the world to come — [of such quality] as to melt the heart of his hearers and fill them with awe of their Creator; R. Joseph the Judge b. R. Isaac b. Sahl; R. Joseph the Judge b. R. Zadok b. Zaddik; R. Judah ha-Levi b. R. Samuel ha-Levi; and R. Abraham b. Ezra. All of them were great and saintly scholars, who have added strength to Israel || with their poems and verses of consolation. Of these it is said, "Blessed be the memory of the righteous," and of those heretics it is said, "May the name of the wicked rot."

Now that we have completed the history of tradition we will recount the history of the kings of Israel during the days of the Second Temple, in order to refute the Sadducees, who claim that all of the consolatory passages in the books of the prophets were fulfilled for Israel in the days of the Second Temple. We deny that and will demonstrate that this is not the case. We shall also interpret the prophecy of Zechariah in which the Holy One, blessed be He, said to him: "Feed the flock of slaughter," and explain the whole passage. In addition to that [we have composed] a history of Rome to show how late their Gospels were composed. May the Almighty, blessed be He, manifest His approval of our desire to study and to teach, to preserve and to fulfill. Amen, Selah.

159   *R. Joseph the Judge b. Zadok*: Cf. VII.358 f. *R. Judah ha-Levi*: Ca. 1075–1141. Cf Baron, *SRH*, Index vol. s.v. Halevi; Baer, *History*, I, 67 f.; Schirmann, *Ha-Shirah ha-Ibrit*, I, 425 f.; II, 684 f.; Guttmann, *Philosophies of Judaism*, pp. 120 f.; the papers by Goitein listed in note to VII.375.
160   *Abraham b. Ezra*: 1092–1167. Cf. Baron, *SRH*, Index vol. s.v. Ibn Ezra, Abraham; Schirmann, *Ha-Shirah ha-Ibrit*, I, 569 f.; II, 686 f; Guttmann, *Philosophies of Judaism*, pp. 118 f. *Saintly*: Cf. note to line 140.
162–163   *Blessed be the memory of the righteous... May the name etc.*: Prov. 10.7; and cf. M. Yoma 3.11. Cf. also Prologue. 8; VI.43; Epilogue. 17.
165   *History of the kings of Israel*: Ibn Daud's work, *Dibray Malkay Israel be-Bayyit Sheni*. Cf. Introduction, pp. xxxiv f.
166   *Sadducees*: Karaites; cf. II.40. However, this view was not shared by most Karaites, but only by certain outlying groups; cf. Nemoy, "Al-Qirqisani's Account etc.," p. 395 on Karaites of Khorasan, and p. 365, where Christians are cited as entertaining this view. Cf. also Saadiah, *The Book of Doctrines and Beliefs*, ed. and trans. by A. Altmann (Oxford, 1946), p. 175 n. 1. It is, of course, possible that the Karaites of Spain also adopted such a doctrine. However, there are weighty reasons for the argument that Ibn Daud was concerned not so much with sectarian abandonment of traditional eschatology so much as with Rabbanite exegesis to that effect; cf. below, pp. 300 f. and Silver, *A History of Messianic Speculation in Israel*, pp. 209, 215 f.
169–170   *Interpret the prophecy of Zechariah... "Feed etc."*: Zech. 11.4 f. Cf. Introduction, pp. xxxv f.
171   *History of Rome*: *Zikron Dibray Romi*; cf. Introduction, pp. xxxii f.
172   *Their*: I.e., Christian.
172–173   *May the Almighty... manifest etc.*: For the style, cf. VII.466 f.
173   *Study and teach, preserve and fulfill*: Abot 4.5.

SUPPLEMENTARY NOTES

Supplementary Notes to Prologue

1 *Students* advanced in rabbinic learning but who have not as yet attained full rabbinic status; see also VII. 45, 50; Mann, *Texts and Studies*, I, 133, lines 133 f.; 401 n. 17; 406 line 6; 410 line 35; Hirschberg, "The Almohade Persecutions and the India Trade" [in Hebrew], *Yitzhak F. Baer Jubilee Volume*, p. 146 n. 24; Goitein, *Jewish Education in Muslim Countries* [in Hebrew], pp. 146 f. See also Alon, *Toledot*, I, 299 f.

6 *School*: Lit., coterie, company of scholars. Collective or collegiate transmission serves as proof that the tradition was not altered in the course of transmission. See also II. 34, 42, 89, 92, 94; *Emunah Ramah*, pp. 80 f.; Maimonides, *Epistle to Yemen* (ed. Halkin), p. xvii; Baron, "The Historical Outlook of Maimonides," *PAAJR*, VI (1934–1935), p. 16 n. 19.

8 *Never did etc.*: Underlying this *a fortiori* clause is the traditional rabbinic assumption of the superiority of the tannaim to the amoraim; see the remark of R. Ze'ira in *B. Shab.* 112b.

11 *Universal agreement*: As far as I can determine, Ibn Daud's view is unprecedented, the general view being that *taqqanot* required only majority approval, not unanimity; see *Tos. Sanhed.* 2.13 (ed. Zuckermandel), p. 418 lines 3–4 and the general survey in Maimonides, *Mishneh Torah*, Mamrim, 1.1–3. Ibn Daud may have based his view on the talmudic statement that certain enactments may never be repealed, inasmuch as they have been *universally accepted*; *B. A.Z.* 36a: הואיל ופשט איסורן בכל ישראל. However, in all likelihood the real source of Ibn Daud's view lies in the Arabic philosophic concept of consensus ('*ijmā*'), which was often interpreted as consisting in unanimity of opinion; cf. Introduction, p. LXI. Ibn Daud may well have adopted this extreme position in view of the Karaite doctrine, promulgated in the eleventh century, that non-Mosaic usage is obligatory only if it has gained universal adherence; cf. Qirqisani, *Kitab al-Anwar* (ed. Nemoy), II, 436 f., and Ankori, *Karaites in Byzantiium*, pp. 208 f., 218 f. In other words, Ibn Daud would be urging the Karaites to accept rabbinic legislation on the basis of their own principles.

13 This charge against the Rabbanite claim to authentic tradition was repeatedly made by Karaite polemicists, the classic statement being "Al-Qirqisani's Account of the Jewish Sects" (tr. by L. Nemoy), *HUCA*, VII (1930), 377 f., 396. See also Pinsker, *Lickute Kadmoniot*, Appendix pp. 24, 26 f. (and the refs. given below, line 16–17); Mann *Texts and Studies*, I, 558 f.; Ankori, *Karaites in Byzantium*, pp. 356 f. Salmon b. Yeruḥim argued that had Rabbanite *qabbalah* indeed been received from the prophets, the opinions in the Mishna would all have been recorded anonymously; Salmon b. Yeruḥim, *The Book of the Wars of the Lord* (ed. Davidson), pp. 40, 43, 46. See further Sultanski, *Zeker Ṣaddiqim* (ed. Poznanski), Introduction, p. 15 n. 2; Margulies, *The Differences Between Babylonian and Palestinian Jews* [in Hebrew], pp.20–23, 52–56.

14 *Rebel*: Technically, this is incorrect here as well as below, VI. 51, for such doubts or even outright violation of rabbinic teachings are insufficient to put one in the category of "a rebellious elder;" cf. *M. Sanhed.* 11.2. Ibn Daud probably adopts the popular usage of the term, which goes back at least to the third century; cf. Alon, *Toledot*, I, 144.

This loose usage probably gained strength in view of the wide use in anti-Karaite polemic of the word "sages" where classical sources had had "Sanhedrin," against which the category would indeed have applied; cf. M. Zucker, "Tegubot li-Tenu'at Abaylay Zion ha-Qaraiyyim ba-Sifrut ha-Rabbanit," *Sefer ha-Yobel le-Rabbi Ḥanok Albeck* (Jerusalem, 1963), pp. 390 f.

16–17 *Principle... details*: Lit., root of a commandament but only with respect to its off-shoots. Although the more usual contrast in rabbinic literature is אב...תוֹלדה, Ibn Daud's usage is well attested; cf. *Yer.* Shab. 2:[5] f. 5a and Ber. *R.* 12.5 (ed. Theodor-Albeck), p. 100 (cf. the parallel usages in Epstein, *Prolegomena ad Litteras Tannaiticas* [in Hebrew], p. 503 n. 28). For its use with respect to rabbinic tradition, see *ISG*, 48.12, 49.20, 52.6–15. Sherira defines a "root commandment" as one which is derived from Scripture by one of the rabbinic hermeneutical rules. The early Karaites were well aware of this argument and laughed it out of court. Whatever Rabbanite unity did exist, they contended, was the product of late machination; Pinsker, *Lickute Kadmoniot*, Appendix pp. 35 f., 42, 68, 101.

19–21 The Sabbath lamp, which the Rabbanites regarded as obligatory and the Karaites as a desecration, became one of the arch-symbols of the Rabbanite-Karaite schism. As noted by Lewin, it is doubtless on that account that Ibn Daud chose this as his first example of Rabbanite law, although no Rabbanite could point with certainty to any explicit source enjoining the kindling of the Sabbath lamp. Ibn Daud would probably have argued that the style of the Mishna, "With what may it be lighted," parallels the style of the Mishna with reference to the *Shema'* (see immediately below) in the case of which the obligation is clearly spelled out. On the whole subject, see Lewin, "Le-Toledot Ner shel Shabbat," *Essays and Studies in Memory of Linda R. Miller*, Hebrew Section, pp. 55–68; Klar, *Meḥqarim we-'Iyyunim*, pp. 242–258; Ankori, *Karaites in Byzantium*, Index s.v. "Sabbath candles"; Nemoy, *Karaite Anthology*, Index s.v. "Sabbath, fire on." See also the marriage contracts between Rabbanites and Karaites in Mann, *Texts and Studies*, II, 158, 160, 173.

24 For Rabbanite disagreements on the first of the two questions on the *Shema'*, see *B.* Ber. 2b. For the source for the obligation to recite the *Shema'*, see *M.* Ber. 1.3. — Ibn Daud probably chose this example because it is the opening law of the Mishna. Although by the twelfth century Karaites were reciting the *Shema'*, they were clearly not reciting it in accordance with rabbinic prescriptions; see Ginzberg, *Genizah Studies*, II, 435 f. and Goldberg, *Karaite Liturgy*, pp. 64 f. However, Ibn Daud may not have been aware of this and may have had in mind the view of his principal targets, Anan and Qirqisani, that prayer should consist only of recitations of verses from the Psalms; see Harkavy, *Zikron la-Rishonim*, VIII, 158 n. 9; Mann, "Anan's Liturgy and his Half-Yearly Cycle of the Reading of the Law," *Journal of Jewish Lore and Philosophy*, I (1919), 339; Qirqisani, *Kitab al-Anwar*, II, 608. Weiss, "Ibn Ezra, the Karaites and the Halakha," [in Hebrew], *Melilah*, III–IV (1953), 195, detects an anti-Karaite allusion in Ibn Ezra's comment on Dt. 6.4. May that be a further bit of circumstantial evidence that Spanish Karaites did not recite the *Shema'*?

Supplementary Notes to Chapter I

4 *52*: Based on a calculation in *B.* A.Z. 9a, this figure represents a Spanish-Jewish tradition on the age of Abraham at the time he forsook idolatry and left home; see S. Abramson, "Imray Ḥokmah we-Amre Inshay," *Minḥah li-huda*, pp. 23 f. In giving this datum on Abraham's first departure from Haran, Ibn Daud follows the rabbinic tradition which interprets Gen. 12.4 as referring to Abraham's second departure; see below and cf. Seder 'Olam 1 (ed. Ratner), p. 5 (ed. Marx, p. 1); Ginzberg, *Legends*, V, 230 n. 115.

14–15 For this legend, which is based on the rabbinic interpretation of Ps. 78.9 and I Chr. 7.20-22, see Ginzberg, *Legends*, III, 8 f.; VI, 2 n. 10; Kasher, *Torah Shelemah*, XIV, 5 n. 234, 6 n. 237, 9 n. 251; Maimonides, *Epistle to Yemen* (ed. Halkin), p. 62 n. 80. — The figure 110 is derived by reckoning the 400 years of subjection to Egypt (Gen. 15.13) from the time of the covenant between the pieces of flesh rather than from the birth of Isaac (see B. N. 16). This, says the legend, is what the Ephraimites did and blunderingly proclaimed the Exodus at what they believed to be the appointed end. — The reading "and Gilead" is puzzling, for none of the available sources mention him. It may be that the reading represents an interpretation of the name "Elead" in I Chr. 7.21. Such a *corruption* does occur in the version of the story in one MS of Midrash Haggadol, Exodus (ed. Margulies), p. 247, line 2 (variants).

17 Although these figures yield but a total of 2448 (as in *B.* A.Z. 9a), Ibn Daud was not diverging from the talmudic date but was tacitly following the Spanish-Jewish interpretation of rabbinic chronology, which required the addition of one year to any talmudic date *Anno Mundi*; see Bornstein, "Ta'arikay Israel," *Ha-Tequfa*, VIII (1921), 314 f.; IX (1921), 223 f.

21–22 *410 years*: For an explanation of this figure, see Seder 'Olam 11 (ed. Ratner), p. 43 and n. 37 there; de' Rossi, *Me'or 'Enayyim*, ch. 35 (ed. Cassel), pp. 299 f. — Ibn Daud thus declares that he dates the destruction of the Temple in 3339 A.M., although in reality it was destroyed twenty-three years later. This is, of course, a blatant internal contradiction in *SHQ*, but one which Ibn Daud follows consistently: all dates are calculated in accordance with the traditional figure of 410 years for the First Temple; on the other hand, the destruction of the Temple is dated in terms of Babylonian chronology in the year 23 of Nebuchadnezzar. Ibn Daud based his unprecedented theory on his understanding of Jer. 52.30, which he said refers to the destruction of the Temple (I. 139-140). *The kingship was not taken into account*: Since the events in Jer. 52.28-30 are dated in terms of Nebuchadnezzar's reign, obviously the Judean monarchy was no longer of any consequence. This apparently was also Daniel's understanding, as explained by Ibn Daud below (I.154 f.).

26 The medieval commentators were baffled by the rabbinic attribution of twenty-eight years to Joshua; see Rashi to Jud. 11.26; Jacob b. Asher to Num. 22.15; Zacuto, p. 7. However, this figure had gained general acceptance even in talmudic times; see Ginzberg, *Die Haggada bei den Kirchenvaetern* (1899), pp. 1 f.

27 This number, too, is not taken from Scripture. As far as I can determine, Ibn Daud, or perhaps *Sefer ha-Yashar* (ed. Goldschmidt), p. 296, is the earliest authority to give this figure. Whoever first arrived at this figure probably did so in an effort to account for the 480 years from the Exodus until the year in which Solomon began to construct the Temple (B. N. to I.47-48).

SUPPLEMENTARY NOTES

47-48 Ibn Daud would probably have rationalized his contradiction of Scripture by pointing out that his chronology is calculated *Anno Mundi*, which is to be reckoned from Tishri (*M. R.H.* 1.1). When the Bible, on the other hand, stated that Solomon began building the Temple in the second month of the fourth year of his reign, it clearly referred to Solomon's fourth regnal year, which is calculated from Nisan. Since according to rabbinic legend David died on Pentecost (see Ginzberg, *Legends*, IV, 114; VI, 271 n. 126), David's fortieth year and Solomon's first overlapped. Solomon's second regnal year, which began the following Nisan, was still his first from the point of view of historical chronology.

50 *Abijah:* So in all MSS and eds., as in II Chr. 13.1 f. Cf. also Kittel-Kahle, eds., *Biblia Hebraica* to I Ki. 14.31.

52 Although the MSS are almost unanimous in reading twenty-eight years here, the error is clearly one of transmission, not that of Ibn Daud himself, as thought by de' Rossi, *Me'or 'Enayyim*, ch. 35.

69 On the reason for Ibn Daud's insistence that the First Temple stood 433 years, see Cohen, *SFC*, p. 102 n. 146; below, pp. 194 f.

71-75 Although this list differs somewhat from the *textus recepti* of Seder 'Olam Zuta, it is attested (but for the inclusion of Neariah) by similar ones; see Lazarus, *Die Haeupter der Vertriebenen*, pp. 18 f., 171. On the significance of twenty-one names, see below, pp. 209 f.

74 I cannot locate any earlier source for this report. At the bottom of this tradition lies the rabbinic genealogy according to which Hillel was a descendant of the house of David; II.120.

77 *Rabban Gamaliel the Elder*: *SHQ* consistently lists him as the son of Hillel; cf. II.125.

82 *Sivan 2449*: Ibn Daud omitted the exact day of the theophany at Sinai, for that was a matter of dispute between the tannaim; *ARN*, I, p. 1; Goldin, *The Fathers According to Rabbi Nathan*, p. 175 n. 3.

88 *Henceforth they did not etc.*: This statement is probably based on the rabbinic interpretation of Deut. 2.16-17, viz., that during all thirty-eight years which the children of Israel roamed the desert after the return of the spies, God did not speak with Moses; Mekhilta de R. Ishmael, *Pisha* I (ed. Lauterbach), I, 13; Sifra 2.13, f. 4b (and Abraham b. David's comments there). Cf. further B.J. Bamberger, "Revelations of Torah after Sinai," *HUCA*, XVI (1941), 109. — This statement may have an anti-Karaite motive, for Ibn Daud, like his younger contemporary Maimonides, seems to be adhering to a widely held rabbinic view that the prophets who followed Moses added nothing to the Law; for a full discussion of this question see E.E. Urbach, "Halacha and Prophecy" [in Hebrew], *Tarbiz*, XVIII (1946-47), 1-27 and esp. 20 f. The Karaites, on the other hand, freely used the post-Mosaic books as sources of legal exegesis to justify their sectarian practices; see Baron, *SRH*, V, 390 n. 5.

89 *Sabbath afternoon*: Professor Saul Lieberman kindly called my attention to the fact that the tradition on the exact hour of Moses' death derives from Midrash Petirat Mosheh (cf. Eisenstein, *Ozar Midrashim*, II, 361 f. and esp. 365 f.) and is hinted at by Yannai, the poet of amoraic times (*Piyyute Yannai*, ed. Zulay, pp. 257 f.). Later on, the exact hour was confirmed by astrological calculation, as may be seen from Abraham bar Hiyya, *Megillat ha-Megalleh*, pp. 121, 124.

91-92 Ibn Daud spells out the meaning of "Torah" in Abot 1.1 in view of the Karaite attack on rabbinic tradition. Cf. Salmon b. Yeruhim's jibes at "the two Torahs" of the Rabbanites in his *Book of the Wars of the Lord* (ed. Davidson), pp. 36 f. and in Mann, *Texts and Studies*, II, 85.

95 *Possible contingencies*: Lit., the events which come up anew. The identical terminology is employed in this sense by Sherira, *ISG* 8.13 ("French" recension), 66.16. — This emphasis on new contingencies for which no explicit provision is made in the Torah is related to the second anti-Karaite argument invoked by Rabbanites, namely, that the Torah does not spell out the details even of the commandments which it enjoins explicitly; cf. I.99 f. The present statement, like the ones which follow, seeks to meet the Karaite query that if "the law of the Lord is perfect (Ps. 19.8)," of what need is there for *qabbalah*? Cf. Pinsker, *Lickute Kadmoniot*, Appendix, pp. 20 f.; Salmon b. Yeruḥim, *The Book of the Wars of the Lord* (ed. Davidson), p. 43; see S.N. to I. 99. *He placed etc.*: The point of the paraphrase of Scripture is that, since Moses appointed judges and gave them instructions, he must have spelled out the proper method of adjudicating contingencies not mentioned in the written Torah. The same verse is cited with the same conclusion by Saadiah, who makes the point much more clearly than Ibn Daud; cf. Halkin, "A Fragment of Saadya's Introduction to His Commentary on the Pentateuch", *Louis Ginzberg Jubilee Volume*, Hebrew Volume, pp. 145, 152 par. 4.

99 I cannot locate any similar classical rabbinic interpretation of this particular verse. However, the root צוה in the Pentateuch is interpreted by the rabbis to denote the oral tradition; cf. *B*. Ber. 5a and the sources listed in the next note. Cf. also Maimonides, *Mishneh Torah*, Introduction, beg., who is doubtless quoting older sources. Jacob b. Samuel, a disciple of Saadiah, argued for the antiquity of the Oral Law on the basis of the same usage in I Chr. 24.19; Pinsker, *Lickute Kadmoniot*, Appendix, p. 22 n. 5.

100 Here again, the proof word is צויתיך; cf. *B*. Hul. 28a. Ibn Daud's wording resembles that of an old source cited both by Rashi, *B. Ḥul.* 28a, *s.v.* כאשר צויתיך and Maimonides, *Mishneh Torah*, Hilkot Sheḥita 1.4. — Ibn Daud singles out the laws of slaughtering, inasmuch as the ritual preparation of meat was one of the principal subjects debated by Karaites and Rabbanites; cf. Ankori, "Some Aspects of Karaite-Rabbanite Relations in Byzantium on the Eve of the First Crusade," *PAAJR*, XXIV–XXV (1955–56), 23 f.; *idem, Karaites in Byzantium*, 285 f. Ibn Daud's argument is an abbreviated and somewhat modified version of the Saadyanic argument for the assumption that an Oral Law had to be given along with the written one. The essence of the argument is that the commandments of Scripture, e.g., Sukkah, Lulab and Ṣiṣith, are merely bare outlines, and the details must have been enjoined along with the broad categories; cf. Lewin in *ISG*, Introduction, pp. X-XI; Halkin, "A Fragment of Saadya's Introduction," pp. 145, 152, 156 f.; M. Zucker, "Le-Pitron Ba'yat Lamed-Bet Middot," *PAAJR*, XXIII (1954), 125 f.; *idem, Rav Saadya Gaon's Translation of the Torah* [in Hebrew] (New York, 1959), pp. 209 f.; N. Wieder, *The Judean Scrolls and Karaism* (London, 1962), pp. 74 f.; M. Schreiner, "Zwei Geniza-Fragmente," *ZfHB*, III (1899), 89, 91 f. and S. Poznanski's note thereto, *ibid.*, pp. 172–177.

102 For the same argument, cf. Judah ha-Levi, *Kitab al-Khazari*, III.39.

109–111 On the association of these men with the great assemblage described in Neh. 8.10, cf. *Targum* Song of Songs 7.7, and Moore, *Judaism*, I, 31 f., III, 7 f.; Ginzberg, *Legends*, VI, 447 n. 56; Finkelstein, *Ha-Perushim ve-Anshe Kenesset Ha-Gedolah*, pp. 45 f. These men are called but the "heads" or "leaders," for rabbinic tradition assumes that the Assembly numbered 120 members.

113 I cannot locate any earlier source for this figure. Scripture speaks of a war of but three years; II Ki. 25.1–2. Ibn Daud may have seized on the statement in Seder 'Olam Zuta (Neubauer, *MJC*, II, 70) that Nebuchadnezzar's siege began in the fifth year of Zedekiah's reign, although this statement, too, is not supported by scriptural data.

SUPPLEMENTARY NOTES

Ibn Daud probably appropriated the figure out of considerations of symmetry whereby the war of destruction corresponded to the period of construction. The suggestion of de' Rossi, *Me'or 'Enayyim*, ch. 35 (ed. Cassel, p. 293), to emend the text to "three" is part of de' Rossi's entire scheme to rescue Ibn Daud's chronology by harmonizing it with orthodox tradition.

117 *To Cyrus*: On the substitution of Cyrus for the scriptural Artaxerxes, cf. *B*. R.H. 36, and Seder 'Olam 30 (ed. Ratner, p. 136), which maintain that Scripture uses the names Cyrus, Darius and Artaxerxes interchangeably. The "Commentary on Ezra and Nehemiah by Rabbi Saadiah," (ed. Matthews, *Anecdota Oxoniensia*, Semitic Series, I, part I), p. 10, and Rashi to Ezra 4.7–8 also maintain that the Artaxerxes of these verses is identical with Cyrus, probably on the basis of the same sources consulted by Ibn Daud.

126 Much of the chronological analysis as well as of the exegetical interpretation of Daniel 9 (below, I.154 f.) parallels that of "Abraham Ibn Ezra's Shorter Commentary on Daniel," *Miscellany of Hebrew Literature*, II, 2, 7 f.

134 For gaonic antecedents of this method of harmonization of contradictory censuses in Scripture, see Zucker, *Rav Saadya Gaon's Translation of the Torah*, p. 35 n. 71. For evidence of the embarrassment caused by the conflict of such data in Scripture, see Rosenthal, "She'elot 'Atiqot ba-Tenak," *HUCA*, XXI (1948), Hebrew section, pp. 42, 66#25.

140–142 *Fractional years*: For this expression, see talmudic dictionaries, *s.v.* קטע. and Seder 'Olam (ed. Marx), p. IX. *Twenty-one complete years*: Since Daniel was exiled in the third year of Jehoiakim, Nebuchadnezzar's reign spanned nine years of Jehoiakim's reign (including the year of exile), + three months (= one year of Jehoiachin) + eleven of Zedekiah = twenty-one years. Ibn Daud's chronology here is fraught with difficulties, which I have discussed at length in *SFC*, p. 96 n. 136.

144 *Evil-merodach*: Heb., Evil-medorach. This metathesis is common in medieval MSS. *Twenty-two years*: Although this figure was originally derived by elimination, it is possible that Ibn Daud found it in one of his sources. Thus, Abraham bar Ḥiyya, *Megillat ha-Megalleh*, p. 85, cites the figure twenty-two in the name of Seder 'Olam, though Seder 'Olam 28 (ed. Ratner, p. 126) and Seder 'Olam Zuta concur with *B*. Meg. 11b, in reading "twenty-three."

146 *Three years*: On the rabbinic method of establishing the extent of a reign from data such as that of Dan. 8.1, see Seder 'Olam (ed. Marx), p. VIII.

191 *420 years*: The mistake in arithmetic is so obvious, for sixty-two weeks are equal to 434 years, that Loeb, *Joseph Haccohen et les Chroniqueurs Juifs*, p. 90, had no hesitation in emending the text to the "correct" figure. However, the plausibility of the correction is counterbalanced by the reiteration of the "error" in the statement immediately following. It appears likely that we have before us a specimen of Ibn Daud's deliberate tinkering with the chronology of the Second Temple as he did with that of the First. On the one hand, he was confronted with the official rabbinic figure of 420 years for the Second Temple, a figure on which all subsequent Jewish chronology was based. On the other hand, Ibn Daud knew that the figure did not square with the "facts," notably the wording of Dan. 9.25. Accordingly, he straddled the issue by citing the official figure as the one that really counts and then quoted Scripture to indicate that in reality the number should be in excess of the traditional one. For a detailed analysis of these figures, see Cohen, *SFC*, pp. 100 f.; below, pp. 196 f.

193 *His step-son, who was called his son*: On this epithet, which casts doubt on Titus' parentage, see Lieberman, *Greek in Jewish Palestine*, p. 164, and esp. *idem*, *Greek and*

Hellenism in Jewish Palestine [in Hebrew], p. 126. As Professor Lieberman proves, Ibn Daud is not the author of the phrase, but copied it from a source which apparently misunderstood a subtle classical rabbinic jibe.

202 On Monobaz the son of Agrippa, see Lieberman, *Tosefta Ki-Fshutah*, Order Zera'im, I, 850; cf. also Epilogue. 112 and variants to Hebrew text 70.398.

204 I cannot determine the original source for this covenant between Vespasian and the Jews. Is it perhaps based on Nero's overtures for peace described in *Josippon* 66, p. 241? That the conception was not peculiar to Spanish-Jewish exegesis may be seen from Judah Hadassi, *Eshkol ha-Kofer*, f. 48b, who gives the same interpretation.

206 For the application of this verse to Vespasian in rabbinic times, see Schuerer, *Geschichte des Juedischen Volkes im Zeitalter Jesu Christi* (3rd and 4th ed.), I, 696 n.; Alon, *Toledot*, I, 258.

207 *The lawless ones*. On Ibn Daud's use of this word and his attitude to the Zealots, see above, p. xxxix.

215 *The queen of the Scythians*: Ibn Daud's is a variant version of the story told by Orosius, *Apology*, II. 7, and *Josippon*, 3, p. 24. On the expression for "emperors," literally great kings," cf. II. Ki.13.19.

223 *The Persian Empire was cut off*: On Ibn Daud's theory of the succession of empires, see Analysis, ch. IV.

Supplementary Notes to Chapter II

3 Although the MSS do not indicate that a new chapter begins at this point, and although Ibn Daud would appear to regard this period to have begun a generation earlier, his chronological scheme (cf. below, p. 210) makes it abundantly clear that a new period begins with Simeon the Righteous when prophecy ceased and a new medium of instruction began. Indeed, beginning with the third generation (II. 141–142), Ibn Daud drops the qualifying epithet "of the Great Assembly" and indicates later on (III. 172) that the generations are not of the Great Assembly but rather of instruction in the Temple.

4 *Simeon... Iddo*: Although the Spanish recension of *Josippon* 5, p. 31, refers to the priest who met Alexander as Hananiah, the name may well have been lacking in Ibn Daud's MS of *Josippon*, as it is in the Mantua-Guenzburg edition, cols. 62–63. This appears all the more likely in view of the fact that both recensions of *Josippon* refer to Manasseh the heretic as the brother of Iddo the high priest; ed. Mantua-Guenzburg, col. 63; ed. Hominer, p. 32. Although Simeon Duran, *Magen Abot* (Leipzig, 1855), f. 4b, repeats Ibn Daud's statement on the basis of *Josippon*, his reference may actually be to *MBSh*. On the other hand, Zacuto, p. 11b, could no longer find the evidence for Ibn Daud's identification. — Iddo's genealogy seems to be the product of Ibn Daud's reasoning on the basis of Hag. 1.1.

20–22 Ibn Daud's invocation of miracles in support of the legitimacy of rabbinic leadership and tradition goes back to Saadiah, *Essa Meshali*, ed. by B.M. Lewin (Jerusalem, 1943), 27.41–45, who in turn employed an argument used in the same way in philosophical circles in Judaism, Christianity and Islam; cf. H.A. Wolfson, *The Philosophy of the Church Fathers*, I (Cambridge, 1956), pp. 19 f.; *idem, Religious Philosophy* (Cambridge, 1961), pp. 218 f. For Ibn Daud's theory of miracles as proof of authenticity, cf. *Emunah Ramah*, p. 80, and cf. Halkin's Introduction to Maimonides, *Epistle to Yemen*, p. xx.

SUPPLEMENTARY NOTES

35 *From Ezra etc.*: Although Ibn Daud does not include Ezra's name among the first generation of the Great Assembly (I.109–111), he doubtless assumed him to be the key figure in that body; cf. Neh. 12.1; Moore, *Judaism*, I, 31 f.

37 *Enacted statutes*: Ibn Daud is not repeating the classical rabbinic contention that the Samaritans falsified the text of Scripture; cf. Sifre Deut. § 56 (ed. Finkelstein), pp. 123 f. Instead, he charges them with substituting their own oral Law for the authentic one. Ibn Daud consistently distinguishes between fabricators of Scripture, such as Mani and Ḥiwi (IV.149 f.; VI. 153 f.), and heretics who fabricate laws on the basis of false exegesis of the true Scripture (VI. 52 f.; Epilogue. 21, 130 f.). By this linguistic device Ibn Daud indicates the connection between the ancient heretics and latter-day Karaites; cf. VI.54 f. and Introduction, p. xxxviii.

40 *Assumed leadership*: This expression is a literal translation of the Arabic usage "became *rayis* (head),"which is employed frequently in other sources to designate communal (i.e., political) as well as religious leadership; cf. Hirschberg, "The Almohade Persecutions etc.," p. 146 n. 28. However, Ibn Daud consistently employs the unqualified term "became head" only in the sense of religious leadership, indeed in the very restricted sense of "became head of the academy", and employs other terms for communal-political leadership; cf. III.32 and S.N. to VII.27, 73. — The divisions of Samaritan society, according to Ibn Daud's view, parallel the divisions within Jewish society: political (Sanballat), priestly (the renegade priests of Judea), academic (Zadok and Boethus); cf. notes to II.131, 143.

42–44 On the reading of the second half of Antigonus' dictum, cf. C. Taylor, *An Appendix to the Sayings of the Jewish Fathers* (Cambridge, 1900), pp. 134 f. For the translation of this passage, as well as for many another in this text, I am indebted to J. Goldin, *The Fathers According to Rabbi Nathan* (New Haven, 1955); for this passage, see p. 35 there.

48 *Though they had been his disciples*: In other words, besides repudiating the authentic tradition at their disposal, these two men had the effrontery to break openly with their master. The identical break with their masters is imputed to Anan and Saul (Epilogue. 16 f.), thus establishing a further connection between ancient and latter-day heresy. On the sin of contradicting the master, cf. *B*. Sanhed. 110a. Cf. further Zucker, "Tegubot," p. 390.

49 The role of the temple on Mount Gerizim as an asylum for heretics parallels the widespread medieval view of Arabia as a haven for Christian heretics; cf. N. Daniel, *Islam and the West* (Edinburgh, 1960), p. 84.

53 *3621*: All of the MSS are incorrect, and I have emended the text in accordance with simple arithmetic and on the testimony of Joseph ibn Zaddik in *MJC*, I, 89; Zacuto, p. 12a (bot.); and Samuel ha-Nagid, MS Sassoon, p. 53, which reads: ומשם עד שמנו לשטרות בימי יון לאלפים כ׳. סימן ג׳ אלפים תמ״ט. ומשם ועד שמרדו במלכות יון ועמדו מלכים מבית חשמוניאי (!) קע״ב. סימן ג׳ אלפים תרכ״א. MS ב apparently had this figure originally, and I cannot determine whether the correction is by the original scribe or by a later hand. The copyist of MS ה doubtless had this correct figure before him, too. The error of the other MSS, which record נתרס״א, is parallelled by a similar variant in the Hebrew text 31.129, where MS אפק read ס for the כ of תתכ״ז. *Mattathias... the high-priest, called Hasmonean*: For the name and title, cf. *Josippon* 20, p. 79; *MBSh*, f. 51a; Pesiqta R. (ed. Friedmann), f. 5a; *Megillat Antiochus* in S.A. Wertheimer, *Battay Midrashot*, I, 320 f.; the על הנסים liturgy of Hanukkah in Masseket Soferim (ed. Higger) 20, p. 346; *Siddur R. Saadja Gaon*, p. 255; I. Davidson, *Thesaurus*

of *Medieval Hebrew Poetry*, III, 269, no. 477. Ibn Daud says that he was "called Hasmonean," because in later sources he is often referred to by that name alone; cf. *Megillat Antiochus*, pp. 325 f.; *Sheiltot de Rab Aḥai Gaon* 27 (ed. Mirsky), p. 186; cf. also talmudic dictionaries, *s.v.* חשמונאי.

57 *The mighty warrior*: MSS ח read: "the warrior, who was the eldest *of his sons*," a gloss which agrees with some earlier traditions; cf. Saadiah in Harkavy, *Zikron la-Rishonim*, V, 150 1.16; *Mishnah of R. Eliezer* (ed. Enelow), p. 103. On the other hand, the gloss is suspect, inasmuch as it is lacking in all of the better MSS and contradicts *Josippon* 20, p. 81, which was Ibn Daud's primary source. In *MBSh*, f. 51b, the reading is: יהודה הגדול הגבור which may mean either "the eldest," as in *SHQ* Epilogue. 98, or "the chief." For a similar ambiguity of the synonymous word in Arabic (*al-kabīr*), cf. W. Fischel, *Ibn Khaldun and Tamerlaine* (Berkeley, 1952), pp. 113 n. 215, 114 n. 219.

62 In *B. Kid.* 66a, the same story is told of Alexander Jannaeus. However, Ibn Daud probably found no difficulty in this, inasmuch as according to one rabbinic tradition John Hyrcanus and Alexander Jannaeus are one and the same; *B. Ber.* 29a.

78 *A sword*: Although the meaning is clear, the construction is odd. *Josippon* understood the cry to be a summons to the royal guard to draw their swords against the Pharisees, and the Spanish version indeed reads: "A sword, a sword, against the Pharisees!" Ibn Daud's rendering may be modelled after Jud. 7.20, and perhaps even more after Jer. 25.29, Ezek. 38.21. Ibn Daud may thus well have taken the word in its Arabic meaning and used it as a cry of "War!" *Violently*: Professor A.S. Halkin kindly called my attention to the blatant Arabism of this form, perhaps from وضربهم ضربا عظيما or وقتلهم شديدا. Good Hebrew usage requires a cognate accusative, והרג... הרג רב instead of והרג... מכה גדולה.

86 *Parable*: The Hebrew is a patent Arabism and mistranslation of مثل, which MSS ח corrected to the simpler וירמז, in view of the senselessness of וכמו in this context, on the basis of *MBSh* f. 50a, 79a.

89 *From Antigonus*: Ibn Daud's text of Abot 1.4 probably read קבלו ממנו; cf. Taylor, *op. cit.*, p. 135.

91 All MSS of *SHQ* concur in the division of the fifth and sixth generations contrary to the chain in Abot and *M. Hag.* 2.2. The impulse to charge Ibn Daud with a *lapsus calami* — owing to the aforementioned events where Joshua b. Peraḥyah and Simeon b. Shetaḥ are associated — is complicated by the statement of Gedaliah ibn Yaḥya, *Shalshelet ha-Qabbalah*, f. 24b, 25a, which implies that Ibn Yaḥya had mishnaic MSS which confirmed Ibn Daud's division. Cf. also Finkelstein, *Ha-Perushim ve-Anshe Keneset ha-Gedolah*, p. 41 n. 133, and below, p. 173.

95 For further literature, cf. L. Ginzberg, *Genizah Studies*, I, 324 f.; J. Klausner, *Jesus of Nazareth*, Eng. trans. (New York, 1925), pp. 47 f.; M. Goldstein, *Jesus in the Jewish Tradition* (New York, 1950), pp. 147 f.

99 The ultimate source of Ibn Daud's information for the Christian chronology was probably an Arabic work, which drew on the Coptic version of *Epistula Apostolorum*, which, in turn, states that Jesus was crucified in the days of Pilate and Archelaus; cf. E. Hennecke *New Testament Apocrypha*, I, Eng. tr. (Philadelphia, 1963), 189 f., and esp. p. 195. I am indebted to Professor E. Bickerman for this information.

100 MSS ח add the following gloss: "It appears that in the days of Hillel and Shammai there was another scholar by the name of Joshua b. Peraḥyah, who also went to Alexandria in Egypt, and Jesus went along with him. It is on that account that they [i.e., the Jewish and Gentile historians] differ." This interpolation contradicts the very thesis

which Ibn Daud maintains in the following sentence. Ibn Daud concedes that there was only one Jesus, but contends that the chronology of his life has been falsified by the Gentile historians out of polemical motives. Ibn Daud's view on the existence of but one Jesus, the student of Joshua b. Peraḥyah, is shared by his contemporary Judah ha-Levi, *Kitab al-Khazari*, III.65. For the later Jewish apologetic, which posited the existence of two Jesuses, first advanced by Jewish apologists of twelfth-thirteenth century France, cf. Loeb, *Joseph Haccohen*, pp. 86 f. — On the apparent contradiction of this thesis by the statement below, cf. notes to IV.127.

100–101 *Indicate the chronology... in several ways*: My translation is doubtful. I have preferred to take the verb and its cognate accusative in the classical Hebrew sense of the root סים, "to define, delimit, give a distinguishing mark to" (cf. talmudic dictionaries), rather than in the secondary sense of "to conclude," which makes little sense here. Though the same root is used by contemporaries of Ibn Daud in somewhat different senses (cf. Ginzberg, *Geonica*, II, 305 n. 4; *Ginze Kedem*, III [1925], 58 n. 2), none of these, as far as I can see, is appropriate here.

105–106 In medieval Christian folklore, Vespasian was widely regarded as God's instrument of revenge against the Jews. Thus, the renowned St. Severinus was said to be descended from Vespasian, while a French medieval poem was entitled, "Vespasian, or the revenge of Jesus on the Jews"; D. Comparetti, *Vergil in the Middle Ages* (Eng. trans., New York, 1929), pp. 314 f.

107 *Which did not distort*: Ibn Daud reaffirms the veracity of rabbinic tradition at this point, because the chronology of Jesus was one of the points of history which Christian polemicists charged the Jews with having deliberately suppressed and distorted; cf. Silver, *A History of Messianic Speculation in Israel*, p. 19 n. 61; Williams, *op. cit.*, pp. 33, 71, 76, 108, 225.

113–114 The manifest purposes of Ibn Daud's aside on the chronology of Jesus are to show that rabbinic tradition was in full control of the authentic data with respect to Jesus and that, consequently, there was obviously no connection between the crucifixion and the destruction of the Temple. This is one of Ibn Daud's efforts at "consolation," for the Christian polemic against the Jews rested largely on the appeal to empirical evidence that God had rejected and dispersed them in retribution for their crime of deicide. In the light of the Jewish chronology, the argument fell to pieces.

122 *Who died*: I cannot locate any earlier source for the statement that Menahem died in Hillel's lifetime. In fact, this statement, which obviously interprets the word יצא in *M. Ḥag.* 2.2, contradicts the explanations given in the Talmuds *ad loc*. It would appear that we have before us a mistaken interpretation of a post-talmudic interpretation of *double entendre*. In *B. Ḥag.* 16b, Abaye explains Menahem's departure as יצא לתרבות רעה, meaning that he left the fold, became an apostate. This could well be rendered by a later paraphrast as יצא מעולמו, which could easily be misunderstood to mean that he had died. Whether it was Ibn Daud or his source that misunderstood the paraphrase of the talmudic tradition, it is, of course, impossible to say. On the expression יצא מעולמו as synonyms for apostasy *and* death, cf. S. Lieberman, "Yaṣa le-'Olamo," *Ginze Kedem* V, (1934), 177 f., and esp. 178 n. 1. As an alternative explanation, I venture to suggest that Ibn Daud's source had an Arabic statement to this effect: וכאן צאחבה מנחם והלך סי איאם הלל. The author of this statement would thus have meant to summarize the talmudic disputes on the interpretation of יצא by utilizing the Arabic verb هلك in one of two senses: 1) "became corrupted"; 2) "went away, no one knew whither." (For these usages cf. Lane, *Arabic-English Lexicon*, I, 8,

p. 3044; Dozy, *Supplément aux Dictionnaires Arabes*, II, 761, where Christian-Arabic usage is cited for هلك in the sense of "to be damned.") The translator of the phrase (Ibn Daud?) understood هلك in its primary sense of "to perish" and rendered it accordingly in Hebrew.

126 *These three etc.*: Ibn Daud's genealogy of the Hillelides patently rests on a reading in *B*. Shab. as quoted by Samuel ha-Nagid (and cited by S.D. Sassoon, *Ohel David*, II, 1068a): דהא תניא הלל ושמאי (!) גמליאל ושמעון נהגו נשיאותן בפני הבית מאה שנה.

129 *Ruled supreme etc.*: This would be a violation of the provisions of *M*. Sanhed. 1.5; 2.4, which require consultation with the supreme Sanhedrin before the declaration of offensive war. It is probably for that reason that Ibn Daud stressed that this state of affairs obtained in the days of the *Second* Temple. His statement was doubtless based on the picture portrayed by *Josippon*, where the high court is not described as having played any role in affairs of state. It is also possible that Ibn Daud interpreted the law of *M*. Sanhed. as ideal law applying only to kings who were anointed legitimately, which, of course, was not the case with the monarchs of the Second Temple period. — The expression המוציא והמביא is taken from II Sam. 5.2; cf. also Num. 27.21 and Ps.-Jonathan *ad loc.*; Sifre Num. § 139 (ed. Horovitz), p. 135; *B*. Yoma 73b, where the biblical ideal is described.

134 Although the Talmud editions do not have "the Elder" (and MSS דלך have been corrected accordingly), Ibn Daud or, more probably, the source from which he copied, may well have had the word in his text of the Talmud; note the presence of וזקנים in the parallels, *Tosef.* Sanhed. 2.6 (ed. Zuckermandel), p. 416 and *Yer.* Sanhed. 1.2, f. 18d. — In any event, in contrast with the Bab. Talmud, which identifies the Gamaliel of this epistle with Rabban Gamaliel II of Jamnia, Ibn Daud correctly inferred that the patriarch named herein must be Rabban Gamaliel I, for he is the only one who could have issued rescripts from the Temple mount. Cf. D. Hoffmann, "Der oberste Gerichtshof in der Stadt des Heiligthums," *Jahres-Bericht des Rabbiner-Seminars fuer das orthodoxe Judenthum pro 5638* (Berlin, 1877–1878), p. 32 n. 1.

143 Besides the obvious evidence offered in the B. N., Ibn Daud could point to other more technical marks as evidence of the offices Rabban Gamaliel held. Thus "sitting before him" (line 133) is often used as a technical phrase denoting the rabbinic authority of the person *before whom* the others are seated; cf. Abot 5.15; *B*. Sanhed. 6b מנין לתלמיד שיושב לפני רבו; Ber. R. 34.15 (ed. Theodor-Albeck), p. 327, and so frequently. That he was nasi or patriarch is demonstrated by the talmudic prescription (*B*. Sanhed. 11a) that the year may not be intercalated without the approval of the nasi. The argument on the exclusive authority of the nasi in matters of calendation is stressed in the "Scroll of Ebiathar," (S . Schechter, *Saadyana* [Cambridge, 1903], pp. 92 line 22, 98 lines 10–11) and in the later account of the calendar dispute between R. Gamaliel II and the tannaim quoted from Rabbanite sources by Karaites (Pinsker, *Lickute Kadmoniot*, Appendix, p. 41 [bot.].) On the Rabbanite origin of this account, cf. H.J. Bornstein, "Dibray Yemay ha-'Ibbur ha-Aḥaronim," *Ha-Tequfa*, XIV–XV [1922], 359 f. and S. Lieberman, *Shkiin* [Jerusalem, 1939], p. 20). Ibn Daud may thus have drawn his story and conclusion from some collection like the *Baraitha de-Sod ha-'Ibbur*.

145 *Neither the king etc.*: This is probably a subtle allusion to *M*. Sanhed. 2.4, which forbids demurral against the king's right of eminent domain. For the same thought in the same context, cf. Ben Meir's letter to Babylonia, H.J. Bornstein, *Maḥloqet R. Saadia Gaon u-Ben Meir* (Warsaw, 1904), p. 51. — On medieval reference to obedience to law as proof of its excellence, cf. Wolfson, *Religious Philosophy*, pp. 218 f.

147–150 For the Karaite contention that the injunction of these verses was not followed in the days of the Second Temple, cf. Pinsker, *op. cit.*, p. 102.

151 *A magistrate of Israel*: There is just a chance that Ibn Daud uses the term "Israel" in this context in the sense of "faithful Jew." For this usage, cf. Hebrew text 66.337, 67.351, where "Israel" is used in contrast with heretics; in classical sources: *M*. Nid. 4.2; scholion to Meg. Ta'an. on 28th of Tebet (ed. Lichtenstein), pp. 342 f. [Is that not indeed the meaning of Israel in *M*. Sanhed. 10.1 as it now reads? Cf. L. Finkelstein, *Mabo le-Massektot Abot ve-Abot d'Rabbi Natan* (New York, 1950), p. 323.] Another related possibility is that Ibn Daud stresses that the judge must be an authoritative Jew, and not necessarily a priest, as Anan inferred from these verses; Harkavy, *Zikron la-Rishonim*, VIII, 15, 22. The whole passage is a polemic against the Karaites, to whom the Rabbanite method of calendation was one of the arch-examples of falsification of the Torah. Besides pointing to the Rabbanite abandonment of regulation of the calendar by observation of the new moon and the barley crop in the Holy Land, the Karaites never ceased taunting the Rabbanites with stories of intra-Rabbanite dissension on the calendar; cf. below, III. 12 f. It was on that account that Ibn Daud stressed the universal acknowledgment of the authority of Rabban Gamaliel — the Karaite *bête noire* on this question — and the scriptural basis for his authority. For the Karaite polemic, see the references to Pinsker, Bornstein and Lieberman in S.N. to line 143; cf. further A.S. Halkin, "Toledot Qiddush ha-Ḥodesh ba-'Adat ha-Qara'im," *Horeb*, II (1935), 87 f., 208 f.; Z. Ankori, "Some Aspects, etc.," *PAAJR*, XXIV (1955), 25 f., XXV (1956), 163 n. 95; *idem*, *Karaites in Byzantium*, Index, *s.v.* "Calculation, Calendar"; M. Zucker, "Shenay Qeṭa'im Neged Qara'iyyim," *PAAJR*, XVIII (1949), 20 f., 23 f., Kasher, *Torah Shelemah*, XIII, 6 f., 13 f.

154–163 I cannot find any earlier source for this account of Abba Siqra's negotiations with Vespasian. The story seems to be based on a confusion of pronouns either on the part of Ibn Daud or of an early transcriber of *SHQ*. The original probably read thus (with my own comments in brackets): הוא [= אבא סיקרא] יצא בלאט אליו [=] אל ריב״ז] ושאל [ריב״ז] ממנו שיצא [ריב״ז] אליו [=אספסינוס] ועשה [אבא סיקרא] בקשתו.
The author or translator, misunderstanding the pronouns, supplied proper nouns in the wrong places! Our reconstruction would make Ibn Daud's version (or source) agree perfectly with the classical rabbinic accounts.

Supplementary Notes to Chapter III

13 *Lydda*: Although the mishnaic source of this account does not record that the witnesses came to Lydda, Ibn Daud, or his sources, may have believed that that was where such witnesses would normally appear; cf. *M*. R.H. 1.6. Or, Ibn Daud may have believed that the Sanhedrin was located in Lydda; cf. *Tosef*. Pes. 3.11, 10.12 (ed. Lieberman), pp. 154, 198, and especially Yad. 2.16 (ed. Zuckermandel), p. 683 and Lieberman, *Tosefeth Rishonim*, IV, 157.18–19. A third possibility is that Ibn Daud had written that the witnesses came לביי״ד, which early in the process of transmission became corrupted by metathesis to בלוד. — In any event, Ibn Daud clearly did not draw his account from the Mishna, for apart from the insertion just discussed, in the latter it is not R. Joshua who disqualifies the witnesses but R. Dosa. What is more, the story in *SHQ* is truncated (cf. B.N. to line 15). It appears that we have another example (cf. S.N. to II. 154–163)

of a story copied from a later source which had the word קאל (Hebrew אמר) for the name of R. Dosa b. Horkinas, a substitution which is common enough in Arabic narrative. A later copyist or translator inserted the name of R. Joshua, in view of the role which he plays later in the story. Secondly, before the words "How can people testify etc." the epitomist had probably inserted an ellipsis, such as עד (cf. I.160; II. 136), which was omitted in the course of transmission, and the result is the story as it appears in the text before us.

15 *"When her belly etc."* MSS ח have corrected the reading to "if on the following day her belly etc." in accordance with *M. R.H.* 2.8. For the reading והרי, cf. Rabbinovicz, *Variae Lectiones*, IV (R.H.), 59 n. 30.

22 For the reading שנפרטה, cf. *B.* Ber. 27b (top) ופרטיה הוצא לשפתיה and the Hebrew translation of this passage cited by Ben Iehuda, *Thesaurus*, X, 5163a from *Halakot Pesuqot* (ed. Schlossberg), p. 10: והכנים ראשו ופרט שפתותיו... Cf. also Kohut, *Aruch Completum*, VI, 421, 423, *s.v.* פרט (1) and פרט (7).

25 Ibn Daud drew his conclusion on the exact nature of the removal of Rabban Gamaliel, and the corresponding appointment of R. Eleazar b. Azariah, from the form of the invitation extended to the latter (*B.* Ber. 27b): ניחא ליה למר דליהוי ריש מתיבתא. A similar distinction in *B.* Ket. 103b confirmed this conclusion; see below, line 103.

31 A totally distorted and much expanded version of the first incident is quoted by the Karaites Sahl b. Masliaḥ, in Pinsker, *Lickute Kadmoniot*, Appendix pp. 41 f., and Judah Hadassi, *Eshkol ha-Kofer*, par. 193-194, f. 77d. (In par. 192, f. 77c, Hadassi summarizes the talmudic version accurately. For an analysis of the "Karaite" version, cf. references at end of S.N. to II.143). The aforementioned Karaites and Qirqisani (*HUCA*, VII, 325 f.) single out this incident as the exclusive cause for the removal of Rabban Gamaliel from office, and represent the other rabbis as disputing his *method* of calendation. Accordingly, Rabbanite apologists were in no position to overlook the incident and the others which follow in *SHQ*. Thus, Sherira alludes to them twice (*ISG* 11.8 f., 75.9 f.), as does Judah ha-Levi, *Kitab al-Khazari* III.65. Ibn Daud felt constrained to give the stories at length, in view of his earlier claim that Rabbanite regulation of the calendar was accepted without question throughout Jewry; II. 130 f. The incidents related here prove his point. In the first place, the difference between R. Joshua and Rabban Gamaliel was not one of principle but of detail. Secondly, in the final analysis R. Joshua accepted Rabban Gamaliel's authority on all questions. Moreover, Rabban Gamaliel was not removed from office because of his procedures in calendation, but because of repeated personal provocation of R. Joshua. Finally, although the sages had supported R. Joshua's insurrection, they rejected his proposal to repeal his decisions, thereby demonstrating that personal grievances played no role in matters of law.

33 Although R. Akiba is not designated as a separate link in the earlier lists of tannaitic succession, such as *STW* and *ISG*, Ibn Daud, or his source, may have drawn the conclusion that he did occupy such a place, inasmuch as he is listed as a *parnas* (guardian) of Israel alongside Moses, Hillel and Rabban Johanan b. Zakkai; Sifre Deut. § 397 (ed. Finkelstein) p. 429. Now since, according to Ibn Daud, Rabban Johanan b. Zakkai succeeded Hillel as head of the academy (see B.N. to II. 153), the listing of R. Akiba in the same context as Hillel and Rabban Johanan meant that he succeeded to the same office. Moreover, R. Akiba is said to have regulated the calendar (*M.* Yeb. 16.7; *Tosef.* Sanhed. 2.8 [ed. Zuckermandel] p. 417; *B.* Ber. 63a), an activity which was the province of the nasi and head of the academy; cf. II. 143. Since R. Akiba did not hold the former office, he must have held the other post. In this connection it may be noted that Nissim

b. Jacob ibn Shahin, one of whose works was probably Ibn Daud's immediate source, calls R. Akiba by the same honorific with which Arabic speaking Jews referred to Moses, السيد المنير; cf. Obermann, *Studies in Islam and Judaism*: *The Arabic Original of Ibn Shahin's Book of Comfort*, p. 127, line 9 and the Hebrew tr., *Ḥibbur Yafeh me-ha-Yeshuʿa*, p. 72, and Hirschberg's remarks in n. 6 there.

34–36 The most cursory glance at *ISG* 11–12 will reveal the independence of Ibn Daud's list from that of Sherira. Ibn Daud's list of colleagues of R. Akiba is made up of two components: The first consists of the three scholars who along with R. Akiba entered "the orchard" (*B. Ḥag.* 14b); the second portion, beginning with the name of R. Tarfon, is apparently taken from a list of "the ten martyrs" who died in the Hadrianic persecutions; see below, lines 53–63. The list most nearly akin to the one in *SHQ* is that of Joseph ibn Abitur (S. Bernstein, "Seliḥot Bilti Yeduʿot le-R. Joseph ibn Abitur," *Sura*, I [1953–54], 30–36), who lists the following nine: Simeon b. Gamaliel, Ishmael, Akiba, Judah, Yeshebab, Tarfon, Eleazar b. Dema, Hananiah, Ḥuspith. A variant substitutes Simeon for Tarfon, while the name of Eleazar b. Shammua, which is found in all other medieval lists, was probably omitted from Ibn Abitur's poem by scribal error. R. Simai's name, for which there is no earlier source to my knowledge, is probably a substitute for Simeon b. Gamaliel, while Eleazar b. Dema's name appears in *SHQ* as Judah b. Tema; see next note. On the older lists of these martyrs, cf. L. Finkelstein, "The Ten Martyrs," *Essays and Studies in Memory of Linda R. Miller*, pp. 29–55.

35 *Known as Ben Dama*: The identification of Ben Tema with Ben Dama is explicable in light of the form בן דימא (Ben Dima or Ben Dema) preserved in Ibn Abitur's list (see previous note) and in a MS of *Yalquṭ Shimʿoni* cited by Rabbinovicz, *Variae Lectiones*, X(A.Z.), 66 n. 300; cf. also the variants to b. Tema in *STW*, p. 20 par. 29 n. 3. The difficulty with Ibn Daud's identification is that Babylonian-Spanish traditions record the name as Eleazar b. Dema (or Dama), as in *Tosef. Ḥul.* 2.22 (ed. Zuckermandel), p. 503, and *Yer. Shab.* 14.4, f. 14d. The name appears in this form in *Siddur R. Saadja Gaon*, p. 329 line 32; Joseph ibn Abitur, *loc. cit.*; Beḥayye b. Asher, *Midrash R. Beḥayye ʿal ha-Torah* (New York, 1948), p. 138 (where Eliezer should be corrected to Eleazar); Bernstein, *ʿAl Naharot Sefarad*, pp. 263 f. (where Spanish usage has altered the Provençal version of the text printed on p. 169, lines 98–101). Cf. also Jellinek, *Bet ha-Midrash*, VI, 20, 30 and similarly *Bet Ab, Seder Ḥamesh Taʿaniyyot ke-Minhag Q.Q. Sefardim* (Leghorn, 1877), f. 114a–120b. The name *Judah b. Dama*, on the other hand, points to Franco-German provenience; cf. Judah b. Kalonymos, *Sefer Yiḥusay Tannaim wa-Amoraim* (MS Jewish Theological Seminary of America, no. 0925), *s.v.* ר׳ יהודה בן דמא where the author states: ר׳ יהודה בן דמא הוא שהיה מעשרה אבירי ישר׳ שנהרגו על ידי לופינוס הרשע שחיק עצמות כמו שכתבתי בסדר בן דמא שנהרג על מצות תפילין *Midrash Eleh Ezkerah* published by Jellinek, *op. cit.*, II, 66, 69, and the *piyyut* for the Day of Atonement, "Eleh Ezkerah" (for references cf. Davidson, *Thesaurus of Medieval Hebrew Poetry*, I, 196 no. 4273). The version of the Midrash published by Loewinger in *Emiek-konyu Dr. Kiss Arnold*, Hebrew Section pp. 40–41 is almost certainly of Franco-German origin, as indicated by the form of the story of "Hannah and her seven sons" appended to it; cf. Cohen, "The Story of Hannah and Her Seven Sons in Hebrew Literature," pp. 118 f. Zacuto, pp. 42a, 67b, records both traditions, stating that one of the ten martyrs was Judah b. Tema, while others state (ויש אמרים) that it was actually Eleazar b. Dama. The most likely explanation of the names given in *SHQ*, it appears to me, is that Ibn Daud knew of the "Ben Dema" (from *B. A.Z.* 27b or some elegy), whom he proceeded to equate with Judah b. Tema.

40-52 On the ten martyrs, see S.N. to lines 34-36. — This bizarre account of the Bar Kokba uprising has no precedent in Hebrew literature, or for that matter, in any other known early tradition on the revolt. Since the names of Koziba and his successors do appear in *Kitab at-Ta'rikh* in *MJC*, II, 109, there is a remote possibility that Ibn Daud drew on some Saadyanic source, which he embroidered with his own synchronizations. On the other hand, in view of the fact that no other Jewish author indicates any awareness of these details, it appears much more plausible to assume that the names of Bar Kokba's son and grandson were interpolated into *Kitab at-Ta'rikh* on the authority of *SHQ*. In the Analysis, ch. IV, I have tried to show that every one of the details in this story derives from earlier traditions either of the Bar Kokba episode or of Jewish eschatological literature, which Ibn Daud proceeded to weave into a highly original tapestry in order to explain the failure of the pseudo-Messiah Koziba. For a discussion of later authors who appropriated this account and amplified it, cf. S. Yeivin, *Milḥamot Bar Kokba* (Jerusalem, 1946), pp. 168 f. For a modern but quite unconvincing effort to vindicate Ibn Daud's version of this episode, cf. S. Krauss, "Ḥayyalotav shel Bar Kokba," *Alexander Marx Jubilee Volume*, Hebrew Section, pp. 398 f.

44 Ibn Daud's chronology of the revolt patently derives from a source which is reflected in the text of the editions of Seder 'Olam 30 (cf. also *B*. Sanhed. 93b, 97b), which reads: ומלחמת בן כוזיבא ב' שנים ומחצה נ״ב שנה אחר חרבן הבית where the ב' was read as כ', and which may be translated: "The war of Ben Koziba, which lasted twenty and a half years, began fifty-two years after the destruction of the Temple," thus setting the end of the war in the seventy-third year after the destruction. For an objection to Ibn Daud's interpretation, see Zacuto, pp. 33a, 83a.

54 For the source of this list, see S.N. to lines 34-36. However, I am at a loss to explain why Ibn Daud did not include the names of all the martyrs of this generation, particularly since he does not indicate the circumstances surrounding the martyrdom of each. That Ibn Daud's list is independent of such earlier lists as Midrash Ekah to 2.2 (in ed. Buber, p. 100); Midrash Tehillim 9.13 (ed. Buber), p. 89; *ISG* 13.3, 16.2, is obvious at once. On the other hand, the list of five martyrs in Zacuto, p. 38a, is clearly drawn from *SHQ*.

65-68 Cf. E.N. Adler, "An Eleventh Century Introduction to the Hebrew Bible," *JQR*, IX (1897), 702; A.E. Cowley, "Bodleian Geniza Fragments," *JQR*, XVIII (1906), 405; "Abraham ibn Ezra's Shorter Commentary on Daniel," (ed. H.J. Matthews) *Miscellany of Hebrew Literature*, II (1877), 13; Ibn Ezra to Dan. 11.33; Zacuto, p. 67b.

73-76 The similarity of Ibn Daud's wording to that of *STW* 12. 2-4, makes some connection between the two passages a virtual certainty. Although Kahan, *ibid.*, German section, p. 36, makes no reference to *SHQ*, it is at least possible that the gloss in *STW* should be traced back to this passage.

81 This interpretation of Dan. 11.34 was probably given in Jewish schools, for Jerome in his commentary on Daniel indicates that the Jews of his day applied the verse to the reigns of Severus and Antoninus; cf. Krauss, *Antoninus und Rabbi*, p. 67.

83 *It is said*: Since Ibn Daud prefaces his information with "It is said" (cf. I. 74), he clearly did not know of the talmudic source for this report. For the reasons suggesting that Ibn Daud's source was Nissim b. Jacob ibn Shahin's *Sefer Seder Meqabbelay ha-Torah*, see below, pp. 174 ff. For an analysis of the complex of rabbinic legends on the intimate relationship between Antoninus and Judah the Patriarch, cf. Krauss' work referred to in the previous note.

87 *Honored and revered*: Or, honored and advanced him; cf. Est. 3.1. This is one of Ibn

SUPPLEMENTARY NOTES 121

Daud's favorite expressions; cf. II.9, 159; V.40; VII.338, 341, 374, 384–385 [Heb. text 10.5–6; 17.106; 34.29; 59.226, 227; 61.250, 257]. In Ch. VII, I have translated "honored and provided for him," for in VII.318–319 [Heb. text 58. 211–212], the verb. נשאו is clearly used in that sense (cf. Ezra 1.4), and that thought best suits the context of those passages; cf. Jawitz, *Toledot Israel*, IX (2nd. ed.), 19 n.l. It may be that that is what Ibn Daud intended here as well, with an eye on the legend reported in *B.* A.Z. 10b.

95 *Composed the Mishna*: Although Ibn Daud uses a neutral term here, חבר, elsewhere he seems to indicate that in his view the Mishna was committed to writing; cf. V.8. For discussions of other medieval views on this question, cf. Epstein, *Mabo le-Nusaḥ ha-Mishna*, II, 693; Lieberman, *Hellenism in Jewish Palestine*, p. 84.

103 It should be noted that Ibn Daud abruptly drops the subject of the patriarchate, although the succession to Judah the Patriarch is mentioned in the Talmud and although Ibn Daud himself earlier listed the successors to that office. Ibn Daud thereby indicates that he is interested exclusively in the history of the rabbinate. His interest in the succession of the patriarchate was confined to the period when the patriarchs also served as heads of the academy.

104–105 MSS פק and Zacuto lack the word "four" and accordingly attribute to Ibn Daud the view that Judah had five sons: the four mentioned in the text and R. Ḥiyya Beribbi.

107 In view of the close relationship between *SHQ* and *ISG*, it should be noted that the question of the community of Qairawan in the latter epistle is predicated on the assumption that R. Ḥiyya is the compiler of the Tosefta; cf. *ISG* 6.8 f.; 31.1 f.; 39.17 (on Bar Qappara). It appears fairly clear that the tradition of Menahem b. Solomon Meiri, *Bet ha-Beḥira... 'al-Abot*, f. 14b, is drawn from *SHQ*.

Supplementary Notes to Chapter IV

7 *Matha Meḥasia*: On the identification of this place with Sura, cf. *ISG* 79.12 and Lewin's note 4 there; *JE*, VIII, 374; Ginzberg, *Geonica*, I, 42 n.; Mann, *Texts and Studies*, I, 70 n. 16. — I have adopted the more popular vocalization, although the form "Maḥseyya" is defended cogently by M. Auerbach, "Die Streit zwischen Saadja Gaon und den Exilarchen David ben Sakkai," *Juedische Studien Joseph Wohlgemut... gewidmet*, p. 8 n. 18.

9 *STW* and *ISG* ("French" recension) report that Samuel died in תקס״ה, 565 Sel. Era [= 4014 A.M.]. The 565 could easily have been corrupted to, or misread as, 561 in Ibn Daud's source, ה and א often being indistinguishable in Sefardic cursive script. If Ibn Daud had a date for the death of Samuel only, coupled with a note that this occurred seven years after the death of Rab, it would account for the disagreement between *SHQ* and the earlier sources on the dates of their deaths, and at the same time for the agreement between all the sources on the relative chronologies of Rab and Samuel.

10 For the earlier meaning of "Greek wisdom," cf. Lieberman, *Greek in Jewish Palestine*, pp. 1 f.

11–12 No matter how one manipulates the MSS, some mistake is evident either in scribal transmission or in Ibn Daud's identification. The simplest, most traditionally correct, and accordingly most suspect transcription is that of MS ד, which reads: רב יהודה ורמי בר יחזקאל. On the other hand, the better family of MSS (= ש) attest the readings רמי בר חמא and בני יחזקאל. Moreover, the ת recension (with the exception of the aforementioned MS ד) corroborates the evidence of MSS אפק that a רב חמא is to be included among בני יחזקאל. This leads to the bizarre conclusion that Ibn Daud (or his scribal transmitters) made Rami b. Ḥama and R. Ḥama, both of whom are of a later period, the brothers of R. Judah! Zacuto, p. 199a, summarizes this line by saying that R. Ezekiel had three sons: R. Judah, Rami and R. Ḥama. Our text obviously contains a confusion of names, for in the first instance Rami b. Ḥama is not Rami b. Ezekiel, and secondly no R. Ḥama b. Ezekiel is otherwise known! Our text and translation are, therefore, open to serious question. Cf. also below, line 41.

13 *Blind*: This characteristic is noted again below, VI. 42. Although in the case of R. Jehudai the subject of blindness was raised in connection with the reliability of statements ascribed to the latter — see note *ad loc.* — in the case of R. Sheshet no such explanation would apply. It may be that Ibn Daud mentioned this handicap simply because of its renown in this case, or because R. Sheshet's devotion to Torah was all the more singular in view of his condition; cf. the statement of R. Sheshet in *B.* Pes. 68b and the sentiments on the devotion of the blind in *Seder Eliahu* 19, p. 110. On the other hand, in medieval histories of the learned, this handicap was often noted, as it had been in classical times, in view of the difficulties suffered by the blind and the singularity of their achievement in overcoming them; cf. A. Esser, *Das Antlitz der Blindheit in der Antike* (Leiden, 1961), pp. 96 f., 104 f.: Pérès, *La Poésie Andalouse*, p. 56.

18 MSS ח add the following gloss: "He composed the Jerusalemite [= Palestinian] Talmud for five orders [of the Mishna], of the [sixth] order of Teharot there being but the tractate of Nidda. The Jerusalemite [Talmud] was composed approximately two hundred years after the destruction [of the Temple]." It is not clear whether Zacuto, p. 199b, had this statement in his text of *SHQ* or knew it from another source. — As for the statement itself, cf. Hamburger, *Maimonides' Einleitung in die Misna*, p. 58 [= *Mishna 'im Payrush R. Moses b. Maimon*, ed. Kafih. Jerusalem, 1963. I, 46]; Maimonides, Introduction to *Mishneh Torah*. If Maimonides' two statements were the ones which inspired the glossator — and the similarity of wording strongly suggests that they did — Maimonides' date of three hundred years was corrected to two hundred as a result of combining Ibn Daud's date for the composition of the Mishna with the length of R. Johanan's activity. On the "five" orders of the Palestinian Talmud, cf. Frankel, *Introductio in Talmud Hierosolymitanum*, f. 47b.

22 *In Nehardea*: Ibn Daud's error in this case, as in others noted below, is easily explained on the assumption that Ibn Daud's source listed the heads of academies in parallel columns. Inasmuch as R. Judah's name stood directly beneath that of Samuel, Ibn Daud assumed that he served as head in the same place. The name of R. Naḥman, who took over as head of Nehardea after Samuel's death, was probably omitted in Ibn Daud's source (as it is in *STW*, p. 4) because of the destruction of Nehardea in 259–260, after which the main body of the academy repaired to Pumbeditha; cf. *ISG* 82.9 f.

25 Here again (cf. previous note) the confusion is directly traceable to columns composed on the basis of *ISG* 86.11–15, where it is stated that, after R. Judah's death, R. Huna b. Ḥiyya presided over Pumbeditha. It should be noted that MS פ of *ISG* 86.14 (n. 25) omits "bar Ḥiyya." Ibn Daud's source looked something like this:

Sura	Nehardea
Rab	Samuel
R. Huna	R. Judah
	R. Huna

R. Ḥisda — who established a school etc. (cf. below, lines 33–35)

Ibn Daud or his source identified the two Hunas and concluded that R. Huna outlived

R. Judah. These columns also explain the error with regard to the succession of R. Ḥisda; cf. *ibid.*

37 *Twenty-two years*: MSS ח add: "He composed Bereshit Rabbah and the other [Midrash] Rabbahs." Although this is the earliest known source for this theory (cf. Albeck, *Einleitung und Register zum Bereshit Rabbah*, p. 94), it would appear that the gloss was not yet known to Israeli, Meiri or Zacuto. The statement in Joseph ibn Zaddik, *MJC*, I, 90 (bot.) should be emended to read רב חבר הרבות, as shown by the context there; cf. also Zacuto, p. 98b.

70 *He began to commit etc.*: However, Ibn Daud does not share Ibn Shahin's view on the one responsible for the final redaction of the Talmud; cf. V. 4–6. — To the statement in the text, MSS ח add: "but was unable to complete it." Cf. next note.

72 *Colleagues*: MSS ח add the following gloss: "They completed the Babylonian Talmud, which was sealed in 4265 A.M. It was disseminated throughout all Jewry, who have accepted its authority. The scholars of every generation have taught it publicly, and all Jewry have given their assent to its teachings. Nothing may be added to it, nor anything taken away from it [Eccles. 3.14]. The Talmud was sealed in the days of Rabbah bar R. Joseph, who was head of the academy of the saboraim. Thus, approximately eighty years elapsed from the time that R. Ashi began to compile it until the time that it was sealed in the seventy-third year after his death." Although the last part of the statement is lifted almost bodily from V.6, the date of compilation contradicts the one given there. Moreover, the name of the sabora was not Rabbah bar R. Joseph but Rabbah Jose; cf. V. 2 f. On the acceptance of the Talmud by the consensus of all Israel and the prohibition against adding to it or subtracting from it, cf. *ISG* 7.4; 30.10–21 and *ibid.*, addenda, pp. XI–XII [= B.M. Lewin, *Otzar ha-Geonim*, VIII, Responsa p. 188]; Yesh'uah b. Joseph ha-Levi, *Halikot 'Olam* (Lisbon? 1490?), end of ch. I.

77 *Tabyomi*: For a discussion on the origin of this epithet with regard to Mar b. R. Ashi, cf. Rapoport, *Erech Millin*, *s.v.* איזדגר, pp. 37 f. However, Rapoport's conjecture, *ibid.*, p. 40, that Ibn Daud could not have had the story about Tabyomi in *B.* B.B. 12b in his text of the Talmud, is totally unwarranted, in view of what we know about Ibn Daud's use of sources. It makes little difference whether Ibn Daud's MS of the Talmud had that story or not, for Ibn Daud probably did not refer directly to the Talmud but relied on his post-talmudic sources and added his own (?) interpretations. It should be noted, too, that Ibn Daud was apparently unaware of the persecutions reported in *ISG* 94.13 f., so that Rapoport's conjecture that Ibn Daud explained the name this way because Tabyomi escaped most of these persecutions is equally invalid.

80 *Like Meremar etc.*: Hyman, *op. cit.*, p. 908, *s.v.* Meremar, cites in evidence of this statement the report in *B.* Ber. 30a, according to which R. Ashi is asked why he does not follow the practice of Meremar. However, it is highly doubtful that this is Ibn Daud's source; cf. the well-taken objections of S. Albeck, "Sof ha-Hora'ah wa-Aḥronay ha-Amoraim," *Sinai*, *Sefer Yobel*, p. 67. For Idi, there is no evidence whatever, as far as I am aware.

93–94 *Its diameter... 120 cubits*: Professor Morris Ettenberg, to whom I am indebted for help in explaining this passage, suggests that Ibn Daud provided two dimensions of a rotund figure in order to convey the idea that the monument was shaped as an ellipse. This explanation is supported by the parallel description of Master Gregory of Canterbury (see B.N.), which likewise reflects the difficulty in describing the dimensions of the monument. I have adopted the reading of MS פ, which is the only one that makes sense. The text of MSS אך is obviously truncated and represents a mathematical absurdity, while the remaining MSS reflect a learned correction that would convert the ellipse into a circle: $2\pi x = 150$.

105 Ibn Daud combined the tradition of *B. A.Z.* 8b, according to which one of the instances of Roman seizure of power occurred in the days of "the Greeks," with the popular notion, reported in Ps.-Callisthenes, that the Romans paid tribute to Alexander; cf. A. Ausfeld, *Der Griechische Alexanderroman* (Leipzig, 1907), I:29, pp. 44 f.; R. Merkelbach, *Die Quellen des Griechischen Alexanderromans* (Munich, 1954), pp. 7 f., 24 f. The Romans had to pay tribute to these world empires in view of Jer. 27.7 and the rabbinic notion that he who rules Israel rules the world; Mekhilta de R. Ishmael, *Beshallaḥ* 2 (ed. Lauterbach), I, 196 f.

111–115 For references to the earlier literature and sources of this etymology, cf. A.S. von Stauffenberg, *Die Roemische Kaisergeschichte bei Malalas* (Stuttgart, 1931), pp. 1, 82 f. Cf. also J. Perles, "Die Berner Handschrift des kleinen Aruch," *Jubelschrift... H. Graetz* (Breslau, 1887), p. 1. The marginal gloss cited there is patently influenced by the story told below, lines 152 f.

116–119 *Extended, branching out*: For this translation, cf. Saadiah on Lam. 1.14 in I. Ratzabi, "The Translation of Lamentations by R. Saadya Gaon," *Tarbiz*, XIII (1941–1942), 96; Jonah ibn Janaḥ, *Sefer ha-Schoraschim* (trans. Bacher), p. 535. — The reading of the editions ד is a correction influenced by Lam. 1.14. — The details on the spits are not found in any of the sources known to me. According to Latin traditions, the obelisk rested on four bronze lions, while Graf cites Abulfeda to the effect that the monument rested on four bronze squares.

125 On the use of the *era* in documents, cf. Pauly-Wissowa, *Real-Encyclopaedie der Classischen Altertumswissenschaft*, I, *s.v.* Aera, pp. 611 (par. IV), 630 (par. XXIX). For documents of Ibn Daud's day, cf. A. Gonzalez Palencia, *Los Mozarabes de Toledo en los Siglos XII y XIII* (4 vols., Madrid 1926–1930); *idem*, "Vento por Deudas en Toledo a fino del Siglo XII," *Al-Andalus*, III (1935), 43–56; Baer, *Die Juden im Christlichen Spanien*, passim. For references to the *era* in Jewish literature, cf. Bornstein, "Ta'arikay Israel," *Ha-Tequfa*, IX, 261.

129 *So they say*: Cf. line 120. The words מלך מלכות פושטת בכל העולם are reminiscent of Rab's statement in *B.* Yoma 10a: אין בן דוד בא עד שתפשוט מלכות הרשעה תשעה חדשים על כל העולם כולו (cited acc. to Rabbinovicz, *Variae Lectiones*, IV, Yoma, p. 22 n. 7). However, the cognate accusative in *SHQ* מלכות פושטת does not appear to be an authentic Hebrew form. Moreover, the words "as they say" indicate an expression of some sort. If Ibn Daud's source stated (ملك ماسكا بسيطا) باسطا the Hebrew מלכות פושטת would be a translation by a similarly sounding word, a phenomenon which is common enough in medieval Hebrew usage. The Arabic term signifies absolute world dominion. In any event, the assumption of an Arabic substratum would account for the ostensible repetition of what has already been stated in lines 120–121. Whereas earlier Ibn Daud described the extent of his dominion, in this instance he was citing a quip. — The relationship of this whole account of Augustus' reign to the one in the Arabic Ps.-Orosius has been noted by Levi della Vida, "The Bronze Era," pp. 187 f., and "La Traduzione Araba etc.," pp. 290, 292; cf. esp. the passage cited by Levi della Vida, *ibid.*, pp. 271–273 and 273–275 n. 3. However, the variations in Ibn Daud, on the extent of Augustus' reign and the date of Jesus' nativity, make it probable, as Levi della Vida has himself suggested, that Ibn Daud drew not from Ps.-Orosius, but from a third source which both authors used.

132–133 *The yoke of the Romans*: Ibn Daud reflects the Sassanid-Arabic conception of the

Arsacids and regional princes of Persia as arms of Alexander's imperial policy; cf. Thaʿalibi, *Histoire des Rois des Perses* (ed. and tr. Zotenberg), pp. 415 f.; I. Friedlaender, *Die Chadhirlegende und der Alexanderroman* (Berlin, 1913), pp. 282, 292 f. Alexander was called "the Roman" in Persian literature; cf. Th. Noeldeke, "Geschichte des Artaschir i Papakan," *Beitraege zur Kunde der Indogermanischen Sprachen*, IV (1878), 36, 56.

136 *Ardashir*: Heb. Azdashir. I have adopted this reading, for it is the one closest to the Arabic spelling which Ibn Daud had before him, the difference between "r" and "z" in Arabic script being only a dot above the letter. *He wrote*: I do not know of any source for this communication to the Persians. What is reported in the Persian and Arabic accounts is Ardashir's written appeal to the kings of Persia to unite with him in overthrowing Ardawan; cf. Thaʿalibi, *op. cit.*, pp. 479, 481.

137 *Five hundred years*: Although the better attested figure in Persian-Arabic tradition is 523, the figure 500 is also given in some MSS of Tabari, *Chronique* (trans. Zotenberg), I, 525, 528; but cf. variants on p. 591 and II, 66. For 523, see Tabari, *Annales* (ed. de Goeje et al.) II, 713; idem, *Geschichte* (trans. Noeldeke), p. 1.

138 *The sword of Aristotle*: That such a "sword" was referred to seems possible in view of the symbols which purportedly figured in Ardashir's conquests; cf. Noeldeke, "Geschichte des Artaschir i Papakan," pp. 44 f., on "the Ram" and the majesty of the Kajanites. On the other hand, the expression may refer to wisdom or specifically to magical spells and powers which Aristotle had taught his pupil; cf. the mystical "Sword of Moses" revealing the powers inherent in uses of the divine names published by M. Gaster, *Studies and Texts*, I, 288 f., III, 69 f. Cf. also Zunz, *Ha-Derashot be-Yisrael*, p. 334 n. 70.

145 The source of this identification is probably to be found in the "Septuagintal" translations of the names of the kings of Persia recorded in Scripture. While the Hebrew Artaḥshast was always rendered in Greek as "Arthasastha," the name Ahasuerus was rendered in the *translation of Esther* as "Artaxerxes." Now, the latter and very similar forms were the ones used by Greek and Roman chroniclers as the equivalent for the later Artakhshast whom the Arabs called Ardashir; cf. Noeldeke, "Geschichte des Artaschir i Papakan," p. 35 n. 1. Hence, Artakhshast-Artaxerxes became Ardashir-Ahasuerus.

152–157 Ibn Daud doubtless incorporated this story as a further illustration of the symmetry of Persian and Roman history. As Rome enjoyed monarchy twice, so did Persia. As Rome had a great monarch who was miraculously extracted from his mother's womb, so did the Persians have a monarch who was crowned while yet *in foetu*. Cf. also the gloss published by Perles, referred to in S.N. to lines 111–115, which indicates that that was how some readers understood the story told here.

161–164 *Huna Mar*: The MSS of *ISG* 96.16–97.1 reflect the error of Ibn Daud's source. Actually, Huna Mar was the son of the exilarch, Mar Zutra; cf. *ibid*. 97.4 and Assaf, *Tequfat ha-Geonim*, p. 28.

164 *4234*: In *ISG* 96.15, Ibn Daud's source probably read תשמ״ה for תשמ״א. Cf. S.N. to line 9; *STW*, p. 6 n. 131.

165 The most plausible explanation of Ibn Daud's date for the death of Rabina is the one proposed by Albeck, "Sof ha-Horaʾah etc.," p. 62, namely, that in Ibn Daud's source the תתי״א [= 811 Sel. Era = 4260 A.M.] became corrupted to ההיא, leading to the conclusion that Rabina rose to leadership in the very same year as the events just described.

167-169 Although the date in *SHQ* coincides with that of *ISG*, I fail to see how Ibn Daud knew that R. Gebihah began his term after the death of R. Ashi.
170 For the variant form of his name, Neḥumi, reported in MSS אפק, cf. *ISG* 70, "French" recension variant 4; p. 96, "Spanish" recension variant 4; p. 98, "Spanish" recension variant 8; Ginzberg, *Geonica*, I, 5 n. 1.

Supplementary Notes to Chapter V

4 *Thirty-eight years, until 4274*: Ibn Daud's dates are traceable to *ISG* 98.2-4, where R Sama b. Judah is said to have died in 815 Sel. Era = 4264 A.M. This name was apparently omitted in Ibn Daud's source, but the date of his death was registered next to his predecessor's name as 825 the תתי״ה of *ISG* being corrupted into תתכ״ה = 4274 A.M.
13-14 *R. Aḥai*: Ibn Daud's chronology is based on the fact that only one year is credited to R. Aḥai in *ISG*, and Ibn Daud merely added this item to the date of Rabbah Jose's death.
20 *Also included*: These two words must be supplied if any sense is to be made of the text. That the text puzzled the copyists is apparent from the variants. The reading we have adopted is supported by Zacuto, p. 204a (bot.).
25-26 *R. Mari, R. Huna, R. Ḥanina, and R. Ḥinena, respectively*: *ISG* lists these men not as succeeding each other but as partly contemporaneous heads of the two academies. Once again (cf. S.N. to IV.25), Ibn Daud's divergence from *ISG* is best explained on the assumption that his source had the names of these men listed in columns, which Ibn Daud took to mean "succeeded each other." *SHQ* diverges in a number of other minor details on the names of these men. Thus, the name of the authority was not Huna, but Mar Rab Mar b. R. Huna. *SHQ* also omits the name of a Mar R. Huna who succeeded R. Ḥinena.
35 *Then Umar*: For this reading, cf. Tyckoczynski (reference in next note), pp. 158, 167.
36-37 For a thorough study of the various versions of this story, cf. H. Tyckoczynski, "Bustanai Rosh ha-Golah," *Debir*, I (1923), 145-179; on Ibn Daud's account, pp. 158 f. Tyckoczynski concludes that Ibn Daud's version goes back to an exilarchic source of the eighth century, which defended the legitimacy of the Bustanaides, but which Ibn Daud, or his source, misunderstood when he called the princess the daughter of Yezdegerd rather than of Khosrau (Chosroes).
38 *King of the Arabs*: For this title, cf. the "Continuatio Byzantia Arabica" [completing the Chronicle of Isidore of Seville] in *Monumenta Germaniae Historica*, XI, 337 f. where Muhammad is styled "princeps" of the Arabs. Ibn Daud may thus have utilized a Mozarabic source. *4374*: This is not Ibn Daud's date for the beginning of Muslim chronology, as Loeb, *Joseph Haccohen*, p. 98, thought. Ibn Daud indicates the correct date in no uncertain terms, above, line 5. For other Jewish traditions on the date of Muhammad's first proclamations, cf. M. Steinschneider, *Polemische und Apologetische Literatur in Arabischer Sprache* (Leipzig, 1877), pp. 305 f.

Supplementary Notes to Chapter VI

12-13 *Began to serve*: I have supplied these words on the basis of *ISG* 102.8. Ibn Daud was understood this way by Samuel ha-Nagid, MS Sassoon, p. 62, where the passage is transmitted thus: הגאונים שהיו בסוריא והיא מתא מחסיא משנת דתמ״ט שבו התחילו בגאונות

תחלתן רב הונא בר יוסף הוקם לראש שנת דתמ״ט. However, it is by no means certain that Ibn Daud understood his source this way; cf. B.N. to line 16.

18–19 For the various theories on the meaning of the name Qayyara, cf. S. Assaf, *Responsa Geonica* [in Hebrew] (Jerusalem, 1942), pp. 38 f.; idem, *Tequfat ha-Geonim*, p. 169, Assaf accepts the suggestion of Epstein, *Kitbay R. Abraham Epstein*, II, 379 n. 2, that the term denotes a dealer in wax. — Most modern scholars have rejected Ibn Daud's assertion that R. Simeon Qayyara preceded R. Jehudai Gaon (cf. below, lines 40–42), for *Halakot Gedolot* displays extensive use of R. Jehudai's work; cf. the literature listed at the beginning of this note and in B.N. to lines 19, 21–22; Mirsky's introduction to *Sheeltot de Rab Aḥai Gaon*, I, 12 f. On the other hand, Ibn Daud's date for Simeon Qayyara's work is not devoid of attestation. In the survey of tradition in the commentary of Nathan Ab ha-Yeshiba, Simeon Qayyara is listed *after* Jehudai, but the compilation of *Halakot Gedolot* is dated 1054 Seleucid Era [= 4502 A.M.]; cf. Assaf, *Tequfat ha-Geonim*, pp. 297 f., and Assaf's n. 14 there, where it is suggested that Ibn Daud and R. Nathan drew from a common source. (I am indebted to Professor S. Abramson for calling my attention to this point.) — Although *ISG* does not mention *Halakot Gedolot* or its author, Ginzberg, *Geonica*, I, 76 f., has made the plausible suggestion that the insertion of the datum on R. Simeon Qayyara at this point in *SHQ* is traceable to *ISG* 103.6–7, where the unusual name R. Samuel bar Rab Mar de-Iqri became corrupted into a statement that in the days of this R. Samuel there lived Mar [Simeon] Qayyara. In any event, the special mention of the work in *SHQ* should occasion no surprise in view of the great popularity of the work, not only as a standard reference work among legal authorities, but also as a school-text for advanced students; cf. Mann, *Jews in Egypt and in Palestine*, I, 119; S.D. Goitein, *Jewish Education in Muslim Countries* [in Hebrew] (Jerusalem, 1962), p. 153 n. 195.

22 *We have no knowledge etc.*: This may be Ibn Daud's guarded way of saying that he is not certain of the authenticity of these passages or of the date he has given for its publication; cf. F. Rosenthal, *The Technique and Approach of Muslim Scholarship* (= *Analecta Orientalia*, 24. Rome, 1947), p. 47 col. b.

27–29 *This book... was examined... not a single error etc.*: This may be a stock stylistic genre; cf. Benjamin of Tudela, *Itinerary* (ed. Adler), Hebrew p. 2, trans. p. 2. On the other hand, Ibn Daud's remark may also be an oblique retort to those who claimed that the work did manifest errors; cf. M. Margaliot, *Hilkhot Hannagid* (Jerusalem, 1962), p. 17 n. 28.

33–34 *R. Natronai*: Although *ISG* does not give any chronological data on R. Natronai, Ibn Daud's statement can be traced to *ISG* 104.1, where R. "Durai" (cf. below, line 63) is said to have become gaon in 4521. Since Ibn Daud's source omitted R. Abraham Kahana of *ISG* 103.14–15, it credited R. Natronai with the years between the death of R. Samuel b. Mari (above, line 17) and the ascension of R. "Durai."

38 *Ada*: The reading is attested by Zacuto, p. 205, and Samuel ha-Nagid, MS Sassoon, p. 60. The reading of MS א here is patently a learned correction; cf. also S. Poznanski, *Studien zum Gaonaeischen Epoche*, p. 51.

42 *He was blind*: R. Jehudai's blindness was a *cause célèbre* in view of the problem of the authenticity of statements ascribed to him; cf. Margaliot, *Hilkhot Hannagid*, p. 17; Mirsky, *Sheeltot*, I, 14. Cf. also above, IV.13 and S.N. there.

43 On the Rabbanite practice of cursing Anan and Saul as one, cf. the fanciful popular exegesis of Job 7.9 discussed by N. Ben-Menahem, "Aggadot ʿAm ʿal R. Abraham ibn Ezra," *Minḥah li-huda*, p. 156; Zucker, "Against Whom did Seʿadya Gaon Write etc.," *Tarbiz*, XXVII (1957–58), 79 f.

46 *Vouchsafed divine assistance*: Cf. *B.* Meg. 6b and *ISG* 21.6–7, from which it appears that whereas knowledge of the Torah can be acquired by human effort, temporal power is bestowed by Heaven. However, one should not overemphasize this distinction, for the same expression is used also in connection with religious success; cf. *ibid.* 22.12, 36.9. On the similar expression often used in legal responsa, cf. Lewin, *Mi-Tequfat ha-Geonim*: *R. Sherira Gaon*, p. 24; A.J. Heschel, "'Al Ruaḥ ha-Qodesh bi-may ha-Baynayyim," *Alexander Marx Jubilee Volume*, Hebrew vol., pp. 206 f. *To become exilarch*: On the principles of succession to the exilarchate, cf. Assaf, *Tequfat ha-Geonim*, pp. 38 f.; F. Lazarus, "Neue Beitraege zur Geschichte des Exilarchats," *MGWJ*, LXXVIII (1934), 279 f.; Baron, *SRH*, V, 5 f.

47 *Because of the sordid envy... he revolted*: Ibn Daud's phraseology represents a combination of two distinct rabbinic idioms: 1) והעלה בלבו טינה, greed (or envy) welled up in his heart; cf. Kohut, *Aruch Completum*, IV, 45 (bot., *s.v.* 3 טן), 46b; IX, 203; S. Lieberman, *Hayerushalmi Kipshuto* (Jerusalem, 1934), p. 526 n. to line 23. 2) The expression translated as "he revolted" is normally employed to describe the eruption of land from the sea; cf. Kohut, *op. cit.* VIII, 166 f. Since the word for "envy" also means "mud," "filth," (*ibid.*, IV, 45 f.) the sentence has the *double entendre* of our translation and of "because of the filth in his heart, he erupted."

52 *Composed books*: R. Natronai speaks of Anan as having "fabricated a Talmud of his own"; cf. B.N. to line 47. R. Moses Taqu cites a further tradition that Anan and his associates forged works and employed devious methods to claim antiquity for them; cited by Lieberman, *Shkiin*, p. 52, from Moses Taqu, "Sefer Ketab Tamim," in *Ozar Nechmad*, III (1860), 62; cf. also Lieberman, "Light on the Cave Scrolls from Rabbinic Sources," *PAAJR*, XX (1951), 402; P. Kahle, *The Cairo Geniza*, 2nd ed. (Oxford, 1959), pp. 15 f., 99. Besides a legal code, a work on the transmigration of the soul is also ascribed to Anan. Whether or not the work is genuine, what matters is that at the time of Qirqisani and later, people believed that he had composed at least two works, which will account for Ibn Daud's use of the plural "books." *Set up disciples*: The style is deliberately patterned after Abot 1.1 to emphasize Anan's responsibility for the rejuvenation of the heresy and for setting up a counter-religion, which sought to imitate the authentically Rabbanite form. Indeed, the tripartite form of the sentence, "composed books, set up disciples, and fabricated statutes," seems likewise to be a deliberate allusion to the style of the rabbinic program advocated in Abot 1.1–2; cf. also B.N. to line 54, end.

52–53 This verse was apparently invoked as a stock rubric against Karaite practice; cf. Maimonides, *Mishneh Torah*, Shabbat, 2.3; that the citation there is directed against Karaites is indicated by Aaron b. Elijah, *Gan Eden* (Eupatoria, 1864), f. 34a. The Karaites, in turn, paid the Rabbanites in kind by citing the verse against them; cf. Yefet b. Ali in Pinsker, *Lickute Kadmoniot*, Appendix p. 20, stanza "waw."

53 Whatever merit modern scholarship may see in Ibn Daud's thesis that Anan did not fabricate a heresy *ex nihilo* but actually organized and reinvigorated dissident elements in the Jewish community (cf. above, pp. xxxvii f.), there can be little doubt that Ibn Daud's observation reflects no such subtlety or sophistication. To Ibn Daud the disciples of Anan are the reincarnation of the ancient Sadducees and Samaritans. His observation that after the destruction of the Temple the *minim* dwindled is probably based on the fact that after the incorporation of the "blessing against the heretics" in the liturgy, talmudic legislation seems to have shown little concern with the community of heretics. That the blessing against the *minim* was not directed against Sadducees and Samaritans

is of no consequence. The issue is what Ibn Daud understood by *minim*; cf. Moore, *Judaism*, I, 292 f.

60   *R. Manasseh... head*: According to *ISG* 108.7-10, R. Bebai joined R. Huna ha-Levi and R. Manasseh, both of whom presided over Pumbeditha (= Sura of *SHQ*), in enacting new legislation on payments of marriage contracts and debts. Does the reading "heads" in MSS אפק indicate that the "Urtext" of *SHQ* mentioned both of these geonim at this point?

72-73   *R. Isaiah ha-Levi*: Despite the confusion of the MSS in the transmission of this line, the text, I believe, can be restored with a fair measure of certainty. Those MSS, of both classes, giving any information on the extent of R. Isaiah's term attest that it lasted two years, in agreement with *ISG* 109.2-6*. What they differ on is whether R. Isaiah's term began in 4556 or ended in that year. The confusion was almost inevitable in view of the fact that Ibn Daud suddenly began to locate geonim in their actual place of service. However, in view of his earlier blunder, he had to make R. Isaiah of Pumbeditha succeed R. Bebai ha-Levi, who in reality had been of Sura. Since the latter died in 4543 (line 60), MSS אפק took the easiest way out by deleting the puzzling "two years," thereby solving the problem of the hiatus in succession by maintaining silence on the extent of R. Isaiah's term. Obviously, there is an alternative course to deletion and that is emendation, which is the one reflected by Samuel ha-Nagid, MS Sassoon, p. 60, who transmits the sentence thus: אחריו רב ישעיה הלוי בר אבא דור ג' י"ג שנה (!) דתקני; cf. also Zacuto, p. 206. MSS בהת, on the other hand, solved the problem by transposing the sentence in *SHQ* completely, while retaining the original words, with the following result: "R. Isaiah ha-Levi bar Abba became the head of the academy in 4556, served for two years and passed away." Although this reading makes the sentence coincide completely with the datum in *ISG* 109.1-6, it must be rejected for *SHQ*. In the first place, this correction solves nothing, for it makes the next sentence in *SHQ* arithmetically untenable; if R. Isaiah's term began in 4556 and lasted two years, how could his successor's term of nineteen years terminate in 4575? However, more important than this consideration is the virtual certainty that the reading of MSS בהת is not based directly on *ISG*, for, as has been repeatedly stressed, Ibn Daud or his source usually understood the dates of accession in *ISG* to refer to dates of death and end of term; cf. B.N. to lines 16, 64, 67-68. Finally, it may be noted that Ibn Daud's regular style is to give the extent of term first and then indicate the date of termination. Thus, the agreement of MSS בהת with *ISG* is pure coincidence and derives entirely from internal considerations of the copyists.

79   On the manifestation of Elijah after his translation to heaven, cf. *Seder Eliahu Rabba und Seder Eliahu Zuta* (ed. Friedmann), Introduction pp. 27 f. and especially 32 f.; A.J. Heschel, "'Al Ruaḥ ha-Qodesh bi-may ha-Baynnyim," pp. 177, 202 f.; Ibn Shahin, *Ḥibbur Yafeh me-ha-Yeshu'ah* (ed. Hirschberg), Introduction p. 51.

82-83   The problematic nature of this sentence is reflected in Samuel ha-Nagid, MS Sassoon, who lists Abraham b. Sherira twice, but in each case without a date. In the first case (p. 60), he is listed, as in *SHQ*, with geonim of Pumbeditha in a way which clearly reflects the difficulty: ר' יוסף ב"ר יהודה... דתקפ"ד. אחריו רב אברהם בר רב שרירא י"ב שנה אחריו רב יוסף בר רב חייא דור חמישי בגאונות ב' דתקפ"ו. Later on (p. 63), he is reckoned among the geonim of Sura: ואחריו דור רביעי רב אברהם בר שרירא י"ב ואחריו דור ה' רב אהילאי... Zacuto, p. 206, had clearly omitted all reference to Abraham b. Sherira; the statement there in brackets is the editor's addition; cf. n. 1 there.

98-99   *R. Hai*: I have consistently adopted the popular transliteration of this name, although the proper pronunciation was probably Hayya; cf. S. Morag, "On the Form and Etymology of Hai Gaon's Name" [in Hebrew], *Tarbiz*, XXXI (1961-62), 188 f.

105 On the frequent confusion in MSS of the names Isaac and Zadok, cf. Ginzberg, *Geonica*, I, 148 n. 1; Mann, "The Responsa of the Babylonian Geonim etc.", *JQR* NS, VIII (1918), 340, XI (1921-22), 444; B.M. Lewin, *Meḥqarim Shonim bi-Tequfat ha-Geonim: Gemara de-Bay R. Yishai 'ow R. Ashi* (Haifa, 1929), p. 7 n. 4; V. Aptowitzer, "R. Chuschiel und R. Chananal," *Jahresbericht der Israelititsch-Theologischen Lehranstalt in Wien*, XXXVIII-XXXIX (1933), 33 n. 10; cf. also below, line 116 and variants to Hebrew text of *SHQ* 70:389.

117 *His maternal brother R. Ṣemaḥ*: S.J.L. Rapoport, *Toledot*, I, 118-119 (reprinted from preface to D. Cassel, *Teshubot Geonim Qadmonim* [Berlin, 1848]), suggests that Ibn Daud misunderstood *ISG*, which states: ובתריה מרב צמח בר מרב חיים אחיו של מרב נחשון גאון שבע שנים. R. Sherira had meant that R. Ḥayyim, not R. Ṣemaḥ, was the brother of R. Nahshon. However, Ibn Daud, believing that Sherira had stated that R. Ṣemaḥ was R. Nahshon's brother, concluded from their different patronymics that they were half-brothers.

124-127 Ibn Daud glides over the events between the appointment of R. Yom-Tob and that of Saadiah; cf. *ISG* 117.4-10; Nathan the Babylonian in *MJC*, II, 80. — Modern scholars are almost unanimous in their judgment that Ibn Daud's statement that Saadiah was invited to come from Egypt to assume the gaonate is based on a misunderstanding of *ISG* 117.11-13; cf. Malter, *Saadia Gaon*, pp. 54, 64 f., 108 n. 231. J.N. Simhoni, in his review of Malter in *ha-Tequfa*, XXII (1924), 497 f., and Marx (see S.N. to lines 129-143) imply that Ibn Daud had reference to Saadiah's second departure from Egypt in response to the Exilarch's invitation. Ibn Daud's source may have related of the Exilarch's summons to Saadiah to come from Egypt to help in some communal dispute or other endeavor, and Ibn Daud then telescoped the account giving the impression that the invitation was to assume the presidency of the academy.

126-127 *A great quarrel and dispute*: This seems to have been a stock expression; cf. Ginzberg, *Geonica*, II, 52 line 22; cf. also I. Friedlaender, "The Arabic Original of the Report of R. Nathan Hababli," *JQR*, XVII (1904-1905), 73 line 5: וקע בינהמא אכתלאף ושרור.

129-143 The dispute between Saadiah and the Exilarch has been treated extensively. For the most thorough analysis of the various accounts, including Ibn Daud's, cf. M. Auerbach, "Die Streit zwischen Saadja Gaon und den Exilarchen David ben Sakkai," *Juedische Studien Joseph Wohlgemut... gewidmet* (Frankfurt a.M., 1928), pp. 1-30; cf. also H. Malter, *Saadia Gaon*, pp. 89 f.; A. Marx, "Rab Saadia Gaon," *Rab Saadia Gaon, Studies in His Honor*, ed. by L. Finkelstein (New York, 1944), pp. 66 f.; S.W. Baron, "Saadia's Communal Activities," *American Academy for Jewish Research: Saadia Anniversary Volume* (New York, 1943), pp. 48 f.; idem, *SRH*, V, 21; J. Mann, "Varia on the Geonic Period" [in Hebrew], *Tarbiz*, V (1933-34), 162 f.; E. Rivkin "The Saadia-David ben Zakkai Controversy; A Structural Analysis," *Studies and Essays in Honor of Abraham A. Neuman* (Leiden, 1962), pp. 388-423.

132 That David b. Zakkai had a son by the name of Judah is now confirmed by the genealogy of Hezekiah the Exilarch, which reads: "From Hezekiah the Exilarch b. David b. Hezekiah the Exilarch b. *Judah* b. *David* the Exilarch b. Zakkai the Exilarch"; cf. B.N. to line 208. However, there is no proof that Ibn Daud was mistaken in his information on the name of the Exilarch's son involved in the altercation with Saadiah. Ibn Daud may well have drawn from a source that had the correct name of another son, and of whom Nathan the Babylonian was unaware.

SUPPLEMENTARY NOTES

134 *I will strike your head etc.*: Although the threat of violence against Saadiah is confirmed by Nathan the Babylonian, and although the Gaon's entourage took the expression literally and retaliated in kind, it is possible that Ibn Daud used this stock expression to point up the drama of the event. Ibn Daud may well have wanted to convey the thought that Saadiah's students took literally an expression that was a graphic but figurative threat to "boot the Gaon out of office." For similar usage, cf. below, VII.72, 82, where the literal meaning of the word translated as "reject" is "boot"; cf. also Kohut, *Aruch Completum*, II, 139b.

138 For the identification of these factions, cf. the studies of Mann and Rivkin listed in S.N. to lines 129–143.

142–143 Mann, "Varia on the Gaonic Period," p. 164 n. 68, indicated that this statement is inaccurate, for R. Saadiah emerged from hiding and dwelt in Baghdad long before the settlement with David b. Zakkai. However, Ibn Daud doubtless equated the period of hiding with the period that Saadiah claimed he had to endure suffering. Since the dispute broke out in 930 and was not settled until 937, Ibn Daud considered that the period of seclusion lasted seven years. For another tradition on Saadiah's "imprisonment" for thirteen years, cf. next note.

143 For a tradition that Saadiah spent thirteen years in prison, where he came in contact with Gentiles who influenced his writing, cf. Malter, *Saadia Gaon*, p. 283.

150 *Black bile*: This statement is generally taken to mean that Saadiah died of *melancholia*, which is the literal Greek translation of "black bile"; cf. Malter, *Saadia Gaon*, p. 128 n. 278. However, I am not certain that Ibn Daud intended the term in its popular sense. According to contemporary sources, black bile was regarded as the cause of several degenerative illnesses; cf. Joseph b. Meir ibn Zabara, *Sefer Shaashuim*, ed. by I. Davidson (New York, 1914), p. 162, lines 65 f., and n. 4 there. That Saadiah died under bizarre circumstances seems to be implied by Sahl b. Maṣliaḥ who says the Gaon died the death of the wicked (II Sam. 3.33); Pinsker, *Lickute Kadmoniot*, Appendix p. 37.

151–152 *Accomplished great good:* This phrase bears a striking resemblance to the eulogistic genre encountered in (Karaite) memorial lists; cf. Mann; *Texts and Studies*, II, 260-270 f., where men are listed as having done כמה חסדים וכמה טובות.

173–176 Ibn Daud's poor estimation of Ibn Sarjada, which is a reflection of the one held by Saadiah and Sherira, is not shared by modern students; cf. Malter, *Saadia Gaon*, p. 241; Marx, "Rab Saadia Gaon," p. 256. On his wealth, cf. Mann, "Varia on the Gaonic Period," p. 152.

176 *4720*: Although this reading occurs in but one MS, I have adopted it out of four considerations: 1) It conforms to the date in *ISG*; 2) the confusion of ב with כ is so simple in medieval MSS that one is often at a loss to know which letter the scribe really intended; 3) the date is attested in no uncertain terms by Samuel ha-Nagid, MS Sassoon, p. 61, which reads: ואחריו ר' אהרן הכהן... י"ט שנה והוא דור ז' דתש"ך. Although the words "nineteen years" are doubtless the epitomist's addition, they represent a "correct" interpolation in view of the date clearly written there; 4) Ibn Daud himself suggests that this reading is correct, as can be seen from the data on Ibn Sarjada's successor; cf. B.N. to line 177.

184 A further indication of the annual commemoration of the day of R. Hai's death may be seen from the fact that Solomon ibn Gabirol composed four elegies in his memory. Cf. *Shiray Solomon b. Judah ibn Gabirol* (ed. Bialik-Ravnitzky), I, 88–90, 188.

186 *He was the last of the geonim*: Ibn Daud might well object to our contention that his own account contradicts this statement. Ibn Daud was careful not to call Hezekiah

a gaon, but confined himself to the statement of fact that Hezekiah was appointed to R. Hai's "see" and in that capacity served as "head of the academy" (cf. lines 208, 213 and S.N. to lines 207–208). As for R. Isaac b. Moses ibn Sakri (VII.362 f.), Ibn Daud would probably have retorted to our objection with the observation that his appointment can in no wise be considered a continuation of the gaonate in view of the fact that about half a century must have elapsed between the death of R. Hai and the appointment of the Spaniard, R. Isaac. — Be that as it may, Ibn Daud's statement must be totally rejected in the light of our present day knowledge on the history of the gaonate after R. Hai. Cf. below, to lines 220–221.

189 *His seal*: For a description of a gaonic seal, cf. Lewin in *ISG*, p. 132 (seal of R. Nehemiah).

196 *Lawless Jews*: For other uses of this term in connection with delators, cf. the letter from the period of the Crusades published by Assaf in *Zion*, V (1940), 120 f. [= *Sefer ha-Yishuv*, II, 82]; Ben Iehuda, *Thesaurus*, X, 5178 (citation from Joseph b. Solomon). What is noteworthy about Ibn Daud's use of this term here is that he normally employs it for Zealots, who refused to collaborate with the ruling powers; cf. above, I.207. — Harkavy, *Zikron la-Rishonim*, I, 173, suggests that Ibn Nagrela alludes to the same events in his elegy for R. Hai, where he compares the enemies of Sherira and Hai to Tobiah and Sanballat of biblical notoriety; cf. *Diwan* (ed. Sassoon), p. 13 lines 63–65 (ed. Habermann, I, part 2, p. 133). There is no indication of the nature of the accusations against them. For conjectures, cf. the references in S.N. to line 199. For a similar occurrence, cf. below, lines 209 f. On delators as part of the machinery of state in the east at that time, cf. M.A. Mez, *The Renaissance of Islam*, Eng. trans. (Patna, 1937), p. 78; on the prevalence of confiscation, pp. 113 f. Cf. also Lewin, *Otzar ha-Geonim*, XI (Nedarim), p. 33.

199 *Did manage to get some aid*: For the many, and unsatisfactory, explanations and emendations of this puzzling expression, along with conjectures on the nature of the charges brought against them, cf. Lewin, *Mi-Tequfat ha-Geonim*, pp. 27 f.; Malter, *Saadia Gaon*, p. 130 n. 281; Assaf, *Tequfat ha-Geonim*, p. 55. — The only explanations which begin to make sense are those which explain the words ב. נתלה... as "he found means of support through, invoked the aid of"; cf. VI.140–141, VII.115 [Hebrew text 40.94, 49.76]. In other words, whatever the exact meaning of the expression, the problematic words ונתלה רב שרירא בידו אחת must be understood as explaining how it came about that Sherira and Hai were able to retain their position. Malter, accordingly, emended the text here to ונתלה במלכות, and explained that "through the intervention of friends [Sherira] 'regained influence with the *government* and was not removed from the gaonate.'" Apart from the violence which this emendation does to our text, it reads into the passage more than the words warrant. My own translation is based on the suggestion that the passage is a literal translation of a perfectly intelligible Arabic expression (which I render in Judeo-Arabic transcription): ותוקף עלי בעץ מואידה "he leaned on (i.e., found support through) some (unspecified source) of help and, accordingly, was not removed from the gaonate." This was corrupted to ותוקף עלי בעץ מן אידיה, which was translated literally into "He found support in one hand of his"!

207–208 Jerahmeel b. Solomon gives the following report: "After R. Hai, no head was appointed over the academy in Babylonia; instead, the Exilarch whose name is R. Hezekiah [was appointed], and he is presently serving as head. He is of the house of David." Poznanski felt that this statement indicates that Hezekiah was merely appointed as acting head of the academy but was not invested with the title of Gaon. This interpretation fits in with our text as well, for Ibn Daud nowhere calls Hezekiah a gaon; cf. above, S.N. to line 186. Cf. also Mann, *Texts and Studies*, I, 209 n. 14; Assaf, "Letters of Babylonian Geonim" [in Hebrew], *Tarbiz*, XI (1939–1940), 152 f.

208 *Grandson etc.*: Poznanski's suggestion, *Babylonische Geonim im nachgaonaeischen Zeitalter*, p. 2 n. 4, to translate בן בנו as "a descendant" appears to me far-fetched; "a descendant" would have been expressed as מבני בניו; cf. above, line 8. — On Hezekiah's parentage, cf. also J. Mann, "Misrat Rosh ha-Golah we-Hista'afutah be-Sof Tequfat ha-Geonim," *Livre d'Hommage à la Mémoire de Dr. Samuel Poznanski* (Warsaw, 1927), Hebrew section p. 21.

211 *Left him no survivors etc.*: In reality, the exilarchate continued through the third quarter of the twelfth century; cf. Poznanski, *Babylonische Geonim*, etc., pp. 111 f.; Mann, *Texts and Studies*, I, 208. See next note.

212–213 According to Jerahmeel b. Solomon, *MJC*, I, 178, David b. Hezekiah was living in Baghdad in 1046! Cf. also Mann, *Jews in Egypt*, I, 111–113; on the possible identification of another son, cf. *ibid.*, p. 129; II, 145 n. 7.

217 *Al-Daudi*: The surname means "the Davidide"; cf. lines 187–188. — Professor Shalom Spiegel graciously drew my attention to the conjecture of S.D. Luzzatto, *Betulat Bat Yehuda* (Prague, 1840), p. 7, that Ḥiyya al-Daudi is to be identified with the first editor of the Diwan of Judah ha-Levi. The gloss in MS ב suggests that Ḥiyya was indeed poetically inclined. Apart from this gloss, I do not know of any source which mentions this Ḥiyya as a redactor of a liturgy, i.e. special prayer(s) for the Day of Atonement. (I am unable to interpret the last three words of the gloss: בשלשלת על אופן.) For poetry by Ḥiyya, cf. Davidson, *Thesaurus*, IV, 381. On Ḥiyya, the editor of ha-Levi's Diwan, cf. A. Geiger, *Divan des Castiliers Abu'l Hasan Juda ha-Levi* (Breslau, 1857), pp. 167 f.

218 *After him there did not remain etc.*: To the end of this sentence, Samuel ha-Nagid, MS Sassoon, p. 64 adds: "except for his son Josiah" (לבד יאשיהו בנו). Whatever Ibn Daud meant by his statement, the fact is that there were persons claiming Davidic descent long after that time; cf. below, p. 293.

220–221 On the academies after Hai and Hezekiah, cf. Poznanski, *Babylonische Geonim im nachgaonaeischen Zeitalter*; Mann, *Texts and Studies*, I, 202 f.; S. Assaf, "Letters of R. Samuel b. Eli and His Contemporaries" [in Hebrew], *Tarbiz*, I part 1 (October, 1929), 104 f.; *idem*, *Tequfat ha-Geonim*, pp. 127 f.

Supplementary Notes to Chapter VII

2 *The income of the academies*: On contributions from Spain, cf. A. Cowley, "Bodleian Geniza Fragments," *JQR*, XVIII (1906), 399 f. [= *ISG*, Appendix pp. XXII–XXV]; A. Marx, "Notes on *JQR*, XVIII, 399 ff.," *ibid.*, pp. 768 f.; Mann, "The Responsa of the Babylonian Geonim etc.," *JQR* NS, XI (1920–21), 448; *idem*, *Texts and Studies*, I, 64 f.; Margalioth, *Hilkhot Hannagid*, p. 5; Dunash b. Labrat, *Shirim* (ed. by N. Allony, Jerusalem, 1947), p. 70 stanzas 35–36 and notes *ad loc.* on p. 134. — On contributions from North Africa, including Egypt, cf. Mann in *JQR* NS, VII (1917), 477 f., and *Texts and Studies*, I, 63 f. — On the possibility of contributions coming from Palestine, cf.

Mann, *JQR*, NS, VII (1917), 474 f., and *Texts and Studies*, I, 92. Ibn Daud may have drawn his inference on the contributions from the Holy Land on the basis of gaonic reports of collections solicited in Syria, which is called in Arabic by the same name often used for Palestine, al-Shamm; cf. S. Assaf, "Letters of Samuel b. Eli and His Contemporaries," *Tarbiz*, I, 1 (Oct. 1929), pp. 118 f. — This list of communities is, of course, not exhaustive; cf. Assaf, *ibid.*; *idem*, "Li-Ṣemiḥat ha-Merkazim ha-Yisraeliyyim bi-Tequfat ha-Geonim," *Haschiloah*, XXXV (1918), 16 f.; *Megillat Ahimaaz*, ed. by B. Klar (Jerusalem, 1944), pp. 44, 47; and especially the report of Nathan the Babylonian in Neubauer, *MJC*, II, 78 f. Above all, however, it should be noted that this list is not a reliable statement of the names of those communities which actually stopped supporting the academies at that time. In the first place, it is highly doubtful that the Palestinian community ever was a major source of support for the Babylonian academies. On the other hand, Ibn Daud himself claimed that contributions from Spain were sent even a generation later; cf. below, line 236. Ibn Daud's statement should, therefore, not be taken as testimony, but rather as a conclusion based on his knowledge of the terrible financial plight of the academies and of the tension between R. Ḥanok and R. Hai; cf. Mann, *Texts and Studies*, I, 157, 187, 202 f. He then proceeded to name in *schematic* fashion the principal areas of the Mediterranean from which the academies drew their support: Spain (north), Maghreb (west), Ifriqiya (south), Egypt and Palestine (east).

3 *Maghreb*: Ibn Daud includes in this term both the further and central Maghreb; cf. below, lines 30, 235; Epilogue. 24–25. On occasion, he uses the term loosely, including what might technically have been considered Ifriqiya or Spain; cf. below, lines 256 f.; *Zikron Dibray Romi*, f. 48a (bot.). There is nothing unusual about this loose usage, as was thought by B. Klar, *Meḥqarim we-'Iyyunim*, p. 326 n. 32. Cf. references to *EI* in B.N.; Mann, "The Responsa etc.," *JQR* NS, VII (1917), 482; W. Fischel, *Ibn Khaldun and Tamerlane* (Berkeley, 1952), p. 76 n. 74.

4 *The Holy Land*: Although "the Beautiful Land" is used in Scripture and explained as well as used in the Talmud, e.g. *B*. Ket. 111a, M. Q. 25b, it does not appear to have been employed *regularly* until gaonic times. In the latter period, it is encountered as the usual designation for Palestine; cf. *Sefer ha-Yishub*, II, ed. by S. Assaf and A. L. Meyer (Jerusalem, 1944), p. 149 s.v. ארץ הצבי, Mann, *Jews in Egypt and in Palestine*, II, 424 s.v. צבי.

6 *Commander*: Heb., *shalish*, which Saadiah and Jonah ibn Janaḥ translate by قواد. Cf. Saadiah, *Oeuvres Complètes*, I, 101; Johan ibn Janaḥ, *The Book of Hebrew Roots* (ed. Neubauer), p. 729. Cf. also *MBSh*, f. 50a, 57b, 58b, where the same Hebrew term is used for the generals of an army. In documents of the Geniza, the term is used for governor as well as commander; cf. Mann, *The Jews in Egypt and in Palestine*, II, 175 line 7, 199 line 15; *idem*, "The Responsa etc.," *JQR* NS, IX (1918), 177 line 32.

8 *To capture the ships etc.*: On piracy and kidnapping as semi-official occupations during the reign of 'Abd ar-Raḥman III, cf. Dozy, *Histoire*, II, 145 (Eng. tr., p. 430); Lévi-Provençal, *Histoire de l'Espagne Musulmane*, II, 154 f.

17 *I do not know his name*: On confession of ignorance as a mark of critical scholarship in Ibn Daud's milieu, cf. von Grunebaum, *Medieval Islam*, pp. 242 f.; Rosenthal, *The Technique and Approach of Muslim Scholarship*, p. 62.

27 *Head [of the academy]*: Although it may be contended that Ibn Daud merely employs here the typical Arabic usage "became head (*rayis*)" as he does in II. 39–40, III. 25–26, 70, the fact is that these men were often called by that title (*ha-rosh*), or referred to as *ha-rab ha-rosh*, the chief rabbi, a title adapted from biblical usage (cf., e.g., Ezra 7.5;)

Lewin, *Otzar ha-Geonim*, V (Rosh ha-Shanah), 9 n. 2; S. Assaf, *Gaonica* [in Hebrew] (Jerusalem, 1933), p. 121 n. 10; Hirschberg's introduction to Nissim b. Jacob. *Ḥibbur Yafeh etc.*, p. 25 n. 12. Whatever the merits of the argument of Mann, *Texts and Studies*, I, 87 n. 70, that the title is a technical one among other titles, Ibn Daud is consistent in employing the term in connection with leaders who served as "head of the academy," which, to Ibn Daud, meant religious head of a community.

33 *The people of Cordova*: "The people" is a literal Hebrew translation of the Arabic "*ahl*" denoting members of an ethnic or religious community; cf. also below, line 59. For the overtones of the term in Muslim Spain, cf. Pérès, *La Poésie Andalouse*, pp. 5 f.

35 *College Synagogue*: On houses of study in, or attached to, synagogues, cf. Mann, *Texts and Studies*, I, 70 n. 16; Goitein, *Jewish Education in Muslim Countries*, pp. 188 f. Cf. also the educational program of "The Laws of the Torah" in Guedemann, *Geschichte des Erziehungswesens und der Cultur der Juden*, I, 94 par. II, 268 (= S. Assaf, *Meqorot le-Toledot ha-Ḥinuk be-Israel*, I, 10). Cf. also the related expression זקני הכנסת והמדרש in Judah b. Barzillai, *Sefer ha-Shetarot*, p. 132.

38–39 *The people of Spain etc.*: Modern scholars have gone to great lengths to square this statement with the unequivocal evidence of a fully developed and talmudically mature community in Spain prior to the arrival of R. Moses: cf. I. Halevy, *Dorot Harishonim*, III, 294; Harkavy, "Le-Toledot R. Samuel ha-Nagid," pp. 1 f.; Margalioth, *Hilkhot Hannagid*, pp. 1 f.; Ashtor, *Qorot ha-Yehudim*, I, 82 f. It does not help clarify matters historically to plead that Ibn Daud is referring only to the Jewry of Cordova or that his scale of judgment is in relation to the creativity of Babylonian Jewry. Granted that Spain could not boast of a R. Saadiah or R. Hai, Ibn Daud's condescending statement is calculated to belittle whatever achievements had been attained in Spain in earlier periods and can be understood only in the light of his general tendency to regard the period of Ḥisdai ibn Shaprut as the dawn of a new era; cf. Epilogue. 150 f., and Cohen, *SFC*, pp. 114 f.

39 *Conducted a school*: For the possible Arabic idiom underlying this expression, cf. Cohen, *SFC*, p. 61 n. 21. However, Professor Isadore Twersky has kindly drawn my attention to the parallel idiom used in Italian-Franco-German sources, לקבוע מדרש, which means the same thing; cf. *Megillat Ahimaaz*, p. 17; Guedemann, cited in S.N. to line 35.

55–56 On the stipend (Heb., *pesiqa*), cf. S.D. Goitein, *Jewish Education in Muslim Countries*, p. 78; *idem*, "Jewish Community Organization in the Light of the Cairo Geniza Documents" [in Hebrew], *Zion*, XXVI (1960–61), 174. The same term is used for fixed allotments contributed to the academies; cf. Assaf, *Tequfat ha-Geonim*, pp. 68 f. The costly garments may have been special robes of office or of the scholarly class; cf. Judah b. Barzillai, *Sefer ha-Shetarot*, p. 132.

61–62 *All the questions etc.*: If Ibn Daud meant to say that all the questions which had formerly been sent to Babylonia from the Maghreb as well as from Spain were now directed to Cordova (cf. line 60), this is incorrect. As pointed out by Halevy, *Dorot Harishonim*, III, 304, during the administrations of Sherira and Hai more questions than ever came from the Maghreb to the academy in Baghdad. It may, to be sure, be true for the communities of Spain. For the responsa of R. Moses and R. Ḥanok, and even some of Ibn Abitur, cf. J. Mueller, *Die Responsen der Spanischen Lehrer des 10. Jahrhunderts* (Berlin, 1899). Cf. also the note by Mueller, *Teshubot Geonay Mizraḥ u-Ma'arab* (Berlin, 1888), f. 54b n. 1. Margalioth, *Hilkhot Hannagid*, pp. 7 f.

64 *The Rabbi*: Aptowitzer, "Rabbenu Chuschiel etc.," p. 27 n. 17, has suggested that this

title, although indigenous to Qairawan, was originally bestowed by the Palestinian geonim.

73 *Nasi*: This title, used earlier in the sense of Davidic patriarch and exilarch (cf. I. 75-76; II.126, 131; III.3, 32; IV.24; VI.127), appears in medieval European communities with a sudden frequency that has not yet been totally clarified; cf. the discussions of Baron, *SRH*, V, 44 f.; Baer, *History*, I, 105 f. As for Ibn Shaprut, Ibn Daud consistently refers to him by that title, suggesting that it was regularly applied to him; cf. VI. 159, Epilogue. 150. The same term is used by al-Ḥarizi, *Taḥkemoni* ch. 18 (ed. Toporowsky), p. 184 (and cf. P. Luzzatto, *Notice sur Abou-Ioussef Hasdai ibn-Schaprout* [Paris, 1852], pp. 21 f.). On the other hand, Ibn Shaprut's contemporaries address him by other titles, such as *nagid*, *alluf* and *rosh kallah*, but never as nasi; cf. Schirmann, *Ha-Shirah ha-Ibrit*, I, 11, 37, 43. Moses ibn Ezra speaks of him as *al-rayis*; Munk, *Notice sur Abou'l Walid Merwan ibn Djana'h*, p. 77 n. 2, and Moses ibn Ezra, *Shirat Israel*, p. 63. It may well be that he was entitled, or recognized as, *rayis al-yahud* (= head of the Jews), which his contemporaries translated as *nagid*, but which later generations rendered by *nasi*. That the latter two terms were regarded as synonymous may be seen from Ibn Gabirol's poem to Samuel ibn Nagrela and from the poem in honor of the Nagid Abraham ibn Ata of Qairawan; cf. *Shiray Solomon ibn Gabirol* (ed. Bialik-Ravnitky), I, 189 f. lines 1, 22; Mann, "Abraham b. Nathan, "*JQR* NS XI (1920-21), 431. The term *rayis* in itself is a nebulous one, and Ibn Daud is careful to avoid its use except in a very technical sense; cf. S.N. to II.40 and VII.27. In all likelihood, he preferred the term nasi in connection with Ibn Shaprut in order to convey the idea that authority in the community of Cordova was patterned along classical lines; cf. notes to II.131-132, 143.

76-79 This entourage seems to have been patterned after that of the exilarch in Baghdad; cf. Benjamin of Tudela, *Itinerary* (ed. Adler), p. 40. That the caliph would decide who would wield rabbinic authority was probably as true with the Jews in Cordova as it was with the Christians in other parts of the Muslim world; cf. below, S.N. to line 372; Cohen, *SFC*, p. 119 n. 202.

78 *Headdress*: *qalansuwa*: Professor D.M. Dunlop graciously drew my attention to Hilal al-Sabi, *Rusum dar al-Khilafah*, ed. by M. Awad (Baghdad, 1964), where interesting details on the history of this form of headdress are supplied, pp. 53, 75 n. 3, 80 f., 91 n. 3, 96. Cf. also Lane, *An Arabic-English Lexicon*, VII, 2558 f.; Dozy, *Supplément aux Dictionnaires Arabes*, II, 401; Mez, *The Renaissance of Islam*, p. 132.

89 *Pointing out his error*: That the Rabbi of Pechina was not alone in employing this form of argument in attempting to make his correspondent retract his position has been shown by D.Z. Baneth, "Ta'uyot be-Shimush Leshon Arab," *Tesoro de los Judios Sefardies*, IV (1961), 14 f.

96 *To Damascus*: There is no evidence that Ibn Abitur left Alexandria for Damascus. On the other hand, it is now well known that he maintained close ties with the gaon of Palestine; cf. reference in note to line 70. It may, therefore, be that Ibn Daud mistranslated a statement that Ibn Abitur went to *al-Shamm* (= Damascus, Syria, Palestine). Was the mistranslation a deliberate one with an eye on Amos 5.27?

100 *Merchants and manufacturers of silk*: On Jews in the silk trade in the Middle Ages, cf. Baron, *SRH*, IV, 168 f., 319 f.; cf. also below, line 300. It may well be that Ibn Daud mentions their source of livelihood pejoratively, indicating obliquely that the Ibn Jaus were not native to the scholarly-courtier class; cf. VI. 122, 174-176. Moreover, the Ibn Jaus attained their power in a way which might be expected of merchants; cf. *ibid.* and VI.128-129, 192-193. Should it be objected that Ibn Daud's heroes, Samuel ibn

Nagrela and his own ancestors, were also peddlers and craftsmen (cf. VII.185, 299), it should be noted that Ibn Daud makes the distinction quite clear: Ibn Nagrela was reduced to peddling by circumstances; his ancestors of Merida were no mere craftsmen, but makers of silk for synagogue curtains, a holy calling indeed. On Ibn Daud's feelings about Ibn Jau, cf. Cohen *SFC*, p. 122.

117 *Pennants*: On the role of pennants and flags in medieval Islam, cf. Ibn Khaldun, *Muqaddimah* (tr. by F. Rosenthal), II, 48 f.; R. Levy, *The Social Structure of Islam* (Cambridge, 1957), pp. 432, 434 f.; Mez, *The Renaissance of Islam*, pp. 132 f.

121 *Issued him a document*: For a specimen of such a document of appointment to a leader of a minority community, cf. Mez, *op. cit.*, p. 35. For the Jewish community's writ of confirmation, cf. the formula reproduced by Judah b. Barzillai, *Sefer ha-Shetarot*, pp. 131, 134. For a discussion of this document, cf. Baron, *SRH*, V, 44 f.

145–147 On this method of presenting a petition, cf. Dozy, *Histoire*, II, 221 (Eng. trans., p. 487). On the state-prison in al-Zahra, cf. *ibid.* pp. 217, 224 (Eng. tr., pp. 484, 489).

157 *In-laws of the Ibn Falija family*: Lit., one of his sons-in-law of the Ibn Falija family. Actually, only one of R. Ḥanok's children was married to an Ibn Falija; cf. line 66. However, Ibn Daud uses the word *ḥatan* in the Arabic sense of an in-law; cf. also VI.205 and the Heb. text 44.138.

166 *Refused to derive any profit etc.*: A comparison of this statement and the one below, lines 279–280, with the commentary of Maimonides to Abot 4.5 will show that Ibn Daud and Maimonides shared the same view on the proper way for a rabbi to earn his livelihood. For similar Muslim sentiments on the subject, cf. Mez, *op. cit.*, p. 184.

180 *One of his outstanding disciples*: Although I have translated the phrase literally, Ibn Daud employs this form regularly to designate the man who took over in the line of rabbinic succession and was his predecessor's outstanding disciple; cf. below, lines 353, 393. The latter instance is most instructive, for R. Baruk ibn Albalia is listed there as "one of the outstanding disciples" of al-Fasi, while on line 357 he is listed as but "one of the disciples of [his father] R. Isaac" ibn Albalia. That is because R. Baruk received his rabbinic "recognition" from al-Fasi, under circumstances described in detail in lines 427 f. Ibn Daud's usage is probably an Arabism, equivalent to ومن أشهر تلاميذه, which Professor Halkin informs me is the form Moses ibn Ezra uses in the case of Joseph b. Sahl; cf. *Shirat Israel*, p. 74 and below, line 353. This way of designating the outstanding authority of a given generation or place probably underlies the form employed regularly by R. Menahem b. Solomon Meiri in his great code-commentary, *Bet ha-Beḥirah*: גדולי המחברים, גדולי המפרשים etc. — On Samuel ibn Nagrela as an arch-disciple of R. Ḥanok, cf. Margalioth, *Hilkhot Hannagid*, pp. 8 f., 22, 32 f., 52.

181 *Cordova*: Actually his ancestors were of Merida, as noted by Harkavy, "Le-Toledot R. Samuel ha-Nagid," p. 2. The matter is of no small consequence, for it helps explain the close ties between the Ibn Nagrelas and the Ibn Albalias, lines 294 f., 313 f.

204–205 *Now the counsel etc.*: This hyperbole, although a cliché appropriated from biblical style, may reflect Ibn Nagrela's own claim to prophetic inspiration; cf. his letter to Hezekiah the Exilarch in his *Diwan* 102.44 (= ed. Habermann, I, 142); Eng. trans. in Baer, *History*, I, 35.

217 For a similar situation in 852 in which 'Abd ar-Raḥman II died without designating a successor, and the issue was decided by the palace eunuchs, cf. Dozy, *Histoire*, I, 346 f. (Eng. tr., pp. 294 f.).

223 For the latest discussion of the classical roots of this form of adoration, cf. E. Bickerman,

"A Propos d'un Passage de Charès de Mytilène," *La Parola del Passato*, XCI (1963), 244 f.

230 For other instances of the use of physicians in Andalusian court intrigues, cf. Dozy, *Histoire*, I, 331 f.; II, 22 (Eng. tr., pp. 281 f., 322).

241 Although the virtues of Ibn Nagrela which are singled out here would have been acknowledged as such in Jewish communities in other lands, taken together they reflect the virtues of an aristocrat of an Arabic milieu. Thus, the amassing of a large library, the lending of books, the maintenance of scribes and the placing of these facilities, as well as of funds, at the disposal of students are all virtues highly regarded by medieval Muslim men of letters; cf. Mez, *op. cit.*, pp. 172 f., 175 f., 183; Rosenthal, *Technique and Approach of Muslim Scholarship*, p. 9. On the great expense of books at that time, cf. E. Ashtor, "Prices of Books from the Geniza" [in Hebrew], *Tarbiz*, XXXIII (1963–64), 214 f. and especially p. 222.

245 *Contributions of olive oil*: The mention of this virtue probably has special overtones in this context, for in Wayyikra R. 9.2 (ed. Margulies), p. 176, and especially in the later form of this passage recorded in Midrash Haggadol, Exodus 27.21 (ed. Margulies), p. 613, the contribution of olive oil for public benefit is lauded as conducive to kingship. In other words, the Nagid or prince of medieval times was fulfilling the obligation of a Jewish surrogate of royalty; cf. also *B*. Sahned. 94b.

248 *Towering above them all etc.*: This is a makeshift translation of a line on which the MSS differ to such a degree as to make the text itself most uncertain. MSS אפק read: And the crown of a good name towering above them by dint of good deeds accompanying each of them (i.e., each of the three preceding virtues). MSS ת read: The crown of good deeds and the crown of a good name over all of them. MSS ב and ה differ in minor points but enough to make it impossible for me to establish some definite reading. Obviously, the copyists themselves were confused by the meaning of the line.

256 Although Halper's translation of Moses ibn Ezra, *Shirat Israel*, p. 68, records the date of Joseph's death as the twentieth of Tebet, Professor Halkin, who is preparing a new edition of the Arabic text and a new Hebrew translation, informs me that Ibn Ezra's datum agrees with that of *SHQ*.

270 *Without exception*: The expression על יד is unclear. MSS קת tailored it to read על יד על יד which would mean *seriatim*, little by little; cf. Kohut, *Aruch Completum*, IV, 109. However, as the text stands, the expression seems to be taken from Prov. 13.11, which is not much help in this case. I have translated it as an Arabism, عن يد, which 'Abdu'l-Waḥid, a Moroccan contemporary of Ibn Daud, uses in the sense of "all, without exception"; Dozy, *Supplément aux Dictionnaires Arabes*, II, 850a. *It was through R. Nissim etc.*: On the scholars of Qairawan as middlemen in the transmission of messages between the academies of Babylonia and other Jewish communities, cf. Mann, *Texts and Studies*, I, 110, 120; Hirschberg's introduction to Nissim b. Jacob, *op. cit.*, p. 30 n. 51. Ibn Daud's picture of the relationship between Ibn Nagrela and R. Hai is probably highly idealized. For a summary and critical appraisal, cf. Margalioth, *Hilkhot Hannagid*, pp. 26 f., 56 f. The use of the talmudic metaphor "the waters of R. Hai" may derive from Ibn Nagrela himself; cf. Ibn Nagrela, *Diwan*, p. 83 line 45.

297 *When Titus overpowered Jerusalem etc.*: This tradition contains two distinct motifs which, as in some parallel legends, have been combined into one story in order to validate the claim of the first Jewish families of Merida — and, of course, of their descendants, of whom Ibn Daud claims to be one — to being of noble stock. The first motif is that the family of Ibn Albalia was descended of the nobility of Jerusalem, the full force of

SUPPLEMENTARY NOTES 139

this claim being explained below, in the case of the Ibn Ezra family, Epilogue. 94 f The claim was made not merely for the sake of vanity, but probably had political implications, for these first families claimed the right to rule over the Jews of Spain internally and to represent them to the Muslim and Christian authorities. The claim of exalted genealogy was invoked in various Jewish communities particularly in time of tension and strife between factions within the Jewish community, or when the occasion arose, to validate the claim to privileged position; cf. VI.144 f., 187 f.; Neubauer, *MJC*, I, 82 (and cf. Aronius, *Regesten zur Geschichte der Juden* pp. 25 f. no. 70); Baer, *History*, I, 105 f. Though there is, therefore, nothing unique about this claim on the part of the Spanish Jewish aristocracy, it is significant that the courtier class of Andalusian Jewry, which in all of its ways reflected profound Arabic acculturation, should make a claim that echoes one made by Spanish Arabs, who made invidious distinctions between themselves and Spanish converts to Islam or Berber Muslims; cf. Dozy, *Histoire*, I, 69, 157 f. (Eng. tr., p. 64, 137 f.); Lévi-Provençal, *La Péninsule Ibérique*, pp. 8 f., 213; Pérès, *op. cit.*, Introduction. Needless to say, the Christians of Spain also laid claim to exalted origins; Dozy, *Histoire*, II, 24 (Eng. tr., p. 325); and the bibliography on Santiago de Compostela in P.E. Schramm, "Das Kastilische Koenigtum und Kaisertum waehrend der Reconquista," *Festchrift fur Gerhard Ritter* (Tuebingen, 1950), p. 102 n. 25. The second motif is that these Jewish nobles had come to their new home by invitation and had indeed been singled out by Gentile authorities precisely because of the nobility of their stock, usually for the sake of ruling over the Jewish community; cf. Neubauer, *loc cit.*; D. Neustadt, "Some Problems Concerning the 'Negidut' in Egypt during the Middle Ages" [in Hebrew], *Zion*, IV (1938–39), 126 f. For a somewhat similar Christian story, according to which Roderic sent to Rome for a man to teach him the Catholic faith, cf. Ps-Isidore, *Chronicon* (ed. Mommsen), in *Monumenta Germaniae Historica*, Auctores Antiquissimi, XI, 382 par. 9. The genre is thus that of religious foundation stories on which cf. Cohen, *SFC*, pp. 75 f. — Since the tradition quoted by Ibn Daud is often cited in connection with traditions on the ancient origins of Spanish Jewry, it may be appropriate to emphasize that Ibn Daud is not referring here to the tradition tracing the beginnings of the Spanish community to the exile of the days of Nebuchadnezzar. The latter tradition is quite discrete from the one cited in *SHQ*. For the one tracing the forebears of Spanish Jewry to the exiles of the days of the First Temple, cf. Cowley, "Bodleian Geniza Fragments," p. 401 [= *ISG*, Appendix, p. XXIII] and the passages collected by Harkavy, "Le-Toledot R. Samuel ha-Nagid," pp. 1, 36 f., 38 n. 3, 41 n. 16, where, however, the traditions are not separated; Margalioth, *Hilkhot Hannagid*, p. 1.

311 *From France*: For a similar occurrence some thirty-five years later, cf. R. Isaac al-Fasi, *Responsa*, no. 123 (ed. Leiter), pp. 125 f., reprinted in part in Assaf, *Meqorot le-Toledot ha-Ḥinuk be-Israel*, II, 21 f. R. Paregoros' arrival in Andalus ca. 1055 occurred shortly after the beginnings of French influence in Christian Spain; cf. M. Defourneaux, *Les Français en Espagne au XIe et XIIe siècles* (Paris, 1949), pp. 19 f.; R. Menendez Pidal, *El Imperio Hispanico y los Cinco Reinos* (Madrid, 1950), p. 77. Cf. also below, S.N. to line 469.

358 *R. Joseph b. R. Zadok b. Zaddik*: Although it has become widely accepted that his full name was Joseph b. *Jacob* b. Zaddik, the question bears review in light of the fact that his name is given by Ibn Daud twice as Joseph b. *Zadok* b. Zaddik; cf. Epilogue. 159. As far as I can determine, no medieval writer ever records the name of his father as Jacob; cf. Moses ibn Ezra, *op. cit.*, p. 75; Zacuto, pp. 213a, 216b, 220b, 229b; A.

Jellinek's introduction to his edition of Joseph b. Zaddik, '*Olam Qatan* (Leipzig, 1854), pp. vi f.; S. Horovitz, *Der Mikrokosmos des Josef ibn Saddik* (Breslau, 1903), pp. 1 f. Indeed, in tracking down the patronymic Jacob, all roads apparently lead to Steinschneider, who recorded the name thus in his edition of *Ozrot Chajim, Katalog der Michael'- schen Bibliothek* (Hamburg, 1948), p. 4 no. 37. It should be noted that Steinschneider's own copy of this catalogue, housed in the Library of The Jewish Theological Seminary of America, has the words "b. Jacob" underlined and enclosed in parentheses, indicating that Steinschneider later had some doubts on the subject. These doubts were hinted at in Steinschneider's *Catalogus librorum hebraeorum in Bibliotheca Bodleiana*, p. 1542. However, Steinschneider persisted in keeping the patronymic Jacob in his *Hebraeische Uebersetzungen des Mittelaters*, p. 407, *Die Arabische Literatur der Juden*, p. 151, and in his article on Ibn Zaddik originally printed in Ersch u. Gruber and recast for his *Gesammelte Schriften*, ed. by H. Malter and A. Marx (Berlin, 1925), p. 180. From Steinschneider's works, it would seem, the name Jacob (or Yaʿqub) as that of R. Joseph's father came into encyclopedias and many monographic works without being questioned. Steinschneider also enjoyed calling attention to the frequent "error" of having R. Joseph's father listed as Zadok; cf. *Heb. Uebersetz.*, *loc cit.*, and *Die Geschichtsliteratur der Juden*, p. 73. These are minor points, to be sure, but the MSS evidence of *SHQ* deserves to be reconsidered by catalogers of his name.

362 [*The third...*] *was a man* [*widely*] *designated etc.*: In view of the fact that Neubauer's edition of *SHQ* in *MJC*, I, 75.13 recorded the reading of the text as והוא נקרא חבר לר' יצחק and noted no variants to the line, it has been the unanimous opinion of authorities that a passage is missing here; cf. Bruell, *Jahrbuecher*, IX (1899), 105; Poznanski, *Baylonische Geonim etc.*., p. 6; Mann, *Texts and Studies*, I, 207 n. 10. These scholars were right in remonstrating that the passage seemed to refer to Joseph b. Zaddik, which made no sense. However, the reading of MSS פק clarifies the sentence and indicates that a new passage begins here. Its structure is that of an Arabic sentence beginning with واما: "As for the one called the colleague of R. Isaac etc." Our construction of this line is confirmed by the epitome of Samuel ha-Nagid, MS Sassoon, p. 66, which reads: והשלישי החבר רב יצחק בר משה הידוע בר חפני (!) מקהל דניא סעמים נקרא רב ופעמים נקרא חבר ולא חבר לאלו וכ'.

364 *Al-Ḥaber*: On *ḥaber* as an official title in the gaonic period, cf. Mann, *The Jews in Egypt*, I, 54 n. 2, 264, 272; for use of the title, which seems to have been essentially a Palestinian one, cf. also Guedemann, *Geschichte des Erziehungswesens*, I, 246; Baron, *SRH*, V, 313 n. 58. On the classical connotation of the term, cf. *JE*, VII, 121 f.

372 *Denia*: In the fragment published by Mann, "Glanures de la Gueniza," pp. 156 f., R. Isaac b. Reuben is said to have received a tradition form "his master Rab... b. R. Moses the Righteous," which Mann restored to read R. Ḥanok b. R. Moses. Accordingly, he suggested that R. Isaac had studied in Cordova under R. Ḥanok, returned to his native Barcelona and migrated from there to Denia. While this is possible, the theory is rather implausible in view of several considerations. In the first place, a full generation intervenes between the death of R. Ḥanok and the generation of the five Isaacs. Secondly, had there been any tradition to the effect that R. Isaac b. Reuben was a disciple of the school of Cordova, Ibn Daud is likely to have known about it and to have reported it. After all, one of Ibn Daud's principal motifs is the crucial influence exercised by the academy of Cordova and its offshoots. Al-Bargeloni's place in Ibn Daud's circle of notables probably derives, at least in part, from his marriage

into the family of Ibn Laktush, which, in turn, was closely associated with the other notables of this generation; see B.N. to line 375. R. Isaac's migration to Denia is more plausibly explained not as a *return* to the vicinity of Andalus, but as an aspect of the close connections between Barcelona and Denia in the eleventh century. Thus, in 1058, the Mozarabic community of Denia and its territories were placed by the Muslim ruler under the jurisdiction of the bishopric of Barcelona. There is every reason to assume that the Muslim king made a similar arrangement for the Jewish community in his domain. Is it, therefore, too far-fetched to suggest further that Ben Sakri's migration from Denia at that time was in some way parallel to the abandonment of Cordova by Ibn Shatnash under similar circumstances about a half century earlier (cf. lines 69 f. and notes there)? Cf. *EI*, I (new ed.), 1054. Indeed, the parallel circumstances between the arrival of R. Moses in Cordova and his marriage into the Ibn Falija family and that of R. Isaac's marriage into the Ibn Laktush family are too striking to be coincidental. On the refusal of Jews to return to Denia after the conquest of the city by James I, cf. Baer, *History*, I, 195.

406 *About fourteen years:* To be sure, this report may be correct. However, in the light of the typological phrases which Ibn Daud applies to Ibn Megash, it may be that he adopted this figure in view of its classical associations; cf. *B.* Meg. 17a, and Ginzberg, *Legends*, I, 316, 340. Note that Ibn Daud says he was "about twelve years old" and that he remained under al-Fasi's care for "about fourteen years." Such approximations in *SHQ* may be symbolic; cf. Cohen, *SFC*, pp. 106 f.

408 *Letter of [appointment]:* On the practice in Spain of issuing such letters of ordination or recognition, cf. Judah b. Barzillai, *Sefer ha-Shetarot*, pp. 132 f., and the report of such a letter issued by Ibn Megash himself in Hirschberg, "The Almohade Persecutions etc.," pp. 143/151 f. lines 18 f.; cf. also Goitein, *Jewish Education*, p. 192. These letters resemble the Arabic *ijaza* (cf. *EI*, II, 446 s.v.) and are quite distinct from official letters of appointment described by S. Assaf, "Le-Qorot ha-Rabbanut, *Reshumot*, II (1926–27), 264 f.

459 *Ibn Tumart:* I have adopted the reading of MSS לך, which, although members of class ח, transmit the correct orthography. For the reading of MS פ, cf. the statement about the same event, ובאותו הזמן בא מזמור הרשע, in A. Neubauer, "Documents Inédits: I. Une Pseudo-Biographie de Moise Maimonide," *REJ*, IV (1882), 173. Note that the writer there indicates that he fled to Toledo "because of that wicked one;" cf. below, line 465. *4783, when he decreed etc.:* Since it is now a virtual certainty that the Almohade onslaughts against the Jewries of the Maghreb and Spain did not antedate 1146/1147, the reading of MS ל, ed. pr., and Zacuto, 4902 [= 1141/1142], does not represent much of an improvement over the "erroneous" date of MSS הפ. However, further consideration of the date we have adopted as the original reading will reveal that it was not erroneous at all, but probably deliberately chosen by Ibn Daud. It is well known that Ibn Tumart was said to have rationalized the alternative of "Islam or the sword" for the Jews on the basis of a tradition that the Jews had promised to convert to Islam if the Messiah did not appear within five hundred years of the beginning of Islam; cf. Baron, *SRH*, III, 124 f.; Dozy, *Histoire*, III, 158. (Eng. trans, p. 721). Now, Ibn Daud had specifically indicated that "Muhammad... had begun to make his pretensions in 4374;" V. 38. This statement was totally unnecessary in the context in which it was placed and must, therefore, be seriously considered as one of Ibn Daud's hints at a "significant" date. In other words, Ibn Daud dates Ibn Tumart's persecutions from the year in which the Jews had to justify their right to existence. — The reading of the

editions and of Zacuto, p. 214a, 4902 (תתק״ב), is obviously a corruption (or correction) of the reading of MS א, Samuel ha-Nagid, MS Sassoon, p. 6 f. and Ibn Verga, *Shebet Yehudah* (ed. Shohet–Baer), p. 21, 4872 (תתע״ב). This would place the date in the 490th year after the Hijra, according to Ibn Daud's dating in V.5., and this figure is also a symbolic number in Ibn Daud's schematology; cf. Cohen, *SFC*, pp. 108 f. and Analysis, ch. III. On the other hand, the reading of MS ק seems to place the event 500 years after the Hijra.

463 *Silves*: Virtually all modern accounts relying on this passage of *SHQ* speak of Sala (or Salé) in Morocco as the westernmost Jewish community mentioned by Ibn Daud to have suffered during the Almohade persecutions. This is probably owing to the fact that Neubauer adopted the reading of MS ה against *all* the others and because of the similarity of Ibn Daud's description of its location to his description of the location of Sala in Epilogue. 23–24. However, there are neat distinctions between the two passages that have been overlooked. In the first place, Ibn Daud describes Sala as being "at the end of the Maghreb," but Silves as "at the end of the world." Now Silves is indeed somewhat west of Sala; but, what is far more important, it was recognized as being the westernmost point of the continent of Europe, as a glance at the map of Ibn Haukal will indicate; cf. his *Opus Geographicum*, 2 vols. ed. by J. H. Kraemers (Leiden, 1938), I, map facing p. 66. Moreover, the reading of the MSS, *shlb*, is a perfect transliteration of the Arabic spelling of Silves, which was a famous town, under the domination of Seville at the time of the Almohade invasion. Since the Almohades made their first headquarters in Spain at Seville, there is little reason to doubt the authenticity of Ibn Daud's report. Nor should we reject what is in reality an attested *lectio facilior* for an incorrect spelling, for Sala is spelled with a ס not with a צ as MS ה has for the variant here. — For a partial list of the communities which were shattered by the Almohades, cf. Abraham ibn Ezra's dirge in S. Bernstein, *'Al Naharot Sefarad* (Tel Aviv, 1956), pp. 114 f., 243 f.; H. Schirmann, "Qinot 'al ha-Gezerot be-Ereṣ Israel, Africa, Sefarad etc.," *Kobez al Jad*, III (XIII) (1939), 31 f.; Hirschberg, "The Almohade Persecutions," pp. 139 f.

469 *We have heard that in France*: Although Ibn Daud gives no indication as to the identity of his informants, the content of his report as well as external evidence enable us to narrow down his possible sources of information with a considerable degree of certainty. It has by now been well established that scholars of Lucena, notably R. Joseph ibn Megash, Judah ha-Levi and possibly even Ibn Daud's uncle, R. Baruk b. Isaac ibn Albalia, corresponded with scholars of Narbonne and exchanged information with them; cf. H. Schirmann, "The Life of Jehuda ha-Levi" [in Hebrew], *Tarbiz*, IX (1937–38), 227 f.; B.Z. Benedict, "On the History of the Torah-Centre in Provence" [in Hebrew], *ibid.*, XXII (1950–51), 90, 98 f. Ibn Daud may thus have heard about these renowned scholars of France from members of the Lucena circle of which he, too, was one and from which he had gained the major portion of his education; cf. above, lines 443–444. This conjecture appears all the more plausible in view of the fact that Ibn Daud reports the names of but three members of the community-court of Narbonne, while he has no inkling of the many other scholars who were active there and whose names appear in other sources. (It need hardly be added that the gloss to *SHQ* in MS א on the Jewry of Narbonne and published by Neubauer, *MJC*, I, 81 f., is not a product of Ibn Daud's pen.) Indeed, we may be reasonably certain that Ibn Daud was not informed of Narbonnese Jewry, let alone of that of all Provence, to the extent that his contemporary confrères of Catalonia and especially Barcelona must have been. This new,

albeit limited, awareness of Narbonnese Jewry reflected by Ibn Daud, and the increased tempo of intercourse between the Jewry of Spain and that of France, are to be explained not only by the annexation of Provence to the county of Barcelona, but by the general permeation of Spanish society, religious as well as military, by French personnel and influence; cf. M. Defourneaux, *op. cit.*, pp. 15 f., 39 f., 125 f., 152 f. On Franco-Jewish migration, cf. Baer, *History*, I, 83 f.; above, S.N. to line 311.

Supplementary Notes to Epilogue

12 The integrity of reporters was vital to the trustworthiness of a tradition, according to the Muslim scientists of *ḥadith*; cf. J. Schacht, *The Origins of Muhammadan Jurisprudence* (Oxford, 1950), pp. 27 f., 37 f. That the Jews also classified the transmission of the tradition and its transmitters in the category of testimony and witnesses has been indicated by Halkin in Maimonides, *Epistle to Yemen*, p. 56 n. 72. Witnesses of unimpeachable character can obviously not be accused of *bid'a* or fabrication; cf. S.N. to Prologue. 13–14. Similarly, Ibn Daud's insistence on the integrity of the chain, which suffered no interruptions, is an old Rabbanite argument, which reflects Muslim thinking on the subject; cf. Schacht, p. 38 and Saadiah's style in S. Atlas and M. Perlmann, "Saadia on the Scroll of the Hasmoneans," *PAAJR*, XIV (1944), 6/7 line 14. See above, pp. LVII f. and below, pp. 155 f. for further elaboration of this point.

22 The Karaites, of course, were willing to accept only unanimity as evidence of consensus and, therefore, distinguished between the text of Scripture, on which there was universal accord, and rabbinic tradition, on which there was not; cf. Pinsker, *Lickute Kadmoniot*, Appendix p. 26; Salmon b. Yeruḥim, *Wars of the Lord*, p. 37. On Karaite sensitivity to this argument, cf. Ankori, *Karaites in Byzantium*, pp. 54 f. — The argument from majority was also construed as an argument from success, numerical as well as financial, as evidence of the truth; cf. Daniel al-Kumisi's remarks in Mann, *Texts and Studies*, II, 80; Mahler, *Karaites*, pp. 277 f., 282 f.

33 *Land of Venice and Genoa*: For earlier efforts to interpret these two obscure names, cf. S. Krauss, *Studien zur byzantinisch-juedischen Geschichte* (Leipzig, 1914,) pp. 77 f.; B.Z. Dinur, *Israel ba-Gola* (2 ed.), I, 270. Orthographically, the closest names to *nbqry* and *ggnt* are Naupaktos and Zakynthos, but why Ibn Daud should single out these two out-of-the-way places has not been explained. The suggestion presented in the translation here requires but slight emendations and, I submit, has the merit of following (Ibn Daud's conception of) the map with a fair degree of order. The scribal evolution in reverse was *nbqry-nbqdy-bndqy* = Venice; or to trace the Arabic to Hebrew evolution of this identification: 1) بندقية 2) mistakenly read as نبدقية 3) by metathesis became נבקדי, נבקרי. The identification of *ggnt* as Genoa requires emending the Hebrew from גגנת to גנות (= جنوة), which may be reflected in the readings of MSS פג. For these names in Arabic, with descriptions of their location, cf. Abu'l Fida, *Géographie. Texte Arabe*, ed. by M. Reinaud and M. de Slane (Paris, 1840), pp. 208, 210. If our interpretation is correct, Ibn Daud takes the two extremes of the central Mediterranean: Venice and Genoa to Constantinople and Byzantium. See also B. N. to next line.

35 *Messena*: Heb. Maginsiya. I have adopted the identification of Dinur, *loc. cit.*, which is endorsed by Krauss, "Die hebraeischen Benennungen," p. 411 n. 99. However, I confess to the same misgivings on the subject which Krauss had. I would suggest Sardinia as a logical point on the map to be named in this context, but this would require radical

emendation of the text for which I can find no support. *Rhone*: Heb., Dorano = Rhodano. For the frequent interchange of "r" and "d" within a word cf. S.N. to I.144; variants to Hebrew text 15.66, 16.85–86 s.v. הורדוס.

47 *Al-Sheikh*: For this title and its Hebrew equivalent, *ha-zaken*, cf. Munk, *Notice sur Abou'l Walid*, pp. 6 f.; Pinsker, *Lickute Kadmoniot*, Appendix p. 144, where he is called *al-sheikh al-kabir*, the great sage; Mann, *Texts and Studies*, I, 384; II, 99; *Sefer ha-Yishub*, II,46 f. Abu'l-Faraj was occasionally called *ha-melammed ha-gadol*, which is almost the identical title which Abu'l-Taras' widow had; below, line 54 and Pinsker, *Lickute Kadmoniot*, p. 217.

48 *Fool*: Ibn Daud adopts the normal practice of Rabbanites of playing on the word *maskil* (learned, illuminated), used by the Karaites for their sages, by converting it to *kesil* (fool, nitwit); cf. below, line 137. On the use of *kesil(im)* for Karaites, cf. Tobiah b. Eliezer, *Leqaḥ Tob*, I to Ex. 21.22, p. 151 and Buber's introduction, pp. 26, 34; cf. also *ibid.*, II on Lev., p. 64 (very bot.), where a Hebrew synonym, *shotim*, is used. Cf. also Nemoy, "Al-Qirqisani's Account etc.," *HUCA*, VII (1930), 321 to nn. 6–7. On the Karaite use of the term *maskil*, cf. Ankori, *Karaites in Byzantium*, index, s.v. maskil; Wieder, *Judean Scrolls and Karaism*, pp. 105 f.

54 On the title *mu'allim* or its Hebrew equivalent *ha-melammed*, cf. S.N. to line 47; Munk, *Notice sur Abou'l Walid*, p. 5 n. 1; Ankori, *Karaites in Byzantium*, Index s.v. teachers. Although the title was most commonly used by Karaites, it also crops up in Rabbanite circles; cf. Poznanski's review of the Berliner *Festschrift* in *REJ*, XLVII (1903), 139 n. 2; *idem*, "Ephraim b. Schemaria de Fostat," *ibid.*, XLVIII (1904), 145 n. 1, 154.

57 *R. Joseph b. Ferrizuel surnamed Cidellus*: The name of Joseph's father as well as his surname are recorded in a hopelessly corrupt fashion by all of the MSS. Nevertheless, the correct orthography is clearly detectable in each of these names. Thus Ferrizuel may clearly be seen to underlie not only the forms recorded by MSS ש but also in the form of MSS ת where the names אל פרונאל קברי should be redivided to קברי אל פרונגאל. As for Cidellus, Baer clearly saw that this name lay hidden in the form מבצירדל, which on the authority of Neubauer he copied as מבצידל; cf. Baer, *Die Juden im Christlichen Spanien*, II, 14, 552. The original form lying behind the corruption of this name is easily discerned. Ibn Daud apparently recorded the name as הנשיא ר' יוסף הנקרא צידל. Over the word הנקרא either the author himself or a copyist inserted the salutation for the dead מ"ב (מנוחתו בכבוד); cf. VI.159. A subsequent copyist mistakenly inserted these two letters *after* the word, "surnamed," and the corruption before us emerged. The form קברי, אלקברי, in MSS ת leaves me utterly baffled.

60 On the knotty question as to whether the Jews did have the right to administer capital punishment in medieval times, cf. Mann, "The Responsa of the Babylonian Geonim," *JQR* NS, X (1919), 129 n. 192, XI (1921), 456 f.; *idem*, "Seqirah Historit 'al Dinay Nefashot ba-Zeman ha-Zeh," *Hazofeh*, X (1926), 200 f.; Baron, *SRH*, V, 45 f.; *idem*, *The Jewish Community*, III, index s.v. capital punishment.

62 *King of kings*: Since, as far as I am aware, Ibn Daud is the first Jew to give this explanation of *imperator*, and since the expression has evoked no little comment among medievalists, it may not be inappropriate to reconsider some of the accepted views on this title. Menendez Pidal, *El Imperio Hispanico*, p. 11, states that "Los arabes conciben el titulo [i.e. imperator] como 'rey de reyes'." This sentence is lifted bodily from E. Mayer, *Historia de las Instituciones Sociales y Politicas de España y Portugal*, 2 vols. (Madrid, 1925–26), II, 17, where the statement is documented in n. 17 with the assertion: "Asi para Alfonso VI en referencia de Dozy, *Recherches*, I." An examination of R. Dozy,

SUPPLEMENTARY NOTES 145

Recherches sur l'Histoire et la Littérature de l'Espagne pendant le Moyen Age, 3rd ed., 2 vols. (Leiden, 1881), I, 105, and Arabic appendix, p. xvii, will reveal that the remark is not by Dozy at all, but Ibn Khaldun's parenthetical observation (probably on the basis of Ibn Ḥayyan; cf. Dozy, *ibid.*, p. 90) on the meaning of the title "Imperator:" ومعناه ملك الملوك (Ibn Khaldun, *Kitab al-Ibar*, Beirut, IV [1958], 391.) Ibn Khaldun himself, however, was not really certain that this was the meaning of the word, for in the *Muqaddimah* he suggested that the term Imperator means crowned; Ibn Khaldun, *Muqaddimah* (trans. F. Rosenthal), I, 481. (Arabic: فيسمى المتوج; ed. Beirut [1921], I, 415). Professor Douglas Dunlop, with whom I discussed this question, graciously drew my attention to the note in M. de Slane's translation, *Les Prolégomènes d'Ibn Khaldūn*, I, 477, where a marginal note in the Bulaq edition is cited indicating that among the French the term pronounced "eimberour" signifies "king of kings." Thus, the evidence in no way warrants the conclusion of Mayer that the title "king of kings" is the usual Arabic interpretation of "Imperator." Professor Dunlop also informs me that Ibn al-Khatib, *Kitab A'mal al-A'lam* (ed. by E. Lévi-Provençal, Rabat, 1934), p. 381, in explaining the imperial title of Alfonso VI, cites the Jew, Joseph b. Waqar of Toledo according to whom the term "imperator" means "sultan of sultans." Ibn Daud, to be sure, may have known of the usage "king of kings" from the east, where it evoked no little disapproval; cf. Mez, *op. cit.*, pp. 24, 126. However, it is more likely an extension of similar titles used by Jews in Egypt, e.g., *sar-ha-sarim, negid ha-negidim*; cf. Mann, *Jews in Egypt*, I, 216, 256. It was all the more appropriately applied to Alfonso, inasmuch as in the Bible the expression is employed of pagan kings; cf. Ezek. 26.7; Dan. 2.37; Ezra. 7.12. — It remains to consider one other immediate source that may supposedly have influenced Ibn Daud, and that is the Christian society of Toledo. G. Post, "Blessed Lady Spain," *Speculum*, XXIX (1954), 210, cites R. B. Merriman, *The Rise of the Spanish Empire* (1918; 1962), I, 90, and Menendez Pidal, *El Imperio Hispanico*, pp. 155 f., in support of the statement that Alfonso VII received permission from Innocent II to style himself "king of kings." Menendez Pidal says nothing of the sort, while Merriman indeed asserts the point but provides no documentation. The baselessness of Merriman's assertion was noted by H. Hueffer, "Die leonesischen Hegemoniebestrebungen und Kaisertitel," *Spanische Forschungen der Goerresgesellschaft*, Erste Reihe, III (1931), 375 n. 1; cf. also Schramm, "Das Kastilische Koenigtum und Kaisertum," p. 108 n. 41. The documents of Alfonso VII, edited and analysed by Rassow, as cited in B. N. to line 63, contain no reference to such a title. To be sure, *imperator* often meant a king over other kings; cf. P.E. Schramm, *Kaiser, Rom und Renovatio* (2nd ed. Darmstadt, 1957), pp. 76, 119, 157 f. However, I can find no other evidence for the use of "king of kings" as an official title, or even as an explicit interpretation of *imperator*.

83 *Fled on foot etc.*: Cf. the similar wording in Judah ha-Levi's elegy יום הגליתי in his *Diwan* (ed. Zamora), III, 473, lines 5 f. The verbal similarities of Ibn Daud's description to the elegy of Judah ha-Levi, coupled with the fact that the portrayal here consists largely of a patchwork of biblical phrases, suggest that at this point Ibn Daud was consciously imitating the elegiac payyetanic style, if not indeed ha-Levi's poem itself.

90 For an interesting episode some seven years prior to the fall of Calatrava, which may have involved Judah ibn Ezra, cf. S.D. Goitein, "The Last Phase of R. Yehuda Hallevi's Life etc." [in Hebrew], *Tarbiz*, XXIV (1954–55), 35.

99–100 *Of royal blood*: However, not necessarily of the house of David. Indeed, Ibn Daud denies explicitly that the Jewish community could claim any survivors of Davidic descent; cf. VI.218–219. *As evidenced etc.*: The overtone here is somewhat different from that in the statement of VII.418, for here Ibn Daud stresses not religious virtues so much as qualities of rule and leadership. For the idea that a man's nobility lies in his blood and will be reflected in his traits, cf. Mez, *op. cit.*, pp. 147 f.; Pérès, *op. cit.*, pp. 18–20, where even Jewish traits are singled out by al-Makarri as a mark of true cultivation.

125 The latter part of this sentence spells out the specific benefits which the Karaites failed to achieve, namely the production of literature that "would fortify the hearts of Israel in the lands of their dispersion" (below, line 149). This may be an oblique reference to the fact that the Karaites often characterized themselves as "those who sigh and cry" (Ezek. 9.4) for Zion; cf. Ankori, *Karaites in Byzantium*, Index s.v. Mourner(s) of Zion, Mourning, Mourning of Zion; Zucker, "Tegubot li-Tenuʿat Abaylay Zion etc.," pp. 378 f. The Karaites are thus contrasted with the Rabbanites whose whole effort was to console and encourage the Jews through poetry, exegesis and exhortation. This concern with consolation and "fortification of the heart" goes back to talmudic times; cf. Zunz, *Ha-Derashot be-Israel*, pp. 165, 462 n. 41, 483 n. 64. However, in gaonic times it becomes a major motif; cf. Saadiah, *Essa Meshali* (ed. Lewin,) pp. 10, 41.87–91; Schechter, *Saadyana*, 5.16 f.; Cowley, "Bodleian Geniza Fragments," pp. 401 f. [= *ISG*, Appendix, pp. XXII f.]; Abraham bar Ḥiyya, *Megillat ha-Megalleh*, p. 1; Cohen, *SFC*, pp. 95 f. Note, too, how concerned R. Saadiah was to refute the charge that his work was an agent of discouragement to the Jewish community; Harkavy, *Zikron la-Rishonim*, V, 162/163.1–2.

127 On the triad, *shiratha tushbeḥatha we-neḥamatha*, cf. D. de Sola Pool, *The Kaddish* (New York, 1929), pp. 61 f. For some early Karaite *piyyutim*, cf. Ankori, *Karaites in Byzantium*, Index s.v. piyyutim; M. Zulay, "Bayn Kotlay ha-Makon le-Ḥeqer ha-Shirah ha-Ibrit," *Alei Ayin: The Salman Schocken Jubilee Volume* (Jerusalem, 1952), pp. 119, 124 n. 43.

132–133 *Folly and ignorance*: For the same style of attack, cf. Saadiah in Lewin, *Otzar ha-Geonim*, I, Responsa, p. 14 # 29; M. Friedlaender, *Essays on the Writings of Ibn Ezra* (= *Ibn Ezra Literature*, IV, London, s.a.), p. 126 n. 1. Cf. also above, note to line 48.

135–136 *Reason requires the following*: Cf. the explicit statement by Qirqisani to that effect in Nemoy, "Al-Qirqisani's Account etc.," p. 396. On Karaite use of reason, rather than tradition, cf. Mahler, *Karaites*, pp. 280 f.; M. Zucker, "Fragments from Rav Saadya Gaon's Commentary to the Pentateuch" [in Hebrew], *Sura*, II (1955–56), 320 f., 327, 329 f.; Ankori, *Karaites in Byzantium*, pp. 327 f. On Abu'l-Faraj's renown within Karaism for the use of reason in exegesis, cf. *idem*, "Elijah Bashyachi," p. 56 n. 42.

144 *These having been forgotten etc.*: Jewish sensitivity to the decline of Hebrew letters, and especially of Hebrew verse, was in large measure a consequence of the vigorous Arabic propaganda for the inherent superiority of the Arabic language; cf. von Grunebaum, *op. cit.*, pp. 36 f. For a similar inferiority complex within the Christian community of Andalus because of the decline of Latin letters, cf. *ibid.*, pp. 57 f.; Dozy, *Histoire*, I, 317, 344 (Eng. tr., pp. 268, 292).

ANALYSIS AND INTERPRETATION

I. THE STRUCTURE OF *SEFER HA-QABBALAH*

Ostensibly, the plan of *Sefer ha-Qabbalah* is a simple one, and assuming the associations inherent in the polemical categories we have described in the Introduction, its contents are easy to comprehend. Apart from an introductory statement and a closing diatribe, the work is manifestly divisible into seven chapters, the titles of six of them being supplied by Ibn Daud himself.[1] Each chapter corresponds to a distinct period in the history of Jewish tradition, and, apart from the first period, each of the ages is subdivided into generations of authorities.

Curiously, the portion of the work which seems to be least consistent with the general plan is the first, the one covering the biblical period and the chain of prophetic succession. Although Ibn Daud had ample precedent and indeed ready models to follow in building his work around a detailed list of prophetic transmitters of tradition,[2] he chose to ignore these, for reasons which will become increasingly apparent, and to construct his opening chapter with a series of distinct units, each of which represented a different genre and different line of attack. The probity of the rabbinic *isnad* had to be demonstrated by (A) reason, (B) a religious genealogy demonstrating an unbroken chain of transmission, (C) accurate data on the chronology of the transmitters and the circumstances under which they worked, and (D) full and accurate data on the lives of the transmitters demonstrating the integrity of their character.

Ibn Daud opened his history of tradition by a statement of the thesis of his work, which was basically an impassioned argument from reason (A), and alluded at the same time to his claim that his reason was supported by an ancient *isnad* (B) deriving from men whose probity was beyond question (D).[3] Without any apparent connection, he then plunged into a detailed chronology of Jewish history from the year of Creation until the destruction of the First Temple.[4] Clearly, what he was doing was to indicate at the very outset of his story that all of his historical data would be coupled with scrupulous attention to exact chronology, of which the Rabbanites were in full possession (C). Since this

---

1 On the division of a work into chapters as a characteristic of Arabic style, cf. Mez, *op. cit.*, p. 194.
2 Cf. *STW*, p. 14.
3 Prologue.4 f.
4 1.2–70.

chronology necessitated giving a list of the kings of Judah along with the length of their reigns,[5] Ibn Daud extended the list to include the Davidic princes who had stood at the helm of Jewish society from the Babylonian exile until R. Judah the Prince II in the amoraic period.[6] This list of princes clearly was meant to serve as demonstrable proof that the Davidic patriarchate of the Rabbanites[7] could boast an attested genealogy that went back to the universally acknowledged kings of Judah and Israel (B). However, this genealogy also served as a convenient means of transition to the genealogy with which *Sefer ha-Qabbalah* was really concerned, namely, the chain beginning with Moses and extending to the last of the prophets and the men of the Great Assembly (B).[8] This latter aspect of biblical history was treated rather summarily, the account being confined essentially to a quotation of the first paragraph of the Ethics of the Fathers, for Ibn Daud felt that he had no need—indeed, there would be little point—to argue the transmission of an unwritten tradition through prophets who were universally acknowledged except on the basis of reason. Accordingly, he wove exegetical arguments from Scripture, which even Karaites would have to acknowledge as arguments from reason (A), into his biblical *tabaqat*.[9] Having disposed of the biblical chain (B), he quickly returned to (C) with a detailed chronological analysis of the periods of the two Temples and especially of the period from the destruction of the First Temple to that of the Second.[10] This third part falls into two distinct sections, the first (Ca)[11] containing a series of "empirical" observations on the chronology of the First Temple and the period of the first exile under the kings of Babylon and Persia. The second (Cb)[12] provides an elucidation of Daniel's oracle on the "seventy weeks" in terms of the actual sequence of events from the first exile until the destruction of the Second Temple.

Now in the light of what we have already indicated about the loose relationship between the expressed purposes of Ibn Daud's other works and their actual contents,[13] it should not surprise us that in this work as well, the author

---

5   I.45–68.
6   I.71–80.
7   II.120.
8   I.81–111.
9   I.92–103. For the Karaite invocation of reason in Bible exegesis, cf. Epilogue.135, and esp. Zucker, "Fragments from Rav Saadya Gaon's Commentary," pp. 316 f.; *idem*, *Rav Saadya Gaon's Translation*, pp. 229 f.
10 I.112–209.
11 I.112–153, 210–223.
12 I.154–209.
13 Cf. Introduction, pp. xxxiii f.

sought to tackle several problems at one and the same time and to convey his multiple message subtly and tacitly, if not too artistically.

The apparent purposes of his chronological expositions, studded with references to problematic statements in Scripture and ostensibly contradictory rabbinic traditions (C), seem to be clear enough. To begin with, the first chronological summary sought to square the traditional rabbinic figure of 410 years for the duration of the First Temple with the data in Scripture, which clearly indicated to Ibn Daud that the total was 433.[14] Whether his solution was felicitous or not is another matter.[15] The point that must be stressed here is that Ibn Daud felt constrained to harmonize authentic historical data of one class, Scripture, with contradictory but no less authentic data of another class, that of rabbinic tradition. This identical aim underlies the analysis of the period from the destruction of the First Temple until the destruction of the Second in the light of Daniel's oracle (Cb). The rabbinic traditions on the periodization of this stage of history had to be squared with the prophecy of Daniel, which was apparently predicated on divergent assumptions. In other words, chronology served Ibn Daud's primary thesis as a case in point. The discrepancies between Scripture and tradition, which Karaites were so fond of playing up, were actually specious, and real only to superficial and uninformed amateurs. How intricate and religiously instructive the seemingly simple subject of biblical chronology really was, Ibn Daud preceeded to show (Ca) by pointing out the rhythmic pattern of certain stages in the history of the Temples, a point which no one apparently had noted before him. Ibn Daud thus validated a cardinal point in rabbinic tradition, a calendar derived from the one and only proper interpretation of scriptural data.[16] In this vein, too, he provided the evidence substantiating the Rabbanite date for the beginning of the Seleucid Era in 3449 A.M. (= 312/311 B.C.E.),[17] as opposed to the Karaite date of 3475 A.M.[18]

The second part of the first chronological excursus (Ca) disposed of another matter regarded as essential by medieval chronographers, and that was the synchronization of Jewish history with the history of the principal Gentile empires.[19] That genre of chronography had been established by Eusebius, Jerome and Isidore and had been taken over from them by later chroniclers,

---

14 I.20–23.
15 Cf. below, pp. 194 f.
16 Cf. above, p. LVI n. 65.
17 II.18.
18 Neubauer, *Medieval Jewish Chronicles*, II, 249; cf. also H. J. Bornstein, "Ta'arikay Israel," *Ha-Tequfa*, IX (1921–22), 230 f.
19 Cf. also above, p. LVI n. 65.

Christian as well as Arab. Since in the case of the period from Nebuchadnezzar to Titus, and especially from the rise of the former until the period of Artaxerxes, this synchronization was fraught with exegetical problems, Ibn Daud broke up this section and inserted his analysis of the prophecy of Daniel (Cb) in the very middle of this survey of Jewish-Gentile history. If momentarily we overlook this diverting footnote on Daniel, the plan of his discussion is clear and consistent.

Quite apart from the two sides of chronology that required treatment—the purely Jewish, and the Jewish synchronized with the Gentile—the first chapter also anticipated two issues that will be seen to run as *leitmotifs* throughout *Sefer ha-Qabbalah*, After enumerating the kings of Judah, which he had to do in connection with the exact number of years that the kingdom of Judah had endured, Ibn Daud, it will be recalled, proceeded without any apparent reason or motive to enumerate the Davidic princes from Zerubbabel to Judah the Prince II.[20] On the face of things, it would seem that Ibn Daud inserted this list (Bb) merely as a means of easy transition to the theme which follows on its heels, namely, the transmission of tradition from Moses to the last of the prophets. Above all, he wished the reader to keep in mind the high-born origin of the Rabbanite leaders. Their nobility was, in his view, as in the view of many another writer of ancient and medieval times, a further proof of the high-mindedness of the bearers of the oral tradition.[21] But, as will also be seen from the subsequent sections of his work, there was a second subtlety embedded in this list, given the context in which it had been recorded. This was the nature of the ideal, ie., divinely ordained, structure of Jewish society. Like Judah ha-Levi and Moses Maimonides, Ibn Daud had indicated in his philosophical exposition of Judaism that the Torah was not only a system of faith and practices leading to the perfection of the individual, but also a blueprint for the most perfect form of political organization.[22] What this system was in operation he proceeded to show in *Sefer ha-Qabbalah*. In subsequent sections of his book, Ibn Daud made it quite clear that in the ideal Jewish state authority and administration were to be divided between political and religious leadership, between nasi, or prince, and rabbi.[23] This neat division, which when violated would set off upheavals and schisms within the Jewish

---

20 Cf. above, n. 6.
21 Cf. Introduction, pp. L f.
22 *Emunah Ramah*, p. 98; Judah ha-Levi, *Kitab al-Khazari*, III, 3 5; Maimonides, *Guide*, III.27-28. Cf. also Berman, *op. cit.*, where the whole literature of, and on, the political philosophy of Maimonides has been collected and analyzed.
23 II.143.

community,24 was not, Ibn Daud indicated at once, a rabbinic innovation but merely an extension of the two-fold character of Jewish society of biblical times, where king (Bb) and prophet (Ba) prefigured the later nasi (Bb) and head of the rabbinic academy (Ba). In certain periods, to be sure, both reins of government were held by one man, e.g., Moses, Joshua and "the elders."25 However, by and large, the two arms of government were distinct and held by different men. This phenomenon, which recurred in Jewish history right down to Ibn Daud's own day,26 was in itself part of the history of the tradition and one of the vehicles by which the purity and continuity of the transmission had been assured.

In the light of this analysis, the first chapter of *Sefer ha-Qabbalah*, which at first glance gives the impression of a rambling and totally disconnected discussion, now emerges as a carefully planned and rigidly pursued treatment divided into six distinct parts. If we follow Ibn Daud's lead and consider the argument from reason and the chain of transmission as two sides of the same argument, the chapter consists of two alternating discussions of tradition and chronology. Beginning with the Prologue—which, of ocurse, Ibn Daud considered as part of his opening section and which we have arbitrarily separated from the body of the work—the sequence of the themes discussed is:

	Theme	Chapter and lines of our translation
A	(The rational basis of tradition)	Prologue
C	(Chronology)	I. 2-70
Bb	(Transition from chronology to tradition through rulers who succeeded the kings)	I. 71-80
Ba	(History of biblical tradition buttressed by reason [A])	I. 81-111
Ca	(Chronology)	I. 112-153, 210-223
Cb	(Footnote on chronology and exegesis)	I. 154-209

Beginning with the second chapter, the various genres and strands of the argument are presented in an integrated and much more simplified form. We do not mean to imply that Ibn Daud abandoned all subtlety in the construction of his work. However, at least to the naked eye, and with but one or two exceptions, the framework of the narrative is rigidly adhered to and easy to follow. Each paragraph begins with an enumeration of the bearer(s) of tra-

---

24 III.3 f., VI.126 f.
25 Cf. also III.31, 70, 78, 79.
26 Cf. VII.75, Epilogue. 57, 63, 89–90; and cf., below, ch. V.

dition (Ba), the other themes being subsumed as interpolations within the major one. To be sure, these other themes have by no means been forgotten. Besides the problem avowedly taken up by the author, each of the chapters makes at least a passing reference to, or includes an extended discussion of, turning points of Jewish chronology (C),[27] the relationship of accepted Jewish dating to problematic evidence in other sources (Cb),[28] and the relationship of the dates of events and turning points in Jewish history to corresponding dates of Gentile history (Ca).[29] Finally, the aristocracy of rabbinic leadership and the recognition of its nobility by the Jewish masses as well as by foreign rulers (Bb) will be recalled to the reader repeatedly.[30]

Moreover, beginning with the second chapter, a new and antiphonal element in Jewish history, which was merely hinted at in the Prologue, is described fully. The new element is presented in terms of historical events, to be sure, but also in such a way as to make its components into counterpoints of the themes characterizing the mainstream of Jewish history. Thus, the various types and stages of sectarianism (A') are dated (C'),[31] and the genealogy of dissident leadership is carefully described (Ba'-b').[32]

Perhaps the best example of the new and simplified framework in which the various themes and counter-themes are woven into a running narrative occurs at the very beginning of the account of the second stage of Jewish history. The section opens with the identification of the head of the generation representing the "link" in the chain of transmission, Simeon the Righteous (Ba). His high-born origin and the author's full awareness of all the vital details of his life are reflected in the identification of Simeon with Iddo, the high priest (Bb). His setting in the chronology of world history—the downfall of the Persian Empire and the rise of the Greek (Ca)—is complemented by a purely Jewish date, the fortieth year of the Second Temple (C). The new form of chronology adopted by the Jews as a result of the encounter between Simeon the Righteous and Alexander the Great (Ca) is quickly shown to have been justified, indeed endowed with the stamp of divine approval, in view of the fact that that very year was a major turning point in purely internal Jewish history. It marked the millennium of the Exodus from Egypt, and it marked the end of prophecy and the beginning of a new form of instruction of religious knowledge to the Jews. Thus, the year in which Rabbinism emerged as the exclusive

---

27 II.18, 164; III.95; IV.70; V.5.
28 II.97 f.
29 III.98 f.; IV.87 (and cf. *ZDR*, beg.); V.5, 38 f.; VII.459.
30 Cf. Introduction, p. LXII.
31 Cf. *ibid.*, p. LIX.
32 Cf. *ibid.*, pp. XXXVII f.

and manifest form of Judaism was also a memorable date from several points of view (C, Ca). All this occurred against the backdrop of Alexander's confessed recognition of the almost supernatural character of the leader of the Jews, who was, accordingly, "honored and exalted" by the Gentile monarch (Bb). Was such recognition ever accorded to heretics and sectarians?[33]

Ibn Daud's last expostulation was not an outburst of uncontrolled emotion. The contrast of Simeon with Anan and Qirqisani was a literary device serving as the transition to the new and antiphonal part of Jewish history, the rise of sectarianism. Samaritanism, which, it will be recalled, Ibn Daud and many Rabbanites regarded as the parent of Karaism, became an institutionalized religion (B') thanks to a grant from the same Alexander who had accorded the correct form of Judaism special honors. However, the leaders of that new form of worship had no basis in tradition. They simply set up a counter form of worship in order to accommodate the base desires of some disaffected priests who had condemned themselves forever by an alliance with the Kutheans, a people of Gentile stock (Bb'). Only after they had set up their secessionist Temple did Zadok and Boethus, two *mis*interpreters of good Jewish doctrine (B'), arrive with a new set of laws and dogmas (A') that posed as tradition. Now in possession of political leaders, a temple, priests and pseudo-teachers, the Samaritans could also pretend to have a Jewish-type, and consequently legitimate form, of government.

But make no mistake about it. These heretics could flourish only so long as they had Greek protection. No sooner did the Jews manage to stabilize their newly won independence, thanks to the revolt of the Hasmoneans (who were, of course, of authentic high-priestly stock (Bb), than the Samaritans began to feel the effects of the policy practiced by all authentic Jewish leaders—persecution and obliteration of heresy. That is why their temple was destroyed scarcely two and a half centuries after it had been established (Ca'). For all we know, Ibn Daud indicated, heresy might have been dead and buried once and for all but for the corruption of the Hasmonean stock as the consequence of illicit marriage (Bb'). Jealous of the powers they had attained, the Hasmoneans refused to give up the reins of that part of the government which they were now disqualified to direct, and they became sectarians themselves. Greed and lust breed heresy, history will show us, not tradition or ingenuous difference of opinion.

Through five stages of Jewish history—the teachers of the Second Commonwealth, tannaim, amoraim, saboraim, geonim—the account in *Sefer ha-Qab-*

[33] II.3-22.

balah proceeds along these clear, and for the most part obvious, lines. Whenever possible, Ibn Daud supplemented his data on the link in the tradition (Ba) with chronology (C), which he synchronized, at major turning points, with other systems of dating, Jewish as well as Gentile (Ca). Each of the major themes and counter-themes is accorded a more extended treatment when necessary. Thus, the invidious implications which Christians elicited from their dating of the crucifixion of Jesus of Nazareth (C') is vigorously refuted, at least by Ibn Daud's standards of evidence, and shown to be unsupported propaganda. The emergence of new religions such as Christianity, Manichaeism and Islam is carefully dated (Ca'); these are shown to be the concoctions of latecomers on the scene of history. The calamities in Jewish history, the destruction of the Temple and the revolt of Bar Kokba, are shown to have resulted from the usurpation of authority by lawless men and pretenders to Davidic stock (Bb'). The most recent tragedy in the history of the tradition, Karaism, was perpetrated by a man who had indeed been learned and of authentic Davidic lineage (Bb). However, he broke with his master and with the truth out of the same motives which had prompted the once righteous Hasmoneans to defect to heresy—the discovery of some personal taint which disqualified him from leadership (Bb'). His subsequent actions proved how right his detractors had been, for he proceeded to act on his envy and to resurrect a heretical movement, which he now strengthened with an *ersatz* law manufactured in the mire of his warped heart (A'). Greed and envy had also generated this perversion; the distortion of Scripture and the flaunting of authority have ever been the hallmarks of this treasonable mob.[34] No wonder that Jews everywhere hold them in contempt, while intelligent Gentile kings permit the Jews to beat them to the ground.

By contrast, the leadership of the rabbinic mainstream has always been accorded the honor it deserves. They have been "honored and exalted" by Alexander and Vespasian, Romans and Persians, Arabs and Christians, not to mention the whole of the Jewish people who have accepted their authority and abided by their teachings. No envy lives in their hearts. Even when they were locked in the most bitter of disputes, they would not alter a jot of the enactments of their opponents.[35] Their history is an open record, and even

---

34 The description of Karaism as a doctrine that thrived on rejection of legitimate tradition out of sheer spite and adolescent contempt for elders was a stock Rabbanite argument going back to the geonim; cf. VI.47 and Zucker, *Rav Saadya Gaon's Translation*, pp. 214 f.; *idem*, "Tegubot li-Tenu'at Abaylay Zion ha-Qaraiyyim ba-Sifrut ha-Rabbanit," *Sefer ha-Yobel le-R. Ḥanok Albeck* (Jerusalem, 1963), pp. 390, 394.

35 III.30–31.

when out of vengeful motives their *names* were suppressed, not without legitimate reason, their views have been recorded and are easily identified.[36] Their deeds and their character, private and public, are ample testimony to the probity of their teaching and the legitimacy of their rule.

Only once, toward the end of his account of the amoraic period, did Ibn Daud interrupt the sequence of his account with a long footnote on the histories of Persia and Rome.[37] However, even this annoying divagation from his straightforward narrative attempted to serve several purposes simultaneously. Ostensibly, it took up the point made in the first chapter on the marvelous implications for Jewish faith to be derived from the history of the Gentiles (Ca). The histories of Rome and Persia revealed a remarkable symmetry, while the history of Persia showed that persecution of the Jews brought about the downfall of its rule. But this was only the external trapping for Ibn Daud's desire to bring his account of the history of the major empires, which he had begun and dropped earlier in his work, down to the parallel stage in Jewish history (C). Later on, he interpolated briefer statements on the subsequent empires, Islam and Christian Spain, thus keeping his account balanced between the history of the Jews and developments in the world at large.

More than a third of the work, and by far its most popular section, surveys the last of the periods in the history of tradition, namely the succession of the rabbinate following the collapse of the gaonate of Babylonia. Although this chapter, too, adheres formally to the structural framework of the preceding five, and weaves in the various themes and counter-themes within the framework of generations, chronicle and catalogue have been replaced by narrative and biography (D). Men and their lives, events and their consequences engage our attention rather than the number of the generations or strings of names, reigns and dates. Indeed, this chapter almost appears to be a work unto itself. Opening with a long and engaging introduction known as the "story of the four captives" (D) it proceeds to recount the history of the three generations of the rabbinate (B, D) and concludes with a general statement—which we have arbitrarily separated and named an Epilogue—that recapitulates the Prologue and brings together all of the arguments for Rabbinism and against Karaism hitherto unmentioned or but obliquely summarized (A).

It is in this section that Ibn Daud showed himself capable of telling an absorbing narrative and even of some historical insight. The shift in the centers of Jewish learning and authority from Babylonia to Egypt, North Africa and Spain is explained almost by purely economic causes. The arrival of scholars to areas

36 III.73–76.
37 IV.83–163.

with sufficient Jewish populations to sustain independent academies brought about the diversion of funds that had hitherto been sent to Babylonia to their own local institutions. Without the financial support of the Jews from abroad, the Babylonian academies were powerless and finally closed down.[38] What little talent and efforts had remained in Babylonia were finally reduced to nought as a result of persecutions and exile.[39]

Ibn Daud was also aware of the indebtedness of the Jews of Andalus to their Muslim overlords for the protection and encouragement they received in developing a center of scintillating personalities and cultural creativity. Were it not for the strong arm of 'Abd-ar-Raḥman III, the achievement of R. Moses the captive would have been frustrated at the outset. Were it not for the judicious intervention of al-Ḥakam II, the Jewish community of Cordova would have been irreparably sundered by the strife and factionalism germinated by Joseph ibn Shatnash. With the rise of Samuel ibn Nagrela to the vizierate of Granada, and thanks to his munificence and encouragement of Jewish savants of diverse talents and interests, Andalusian Jewry came into full flower. This golden age, spanning three generations of Jewish learning and literature, came to an end only as a result of the collapse of the traditional Muslim form of government in the south, the Jews being swept out along with the many victims of the Almohade "rebels." While Ibn Daud was obviously grieved at having to write an epitaph for a glorious community, his nostalgia for which he made no effort to conceal, he brought his account to a close with a faint expression of hope that the rise of Jewish learning in France and in Christian Toledo augured well for the future. He ended on the note he had begun, with an impassioned affirmation of the tradition of his faith (A).

What we hope has become clear is that for all of its stylistic and technical shortcomings—and these, too, are obvious enough—*Sefer ha-Qabbalah* was not the product of haphazard jotting. Carefully planned and structurally integrated, Ibn Daud's work suffered from the same pitfalls as the Talmud and many other ancient works. The footnote or the appendix had not yet been discovered. What the modern would normally reserve for the margin, Ibn Daud felt it necessary to weave into the body of his work. These distractions may annoy us and divert our attention, but they should not obscure his own plan and its unmistakable adherence to the subject of his work.

---

38 VII.2 f., 59, 93, 369.
39 VI.209 f.

II. IBN DAUD'S SOURCES

Torah and "Greek Wisdom"

While *Sefer ha-Qabbalah* is primarily a history of rabbinic tradition and was written from beginning to end in the spirit and defense of Rabbinism, it reflects the same synthesis of two different traditions as Ibn Daud's philosophical work.[1] His historiography, like his theology, drew on two discrete types of sources—Jewish and Gentile—and blended them into a unified and ostensibly harmonious account that traced the history of Jewish leadership in the wider setting of world history. In other words, Torah and "Greek wisdom" were combined to give a chronicle that would make Jewish history intelligible.

In the category of Torah, or Jewish sources, must be included not only the biblical, talmudic and rabbinic material but the method and content of the attack on Karaism. Although, as we have already seen, the Rabbanite polemical technique and canons of reasoning derived largely from the literature of Muslim jurisprudence and historiography, by Ibn Daud's day this form of apologetic had become so accepted a part of orthodox Jewish idiom as to be considered a native Jewish technique and genre.[2] Indeed, the very phraseology of the obviously polemical sections of *Sefer ha-Qabbalah* is so similar in wording to passages in the work of Ibn Daud's older contemporary, R. Tobiah b. Eliezer of Thessalonica, that the conclusion forces itself upon us that either both drew on a common source, or Ibn Daud utilized the work of R. Tobiah.[3] In any event, the ultimate source of inspiration for the anti-Karaitic passages of both writers was the anti-sectarian literature of Saadiah Gaon and his disciples, which had been circulated in Byzantium no less than throughout the Judeo-Arabic world.[4]

In Ibn Daud's case, the spirit of the Gaon is discernible in all of his work.

1 Cf. Introduction, ch. II.
2 Cf. *ibid.*, ch. III.
3 Cf. Prologue, 4 f., Epilogue, 12–14 with Tobiah b. Eliezer, *Leqah Tob*, 2 vols., vol. I, Genesis-Exodus, ed. by S. Buber (Vilna, 1880); vol. II, Leviticus-Deuteronomy, ed. by A.M. Padua (Vilna, 1884), II, Leviticus, pp. 32, 38 f., 125 f.; Prologue.19 f. with *Leqah Tob*, I, Exodus, pp. 106, 211. Cf. also Ankori, "Some Aspects of Karaite-Rabbanite Relations," *PAAJR*, XXV (1956), 170; idem, *Karaities in Byzantium*, pp. 269, 356 f. For a full discussion of R. Tobiah's work, cf. *ibid.*, pp. 261 f.
4 On Saadiah's acknowledged influence on Tobiah, cf. *Leqah Tob*, I, Introduction, p. 43.

In rationalizing Judaism by means of philosophy, he openly invoked the example of Saadiah.[5] Moreover, Ibn Daud's interest in chronology, his vigorous reaffirmations of the messianic hope of Judaism, and his impassioned polemic against Jewish sectarians and other religions were all anticipated by the great head of the academy of Sura.[6] To this must be added Ibn Daud's unconcealed interest in the life of the Gaon and his partisan endorsement of the Gaon's position in intra-Babylonian disputes.[7] To Ibn Daud, a Saadyanic statement represented the confirmation of a fact.[8] What Saadiah had condemned was to Ibn Daud anathema, and the Spaniard had doubtless "imbibed the waters of the Gaon"—to use Ibn Daud's own figure of speech[9]— no less than some of his forebears.

On the other hand, it is not all impossible that Ibn Daud appropriated some of his *phraseology* from the biblical commentary of R. Tobiah, composed around 1100. The suggestion that Ibn Daud actually saw and drew upon R. Tobiah's work becomes all the more plausible in view of the fact that in Toledo he apparently became familiar with a second Byzantine Hebrew work, a great compendium of Karaite lore by Judah Hadassi. The latter's *Eshkol ha-Kofer*,[10] although basically a code, also contained considerable anti-Rabbanite polemic and pro-Karaite apologetic. One long passage of the latter type consists of a detailed excursus on the chronology of the First and Second Temples that has some marked points of affinity with Ibn Daud's disscusions. The most striking resemblance between the two works is the interweaving of religious polemic with a chronology of the biblical and Second Temple periods coupled with detailed exegeses of biblical passages dealing with the dates of building and destruction of the two Temples.[11] While it is possible that

---

5 Cf. above, p. xxix.
6 Cf. Malter, *Saadia Gaon*, pp. 172 f., 353 f.; above, pp. LII, LVI.
7 VI.126 f.
8 VII.303 f.
9 VII.271.
10 For an exhaustive bibliography on this work, cf. Ankori, *Karaites in Byzantium*, pp. 28 f.
11 Cf. I.18 f., 114–209 with Judah Hadassi, *Eshkol ha-Kofer* (Eupatoria, 1836), f. 46b, par. 125 and following. Several points of correspondence are particularly worthy of note. Both authors agree that the real exile of the Jews by Nebuchadnezzar is to be dated from the latter's twenty-third regnal year; cf. I.139–140 and Hadassi, f. 48a, par. 128; however, Hadassi does not seem to have drawn the same mistaken conclusion as Ibn Daud that the Temple was destroyed in that year. Both authors have a detailed and similar exegesis of Dan. 9; cf. I.154 f. and Hadassi, *loc. cit.* While Ibn Daud probably drew the interpretation of the chapter from Rabbanite, and more specifically Saadyanic, sources, it is remarkable that he should go off on this kind of exegetical tangent precisely as Hadassi does. Both of them invoke scriptural words as chronological mnemonics; cf. below, pp. 171, 194 f. and Hadassi, f. 47c. Both of them consistently refer to Titus as Vespasian's step-

both Ibn Daud and Hadassi drew on the same earlier source, the fact that the former's work betrays points of almost verbal identity with two Byzantine works of the twelfth century can hardly be pure coincidence. Hadassi's work was composed only some twelve years prior to *Sefer ha-Qabbalah*, and may well have come to Toledo—where, it will be recalled, Karaites were concentrated—along with other works, such as those of the Rabbanite Tobiah, in time for Ibn Daud to absorb them and take some cues from them. A new corpus of literature had apparently recently arrived in Spain, and Ibn Daud drew on the latest material available to him.[12]

Ibn Daud, to be sure, did not refer explicitly to either of these works, but that should not surprise us. Ibn Daud was no different in that respect from most medieval writers, and, as already noted, he did not indicate in his philosophical work the names of those authors who had obviously stimulated him most.[13]

Neither R. Tobiah nor Judah Hadassi can be credited with serving as any more than stimuli or sources for bits of information and phraseology. At most they influenced the wording in the Prologue and Epilogue of *Sefer ha-Qabbalah*, and some aspects of Ibn Daud's history of the period of the Second Temple. However, the assumption that these two works were before him would account not only for the points of coincidence between the two Byzantine works and *Sefer ha-Qabbalah*, but also for the structure of the first chapter of *Sefer ha-Qabbalah*, which differs so remarkably from the pattern followed in the remainder of the work. Hadassi's work may well not only have irritated Ibn Daud, but also inspired him to construct his chapter on the biblical period along a similar pattern, but with, of course, a diametrically opposed point of view.

The other half of Ibn Daud's reference shelf, no more acknowledged than the first, consisted of Gentile works of history from which he drew his infor-

son; I.193 and references cited there. Now this is a particularly revealing point, for this pejorative form of reference to Titus, which Lieberman has shown Ibn Daud misunderstood, is fairly rare in Hebrew literature. That both authors should be very concerned with the future messianic redemption is in itself not remarkable, but that both should be very much concerned with the physical signs of the end of time, earthquakes and the like, and in reaffirming that the restoration of the days of the Second Temple was only a partial one, are again interesting coincidences; cf. *MBSh*, end and Z. Ankori, "Studies in the Messianic Doctrine of Yehuda Hadassi" [in Hebrew], *Tarbiz*, XXX (1960–61), 186 f. No one of these parallelisms would in itself be of significance, but the aggregate suggests some connection between the two works.

12 On the channels of trade making the importation of these books possible *ca.* 1150, cf. A.A. Vasiliev, *History of the Byzantine Empire*, 2 vols. (Madison, 1958), II, 487.

13 Cf. Introduction, p. XXIV.

mation on ancient Rome and Persia. Here again, Ibn Daud reflected tendencies that are often associated with twelfth-century European historiography: a renewed interest in antiquities, especially architectural marvels, in bizarre phenomena of the Orient and etymologies,[14] and a fascination with the symmetry of history.[15] His outline of Roman history, where due reference was made to plagues, earthquakes, assassinations, Latin etymologies and, above all, the length of reigns of emperors, the spread of Christianity, and the renown of Gregory the Great and Isidore and Leander, made it quite clear to modern scholars that Ibn Daud had not confined his reading exclusively to Andalusian Jewish and Arabic sources, but had begun to tap the new sources available to the Jews of Toledo from Christian manuals on ancient history. No wonder, then, that scholars saw in Ibn Daud's works the traces of Paulus Orosius and of Isidore of Seville, the two Spaniards whose historical and etymological writings exercised the greatest influences on medieval historiography both in Spain and elsewhere.[16] Although detailed comparisons of Ibn Daud's works with the *Apology* of Orosius, as well as the augmented Mozarabic version of this work, and with the *Chronicon* of Isidore of Seville make it virtually certain that Ibn Daud did not use those works, there can be little doubt that his knowledge of Gentile history derived from these men by way of intermediate channels.[17]

Despite Ibn Daud's very fragmentary and highly inaccurate knowledge of Roman and Persian history, to modern students of Jewish literature he represented a breath of fresh air. In displaying at least an awareness of the importance of non-Jewish history, and in making an effort at enlivening the Jewish side of the story by the use of biography and information from unorthodox sources, he echoed faintly some of the new notes that were being sounded in the renascent European interest in the past and in the non-Christian world.[18]

---

14 Cf. IV.87 f. For Ibn Daud's allusion to his use of Gentile works, cf. below, p. 165.
15 I.121 f. and below, ch. III.
16 Ibn Daud's sources were studied by M. Klein and E. Molnar, "Ha-Rabad be-tor Ḥoqer Dibray ha-Yamim," *Hazofeh*, V (1921), 93 f., 165 f.; VIII (1924), 24 f.; IX (1925), 85 f. Cf. *ibid.*, V, 96 f. and esp. VIII, 24 f., where they list the points of correspondence between Ibn Daud and Orosius, Isidore and others. What these scholars apparently failed to realize was that by taking note of points of agreement and ignoring the basic disagreements on every line of Ibn Daud's parallel sections, all they have shown is that Orosian-Isidorian ideas had gained such wide circulation in the Middle Ages as to have influenced even some Jews. Elbogen, "Abraham ibn Daud als Geschichtsschreiber," p. 199, was much more circumspect.
17 Cf. IV.120–129 and references cited there.
18 For a short but lucid summary, cf. C.H. Haskins, *The Renaissance of the Twelfth Century* (New York, 1957), pp. 232 f.

The Problem

Strangely enough, it is not the new unidentifiable sources of information that have challenged most modern students of Ibn Daud; for whatever the results of the investigation, they would at best yield a new and more accurate footnote. Orosius might be replaced by Pseudo-Orosius, Isidore by Pseudo-Isidore, Tobiah b. Eliezer by some other disciple of Saadiah. It was in the area of the traditional that *Sefer ha-Qabbalah* presented some fascinating problems.

Students of medieval Jewish literature have often been puzzled by several sections of the work, for Ibn Daud blandly put forth original and occasionally highly unorthodox statements in some of the very areas where an orthodox Rabbanite would be least expected to do so. One would assume, for example, that if a medieval Rabbanite, who summarized the history of ancient Israel, did not defend the talmudic chronology of biblical times, he would at least represent it faithfully as the correct reconstruction of events—especially since the traditional Jewish chronology was a favorite target of the very sectarians whom Ibn Daud had set out to refute. However, not only did Ibn Daud diverge from the classical interpretations of biblical history dispersed throughout talmudic literature, but he frequently contradicted even biblical data outright without so much as an oblique apology. Moreover, his summary of post-biblical history is on occasion no less original and puzzling. Some elementary data are so distorted as to be inexplicable by the assumption normally invoked in the case of medieval quotations of the Talmud, to wit, "a variant reading" in Ibn Daud's sources. These individual deviations in the talmudic period are climaxed by a fantastic blunder in the gaonic age when he consistently locates the authorities of the first three generations in the wrong academy, the geonim of Sura being made heads of Pumbeditha, and vice versa. Closely related to this error are mistakes in simple arithmetic and inconsistencies in chronology and in the enumeration of generations with which the work is generously sprinkled. Finally, the very periodization of Jewish tradition in *Sefer ha-Qabbalah* apparently differs markedly from that found in earlier sources, for in Ibn Daud's account the dates of the redaction of the Mishna and of the end of the amoraic and saboraic periods do not correspond with those found in earlier Rabbanite sources.

Ibn Daud himself did not provide too much help in this respect. As was to be expected, he quoted Scripture repeatedly, often as a proof text for a fact or interpretation which he advanced.[19] Secondly, Ibn Daud cited the Talmud

---

19 I.96 f., 100, 117 f., 148, 150, 154, 157 f.; II.147; III.65 f., 79 f.; IV.98, 103. Scriptural

as a reliable, indeed as an unimpeachable historical source.[20] His work is saturated with biblical and talmudic vocabulary, and despite his unorthodox use of the Bible, his quotations from Scripture often reflect midrashic literature in substance as well as in form.[21] Apart from the Mishna and the Talmud, Ibn Daud referred by name to but one other rabbinic work, which he believed to derive from antiquity. However, that single reference to *Megillat Ta'anit* was taken in reality from a medieval gloss to the original scroll and scholion.[22]

As regards post-talmudic literature, Ibn Daud apparently consulted R. Simeon Qayyara's *Halakot Gedolot*,[23] R. Saadiah's *Sefer ha-Galuy*,[24] and an epistle written by R. Dosa to Ḥisdai ibn Shaprut.[25] Although nowhere in *Sefer ha-Qabbalah* did the author refer to his extensive use of *Josippon*, he did state elsewhere that the Hebrew pseudepigraphon was one of his prime tools,[26] and this work must, therefore, be included in his list of acknowledged sources. He also mentioned the works of Jewish historians without, however, specifying which ones he meant.[27] Moreover, Ibn Daud cited documents which he saw himself or heard about from others, and reported data of which he learned in the course of conversation.[28] Finally, he cited traditions in the name of others, without indicating the identity of his informants.[29]

As regards Karaite literature, he claimed to have seen at least portions of the commentary on the Pentateuch by Abu'l-Faraj Furqan ibn Asad.[30] Ibn Daud reported that Abu'l-Taras, the Castilian disciple of Abu'l-Faraj, had compiled a work under the direction of his master and brought it to Spain. Although Ibn Daud did not describe the work, nor even say explicitly that he saw it, it probably contained at least portions of Abu'l-Faraj's commentary on the Pentateuch, and perhaps portions of a code in which the names of

phrases and clichés abound, especially from the end of VI to the end of the work; cf. below, ch. V.

20 Prologue; II.107, 133.
21 Cf. I.173; III.65; VII.452; Epilogue.87.
22 VII.260.
23 VI.19 f., and cf. also line 26 on the *She'eltot*.
24 VI.158.
25 *Ibid.*
26 Cf. above, p. xxxv.
27 II.95.
28 VI.189; VII.302 f., 428 f. Under this category must also be included the documentary sources which Ibn Daud used for his history of the Andalusian rabbinate. These documents are nowhere acknowledged, but that they must have existed is seen from the fact that Moses ibn Ezra also had copious chronological information, which he utilized in his work on prosody; cf. above, p. xxii n. 23.
29 I.74; III.83 f.; Epilogue.94.
30 Epilogue.130 f.

Anan and Qirqisani figured prominently.³¹ Of Abu'l-Taras' widow and her activity as a Karaite leader (*al-Muʿallima*),³² Ibn Daud seemed to be informed from contemporary reports. Although other prominent sectarians are mentioned by name,³³ he made no claim that their works were examined first-hand.

In the third and final category of sources are those Gentile works upon which Ibn Daud acknowledged that he had drawn. Contrary to his practice in *Emunah Ramah*, where a number of Gentile authors and their works were singled out by name, he referred to them in *Sefer ha-Qabbalah* only in the most general terms.³⁴

To sum up, Ibn Daud drew upon the Bible and the works of Rabbanites, Karaites and Gentiles, which he supplemented with oral reports. However, all of the sources he mentioned do not account for the information contained in the major portion of *Sefer ha-Qabbalah*, not even for his account of the "pre-Spanish" periods. Manifestly, he must have derived the bulk of his information from works at which he vaguely hinted on one occasion but did not identify.³⁵ Only after a thorough investigation of the data which he absorbed can his method and the historical value of the work as a whole be appraised. We shall, accordingly, begin by approximating Ibn Daud's order of chapters, enumerate the obvious sources, as well as those which scholars have often claimed that he used, and then try to identify those he did not acknowledge

A. Biblical Chronology

At first glance, Ibn Daud's summary of biblical dates gives the impression of a typically rabbinic tabulation of events that are undated in Scripture. "From Adam until the Flood 1656 years... From the birth of Abraham until his first departure from Haran 52 years. From his departure from Haran until the covenant between the pieces of flesh 18." And so on.³⁶ Since many of the chronological figures in this chapter are plainly non-scriptural and derive from earlier rabbinic tradition, virtually all modern scholars who have expressed an opinion on the subject have agreed that his primary source for the biblical period was the tannaitic-midrashic chronicle, Seder ʿOlam.³⁷ This judgment

---

31 *Ibid.*, 47 f.
32 *Ibid.*, 54 f.
33 Cf. above, p. XLIX.
34 II.97; IV.125.
35 IV.57.
36 I.2 f.
37 B. Ratner, *Mabo le-ha-Seder ʿOlam Rabba* (Vilna, 1894), p. 129 n. 94; A. Marx, *Seder ʿOlam (Cap. 1–10)* (Berlin, 1903), p. viii; Steinschneider, *Geschichtsliteratur*, p. 46; Klein and Molnar, *op. cit.*, *Hazofeh*, V (1921), 96 f.

is most curious, since even a cursory comparison of the two works will disclose fundamental discrepancies between them. Abraham Zacuto, writing in the sixteenth century, noted these disagreements and concluded that Ibn Daud had not consulted Seder 'Olam.[38] As will be seen, there can be no question that Zacuto was perfectly right.

Sefer ha-Qabbalah credited "the elders who outlived Joshua" with a reign of seventeen years,[39] while Seder 'Olam expressly stated that no years are to be reckoned for these elders.[40] Now this divergence represents a disagreement not in mere detail, but a difference in approach to the explanation of the 300 years mentioned in Judges 11.26 and of the 480 years mentioned in I Kings 6.1.[41] Moreover, Ibn Daud reckoned his chronology solely from the reigns of the kings of Judah, despite the rabbinic principle—which the Seder 'Olam demonstrated—of arriving at a total only after synchronizing the reigns of the kings of Judah with those of the kings of Israel.[42] Ibn Daud's unawareness of the Seder 'Olam becomes even more manifest after a comparison of their divergent explanations of the last days of the Judean monarchy. Whereas Ibn Daud resolved the contradiction of Daniel 1.1 and Jeremiah 25.1 by assuming that Daniel suffered exile in Jehoiakim's third-fourth year,[43] Seder 'Olam explained the events of Daniel 1.1 as taking place in the eleventh or last year of Jehoiakim's reign.[44] Ibn Daud took the number of captives in Jeremiah 52.28 to refer only to heads of families, and the numbers in II Kings 24.14, 16 to refer to the total number of persons actually exiled;[45] Seder 'Olam, on the other hand, accounted for these very same figures quite differently.[46] Ibn Daud explained Jeremiah 52.29 as taking place five years before the destruction of the Temple (thereby contradicting Jeremiah 32.1);[47] Seder 'Olam interpreted the verses correctly.[48] Ibn Daud explained Jeremiah 52.30 with reference to the fall of Zedekiah and the destruction;[49] Seder 'Olam took the verses to refer to

---

38 Zacuto, *op. cit.*, p. 18b.   39 I.27.
40 Seder 'Olam 12 (ed. Ratner), pp. 51 f.
41 *Ibid.*, p. 55 and n. 23. Ratner's conclusion in note 7 there that Ibn Daud and other authorities had 17 in their MSS of Seder 'Olam is totally unfounded. The chronological scheme of Seder 'Olam precluded the attribution of any years to these elders, while Ibn Daud's scheme required it.
42 Bornstein, "Ta'arikay Israel" *Ha-Tequfa*, IX (1921), 216 f.
43 I.126 f.
44 Seder 'Olam 25 (ed. Ratner), p. 110.
45 I.131 f.
46 Seder 'Olam 25 (ed. Ratner), pp. 111 f.
47 I.138.
48 Seder 'Olam 27 (ed. Ratner), p. 121, where although the 18 is dated from "the capture of Jehoiakim," the basic approach to the text is correct.
49 I.139.

the invasion of Nebuchadnezzar long *after* the destruction of the Temple when he banished the Jews living in the environs of Palestine.[50] So, too, Ibn Daud's figures for the reigns of Evil-merodach and Ahasurerus differ from those of Seder 'Olam.[51] Finally, Ibn Daud did not make the slightest effort to harmonize his account of post-biblical history with the figures in Seder 'Olam 30.[52]

Accordingly, the evidence compels us to conclude that Ibn Daud made no use of Seder 'Olam in his chronological scheme. To this we may add the weighty consideration that a Rabbanite Jew would not lightly have ignored a rabbinic classic had it been available to him. The few statements which ostensibly do derive from Seder 'Olam may well have come to him from some intermediary source, such as Saadiah's *Kitab at-Ta'rikh*.[53]

Very similar considerations make it equally difficult to subscribe to the view that Ibn Daud drew from the later rabbinic chronicle Seder 'Olam Zuta.[54] The only points in common between *Sefer ha-Qabbalah* and this little tract are the enumeration of the reigns of the kings of Judah, without synchronizing them with the kings of Israel, and the list in *Sefer ha-Qabbalah* of thirteen Babylonian exilarchs prior to Hillel's departure for Palestine. However, in the case of Seder 'Olam Zuta, too, we must single out its basic dissimilarities of aim and style—not to mention chronological and historical details—from the work of Ibn Daud. Seder 'Olam Zuta is concerned essentially with Palestinian nesiim of Babylonian exilarchic extraction, whom Ibn Daud did not even so much as mention. Moreover, had Ibn Daud known Seder 'Olam Zuta, he could hardly have failed to notice that Hezekiah, "the brother" of Hillel, is said

---

50 Seder 'Olam 26 (ed. Ratner), pp. 119 f. For the possible source of Ibn Daud's error, cf. above, n. 11.
51 I.144 f., 152; Seder 'Olam 28–29.
52 According to rabbinic tradition, the Jews were under Persian domination for thirty-four years after the rebuilding of the Temple; cf. Seder 'Olam 30 (ed. Ratner), p. 141, but according to Ibn Daud the Persian empire fell thirty years after the rebuilding; I.219–220. Cf. also Seder 'Olam, *loc. cit.*, with III.44, 50.
53 Cf. above, n. 6.—The question as to whether Seder 'Olam was available in Spain requires further investigation. In the preparation of a new edition of Seder 'Olam, in which I collaborated with the late Professor Alexander Marx, all available medieval works were examined for quotations of this work. Prior to Abraham ibn Ezra, who may well have come across this book in the course of his travels, the only Spanish authority known to me to quote Seder 'Olam is R. Joseph ibn Megash (cited by Bezalel Ashkenazi, *Shittah Mequbeṣet* to B.B. 28b). The quotation by Abraham bar Ḥiyya in the name of Seder 'Olam (cf. S.N. to I.145) is not attested by any known MS of that work and may come from another tract with a similar name. Judah ibn Bal'am was patently unaware that a problematic statement of Saadiah derived from Seder 'Olam; cf. Neubauer, *Medieval Jewish Chronicles*, II, xi and Seder 'Olam 12 (end) (ed. Ratner), p. 55.
54 So Klein, *op. cit.*, *Hazofeh*, V, 97.

in that work to have died after the destruction of the Second Temple![55] On the other hand, the bare list of the names of exilarchs in *Sefer ha-Qabbalah* manifestly served but as an introduction to the establishment of the Hillelite dynasty as one of legitimate, i.e., Davidic, lineage. Ibn Daud's list may well have derived from one of a number of sources: from Saadiah's *Kitab at-Ta'rikh*; from the latter's *Sefer ha-Galuy*, which contained a chronological section; from Ibn Daud's prime source for rabbinic chronology (to be discussed presently); or even from Ibn Daud's own study of the Book of Chronicles. To be sure, the *ultimate* source for any one of these possibilities, other than the last, was a recension of Seder 'Olam Zuta. But by the time the list reached Ibn Daud, the original had become so truncated as to make Ibn Daud's data only a pale reflection of it. For lack of further evidence, we shall have to leave the matter an open question with the qualification that of the four possibilities mentioned, the latter two appear to be the more plausible ones. The identity of method in computing the reigns of the kings, even if not fortuitous, is of no real consequence. For Seder 'Olam Zuta does not manifest any concern with the totals of these reigns—which, incidentally, diverge radically from those of *Sefer ha-Qabbalah*—while Ibn Daud, as we shall see, considered the totals of crucial significance. It is, therefore, most unlikely that Ibn Daud utilized any recension of Seder 'Olam Zuta.[56]

Inevitably, we are forced to the conclusion that for his biblical chronology, Ibn Daud used principally the Bible itself, which he interpreted in accordance with views of Andalusian exegetes, without recourse to classical rabbinic works on problematic dates. However remarkable this may appear in the case of a vehement Rabbanite polemicist, the fact of the matter is that Ibn Daud was not alone in the Middle Ages generally, and certainly not in Andalus, in venturing to examine biblical data along independent lines. Some of his confrères had displayed far greater boldness in this respect. Although understandably enough such deviation evoked the pious protests of more conservative expositors, original exegesis was never totally suppressed.[57]

However, Ibn Daud's un-rabbinic reconstruction of biblical chronology is the least troublesome aspect of this section of his work. Even the most orthodox Jew could permit himself a certain amount of latitude with rabbinic exegesis, particulary if his speculation did not seem to suggest deviations in

---

55 Cf. Neubauer, *Medieval Jewish Chronicles*, II, 68–73, and for Hezekiah, p. 71; Lazarus, *Die Haeupter der Vertriebenen*, p. 162.
56 Cf. also below, pp. 215 f.
57 Cf. Baron, *SRH*, VI, 309 f. For a religious protest against these "Scripturalists," i.e., men who studied the Bible without the aid of rabbinic interpretation, cf. Judah b. Barzillai, *Commentar zum Sepher Jezira*, p. 5.

behavior or basic doctrine. Chronological vagaries especially could be easily shrugged off as deriving from "lost sources" or personal speculation. But what is one to say about outright contradictions of the Bible? To cite examples: Ibn Daud offered no explanation for the statement, which he repeated, that Solomon began to build the Temple in the *third* year of his reign, a flat contradiction of explicit scriptural statements that the building of the Temple was begun in the fourth year of Solomon's reign.[58] Secondly, he stated that the First Temple was destroyed after a war of seven years, although Scripture plainly indicates that the siege of Jerusalem lasted but three years.[59] Further, his synchronizations of the reigns of Nebuchadnezzar and Zedekiah are such blatant divergences from Scripture as to give the impression of slips of either pen or memory.[60] That Ibn Daud was not incapable of outright misquotation or of mistakes in simple arithmetic seemed to be clear and lent added weight to this impression.[61] Abraham Zacuto flatly charged Ibn Daud with distorting Scripture, while Azariah de' Rossi tended to the more generous solution of emending Ibn Daud's text.[62] Most modern scholars, apparently, shared the sentiments of de' Rossi, for they virtually ignored these howlers completely. After all, there is no limit to the destructive work of copyists, and why should Ibn Daud's work have escaped the ravages of scribes? And there the matter rested. We shall have to reopen the question later on, in the context of Ibn Daud's historiography as a whole.

B. *The Period of the Second Temple*

Ibn Daud surveyed the events of the Second Temple in two passages. The first consists of a historical elucidation of Daniel 9.24–27,[63] in which the chronological interpretations were derived principally from Saadiah's commentary on Daniel and supplemented by historical data from *Josippon* and homiletical applications of classical rabbinic sources.[64]

Having completed his very general survey of the Second Temple from the biblical sources, Ibn Daud proceeded to set forth the *isnad* or chain of rabbinic Judaism.[65] His method for each of the ten generations of "instruction in the Temple" was to cite verbatim a rubric from the Ethics of the Fathers and then

58 I.47–48, 69.
59 I.113.
60 I.137 f.
61 Cf. below, pp. 189.
62 Zacuto, *op. cit.*, p. 81b. Azariah de' Rossi, *Meor 'Enayyim*, ch. 35, ed. by I. Ben Jacob 2 vols. (Vilna, 1863–65), II, 19; *idem*, ed. by D. Cassel (Vilna, 1864–66), p. 293.
63 I.154–209.
64 Cf. notes *ibid*. For another possible stimulus, cf. above, n. 11.   65 II.1 f.

to fill in relevant data, principally from the Talmud, midrashim and *Josippon*. In connection with the latter work, two observations must be made. In the first place, Ibn Daud almost certainly had a recension of *Josippon* which differed in chronological details from the Spanish recension currently available.[66] In the absence of a critical edition of *Josippon*, it is fruitless to speculate on the provenience of each date in *Sefer ha-Qabbalah* that diverges from *Josippon*. Certainly the agreement of *Sefer ha-Qabbalah* with one version of Seder 'Olam Zuta on the date of Antiochus Epiphanes' spoliation of the Temple does not permit us to assume that Ibn Daud doctored *Josippon* from the little chronicle.[67] All other dates which diverge from *Josippon* diverge from Seder 'Olam Zuta as well.[68] It would have been most unlikely for Ibn Daud to select one date for this period from Seder 'Olam Zuta and ignore all others. The agreement on the date of the invasion of Antiochus (and the uprising of the Maccabees) is probably quite fortuitous and derives from other considerations.

However, the figures on the reigns of the Hasmoneans are of no little interest in this connection, for while they cannot be traced definitely to earlier sources, they nevertheless afford us some insight into Ibn Daud's criteria in his selection of data. It happens that the figures on the reigns of the Hasmonean kings were repeated by Ibn Daud in his sermon on Zechariah 11.4 f., which was appended to his history of the kings of the Second Temple.[69] From that passage it is clear that Ibn Daud saw in the thirty-one years of the reign of Mattathias, Judah, Jonathan and Simeon the true meaning of the thirty pieces of silver mentioned in Zechariah 11.12. In other words, this sermon indicates that, while Ibn Daud may have drawn the figures on the Hasmonean reigns from a source such as *Jossippon*, what was uppermost in his mind was his desire to interpret these reigns as fulfillments of Zechariah's prophecy. Allegory and historical midrash were so important to him that he was even willing to disregard the fact that the total of thirty-one years did not tally exactly with

---

66 According to II.58, Jonathan the Hasmonean ruled 6 years, but according to *Josippon* 26, (ed. Hominer), p. 101, 7 years, and *ibid.*, 65, p. 239, 8 years. According to II.59, Simeon ruled 18 years, but according to *Josippon, locis citatis*, pp. 102, 239, he ruled 8. In late editions, the figure was corrected *ibid.*, p. 239, to 18.—On Ibn Daud's *Josippon*, cf. above, p. xxxv.

67 Zacuto, *op. cit.*, p. 92b. Neubauer, *Medieval Jewish Chronicles*, II, 74b. The quotation in Zacuto, p. 82b, is from *Sefer ha-Qabbalah*.

68 The recension in Zacuto, *op. cit.*, p. 92a, credits Jonathan with 7 years, while earlier, pp. 90a, 91b, Zacuto quotes sources crediting him with 9; cf. II.58. The same recensions cited by Zacuto credit Simeon with 12 and 7 year terms. In *MBSh*, f. 54b, John Hyrcanus is said to have ruled 31 years, while the recensions of Seder 'Olam Zuta credit him with 16, 26, 31 and 37! Cf. Zacuto, *loc. cit.* and Lazarus, *Die Haeupter der Vertriebenen*, p. 161.

69 *MBSh*, f. 79b.

the thirty pieces of the prophecy. In any event, the fact that homiletical considerations were so vital to him makes it most likely that the date of 212 of the Second Temple for the Maccabeean uprising, in the face of the figure 213 of *Megillat Antiochus*,[70] is a slightly tailored figure to give the mnemonic ריב, meaning "battle," "controversy" and even "vengeance." Although in the absence of evidence it is hazardous to speculate on the origin of mnemonics, there exists some evidence to warrant a guess that the mnemonic is a midrash on Isaiah 34.8, where the word occurs in the context of God's avenging Zion, i.e., the Temple.[71] That midrashic considerations were uppermost in Ibn Daud's mind is further indicated by the fact that he was seemingly untroubled by the contradiction between his Maccabeean chronology and the date which he considered to be the authentic one for Jesus' birth.[72]

However, one remarkable fact emerges from an examination of Ibn Daud's combination of rabbinic sources and *Josippon*. Whereas Ibn Daud adhered religiously to the chain of authorities reported in rabbinic sources, he was quite eclectic about his incorporation of other historical data from rabbinic literature. Thus, he ignored completely the chronological data transmitted in *B. Abodah Zarah* 8b–9a on the division of the days of the Second Temple into periods. He even omitted the miracle of Hannukah as told in *B. Shabbat* 21b, although this festival was a major point of dispute between Karaites and Rabbanites.[73] The reason for this omission was, in all likelihood, that the story did not appear in *Josippon*. The latter source, on the other hand, Ibn Daud often followed almost slavishly. As noted earlier, he adopted *Josippon*'s evaluation of the causes of the calamities that befell the Jews,[74] and where *Josippon* made an absurd statement on ancient Jewish custom, Ibn Daud followed suit.[75]

The survey of the history of tradition in the days of the Second Temple is interrrupted by a brief and avowedly polemical excursus on the dates of the activity of Jesus.[76] Ibn Daud revealed that he was quite aware of the invidious associations which Christian historians drew from the proximity of the date

---

70 S.A. Wertheimer, *Battay Midrashot*, 2 vols. (Jerusalem, 1950–53), I, 319; M. Gaster, "The Scroll of the Hasmoneans," *Studies and Texts*, 3 vols. (London, 1925–28), I. 179, III, 34.
71 For a full explanation, cf. Cohen, *SFC*, p. 103 n. 146.
72 II.112.
73 Cf. *MBSh*, f. 52a; Atlas and Perlmann, *op. cit.*, p. 22; Ankori, *Karaites in Byzantium*, p. 282; Zucker, "Against Whom did Se'adya Ga'on Write the Polemical Poem *Essa meshali*?" p. 70.
74 Cf. Introduction, p. xxxix and below, pp. 221 f.
75 II.74 f.
76 II.95 f.

of the crucifixion to that of the destruction of the Temple. Although he did not identify his sources by name, it is most likely that he drew on some Mozarabic work, which probably also served as his basic source of information on Roman history.[77] However, while he was content to accept the testimony of Gentile historians on neutral matters, even if their account implied a rejection of talmudic tradion, in this case he rejected Gentile claims out of hand in favor of a traditional Jewish point of view. He derived his "Jewish" date for Jesus from the Talmud and other Jewish sources, which, although unidentified by him, were in all likelihood a version of the *Toledot Yeshu*, which circulated in various forms in the medieval world. Uncritical adherence to some version of this work was probably responsible for the dates of the Jewish kings given in this passage of *Sefer ha-Qabbalah*, which, as indicated above, contradict Ibn Daud's own Hasmonean chronology. Ibn Daud apparently never bothered to harmonize the dates in the passage on Jesus with those given in other parts of his work, and this inner contradiction remains one of the few puzzling passages in his book.

C. *The Talmudic Period (Tannaim and Amoraim)*

Like the period on the authorities of the Second Temple, the four subsequent divisions of Jewish history—the tannaitic, amoraic, saboraic, and gaonic—are built according to a strict pattern: an introductory phrase identifying the head of each generation is supplemented by relevant historical material. However, beginning with the tannaitic period, the pattern is developed further by the listing of the students and colleagues alongside the master of each generation.[78] This slight change in pattern is very significant, for the nature of the sources utilized by Ibn Daud for the post-biblical periods now becomes quite clear. But since Ibn Daud's prime source has become a *cause célèbre* in the annals of modern Jewish scholarship, and that particularly in connection with the saboraic and gaonic periods, we must postpone our analysis of this source to our discussion of Ibn Daud's post-talmudic history.

In addition to the framework material, Ibn Daud supplied considerable information on the tannaitic period, which, as we would expect, was drawn principally from the Talmud. But in fact, the talmudic information itself falls into two categories. The first consists of verbatim quotation and paraphrastic summary of events recorded in rabbinic literature. The second type of data

77 Cf. references in notes to II.99; IV.120–129.
78 In the chapter on the period of the Second Temple, the lack of such precise information impelled Ibn Daud to refer to the disciples and colleagues of the various authorities by the general term "and his (or, their) school;" cf. II.34, 42, 89 etc.

consists of information based on *interpretation* of talmudic statements; that is, information which is based on the Talmud but which is not explicitly recorded in the sources.

An examination of the first category of talmudic material will yield results that are at first astounding because of statements encountered which are very similar in character to the ones found in the summary of the biblical data. To be sure, a basic distinction must be made with regard to talmudic literature, for the latter has no masoretic text, and variants from the *textus receptus* of the Talmud are to be expected.[80] The outstanding case of such a variant is Ibn Daud's paraphrase of a *baraita* in *B. Shabbat* 15a, on the Hillelite dynasty, which, at least in Ibn Daud's copy, clearly contained no reference to Simeon b. Hillel.[80] As far as I can determine, Ibn Daud is the only early authority to assert unequivocally that Hillel's successor was Gamaliel I; all other sources quote this *baraita* as it appears in the printed editions.[81]

However interesting talmudic variants may be, they will cause no surprise. What will occasion astonishment is the ostensible misquotation, or distorted paraphrase, of three well-known talmudic passages. The first instance is Ibn Daud's coupling of Judah b. Tabbai with Nittai the Arbelite and of Joshua b. Peraḥyah with Simeon b. Shetaḥ, a blatant contradiction of all known manuscripts of the Mishna.[82] Although Gedaliah ibn Yaḥya, who took note of Ibn Daud's strange pairs, cautiously refrained from passing judgment on them as misquotations,[83] I think it is rather far-fetched to seek these couplings in a variant reading of the mishnaic text. It appears far more likely that we have either 1) a *lapsus calami* or *memoriae*; 2) a scribal corruption early in the history of the transmission of *Sefer ha-Qabbalah*; 3) an overly faithful adherence on the part of Ibn Daud to his prime source, which had previously recorded this corruption in the chain of authorities; or 4) a deliberate correction of the mishnaic chain by Ibn Daud in line with the talmudic story, according to which Simeon b. Shetaḥ interceded with Alexander Jannaeus on behalf of Joshua b. Peraḥyah.[84] Since the story of this intercession was related to the Jewish date for Jesus, Ibn Daud may have altered the traditional coupling of authorities in keeping with his polemical excursus on Jesus, the student of Joshua b. Peraḥyah.

The second and third instances of distortion are basically similar in charac-

---

79 Cf., e.g., I.43; II.42–44, 71, 133; III.15, 22, 55 f.
80 I.76 f.; II.118, 125.
81 See S.N. to II.126.
82 II.91, 93.
83 Cf. S.N. *ad loc.*
84 II.80, 95.

ter and will enable us to arrive at more positive conclusions on Ibn Daud's source. The first of these is encountered in Ibn Daud's version of the story of R. Johanan b. Zakkai's escape from Jerusalem, where the *dramatis personae* have been confused.[85] However, a careful examination of Ibn Daud's version reveals that the account of events itself has suffered no changes or distortions. By a simple transposition of the names of the persons involved in the narrative, we can readily restore the story to an original which was identical with that of the Talmud and Midrashim.[86]

Our suggestion seems to us to be supported by the third instance of distortion, namely, the dispute between R. Joshua and R. Gamaliel II.[87] In that story we can clearly discern a lacuna and a resultant confusion of the identity of one participant in the story. In other words, here, too, the story *per se* will be seen to be identical with the one in the Mishna, except for the substitution of the name of R. Joshua for that of R. Dosa.

Now the fact that in two cases of distortion the narratives themselves remained untouched, and only the proper nouns were confused, cannot be dismissed as mere coincidence. The evidence points to the likelihood that Ibn Daud drew his information not from the Talmud itself, but from a post-talmudic work where some of the personal names, which were later inserted into places inappropriate to them, were originally lacking. That Ibn Daud took at least some of his talmudic data from secondary works is indicated by a number of other statements: in his report on Hillel's fraternal relationship to Hezekiah;[88] in his account of the defection of Antigonus' disciples;[89] in his statement that Menahem, the colleague of Hillel, died during the latter's lifetime;[90] and in the amazing account of Ben Koziba's revolt against Rome.[91] Happily, we are able to point to one such source, the nature of which will account for some of the major peculiarities of Ibn Daud's post-biblical and pre-Spanish history.

As was noted earlier, R. Nissim b. Jacob ibn Shahin of Qairawan composed a work entitled *The Sequence of the Recipients of the Torah (Sefer Seder Meqabbelay ha-Torah)*.[92] In one of his other works, R. Nisim promised that in this

---

85 II.154 f.
86 Cf. S.N. *ad loc.*
87 III.12 f.
88 I.75.
89 In *ARN*, I, 5, p. 26, Zadok and Boethus are represented as having learned the doctrine of Antigonus from the latter's disciples. Cf., Maimonides to Abot 1.3, where the same discrepancy with the original story is reflected.
90 II.123.
91 III.40 f., and cf. below, pp. 241 f.
92 Cf. Introduction, p. LIV n. 50.

work on the history of tradition he would furnish some of the details concerning the esteem in which R. Judah the Patriarch was held by Antoninus, the emperor of Rome.[93] Since a *Seder ha-Qabbalah* of Rabbi Nissim was later cited by R. Menahem Me'iri,[94] there is every reason to believe that he completed his project. To return to the problem at hand, in his account of the cordial relations between Antoninus and Rabbi Judah, Ibn Daud states, "And it is said that R. Judah converted Antoninus secretly."[95] This cautious qualification, "and it is said," clearly indicates that Ibn Daud knew of no classical source for this information, but learned of it only from some non-canonical work, as it were. Now the ultimate source of this report is a passage in the Palestinian Talmud of which R. Nissim made extensive use in his talmudic compilations.[96] Moreover, R. Nissim had close associations with the Jewish community of Spain, and his works were well known there.[97] Is it not plausible that Ibn Daud, who was himself writing a history of the recipients of the Torah, took over this information from an earlier work on the very same subject?

Since the character of R. Nissim's works has become fairly well known in recent years, there is one further assumption that we can make with virtual certainty, and that is that R. Nissim's work was written in Arabic and liberally sprinkled with Hebrew and Aramaic quotations from rabbinic classics.[98] The peculiarities of Ibn Daud's stories about R. Johanan b. Zakkai and R. Joshua are best explained if we assume an Arabic substratum for them. Arabic narrators often omitted proper nouns and wrote simply "he did" or "he said," without specifying which of the two persons involved was the "doer" or "sayer." The reader could presumably be trusted to understand the subject of the verb from the context. This would be particularly true in the case of Judeo-Arabic quotations from classical sources, such as the Bible and the Talmud, which would be quoted briefly and with ellipses, inasmuch as they were considered well known. Now we have seen that the essential features of Ibn Daud's two misquotations are their confusion of names, that is, the imperfect reintroduction

---

93 Nissim b. Jacob ibn Shahin, *Clavis Talmudica*, f. 2b.
94 Poznanski, *Esquisse Historique*, p. 38.
95 III.83.
96 Cf. S. Assaf, " 'Megillath Setharim' of R. Nissim b. Jacob of Kairuwan" [in Hebrew], *Tarbiz*, XII (1940–41), 29. Nissim b. Jacob ibn Shahin, *Ḥibbur Yafeh me-ha-Yeshu'ah* (ed. Hirschberg), Introduction, p. 30.—Incidentally, this "report" should serve as virtually conclusive proof that Ibn Daud did not consult the Palestinian Talmud; cf. also above, n. 42, and *Yer. R. H.* 1.1, f. 56b.
97 Cf. VII.270 f. and notes there.
98 Cf. Steinschneider, *Arabische Literatur der Juden*, pp. 103 f.; B.M. Lewin, "Payrush R. Nissim le-Erubin," *Festschrift Dr. Jakob Freimann* (Berlin, 1937), Herew section, p. 75; Nissim b. Jacob, *Ḥibbur Yafeh me-ha-Yeshu'ah* (ed. Hirschberg), pp. 36, 47 f.

of the very items that were the most likely to have been omitted in an earlier learned work. R. Nissim b. Jacob's work provides a likely possiblity for just this kind of a Judeo-Arabic susbtratum for Ibn Daud's work. The assumption that R. Nissim's work served as Ibn Daud's prime source for the post-biblical periods of Jewish history will also explain much of the other problematic material in *Sefer ha-Qabbalah*.[99]

The only quite baffling account reported in rabbinic literature, which has hitherto eluded all attempts at explanation, is Ibn Daud's version of the revolt of Ben Koziba and his dynasty.[100] The story may be older than Ibn Daud's *Sefer ha-Qabbalah*, for the enumeration of Ben Koziba's successors appears in much briefer form in *Kitab at-Ta'rikh* and, therefore, may go back at least in germ to Saadiah Gaon.[101] By the time the story appeared in *Sefer ha-Qabbalah*, it had been amplified either by Ibn Daud or by some other source into the fantastic form it now has.[102] But whatever the source of the present version, it will soon be seen that it was tailored to fit into the schematic portrayal of history of which Ibn Daud was so fond.[103]

The second category of talmudic information in *Sefer ha-Qabbalah* consists of material not contained in classical rabbinic literature but manifestly based on it. The obvious source of such information, if not indeed a written work, was the oral instruction which Ibn Daud had received in the Jewish academy and synagogue or by way of conversation. Ibn Daud's habit of advancing dates *Anno Mundi*, and accordingly of the Seleucid Era, by one year over those recorded in the Talmud reflects the astronomical presuppositions of Spanish-Jewish experts on the calendar, which became stock usage in all Spanish references to chronology.[104] The lectures of the school-house were doubtless the source for the mnemonics,[105] the dating of certain biblical events,[106] and the application of scriptural verses to post-biblical events.[107] Ibn Daud's unique and, on occasion, even brilliant insights into talmudic history probably

---

99 If part or all of *Sefer ha-Qabbalah* was written in Arabic (cf. below, Appendix), the mistakes may have to be blamed on the translator of Ibn Daud. However, that does not alter in the least the explanation we have suggested for these mistakes. It merely pushes the blame on to a third party.
100 III.40 f.
101 Cf. S.N. *ibid*.
102 For a full discussion, cf. below, pp. 241 f.
103 Cf. below, ch. IV.
104 Cf. S.N. to I.17.
105 Cf. above, to n. 71 and below, pp. 194, 201 f.
106 I.4, 89. Cf. aslo I. 134.
107 III.65 f., 79, 81 f. On the Saadyanic precedent for this, cf. Atlas and Perlmann, *op. cit.*, pp. 7 f.

derived from the lectures he had heard from his uncle or other Andalusian scholars.[108] His puzzling list of contemporaries of R. Akiba has been sufficiently illuminated by recent publications to be associated with a hitherto unknown Spanish list of the "ten martyrs."[109]

To sum up, Ibn Daud drew his information on the talmudic period from a post-talmudic summary of rabbinic tradition, from a Spanish recension of the talmudic text itself, and from the conversation in the Jewish milieu in which he had been nurtured. Since the second and third sources of information were in the final analysis merely ancillary to his prime source on all of rabbinic tradition from the days of the Second Temple to the end of the gaonic period,[110] we must attempt to identify that work and describe its contents precisely.

D. *Ibn Daud's Principal Source for the Talmudic and Gaonic Ages*

Two medieval lists of the bearers of rabbinic tradition from the age of the tannaim to the end of the gaonic period have survived into modern times. The first is contained in the *Epistle* of R. Sherira Gaon, which begins its chain with Hillel the Elder and concludes with the term of the author and his son, R. Hai.[111] The second is the *Sefer ha-Qabbalah* of Abraham Ibn Daud. Since the latter work includes very much the same material as the former, and since Sherira's work antedates that of Ibn Daud by almost two centuries, it would be natural to assume that Ibn Daud drew his information principally from Sherira.

However, a careful comparison of the two works reveals major descrepancies between them. As regards the tannaitic period, Sherira listed four members of the Hillelite dynasty as having functioned in Temple days, while Ibn Daud named only three.[112] Ibn Daud listed R. Akiba as successor to R. Gamaliel as head of the academy,[113] while Sherira made no mention of him in this connection. In the parallel sections on the amoraic period the differences become more pronounced, for Ibn Daud's dating of authorities more often than not disagreed with that of Sherira.[114] The glaring discrepancy between the two works

---

108 Cf. III.25. Modern scholars have revived Ibn Daud's explanation of that event; cf. L. Ginzberg, *A Commentary on the Palestinian Talmud*, 4 vols. (New York, 1941–61), III, 193 f.; C. Albeck, "Ha-Sanhedrin u-Nesi'ah," *Zion*, VIII (1942–43), 166, n. 3, where Ibn Daud is cited in support of a redefinition of the office of nasi.
109 II.34 and S.N. there.
110 From II.1 f., but esp. from II.117 f. to VI, end.
111 *ISG* 74.5–121.4. Cf. above, p. LIII.
112 I.76–78; II.125–126; *ISG* 74.7–16.
113 III.33.
114 Cf. IV.8, 9, 28–29, etc.

on the dates of Rabina's death and the redaction of the Talmud has evoked considerable discussion among modern scholars.[115] Ibn Daud lumped the successors of Samuel under the category of Nehardea, while Sherira was punctilious in naming their actual place of service.[116] Finally, both in the tannaitic and amoraic sections, Ibn Daud's lists of students and colleagues of the leaders of each generation differ very markedly from those of the Gaon.[117]

Should any doubts linger on the independence of *Sefer ha-Qabbalah* from Sherira's *Epistle*, they will most assuredly be dispelled by a comparison of their respective accounts of the saboraic and gaonic periods. Whereas Sherira described the age of the saboraim as one of short duration, Ibn Daud divided the age into five generations lasting over a period of 187 years. Whereas according to *Sefer ha-Qabbalah* the saboraic period began in 4237 A.M. and ended in 4449 A.M., according to Sherira the terminal points of the period were apparently 4260 and 4349.[118] Moreover, Ibn Daud supplied chronological information lacking in Sherira, omitted authorities mentioned by the latter, and understood the sequence of those he did list differently fom the Gaon.[119] Ibn Daud's periodization seems to parallel that of the *Seder Tannaim wa-Amoraim* in treating the rise of Islam within the saboraic section, while Sherira clearly believed that by the time of Muhammad the gaonic age had already begun. More precisely, Sherira dated the beginning of the gaonic period in 900 Seleucid Era (4349 A.M., 589 C.E.), while Ibn Daud put it exactly one century later.[120] Above all else, nothing has cast discredit on Ibn Daud's chronicle so much as his survey of the gaonic period. In addition to all the discrepancies encountered in the earlier sections, his list of the first three generations of geonim is, as we have noted, topsy-turvy; the geonim of Sura are placed in Pumbeditha, and vice versa![121] To this must be added the fact that modern research into the history of the geonim has confirmed the trustworthiness of Sherira, but virtually shattered the credibility of Ibn Daud whenever he makes an otherwise unattested statement.[122]

To all these considerations, modern scholars have reacted in different ways. Isaac Halevy, motivated at least as much by considerations of piety as he was by the desire for historical objectivity, concluded that Ibn Daud had never seen the *Epistle* of Sherira and that his errors derived from faulty sources.

115 Cf. IV.165 and S.N. there.
116 Cf. IV.22, 25 and S.N. there.
117 Cf. III.5 f., 34 f., 90, etc.
118 Cf. V.3–4, 44; *ISG* 97.14–15, 99.16–100.2.
119 Cf. V.4; VI.*passim*; for information not in *ISG*, cf. VI.17 f., 26 f., 41. f, 129 f.
120 Cf. V.38; VI.2; *ISG* 99.16 f.
121 Cf. VI. 3.
122 Cf. VI.18–19, and S.N., 41, 143, 154 f.

On the other hand, Halevy stoutly defended some of Ibn Daud's dates as superior to Sherira's.[123]

Most other scholars, however, have recognized that the problem is not so easily solved; for in spite of the veritable mountain of discrepancies between the works of Sherira and Ibn Daud, the affinities between the two works are much too marked to be dismissed as mere coincidence. In the first place, the disagreements between them remain far fewer in number and importance than the points of basic agreement. In the great majority of instances the links of Ibn Daud's chain correspond to those of Sherira's, and even where their chronilogies disagree, the *extent of the terms* they credit to each authority is generally identical. This could perhaps be dismissed as inevitable, since two men covering the same period are bound to agree on basic facts. However, there are incidental points of correspondence which are not necessary for Ibn Daud's account, but which do appear in his chronicle in places that parallel their appearance in Sherira. These can in no wise be dismissed as coincidental or the product of independent parallel research. Thus, Ibn Daud departed from the chain in M. Abot and inserted the name of Hillel's successors exactly at the point that Sherira does.[124] Ibn Daud's inclusion of an account of the disputes between R. Joshua and R. Gamaliel will be seen to be an amplification of a brief reference by Sherira, and appears at the point of the narrative corresponding to that of the Gaon's *Epistle*.[125] Moreover, Ibn Daud's account of Rab's first years in Babylonia disagrees blatantly with that of *Seder Tannaim wa-Amoraim* but mirrors that of Sherira.[126] Ibn Daud's introduction of the name of R. Aḥa of Shabḥa at the very point that Sherira brings him in is unnecessary to the story of *Sefer ha-Qabbalah*, but perfectly explicable in the light of the *Epistle*.[127] As A. Epstein noted in a classic study on these two works, Ibn Daud's account of the miraculous events which R. Joseph b. Judah experienced could only have derived from Sherira.[128] Indeed, one need only read the two works side by side to discover their affinities and the obvious dependence of Ibn Daud on Sherira.

The most plausible solution for two such contradictory sets of evidence is to assume that Ibn Daud utilized two sources for his rabbinic history: the *Epistle* of Sherira and some other source. The advocates of this solution did

123 I. Halevy, *Dorot Harischonim*, 4 vols. (Pressburg and Frankfurt a.M., 1897–1918), III, 7 f., 15, 35 n. 11, 54 f., 101, 159 f., 172 f., 178 f., 202 f. Halevy's conclusions were repeated, in much shoddier form, by Klein and Molnar, *op. cit.*, *Hazofeh*, V (1921), 165 f.
124 II.125 f., 153, 164 f.; *ISG* 74.7 f.
125 III.12.
126 IV.2; *STW*, p. 4; *ISG* 78.9 f.
127 VI.25 f.
128 VI.78 f. For Epstein's study, cf. below, n. 133.

not have to hunt very far, for David Conforte, in his work *Qoray ha-Dorot* (written *ca.* 1650), took note of some of the major peculiarities in *Sefer ha-Qabbalah* and stated that they were taken from Samuel (ibn Nagrela) ha-Nagid's *Mebo ha-Talmud* (Introduction to the Talmud).[129] The first part of this introduction, which treats talmudic methodology, is well known, having been printed several times;[130] but the second portion, which contains rabbinic chronology, has remained in manuscript and is known only from a few citations. These quotations proved, indeed, to be identical with statements in *Sefer ha-Qabbalah* which were independent of Sherira and confirmed Conforte's conjecture that Ibn Daud was but following in the footsteps of his Spanish precursor, Samuel ibn Nagrela.

Accordingly, to account for the contradictory evidence within *Sefer ha-Qabbalah*, S.J.L. Rapoport advanced the following theory: Ibn Daud's basic source for his rabbinic chain was Sherira's *Epistle*. This holds true even for the first three generations of geonim. Ibn Daud's mistake on the places of service of these generations of geonim could be easily accounted for by assuming that in the text of the *Epistle* which he consulted, the name Sura had been omitted in one spot.[131] This error in his source caused Ibn Daud to compound error upon error, in view of the requirement he felt to square the limits of Sherira's chronology with his own. Hence, within the various terminal points mentioned by Sherira, Ibn Daud corrected dates liberally. However, in those cases where Samuel ibn Nagrela's *Introduction to the Talmud* differed with the *Epistle*, Ibn Daud abandoned Sherira and followed his own countryman.[132]

A. Epstein attempted to refine this theory even further by defining the sources of the various portions of Ibn Daud's work more precisely.[133] To begin with, he justifiably found Rapoport's explanation of Ibn Daud's major error in the first three generations of geonim flimsy and untenable.[134] Even if one could assume that such an error had existed, the remainder of Sherira's discussion would of necessity have set the error right. Accordingly, Epstein concluded that Ibn Daud had no text of Sherira for the first three generations of geonim

---

129 David Conforte, *Qoray ha-Dorot*, ed. by D. Cassel (Berlin, 1846), f. 2a f.
130 Cf. Kasher and Mandelbaum, *op. cit.*, p. 113.
131 *ISG* 106.3.
132 S.J.L. Rapoport, Letter 24 in *Kerem Chemed*, IV (1839), 208 f.; *idem*, *Erech Millin* (Prague 1851–52), s.v. Antoninus, pp. 137 f.; *idem*, "Toledot R. Nathan Ba'al he-'Aruk," *Toledot* (Warsaw, 1913), part 1, pp. 42 n. 24, 124; *ibid.*, "Toledot R. Hai Gaon," pp. 168 f. nn. 1–2.
133 A. Epstein, "Meqorot le-Qorot ha-Geonim vi-Yeshibot Babel," *Kitbay R. Abraham Epstein*, II, 410 f. Epstein's conclusions were repeated, without credit to their author, by Klein and Molnar, *op. cit.*, V, 166 f.
134 He had been anticipated by Halevy, *op. cit.*, III, 160; cf. also below, n. 142.

and, presumably, for the preceding periods. It was only when Ibn Daud came to the fourth generation that he was able to draw upon a manuscript of the *Epistle*! As for the earlier sections of *Sefer ha-Qabbalah*, Epstein considered the internal evidence sufficient to identify Ibn Daud's sources. In the first instance, there was the *Introduction* of Samuel ibn Nagrela, upon whom it was but natural for Ibn Daud to have drawn. But in the second place, the medieval quotations from the Nagid's work, coupled with the material of Ibn Daud, enabled Epstein to point to the ultimate roots of the historical notions of both Spaniards.

Sherira, Epstein noted, had possessed copious information on the history of his own academy of Pumbeditha. It was only when he came to give the history of Sura that the Gaon was often admittedly wanting in information and shaky on dates.[135] The very opposite was true of *Seder Tannaim wa-Amoraim*, which, with its abundance of knowledge on Sura and dearth of material on Pumbeditha, must have emanated from the former. Since the academy of Sura had progressively declined from the early part of the tenth century, its records must have fallen into disorder and could not measure up to those of its sister institution.[136] If any proof was needed on the sad state of Sura's archives, *Sefer ha-Qabbalah*, which drew upon Suran records, perhaps by way of Samuel ibn Nagrela, provided overwhelming evidence.

Three salient characteristics of Ibn Daud's data enabled Epstein to classify the sections before the fourth generation of geonim as reflecting a Suran point of view: 1) Ibn Daud's chronology reflected Sura's traditions with respect to two crucial dates. The tradition of Pumbeditha stated, according to Rapoport's emendation of Sherira's *Epistle*, that Rab had migrated to Babylonia in 500 Seleucid Era.[137] Ibn Daud, on the other hand, clearly stated, as did *Seder Tannaim wa-Amoraim*, that the date was 530 Seleucid Era.[138] To be sure, the new date of 500 Seleucid Era in Sherira's *Epistle* was the result of Rapoport's emendation of the 530, recorded in all manuscripts of Sherira's *Epistle*, from *Sefer ha-Qabbalah*, which was the sole witness to anything of note having happened in 500![139] But that was a minor point, which Epstein conveniently overlooked in view of Ibn Daud's second chronological characteristic. Ibn Daud, following Samuel ibn Nagrela and *Seder Tannaim wa-Amoraim*, had extended the saboraic period to 689 C.E. against the 589 of Sherira.[140] Here

---

135 *ISG* 105.10 f.
136 VI.121 f.
137 Cf. references in n. 132.
138 IV.3.
139 III.95.
140 Cf. above, n. 120.

was positive evidence of the alignments of traditions. 2) Ibn Daud's early gaonic data, with their plethora of errors, reflected the shabby state of the archives of Sura, as did the *Seder Tannaim wa-Amoraim.* 3) Ibn Daud did have information on Sura, which Sherira did not, notably on the authorship of the *Halakot Gedolot* and the *She'eltot*,[141] although, even in the case of the former work, his chronology was obviously faulty. In short, Sura and its traditions, by way of Samuel ibn Nagrela, were the sources of Ibn Daud's errors. When Ibn Daud followed the Nehardean Sherira, he had obviously returned to more solid ground.[142]

Epstein's theory had all the earmarks of brilliant insight coupled with meticulous textual analysis. Accordingly, until this day it remains the last word on the subject. However, the evidence compels us to reject every one of his identifications and, with them, the whole of his water-tight theory. To begin with Ibn Daud's supposed prime source, Epstein predicated his theory on the statements of Conforte that Ibn Daud drew from Samuel ibn Nagrela's *Introduction to the Talmud.* Although Epstein himself admitted that this testimony is fraught with serious difficulties, he cavalierly dismissed the problems in deference to his ingenious theory. As he himself noted, no Spanish authority of the Middle Ages ever mentions an *Introduction to the Talmud* by Samuel ibn Nagrela, though many Spanish talmudists cite his talmudic code and the *Introduction to the Talmud* of Samuel b. Hofni, gaon of Sura. The earliest citation from Ibn Nagrela's *Introduction* comes from the work of Estori ha-Parḥi, whose *Kaftor wa-Peraḥ* was written in Palestine in the fourteenth century.[143] On the other hand, Joseph Sambari, an Egyptian Jew of the seventeenth century, stated flatly that the *Introduction* ascribed by many to Samuel ibn Nagrela was in reality the work of Samuel ibn Hananiah the Nagid of Egypt, who was a contemporary of Ibn Daud.[144]

These serious objections, which were recognized but disregarded by Epstein, can now be compounded by the results of Professor Mordecai Margalioth's study of the remnants of the talmudic code of Samuel ibn Nagrela.[145] Compari-

---

141   VI.19, 26.
142   Epstein, as far as I am aware, never acknowledged the fact that he was anticipated in this division of Suran and Pumbedithan sources, albeit with less detail, by Halevy, *op. cit.*, III, 54 f.
143   Estori ha-Parḥi, *Kaftor wa-Peraḥ*, ed. by A.M. Luncz (Jerusalem, 1897), p. 51; *idem*, 2 vols., ed. by J. Blumenfeld (New York, 1958-64), I, 159. Actually, the statement quoted by Parḥi does not appear in Samuel ha-Nagid's chronology at all. Filipowski's conjecture that its real source was the Introduction of Samuel b. Hofni is quite plausible; cf. Cohen, *SFC*, p. 126 n. 224.
144   Neubauer, *Medieval Jewish Chronicles*, I, 156.
145   Margalioth, *Hilkhot Hannagid*, pp. 68 f.

son of the manuscript fragments and medieval citations of the latter's work with the published section of Samuel ha-Nagid's *Introduction* drove Margalioth to the conclusion that the two are not the work of the same man. As had long been recognized, the *Introduction to the Talmud* was drawn largely from Samuel b. Hofni's work of the same title. In contrast with Ibn Nagrela's method of meticulously documenting each statement by its source, these two works generally did not mention the sources of their data. Furthermore, Margalioth has shown that there are distinct differences of linguistic usage between Samuel ibn Hananiah's work and that of Ibn Nagrela. Finally, a comparison of *Sefer ha-Qabbalah* with the unique manuscript of the chronological section of Samuel ibn Hananiah's *Introduction* has revealed beyond the shadow of a doubt that the Egyptian Nagid's chronology is nothing but an epitome of Ibn Daud's work. Whatever the identity of the real author of this epitome, there is no question but that his work drew on Ibn Daud's book and, therefore, cannot possibly have been the work of Samuel ibn Nagrela![146] Accordingly, Conforte's statements on Ibn Nagrela as Ibn Daud's source must be rejected.

There remains the possibility that Ibn Daud drew his information directly from Suran sources, such as the work of Samuel b. Hofni, a possibility at which Epstein indeed hinted. However, for some reason which I cannot fathom, it never occurred to Epstein that, even if that academy's archives were a shambles, its official statements could not possibly have exchanged the names of its presidents with those of Pumbeditha! Ibn Daud's mistake on the place of service of those geonim has to be accounted for independently of his sources.

Ibn Daud's blunder on the first three generations of geonim can actually be explained much more simply. A comparison of the *whole* of the gaonic section with the parallel section of Sherira will prove at once that Sherira is no more or no less the source for the last five generations than he is for for the first three. To cite a major error from the fourth and fifth generations, the generations where Epstein maintained that Ibn Daud had returned to *terra firma* (i.e., Sherira), Ibn Daud believed that Abraham b. Sherira of Pumbeditha was a gaon of Sura![147] The same types of omission, distortion and chronological confusion that appear in the first three generations of *Sefer ha-Qabbalah* are reflected in the last five.[148] Conversely, but for the confusion of academies,

---

146 Cf. Cohen, *SFC*, pp. 124 f. Whether the epitome is to be ascribed to Samuel b. Hananiah is a moot point, in view of the fact that the latter may have died in 1159, or two years before the writing of *Sefer ha-Qabbalah*; cf. Baron, *SRH*, V, 42 and Margalioth, p. 72. But that is a problem that is not germane to our study. Whoever the epitomist was, he copied from Ibn Daud and not vice versa.
147 VI.82–83.
148 Cf. VI.84 f.

the first three generations of Ibn Daud's work are faithful replicas of Sherira's list. The story and actors are identical; only the places have been exchanged. What is more, although Ibn Daud confused the academies, he consistently followed Sherira's scheme in listing "Pumbeditha" first.

Granted that Ibn Daud's error is an egregious one, it is still only an accident of but one or two leaves in a medieval manuscript. Assuming that Ibn Daud's source had listed the geonim of Sura and Pumbeditha in parallel columns,[149] it becomes apparent that the error of the first *four* generations could have occurred in a number of ways: by a misunderstanding of the headings; by a simple *lapsus calami* of the scribe writing the headings first and then both lists of geonim; by a torn page that had been wrongly pasted together. Somehow, the name of Abraham b. Sherira, the last of the fourth generation of Pumbeditha, was transferred to the wrong column, and he was accordingly placed in Sura.

Ibn Daud clearly had but one source for his *isnad* of the whole gaonic period. We may be fairly certain that it was a defective copy or, more probably, a digest of Sherira's *Epistle*. This list suffered omissions, particularly of the homoioteleuton type to which Sherira's *Epistle* was especially susceptible, as well as normal scribal corruptions.[150] This source always had dates for the authorities of Pumbeditha, but not always for Sura, precisely as in Sherira's *Epistle*. Where Ibn Daud found that the dates in his source did not tally with the length of the terms, he doctored the *dates* freely. After all, he had not hesitated to do so with biblical and talmudic dates; why should he not do so for amoraim, saboraim, and geonim? To this source, the digest of Sherira, he added information from other sources, to which we shall return presently.

Having seen that Ibn Daud wrote all of his gaonic history on the basis of one lineal descendant of Sherira's *Epistle*, we must return to the earlier sections to see whether they, nevertheless, reflected Suran, rather than Sherira-Pumbedithan orientation.

The first example of evidence offered by Epstein is the divergence between *Seder Tannaim wa-Amorian* and Sherira on the date of Rab's migration to Babylonia. We have already indicated that this difference is in reality a modern myth based on Rapoport's emendation of Sherira. Now this emendation was not necessitated by Sherira's text, but by Rapoport's efforts to identify the Antoninus mentioned in the Talmud with Marcus Aurelius (161–180 C.E.). Since Rapoport contended that the Antoninus of the Talmud was "the philosopher" and that in the days of later emperors known as Antoninus, namely Caracalla and Elagabalus, R. Judah the Prince was no longer living, he could

149 Cf. S.N. to IV.25.
150 Cf. VI.14–15, 34, 74–75.

not permit Sherira's *Epistle* to extend R. Judah's lifetime down to 530 Seleucid Era (218/219 C.E.). Accordingly, taking his cue from Ibn Daud's date for the redaction of the Mishna, Rapoport emended the date 530 in Sherira's *Epistle* to 500.[151] However, it stands to reason that no modern historical exigencies can legitimately demand the emendation of a date, which is attested by all manuscripts of the *Epistle*, by *Sefer ha-Qabbalah* and by virtually every other medieval source, and thereby validate an "authentic" tradition. To proceed after that to classify sources on the basis of an emendation, as did Epstein, is to juggle texts a bit too liberally. In reality, therefore, the medieval Jewish texts are unanimous in dating the death of Judah the Prince in 530 Seleucid Era.[152] There are no disagreements on this point between the historians of the two academies.

The same conclusion holds for the second of the three typical Suran traditions supposedly appropriated by Ibn Daud; to wit, that the amoraic period terminated and the saboraic period began in 4237. To a certain extent, it must be conceded, Ibn Daud was partially to blame for the impression he made on Conforte and Epstein on this point, for he began his chapter on the saboraic period with the ascension of Rabbah Jose to the presidency of academy in 4237.[153] However, Ibn Daud made it quite clear that the saboraic period, as distinct from Rabbah Jose's term, did not begin in that year, but some twenty-three to twenty-five years later in 4260-4262. At the end of the chapter of the saboraim, he indicated in no uncertain terms that this period came to an end in 4449 after a duration of but 187 years.[154] If anything, then, Ibn Daud deferred the beginning of the fifth period of Jewish history to 4262, or two years later than the Pumbedithan Sherira. We shall soon see that, although in reality Ibn Daud agreed with Sherira that the turning point in the transition from the period of amoraim to that of saboraim was to be dated in 4260, the actual date was far less significant to him than the lesson to be derived from the change of periods.

This leaves us with one final tradition of Sura in *Sefer ha-Qabbalah*: the tradition that the age of the geonim began in 689 C.E., rather than 589 C.E. as in the *Epistle*.[155] Ibn Daud, it is said, must have derived this tradition from *Seder Tannaim wa-Amoraim*, for he reflected the latter's placement of the rise of Islam within the saboraic age, while Sherira indicated that by the time of Muhammad the gaonic period had already begun. However, in reality,

151 Cf. above, n. 132.
152 Cf. S. Krauss, *Antoninus und Rabbi* (Frankfurt a.M., 1910), pp. 142 f. Cf. also below, p. 211.
153 V.2 f.   154 V.46.
155 Cf. above, n. 120.

Sherira nowhere explicitly indicated at what point the gaonic period began, for he used the term "geonim" even of amoraim.[156] In the absence of a clear-cut statement to the contrary, the medieval (indeed, even the modern) reader of the statement that the following "geonim" reigned in Pumbeditha could have understood the term merely as "presidents," amoraic, saboraic, or gaonic. Moreover, even if Ibn Daud had understood Sherira as Conforte, Rapoport, Halevy and Epstein did, he would still not have been bound by this limitation. He had not hesitated to diverge from older texts; why should he feel diffident about so trivial a matter as the date of the first gaon? The sacred chain (*isnad*) that he wished to establish was there in any case!

To all this must be added that there is absolutely no ground for the contention that *Seder Tannaim wa-Amoraim* emanated from Sura. On the contrary, recent analysis of that work has shown that it represented the historical thinking of neither of the two great academies.[157] But even if the Suran provenance of this little tract should be demonstrated, we would be in no better position as far as Ibn Daud's work is concerned, for *Sefer ha-Qabbalah*, with all its divergences from Sherira's *Epistle*, is far more closely related to the latter than to *Seder Tannaim wa-Amoraim*.

The evidence points overwhelmingly to the conclusion that for the framework of the whole of his rabbinic chain, Ibn Daud was guided by one post-talmudic source, which was closely related to Sherira's *Epistle* but not identical with it. This source had incorporated some material from other works, such as the Talmud, *Seder Tannaim wa-Amoraim* and Seder 'Olam Zuta, and had further reworked Sherira's lists by reducing them to parallel columns. It is in connection with this point that a number of coincidences about Ibn Daud's rabbinic list begin to assume importance. In the first place, Ibn Daud's detailed knowledge of the geonim comes to an end with the contemporaries of Nissim b. Jacob ibn Shahin of Qairawan.[158] Ibn Daud was patently unaware of the names of the successors of Samuel b. Hofni to the presidency of Sura or of the later appointments to Pumbeditha, although he knew that the latter continued to flourish.[159] In other words, Ibn Daud brought his account of the geonim to a close at the very point that his source did. One further coincidence must be stressed. Nissim ibn Shahin was the son of the recipient of Sherira's *Epistle*, and Nissim carried on his father's intimate relationship with the gaonate of Pumbeditha.[160] On the other hand, Nissim maintained close contact with Sam-

---

156 Cf. *ISG* 89.16, 90.15. The point was noted by Ginzberg, *Geonica*, I, 48.
157 Cf. Kahan's introduction to *STW*, pp. xiv f.
158 VI.177 f.   159 Cf. notes to VI.186, 220.
160 Cf. Nissim ibn Shahin, *Ḥibbur Yafeh me-ha-Yesh'uah* (ed. Hirschberg), Introduction, pp. 24 f., 30 f.

uel ibn Nagrela of Spain, who was the guiding image of Ibn Daud's school of thought.[161] Is it not, therefore, plausible to conjecture that Ibn Daud's prime source for the gaonic age was the history of tradition of Nissim ibn Shahin? We have already indicated other considerations pointing to the work of Ibn Shahin as Ibn Daud's guide. The evidence of *Sefer ha-Qabbalah* on the gaonic age seems to us to confirm our suggestion.[162]

Ibn Daud does diverge from Sherira's *Epistle* within the tannaitic and amoraic sections with respect to the students and colleagues of the master of each generation. However, this would merely indicate that his basic source was a *digest* of Sherira, rather than a corrupted text of the *Epistle* itself. This additional material may have been drawn in part from Nissim ibn Shahin's history and in part from Ibn Daud's own conclusions from the texts of the Talmud or of Spanish martyrologies.[163] But in at least one instance Ibn Daud indicates that he had a second source. "The fifth generation [of amoraim]," Ibn Daud writes, "was that of R. Nahman b. Isaac, R. Papa, and R. Huna b. R. Joshua.... As for R. Huna b. R. Joshua, his name is not recorded among the heads of the academies."[164] This statement can only mean that R. Huna b. Joshua's name was recorded in one work, but not in Ibn Daud's prime source on the links of the rabbinic chain. This second work was doubtless a recension of *Seder Tannaim wa-Amoraim*, where the chain of amoraim lists one link as consisting of R. Papa and R. Huna b. R. Joshua.[165] Only in one other instance does *Sefer ha-Qabbalah* reflect use of this work, and that is in the list of patriarchs from Hillel to R. Judah II.[166] The style of this bare list clearly indicates that it was lifted *verbatim*—perhaps by way of Ibn Shahin—from that early work on talmudic chronology and method. It may, therefore, be that Ibn Daud lifted the remainder of the sentence on R. Huna b. Joshua from Ibn Shahin, who had been puzzled by the fact that Sherira's *Epistle* did not credit this amora with the presidency of an academy.

Be that as it may, the indirect dependence of *Sefer ha-Qabbalah* on Sherira's *Epistle* is undeniable, no less for the talmudic age than for the saboraic and gaonic periods; no less for the first three generations of geonim than for the

---

161   VII.270 f. On the centrality of the image of Ibn Nagrela in Ibn Daud's work, cf. below, pp. 269 f.
162   Cf. above, pp. 174 f. That Nissim's chronological work served as one of Ibn Daud's sources was also conjectured by Elbogen, "Abraham ibn Daud als Geschichtsschreiber," p. 197.
163   Cf. above, pp. 172 f.
164   IV.47–48, 56–58.
165   *STW*, p. 10, line 3.
166   I.76–80; *STW*, p. 2, lines 5 f., p. 3, par. 3 and 2b.

last five. Ibn Daud's discrepancies with well-known stories in the Talmud and with the traditions of Sherira are most easily explained as the result of his immediate reliance on a work that had somewhat revised Sherira's presentation and that had, in turn, suffered at the hands of copyists. Nissim ibn Shahin's *Sefer Seder Meqabbelay ha-Torah*, it appears to us, offers the most likely solution to the major problems we have discussed.

III. THE SYMMETRY OF HISTORY

After all of Ibn Daud's work on pre-Andalusian history has been dissected and traced to its sources, there remains a small but hard core that simply cannot be accounted for in this manner. Granted that Sherira's *Epistle* does not openly contradict Ibn Daud's statement that the redaction of the Mishna occurred in 500 Seleucid Era (= 3449 A.M.); granted, too, that the *Epistle* is not unequivocally definite about the date of transition from saboraim to geonim. We are still left with the problem of determining *Ibn Daud's* reasons for dating these two pivotal points in Jewish history.

To be sure, were these two dates the only problematic ones in *Sefer ha-Qabbalah*, we could afford to leave the matter open until some fresh discovery would provide us with the appropriate footnotes. But the fact of the matter is that these two dates, which have so troubled modern scholars, are the least disturbing aspect of Ibn Daud's chronology, for they neither contradict otherwise well-established traditions, nor do they contradict material within *Sefer ha-Qabbalah* itself. However, as we have indicated, the book is liberally dotted with statements that do contradict matters of common knowledge and even of common sense. We have already noted some examples of such shocking violations in Ibn Daud's treatment of the biblical period. But those were by no means all. What is one to make of a statement, repeated for emphasis, that $62 \times 7 = 420$![1] Or that $4449 - 187 = 4260$![2] Or that $4798 - 13 = 4775$![3] Or, to turn to matters that were common knowledge in Ibn Daud's milieu, that ʿAbd ar-Raḥman III was still alive in 4750 (= 990 C.E.)?[4] That the Almohade persecutions began in 4873 (= 1112/13 C.E.)![5] These are not mere cases of slovenliness. They appear to be deliberate distortions. Granted, once again, that Ibn Daud was a medieval man; he was not a fool!

Perhaps, therefore, it would be better to deviate from the line of attack hitherto taken by modern analysts of *Sefer ha-Qabbalah* and to try to tackle the work as a whole. Perhaps many of the puzzling elements of Ibn Daud's work eluded his readers because they concentrated on isolated details rather

1 I.191, 200–201.
2 V.5, 46 and cf. above, p. 185.
3 VII.168.
4 VII.7, 64.
5 VII.459.

than on Ibn Daud as a historian and on his method—of which the specific problems are but instances. In the final analysis, a work must be understood phenomenologically, i.e., as an independent statement that conveys a message of its own. The discovery of sources for every single statement in *Sefer ha-Qabbalah* will not account for the method and intent of the author. These can be elicited and determined only by examining the work as a unit and as the product of a man who wished to say something that for reasons of his own he did not immediately make obvious to his reading public.

Indeed, the real literary problem of *Sefer ha-Qabbalah*, we suggest, should consist not of unattested traditions, but of statements that contradict either established sources or other statements within Ibn Daud's work itself or facts that were well known to Ibn Daud and his audience. To be sure, internal contradictions are not a phenomenon peculiar to Ibn Daud, but in the context of his intellectual world they had some very definite connotations. The significance of internal contradictions was spelled out in considerable detail by Ibn Daud's contemporary countryman and intellectual kinsman, Moses Maimonides.

In the Introduction to his *Guide of the Perplexed*, Maimonides indicated that contradictions within a carefully written book, one expressing an integrated point of view, are often deliberate and reflect meaning that is not immediately manifest. One or both of the contradictory terms may be symbolic of some hidden meaning. On occasion, Maimonides warned, apparent contradictions must be introduced in order to obscure certain matters in accordance with the demands of the subject itself. This would be particularly true when one must deal with matters which religion—or prudence—prohibits as subjects of open or public discussion.[6] While we shall have to suspend judgment for a while on the factors which prompted Ibn Daud to adopt such usages in his writing, we can at least assume that a philosopher of the same general school of thought as Maimonides, who, at the very least, wrote with deliberation and precision, would not lightly permit glaring blunders to creep into his work. They must have had some purpose.

Now we have already seen that to Ibn Daud history was not a neutral discipline, but a weapon for religious polemic. History, in other words, proves or disproves the validity of religious claims, be they Rabbanite, Karaite, or Christian.[7] But this is not all that history can do. According to Ibn Daud, history not only legitimizes the past and the present; it also comforts and, by implication, gives hope for the future. History is a kind of sermon, a medium of insight into the workings of Providence and, accordingly, a vehicle of solace

---

6 Moses Maimonides, *The Guide of the Perplexed* (tr. Pines), pp. 17 f.
7 Cf. Introduction, pp. xxviii f.

for Israel.⁸ To demonstrate this point, Ibn Daud deliberately interrupted his perfectly intelligible account of biblical history with an extended and somewhat opaque analysis of the sequence of events from the destruction of the First Temple to the rebuilding of the Second.⁹ Upon closer examination of this passage, it will be seen that the author has abandoned the genre of historiography for the style of homiletics.

"Behold how trustworthy are the consolations of our God, blessed be His name, for the chronology of their exile corresponded to that of their redemption. Twenty-one years passed from the beginning of their exile until the destruction and the cessation of the monarchy. Similarly, twenty-one years passed from the time the rebuilding of the Temple was begun until it was completed."¹⁰ In other words, at least one purpose of the study of history was to discern through chronology the hints of divine providence over Israel. And for Ibn Daud the surest sign of Providence, or as he calls it, of divine consolation, was to be found in the rhythmic workings of history: construction, destruction, and reconstruction of the two Temples were decreed from Heaven to occur in periods that were equal in length and, therefore, symmetrical. It is in the symmetrical periodization of history, then, that we may discern the transcendent plan of history. It matters not that Scripture did not supply all the necessary data for such a symmetry, or even that Ibn Daud's symmetry contradicted the manifest data of Scripture. The function of the historian was to find the plan and rewrite the chronological facts where necessary.

The view that the meaning of history could largely be discerned in its symmetrical pattern was not, of course, Ibn Daud's own discovery, but an ancient doctrine which Ibn Daud merely appropriated and tailored to his own subject matter. Classical midrash had often taken note of the symmetrical balance in the story of creation, the events in the second day of creation being balanced by the events of the third, the creation of the fourth day being balanced by that of the fifth.¹¹ As ancient Hebrew poets had versified within a fixed framework of *parallelismus membrorum* (the parallel stichs being synonymous, antithetical or progressive), so the later homilist saw in the phenomena of nature and the events of history counterparts of other phenomena. These phenomena or events might be repetitions of earlier occurrences (exile, destruction, restoration, etc.) or they might be totally unrelated phenomena, whose inner connection was discovered—we would say, artificially drawn—because they occurred at parallel points in the year. Parallelism and symmetry were second nature to

---

8 Cf. *ibid.*, p. xxxv.
9 I.114 f.
10 I.121–125.
11 Ber. R. 12.8 (ed. Theodor-Albeck), p. 106.

a rabbinically trained mind, and Ibn Daud's collation of historical events was thus but a continuation of a well-established literary-theological scheme.[12]

Indeed, the very phraseology in Ibn Daud's introduction to his excursus on symmetry is reminiscent of a classical homily on the verse in Psalms (92.6): "How great are Thy works, O Lord." On this verse an ancient preacher had observed: "Behold the wonders of the Holy One, blessed be He, who created worlds within worlds. He created worlds and created mankind within one of them. He created harmful spirits and created the ministering angels."[13] In other words, every detail of creation is balanced by another. "Another interpretation of the verse 'How great are Thy works, O Lord, Thy thoughts are very deep.' What is the significance of the words 'Thy thoughts are very deep'? R. Hanina said: Although the work on the Tabernacle was completed on the twenty-fifth of Kislev, the Tabernacle was not erected by Moses until the first of Nisan... for Moses wished to associate the festivities of the Tabernacle with the month in which Isaac was born."[14] Put differently, R. Hanina saw significance in the date of one historical event through its association with the approximate date of an entirely different, indeed chronologically quite remote, occurrence. One event fitted in with another.

R. Hanina himself was only applying to one more instance in Scripture a homily which other sages had applied to major turning points in history. Thus, rabbinic tradition had decided that the First Temple could only have stood 410 years, for when added to the seventy years during which there was no Temple, the total equalled, i.e., was symmetrical with, the 480-year period from the Exodus to the building of the First Temple.[15] Similarly, the classical Seder 'Olam saw detailed points of correspondence between the two great exiles of biblical days: "If you examine the data in detail, [you will find that] as the ones [i.e., the northern kingdom of Israel] fell by dint of a revolt [against Assyria], so, too, the others [i.e., the kingdom of Judah] fell by dint of a revolt [against Babylon]. The ones sought help from the kings of Egypt, and

---

12 Cf. I. Heinemann, *The Methods of the Aggadah* [in Hebrew] (Jerusalem, 1949), pp. 60 f.; A. Mirsky, "The Origins of the Forms of Liturgical Poetry" [in Hebrew], *Studies of the Research Institute for Hebrew Poetry in Jerusalem*, VII (1958), 1 f. For the stress on the symmetry of history in medieval historiography generally, cf. Cohen, *SFC*, pp. 103 f. For an excellent example of schematological chronology in Josephus, cf. A. Shalit, "Two Traditions Concerning the Time of Isaiah's Prophecy on the Destruction of the Temple and the Return to Zion" [in Hebrew], *I.F.Baer Jubilee Volume* (Jerusalem, 1960), pp. 69 f. There, too, the schematology is based on symmetry and multiples of "seven."
13 Pesikta Rabbati (ed. Friedmann), f. 24a.
14 *Ibid.*
15 Cf. I Ki. 6.1; *Sefer ha-Qabbalah* I.21. The reason for the figure 410 was pointed out to me orally by Professor H.L. Ginsberg.

so did the others. The former ones suffered three exiles, and so, too, the latter ones. The former were besieged for three years, and so the others were besieged for three years. The former ate of the flesh of their sons and daughters, and so did the latter. The former were driven into captivity three times, and so, too, the latter, thus fulfilling the prophecy of Scripture: 'In the way of thy sister hast thou walked; therefore will I give her up into thy hand (Ezekiel 23.31).' "[16] To cite but one more specimen of symmetrical historical midrash: "R. Jose said: Good things are brought about on a meritorious day and evil things on a day of evil. Thus, when the First Temple was destroyed, it was the ninth of Ab, the first day of the week, and the beginning of a new sabbatical cycle. The priestly watch on duty was that of Jehoiarib. So it was also at the time of the second destruction."[17]

Once again, it does not matter in the least whether there is any substantive basis for these homilies. The fact is that they were part of the classical rabbinic tradition and, no less germane to our point, but a minute fraction of a vast genre of homily and exegesis portraying the manifestations of symmetry in nature and history. Ibn Daud was no innovator in this respect. If there was any novelty in his appropriation of this pattern of thinking, it lay in his almost concealed employment of it as a law of history, Jewish as well as general history. History could now be structured schematically, thus giving it a form and rhythm which were otherwise not apparent.

Ibn Daud coupled this schematology with several other considerations and techniques, which he felt the authority of precedent gave him license to appropriate. The first was the use of symbolic biblical words, which could be assigned appropriate numerical, i.e., chronological, value. An example of such usage was the derivation of a date for the Hasmonean uprising from a word in Isaiah.[18] Such symbolism is found frequently in the Talmud and was invoked by many a medieval writer.[19] The second and by far more important principle was that biblical dates and chronological data are not always accurate, for they may have been corrupted in the wake of the calamity of exile.[20] Although

---

16 Seder 'Olam 26 (ed. Ratner), p. 117.
17 *Ibid.*, 30, p. 147.
18 Cf. above, p. 171.
19 Cf. Kasowski, *Thesaurus Talmudis*, VII, 264; Cohen, *SFC*, p. 104. For an impassioned defense of *gematriaot* a century after Ibn Daud, cf. Moses Nahmanides, "Sefer ha-Geulah," *Kitbay R. Moses b. Nahman*, ed. by H.D. Chavel, 2 vols. (Jerusalem, 1963), I, 262.
20 *Yer.* Ta'an. 48, f. 68c; Tosafot to *B.* R.H. 18b. Such a principle is, of course, a dangerous one, and Ibn Daud used it with the utmost caution. He departed from traditional figures only when the evidence drove him to his own conclusions. However, even in those instances his emendations turned out to be minor ones. Thus, his emendation of Zedekiah's tenth year to his sixth (I.137) meant reading a י as a ו. The opposite was done in per-

this conclusion was invoked by the rabbis of Talmud most cautiously and only as a last resort, it opened the door to further speculation. Ibn Daud felt perfectly free to invoke this principle, in view of the fact that when he did employ it his conclusions did not imply any break with the traditional calendar. In fact, he applied the principle in the service of what he considered a highly significant end: deriving consolation for his people by eliciting new relevance from Jewish history. In any event, he felt free to alter dates if he could thereby verify the sermon of history for his audience. Schematology and symbolism took precedence over bald fact.

If we keep these various considerations in mind, the bizarre and often self-contradictory chronology in *Sefer ha-Qabbalah* begins to take shape and meaning.

In connection with the chronology of ancient Israel, Ibn Daud began with two *rabbinic* presuppositions, both of which he considered of equal weight and both of which he felt constrained to harmonize with the chronological data of Scripture. The first and well-attested tradition stated that the First Temple had stood for 410 years.[21] A second tradition, based apparently on a mnemonic for the word for exile (גלה = 433) in the twentieth verse of the prophecy of Obadiah, stated that the Temple had stood for 433 years.[22] However, neither of these traditions tallied exactly with the data contained in Scripture.[23] Consequently, the pertinent verses in the Bible had to be treated midrashically; that is, they had to be reinterpreted and tailored to fit the two traditions.

The earliest terminus for which Ibn Daud could find some foothold for the classic talmudic figure of 410 was the exile of Daniel in the third year of Jehoiakim.[24] This left Ibn Daud with the task of accounting for the excess of twenty-three years deriving from the second number, 433, which he considered to be of equal traditional weight. Ibn Daud doubtless knew quite well that the reigns do not add up to 433. Accordingly, he (or his sources) contrived some method to find three additional years over the total of 430 (actually, 429 1/2). He did this by *reinterpreting* the date of Solomon's construction of

---

mitting ten years to elapse between the downfall of the Persian Empire and the beginning of the Seleucid Era, instead of the six normally accepted in Jewish literature; cf. I.222; II.8; *B*. A.Z. 10a. Similarly the change of 2 1/2 to 20 1/2 in the Ben Koziba story (III. 44, 50) could result from reading (deliberately ?) a ב as a כ. Cf. also note to VII.250.

21 I.21.
22 Cf. Ibn Ezra to Obad. 20; Moses Nahmanides, *op. cit.*, p. 275.
23 Cf. Azarah de' Rossi, *op. cit.*, ch. 35 (ed. Cassel), pp. 299 f., where the various possible totals are given.
24 I.126–129, 135–136.

the Temple[25] and by reckoning a year each for Jehoahaz and Jehoiachin.[26] But what was Ibn Daud to make of the excess of twenty-three years over the tradition of 410, if he was to account for them in terms of biblical dates? By no stretch of the imagination could he find an interval of twenty-three years between the third year of Jehoiakim and the eleventh year of Zedekiah. It would have been more convenient if Nebuchadnezzar's reign had begun in the first year of Jehoiakim. Ibn Daud would then not have been compelled to contradict the synchronistic data of the Bible. Unfortunately, this was not the case, and Ibn Daud had to begin with the actual ascension of Nebuchadnezzar to the throne in the third year of Jehoiakim.[27] However, Scripture did give another terminus for Nebuchadnezzar's invasion of Judea. That was the report of Jeremiah 52.30 that Nebuchadnezzar invaded Judea in the twenty-third year of his reign. Here was a partial way out of the difficulty. By identifying the invasion in the twenty-third year of Nebuchadnezzar as the year of the destruction of the Temple, and by adding the twenty-three to the year 410, which was when Ibn Daud dated Nebuchadnezzar's ascension to the throne, he found documentary confirmation of the tradition that the Temple was destroyed after having stood for 433 years![28]

Ibn Daud then proceeded to work backwards from that figure. Since the twenty-third year of Nebuchadnezzar was the year of the final invasion, it had to be equated with Zedekiah's eleventh year, and hence Nebuchadnezzar's eighteenth year patently corresponded to Zedekiah's sixth.[29] However, since the twenty-three years of Nebuchadnezzar did not tally with the corresponding number of years of the reigns of the Jewish kings, Ibn Daud concluded that the figure in Jeremiah 52.30 was a Babylonian figure of official regnal years, which really amounted only to twenty-one calendrical years.[30] It is pointless to theorize about how Ibn Daud would have resolved this weird chronology with that of Scripture in complete detail. The essential point is that Ibn Daud was trying to reconcile the *terminal* points of rabbinic tradition with those of the Bible on the basis of the data furnished by Scripture itself.

A further glaring contradiction of Scripture, as we have noted, is Ibn Daud's statement that the First Temple was destroyed after a war of seven years.[31] However, it was in connection with these doctorings of Scripture that Ibn

---

25   I.48, 69.
26   Cf. note to I.70.
27   Dan. 1.1 and cf. above, n. 24.
28   I.139–140.
29   I.137–138.
30   I.140–142.
31   I.113.

Daud revealed his schematological conception of history: "Behold how trustworthy are the consolations of our God, blessed be His name, for the chronology of their exile corresponded to that of their redemption."[32] In other words, construction, destruction and reconstruction should be understood as having been decreed from Heaven to occur in periods that are symmetrical. That Scripture did not supply all the necessary data for such a symmetry, or even that the symmetry contradicted the manifest data of Scripture, was of no consequence. The function of the historian was to find the plan and rewrite the chrolonogical facts where necessary. Hence, since the Temple had been seven years in the building,[33] it had to endure a seven-year siege before its destruction. Since the Second Temple had not been built until twenty-one years after the Jews came under Persian domination,[34] the twenty-three year subjection to Babylon (i.e., to Nebuchadnezzar) before the destruction of the First Temple had to be pruned to twenty-one! The fate of the Second Temple also had to parallel that of the First, and, accordingly, its period of subjection to foreign pressure also lasted for seven years.[35]

The identical concerns and methods of resolution of contradictory traditions are manifested in Ibn Daud's summary of the chronology of the Second Temple. In his excursus on the chronology in the book of Daniel, we learn that the Second Temple stood from the time its foundation was laid until its destruction, for a total of sixty-three weeks, or 441 years.[36] Of these, one week (or seven years) was spent in the war with Vespasian and Titus, leaving sixty-two weeks, or 434 years, during which the Second Temple could be said to have stood in peace.[37] Ibn Daud could not accept this as quite true, for according to talmudic tradition, the Second Temple had stood for 420 years.[38] How was he to harmonize an authoritative rabbinic tradition, one which was basic to all Rabbanite chronology, with the text of Daniel, which credited the period of the Second Temple with 434 years? The talmudic tradition could be explained simply enough as referring to the period during which the Temple had stood after its completion. Since from the time of Cyrus' edict until the destruction sixty-three weeks had passed, and of these, three weeks, or twenty-one years, elasped during which work on the Temple had been suspended, the Second Temple could properly be said to have stood for 420 years.[39] However,

32 Cf. above, n. 10.
33 I Ki. 6.38.
34 I.124–125, 214–219.
35 I.192, 204 f.
36 I.190.
37 I.191–192, 200 f.
38 Cf. note to I.164.
39 I.188.

since the book of Daniel had plainly indicated that the period during which the Second Temple had stood in peace was one of sixty-two weeks, Ibn Daud hinted that the traditional figure of 420 was an ambiguous one, for it could also be said to have referred to the period before the pact with Rome, when the Temple was no longer independent.[40] Such a situation had its parallel in the days of the First Temple, for the kingdom of Judah was considered to have been ended from the moment of Nebuchadnezzar's first invasion.[41] Hence the 420-year period of the Second Temple could be said to have begun fourteen years after the edict of Cyrus, or seven years before the Temple was actually completed. To be sure, Ibn Daud had no basis for this conclusion either from Scripture or from rabbinic tradition. But he insisted on retaining the rabbinic figure 420 as well as the expression from Daniel of "sixty-two weeks," thereby giving the impression that he thought that $62 \times 7 = 420$.[42] He knew the the truth of simple arithmetic full well. Futhermore, no scribe would have been likely to emend the correct figure of 434, if it had been in Ibn Daud's text. He chose to pass over this problem in silence. However, his arbitrary dating of the beginning of the 420-year period 427 years before the destruction of the Second Temple did yield him one further result, which doubtless pleased him. Now the First and the Second Temples could be seen to have stood for 427 years, from the time they had been completed until their destruction.[43] The periods were symmetrical despite the apparent difference in the periods of their existence.

Now if we put some of Ibn Daud's biblical data together, a remarkable pattern emerges. The First and Second Temples stood for 427 years. The First Temple was built in seven years and destroyed after a siege of seven years. The Second Temple, too, was destroyed after a seven-year period of Jewish subjection to Rome and revolt against it. The period of destruction of the First Temple began twenty-one years before its actual end; this period was balanced by the twenty-one-year period of construction of the Second Temple. If we consider the fact that the common denominator of all these figures is the number seven, which is the number underlying the prophecies of Daniel, we begin to glimpse Ibn Daud's real conception of historiography. Ibn Daud's pen has identified history with apocalyptic literature.

However bizarre and unwarranted such tinkering with historical data may appear to the modern—and it was no less objectionable to Zacuto[44]—the fact

---

40 I.166, 192, 200 f.
41 I.21–23.
42 I.191, 200 f.
43 Cf. *ibid.* and I.112.
44 Zacuto, *op. cit.*, pp. 81b f.

is that the principle of symmetry, coupled with the underlying commitment to the defense of official traditions, was very dear to Ibn Daud and, as we shall see, will serve to elucidate some of the more puzzling passages in other parts of his work. The important thing is that we are confronted not by a chronicler bound to facts but by a medieval homiletician on history, who often tailored his facts to suit his own midrash.

On the other hand, the remarkable thing about this game with numbers is that Ibn Daud ignored them completely in his exoteric chronology. Jewish chronology, *Anno Mundi*, is always reckoned by him in accordance with the orthodox tradition that the First Temple was destroyed 410 years after its foundation had been laid, rebuilt seventy years later, and destroyed a second time 420 years after that.[45] Not that, Ibn Daud hints, these figures are only official; they were indeed based on historical fact, but they were not always meant literally. Since official Jewish dating was in itself based on an interpretive reading of rabbinic totals, which did not always tally with actual fact, the door was open for further theorization and intepretation of dates. Indeed, the later historian could indulge in a certain amount of symbolic dating in order to guide the more attentive student to a profounder understanding of the rhythm of Jewish history. Dates could, therefore, be of several types. Some dates, indeed most, were merely factual and of no significance. Others were based on facts but were deliberately applied inaccurately for the sake of symbolism: e.g., 410 years for the First Temple and 420 for the Second. Still other dates might be factual and symbolic but not applied in official chronology: e.g., 433 years for the First Temple. However, such a number (433) might well crop up again in Jewish history, as we shall see immediately. Finally, it was quite possible for a date to be correct, official and symbolic at the same time, as will also become apparent in the course of our survey of Ibn Daud's later chronology.

In any case, the profound and truly significant aspect of Jewish chronology was that which revealed the key to the meaning of chronology, namely, symbolic numbers and dates. Meaning, as we know, was often expressed through internal contradiction, and it was this category of numbers—those which contradict official ones—which was, accordingly, the most revealing.

At the end of the saboraic period, Ibn Daud tells us that the length of that age was 187 years.[46] This figure is arithmetically untenable from any point

---

45 I.19—First Temple built in 2929.
   I.21—First Temple stood 410 years [i.e.First Temple destroyed in 3339].
   II.8, 18—Second Temple rebuilt 70 years later in 3409.
   II.164—Second Temple destroyed 420 years later in 3829.
46 V.46.

of view. If one reckons from the beginning of the term of the first of the saboraim, Rabbah Jose, the figure must be 213 years.⁴⁷ However, if one reckons from the date of the redaction of the Talmud, the difference is one of 189 years.⁴⁸ The temptation to emend a figure transmitted by all manuscripts will be quickly checked if one bears in mind that we are dealing with a man who will blandly tell us that 62 × 7 = 420. Let us, therefore, follow Ibn Daud's directions and subtract 187 from 4449 and we arrive at 4262 A.M., which would make that year the turning point from amoraic to saboraic ages. Expressed otherwise, the *symbolic* date of the redaction of the Talmud is not 4260, which is what tradition states, but 4262. The suspicion that the date of the redaction of the Talmud is pregnant with symbolic meaning grows deeper when we note that in connection with that event Ibn Daud gave not one but *seven* dates: 1) *Anno Mundi*; 2) Seleucid Era; 3) year *before* the *Hijra*; 4) from the death of R. Ashi; 5) the redaction of the Mishna; 6) from the redaction of the Mishna until the year in which Ibn Daud was writing; 7) from the redaction of the Talmud until Ibn Daud's writing.⁴⁹ This is not mere pleonasm but sheer superfluity, unless we concede that Ibn Daud is alerting us to something. And now to Ibn Daud's clues: "Thus," he says, "there were 311 years from the time of the writing of the Mishna until the sealing of the Talmud."⁵⁰ If one adds the two additional years now gained from the symbolic date of 4262 to Ibn Daud's statement on the date from the redaction of the Mishna, it follows that the Talmud was really completed 313 years after the Mishna. Now in connection with the date of the redaction of the Mishna, Ibn Daud had supplied not only the date *Anno Mundi* but also the date of the Seleucid Era and the reckoning from the destruction of the Second Temple.⁵¹ As pleonasms, each of these two additional reckonings must have some significance. If one combines the last datum, namely that the Mishna was redacted 120 years after the second destruction, with that of the symbolic date of the redaction of the Talmud, it follows that from the destruction of the Second Temple until the redaction of the Babylonian Talmud, there were 433 years. But 433 is one of the symbolic figures of the chronology of the First Temple!⁵² Or, we may approach this figure for the redaction of the Talmud from a different angle: In connection with the first exile, Ibn Daud indicated that, although it occurred in the year 433 of the Temple, in reality that figure should be tailored to 431.⁵³ If we do just that, the figure is all the more relevant in the present context, for from the second destruction (3829 A.M.) until the *official date* of the re-

47 V.3–4.
48 V.5.
49 V.5–11.
50 V.7–8.

51 III.95–96.
52 Cf. above, n. 22.
53 Cf. above, to n. 30.

daction of the Babylonian Talmud (4260 A.M.), 431 years passed. From whichever angle you look at it, Ibn Daud hinted, the redaction of the Talmud was a divine consolation, for the same number of years elapsed from the destruction of the Second Temple to the redaction of the Talmud as from the building of the First Temple until its destruction. The two periods are symmetrical; in other words, the Talmud is religiously symmetrical with the Temple. At last we begin to discern the meaning of the statement that from 4260 until 4449, 187 years passed. "Behold how trustworthy are the consolations of our God." History will prove, according to Ibn Daud, that the Guardian of Israel "doth neither slumber nor sleep (Ps. 121.4)."

The problem with this method of dating and counterdating is that the modern student is never quite sure that he has read Ibn Daud's code correctly, and that he himself has not been sucked into a trap of fantastic numerology. Fortunately, we are not compelled to pluck dates out of the air, but, as we have seen, are frequently provided by Ibn Daud with little hints as to what constitute symmetrical turning points. In a separate study we have tried to prove that the absurd synchronization of the story of the four captives is construed along these very lines of historical symmetry.[54] Into this tale on the spread of Jewish learning to Egypt, North Africa and Andalus, Ibn Daud wove several motifs which appear in classical sources and which illustrate the point that the Almighty does not permit the sun of one community (in this case, Babylonia) to set before providing adequate illumination from some other quarter (i.e., Spain). Moreover, the human agent in that divine plan achieved recognition and rabbinic authority in a way very reminiscent of the way Hillel the Babylonian had attained the presidency over the academy in Jerusalem much earlier.[55] Now although Ibn Daud knew full well, as did his learned audience, that R. Moses the captive came to Cordova in the reign of 'Abd ar-Raḥman III, and rose to power through the patronage of 'Abd ar-Raḥman's Jewish courtier, Ḥisdai ibn Shaprut, he threw scholars off by dating the event "in approximately 4750, somewhat more or less." If we take Ibn Daud seriously and date the event somewhat less, i.e., 4749, the date of R. Moses' rise to power occurred 980 years after Hillel.[56] 980 years is twice 490, or twice seventy weeks of years, and is thus not only a symmetrical figure but also a consolatory one; for Daniel had prophesied the great destruction for 490 years after the first exile.[57] Now the Almighty had shown that the same number could be a sign of regeneration

---

54 Cohen, *SFC*, pp. 106 f.; cf. also below, n. 70.
55 Cohen, *SFC*, pp. 90 f., 107 f.
56 Hillel attained the title of Nasi in 3729; cf. I.76–77. However, he did not become "head of the academy" until forty years later; II.119 and cf. Cohen, *SFC*, pp. 107 f.
57 I.160 f.

through Torah. (Once again we see the Torah filling the breach, as it were, created by the loss of the Temple.) Accordingly, if we follow Ibn Daud's second instruction and add one year to the date, so that R. Moses' rise to office occurred in 4751, an even more demonstrable symmetry emerges. The Talmud, Ibn Daud recorded, was redacted according to official reckoning in 4260, or 491 years after Hillel, the emigrant from Babylonia, attained the presidency of the academy in Jerusalem.[58] R. Moses, the emigrant from Italy, attained the same position in Cordova in 4751, or 491 years after the redaction of the Talmud. In other words, R. Moses is the Hillel of Spain, and the dynasty of rabbis that was filiated by his school was thus shown to have the stamp of divine approval. Secondly, the Jewish number of doom and destruction, 490, was now seen to bear within itself the balancing and restorative seeds of comfort and consolation. "Behold how trustworthy are the consolations of our God, blessed be His name, for the period of their redemption corresponded exactly to that of their exile." The date 4750 was all the more consolatory, for it itself spelled out a mnemonic תד"שין, meaning to anoint and hence to legitimate.[59]

In the same study on the story of the four captives, we also tried to show that the tale bore not only a message of consolation, but also some invidious overtones on the authority of Babylonia over the Jews of the world. With the death of R. Hai, according to Ibn Daud, the gaonic period came to an end, and the age of the rabbinate began. Now although Ibn Daud introduced the history of the post-gaonic rabbinate with the story of the captives, he was careful to indicate that the new period of Jewish history actually began only after the death of R. Ḥanok and with the succession of Samuel ibn Nagrela.[60] Thus, the deaths of R. Hai and R. Ḥanok were turning points in Jewish history, and significantly enough, Ibn Daud committed a sloppy "blunder" in recording the dates of their deaths. On the one hand, we are told that R. Hai died in 4798 A.M., and on the other that R. Ḥanok died "in 4775, *thirteen years prior to the demise of R. Hai!*"[61] By now we should suspect a hint of some symbolism, and this suspicion, like earlier ones, becomes stronger in view of the fact that the date of R. Hai's death is given not only *Anno Mundi* but also in terms of the Seleucid Era. Moreover, the Seleucid date has the curious "coincidence" of being a Hebrew word that corresponds perfectly to what Ibn Daud tells us the Almighty did to gaonic authority with the death of R. Hai;

---

58 V.5 and cf. n. 57.
59 Cohen, *SFC*, pp. 109 f.
60 Cf. VII.287–288.
61 VI.185; VIII.168.

He *withdrew* (שמ״ט) that power.⁶² Thus, we have a pleonasm of dates coupled with a mnemonic, urging us, as it were, to discern the symbolism underlying the contradiction in Ibn Daud's information.

Following Ibn Daud's hint that R. Hai died thirteen years after R. Ḥanok, the end of the gaonic period must be antedated by ten years to 4788 or in the 980th year after the death of Hillel in 3809.⁶³ Suddenly, the fact that R. Hai's term as gaon parallelled in length the term of Hillel⁶⁴—which, by the way, was not really the case⁶⁵—takes on added significance. Ibn Daud had not assigned R. Hai Gaon a term of forty years merely because of his penchant for round numbers.⁶⁶ The figure of forty years was useful to Ibn Daud's story, for it added one more flourish to his portrayal of the rise of R. Moses of Cordova, the nemesis of Babylonian power, in terms of the rise of Hillel the Elder. The passing away of R. Hai Gaon, the Babylonian "Hillel" of latter days, marked the end of the gaonic age and the beginning of the age of the rabbinate, who where the successors of the Spanish "Hillel," R. Moses.⁶⁷ It was for this reason, too, that Ibn Daud wished to date the symbolic death of R. Hai 980 years after the death of Hillel. The same number that had symbolized the rise of Spanish Jewry "in 4750 more or less" now symbolized the end of the lifespan of the gaonate.

Ibn Daud, of course, could not let matters rest there, for even in terms of his own cryptography, the mere death of R. Hai could provide no message of consolation. What is more, by Ibn Daud's own account, R. Ḥanok's death had preceded that of the Babylonian Gaon's by at least thirteen years. Where was one to discern the orderly transmission of the mantle of authority from generation to generation? This was particularly a problem in view of the fact that according to Ibn Daud's account, no one succeeded to the seat of R.

---

62 VI.185. Note that Zacuto, *op. cit.*, p. 201b, understood the Seleucid date of R. Ashi's death as a reference to Ps. 80.12.

63 Hillel came to Palestine in 3729 and died eighty years later; II.118–119.

64 Hillel served as nasi eighty years but as head of the academy (= gaon) only forty; cf. above, n. 56. For R. Hai's term, cf. VI.202.

65 Cf. note *ibid.*

66 Cf. Mann, *Texts and Studies*, I, 109, n. 2. Ibn Daud was careful to designate that his figures were only approximate when he was not being precise; cf. II.50; V.22; VII.63, 405–406.

67 Cf. further in Cohen, *SFC*, pp. 93 f. Obviously, Ibn Daud could not extend the term of R. Moses of Cordova to forty years, for the distortion would have been too obvious; cf. above, n. 20. In describing R. Hai in terms reminiscent of Hillel, Ibn Daud inevitably evoked the association of Moses, who led the children of Israel for forty years; cf. Sifre Deut. par. 357 (ed. Finkelstein), p. 429, and cf. also Ibn Daud's style in VI. 185 f. The comparison of R. Hai with Moses had already been made in a somewhat different sense by Samuel ibn Nagrela, *Diwan* (ed. Habermann), I, part 2, p. 132. However, that may have been sufficient clue for Ibn Daud; cf. below, ch. V.

Ḥanok.⁶⁸ Following the latter's death, Spanish Jewry had, it would appear, remained without rabbinic leadership. The obvious place to turn for a solution is the next link in the rabbinic chain of succession, and that is the life of Samuel ibn Nagrela.

At this point, all the techniques which we have encountered as hints of symbolic meaning will immediately alert us to the suspicious circumstances in Ibn Daud's biography of the first nagid of Andalus. Ibn Daud's account of the Nagid's rise to power has long been recognized as a delightful but historically unlikely tale.⁶⁹ What has not been noted, as far as I am aware, is that the story is a fitting sequel to the story of the four captives. Both anecdotes portray the rise of men from rags to riches, from obscurity and penury to fame and power. In both stories the heroes achieve *recognition* of their high deserts by dint of their learning, a motif which goes back to classical times but which enjoyed renewed popularity in Arabic and Hebrew literature in Andalus as well as elsewhere.⁷⁰ Recently the specific Arabic model on which Ibn Daud drew for his story of Ibn Nagrela's graduation from peddler to vizier was located and identified.⁷¹ In dismissing the validity of Ibn Daud's story of Samuel ibn Nagrela's miraculous emergence onto the stage of history, we are not merely displaying the usual judgment of latter-day skeptics, but deferring to the evidence of documentation. Ibn Daud, however, more than anyone else, was in a position to know that his biography of Samuel ibn Nagrela was a plagiarized and somewhat doctored fable. He, more than most persons of his day, had access to better information, which he shunned for reasons that were all too cogent; the facts were probably drab enough and, therefore, of no consequence to the moralizing historian. Accordingly, where history was lacking, the homiletician filled the gap.

In the light of all this, it should occasion no surprise that modern scholars have questioned, out of considerations quite remote from our own, two of the key dates in *Sefer ha-Qabbalah* with respect to the life of Samuel ibn Nagrela. Thus, Harkavy and Schirmann have rejected the date of 4780 for Samuel's

---

68 Cf. VII.179 f. Although Ibn Daud referred to Ibn Nagrela by the term he usually employed for rabbinic "successors" (cf. S.N. to VII.180 f.), the fact is that Ibn Nagrela is nowhere said to have succeeded R. Ḥanok as rabbi, for he could not possibly have done so; cf. VII.185 f.
69 Cf. H. Schirmann, "Isaac ibn Halfon" [in Hebrew], *Tarbiz*, VII (1935–36), 300; idem, "The Wars of Samuel ha-Nagid" [in Hebrew], *Zion*, I (1935–36), 266 f.
70 Cf. Cohen, *SFC*, pp. 111 f.; A. Scheiber, "Die Parabel vom Schatz des Gelehrten," *Acta Antiqua Academiae Scientiarum Hungaricae*, X (1963), 233 f.
71 Cf. note to VII.192–205.

rise to political office.[72] Assaf has shown that Ibn Daud's date for the death of Samuel ha-Nagid is short by at least one year.[73] Long before documentary contradiction of Ibn Daud's dating of Samuel's death was available, scholars had questioned—again on documentary grounds—Ibn Daud's unmistakable hint that Ibn Nagrela had lived until the age of seventy.[74] While the date of Samuel's appointment as nagid, 4787, has not been questioned, his attainment of that title is also somewhat enigmatic. Who promoted him to that honor? Exactly what did it imply? From Ibn Daud's account alone we would have no idea that the title was held by other men in other parts of the world almost at the very same time.[75] But Ibn Daud almost certainly knew this. Surely Ibn Daud's emphasis of Ibn Nagrela's attainment of this title must have some significance.[76] While I am unable to decipher the purpose behind the two other dates,[77] the significance of the date 4787 for the appointment of Samuel ibn Nagrela to the position of nagid does seem to me to be clear. Since the symbolic date for the death of R. Hai is 4788, the fact that Samuel attained the position of nagid a year earlier is a bit too coincidental. Is it not to be interpreted as one more fulfillment of the rabbinic lesson that the Almighty never permits the sun of learning to set in one area (or person) before causing it to rise in another?[78] Here was consolation indeed, for the affliction of the death of R. Hai, and with him of Babylonian hegemony as a whole, was anticipated by the appointment of Samuel to a position that connoted the authority of a new leadership over the Jewish community.

We have gone to great lengths to analyze Ibn Daud's "mistakes" and internal contradictions in order to show that we are confronted not by a careless and uncritical compiler of traditions, but by a subtle schematologist, who played

72 Cf. note to VII.215; A.A. Harkavy, "Le-Toledot R. Samuel ha-Nagid," *Meassef*, ed. by L. Rabinowicz (St. Petersburg, 1902), pp. 8, 48 n. 2 *ad loc.*
73 Cf. note to VII.250.
74 Harkavy, "Le-Toledot R. Samuel," pp. 36, 56 n. 3 *ad loc.*
75 Cf. note to VII.234 where the latest discussions are listed. However, I cannot help but feel that the issue is by no means settled. Margalioth, *Hilkhot Hannagid*, p. 58 n. 45, has correctly remonstrated against the suggestion that Ibn Nagrela was appointed nagid by R. Hai; cf. also Cohen, *SFC*, p. 119 f. Above all, the question remains as to the meaning of the term. Was he nagid of the Jews of the kingdom of Granada? Was his authority recognized beyond the borders of that kingdom?
76 On the significance of biblical titles in *Sefer ha-Qabbalah*, cf. below, ch. V.
77 It is possible that the Nagid's rise to political power in 4780 was dated 1440 years (= 3 × 480) after the destruction of the First Temple in 3339. The difficulty with this solution is that we cannot point to another instance where this symmetry is used by Ibn Daud.
78 Ber. R. 58.2 (ed. Theodor-Albeck), pp. 619 f. For a clear example of Ibn Daud's belief in the providential character of Jewish history, cf. Epilogue. 86 f. Cf. also Cohen, *SFC*, pp. 90 f.

with history as he saw fit. Ibn Daud considered every item in his work carefully and arranged his account in such a way that the attentive reader, the one who was concerned with the inner workings of his message, would be able to unravel his code.

Ibn Daud did not confine his schematology to tinkering with dates. Upon close examination, it will be seen that the whole of *Sefer ha-Qabbalah* is structured on schematic lines, which have much in common with some of the problematic dates. One such notable scheme is the common denominator "seven." Ibn Daud divided history into seven stages: the succession of 1) prophets, 2) teachers in the days of the Second Temple, 3) tannaim, 4) amoraim, 5) saboraim, 6) geonim, 7) rabbis. Now this division of the development of Jewish tradition has become so much a part of historical vocabulary that we may easily overlook the fact that, however logical it appears to us, it is largely the product of schematological reduction. Surely Ibn Daud recognized how arbitrary it was. Thus, the second stage of Jewish history begins not with the first post-prophetic generation but with the second, for in accordance with classical tradition Ibn Daud reckoned the first generation of the men of the Great Assembly as part of the prophetic, i.e., biblical, chain.[79] However, when it came to giving totals of generations within each stage of Jewish history, Ibn Daud equivocated. In two passages he included that first generation in the category of post-biblical history.[80] On a third occasion, he contradicted himself and reckoned only nine generations for the second stage, indicating that the first generation was really part of biblical history, and that the new stage of Jewish history began only with the second generation![81] Moreover, he quietly glossed over his change of name for that second stage of Jewish history, for while he began his description of the second stage by describing it as that of the men of the Great Assembly,[82] in the third generation he quickly dropped this label.[83] Only later on did he indicate that he had changed its name completely to that of "Teachers in the Days of the Second Temple."[84] To be sure, Ibn Daud tried to adhere to categories and divisions that were implicit in classical sources, but the actual division he did adopt was not the only possible one.[85]

79 I.109 f.; II.3.
80 II.169; Epilogue.1.
81 IV.173.
82 II.3.
83 II.42.   84 IV. 124
85 According to Ibn Daud, Hillel, Shammai and R. Johanan b. Zakkai are not to be reckoned as tannaim, for the period of the latter began only after the destruction of the Second Temple; cf., however, *STW*, pp. 8, line 4, 9 par. 7. Cf. also below, n. 87.

The same stricture applies to the last stage of Jewish history, namely the succession of the rabbinate following the end of the gaonate. It cannot be overemphasized that Ibn Daud had ample evidence of the fact that the Babylonian academies had not closed down by his time, and that the period of the gaonate had, strictly speaking, not come to an end even in his day, let alone with the death of R. Hai.[86] Ibn Daud was not the only Andalusian who expressed the feeling that the authority of the Babylonian geonim was not exclusive and binding over all of Jewry. However, there were other ways of expressing the same theory. Moses Maimonides, for example, concluded that the term geonim included all sages who flourished after the redaction of the Talmud, including the saboraim, geonim and rabbis of Palestine, Spain and France.[87] In other words, Ibn Daud's separation of the saboraim and the rabbinate from the geonim into quite separate stages was not necessary to history, but must have been to Ibn Daud's historiography and its seven-fold scheme.

Within the seven stages of history, there were significant developments that also unfolded in patterns of seven. According to a well-known gaonic tradition, R. Judah the Prince was the seventh in line of the Hillelite dynasty. This was usually understood to mean that Rabbi Judah was the seventh direct descendant of Hillel, the chain being: Hillel, Simeon, Gamaliel I, Simeon b. Gamaliel I, Gamaliel II, Simeon b. Gamaliel II, Judah.[88] However, according to Ibn Daud, Hillel's immediate successor and son was Gamaliel I.[89] Accordingly, Ibn Daud invoked a distinction which he followed throughout his account of the tannaitic period,[90] and made R. Akiba "head of

86 VII.367 f.
87 Maimonides, *Mishneh Torah*, Introduction. The definition, while first publicized by Maimonides, is probably derived from the Andalusian school and reflects the view of Samuel ibn Nagrela; cf. Margalioth, *Hilkhot Hannagid*, pp. 26 f. Moreover, had the division between saboraim and geonim and the definition of the geonim as a specific group been universally accepted as *official* categories, it is unlikely that Maimonides would have ignored them.
88 As far as I can determine, the earliest authority to cite this tradition explicitly is Nissim b. Jacob, *Clavis Talmudica*, f. 19a. However, the same view is clearly reflected in the division of generations in *ISG* 17.13, 31.20, where the generation of Rabbi Judah the Prince is described as the third after the destruction of the Temple. Prior to the Destruction, there had been four generations of scholars; *ibid.*, 74.13. Even if Kahan's criticism of Rapoport is well taken, *STW*, German section, p. 19, Rapoport's contention that this seven-fold division is already reflected in *STW* seems to be correct; cf. *Kerem Chemed*, IV (1839), 205.
89 I.77 f.; II.125.
90 II.143; III.3, 32 f., 70–71, 78–79, 102 to n. 90— Incidentally, this distinction enables us to resolve one other puzzling internal "contradiction" in Ibn Daud's works. On three separate occasions, Ibn Daud reported that John Hyrcanus turned Sadducee after having served as high priest for forty years; II.71; *MBSh*, f. 54b, 79a. However, in the very same paragraph he was able to write: "Now the years which Hyrcanus ruled over Israel num-

the academy" after the death of R. Gamaliel I,[91] thus producing a chain of seven *heads of the academy*: Hillel, Gamaliel I, Johanan b. Zakkai,[92] Gamaliel II, Akiba, Simeon b. Gamaliel II, Judah the Prince.

Somewhat later in his work, Ibn Daud informs us that "from the days of Rabbi [Judah the Prince] until R. Ashi, Torah and high office had not been combined in one person."[93] Although this remark is a verbatim quotation from the Talmud, its inclusion in *Sefer ha-Qabbalah* is significant, for Ibn Daud does not usually cite such *laudes*. Obviously, this one must have had some special overtone. Is it, therefore, a mere coincidence that as Judah was seventh in the line of Hillel, R. Ashi's generation was the seventh after the death of Judah? This chain begins with R. Hanina b. Hama, who succeeded "Rabbi" as "head of the academy" and marked the beginning of the fifth and last generation of tannaim, and concludes with R. Ashi, whose succession to the same office began the sixth generation of amoraim.[94] The significance of this sequence of seven generations lies not only in its heptadic character, but primarily in the fact that the culminating point of each stage, i.e., the seventh generation, bears a symmetry with the earlier counterpart in the chain. Thus, in the seventh generation of the Hillelite chain, the Mishna was redacted.[95] In the seventh generation of the subsequent chain, the redaction of the Talmud was begun.[96] Fourteen generations after that, or twice seven, from Meremar and Mar b. R. Ashi until Hai, the gaonic period came to a close.[97]

We are now in a position to account for one more bit of "slovenly" internal contradiction in *Sefer ha-Qabbalah*. According to Ibn Daud, Hillel and Sham-

> bered thirty-one, after which he died;" *ibid.*, f. 54b. It does not help us to say that the first figure was taken from Ibn Daud's text of the Talmud, and the second from his text of *Josippon*. Surely, he would have noticed the contradiction. However, Ibn Daud probably saw no contradiction between the two figures. The figure forty represented his term as high priest or religious leader, while thirty-one was the extent of his political leadership as "king."

91 III.33.
92 In other words, R. Johanan b. Zakkai, according to Ibn Daud, had not been a nasi but only a head of the academy; for a survey of the problem, cf. G. Alon, *Studies in Jewish History* [in Hebrew], 2 vols. (Tel Aviv, 1957-58), I, 253 f.
93 IV.59-60.
94 The generations are: 1) R. Hanina bar Hama (III.102); 2) Rab and Samuel (IV.2); 3) R. Judah and R. Huna (IV.21); 4) R. Hisda, Rabbah and R. Joseph (IV.32); 5) Abaye and Raba (IV.43); 6) R. Nahman bar Isaac, R. Papa and R. Huna b. Joshua (IV.47-48); 7) R. Ashi (IV.58).
95 III.95-97.
96 IV.70.
97 The fourteen generations are 1) Meremar *et alii* (IV.71, 173); 2-6) five generations of saboraim (V.45-46); 7-14) eight generations of geonim (VI.203 and cf. VI.186).

mai represented the eighth generation of teachers in the days of the Second Temple.[98] However, after proceeding to tell of Hillel and his dynasty, Ibn Daud then listed Hillel a second time with the statement that "Hillel and his school represent the ninth generation."[99] How can Hillel represent two generations?[100] But Hillel had to be put in that position if 1) he was to be the seventh in line in the new period begun by Simeon the Righteous, and at the same time 2) was to be the first in the line of seven culminating with Judah the Prince.[101]

Schematology, not tradition or the material itself, is the governing consideration in the division. The division of amoraic generations, for example, is quite uneven and arbitrary. By a generation, Ibn Daud usually means leadership exercised by students of the master of a preceding "generation." But this is not always so. Thus, the fifth generation of amoraim is initiated by a colleague of the master of the third generation, and though his activity began within the fourth generation, the fifth link in the chain is not dated until the death of the masters of the fourth![102] The schematology is even more blatant in the classification of the saboraim, for in that age Ibn Daud reckoned two separate second generations! What would Ibn Daud have lost had he added another generation, that of the disciples of R. Simona and R. 'Ena, which he claimed lasted fifty years?[103] Clearly Ibn Daud was eager to limit the number of generations, and since the names of the disciples of R. Simona and R. 'Ena were not disclosed in the sources, and the academies had closed down for about fifty years, he classified the leaders of this generation with their masters as being of one generation. However one interprets the word "generation," the leaders of the third generation of saboraim should clearly have been classified as the fourth. Furthermore, the criteria for the division of generations in the saboraic and gaonic periods are nowhere made clear, and they can in no wise be equated with those implied for the tannaitic and amoraic periods. Ibn Daud had to improvise in order to obtain results in multiples of seven.

The results must have been highly satisfactory, for they illustrated the rhythmic pattern of history no less than its symmetry. If, on the one hand, there were twenty-one links from the post-mishnaic generation to the close of the gaonic age, there were, from another point of departure, twenty-one generations from Simeon the Righteous, the leader of the first post-prophetic genera-

---

98 II.117–118.
99 II.152.
100 It cannot be argued that in the first instance, Hillel is listed as nasi and in the second as head of the academy, for the recipients in ch. II were all "heads of the academy." Hillel's patriarchate is treated separately by Ibn Daud; cf. above, n. 56.
101 For the antiquity of this tradition, cf. Finkelstein, *Mabo*, pp. 7 f.
102 IV.49–50.
103 V.12, 19–20.

tion, until the close of the amoraic period.[104] Here, again, we note that Ibn Daud's division was not a necessary one, and indeed, other classifications were known in the medieval period.[105]

The immediate advantage that we gain from discerning Ibn Daud's method of dividing generations is that otherwise totally unintelligible phenomena in his work begin to make perfect sense. Thus, the very beginning of *Sefer ha-Qabbalah* is puzzling, for though the express purport of the work is to trace the history of the chain of tradition, the opening historical section deals exclusively with matters of chronology and with the succession of policital rulers from Moses through R. Judah the Prince II. Only after this political chronology and enumeration of leaders does the work finally turn to the subject its author proclaimed to be the burden of the work—the transmission of the Torah from Moses to Joshua to the prophets, and so on.[106] Ibn Daud could easily have omitted the opening section on chronology and on kings and princes in Babylonia, and given a list of transmitters of the *tradition* such as those found in *Seder Tannaim wa-Amoraim* or the *Mishneh Torah* of Moses Maimonides. But Ibn Daud obviously had more than one aim in mind. We have suggested as the purpose of the opening chronological statement the explanation of official and lesser known Jewish chronologies with a view to illustrating the consolation in history through its symmetry. But why the detailed list of judges, kings and princes, whose chronological details, where they were known, were readily available from Scripture? Exoterically, the passage demonstrated the royal lineage of Hillel and his patriarchal descendants. However, this explanation only begs the main question, for the Davidic origin of the Hillelites was nowhere an issue in his work; what is more, this lineage was demonstrated in the first instance only by hearsay and finally affirmed on the basis of tradition.[107] Why, then, this long and detailed—indeed, virtually pointless—list? But once again we are confronted by a strange coincidence. From Moses to Solomon, in whose reign the Temple was built, there were twenty-one "generations." From Solomon until Zedekiah, when the Temple was destroyed, there were again twenty-one generations.[108] Is it, therefore, a mere coincidence that Ibn Daud then

---

104 Cf. IV.174 and Epilogue.4, which contradict each other! Clearly, the first passage is traditionally correct, i.e., schematological, while the second is "factually" true.

105 Joseph ibn Aknin, *Einleitung in dem Talmud* [in Hebrew], ed. by H. Graetz (Breslau s.a.), pp. 17 f., reckons Simeon the Righteous as the first generation of tannaim and Hillel as the seventh. The same scheme is followed by R. Yesu'ah b. Joseph ha-Levi, *Halikot 'Olam*, ch. 2. Ibn Aknin reckons eight generations following R. Judah the Prince to the end of the amoraim.

106 Cf. above, pp. 149 f.   107 I.74; II.120.

108 I.25 ("In the desert" = Moses) - 46, 46–68. Solomon is probably to be reckoned twice, for the building of the Temple marks a dividing point in biblical history; cf. I.47, 69–70.

proceeded to give a list of twenty-one princes from Jehoiachin until R. Judah the Prince II?[109] Indeed, it cannot be a coincidence, for Ibn Daud doctored the traditional lists of princes to yield the necessary total. In no other list of princes does the name of Neariah appear.[110] On the face of things, Ibn Daud was quite innocently filling in a lacuna on the basis of I Chronicles 3.22–23. However, that explanation is much too simple, for the whole list of Babylonian princes is derived from so arbitrary and eclectic a reading of that section of Chronicles that Ibn Daud could either have ignored the omission or, better yet, omitted other names which he did include. But Ibn Daud found the traditionally accepted names convenient and added one more from Scripture, thus again proving a thesis.[111]

One further circumstance must be noted. The number twenty-one, which figures so prominently in Ibn Daud's schematization of generations was also, it will be recalled, one of the basic numbers in Ibn Daud's highly artificial construction of the symmetry of the chronologies in the First and Second Temples.[112] The consolation of history was thus seen to be manifest not only in the numbers of years, but in numbers of links of Jewish political and religious leaders as well.

We have travelled far afield from our orignial point of inquiry in order to demonstrate in no uncertain terms the kind of work confronting us. If Ibn Daud's periodization of history has been a problem, it is because scholars have sought respectable literary sources and rational criteria to account for the vagaries of a man who never felt bound by such canons. Ibn Daud was far too original a man to be confined to dry data. He had his own wellsprings of inspiration, and it is the nature of these that we have tried to uncover.

An examination of important dates in Jewish history, according to Ibn Daud's description, reveals another pattern, and that is that almost every major turning point in that history occurred in the year "nine" of a decade. Thus, the Exodus occurred in 2449 A.M.; the building of the First Temple in 2929; the first Destruction in 3339; the building of the Second Temple in 3409; the end of prophecy and the beginning of the Seleucid Era in 3449; the destruction of the

---

109   I.71–80.
110   Cf. Lazarus, *Die Haeupter der Vertriebenen*, p. 161; cf. also pp. 171–172, where only David b. Hodaya gives the name of Neariah.
111   This is all the more evident in that in Ibn Daud's scheme Hillel is the fourteenth name in the list; moreover, Ibn Daud listed two princes after R. Judah the Prince I about whom he had no chronological information, as can be seen from the fact that he nowhere mentioned them again. They were inserted simply to fill the seven names needed for a schematological list.
112   Cf. above, pp. 195 f.

Second Temple in 3829.[113] And so on. History is thus possessed not only of rhythm but of rhyme, too.

Can any rhythm be found within a group of dates that rhyme? The first major turning point in the history of Jewish tradition was unquestionably the end of prophecy and the beginning of "instruction," i.e., exegetical interpretation, in the days of the Second Temple. This change, we have seen, was Ibn Daud's clue to the beginning of a new chapter in his work. According to tradition, the year of the cessation of prophecy was 1000 after the Exodus.[114] The redaction of the Mishna is dated by Ibn Daud—and, it will be recalled, only by Ibn Daud—500 years after the cessation of prophecy.[115] The transition from the saboraim to the geonim is dated by Ibn Daud—and, again, only by Ibn Daud—500 years after the redaction of the Mishna.[116] Thus, the changes in the cornerstone of tradition occurred in periods that were units

---

113 Cf. above, n. 45.
114 II.18–19. Saadiah calls the period initiated by the Seleucid Era "the period of the dominion of the sages;" cf. Bornstein, "Ta'arikay Israel," VIII, 293, where sources are cited. For the origin of this theory, cf. Seder 'Olam 30 (ed. Ratner), p. 140.
115 Cf. above. pp. 181, 184 f.—There are basically two medieval traditions on the date of the redaction of the Mishna. The one tradition, followed by Nissim b. Jacob ibn Shahin and Judah ha-Levi, equates the date of the redaction of the Mishna with that of R. Judah the Prince's death and/or Rab's migration to Babylonia, in the year 3979 A.M., or 530 Seleucid Era, or 150 after the destruction of the Second Temple. A second tradition is that of Ibn Daud, which may go back to Saadiah's *Sefer ha-Galuy*, according to which the Mishna was redacted in the year 3949, or 500 Seleucid Era, or 120 of the destruction of the Second Temple. In the introduction to that work, the Gaon promised to survey the thousand years of prophetic and five-hundred years of post-prophetic instruction; cf. above, pp. LII f. ; note, too, that in Malter's text referred to there, the figure "500 years" is spelled out in full. The difficulty with this suggestion is that a Karaite quotation of *Sefer ha-Galuy* in Harkavy, *Zikron*, V, 194, ascribes to Saadiah the statement that the Mishna was complied 150 years after the destruction of the Temple and 510 years after the cessation of prophecy. Since these two dates are self-contradictory, Harkavy corrected the latter figure to 530, thus bringing Saadiah's dating into consonance with the more prevalent view. However, S. Poznanski, *The Karaite Literary Opponents of Saadiah Gaon* (London, 1908), p. 41 n. 1, chose to uphold the date of 510 and to correct the figure of 150 to 130. In support of his suggestion, he cited a fragment of a work by Saadiah where the redaction of the Mishna is explicitly said to have taken place 130 years after the desctruction of the Temple. Poznanski's view seems to be supported by *STW*, pp. 7, par. 4c, 8, par. 6a, where the tannaitic period is said to have begun 180 years before the Destruction and to have ended 311 years later, i.e., 131 after the Destruction; but the text there is fraught with difficulties; cf. Kahan's note, pp. 30 f. Whatever the case, Ibn Daud may well have seized on Saadiah's round number, because it fitted into his own scheme. All of these figures are reviewed by Krauss, *loc. cit.* above, p. 185 n. 152.
116 Cf. above, pp. 178, 185.

or fractions of one thousand: 1000 years of prophecy; 500 years of instruction (in the Temple and by tannaim); 500 years of mishnaic instruction (amoraim and saboraim). Or, to summarize the matter from the point of view of a medieval Rabbanite: 1000 years of prophetic revelation and 1000 years of instruction incorporated in rabbinic literature. It is no coincidence that these are the crucial turning points in the history of tradition. These moments in Jewish history were the major bones of contention between Rabbanites and Karaites. Once again, the validity of the Jewish claim to legitimacy was seen in the symmetry of religious developments.[117]

But obviously, history did not end with the beginning of the gaonic period. What was to happen 500 years after that, in 4949 A.M.? Was that year also to be a turning point? Consider the fact that 4949 A.M. was the equivalent of 1188-89 C.E., or *twenty-eight* years after the time Ibn Daud claimed to have been writing, that is in Ibn Daud's own generation, and we are somehow driven to ask what it was that Ibn Daud expected to happen in that year. That something was bound to happen is clear from the purpose of his whole work, which was to demonstrate that the hand of Providence moves unceasingly. Did Ibn Daud hint in any way as to what it was that he was looking forward to?

The Meaning of Symmetry

"Behold how trustworthy are the consolations of our God, blessed be His name, for the period of their redemption corresponded to that of their exile."[118] In proving that a period of exile is balanced by a period of redemption, Ibn Daud demonstrated that the Almighty had granted the prayer of Moses: "Make us glad according to the days wherein Thou has afflicted us, according to the years wherein we have seen evil (Ps. 90.15)." This verse had some very definite overtones in the mind of a rabbinically oriented Jew, since the ancient tannaim had already cited this verse to support their prediction that the messianic age would correspond in length to the days of ancient affliction.[119] While some sought other clues to the denouement of history, these clues, too, were predicated on the assumption of the symmetrical pattern of events. "R. Jose b. Ḥalafta said: Whoever knows the number of years that the people of Israel served idols, knows when the son of David will come," for the days of the exile will serve as retaliation for the days of their idolatry.[120] "R. Ḥanina

117 Cf. above, pp. 199 f.
118 Cf. above, n. 10.
119 *B.* Sanhed. 99a; Pesikta R. (ed. Friedmann), f. 4a.
120 Midrash Ekah, Petiḥta 21 (ed. Vilna, f. 4d; ed. Buber, p. 16).

b. R. Abbahu said: That dastard [Balaam] stood just about midpoint in the history of the world. How so? [For thus it is written] 'Of a period *corresponding to this one* it is revealed to Jacob and to Israel what God has planned (Num. 23.23)."[121] "R. Berekiah said in the name of R. Levi: The final redeemer will come as the first one did."[122] It was not out of love for the art of history that the rabbis sought symmetry, but out of a passionate longing for the messianic redemption. Schematology always betrays a very superficial interest in the events themselves, but a deep desire to unravel their meaning and their place in the plan of history as a whole. If the gates of prophecy had been closed, the avenues of exegesis and wisdom were still wide open. The perspicacious student of the past could gain a reliable glimpse into the future.[123]

Ibn Daud did not conceal the identity of his motives with those of the more ancient homilists. Time and again he proclaimed in the clearest terms that the purpose of historiography is to bring consolation to the despised and persecuted nation of which he was a member.[124] His "History of the Jews in the Days of the Second Temple" begins and ends with the assurance that the scriptural prophecies of consolation-redemption have not yet been fulfilled and that, accordingly, their capital has not yet run out.[125] Comfort and consolation, albeit of somewhat different natures, are also behind his work of philosophy and his brief treatise on the history of Rome. The polemic they advanced would help sustain the Jew in the long period of trial which he was fated to endure. *Sefer ha-Qabbalah*, it should be recalled, was but one part of a four-pronged polemic which Ibn Daud had issued in 1160–1161.[126] While along with the other three of his books it, too, sought to defend and legitimize a particular way of life, this work went one step further. It furnished the substantive basis for hope for the future. In keeping with classical rabbinic teaching, Ibn Daud showed that history was pointing to a new stage and to a new fulfillment.[127]

That it is not *our* imagination that is at work here but Ibn Daud's becomes all the more clear in view of his constant admonitions to distinguish between those prophecies which had already been fulfilled and those which were yet to be realized. The prophecy of Zechariah, "Feed the flock of slaughter," etc., is explained in detail in his sermon on that section to prove that all of its pre-

---

121　*Yer.* Shab. 6 (end), f. 8d.
122　Num. R. 11.2. I.e., at a point in time corresponding to when Moses did. For the tannaitic origin of this symmetry, cf. *B. R.* H.10b–11a (R. Eliezer and R. Joshua).
123　Cf. Wolfson, *Philosophy of the Church Fathers*, pp. 26 f.
124　II.87; Epilogue.125 f., 165 f.
125　Cf.above, p. xxxv.
126　Cf.pp. xxviii f.
127　Cf. VII.467–68, which shows clearly that the "present age" is nearing its end.

dictions had already come to pass. However, his sermon concludes with the assurance that "the remainder of the consolations of Zechariah (as well as those of all the other prophets), such as the prophecy 'Behold a day of the Lord cometh' (Zech. 14.1) and his prophecy concerning 'every one that is left of all the nations that came against Jerusalem shall go up from year to year to worship the King, the Lord of hosts, and to keep the feast of Tabernacles' (*ibid.*, 14.16), and the war of Gog and Magog, concerning whom Ezekiel and Zechariah, may he have peace, had prophesied, and the earthquake which will take place at the time of the arrival of Gog and Magog, when the Mount of Olives will be cleft in its center, and the rule of the house of David, *the return of which is imminent in our day*, [all these] have not yet been witnessed nor heard, and they remain to be fulfilled. May the Holy one, blessed be He, cause [all] this to come to pass speedliy, for our God is faithful and His words are trustworthy...."[128] Ibn Daud's history concludes on the note on which it began, on the trustworthiness of the divine consolation. What could that consolation be to a medieval Jew but the promise of the Messiah and of the redemption?[129] And where should the signs of that consolation be found if not in the meaning of events and their sequence? Ibn Daud, it will be recalled, was in the first instance a philosopher, and as a member of the philosopher class he probably had little concern with, or even respect for, history and historical writing as such. After all, what was pure history to a philosopher but a series of anecdotes that suited the mentality of the vulgar masses?[130] However, as a philosopher, Ibn Daud took very seriously the obligations of *philantropia*, which that noble station imposed on him.[131] Did he not berate the Karaites for the lack of this particular quality, for their failure to bring any benefit or consolation to their brethren?[132] He, by way of contrast, was living up to the criteria of the father of philosophy, who stipulated that the true philosopher is a man of noble soul who contemplates all *time* as well as all existence.[133]

Having defined the state of mind underlying Ibn Daud's writing and above all his historiography, we must return to the unspecified future date of 4949

---

128 *MBSh*, f. 79b.
129 Cf. S. Schechter, *Aspects of Rabbinic Theology* (New York, 1961), ch. VII, pp. 97 f.; G.F. Moore, *Judaism*, 3 vols. (Cambridge, 1927-30), II, 323 f.; above, p. xxxvi n. 97.
130 Cf. Baron, "The Historical Outlook of Maimonides," pp. 7 f.; M. Friedlaender, "Ibn Ezra in England," *Transactions of the Jewish Historical Society of England*, 1894-95 p. 46 n. 1.
131 Cf. above, p. LX.
132 Epilogue.124 f.
133 Plato, *Republic*, VI, 486A.

[1188–1189] to see if it has some peculiar qualities. In the first place, the number is internally symmetrical: 49–49. In the second place, that year was the end of the fiftieth jubilee cycle following the first redemption of 2449. 4949 = 2449 + (50 × 50). The jubilees were thus approaching a grand jubilee, and would be initiating a new stage at the time they "balanced" themselves. Would the appropriate moment to proclaim the ultimate liberty not be the one parallel to the time when liberty was proclaimed for the slaves of antiquity, to wit, in the jubilee year?[134] Thirdly, the year 4949 was the end of the 707th sabbatical cycle since creation, and this sabbatical cycle itself was a symmetrical one: 7–0–7. Was it not an established tradition that the redemption would come at the beginning of a new sabbatical cycle?[135] Have we not had overwhelming evidence of the centrality of the number seven in Ibn Daud's schematology?[136] What would be more appropriate than the fulfillment of the redemption in a year that rang so much with the echoes of Daniel's prophecies of seventy weeks of years? Did this year not have further merit in that it combined *two* of the key factors of Ibn Daud's numerology, for it was a multiple of seven and fell into the scheme of five-hundred (or one-thousand) year cycles. Finally, in that year all of Jewish history would achieve its goal of ultimate symmetry, for, in accordance with the prophecy of Balaam, it was exactly twice the midpoint at which meaningful history had begun. The beginning and midpoints of significant history were ever considered a basic clue to the fullness and end of time.[137] However, to demonstrate this aspect of his chronology we must return to that enigmatic section at the very beginning of *Sefer ha-Qabbalah*.

The opening lines of the first chapter of Ibn Daud's work consist of data very reminiscent of Seder 'Olam and Seder 'Olam Zuta. Although, as we have seen, Ibn Daud probably did not consult these works, his source had doubtless

---

134 Cf. Lev. 25.10. According to talmudic tradition, the reckoning of sabbatical and jubilee cycles was not begun until fifty-four years after the Exodus; Seder 'Olam 11 (ed. Ratner), pp. 48 f. However, Ibn Daud's scheme was not a halakic one but a historical one and would, accordingly, not necessarily have been bound by such considerations. Judah b. Barzillai, *Commentar zum Sepher Jezira*, p. 238, also considered the fiftieth jubilee, which he calculated from the time of the erection of the Tabernacle, a clue to the date of the redemption. The likelihood, therefore, is that calculation by jubilees goes back to gaonic if not classical tradition; cf. *B. Sanhed.* 97b.

135 *B. Meg.* 17b, Sanhed. 97a. The redemption was doubtless predicted for that time not only because of the association of the messianic age with the rest of the Sabbath (*M. Tamid* 7.4, end) but also as a symmetrical balance to the time of the exile; p. 193 n. 17.

136 Cf. above, pp. 197 f.

137 Cf. above, n. 121; Judah b. Barzillai, *Commentar zum Sepher Jezira*, pp. 237 f.; Moses Maimonides, *Epistle to Yemen*, pp. xxii, 82 f.

incorporated a summary of the major chronological traditions of rabbinic Judaism. The comparison between these tracts and Ibn Daud's will prove most instructive.

Seder 'Olam	*Seder 'Olam Zuta*	*Sefer ha-Qabbalah*
"From Adam until the Flood 1656 years... From the Flood until the Dispersion of peoples 340 years... At the time of the Dispersion, Abraham was 48 years old... Abraham our patriarch was 70 years old when the Lord spoke with him etc."	"From Adam until the Flood 1656 years. From the Flood until the Dispersion of peoples 340 years. From the Dispersion until the birth of Isaac 52 years."	"From Adam until the Flood 1656 years. From the Flood until the birth of Abraham 292 years. From the birth of Abraham until he left Haran the first time 52 years."

The most striking thing about Ibn Daud's summary is the total omission of any reference to the chronology of the Dispersion of peoples at the Tower of Babel. Obviously, Ibn Daud was not concerned with the chronology of biblical events in themselves but in events that were significant to his own work. The first significant turning point after the first stage of creation was the date of the birth of Abraham, which simple arithmetic will tell us occurred in 1949 A.M.,[138] or 500 years before the Exodus. In other words, from the birth of Abraham until the termination of prophecy in 3449, 1500 years elapsed.[139] From the termination of prophecy until 4949, another 1500 years would have passed. The full symmetry of Jewish history becomes manifest if one begins from the birth of Abraham, the father of the Jewish people. "Behold how trustworthy are the consolations of our God, blessed be His name."

Now, in establishing that the rhythm of history was leading to a culminating date of 4949, it is obvious that Ibn Daud had superimposed two distinct methods of calculation one upon the other. On the one hand, he reckoned according to sabbatical and jubilee cycles, which were predicated on a heptadic scheme and which were, accordingly, in general consonance with the apocalyptic calculations of Daniel. On the other hand, he invoked a totally different scheme, which had no obvious connection with the first one, according to which history

---

138 It will be recalled that every traditional total must be augmented by one year. Hence, 1948 = 1949; cf. I.17.
139 Cf. above, nn. 114–115.

moved in 500-year cycles. This problem should not be lightly dismissed, for a messianic mathematician must work with a vocabulary that will be intelligible to his audience, unless he is to be accused of promiscuous eclecticism.

However, in this case, as in so many others, Ibn Daud took for granted that his audience would immediately sense the classical foundations on which his second scheme was predicated. In messianic calculations, history was frequently divided into six days of time, corresponding, of course, to six days of the week, and equalling in human terms six thousand years. This method of division and historical reckoning was given universal renown by Augustine and Isidore. In ways which are still not clear it also permeated Rabbanite circles, and was given its most famous Jewish formulation by Ibn Daud's contemporary, Abraham bar Ḥiyya.[140] The latter, however, did not accept the division without tailoring the scheme to more exact figures, which were considerably less than 1000. In any event, 500 may well have been invoked by Ibn Daud as "half a day" of the Almighty along with the 1000-year or whole-day cycles of prophetic and talmudic-gaonic ages which he had used. Not the least significant aspect of this cycle of 500 years is the Muslim testimony, hardly fabricated out of thin air, that the Jews of Arabic speaking lands had a tradition that the Messiah would appear 500 years after the *Hijra*. Ibn Daud himself hinted at that tradition in his deliberate misdating of the Almohade uprising.[141] Clearly, then, the 500-year cycle had gained wide currency in Ibn Daud's milieu, and he felt free not only to invoke it but to weave it in with other accepted methods of calculation.

However, even with this symmetry we have not yet exhausted Ibn Daud's apparently inexhaustible supply of messianic hints. As we have seen, Ibn Daud took considerable pains to keep his reader informed on the exact number of links or generations between one major stage and another. At the end of his work he reviews the data with a sum total. "Thus there were thirty-eight generations from Haggai, Zechariah and Malachi until R. Joseph ha-Levi, of blessed memory."[142] Now, if the generation of Joseph ibn Megash was the thirty-eighth since the construction of the Second Temple, Ibn Daud must have been writing in the thirty-ninth generation. That this was the case Ibn Daud hinted by telling us that at the time of his writing the academy of Lucena was being presided over, in its newly found home of Toledo, by the sons of Ibn Megash.[143] Is it too far-fetched to suggest that twenty-eight years later, i.e.,

---

140 Cf. *B.* Sanhed. 97a, and Guttmann's introduction to Abraham bar Ḥiyya, *Megillat ha-Megalleh*, ed. by A. Poznanski (Berlin, 1924), pp. x f.
141 Cf. VII.459 and notes there. For other 500 year cycles, cf. below, pp. 233 f.
142 Epilogue.2 f.
143 VII.464 f.

in 4949, the fortieth generation would begin? If that is so we have another messianic hint, for the number forty is particularly rich in messianic overtones in Jewish tradition, the reason, of course, being its symmetrical character. The children of Israel had been in the desert for forty years. While some rabbis speculated that the messianic age would last forty years, others extended it to four hundred.[144] What is relevant to our purpose here is the fact that forty was a symbolic number.[145] Perhaps not the least significant phenomenon in this context is Maimonides' list of the transmitters of Jewish tradition as a chain of forty links, symmetrically divided into two halves of 890 years each. According to Maimonides, each twenty links in the tradition spanned the amount of time that elapsed between the Exodus and the destruction of the First Temple.[146]

Although Ibn Daud had his own scheme, the orientation which he shared with Maimonides is clearly discernible, for both were concerned to portray Jewish history in terms of a scheme of forty generations and in terms of chronological symmetry. In any event, the idea that the number of generations that would pass in history was a clue to the appointed end of time was a doctrine which many a medieval considered to be officially codified by the Mishna and Tosefta. "The number of generations is appointed by Him for the [end of] time, as it is written 'He that called the generations from the beginning (Isa. 41.4).' Although it is written 'And they shall be enslaved and oppressed four hundred years (Gen. 15.15),' it is also said 'They shall return here in the fourth generation.' "[147] What concerns us is not what this tannaitic tradition meant to its author, but how this statement was understood in circles on whose traditions Ibn Daud was likely to draw. R. Hai Gaon explained this passage to mean that the patriarch Abraham had gained for his descendants, the people of Israel, the divine promise of "a fixed [i.e., limited] number of generations that would rise after him before the Holy Land would be occupied ...That was the appointed time which was decreed for the redemption from Egypt. Similarly, Jacob gained for the people of Israel [the promise of a fixed] number of generations, which were known to the Holy One, blessed be He, and which would pass until the time of their redemption." He also cited the interpretation of reliable bearers of tradition that it was Adam who gained that promise for the "time of the Messiah and for the time when the whole

---

144 B. Sanhed. 99a.
145 On the significance of forty and its multiples, cf. Cohen, *SFC*, pp. 87 f. nn. 114–116.
146 Baron, "The Historical Outlook of Maimonides," pp. 96 f. On the messianic overtones of the number 890, cf. Cohen, *SFC*, p. 104 n. 150.
147 *M*. 'Eduyot 2.9. I have translated this passage according to the transcription of R. Hai and R. Nissim b. Jacob; cf. following notes.

world would be destroyed."[148] R. Nissim b. Jacob ibn Shahin explained further that "although all hidden things and future events are known to the Holy One, blessed be He, even with regard to each day, hour and moment, the appointed times [of redemption] were set in terms of generations. The exact day, year and moment of the appointed time, although known to Him, were not revealed. Instead He stipulated the times in terms of generations, as it is written 'He that called the generations from the beginning.' This verse means to say that ever since the creation of the world, He had established an appointed time [by stipulating] that such and such a generation will rise. That this is so may be seen from the time appointed for the redemption from Egypt when, although He had decreed the end to come four-hundred years later, He further defined this date by saying 'The fourth generation shall return here.' This teaches us that 'the number of generations is appointed by Him for the [end of] time.' Nevertheless, He, exalted be His name, knows when the end will come in terms of the exact day, hour and moment."[149] Not the least important aspect of this tannaitic tradition was the role of the "fourth" generation, for to later eschatologists four could easily be a symbol for forty.[150] Put differently, the number of years spent in the desert could be balanced symmetrically by an exile of forty generations, for the days appointed to man are appointed in terms of generations rather than years.[151]

Thus, it was not faulty Suran sources that made Ibn Daud date the redaction of the Mishna and the beginning of the gaonic period when he did, but the inspiration of the messianic dream. Ibn Daud's calculations are in reality but one echo of a virtual chorus of messianic calculations that have come down to us from the twelfth century,[152] a number of which were based on the same type of symmetrical calculation.[153]

In the light of the frightful persecutions and upheavals that the Almohades had brought on Andalusian Jewry, Ibn Daud doubtless believed that his own day was ripe for the appointed end. He felt very deeply that he was witnessing

148 Harkavy, *Zikron la-Rishonim*, IV (= *Teshubot ha-Geonim*), p. 176, par. 348.
149 S.A. Poznanski, "Liqqutim min Sefer Megillat Setarim le-R. Nissim b. R. Jacob mi-Qairawan," *Hazofeh*, V (1921), 300, VI (1922), 331. On Ibn Daud's relationship to R. Nissim's work, cf. above, pp. 174 f.
150 Cf. above, n. 143.
151 I.e., beginning with the first generation of the Men of the Great Assembly.
152 Cf. Introduction, ch. II, n. 97. J. Mann, "Ha-Tenu'ot ha-Meshihiyot bi-may Mas'ay ha-Ṣelab ha-Rishonim," *Ha-Tequfa*, XXIII (1924–25), 243 f., 251 f.; XXIV (1928), 335 f.; Baron, *SRH*, V, 138 f., 197 f.; Ankori, "Studies in the Messianic Doctrine of Yehuda Hadassi."
153 Cf. Cohen, *SFC*, p. 104 n. 150; above, n. 137.

a Jeremianic age when men were enduring the fulfillment of the prophecy "Such as are for death, to death; and such as are for the sword, to the sword; and such as are for the famine, to the famine; and such as are for captivity, to captivity." Indeed, Ibn Daud felt that the Jews of his day had endured all this and more, for he adds the affliction of being compelled to leave the fold.[154] Terrible upheavals and persecutions were ever considered sure signs of the approaching end,[155] and Ibn Daud took pains to elucidate the workings of Providence in the changing attitudes which empires displayed toward the Jews as well as in the internal history of his people.

Nor was the date we have suggested for Ibn Daud's view of the appointed end only his personal view of things. His older contemporary, Abraham bar Ḥiyya, had sought to prove on the basis of the book of Daniel, that the end of the second stage of history would occur in 4948 A.M., and in that year the first signs of the final redemption would become manifest to all.[156] This may be only a coincidence; but the fact is that Abraham bar Ḥiyya's date 4948 is identical with Ibn Daud's Judeo-Arabic calculation of 4949.[157]

Exactly what kind of change Ibn Daud anticipated for 4949 he did not indicate. It may have been the restoration of prophecy or of some new source of religious knowledge that would initiate the messianic movement. It seems more plausible to think in these terms rather than in terms of some major political upheaval,[157a] for Ibn Daud's symmetry of five-hundred-year stages and his calculation of fifteen-hundred years since the end of prophecy also suggest a change in the type of religious instruction rather than any relocation of the Jewish community. Maimonides himself had predicted—on the basis of symmetrical calculation—that the first major change in the Jewish situation would be the introduction of prophecy.[158]

154 VII.443 f.; Epilogue.73 f.
155 Cf. R. Johanan's remark on a generation flooded by woes in *B.* Sanhed. 91a; cf. esp. the signs of the end in the various texts in Even-Shmuel, *op. cit.*; Baron, *SRH*, V, 143 f.
156 Abraham bar Ḥiyya, *op. cit.*, p. 108.
157 Bornstein, "Ta'arikay Israel," IX, 223 f.
157a However, cf. below, pp. 234 f., 259 f.
158 Moses Maimonides, *Epistle to Yemen*, pp. 82–83. Maimonides' calculation, or more exactly the tradition which he received on the calculation, is most instructive, for it is predicated on symmetry and on a doubling of the time from the midpoint of history. Now in connection with the date of the midpoint, Maimonides invoked the talmudic mnemonic of 2448 A.M., although in legal contexts he himself worked with the Andalusian date which augmented the traditional date by one year to 2449. In other words, the facts of history were irrelevant in the calculation of the messianic age; what was crucial was the traditional and schematic date. Here we have a clear reflection of Ibn Daud's juggling of traditional and factual dates depending on the problem at hand.—Although Maimonides gives a lucid statement on the method of calculation underlying his tradition, the Arabic

However, we are really in the dark on this point, for Ibn Daud did not furnish any clear hints, as far as we can see. His esoteric method stands out in marked contrast to the explicit messianic speculation of some of his contemporaries. The fact that until modern times no one suspected that this bizarre book is really a kind of secret code shows Ibn Daud's implicit view of open eschatological discussion. Indeed, in the very opening chronological section of his work he inserted a datum not encountered in earlier chronological works, namely, the calamity which the false prophets of Ephraim and Gilead had perpretated on the children of Israel by the promulgation of what subsequently proved to be an erroneous calculation of the end.[159] What purpose could such a statement in that chronological summary serve if not as a covert admonition to his contemporaries: "Sages, watch your words!"[160] Such matters should be discussed only with the discreet, and those who understand them with their own intelligence.[161] Ibn Daud followed in the footsteps of all great teachers of esoteric lore in uncovering one handbreadth and concealing two.[162] It may well be that his very method of writing was intended as a covert reproof to men like Abraham bar Ḥiyya, Johannes Avedahut, Judah ha-Levi and others who openly discussed what official religion had prescribed must be kept hidden.[163] Philosopher that he was, he applied to history the very method that the great teachers of philosophy had employed before him and would continue to employ after him.[164]

Finally, we are in a position to understand the great paradox of Ibn Daud's

text of Maimonides' *Epistle* and the Hebrew translations give different figures for when the reinstitution of prophecy would occur. Most scholars have accepted the figure given in the translation of Jacob b. Nahum, and reported by R. Nethanel b. Isaiah, that the date was 4976. However, the material collected by Professor Halkin in his edition clearly shows that ben Nahum's translation is self-contradictory in that passage and that R. Nethanel's report is quite fragmentary. On the other hand, the Arabic text has preserved a date that is quite consistent with Maimonides' argument there. According to the Arabic text, Balaam's prophecy was spoken in 2485 A.M., a statement which Ibn Ḥisadai's translation there renders correctly. If that figure is doubled, as Maimonides says it should be, the date of the great event is to be placed in 4970 A.M., which would made it the 710th sabbatical cycle of creation. That date, attested by the Arabic text, thus has the merit of being predicated on two crucial principles of messianic calculation, symmetry and heptads.

159 I.14–15.
160 Abot. 1.11. (The translation is taken from Goldin, *The Living Talmud*, p. 64.)
161 B. Ḥag. 13a (on the divine mysteries).
162 On the opposition to open messianic calculation, cf. Silver, *op. cit.*, pp. 195 f., and esp. Halkin's introduction to Maimonides' *Epistle*, pp. xxii f., xxviii f.
163 Cf. *ibid.*, pp. 108 f.; Silver, *op. cit.*, pp. 67 f.
164 Cf. the clear statement of Moses ibn Ezra, *Shirat Israel*, pp. 197 f.; cf. also Cohen, *SFC*, p. 123 n. 218.

defense of Rabbinism coupled with an apologia for Rome. Ibn Daud plucked from *Josippon* not only his facts on the history of the Second Temple, but appropriated lock, stock and barrel *Josippon*'s point of view on political quietism and resentment of open messianism. Ibn Daud abandoned totally the rabbinic view of Vespasian and Titus and even of Hadrian, blamed major Jewish calamities on the Jewish Zealots in terms even more vigorous than his source, and defended Roman emperors with greater consistency.[165] Where *Josippon* had castigated Tiberius, Ibn Daud praised him.[166] Where the rabbis had pictured Titus as a vulgar blasphemer, Ibn Daud portrayed him as a mild and highly cultured man.[167] Though he, too, recognized that the revolt against Rome was brought about by Roman provocations, the Jews in his view were none the less guilty. Eleazar b. Ananias "brought about all the woes [that befell the Jews] by his insurrection against the Roman procurator and by seducing the Jews to rebellion. It appears plausible that the emperor Nero alone hated the Jews, and that, had they tolerated his yoke until his death, Vespasian and Titus would have ruled them with kindness, as Octavian had done, and would have set up Jewish kings over them."[168] When the Temple was destroyed, "Joseph b. Gorion composed bitter dirges over Jerusalem, though he was able to recount but one thousandth of the tragedy which befell Jerusalem *thanks not to its enemies but to its lawless ones*. See now how much more harmful the lawless Jews were to them than the lawless men among the Gentiles."[169] Could Ibn Daud have more openly endorsed *Josippon*'s view of the past and its implications for Jewish policy in the present? These were not mechanical and unwitting paraphrases of the views of his model and source. Ibn Daud went out of his way to reiterate what had clearly become his own view in his defense of rabbinic tradition and in his history of Rome. His emphasis in *Sefer ha-Qabbalah* that the destruction of the Second Temple and the calamities in the days of Bar Kokba were brought about by Jewish provocations of the Romans was an almost open warning that it is not for man to decide when to take action.[170] The empires of the world, too, have their appointed times, and any effort to hasten the end is doomed to failure.

---

165 Cf. above, p, xxxix.
166 *Josippon* 62 (ed. Hominer), p. 224; *ZDR*; *MBSh*, f. 69a.
167 *ARN*, I, 1, p. 4; *B.* Git. 56b; *ZDR*; *MBSh*, f. 74b, 75b.
168 *MBSh*, f. 72b. The opening words of this sentence, ונראין הדברים, make me suspect that it is an interpolation by the same glossator who doctored Ibn Daud's statement on Jesus; cf. II.100 and S.N. there. However, *this* gloss is very much in consonance with Ibn Daud's general message in *MBSh*.
169 *Ibid.*, f. 73a.
170 I.207–208; III.63; *ZDR*. For the basic benignity of the Romans, cf. also II.163.

IV. THE FOUR EMPIRES AND JEWISH HISTORY

A. The Chronology of the Gentile Nations

To the the superficial reader, who does not take the trouble to examine *Sefer ha-Qabbalah* for inner consistency and accuracy, the work appears to be a well planned and fully integrated treatise. The treatment of its subject matter is strictly chronological, and the author occasionally departed briefly from its central theme only when ancillary material seemed necessary to clarify the history of the tradition. However, there was one exception, consisting of a long passage on the history of Persia and Rome, which even the most generous critic must concede sticks out like the proverbial sore thumb.[1] Those scholars who did pay attention to this long digression saw in it merely a reflection of the interests of a twelfth-century antiquarian, whose intellectual curiosity impelled him to incorporate entertaining material on subjects that were very much in vogue among the learned of his day. After all, Ibn Daud was so much taken up with the place of Rome in history that he composed a separate little treatise on the history of that empire.[2] Like many another medieval writer, he was fascinated by antiquity—particularly by the stories of its marvels— and his pen simply carried him away even in a purely religious work. We would be content to leave matters at that, were it not for several considerations that cause us to be less condescending to Ibn Daud.

To begin with, the long digression on Rome and Persia is placed in the section on amoraic history, where it interrupts the flow of the narrative. Ibn Daud could well have relegated all this material to an appendix, or to an earlier chapter, or, better still, to his history of Rome, where indeed some of the material in the digression is repeated. If the annoying digression on Persia is at least understandable in view of the context, no such excuse can be made for the inclusion of Rome, unless some comparison between the two histories was intended. Moreover, instead of proceeding with an account of the Persian background of the persecutions, which served as the immediate stimulus for this passage, Ibn Daud went off on a long excursus on Rome and returned

---

1 IV.83 f.
2 Cf. above, pp. xxxii f., 162.

to the original theme of Persia only after he had done with the secondary parenthesis![3]

In the light of all that we have already seen about Ibn Daud's method, these circumstances give us cause to suspect some undisclosed motive behind the passage. But this is not all. Can it be pure coincidence that this material, which, we emphasize, has no place in its present context, occurs in the *seventh* section of the *fourth* stage of Jewish history? "Seven" and "four" represent especially symbolic numbers in Ibn Daud's scheme of things, and it can hardly be fortuitous that the history of the great empires should be discussed at a formal point in the work which combines the two numbers which the prophet Daniel had forever associated with the historical process.[4]

Indeed, the very beginning of the passage in question virtually announces that the histories of these empires are to be understood in terms of symmetry and that the major changes which befell them reflect the fulfillment of the divine plan.

"In the year of Rabbah Tosefa'ah's death the Persian Empire decreed frightful persecutions against the Jews. [This was at the time] when the second calamity of the Persians *was at hand*. [This was "the second calamity"] for the Persians had a monarchic government twice in their history, and so too the Romans."[5]

That we have before us a passage illustrating Ibn Daud's characteristic reading of history becomes all the more probable in view of two circumstances mentioned in the opening words of this passage. The first significant point enunciated by this introduction is that the downfall of the second Persian monarchy was associated with persecutions against the Jews, although by Ibn Daud's own admission that downfall did not occur until some 186 years later.[6] Ibn Daud clearly wanted to give the impression that the downfall of the Persian Empire was a consequence (i.e., divine punishment) of its persecution of the Jews, although a plain reading of the chronology would demonstrate that the retribution was mighty slow in coming. Furthermore, the words announcing the "imminent" doom in store for Persia are reminiscent of a passage of Scripture that adds support to our suspicion:

"Is not this laid up in store with Me, sealed up in My treasuries? Vengeance is Mine, and recompense, against the time when their foot shall slip; *for the day of their calamity is at hand, and the things that are to come upon*

---

3 IV.87–129 (Rome), 130–158 (Persia).
4 Cf. previous chapter and Cohen, *SFC*, pp. 90 f.
5 IV.82 f.
6 The persecutions began in 4234 (IV.82, 164), and the Persian Empire fell in 4420 (V.30-31, 40).

them shall make haste. For the Lord will avenge His people, and repent Himself for His servants (Deut. 32.34–36)."

If these obscure verses are read in the light of early rabbinic interpretation, which understood them as a warning of vengeance against the Gentiles,[7] Ibn Daud's reading of history turns out to be no more than a "historical predictive interpretation of Scripture."[8] Since these verses proclaim that the downfall of the nations has long since been laid up in store in the divine treasury[9] in retribution for Gentile behavior, and to no small extent for Gentile mistreatment of the Jews, clearly this could be taken to mean that the cycles of Gentile history have been fixed and are as schematologically determined as the cycles of Jewish history, and that the clue to the rise and fall of an empire should be sought at least in part in the history of the Jews. That this is so emerges at once from the full story of Roman chronology to which, following Ibn Daud's lead, we turn first.

"The great city of Rome," Ibn Daud tells us immediately after the preliminary statement quoted above, "was founded in the days of Hezekiah king of Judah."[10] In his history of Rome, Ibn Daud was more specific and indicated that the exact time of the foundation was the sixth year of Hezekiah's reign and that the monarchic form of government continued in Rome for some 210 years, until the year of the foundation of the Second Temple.[11]

From an Arabic source that utilized Pseudo-Orosius,[12] Ibn Daud knew that both Romans and Persians had each enjoyed two periods of monarchic government, and it was from this source that he drew support for his chronology, which, however, he tailored in the light of the *meanings* he elicited from rabbinic sources.[13]

---

7 Sifre Deut. par. 325–326 (ed. Finkelstein), pp. 376 f.
8 The phrase is Professor Wolfson's, *The Philosophy of the Church Fathers*, p. 27.
9 Note the conjunction of "calamity" and "punishment, bringing to account" in Jer. 46.21; 49.8.
10 IV.87.
11 *ZDR*, beginning. From this passage it becomes clear that Ibn Daud did not always use the verb מלכו in the sense of "held *imperium*" but, at least in these contexts, in the restricted, and indeed unprecedented, sense of "had a monarchic form of government." The verb מלכו is further explained in *ZDR* by the oath the Romans took after the deposition of Tarquinius, "that never again should a king rule over Rome." Hence, the phrase in *Sefer ha-Qabbalah* IV.97 "and there was no one on earth who ruled over them" does not define the verb מלכו, but merely adds another fact about their early situation.
12 Cf. Levi della Vida, "La Traduzione Araba," pp. 280, n. 1, 286; on the relationship of this source to Ibn Daud's account, cf. *ibid.*, pp. 290 f.
13 Ibn Daud did not hesitate to adopt the conception of two periods of Roman monarchy as significant for his schematology, for it had been confirmed by *Josippon* and the Talmud; cf. *B. A.Z.* 8b and Lieberman, *Greek in Jewish Palestine*, pp. 9 f.; *Josippon*, ed.

A talmudic legend on the stages by which Rome rose was obviously pregnant with meaning: "R. Levi said: On the day that Solomon married the daughter of Pharaoh Necho, king of Egypt, the angel Michael descended, plunged a reed into the sea and raised a marsh, which became a thick orchard, and that is the site of the great city of Rome. On the day that Jeroboam established two calves of gold, Remus and Romulus came and built two domes in Rome. On the day that Elijah was removed, a king was enthroned in Rome."[14] This tradition clearly established the history of Rome as a series of stages corresponding to unfavorable turns of events in Jewish history. Although in view of the inconsistency of the rabbinic sources[15] Ibn Daud felt free to supply his own chronology without even an oblique apology, he remained loyal to the talmudic view that the date of the foundation of Rome corresponded to some pejorative turning point in Jewish history. Aware that Christian chroniclers had dated the begininng of Romulus' rule in the reigns of Ahaz and Hezekiah,[16] Ibn Daud found a scriptural datum that squared with his needs perfectly: "In the fourth year of King Hezekiah... Shalmaneser king of Assyria came up against Samaria and besieged it. At the end of three years they took it; *in the sixth year of Hezekiah... Samaria was taken* (II K. 18.9-10)." Thus, the day that Israel fell, Rome was born.

This correspondence of dates is hardly fortuitous, for as far as I am aware Ibn Daud is the first authority to date the foundation of Rome in that particular year. The significance of this date may have been suggested to Ibn Daud by the *Midrash 'Eser Galuyot* which, as already noted, he appended *in toto* to his work on the Second Commonwealth. When this little tract comes to speak of the third of the ten exiles which Israel suffered, i.e., the fall of Samaria, it dates the event by the reign of Hezekiah without so much as mentioning

---

Mantua-Guenzburg, col. 117. Ibn Daud merely explained the term *malkut* in that talmudic source in accordance with his own scheme. In the first place, not all the talmudic sources were consistent on the meaning of the term *kratesis*, which was the source of the explanation of two seizures of *malkut* by the Romans; cf. *Yer.* A.Z. 1.2, f. 39c. Moreover, *Josippon. loc. cit.*, had spoken of the two times in which Rome had gained dominion with totally different explanations from that given in the Talmud.

14 *Yer.* A.Z. 1.2, f. 39c. Cf. also Ginzberg, *Legends*, IV, 128; S. Krauss, "Griechen und Roemer," *Monumenta Talmudica*, V, part 1 (Vienna, 1914), p. 9, no. 16, where the passage is translated and discussed; idem, *Paras we-Romi ba-Talmud u-ba-Midrashim* (Jerusalem, 1947–48), pp. 14 f. On the genre of the talmudic legend, cf. R. Rieger, "The Foundation of Rome in the Talmud," *JQR*, NS, XVI (1925–26), 227 f.

15 Cf. e.g., *B.* A.Z. 8b and *Yer.* A.Z. 1.2, f. 39c.

16 Cf. Augustine, *City of God*, XVIII, 22; Isidore "Chronicon," *MGH*, AA, XI (ed. Mommsen), p. 443; Lucas (El Tudense), "Chronicon Mundi", *Hispania Illustrata*, IV, 16; Ps.-Orosius, as referred to above, n. 12; Otto of Freising, *Chronica*, II.3 (ed. Hofmeister), p. 71 and references cited there.

Hoshea, king of Israel, although it was in the latter's reign and territory that the calamity occurred. Clearly, Hezekiah's date was the significant one, and to Ibn Daud significant meant *symbolic*. Apart from the fact that the symbolic hint came from a text that had obvious messianic overtones,[17] the name Hezekiah itself bore the meaning of Messiah in rabbinic tradition.[18] Moreover, an old rabbinic tradition stated that on the day the Temple was destroyed the Messiah was born and dwells in Rome.[19] Was it too far fetched for Ibn Daud to reinterpret this somewhat and to conclude that the day Israel fell its archenemy was born, the very one who would destroy the Temple and the very one whose fall would signalize Israel's rebirth? This reading of Ibn Daud is supported by his statement that from the days of Romulus, the Roman monarchy continued for some 210 years *until the establishment of the Second Temple.*[20] Translated symbolically, this means that just as Roman monarchy had risen with the fall of Israel, so it fell correspondingly as Jewish glory rose.

17   Cf. Introduction, pp. xxxv, xl; below, p. 251.
18   Cf. *B.* Sanhed. 94a; Even-Shmuel, *op. cit.*, Introduction, p. 47; J. Neusner, *A Life of Rabban Yohanan ben Zakkai* (Leiden, 1962), p. 173. Obviously, what matters is not what R. Johanan b. Zakkai meant, but how later generations could have understood him.
19   Ginzberg, *Legends*, VI, 406, n. 53, 426, n. 106. This combination of legends was well known even to Christians; cf. B. Blumenkranz, *Les Auteurs Chrétiens Latins du Moyen Age sur les Juifs et le Judaisme* (Paris, 1963), sec. 165, p. 197; O.L. Rankin, *Jewish Religious Polemic* (Edinburgh, 1956), pp. 184 f.
20   *ZDR*, beg. The synchronization of the beginnings of the Roman republic with the first year of Cyrus goes back to Orosius, *History* II.2.—Ibn Daud's statement on the 210 years is of no mean interest, for it reflects the kind of chronological shenanigans which he occasionally allowed himself. Ibn Daud probably appropriated the figure 210 from some chronicle (*Josippon* ?), which had taken it from Josephus, who, in turn, had adapted the number out of religious schematological considerations; see Shalit, *op. cit.* Furthermore, it will be recalled that the unit of 21 years plays a significant role in *Sefer ha-Qabbalah* in connection with the chronologies of both Temples, and that $210 = 10 \times 21$ or $10 \times 7 \times 3$, all combinations of which are stock schematological figures in Ibn Daud's chronology; cf. Analysis, ch. III. In other words, the fortunes of Rome corresponded in multiples of ten to the fortunes of Israel. (See also below, where the number 21 figures in the struggle between Bar Koziba and Rome.) Had Ibn Daud been asked to rationalize the figure 210 in detail he would doubtless have pointed to the detailed enumeration in I.61 f., which would yield the following figures from the sixth year of Hezekiah: 24 of Hezekiah + 55 of Manasseh + 2 of Amon + 31 of Josiah + 1 of Jehoahaz + 26 [sic!] from the ascension of Jehoiakim to the destruction of the Temple [see I.126, 139 f.] + 70 of exile = 209. Although this total is one year short of the 210 required, Ibn Daud was careful to note that the period of Roman monarchy lasted "*approximately 210 years.*" On the importance of the word "approximately" in Ibn Daud's works, cf. Cohen, *SFC*, p. 106. However, that little cipher of 26 years from the beginning of Jehoiakim's reign until the destruction of the Temple is itself a contrived figure that is fraught with difficulties; cf. above, p. 195.

Ibn Daud's way of dating the origins of Rome had polemical overtones, for Christian chroniclers had often claimed that Rome rose as Babylon fell.[21] But this was inadmissible to Ibn Daud, for it would have made Roman history independent of Jewish history, a view to which he could not subscribe. Ibn Daud's tacit but nonetheless firm insistence on the pivotal imporance of Jewish history for the varying fortunes of Rome is reflected in his statement that the Romans paid tribute to Nebuchadnezzar and to his successors, including the Medes and the Persians, and subsequently to the Greeks, until they were able to break the Greek yoke in the wake of the Maccabean revolt.[22] This last item clearly established that the fluctuations in Roman fortune were connected with parallel developments within the Jewish community. However, by making the first period of good fortune extend down to the foundation of the Second Temple, Ibn Daud indicated that he measured Roman good fortune by the institution of monarchy. So long as the Romans had a king, as far as Ibn Daud was concerned, even though they paid tribute to the Babylonians and Persians, they were still in the age of monarchy and dominion. With the removal of the monarchy, the Romans fell into a period of insignificance. However, focusing our attention for the present on chronology, since the Hasmonean uprising occurred approximately 210 years after the building of the Second Temple,[23] the years of Roman subjection to the Greeks corresponded in number to those of the initial period of monarchy and good forture.[24] Thus the period of Roman insignificance was symmetrical with the period of Roman monarchy, and both periods were determined by the fortunes of the Jews.[24a]

21 See beginning of previous note and cf. Augustine, *City of God*, XVIII.21; Otto of Freising, *Chronica*, I.30, Prologue to II, II.2. Obviously, Ibn Daud did not know the work of his contemporary Otto, but the latter attested to the persistence of classical Christian chronological conceptions.
22 IV.105 and S.N. there.
23 II.52. Although the Maccabean uprising is dated in the year 212 of the Second Temple, that figure was in itself a tailored one; cf. above, p.171. Moreover, Ibn Daud indicated that the waves of early Roman history were only measured in round numbers; cf. n. 20.
24 Should it be objected that by the line of reasoning earlier attributed to Ibn Daud, the fortunes of Rome should hardly have risen at the time of the Hasmonean triumph, it should be noted that Ibn Daud repeatedly stressed that the ensuing Maccabean rule was not one of true dominion and hence of consolation for the Jews, for the Maccabean house was not Davidic. Consequently, the fortunes of Israel cannot really be said to have risen at that time; cf. below, pp. 236 f. Furthermore, although Rome was able to shake off the yoke of Macedon at that time, it did not achieve a monarchic form of government until considerably later, at a time in Jewish history that was symbolically appropriate (see below), and it was only at the point that Rome achieved a monarchy that its chronology—i.e., its history—became of any real consequence, as far as Ibn Daud was concerned.

However, the second Roman monarchy did not begin until some time later. "In the days of Jannaeus king of the Jews, the second period of Roman monarchy began. Their first king, Julius, called Caesar... restored the monarchy to the Romans."[25] In this instance, Ibn Daud seemed to give no hint at what point the monarchic form of government was re-established in Rome. Futhermore, the statement contradicted Ibn Daud's own more accurate knowledge that Julius Caesar did not attain power until somewhat later, in the days of Aristobulus and Hyrcanus II.[26] As already indicated, such lapses on the part of Ibn Daud are almost always an alert to esoteric meaning, and as usual he did not leave us completely in the dark. If Roman monarchy began a second time in the days of Jannaeus, it can only be that Jannaeus' rule was a kind of calamity in Jewish history. Of Jannaeus' reign Ibn Daud relates two "facts:" the first that Jannaeus butchered the sages of Israel; the second that in his days Jesus of Nazareth flourished. Clearly, there must have been a connection in Ibn Daud's mind between the massacre of the sages, the appearance of Jesus, and the renewal of Roman ascendency.[27]

> That there could be a hiatus between the point at which a people gained its freedom and the time its monarchy, or true period of government, began is made quite clear from Ibn Daud's history of Persia; cf. below, pp. 232 f. Put differently, Rome's partial good fortune at the time of the Maccabean uprising was commensurate with that of the Jews.
>
> 24a For the talmudic roots of this notion, cf. *B*. Meg. 6a and Rashi to Gen. 25.23. Although the verse cited there (Ezek. 26.2) was said originally of Tyre, the latter is clearly a disguise for Rome.
>
> 25 IV.110–113.
>
> 26 *MBSh*, f. 59a.
>
> 27 II.73 f., 95 f. That the wickedness of Jannaeus was mentioned because of its symbolic significance was indicated by Ibn Daud's confession, II.83 f., that the story of Jannaeus is not germane to his chronicle. The talmudically oriented reader, the author knew, would not fail to associate Jannaeus' brutality to the sages with the flight of Joshua b. Peraḥyah and the defection of Jesus. Although Ibn Daud protested repeatedly in *Sefer ha-Qabbalah*, *ZDR* and *MBSh* that Jesus lived long before the Gentile historians claim he did, Ibn Daud's real opinion on the subject must remain an open question, for else how could he possibly have blandly inserted the unqualifiedly contradictory statement that Jesus was born in the 38th year of Augustus' reign; IV.127! Moreover, as will be seen from section B of this chapter, Ibn Daud hinted that the tannaim had thought the Christian date the correct one. (We must reassert our refusal to patronize Ibn Daud as an uncritical medieval, who would blindly copy his sources and incorporate their data no matter how self-contradictory the results. He who would portray Ibn Daud as so artless and unwitting a chronicler will have to account for the highly original and contrived chronology and other symbolic devices that are neither copied nor the result of chance.) Whatever Ibn Daud's true opinion, self-contradictory chronology was utilized by him as an alert to a symbolic presentation. The dating of the activity of Jesus in the context of Jannaeus' reign served as a further indication that Jannaeus' reign was a calamitous one. That Jesus' activity should have as its counterpart the rise of Roman royal government was probably

Proceeding from this assumption, we are in a position to suggest the exact symbolic date of the renewal of the Roman monarchy. In another passage, where Roman seizure of world dominion through the conquests of Pompey is "accurately" dated, Ibn Daud added: "In those days Jesus the Nazarene was apprehended."[28] Obviously, the event was important enough in Ibn Daud's view to merit special mention, although he had discoursed on it at length elsewhere,[29] and although its insertion in the passage on Pompey represented a digression from his story. Since the crucifixion became the central motif of Christianity and thus boded ill for the Jews, the year of Roman renewal might well have coincided with the crucifixion, which was explicitly dated by Ibn Daud in 3708 A.M.[30] If by Ibn Daud's principle of symmetry one allows the Romans 210 years for their second dominion, one arrives at a terminal date of 3918 or 158 C.E. From Ibn Daud's history of Rome we learn that the latter date corresponds to the year after the death of Antoninus Pius,[31] an event which, Ibn Daud reminded us, Rabbi Judah the Prince described as a major catastrophe to the empire.[32] In other words, Roman *exclusive dominion* came to a complete end in the days of Judah the Prince, a period which Ibn Daud represented as one of Jewish *ascent*.[33]

It may be objected that, as the terminal point for this last symmetrical datum, we have shifted ground from the period during which the Romans possessed a monarchic form of government to a period in which Roman *imperium* over the world came to an end. This is particularly questionable, it would seem, for Ibn Daud did not consider Roman "rule," i.e., its monarchy, at an end even in the period when the Romans were paying tribute to Nebuchadnezzar. Consequently, the termination of a Roman period with the death of Antoninus would appear to be quite arbitrary on our part, since Roman monarchy con-

---

plausible to Ibn Daud, in view of the fact that Rome was destined to become Jesus' standard-bearer; see *ZDR*.

28 *MBSh*, f. 57b. In ed. Amsterdam the sentence בימים ההם נתפש ישו הנצרי has been deleted just before the last paragraph beginning with the words ואחרי כן.
29 II.95 f.
30 II.113.
31 Since the Temple was destroyed in 3829 (II.164), 121 years passed from the crucifixion until the destruction of the Temple. 73 years later Bethar fell (II.50; note that this figure of 73 diverges from the traditional one!). According to *ZDR*, Antoninus Pius reigned 15 years, yielding a total of 209 years from the crucifixion to the death of Antoninus. For the symmetrical figure of 209–210, see above, n. 20. It is futile to try to square these results with the detailed chrolonogical data of *ZDR*, for Ibn Daud does not say how long Julius Caesar reigned. Moreover, Ibn Daud's chrolonogy of the emperors in *ZDR* can in no wise be squared with the statement that Bethar fell 73 years after the Destruction.
32 IV.134.
33 III.79 f.

tinued for centuries afterward, as Ibn Daud knew quite well. While this objection is technically pertinent, the fact is that Ibn Daud expressly indicated that in his understanding of Judah the Prince's lament at the time of the death of Antoninus, that year was a turning point in Roman history. What had happened in the course of the second period of Roman royal goverment was that Roman monarchy had become coextensive with world dominion, with *imperium*. *Regnum* and *imperium*, it is by now quite obvious, were not identical in Ibn Daud's scheme of things. *Regnum* could be, and was, held without total *imperium*.[34] Thus, in the first stage of Roman history, when the Romans had a *regnum* and domination over the West, the *imperium* was held by the kingdoms enumerated in the book of Daniel—Babylon, Media, Persia.[35] However, once a *regnum* attained total *imperium* and was then dislodged from its latter state, a new stage in its own history must properly be said to have begun.[36]

To be sure, these distinctions are only implied, but without them Ibn Daud's account makes little sense. Ibn Daud did not make these fine points explicit, for Hebrew makes no clear distinction between *regnum* and *imperium* and uses the same word for both.[37] However, as we shall see, Ibn Daud did use certain key terms to indicate which *regna* had also attained complete *imperium*. The point to note here is that he also indicated by his statements on the transfer of power from one people to another that *regnum* was indispensable for a people claiming to hold the *imperium*. At the particular historical juncture symbolized by the death of Antoninus, Rome lost its exclusive hold on the *imperium*, for in the following stage of history it shared the dominion with Persia. Thus, 21 years after the end of the second Roman period a new stage in the history of world empires began.[38]

In the introduction to his excursus, Ibn Daud had declared that there was a striking correspondence between the histories of Rome and Persia in that each had possessed royal forms of government twice.[39] Since we have seen that the periods of Roman government were symetrically construed and were connected with developments in Jewish history, it is a plausible assumption

---

34 On the distinction between the two concepts, cf. R. Folz, *L'Idée de l'Empire en Occident* (Paris, 1953), pp. 14 f.; C. Erdmann, *Forschungen zur Politischen Ideenwelt des Fruehmittelalters* (Berlin, 1951), pp. 8 ff.
35 IV.90-91, 104-105.
36 IV.121, 131-134.
37 Cf. I.223 and IV.100 where the same Hebrew word, *malkut*, signifies "empire," "kingdom" and "*imperium*" (dominion). However, *melukah* always signifies monarchy alone; cf. IV.113; *MBSh*, f. 50a.
38 On 21 year spans as periods of transition in history, cf. n. 20.
39 Cf. n. 5.

that Persian chronology, in Ibn Daud's presentation, will display similar characteristics.[40]

The first time that the Persian monarchy was uprooted was in the thirtieth year of the Second Temple, i.e., in 3439 A.M.[41] In his sermon on the prophecy of Zechariah, Ibn Daud indicated that shortly after the deaths of Zerubbabel and Nehemiah, the cordial relations that had existed between the Jews and the Persians were irreparably sundered: "Love was cut off and the covenant between the Jews and the kings of Persia was broken."[42] Translated symbolically, this would mean that there was a basic connection between the fall of Persia and its poor treatment of the Jews in the last days of its first empire. This interpretation of Ibn Daud's meaning is indicated in the first instance by the fact that Ibn Daud had no clear knowledge of any Persian persecution of the Jews in the final stages of the empire's existence. Indeed, the sequence of events in *Sefer ha-Qabbalah* indicated the very opposite: namely, that the Persian government rescinded the prohibition against the construction of the Temple and re-enforced Cyrus' decree, so that the Temple was completed thirty years before the Macedonian invasion.[43] In other words, the exegesis of the prophecy in Zechariah is forced and is governed by schematic considerations. This estimate is confirmed by Ibn Daud's parallel observations on the second downfall of Persia with which, it will be recalled, the passage on Persia and Rome opened. Thus, the history of Persia was shown to be significant in relation to the Jews, for the downfall of the Persians was determined in each instance by Persian treatment of the Jews. Moreover, each time the Persian Empire fell, the empire succeeding to its rule received the leader of the Jewish community warmly and honored him. 'Ali's treatment of R. Isaac paralleled Alexander's treatment of Simeon the Righteous.[44] It stands to reason that the chronology of Persian history would exhibit, no less than the history of the Roman monarchies, characteristics that would reflect symbolism and inner meaning.

---

40 Only the principle of symmetry will account for Ibn Daud's inclusion of the fantastic story of the coronation of Bahram; cf. S.N. to IV.152–157.

41 I.222. That there was a hiatus between the end of Persian dominion and the chronology of the Greek empire, which began according to Ibn Daud in 3449, is recorded in *B.A.Z.* 10a: שש שנים מלכו בעילם ואח״כ פשטה מלכותן בכל העולם. The deviation by Ibn Daud or his source from this figure by extending the hiatus to 10 years amounts to a variant of י for ו; cf. above, p. 193 n. 20.

42 *MBSh*, f. 79b.

43 I.115 f., 219.

44 Cf. II.9 and V.40, where "honored and revered" is the key phrase. Although the Persian Empire was uprooted in 3439, "Greek chronology," the Seleucid Era, did not begin until Alexander "honored and revered" the leader of the Jews; cf. also below, n. 50.

However, before proceeding to Persian chronology, it must be indicated that, in Ibn Daud's scheme, the periods of Roman and Persian rule were not completely parallel. In contrast with the Romans, each time that the Persians possessed *regnum* they were also in control of the world *imperium*. That distinction was indicated by Ibn Daud in his statement that the Persians had *malkut*, which, as shown by the contexts of Ibn Daud's usage, meant not only a monarchy but control over the whole world. Significantly, too, when writing of the downfall of the two Persian Empires, he employed highly charged terms such as "cut off," "destroyed from under the heavens," "uprooted from the earth." Needless to add, the power that effected such destruction and took over was no less an empire than the one that had suffered displacement. Consequently, "when the Persian *Empire* was cut off, the Greek *Empire* began."[45]

The Greek Empire, which followed the Persian, began in 3439,[46] endured for 500 years, and was then overthrown.[47] In other words, the second date of imperial upheaval and change is 3939. It will be recalled that the second Roman monarchy and its tenure of the *imperium* fell within this period.[48] Accordingly, by chronological categories the rule of Rome must be considered as an aspect of the *Greek stage of history*. Ibn Daud emphasized that this stage was Greek by telling us that when the Persians were rallied to revolt against the Romans, they were encouraged to break "the sword of Aristotle" that had been subjecting them for the past five centries!

At this point, the dominion over the world was divided between Persia and Rome, and this state of affairs endured for 480 years, i.e., until 4420, when the Persian half of the Empire was extirpated and the Muslim Empire began.[50] Thus, in connection with the succession of empires from the time of Alexander the Great until the rise of Islam, Ibn Daud provided us with highly detailed chronological information, coupled, to be sure, with little asides to remind us that for the purposes of symbolic periodization we must not hold him to

---

45 I.223; II.5-6; IV.103;V.31. The wording in IV.100, 105 does not refute the distinction we have made between Ibn Daud's use of the verb *maleku* and the noun *malkut*. The fact of the matter is that Babylon had *malkut* or dominion over the world, and that is why its dominion could be said to have "passed" to the Medians and Persians; cf. also n. 37.

46 Cf. n. 41.

47 IV.137.

48 Cf. above, p. 230.

49 IV.137-139.

50 IV.140-144. V.30-31. Although "King" Muhammad began his activity earlier, the Muslim Empire did not begin until after the Persian Empire had been uprooted in 4420; V.40. On Ibn Daud's selection of that date as the year of transition, cf. n. 44.

too strict an account; the second Persian monarchy did not really begin until somewhat after 3939,[51] but the latter date is the one that counts.

Proceeding now on the principle of symmetry, in accordance with which the first period of the Persian Empire would correspond to its second, we would allow 480 years to the first Persian Empire and thus find that it began in 2959 A.M., which was the thirtieth year of the Solomonic Temple.[52] The symmetry is blatant: the first Persian Empire would thus have risen in the thirtieth year of the First Temple and have fallen in the thirtieth year of the Second.[53] Moreover, the 480 years of the first Persian *imperium* would have corresponded in extent to the number of years which passed from the time of the foundation of the First Temple to the foundation of the Second.[54] What is more, in each instance the dominion of the Persian Empire came to an end after (and *because of*) its persecution of the Jews. If we read between Ibn Daud's lines correctly, the consolation to be derived from Persian history seemed to be even greater than the one to be drawn from that of Rome. Whereas the fortunes of the latter corresponded in *inverse ratio* to those of the Jews, in the case of Persia the fortunes of the *imperium* took a turn for the worse as the attitude of the Persians toward the Jews degenerated. Put differently, as Israel fell, Rome rose; as Israel rose, Rome fell. However, as Persia favored Israel, Persia was blessed; as Persia persecuted Israel, Persia suffered.[55] Furthermore, Ibn Daud now provided an instance demonstrating that world history was governed by the same rhythm as that characterizing the periodization of Jewish history, for the 980 years of any two consecutive imperial periods were equivalent to 2 × 70 "weeks" of history. The 980-year period, it will be recalled, had been especially significant in Jewish history,[56] and Ibn Daud proceeded to show that this scheme was operative not only within the Jewish community, but for other great waves of history as well.

If we turn now to the end of the series of empires and allow Ishmael 500 years from the moment at which it replaced the Persian empire, we find that we should stand in 4920 A.M., or 1159–1160 C.E., the year before the publication of Ibn Daud's works.[57] In other words, Ibn Daud's books had come to herald esoterically the beginning of a new era in history. Indeed, the progress of events in Spain gave him every reason to believe that the empire of Ishmael

51 Cf. IV.131–134.
52 The First Temple was founded in 2929; I.19, 112.
53 I.222–223.
54 Cf. above, pp. 192, 198.
55 Cf. above, pp. 224, 232.
56 Cf. above, pp. 200, 202.
57 Cf. Introduction, p. xxxii.

had already come to an end.[58] Moreover, his dwelling at length and with manifest pessimism on the deteriorated condition of the Jews in Spain now takes on new significance.[59] It was not only the plight of the Jews that concerned him, but the momentous and world-shaking consequences which, as earlier stages of Jewish history had demonstrated, such changes forbode. That he in-indeed felt that the Jews and the world at large were standing on the threshold of a new era, we have already seen from the decipherment of his rabbinic cycles.[60] If it should be objected that the latter pointed, according to our interpretation, to a culminating date of 1188–1189, or some twenty-nine years after our interpretation of the fullness of time for Islam, we must insist that from the point of view of a Jewish eschatologist, particularly of the twelfth century, that was no problem at all. Abraham bar Ḥiyya and Moses Maimonides, both of whom publicly theorized on the imminent end of time, indicated that the end would come in stages. In fact, the former writer felt that the unfolding of the end would span several centuries, beginning in 1188–89 and culminating in 1464.[61]

However, the most striking thing about Ibn Daud's chronology is that it tacitly but quite unequivocally had departed from the classical Jewish enumerations of the four empires of the Book of Daniel. According to talmudic tradition and all Jewish exegesis following its guidelines, the sequence of four empires had been: Babylon, Persia (including Media), Greece, Rome.[62] However, if Ibn Daud's chronology is any clue to his interpretation of the sequence of world empires, the order was Persia (including Babylon and Media),[63] Greece, (including Rome),[64] Persia-Rome, Islam.[65] Now inasmuch as we have seen that Rome held monarchy within the first stage of the succession of empires, and that Babylon,

---

58 Cf. Epilogue.73, 78 on "the rebels."
59 VII.448 f.; Epilogue.73 f. Of course, I do not mean to deny or even belittle Ibn Daud's genuine concern with the plight of the Jews of Spain. On the other hand, he was by no means the only one who saw in the terrible sufferings of the Jews of his day a premonition of the messianic era; cf. Silver, *op. cit.*, pp. 48, 74 f. Maimonides, *Epistle to Yemen*, pp. xxvii f.; Baer, *A History of the Jews in Christian Spain*, I, 65 f.
60 Cf. Analysis, ch. III.
61 Cf. Silver, *op. cit.*, pp. 72 f.; Halkin's introduction to Maimonides, *Epistle to Yemen*, pp. xxvi f.
62 Cf. Wayyik. R. 13.5 (ed. Margulies), pp. 281 f.; Ginzberg, *Legends*, V, 223, n. 82; the sequence is assumed in such passages as *B*. Meg. 11a (and variants in the order of empires recorded by E. Z. Melamed, *Halachic Midrashim of the Tannaim* [in Hebrew], I (Jerusalem, 1943), p. 323, no. 987); Midrash Tehillim 22.9 (ed. Buber), p. 185; *Mishnah of R. Eliezer* (ed. Enelow), p. 103.
63 Cf. above, to nn. 52–54.
64 Cf. to nn. 46–47.
65 Cf. to n. 50.

Media and Persia all held the reins of the first empire, it follows that the significant stages of world history were not necessarily identical with the monarchies that held the reins of empire at any given moment. Indeed, if one may judge from Ibn Daud's description of the second stage of history, namely the Greek one, what we have been calling *imperium* was really but a stage in world history. Control was held by the Greeks and then by the Romans. Consequently, not only was Rome not the fourth "kingdom" in the classical sence, but it had achieved unqualified world dominion only for a very brief period, and even that was within the *Greek* stage of history. Clearly, in Ibn Daud's view the kingdoms named in the Book of Daniel were only monarchies; however, they were named in Scripture because they were the ones that held the reins of empire in certain periods of history. Nevertheless, in fact they were only sub-categories of empires which represented the larger stages of history.

Ibn Daud's new distinction between *regnum* and *imperium* was defensible exegetically as well as historically. Exegetically, the Bible itself indicated that kings who were really Median or Persian could also be designated as kings of the Chaldees or kings of Babylon.[66] Obviously, then, Babylon, Media and Persia were basically identical. Moreover, Ibn Daud's understanding of the succession of empires would seem to indicate that he followed in the wake of medieval historians gerenally in regarding Assyria as the first of the four world empires and then rendering the name Assyria in the form current among Arabic-speaking peoples, namely by that of Persia.[67] The talmudic understanding of the succession of empires was no stumbling block, for such aggadic exegesis was not doctrinally binding, and Ibn Daud felt as free, indeed required, as other medieval exegetes to adjust his interpretation to the facts of history.[68]

Actually, Ibn Daud's reinterpretation of the sequence of empires and his implied distinction between *regnum* and *imperium* was consistent with his political theory on the relative merits and distinctions of different forms of government. It will be recalled that the stated thesis of Ibn Daud's history of the Jews in the days of the Second Temple was that the consolatory prophecies of restoration of the Jews contained in Scripture had not been fullfiled in the days of the Second Temple. The Jews could accordingly have every confidence that these prophecies would yet come to fruition.[69] If it was objected that the

66 Dan. 9.1; Ezra 5. 13, 8.1
67 Cf. J.W. Swain, "The Theory of the Four Monarchies," *Classical Philology*, XXV (1940), 12 f.; Otto of Freising, *Chronica*, pp. 5, 66 and Hofmeister's notes there; R. Kirchheim, *Karmay Shomron*, (Frankfurt a.M., 1851) p. 81 n. 4; cf. also references to Ibn Khaldun in note to IV.85; below, n. 81.
68 Cf. below, pp. 237 f.
69 Cf. Introduction, p. xxxv.

principal promise of restoration, namely national independence, had indeed come to pass in that period, Ibn Daud retorted that such was not the case; for in the days of the Second Temple, the two essential conditions of true national restoration did not obtain, at least simultaneously. The first condition was a Davidic monarch, and the Maccabees were not Davidides. Secondly, and no less vital, Zerubbabel, who was a scion of the Davidic kings, had never attained monarchy (*melukah*), but only administrative authority (*serarah*), which was a pale shadow of royal status.[70] Authority (*serarah*) and been held by many different kinds of officials throughout the ages,[71] but no one in his right mind would confuse them with kings. Davidic monarchy had simply never existed within the Jewish community since the destruction of the First Temple. That consolation and, of course, all the others that went with it were yet to come.

Now the distinction between *serarah* and *melukah* within the Jewish community is the counterpart of the difference between *regnum* (*melukah*) and *imperium* (*malkut*) in world empires. Underlying this distinction was the political theory, to which Ibn Daud apparently subscribed, that the ideal form of government was monarchy. Only royal rule gave a people the distinction of having some form of dominion, whether global or only partial.[72]

Close examination will reveal that Ibn Daud was not the only Jew, perhaps not even the first, to feel that the traditional scheme of four empires required correction. Ibn Daud's new scheme clearly reflected the influence of the revised interpretation of Daniel advanced much earlier by the leading Jewish exegetes of Muslim countries. After the conquests of Islam, all traditional exegesis had to be recast to make room for the new empire whose dominion extended from Spain to Persia. Saadiah and Ibn Aqnin maintained that the fourth kingdom consisted of a dominion shared by Rome (Edom) and Islam (Ishmael)—a common designation of Islam in Judeo-Arabic sources is "the partner" (i.e., of Rome)—while Abraham ibn Ezra, adjusting exegesis to the facts of life, eliminated Rome completely from the fourth dominion and designated the latter as the exclusive legacy of Ishmael.[73] Rome, in Ibn Ezra's scheme, was identical

---

70 *MBSh*, f. 50a. This distinction between *melukah* and *serarah* was eagerly seized by Jewish apologists; cf. Abraham b. Moses Maimonides, *Payrush ha-Torah*, ed. by S.D. Sassoon, tr. into Hebrew by E.J. Wiesenberg (London, 1959), p. 204; Posnanski, *Schiloh*, pp. 140 f.

71 Cf. talmudic dictionaries, s.v. שררה; *Mishnah of R. Eliezer* (ed. Enelow), p. 122.

72 Cf. Aristotle, *Nich. Ethics*, VIII.10 and L. Strauss, "Maimonides' Statement on Political Science," *PAAJR*, XXII (1953), 121 f.; E.I.J. Rosenthal, *Political Thought in Medieval Islam* (Cambridge, 1958), pp. 119, 144. For the same point of view by a later philosopher of the same school of thought, cf. M. Mahdi, *Ibn Khaldun's Philosophy of History* (Chicago, 1957), pp. 206 f.

73 Cf. Ibn Ezra to Dan. 2.39 and esp. "Abraham ibn Ezra's Short Commentary on Daniel," ed. by H.J. Mathews, *Miscellany of Hebrew Literature*, II (1877), 3, 7; Joseph b. Judah

with the biblical Kittim, and was ethnically a sub-group of the one which included the Greeks. Consequently, Rome was to be classified as an offshoot of the third empire, which was clearly that of Greece. Maintaining a rigid consistency, Ibn Ezra protested emphatically against the popular view that the people of Edom should in any way be implicated in the destruction of the Temple. That calamity had been the work of the wicked Greek empire, *which exists to this very day*.[74] The subordination of Rome to Greece and its reclassification within the third empire did not necessarily lessen the role of Rome in the eschaton, for, Ibn Ezra noted, the third empire was destined to play a crucial role in ushering in the end of days. That end would be heralded by the mortal combat between the third and fourth empires, i.e., between Rome, the Christian standardbearer of Greece, and the eleven horns or petty kingdoms of Ishmael-Islam. Moreover, he pointed out, Daniel had not claimed that any but the fourth empire would be utterly destroyed. The others would survive, although denuded of their power.[75] Ibn Ezra's Andalusian-Jewish orientation did not require that the Christian nations be destroyed. It was enough that their *power* would be shattered in the fullness of time, and that Israel would then be redeemed. Thanks to this exegesis, medieval scientific genealogy,[76] the facts of history, and the needs of eschatology had been brought into perfect harmony.

By making the Roman Kittim a sub-category of the Greeks, Ibn Ezra had also clearly distinguished between an empire and the specific monarchy in control of it at any given moment. The Greek empire remained Greek whether its representative power was a Greek or a Roman people.

Ibn Ezra's interpretation of Daniel reflected a second motif shared by a number of exegetes-eschatologists of the twelfth century, who saw in the Muslim-Christian conflicts of the Crusades a sign of the approaching end of time. This was the view articulated by Maimonides, Abraham bar Ḥiyya and others: the messianic era would be ushered in by a final war between Esau and Ishmael,

---

ibn Aqnin, *Divulgatio*, pp. 414 f. The Yemenite anthologies *Midrash ha-Gadol*, Genesis (ed. Margulies), p. 254 and *Maor ha-Afelah* (ed. Kafih), p. 87 also refer to Edom and Ishmael as partners in the fourth empire.

74 Ibn Ezra to Gen. 27.40; Zech. 11.5. The conception of the Romans as a Greek people may have been stimulated or confirmed for Andalusian authors by Sassanian views, which came to them by way of Arabic chroniclers; cf. S.N. to IV.132.

75 Ibn Ezra to Dan. 7.14; *idem*, "Short Commentary," p. 4.

76 Medieval exegetes knew very well that the talmudic identification of Edom with Rome was insupportable on historic grounds. I have dealt with the history of this problem and the various medieval Jewish solutions to it in the paper referred to in the Introduction, p. xxxiii n. 83.

i.e., between Christendom and Islam, after which the kingdom of God—and of course, the redemption of Israel—would begin.[77]

Ibn Daud's reading of history thus represented an extension and modification of Ibn Ezra's theory. Imperial Rome, he agreed, was part of the third empire, since the world in the third stage of history had been divided between Persia and Rome.[78] What is more, the western section of the third empire continued to exist even after Islam had uprooted the Persian section and inaugurated the fourth stage of history.[79] However, whereas Ibn Ezra had seen the succession of empires as successive replacements by different points of the compass—Babylon/North, Persia/East, Macedon/West, and Islam/South[80]—Ibn Daud saw the succession (and conflicts) in terms of East versus West: (1) Persia to (2) Greece to (3) Persia and Rome, followed by (4) oriental Ishmael and the Roman or occidental residue of the third empire.[81]

Ibn Daud's departure from the rabbinic scheme as well as from Ibn Ezra's slight modifications of tradition was an effort at improvement on several fronts. The rabbinic interpretation had clearly ignored many changes in the control of world dominion, while Ibn Ezra had only readjusted those stages that were of direct concern to him without showing any consistent theory. In Ibn Daud's view, all of the Gentile kings named in the Book of Daniel fell within the first stage of world history, the Chaldean-Persian.[82] Secondly, Ibn Daud's reinterpretation of the Danielian scheme coincided far better with the regnant notions of his day on the history of the world, which were derived from medieval political theory and which in turn affected scriptural exegesis. In the twelfth century, *imperium* was variously defined as world-embracing dominion, or control of

---

77 Cf. Silver, *op. cit.*, pp. 58 f.; Baer, *History of the Jews in Christian Spain*, I, 66 f.
78 Cf. nn. 50, 65.
79 Cf. *ibid.*; note that only the Persian section of the third stage was uprooted by the Arabs.
80 Ibn Ezra, "Short Commentary," p. 4.
81 Behind Ibn Daud's description of the succession of empires one may detect the faint traces of Isidore's scheme. According to Isidore, *Etymologiae*, IX, 3.2-3, the nations having *regnum* were the Assyrians, Medes, Persians, Egyptians and Greeks. However, of these only two were glorious ones, and it was from them that *regnum* was transmitted to the others. These two were the Assyrians and later the Romans. Moreover, a symmetry may be detected in the rule of these two kingdoms: one was in the east, the other in the west; one was earlier, the other later; the limits of the one began where those of the other terminated; the other kingdoms and rulers were reckoned as the appendages of each of these two. For the Augustinian source of this schematic division, cf. H.A. Deane, *The Political and Social Ideas of St. Augustine* (New York, 1963), p. 31. Clearly, Ibn Daud's portrait is far removed from this one, but it is also no less apparent that Ibn Daud's sources ultimately owed some of their inspiration to Isidore or his disciples.
82 Cf. above, to n. 66.

the Holy Roman Empire, or even as dominion over Italy.[83] However, one of the most widely accepted prerequisites was control over a plurality of nations, which would substantiate the appearance of world-dominion.[84] Since, as noted earlier, classical Hebrew did not distinguish between *regnum* and *imperium*, Ibn Daud took the same root to designate control of the *imperium* through *regnum* at any particular moment. We shall soon see that this was not a mere verbal or intellectual exercise for Ibn Daud, but a vital element in his message of consolation to the Jews of Spain.

Finally, Ibn Daud's schematological division of Jewish history had demonstrated that Jewish history operated basically in cycles of 500 and 980 years. If Jewish history is the key to all of history, the chronological schematology of world empires should in some way parallel the Jewish one. Now, according to Scripture or tradition, Babylon reigned only seventy years;[85] Persia but fifty-two; Rome but some 210.[87] These were hardly fitting terms for empires, i.e., for historical cycles. Accordingly, Ibn Daud readjusted some of the formal aspects of classical exegesis to coincide with the long-term waves of history with which he was primarily concerned.

B. *The Prices of Miscalculation and Indiscretion*

Our own long digression on Ibn Daud's symbolic chronology and his reclassification of the four empires has been necessary in order to establish his real motives for recording some major dates of world history. There can be little doubt that Ibn Daud was concerned with the events of the Gentile past only to the extent that they shed light on the Jewish hope for the future.

While, on the one hand, Ibn Daud constructed a new esoteric schematology of world history, he carefully indicated the fulfillment of a number of prophetic oracles with regard to Babylon, and especially the way in which Daniel's visions were fulfilled in the events of the Second Commonwealth and after.[88] Like may another medieval exegete, Ibn Daud was careful to indicate which prophecies of Scripture had already been fulfilled and could, therefore, no longer serve as sources of hope and consolation for the future, as well as those which, conversely, had clearly not yet been fulfilled, and therefore had to be

---

83   Cf. R. Koebner, *Empire* (Cambridge, 1961), pp. 31, 313 n. 2 to p. 49.
84   P.E. Schramm, *Kaiser, Rom und Renovatio*, 2 vols. (Leipzig and Berlin, 1929; I², Darmstadt, 1957), I, 76, 119, 157 f.
85   I.151–153.
86   I.215–220.
87   Cf. above, p. 225.
88   I.154 f.; III.65 f.

understood as oracles of promise.[89] Ibn Daud's excursus on Daniel indicates in no uncertain terms that Daniel's prophecies had all been fulfilled and could no longer be applied for the future, as other exegetes attempted to do.[90]

This was no idle matter for Ibn Daud, for he went out of his way to remind his readers that nothing but heartache and worse had occurred in Jewish history because of misguided decisions to act on erroneous eschatological calculations or on the basis of misapplied exegesis of supposedly eschatological prophecies.[91] Nor could these admonitions have been too indirectly expressed to readers of Ibn Daud's works. The twelfth century, and particularly Ibn Daud's milieu, it will be recalled, abounded with messianic theories and movements, Jewish as well as Christian.[92] Ibn Daud's esoteric method of speculating on the end of time, coupled with his blatant reaffirmation of *Josippon's* denunciation of the Zealots and eulogy of the Roman emperors were a patent warning that eschatological conclusions may not be promulgated, and action may not be taken on them even in the face of supposedly clear exegetical proof.

What better example do we need, Ibn Daud hints, than the tragic blunder of Ben Koziba and his arch-supporter, R. Akiba? Modern scholars have thrown up their hands in despair of determining the source of Ibn Daud's fantastic account of the Bar Kokba revolt.[93] However, if we read the story in the light of Ibn Daud's categories and of traditional eschatological symbolism, it seems to take on new significance. According to Ibn Daud, the revolt began in the days of Domitian under the leadership of a Jewish pretender by the name of Koziba. The latter succeeded in breaking free from Roman control and bequeathed his power to his son Rufus b. Koziba, who, in turn, was succeeded by his son Romulus. The revolt was crushed by the Romans in the days of "Hadrian,"[94] who put many of the leading rabbis of the generation to death. "All this happened to them . . . because of the provocation of Ben Koziba.

---

89 *MBSh*, f. 50a, 79a-b; cf. also Epilogue.167 f.
90 Wherever Ibn Daud cites Daniel it is in the specific context of some past event. On the other hand, when he wished to indicate those prophetic books whose promise is yet to be fulfilled he referred to Ezekiel and Zechariah, not to Daniel; *MBSh*, f. 79b.
91 Cf. above, p. 221. Note also his emphasis on Daniel's erroneous exegesis of Jeremiah; I.180 f. Ibn Daud doubtless objected to applications of Dan. 11.33 to events of his own age as had been done by Abraham b. Ḥiyya, *Megillat ha-Megalleh*, p. 100.
92 Cf. above, p. 219.; N. Cohn, *The Pursuit of the Millennium* (New York, 1961), pp. 33 f.
93 III.40 f. For the parallel account, see *ZDR*. For recent discussions, cf. end of S.N. to III.40.
94 Cf. III.48 and note there.

Then there was fulfilled for them what had been written by Daniel: 'And they that are wise among the people shall cause the many to understand; yet they shall stumble by the sword and by flame, by captivity and by spoil, many days.' "95

The great blunder of that generation headed by R. Akiba, Ibn Daud tells us, was the error of the wise, of the scholars, in allowing "the many to understand." That is, the wise had promulgated the signs of the end and thereby encouraged the people to act.96 Ibn Daud spells out what these signs were in an effort to account for the support which sages like R. Akiba tragically and ingenuously gave the perpetrator of a calamity only 52 years after the destruction of the Temple. The citation from Daniel clearly lays at least part of the blame for the tragedy on the sages, and Ibn Daud felt obligated to spell out the specific errors of judgment which they committed, in order to account for *their* behavior and as an admonition to his own generation. However, since these were among the outstanding rabbis of the talmudic period, Ibn Daud would hardly charge them in any way but with the most circumspect indirection.97 A frank discussion of the blunders which led R. Akiba to point at Ben Koziba with the statement, "This is the anointed king,"98 would have been an open invitation to Karaite attacks. Nevertheless, the errors Ibn Daud laid at the door of the rabbis become clear enough in the light of classical Jewish symbolism. The first erroneous assumption of that generation was that Rome was the fourth beast or empire which Daniel had seen in his vision.99 This error is explicable by reference to certain details of Roman history, which would seem to have indicated to the wise that the Rome of their generation was the long-awaited cosmocrator with the tell-tale marks of the final empire.

The rabbis knew very well, Ibn Daud said by implication, that Rome was destined to have two periods of royal dominion.100 The first was in the days of Romulus, while the second began in the days of Julius Caesar and came to full flower in the reign of Augustus. In explaining this view, Ibn Daud spoke of three architectural curiosities of Rome, of the ilk which had gained wide currency in his day in the *Mirabilia Urbis Romae*.101 The three antiquities were

---

95 III.63–68.
96 Cf. notes to III.65–68. That "allowing the many to understand" refers to the disclosure of the messianic date is suggested by Abraham bar Ḥiyya, *Megillat ha-Megalleh*, p. 100.
97 The blunder of the sages in general and of R. Akiba in particular is openly expressed by Maimonides, *Mishneh Torah*, Melakim, 11.3 (based, of course, on the Talmud).
98 *Yer*. Ta'an. 4.8, f. 68d; Midrash Ekah to 2.2 (and in ed. Buber, p. 101).
99 Cf. above, n. 62.
100 Cf. above, n. 13.
101 On the *sitz im leben* as well as popularity of the *Mirabilia* literature, see Schramm, *op. cit.*, I, 193 f., 293 f.; II, 45 f., 105 f. In view of Schramm's forceful arguments for a mid-

the *Meta Romuli*, the tomb of Julius Caesar (the Vatican obelisk), and the paving of the Tiber by Augustus.[102] On the face of things, these brief digressions seem innocuous enough, particularly for a man who had a cultivated interest in antiquity and etymology. Thus, the account of the paving of the Tiber is perfectly explicable in the light of Ibn Daud's desire to explain the origins of the Bronze Era current in Spain and in the light of *Josippon's* "erroneous" account of the marvel.[103]

However, the fact remains that Ibn Daud did not describe all the marvels known to him and his contemporaries, although he hinted at some of them elsewhere in his writings. Descriptions of many more such curiosities must have been available to him.[104] Consequently, his choice of three marvels connected with the three greatest figures of Roman history cannot be dismissed as pure coincidence. In the case of each of these personalities, Ibn Daud had carefully indicated his significance in connection with Roman *regnum* and its relationship to *imperium*. Romulus was the first Roman king, and he brought all of the west under Roman control. Julius Caesar restored the monarchy to Rome. Augustus ruled over all the world. It is, therefore, reasonable to assume that the very marvels associated with their names were meaningful, i.e., symbolic. That this was so Ibn Daud disclosed by the use of tell-tale words and phrases in connection with each phenomenon.[105]

> twelfth century date for the *Mirabilia*, I would not want to argue that Ibn Daud drew from a recension of that particular work. However, Ibn Daud's extended descriptions of these phenomena reflect twelfth-century tendencies generally in their concern with these specific antiquities and in their concern with the fantastic; cf. J.B. Ross, "A Study of the Twelfth-Century Interest in the Antiquities of Rome," *Medieval and Historiographical Essays in Honor of James Westfall Thompson*, ed. by J.L. Cate and E.N. Anderson (Chicago, 1938), pp. 302 f. and esp. 312 f. Cf. also J.W. Spargo, *Virgil the Necromancer* (Cambridge, 1934), pp. 36, 48, where the later Spanish "evolutions" of the marvels described by Ibn Daud are traced. For contemporary Jewish interest in such phenomena, cf. the renowned *Itinerary of Benjamin of Tudela*; F.P. Bargebuhr, "The Alhambra Palace of the Eleventh Century," *Journal of the Warburg and Courtauld Institutes*, XIX (1956), 227 f., 233 f.

102 IV.92 f., 116 f., 121 f.
103 Cf. *Josippon* 3 (ed. Hominer), p. 6.
104 Cf. *ibid.*, 2–3, pp. 3–6; *ZDR*, s.v. Commodus, on the Capitol.
105 I am not unmindful of the possible objection that our iconographic reading of Ibn Daud's history is totally unwarranted on two accounts: in the first place, Ibn Daud himself did not in any way hint that these descriptions were symbolic and were intended as anything other than purely factual accounts of phenomena that aroused his interest. Secondly, it may be asked, can another instance of such symbolism on the part of a medieval Jewish author be indicated? Indeed, everything should predispose us to doubt our proposed interpretation of Ibn Daud in view of the general Jewish remoteness from the world of pagan or Christian art, which was *tabu* to Judaism and therefore abhor-

After the death of Romulus, Ibn Daud tells us in the excursus on Rome and Persia, "the Romans paid him a great tribute by building a great cone over his grave. Its diameter was approximately fifty cubits at the base, while its perimeter extended to 120 cubits. At the top it narrowed into a sort of cone. This structure of great height stands intact in Rome until this very day."[106] The description of the edifice as narrowing into a dome or coned hut (Hebrew: *ṣerif*) is a clear allusion to the huts built by Romulus and Remus, according to talmudic legend, at the time that Jeroboam had set up the golden calves in Bethel and Dan.[107] On the other hand, the dimensions of the *meta* are described in phrases taken almost verbatim from the biblical description of "the Sea" that Solomon

> rent to devout Jews. Even if Ibn Daud himself had overcome Jewish inhibitions about artistic symbolism, would the point not have revolted, or at least been lost on, his Jewish audience? These objections, although real enough, are not very difficult to meet. Ibn Daud, it cannot be overemphasized, lived in a society where symbols and symbolism were part of the atmosphere. His own historiography, we have seen, was saturated with traditional Jewish symbolism, which he employed with originality and for his own purposes. Nothing prevented him from extending the field of his symbolism to phenomena outside the circle of traditional Jewish literature. Ibn Daud was careful to select items that could in no way offend religious sensibilities, for these structures were not religious ones; they were mere funerary monuments. Moreover, recent research has made it very likely that Ibn Daud was not the first Jew of his milieu to see symbolic significance in architectural curiosities. The study of F.P. Bargebuhr on the Alhambra palace, built by Joseph ibn Nagrela, and the poem by Solomon ibn Gabirol, possibly composed in honor of this Ibn Nagrela and his fortress, has made a highly convincing case at least for his contention that Solomonic symbolism, with its implications of power and rule, was very much on the mind of the Jewish courtier circle of which Ibn Daud was an offshoot; cf. n. 101. Ibn Daud's reading of works containing descriptions of these and other marvels—and descriptions of such marvels abounded in the literature of his day—or his discussion of them with learned men of his environment doubtless alerted him to the symbolic importance of round cities, domes, revolving palaces and the like; cf. H.P. L'Orange, *Studies on the Iconography of Cosmic Kingship in the Ancient World* (Oslo, 1953). Since the symbolism of these monuments dovetailed with little hints in rabbinic literature, he did not hesitate to use these accounts as symbolic of turning points in Roman history. In talmudic descriptions of the glory of Rome, it was the architectural and engineering achievement that impressed the rabbis, as indeed it has impressed so many others; cf. Krauss, "Griechen und Roemer," *Monumenta Talmudica*, pp. 10 f., 46 f. Finally, there is the indisputable fact that iconographic symbolism would have been well known to a rabbinically oriented Jew from Jewish literautre; cf. Ginzberg, *Legends*, III, 148 f. Ibn Daud was expatiating on a theme long since attested by classical Jewish authorities. It goes without saying that Ibn Daud's interpretation of these symbols need not necessarily reflect the interpretations of others of his environment; cf. the very apposite observations of E. Panofsky, *Renaissance and Renascences* (Stockholm, 1960), p. 84.

106 IV.91–95.
107 Cf. above, n. 14.

built for the Temple, except that the perimeter of *Meta Romuli* is four times the size of that of the Sea of Solomon.[108] Now a rabbinic midrash explained the Sea of Solomon as symbolic of world dominion and compared it to the ball or *globus* which emperors used as symbols of their authority.[109] In other words, Ibn Daud selected the earliest architectural marvel of Rome, significantly associated with its founder, because that edifice symbolized that first period of Roman monarchy and dominion over the west.

The second period of Roman glory was initiated by Julius Caesar, who wrested control of the empire from the Greeks and restored it to the Romans. In his honor the Romans called all subsequent rulers "Caesar," and "after his death accorded him an honor the like of which was never granted to any other king in the world: an exceedingly high tower with iron spits inserted at the base, which extended, branching out, to the top. Above them was a great casket of thick brass, and in it Julius was interred. This casket may be seen to this day."[110] Clearly, the honors which the Romans accorded Caesar were meant to be symbolic of, and commensurate with, his uniqueness. Indeed, other reports of Caesar's tomb described the casket at the summit of the obelisk as a ball, which again brings to mind the symbol of royalty.[111] Whether Ibn Daud omitted these details and substituted others, or adhered to the details given in his source, it is impossible to say. What is clear is that the wording of his description gives the impression of a tremendous hut or pyramid-like structure, thereby suggesting the second of the two Roman huts of talmudic legend. On the surface, Ibn Daud was merely restoring the historical foundations behind the talmudic legend. More subtly, he was indicating the reason for the supposed rabbinic equation of Julius Caesar with a cosmocrator.[112]

---

108   II Ki. 7.23.
109   Num. R. 13.12 (ed. Vilna, p. 106b and *seq.*). To be sure, it is hazardous to support an interpretation of Ibn Daud by reference to a passage in the first part of *Bemidbar Rabbah*, which at its earliest is not much older than *Sefer ha-Qabbalah*. Indeed, the style and content of the passage bear the tell-tale marks of R. Moses ha-Darshan and of the *Midrash Tadshe*, although I cannot locate this particular passage in any other work associated with these names; cf. A. Epstein, "Mi-Qadmoniot ha-Yehudim," *Kitbay R. Abraham Epstein*, 2 vols., ed. by A.M. Habermann (Jerusalem, 7510–5717), II, 64 f.; Moses ha-Darshan, *Midrash Bereshit Rabbati*, ed. by Ch. Albeck (Jerusalem, 1940), pp. 9 f. However, Ibn Daud could well have had access to this particular homily from some midrashic compilation no longer extant. This is all the more likely in view of the fact that this particular homily does not appear in the homiletical collections associated with Moses ha-Darshan and may, therefore, be independent of him. The symbolic character of certain figures like the globus or sphere was recorded in talmudic literature; *M.* A.Z. 3.1 and Talmuds, *ad loc.*, esp. *Yer.* A.Z. 3.1, f. 42c.
110   IV.115–119.   111   Cf. notes to IV.116–119.
112   On cosmocrators in Jewish literature, cf. Ginzberg, *Legends*, V, 199 f To be sure, Julius

The third marvel was erected by the very man who allegedly achieved dominion over the whole world, thereby giving the impression that Rome was the fourth empire: "Julius Caesar was succeeded by his brother's son, the emperor Augustus. It is said that he ruled over the whole world. In the fourth year of his reign, he imposed a tribute of bronze on the whole world, Then he paved the Tiber River, on which Rome is situated, for twenty miles with very thick plates of bronze, although the river was very wide. To this day they continue to reckon according to the Bronze Era. The Romans possess many books in which his praises and wisdom are recounted. They also claim that there never was a king like him in any nation in the world. In the thirty-eighth year of his reign Jesus the Nazarene was born, for he ruled for fifty-two years over an empire that extended over the whole world; so they say."[113]

Note how many times within one paragraph Ibn Daud stressed what "they say" or what "they claim" about his rule, implying his doubts about what the Gentile historians say.[114] Note, too, that in the final instance he used a phrase for absolute dominion that is used in the Talmud as a sign prefiguring the messianic era.[115] Note, again, how blandly Ibn Daud reported that Jesus of Nazareth was born in the reign of Augustus, though he repeatedly insisted elsewhere that this is untrue.[116] Obviously, some early tannaim had seen in the various signs of Augustus' reign clear proof that his rule was a sign of the impending end. In the first place, they had erroneously believed that Jesus, the incarnation of evil, must have been born just before the "end."[117] Secondly, the Gentile historians had openly claimed that Augustus was a cosmocrator and that there was a connection between his world-wide dominion and the birth of Jesus.[118]

Finally, the Jews had been misled by the demonstrable proof which Augustus gave of his rule when he built a marvel symbolizing his *cosmocratia*, for Augustus paved the Tiber with bronze. Of course, the tribute exacted from the

> Caesar is nowhere specifically mentioned among them; but since Rome as a whole was, Ibn Daud could easily have attributed to the tannaim the view that the man who first established Rome as a cosmocratia was a world-ruler.

113 IV.120-129.
114 Cf. also II.95 f.
115 Cf. S.N. to IV.129.
116 II.95 f.
117 That the ultimate enemy of God would arise just before the end was, of course, a basic notion in all messianic theory; cf. Even-Shmuel, *op. cit*,. pp. 31 f.; W. Bousset, *The Antichrist Legend*, tr. by A.H. Keane (London, 1896).
118 Cf. T.H. Mommsen, *Medieval and Renaissance Studies*, ed. by E.F. Rice, Jr. (Ithaca, 1959), pp. 278, 282 f., 308 f. Cf. also our note to IV.127-128, from which it will be seen that Ibn Daud may have deliberately distorted a chronological datum in order to date the birth of Jesus from the time of Augustus' cosmocratia.

whole world in itself demonstrated the extent of Augustus' authority. However, Ibn Daud trusted his readers to recall that according to rabbinic lore another king with cosmocratic pretentions, Nebuchadnezzar, had buried the treasures of the world at the bottom of the Euphrates in bronze ships.[119] Bronze at the bottom of a river was thus a figure of speech for a pretender to world rule. Ibn Daud had merely tailored the details of classical symbolism to convey his own point.

Having established, as it were, that Rome had mainfested some marks characteristic of a cosmocrator in the days of the early tannaim, Ibn Daud proceeded to enumerate the other presumed signs, which would account for the egregious miscalculation of the generation of R. Akiba and his colleagues. A striking point about Ibn Daud's account of the Bar Kokba revolt is the chronology of the event. Although talmudic sources always spoke of the persecution as having occurred in the days of Hadrian,[120] Ibn Daud corrected the tradition and relocated the beginning of the insurrection in the days of Domitian. Now, after all the evidence that has been adduced to show the import of chronology, and particularly of unattested chronology, in the writing of Ibn Daud, it is a fair assumption that the chronological deviation in this case too is of symbolic significance.

The fourth beast in Daniel's vision, it will be recalled, had ten horns and an eleventh little one which sprouted among them. According to classical interpretations, Daniel's vision indicated that the end of time would be ushered in only after the rule of ten kings of the fourth empire.[121] Since Ibn Daud had emphasized that Julius Caesar was the first of the kings of Rome during its second period of monarchy, his history of Rome supplied the names of the other nine: Augustus, Tiberius, Gaius, Claudius, Nero, Galba, Vespasian, Titus, Domitian. The eleventh little horn was probably equated with Nerva, who ruled but one year. Ibn Daud, accordingly, stressed that Koziba rose in the days

---

119 Ginzberg, *Legends*, IV, 367; H.L. Ginsberg, *Studies in Daniel* (New York, 1948), p. 75 n. 7.
120 They have been collected and analyzed by S. Lieberman, "The Martyrs of Caesarea," *Annuaire de l'Institut de Philologie et d'Histoire Orientales et Slaves*, VII (1939–1944), 423 f.; Alon, *Toledot*, II, 42 f.
121 See the recensions of *Sefer Zerubbabel* in Even-Shmuel, *op. cit.*, pp. 382, 384. Even-Shmuel's text on p. 76 is based on the second recension. Although the two versions disagree on what exactly will be performed by the tenth king—for that matter, by the ten kings—the fact is that in both recensions the number 70, based on Dan. 7.7, plays a basic rule. —I do not mean to imply that this interpretation of the ten kings was *the* official one. Obviously, there are no official interpretations in such aggadic matters, and other views were current. What is relevant is that Ibn Daud had the theory, put forth here, available to him in a text that by his time had gained classical stature.

of the tenth king, Domitian, but only *assumed the throne* after the death of Nerva, i.e., after the conditions of the end had been fulfilled.[122]

At this point, Ibn Daud turned to the interpretation of details in the rabbinic accounts of the revolt. According to most rabbinic sources the revolt against Rome was led by "Ben Koziba," the son of Koziba.[123] However, in one or two passages R. Akiba is cited as calling him simply "Koziba."[124] This was all the more plausible to Ibn Daud, for the name Koziba suggested "impostor," and if there was a King Son-of-the-Impostor, it stands to reason that there had been an original King Impostor, Koziba. Hence, it came about that Ibn Daud designated Koziba as the first of the Jewish rulers.

The name of the second of the Jewish rulers was Rufus, which, Ibn Daud made a point of explaining, means "red" or "ruddy."[125] Now there are only two personages in the Bible who are described as "ruddy," and they are Esau and David (Gen. 25.25; I Sam. 16.12). Obviously, Ibn Daud reasoned, it was fitting that a messianic pretender, who had set himself up against Edom, the children of ruddy Esau (as Rome was known in rabbinic Hebrew), should look like the reincarnation of the Judean anointed of the Lord, David the ruddy. Moreover, Rufus' son was named Romulus, and the men of that generation would doubtless have thought it most fitting that Armilus (Romulus) should be destroyed by the Romulus of Israel; for did not the latter's very name signify kingship and conquest![126]

To be sure, Ibn Daud did not create this fantasy *ex nihilo*. Ibn Daud's story represents a distortion of generally accepted and known facts that are clearly discernible behind his tale. The statement that the revolt began in the days of Domitian reflects the Christian report that Domitian had attempted to wipe out the remnants of the house of David because of his fear of a messianic uprising.[127] Ibn Daud was doubtless familiar with this story, inasmuch as Christian polemicists invoked it as proof of the revocation of the divine

---

122 *ZDR*. It will be noted that in the account in III.41 f. Ibn Daud does not say that Ben Koziba began to reign in the days of Domitian, but merely that he revolted in his days. In *ZDR*, he explicitly begins the reign of Ben Koziba in the days of Nerva.

123 Seder 'Olam 30 (ed. Ratner), p. 146 and parallels. Ratner, n. 80 there, calls attention to the variant reading *Bet Koziba*, the house of Koziba, in the transcription of *Yalqut Shim'oni*.

124 *Yer.* Ta'an. 4 f. 68d; Midrash Ekah (Buber) p. 101. One wonders if Ibn Daud found further support for his contention that there was a Koziba, who was to be distinguished from Ben Koziba, in the talmudic report of "Kozibian coins," *B.B.K.* 97b, i.e., assuming that Ibn Daud was aware that these were coins of the Ben Koziba regime; cf. also previous note.

125 III.45.

126 Cf. above, pp. 244 f.

127 Eusebius, *Ecclesiastical History*, III, xix.

covenant with the Jews.[128] The Jewish king Rufus is clearly an adaptation and appropriation of the Roman governor, Tineius Rufus, who, Eusebius reports, led the war against the Jews and then subjugated the country.[129] Finally, Ibn Daud combined this data with the popular eschatological folklore on the symmetry of the Christ and Antichrist. According to these traditions, the false messiah would resemble the true one in a sufficient number of characteristics so as to deceive the people. Hence, he posed Rufus versus Edom and Romulus against the kingdom of Armilus. He was also doubtless acquainted with the Arabic name for the Antichrist, *al-Dajjal* or the Deceiver, who had red frizzy hair and combined many of the features of Gog and Magog and of the Christian Antichrist. It is no coincidence that Ibn Daud's first leader of the uprising is a man whose name is an Aramaic-Hebrew synonym for *al-Dajjal*, "the Impostor."[130] Thus, Ibn Daud's account of the Bar Kokba uprising is a highly doctored version of the Jewish and Christian ones, but one which was fashioned out of older materials and on the basis of beliefs that had gained wide currency.

How and why did Ibn Daud arrive at the conclusion that the Jewish revolt in the days of R. Akiba had endured during the reigns of *three* Jewish kings? This theory, I venture to suggest, was elicited from exegesis of the oracle of Balaam. It was a verse in Balaam's prophecy that R. Akiba had applied to Bar Kokba.[131] If we re-examine that verse along with the others that follow it (Num. 24.17, 19), and scrutinize the older exegesis of this oracle, I suggest that we can detect the traces of the midrash which provided Ibn Daud with the evidence that the Jews would be ruled by three kings in the last war with Rome. This exegesis, which we have inserted in brackets, probably read something like this: "*A star rises from Jacob* [Koziba], *a meteor comes forth from Israel* [Rufus ben Koziba] ... *A victor issues from Jacob* [Romulus ben Rufus ben Koziba] *to wipe out what is left of the city* [of Rome]."[132]

128 Cf. Blumenkranz, *Les Auteurs Chrétiens*, p. 93, for Isidore of Seville; Otto of Freising, *Chronica*, III.19; Posnanski, *Schiloh*, pp. 302 f.

129 Eusebius, *Eccles. History*, IV, vi; on the name "Rufus," cf. E. Schuerer, *Geschichte des Juedischen Volkes* I (3rd ed. Leipzig, 1901), 647 f.

130 Cf. Bousset, *op. cit.*, pp. 29, 134 f., 162; 176 f.; Gibb and Kramers, *Shorter Encyclopaedia of Islam*, p. 67.

131 Cf. above, n. 98.

132 That Balaam foresaw the rise of two great kings in Israel is attested by an old midrash, the original source of which I do not know, but which is quoted virtually identically by such unconnected sources as Rashi, *ad loc.*; Maimonides, *Mishneh Torah*, Melakim 11.1; *Midrash Haggadol, Numbers*, 2 vols., ed. by S. Fisch (London-Jerusalem, 1957–63), II, 193 f. However, other traditions also interpreted the whole verse messianically; cf. R. Akiba in *Yer*. Ta'an. 4, f. 68d; Deut. R. 1.20. Ibn Daud could have easily coalesced the two traditions and read two messianic kings into the first verse and a third king (cf. Rashi) into v. 19. Cf. also Nahmanides, "Sefer ha-Geulah," p. 266 and the note by

Once the midrashic-symbolic character of this historical fantasy is acknowledged, all the other phenomena which Ibn Daud associated with the tragedy fall into place. In the days of Hadrian, Ibn Daud reports, there were violent earthquakes in Greece and Asia, along with other heavenly portents that made people believe "that the Lord was of a mind to destroy the world."[133] These heavenly portents, a stock theme in eschatological literature,[134] obviously must have influenced the thinking of R. Akiba; for had he not quoted Haggai 2.6, perhaps in connection with Bar Kokba: "Once again, in a little while, I will shake the heavens and the earth and the sea and the dry land!"[135] Finally, Ben Koziba succeeded in rallying to his banner Jews from all over the world, a phenomenon predicted by Jewish and Christian literature of the Christ and Antichrist.[136] All these phenomena duped the generation and led to the costly blunder of men who, alas, had not understood that their very tragedy had long since been foreseen by Daniel.[137]

To sum up this analysis, Ibn Daud's excursus on Roman antiquity turned traditional symbolism on its head. The signs of medieval eschatological literature had been tragically invoked in the past when the time seemed ripe. The implication was obvious that, if so great a man as R. Akiba had misjudged the signs, Ibn Daud's generation should not presume that it could predict on a matter in which R. Akiba had erred. Ibn Daud thus became *Josippon's* standard-bearer par excellence.[138]

C. *Edom Rediscovered*

Of course, Ibn Daud could not let matters rest at this point. He himself had set consolation of his people as the driving principle behind all of his work. Moreover, he vigorously protested against those who undermined the morale of

    I.M. Aronson in his edition of this work (Jerusalem, 1958), p. 16 n. 88. It is interesting to note that even the Dead Sea Sect understood the star and the meteor of Num. 24.17 as two different persons; cf. *Scroll of the War of the Sons of Light Against the Sons of Darkness* [Hebrew], ed. by Y. Yadin (Jerusalem, 1955), pp. 194 n. 58, 322.6–7 and Yadin's notes thereto.

133 *ZDR*. To be sure, the same portents are reported by Orosius, *Apology* VII.12, with the same overtones, namely that the portents stimulated the Jews to their madness.

134 Cf. Ezek. 38.19; Joel 4.15–16; Hag. 2.6–7; Zech. 14.4 f.; Even-Shmuel, pp. 42, 87; Bousset, 238 f.; L. Ginzberg, "Mabul shel Esh," *ha- Goren* VIII (1914), 35–51, reprinted in L. Ginzberg, '*Al Halakah wa-Aggadah* (Tel Aviv, 1960), pp. 235 f.; Baron, *SRH*, VI, 45 f. That Ibn Daud himself regarded earthquakes and divine portents as a sign of the end is clear from his sermon on Zechariah; *MBSh*, f. 79b.

135 B. *Sanhed.* 97b.

136 Even-Shmuel, *op. cit.*, pp. 43 f.; 52; Bousset, *op. cit.*, pp. 25, 28, 167, 191 f.

137 III.65 f.   138 Cf. above, p. xxxix.

the community by claiming that all of the prophecies of consolation had already been fulfilled. If it were true that the prophecies had been fulfilled there would be no point in continuing adherence to Judaism in the face of Christian and Muslim claims that the path to redemption lay elsewhere. Side by side with his disqualification of certain classical theories, he therefore put forth an esoteric message of messianic hope of his own, indicating that the best was yet to come—indeed, might well be right around the corner.

As indicated earlier, the first aspect of this message of hope is a complex schematology of Jewish history which was to culminate in the year 1189.[139] The second and quite explicit statement that the good had not yet been realized came in a brief statement at the beginning and end of his history of the Second Temple. To these brief affirmations, Ibn Daud added documentary support by incorporating *in toto* a little tract known as the *Midrash on the Ten Exiles*.[140] Whatever the original date of this tract, which enumerated the "ten exiles" the Jews had suffered, by the ninth century it had achieved official recognition and had been cited by R. Ṣemaḥ Gaon in connection with that bizarre character, Eldad ha-Dani.[141] In the context of Ibn Daud's work it served a twofold purpose. Primarily, it gave assurance that the ten major exiles which the Jews were destined to endure had already come to pass and that, accordingly, no future ones need be feared. Secondly, the account of the last of the exiles, that of Hadrian, indicated that many exiles were driven to Spain, thus fulfilling the prophecy of Obadiah (v. 20): "The captivity of Jerusalem that is in Sepharad [=Spain] shall possess the cities of the South." Since the same verse which spoke of the exile of Spain assured that the exiles of that quarter would inherit the land of Judah, the consolation to Ibn Daud's immediate audience was evident.[142]

---

139   Cf. Analysis, ch. III.
140   *MBSh*, f. 77b–79a. For editions, cf. Kasher and Mandelbaum, *Sarei ha-Elef*, p. 35 n. 35.
141   A. Epstein, *Kitbay*, I, 40.
142   On the "South" as Judah, cf. Daniel al-Kumissi, *Commentarius in Librum Duodecim Prophetarum*, ed. by I.D. Markon (Jerusalem, 1957), p. 40; Kimhi to Obad. 20. This interpretation dovetails perfectly with Ibn Daud's stress on the Judean origins of the Ibn Ezra family; cf. below, ch. V.—To be sure, the *Midrash 'Eser Galuyot* is not the only text that spoke of the exile to Spain; cf. Seder 'Olam Zuta in Neubauer, *Medieval Jewish Chronicles*, II, 71; Lazarus, *Die Haeupter der Vertriebenen*, p. 162. However, the theme of ten exiles had assumed eschatological overtones, for there was a widely held view that the redemption would only follow the completion of ten calamities (based of course, on Dan. 7.7.); cf. Even-Shmuel, *op. cit.*, pp. 311–323; Bousset, *op. cit.*, pp. 98 f. The schematic character of the parallel Christian theory of ten persecutions was noted by Edward Gibbon, *Decline and Fall of the Roman Empire*, ch. XVI, text to n. 105 (Modern Library ed. I, 447; Bury ed. II, 108).

The full implication of this message of consolation is, I believe, the burden of the last portion of Ibn Daud's history of Rome. Toward the end of this little tract, Ibn Daud abandoned the history of the Roman Caesars very abruptly and shifted all his attention to Spain. He then proceeded to recount the story of the Gothic invasions and of the subsequent Christianization of the country. Once again, Ibn Daud is best represented by direct quotation: "Honorius Caesar lived six years and died. In his days the people of Uz, i.e., the Goths, entered Spain in three groups: Vandals, Alans and Suevi. (It is after the Vandals that Spain is called Andalus.) They seized the country from a people known as Ispan [Hispani], after whom the country has been called Espania [Hispania], who were descended from Tubal the son of Japheth. The Uzides defeated them, wiped them out, and settled in their place."[143]

This little statement on the genealogy of the early inhabitants of Spain is most significant, for it established by historical "evidence" the fact that Christian Spain may be classified as an offshoot of the seed of Edom. Ibn Daud had to do this on two mutually contradictory accounts. On the one hand, he had inherited the traditional view, affirmed in Scripture and reaffirmed by the rabbis, that the final war, the one inaugurating the messianic era, would be with the armies of Edom.[144] On the other hand, as an Andalusian, and like Ibn Ezra, he subscribed to the scientific Andalusian exegetical ethnology which indicated that Rome was not originally of the seed of Edom.[145] Accordingly, in an effort to rescue the rabbinic identification of Rome with Edom, the Andalusians had come up with a novel theory. Rome was basically of the same family of peoples as the Greeks, Japhethides and offshoots of the Kittim. However, Constantine had merely adopted the religion of the priests of Edom, i.e., Christianity, and grafted it on to the Roman way of life. Hence, the name of Edom could be applied to Rome, albeit only secondarily, as a consequence of Constantine's conversion.[146] The same stricture would seem to hold true for Spain, for Ibn Daud clearly indicated in his history of Rome that the "Torah of Edom," i.e., Christianity, did not become the official religion of Spain until long after the Gothic invasion, in the days of Reccared. However, a closer examination of the facts, Ibn Daud indicated, will reveal that the name of Edom actually applied to the peoples of Spain far more than it did originally to the Romans.

---

143 *ZDR*; for the genealogy, cf. Isidore, *Etymologiae* (ed. Lindsay) IX, 2.29; Ps.-Isidore, *Historia*, *MGH*, AA, XI, 379; al-Himyari apud Lévi-Provençal, *La péninsule Ibérique*, French tr., pp. 3, 25 f.
144 Cf. Obad. 15 f., and cf. above, n. 76.
145 Cf. *ibid*.
146 Cf. J. Rosenthal, "The Law of Usury Relating to Non-Jews" [in Hebrew], *Talpioth*, VI (1953), 141 f.; Halkin's note in Maimonides, *Epistle to Yemen*, p. 14 n. 15.

Since the Goths were descendants of Uz, they were of authentic Edomite stock,[147] and in coming to Spain Christianity had finally returned to its native and rightful soil. Ibn Ezra's contention that the Jews of his day were not dwelling in the exile of Edom was now shown to be null and void. The Jews of Spain *were* in Edom, and not merely figuratively. They were living in the very midst of the seed of the ancestral enemy of the house of Jacob, the children of Esau.[148]

Here was a twofold consolation for Spanish Jewry. Edom had been rediscovered, and the Jews dwelling within it would be the first to enjoy the consolation of Obadiah. Indeed, the Jews of Spain were dwelling in the very land where the third and fourth empires of Daniel's visions, Esau and Ishmael, were already locked in a battle to the death. It may be noted in this connection that medieval ethnologists and apocalyptists had often identified the Goths with the biblical Gog and Magog, the appearance of whom, according to Jewish as well as Christian theory, would precede the arrival of the ultimate Antichrist, Armilus.[149] Although Ibn Daud patently rejected this classification of the Goths, he was not alone in considering Spain as the scene of the events of the last days. Prof. Yitzhak Baer has called attention to the significant role which the symbols of Edom and Ishmael played in Judah ha-Levi's messianic dreams and how great the likelihood is that the assumption of the title "*imperator totius Hispaniae*" by Alfonso VII in 1126 played a major role in his speculation on the date of the end. Baer has also called attention to the messianic ferment which spread in a number of Jewish circles, the outstanding examples being the astrological prediction by Johannes Avedahut of Toledo on the coming of the end in 1186-87, and Abraham bar Ḥiyya's exegetical-astrological *Megillat ha-Megalleh*.[150] In this connection, we note that Abraham bar Ḥiyya

---

147 See Gen. 36.28 and esp. Lam. 4.21. The identification of the Goths with the children of Uz derives from the Arabic spelling, الغرط; Levi della Vida, "La Traduzione Araba," p. 268 n. Uz is, to be sure, also a name of Arameans; Gen. 10.23 and esp. Gen. 22.21. However, in view of Lam. 4.21, the more common association with Uz as a gentilic would inevitably be with the Edomites; cf. Ibn Ezra to Job 1.1. Cf. further L. Zunz, *Die Synagogale Posesie des Mittelalters*, 2nd ed., ed. by A. Freimann (Frankfurt a.M., 1920), p. 455.

148 The seed, not the present name of a nation, is, of course, what counts; cf. Maimonides, *Guide*, II.29 (tr. Pines, p. 342).

149 Bousset, *op. cit.*, pp. 194 f.; cf. also Isidore, *Etymologiae*, IX, 1.89. Alfonso X el Sabio, *Primera Cronica General de España*, 2 vols., ed. by R. Menedez Pidal *et al.* (Madrid, 1955), I. 5.41 f.; O.A. Machado, "La Historia de Los Godos Segun Ibn Jaldun," *Cuadernos de Historia de España*, I–II (1955), 147.

150 F. Baer, "Eine juedische Messiasprophetie auf das Jahr 1186 und der dritte Kreuzzug," *MGWJ*, LXX (1926); 113 f.; *idem*, "The Political Situation," p. 20; *idem*, *History*, I, 66 f. Cf. also Halkin's introduction to Maimonides, *Epistle to Yemen*, pp. xxix f.

suggested in his work that God's real motive in driving the Jewish people into exile and keeping them there was to permit them to increase their numbers—the dead as well as the living—until they should have attained a number sufficient to occupy the lands to which they had been exiled. At that point the Almighty would destroy the Gentiles, quicken the dead, and hand over the lands of the Gentiles to the Jews![151] Although this event was prudently cast for the remote date of 1448, the implication was clear. The Jews of Spain would have no need to cross land and sea to enter the Holy Land. The whole process of redemption could take place in Leon, Aragon and Castile.

One further aspect of the setting in which Ibn Daud's symbolism was conceived was the increased interest in Spanish circles in the mythological origins of the Spanish Christians. In the thirteenth century the Spanish historian and archbishop of Toledo, Ximenez de Rada, known as Toledano, invoked the myth of Hercules' arrival in Spain in order to link the antiquity of Spain with the classical world—an effort which a modern student of Toledano, R. B. Tate, has associated with the political aspirations of Christian Spain. Tate cogently notes that myths of origin were not mere fancy; they were projections of a political image.[152] Ibn Daud, writing somewhat earlier, thus already reflected the concern with Spanish history which was to engage other Hebrew literati not much later.

Not the least revealing feature of the message of Ibn Daud's tract on Roman history is the way in which he referred to his work: *Zikron Dibray Romi*, the History of Rome. The fact that the center of attention of this tract shifts very abruptly from Rome to Spain and remains fixed on Spain to the conclusion of the book indicates that in Ibn Daud's view Spain was the authentic continuation of ancient Rome. The Spanish claim to succession, Ibn Daud's *Zikron* explained, was legitimized through the marriage alliance concluded between Theodosius and the king of Uz, to which the former had agreed after the king of Uz had conquered all of the territory of Spain claimed by Rome. Sisebut Caesar was thus in the direct line of succession to Theodosius and Marcianus.[153]

---

151 Abraham bar Ḥiyya, *Megillat ha-Megalleh*, pp. 76 f., 110.
152 R.B. Tate, "Mythology in Spanish Historiography of the Middle Ages and the Renaissance," *Hispanic Review*, XXII (1954), 1 f.
153 *ZDR*. The howler which Ibn Daud committed in passing from Marcianus to Sisebut is really an intelligible homioteleuton, if one but compares the texts of Isidore's *Chronicon* and *ZDR*. Ibn Daud's *source* had skipped from Marcianus to the somewhat similar name of Mauricius, in whose reign Leander of Seville and Gregory the Great flourished; cf. Isidore, *Chronicon* (Mommsen), *MGH*, *AA*, XI, 472 par. 380–477 par. 408a–b. The epitomist of Isidore's *Chronicon*, who served as Ibn Daud's source, finding a reference to Leander but none to Isidore, then appropriately inserted the latter's name. Subsequently, the statement on Sisebut and Muhammad was advanced to a position following Marcia-

THE FOUR EMPIRES AND JEWISH HISTORY 255

Spain was thus not only the new home of the people of Edom; it was on Spanish soil that Edom and Rome had been reunited.

In identifying Spain as the authentic heir of Edom and Rome, Ibn Daud apparently drew support for his Jewish aspirations from the sentiments of Spanish nationalists that Spain was not subject to the jurisdiction of the Holy Roman Empire and its imperial authority. Spain, the Spanish theoreticians claimed, was independent of the Empire, for it had been Gothic country and as such was beyond imperial jurisdiction. In indicating the specific steps by which Spain became Romanized, Ibn Daud was echoing the formal Visigothic genealogies invoked by the kings of Leon and Asturia in support of their claims to being the rightful heirs to the dominion of Christian Spain. The nationalist as well as the religious overtones of this neo-Gothic tradition, intimately bound up with the name of Isidore of Seville (with whose activity Ibn Daud concluded his survey of Roman history),[154] were given renewed emphasis and vitality in the latter part of the eleventh century, when the prelates of Santiago de Compostela joined forces with the rulers of Castile to claim their respective independence of, and equality with, the see of Peter and the Holy Roman Empire. Ibn Daud's seemingly innocent meanderings into the

---

nus, since once the name of Mauricius had been omitted, the next known Gothic ruler was Sisebut. Accordingly, the latter was put after Marcianus with Isidore and Leander under his reign, yielding a text which read: "Sisebut Caesar ruled after him. During his reign, Muhammad came into the world. Moreover, in his reign Gregory, a great philosopher, was bishop of Rome. In his reign there lived in Spain Isidore and Leander both of whom were bishops in the city of Seville. The name of his city was Luciliardus [sic!]." The last statement is unintelligible. However, in the Epitome Ovetensis of 883 of Isidore's *Chronicon*, one of the achievements of Sisebut's reign is summarized as follows: "*Ecclesiam quoque sanctae Leocadiae Toledo mire fundavit*" (*ibid.*, p. 480 no. 416a). Since the word for "monastery" in Arabic is دير, Ibn Daud's source probably had a datum in conjunction with the reign of Sisebut stating: واسم ديره لوقدية. However, while the statement on Sisebut was shifted to its present position, the datum on Leocadia was left in its original place, resulting in the sequence we now have in *ZDR*. A copyist probably mistook دار for دير, which *ZDR* translated as עירו, "his seat." I also cannot help feeling that the name Leocadia had been corrupted under the influence of a learned copyist, who, not knowing of any connection between Leander and the church of St. Leocadia, corrected the name to Lucinianus, which is the name appearing after that of Leander in Isidore's *De Viris Illustribus* (Migne, *PL* 83:1103–04), and which became Luciliardus in Hebrew.

154 On the dominating influence of Isidore of Seville in medieval Spain, see the summaries by various scholars in *Miscellanea Isidoriana* (Rome, 1936), pp. 151 f., 221 f. and esp. 323 f.; *Isidoriana*, ed. by M.C. Diaz y Diaz (Leon, 1961), pp. 60 f., 317 f. and esp. 345 f., 401 f.

history of Visigothic Spain become clear when viewed against the background of the Spanish-Christian drives and claims of his own day.

It is by now a commonplace that the protagonists of the Spanish Reconquista adopted and re-emphasized religious and political forms which gave expression to the theory that the lands held by the Muslims of Spain were rightfully Christian, and therefore unlawfully occupied by the Saracens. Particularly prominent among these public gestures was the deliberate adoption of Visigothic usages in the ceremonies of government as well as in the symbolism of the Spanish Church.[155] Moreover, kings who succeeded in expanding their hegemony over more than one province began to adopt the pretentious titles of *imperator* and *magnus rex*.[156] It is questionable whether in the early part of the tenth century the title of *imperator* actually represented imperial aspirations, as maintained by Menendez Pidal, or was merely symbolic of an expanded territorial hegemony or even only of military leadership, as suggested by Schramm. The fact is, however, that these titles did not remain isolated signs of possible imperial dreams.[157] Contemporaneously, the leadership of the Church of Santiago de Compostela began to lay claims to a religious authority that paralleled and complemented the claims of the temporal rulers. Thus in 954, Ordoño III, who himself adopted the title of *imperator* as well as other highly pretentious nomenclature, addressed the bishop of Compostela as "*antistes totius orbis*." Twenty years later, the bishop of the same Church went a step further and proclaimed his office an "*apostolica sedes*."[158] In 992, Bishop Arnulf of Orleans buttressed these episcopal claims by contending openly that the Spanish Church was independent of the jurisdiction of Rome.[159] To the claims of the papacy that only Rome merited the title of "apostolic see" because of the commission of St. Peter, and as a consequence had the right of magistracy over all of Christendom,[160] the hierarchy of Compostela retorted that its own seat derived its authority not from Rome but from the apostle

---

155 H. Hueffer, "Die leonesischen Hegemoniebestrebungen und Kaisertitel," *Spanische Forschungen der Goerresgesellschaft*, Erste Reihe, III (1931), 341; R. Menendez Pidal, *El Imperio Hispanico y los Cinco Reinos* (Madrid, 1950), pp. 21 f., 25 f.; M. Defourneaux, *Les Français en Espagne aux xi et xii siècles* (Paris, 1949), p. 13.

156 Hueffer, *op. cit.*, pp. 346 ff.; Menendez Pidal, *El Imperio Hispanico*, pp. 34, 48 f., 58, 66.

157 *Ibid.*, pp. 11, 28 f.; idem, *La España del Cid*, 5th ed., 2 vols. (Madrid, 1956), I, 24 f., 55 f. P.E. Schramm, "Das Kastilische Koenigtum und Kaisertum waehrend der Reconquista," *Festschrift fuer Gerhard Ritter* (Tuebingen, 1950), p. 91.

158 Hueffer, *op. cit.*, p. 355; Menedez Pidal, *El Imperio Hispanico*, pp. 49 f.

159 Schramm, *Kaiser, Rom u. Renovatio*, I, 123.

160 For a systematic history of this claim, cf. W. Ullmann, *The Growth of Papal Government in the Middle Ages*, 2nd ed. (New York, 1962), and see esp. pp. 5 f., 192 f.

James the son of Zebedee and, therefore, had sole jurisdiction over itself.[161] On December 23, 1063, Ferdinand of Castile, who may have styled himself *imperator magnus*, ceremoniously brought the remains of Isidore of Seville—the arch-symbol of the Gothic tradition of Spanish Christendom—to rest in Leon, the city where Spanish imperial coronations were celebrated.[162]

The papacy obviously could not watch the steady growth of these Spanish pretensions with equanimity. In an age when the Church of Rome was reemphasizing its claim that only he who had been crowned by the pope merited the title of *imperator*,[163] the increased tempo in the revitalization of the Visigothic tradition and the adoption of imperial titles inevitably evoked protests from Rome. In 1049, Pope Leo IX formally excommunicated the bishop of Compostela for his appropriation of the apostolic title. However, the anathema had no effect. Legates of Rome in Spain were treated with such undisguised abuse that Pope Gregory VII threatened Alfonso VI with a punitive war to be led personally by himself. Relations between the two were strained even further when shortly after his accession Gregory VII proclaimed Petrine jurisdiction over all lands conquered from the Saracens. There can be little doubt, therefore, that the adoption by Alfonso VI in 1077—eight years before the conquest of Toledo—of the new title *imperator totius Hispaniae* was at least in part a retort to the Roman curia.[164]

To be sure, thanks to the vigorous activity of the Cluniac representatives of the Church of Rome, Spanish nativism did not go unchecked. The Visigothic tradition was severely shaken by the abolition of the Mozarabic rite and the institution of the Ordo Romanus as the sole liturgical form. With the transfer of the capital from Leon to Toledo, a papal legate was attached to the new capital, and in 1102 a Cluniac monk was made archbishop of the city and primate of all of Spain.[165] The reinvigorated concept of "Romanitas" as synonymous with orthodox Christendom had made successful inroads into

---

[161] Hueffer, *op. cit.*, p. 361; Schramm, "Das Kastilische Koenigtum," p. 102 for bibliography on the cult of St. James.

[162] Hueffer, *op. cit.*, pp. 357 f.; Menendez Pidal, *El Imperio Hispanico*, p. 88; idem, *España del Cid*, I, 135 f.; II, 669 f., 706; A. Vinayo Gonzalez, "Cuestiones Historico-Criticas en Torno a las Traslacion del Cuerpo de San Isidoro," *Isidoriana*, pp. 285-297.

[163] Ullmann, *op. cit.*, p. 270 n. 2.

[164] Hueffer, *op. cit.*, pp. 355, 361 f.; Schramm, "Das Kastilische Koenigtum," pp. 94 f., 102 f.; Ullmann, *op. cit.*, p. 304; Menendez Pidal, *España de Cid*, II, 726 f.; idem, *El Imperio Hispanico*, pp. 101 f. On the decline of papal power in the tenth and first half of the eleventh centuries, see Ullmann, ch. VIII (pp. 229-61).

[165] Hueffer, *op. cit.*, pp. 361 f.; Defourneaux, *op. cit.*, pp. 18f., 32.

Spain and brought the country's oligarchy into the framework of Roman religious authority.[166]

On the other hand, the countervailing tendencies of Spanish nativism did not fall by the wayside. In 1088, the bishop of Compostela was still asserting the title expressive of his episcopal authority.[167] In 1111, the bishop of the same see crowned the young Alfonso VII in a ceremony that was clearly meant to rival the coronation of a Holy Roman emperor, and subsequently followed this up with further ceremonies that were no less symbolic of independent authority. Although in 1135 Alfonso VII himself cleverly initiated a ceremonious coronation of his own and thus independently legitimized his new title "*dei gracia totius Hispaniae imperator*," not only did he not strip Compostela of its pristine rights, but he even conferred new dignities on it with specifically political overtones.[168] By means of dexterous maneuvering and compromise, Compostela, while outwardly submitting to the papacy, actually gained even greater authority within Spain during Alfonso's reign. In any event, in the eyes of the Spanish nobility, the Emperador was master of the situation and had strengthened the political and imperial stature of "mother Spain." The political effort of the papacy in Castile had failed completely. By falling into line with Rome formally, Alfonso VII managed to draw the curia to the support of his own political supremacy and to persuade it to make the archbishopric of the former Gothic capital, Toledo, the supreme authority of Spansh Christendom. Thus Alfonso VII, the Emperador, brought Spanish imperial dreams to a climax.[169]

Although after the death of Alfonso VII in 1157 the power of the Castilian court suffered severe setbacks, the theory of Spanish independence did not. Spanish historiography and literature of the first half of the thirteenth century gave new expression to the Isidorian ideal of the indivisibility of Spain.[170] The theory of Spanish independence of the jurisdiction of the Holy Roman

---

166 On "Romanitas" as a driving motif in this age, see Ullmann, *op. cit.*, pp. 277 f., 292. The effect of this spirit on the Jews of Spain in the eleventh and twelfth centuries has been described eloquently by Y. Baer, "The Political Situation of the Spanish Jews in the Age of Judah Halevi," pp. 6 f. Cf. also Schramm, "Das Kastilische Koenigtum," p. 103, who shows the effect of Romanization on the coronation form used for Alfonso VII in 1111.

167 Hueffer, *op. cit.*, p. 355.

168 Schramm, "Das Kastilische Koenigtum," pp. 102 ff.; Hueffer, *op. cit.*, pp. 357 ff.; Menendez Pidal, *El Imperio Hispanico*, pp. 139 f., 146 ff.

169 Cf. Schramm, "Das Kastilische Koenigtum," pp. 114 f.; Hueffer, *op. cit.*, pp. 369 f., 378 f. On papal avoidance of the use of imperial titles in communications with Castilian monarchs, see Schramm, *loc. cit.*, p. 112 and Hueffer, p. 363.

170 Cf. G. Davis, "The Development of a National Theme in Medieval Castilian Literature," *Hispanic Review*, III (1935), 149 f. on Lucas el Tudense.

Empire was advanced by canonists so successfully that even the papal decretal of 1202 conceded that the translation of Roman imperium from the Greeks to the Germans covered all countries "*excepto regimine hyspanie.*" Vincentius Hispanus argued that Spain was independent of the Empire *de jure* and had always been outside the Empire, indicating thereby that his native land had claims to its own *imperium*.[171]

It is in the light of this flourishing Spanish nationalism that one must read Ibn Daud's history of Rome and his description of the conquest of all of Spain by the Goths. Though he had probably come to Toledo only shortly before writing his works, his residence in that city and his connections with Jews highly placed in the Spanish government gave him access, and won him over, to the Spanish view of things.[172] He lent his ear to these aspirations, for they suited his spiritual needs perfectly. Spain to Ibn Daud was the Empire, the rightful heir of Rome, for the *imperium Romanum* had a great role to play in Ibn Daud's Jewish scheme of things.

Now it may be objected that we are pressing our point too far. Ibn Daud, it may be claimed, reported what he knew or found in his sources and added characteristic Jewish asides to his basic account. However, these objections cannot override the fact that Ibn Daud's excursus on the history of Rome and Visigothic Spain is quite in key with his asides on Spanish affairs of his own day. Ibn Daud, it cannot be overemphasized, was not particularly interested in the history of any people, let alone the history of Gentile peoples, out of mere intellectual curiosity. History was a tool to him, and he would use it only to the extent that was necessary for his own purposes.

Such an opportunity arose for Ibn Daud again when in *Sefer ha-Qabbalah* he came to the events of the Jewish community of Spain of his own generation and had occasion to mention "King Don Alfonso, the son of Raimund, king of kings, the Emperador."[173] Ostensibly, Ibn Daud's summary of the glorious reign of Alfonso VII merely served as background for the circumstances in which the heretical Karaites had been thoroughly suppressed in Christian Spain thanks to the activity of the Jewish courtier, Judah ibn Ezra. However, even the most cursory reading of this section in *Sefer ha-Qabbalah* will indicate that it contains two further digressions within this larger digression from the history

---

171 Cf. G. Post, "Two Notes on Nationalism in the Middle Ages," *Traditio*, IX (1953), 300 f.; idem, "Blessed Lady Spain—Vincentius Hispanus and Spanish National Imperialism in the Thirteenth Century," *Speculum*, XXIX (1954), 198. Cf. also Koebner, *op. cit.*, p. 308 n. 1 to p. 35.

172 Cf. Epilogue.89 f.

173 Epilogue.62 f.

of rabbinic succession. Within the larger parenthesis on the rise and fall of Karaism in Spain, Ibn Daud paused to tell us how Judah ibn Ezra succeeded in providing succor and relief to many of his Jewish brethren who were in flight from the Almohade hordes in the south. This in turn impelled him to pause and describe the exalted genealogy of the Ibn Ezra family and of its ancient association with royalty. These digressions were hardly necessary in a work presumably dedicated solely to a description of the history of Jewish rabbinic leadership. We shall soon see that even these digressions were not idle encomia on a Jewish philanthropist, but were in keeping with the general tone of his esoteric thesis. For the moment we must concentrate on Ibn Daud's rather lengthy aside on Alfonso VII. There was certainly no need for Ibn Daud to amplify on the reign of the Christian king, Alfonso VII, as he did in the opening of this passage, unless we see the very clear hints contained in the data presented and in the style in which they are transmitted.

"The following," Ibn Daud writes, "are the circumstances under which the heretics [the Karaites] were suppressed in Castile. This king, Don Alfonso, son of Raimund, was a king of kings and a righteous king. He prevailed over all the Ishmaelites living in Spain and compelled them to pay tribute. His kingdom grew mighty, 'and the Lord gave him rest from all his enemies round about.' Now the time that he reigned over Edom was thirty-eight years."[174]

What is striking about this passage is the series of phrases suggestive of biblical models. Alfonso's reign is described in terms reminiscent of that of David (II Sam. 7.1). Once again, the characterization of Alfonso as a righteous king is done in terms employed by the Psalmist of David (Ps. 110.4). The chronology of his reign is given in terms imitative of the way in which reigns are reported in the books of Kings and Chronicles. Finally, the length of Alfonso's reign was measured from the time the Emperador had entered Toledo victorious over his enemies in the north, for possession of the Visigothic capital was traditionally, and especially from the point of view of a Toletanian, the sign of dominion over "all of Spain."[175] It is in the light of the style of this whole digression that we should understand Ibn Daud's repeated emphasis of Alfonso's inflated title, and his insistence that Emperador means "king of kings."[176] Emperador, to be sure, meant just that, and Ibn Daud may have been aware of the fact that in the later documents of Alfonso's chancellery, where the imperator himself signed as "*Adefonsus Raimundus dei gracia totius Hispaniae imperator*," the count of

---

174 *Ibid.*, 65 f.
175 Cf. note to Epilogue.70.
176 Cf. note to Epilogue.62.

Barcelona and the king of Navarre were then listed as *"vasalli imperatoris."*[177] On the other hand, there can be no overlooking the fact that Ibn Daud and his readers thought in biblical terms, and the expression "king of kings" appears in the Bible in connection with emperors who effected great changes in the political situation of the Jews. What more apt characterization could one find for the Spanish king of the north, who swooped down on the Moors of the south with horses and chariots, with horsemen and a company and many people? If Alfonso was a modern Nebuchadnezzar or Artaxerxes, was he not so at least in part because he sat on the throne of an empire which was destined to play a role in the ultimate denouement of history? Had not rabbinic literature on occasion used the name Babylon for Edom?[178] Was Alfonso not indeed a "king of kings" because he held the significant *regnum* in the *imperium* which was to usher in the last days? Might Ibn Daud not have characterized Alfonso VII in terms reminiscent of David because Alfonso VII, or more likely his seed, was destined to play the role of Armilus, the last king of Edom? What need was there for Ibn Daud to stress repeatedly that Alfonso was the Emperador unless he wanted his audience to keep in mind the special place of Alfonso or his house in the Jewish scheme of things? Clearly it was this king or his standard-bearer who would shatter the fourth empire and then . . . then, in turn, be shattered with the inauguration of the messianic period. Had not the rabbis indicated that the Messiah sits in the gates of Rome, and where was Rome if not in Spain, indeed in Toledo, the capital of all Spain?

We need not be taken in by Ibn Daud's unqualified praise of Alfonso VII. It surely could not have escaped Ibn Daud that the legislation of this "righteous" king with regard to the Jews was far more Christian than it was righteous. He could not have failed to see the fact that the Jews were legally no better off in the Christian part of Spain than they were anywhere else in Christendom.[179] Furthermore, we need not be deflected from this line of symbolic reasoning because at the time of Ibn Daud's writing Alfonso VII had been dead for four years and his empire was divided between Ferdinand II and Alfonso VIII, neither of whom held the title of Emperador.[180] The fact is that the ecclesiastical circles of Spain had characterized the division of the *imperium* as "calamitous," and Ibn Daud may well have regarded the *imperium*-divided as a temporary state of affairs. Moreover, his own chronological hints as to the time of the impending redemption indicated that it was still some twenty-seven years off,

---

177 Cf. Rassow, "Urkunden," *Archiv*, X, 410, where references are listed.
178 Cf. Ginzberg, *Geonica*, I, 29; Strack and Billerbeck, *Kommentar*, III, 816; Baer, *History*, I, 392 n. 49.
179 Baer, "The Political Situation of the Spanish Jews," pp. 7 f.; *idem*, *History*, I, 51 f.
180 P. Agaudo Bleye, *Manual de Historia de España*, I, 637b.

and by that time Spain could well have been reunited. He had every reason to hope that Alfonso VIII or Ferdinand II would soon replace their respective titles of "*rex Hispanorum*"[181] with "*imperator totius Hispaniae.*" Alfonso VII himself was thus but a symbol of the role of the royal house of Castile, and of the destiny appointed for the Jews associated with it.

Finally, one further detail in Ibn Daud's reading of the past now takes on added significance in the context of his message to his contemporaries. Ibn Daud, it will be recalled, had shown that the fate of the Gentile empires, although intimately connected with the fortunes of the Jewish people, was determined by different aspects of the Jewish situation. Whereas the fate of the eastern empire had been determined by its treatment of the Jews, the fate of the western empire had varied in inverse ratio to the situation of the Jews.[182] Was that not indeed the case at the very time that Ibn Daud was writing? In the wake of Almoravide and especially of Almohade persecution of the Jews, the Reconquista had regained its momentum, and the Christians of the north were planning the complete elimination of the Muslim hold over Andalus. Conversely, in the very years that the Jews had been falling from power, the Christian kingdom of the north, Ibn Daud's Edom, had been regaining its might and was emerging as a true Roman *regnum*. Did not all the signs point to the end at which Ibn Daud had been hinting?

If we have read Ibn Daud's message correctly, the scheme of four empires had been restored and vindicated. Edom was back on the scene, and the Danielian-rabbinic scheme was still relevant. Indeed, it was now seen to be more relevant than ever before.

---

181 Cf. Menendez Pidal, *El Imperio Hispanico*, p. 184.
182 Cf. above, p. 234.

V. THE TYPOLOGY OF THE RABBINATE

A. The Noble Types of Andalus

In his digressions on the Bar Kokba debacle and the histories of Persia, Rome and Spain, Ibn Daud shifted the focus of his attention from chronology to typology. The errors of previous messianic efforts were shown to have derived not only from miscalculations of the fullness of time, but also from a mistaken identification of the awaited Messiah and his countervailing force, the Antichrist. If Ibn Daud could now cautiously suggest that there was room for renewed hope and for success, the source of this hope lay in the convergence of chronology and typology, i.e., in the new, "ethnographically demonstrated" identification of the people of Edom, the source of the Antichrist, with Christian Spain. In carefully cloaked but typologically clear vocabulary, Ibn Daud had announced that the climax of history, the time and setting in which the unfolding of the divine plan would be witnessed, would take place in the land of the children of Uz—Leon, Aragon and Castile—where the remnants of Andalusian Jewry had found a haven.

This esoteric message embedded in *Sefer ha-Qabbalah* gives a totally new significance to Ibn Daud's disproportionate treatment of the later rabbinate. Spanning scarcely two centuries of Jewish history, his treatment of this stage of history covers almost forty percent of his work. If Ibn Daud felt that a major turn in Jewish history was imminent, and that the scene of the denouement was to be his native country, it stands to reason that the Jewish leadership of his age and land would have to play a major role in that momentous change. If Spain was Edom, and from its loins would spring Armilus, it was only logical to expect that Spanish Jewry was the center of Israel, and from its seed there would emerge the herald and messenger of the new redemption. I believe that Ibn Daud afforded us clear indications that this was indeed his view, and that the rabbinate, of which he and his contemporaries constituted the fourth generation, had been singled out to play such a glorious role.

The final sections of *Sefer ha-Qabbalah*—which we have labelled as Chapter VII and Epilogue—betray a distinct change in style from that of the first six chapters. The innovation lies not so much in the expanded and engaging narrative as in the new polemical overtone that permeates the entire story. Andalusian Jewry is manifestly represented as the center of the world and as the climax of Jewish history. Apart from some very brief and token acknowledgments of other Jewish centers of learning, the almost exclusive dominion of the Andalusian rabbinate over all the various branches of Jewish knowledge is proclaimed at every opportunity.

The rabbinate of Spain is introduced with the announcement that even before the curtain had fallen on Babylonia, "it was brought about by the Lord that the income of the academies [there] . . . was discontinued," and that consequently "the academies were reduced to poverty."[1] Never again would the Jewish world "resume the sending of gifts to the academies, inasmuch as these scholars [of Spain] raised many disciples," and the Jews of the world "no longer had need of the people of Babylonia."[2] Although the termination of Babylonian hegemony was brought about by the simultaneous establishment of academies in Spain, Africa and Egypt, the institutions outside of Spain were destined to be short-lived. Talmudic learning soon came to an almost total end in Africa and rested exclusively in Spain.[3] Whatever major rabbinic talent was left outside Andalus soon saw the handwriting on the wall and migrated to Spain.[4] When the community of Babylonia did decide to rear its head, it could now do so only by importing leadership from Andalus![5]

Ibn Daud thus assured us that it was not his local patriotism or personal attachments that compelled him to describe what was after all but one rabbinate as *the* rabbinate. He had merely described the "facts," which were indeed so marvelous that they could only be explained as "having been brought about by the Lord." In short, history demonstrated that Providence had elected Spanish Jewry to play a special role in the last age.

The providential character of that history was established at the very outset by the way Jewish learning took root in Spain. "Four" scholars, veritable messengers of Heaven, brought the knowledge of the Torah to the four corners of the earth, thereby cutting the umbilical cord that had stretched from Baghdad to Cordova.[6] Moreover, the very way in which they severed their attachment to the Babylonian womb demonstrated that these men wrought merely as God had willed. An Arab pirate, driven by greed and lust, served as the channel of God's comfort to the dispersed of Israel at the very ends of the earth. Indeed, nothing but divine will could possibly explain the miracle of the sudden and

---

1 VII.2–3, 94.
2 VII.58–59, 170–171.
3 VII.282–283, 289.
4 VII.291–292.
5 VII.367–370.
6 Cf. Cohen, *SFC*, pp. 73 f.

simultaneous emergence of mature Jewries in Cairo, Qairawan and Cordova.[7] If the other communities did not have the lasting good fortune of that of Spain, was it not because clearly they were not *meant* to have it? Did the felicity of Spanish Jewry not indicate that it was the culmination of the continuing sacred chain that began with Moses and was brought to its own shores by another R. Moses! Did not the very date of the event and the way in which this new Moses attained leadership demonstrate that he was the new counterpart of ancient Hillel who, in classical typology, had been described in terms reminiscent of Moses?[8] In other words, the story of the four captives not only established the divine election of Andalusian Jewry, but also showed that this election was typologically demonstrable. Suddenly, therefore, the innocent-looking clichés that make their appearance for the first time in the whole of this section of the work begin to assume a new significance.

The first major change in style that engages the reader's attention in the last portion of *Sefer ha-Qabbalah* is the regular refrain that summarizes the life of each figure by an enumeration of his virtues. Careful scrutiny of these *laudes* will show that they are not indiscriminately patched on to a biography, but scrupulously selected in keeping with a man's activities. While the claim of *rabbis* to immortality lay in their "having spread the knowledge of the Torah and having raised up many disciples,"[9] that of rabbinic *courtiers* lay in the added virtue of "having accomplished great good for Israel."[10] On the other hand, rabbis who had not been heads of academies but served only as local communal leaders are described as merely "having judged Israel."[11] Interestingly enough, none of these virtues are listed after the lives of the leaders of North Africa.[12]

Secondly, the virtues associated with each figure are drawn almost exclusively from catalogues of ideal qualities enumerated in the tractate of Ethics of the Fathers. Thus, the three virtues of spreading Torah abroad, raising up many disciples, and accomplishing great good for Israel are manifestly concretizations of the three principles on which the father of rabbinic Judaism had said that

---

7   VII.6 f.
8   Cf. above, pp. 200 f. and esp. p. 202 n. 67.
9   VII.171–172, 179, 246 (the raising up of disciples is included in the virtues enumerated in lines 236 f.), 263, 334, 352, 388, 415, 443, 466, 470 f.
10 VII.234, 334, 421–422; Epilogue.100 f. Although Ibn Daud gave no indication of the source of Ibn Ezra's religious authority, he nevertheless went out of his way to accord him recognition as a rabbi, *ibid.*, 89.
11 VII.356, 360 376.
12 The recognition accorded them in VII.171 was a token one, and was not repeated in VII.265 f., as it was in the case of R. Ḥanok in VII.179.

the world stands, "on the Torah and its cultivation and deeds of kindness."[13] Some of the rabbis of Spain had added qualities that are also drawn from this tract, where the characteristics of the ideal man are enumerated. Thus, Samuel ibn Nagrela earned the four crowns representing the totality of achievement possible for a Jew.[14] Other scholars were learned in Greek wisdom over and beyond their knowledge of Torah, thereby covering the whole range of the curriculum of learning praised in the Mishna.[15] Some were distinguished by their humility, their generosity (especially to scholars), their forbearance. For the sake of Torah, they suffered deprivation willingly and would not stoop to use the Torah for personal ends.[16]

Ibn Daud's Spanish rabbinate is thus the incarnation of the ideal rabbinic type, and the last section of *Sefer ha-Qabbalah* is a brief "mirror of princes." It is no accident that men of earlier generations are but sparingly characterized, even when there was copious material available for Ibn Daud to have incorporated at least a statement or two on their lives or characteristics. Ibn Daud was no more interested in the stories of the lives of persons than he was in the histories of nations, except where the "facts" illustrated a thesis of some kind. And if the facts were too drab or too meager, Ibn Daud filled the gap by drawing on the stories of other men and applying them to the man he was describing. The lives of the rabbis of Andalus are thus not real biographies but rather aretalogies and typologies, which serve to prove the thesis pleaded through the story of the four captives.[17] In Ibn Daud's view, the land chosen by

13 Abot 1.2. For my translation of *'abodah* (lit., the Temple service) as "the cultivation of the Torah," cf. Sifre Deut. sec. 41 (ed. Finkelstein), p. 87, from which Ibn Daud found license to equate the second clause of the maxim of Simeon the Righteous with the parallel clause in the maxim of the men of the Great Assembly in Abot 1.1. For Ibn Daud's equation of "deeds of kindness" with *philanthropia*, cf. Introduction, p. LX n. 83.
14 VII.247-248 and notes there.
15 VII.327, 331, 351, 443; Epilogue.156. That the study of "Greek wisdom" was legitimate was shown by Ibn Daud by his reference to that virture in classical figures; II.171-172; IV.10.
16 VII.25, 43, 159-167, 184 (Ibn Nagrela's original state), 234-246, 271-273, 276, 279-280, 314-315, 418-421, 436-438; Epilogue.102-116. Cf. Abot 1.3, 5, 13; 2.9; 4.4, 5, 9, 10, 19 and esp. ch. 6 (= *Pereq Qinyan Torah*). The downfall of Joseph ibn Nagrela is explained as having derived ultimately from his having failed to endure a life of deprivation as his father had; VII.53. Accordingly, having failed to experience the life prescribed in Abot 6.4, he failed to achieve the characteristics that would have inevitably followed.
17 For classical paradigms for Ibn Daud's biographical technique, cf. ARN, I, 6 (ed. Schechter), pp. 28 f. Cf. also Hirschberg's introduction to Nissim ibn Shahin, *Ḥibbur Yafeh*, pp. 50 f., and Baneth's note in *Tarbiz*, XXV (1955-56), 335 n. 10. As a member of the Andalusian school of philosophy, Ibn Daud probably shared the view of Maimonides on the types of stories that a person of good character should tell; cf. Maimonides to Abot 1.17, "type 4." Cf. also above, p. 114.

Providence to lead the Jewish people in the final age had been blessed with leaders who embodied the ideal characteristics which the rabbis of old had laid down as goals of life. The "people of Andalus" were the nobles of the Torah *par excellence*.[18]

The achievements of the leaders of this community were in keeping with the destiny assigned to their age. No communal responsibility obsessed Ibn Daud so much as that of bringing consolation to his people.[19] Consolation, to be sure, was especially appropriate to Ibn Daud's day, when the Jewish community was still reeling under the impact of the Almohade blow. But Ibn Daud saw this reponse to duty manifested even in earlier days. Like all intellectuals living in Arab countries, Ibn Daud was deeply sensitive to the political implications of language and poetry. To many a Jew of Andalus, the lowly state of the Jews was graphically reflected in the decline of creativity in the Hebrew language, a decline which was all the more painful in view of the self-conscious and proud literary productivity of the Arabs of Spain.[20] Ibn Daud's boast that the grammarians and exegetes of Spain had revived the Hebrew language after it had fallen into almost complete oblivion is an unjustified one, if taken literally.[21] Moreover, the philological advances made by the Rabbanites of Spain were in no small measure stimulated by the studies of Karaite exegetes, who used philology as a weapon for their sectarian polemic.[22] However, we miss the point completely if we think that Ibn Daud was flaunting pure scholarly advancement. To Ibn Daud the "revival" of Hebrew in Spain was intimately bound up with the new flowering of Hebrew poetry, and Ibn Daud regarded poetic creativity as one of the great blessings of the rabbinic community to which he belonged.[23] But, once again, it was not poetry as such which he admired, but poetry of a specific genre. This is demonstrated by his omission of some of the outstanding poets of Spain and his inclusion of names of men he disliked intellectually or who were relatively minor figures in this field.[24] As an outstanding case in point,

---

18 For the "people of Spain," cf. VII.37, 291, 293; Judah b. Barzillai, *Sefer ha-'Ittim*, p. 267 and the Arabic expression "ahlu 'l-Andalus." For the invidious overtones of this latter expression, cf. Pérès, *op. cit.*, pp. 7, 19. For the feelings of the Jewish nobility on the exalted station of Torah in Spain, cf. Samuel ibn Nagrela *apud* Judah b. Barzillai, *loc. cit.*, and the references in S.N. to VII.297.

19 Cf. Analysis, ch. III.

20 Cf. note to Epilogue.144.

21 Cf. Baron, *SRH*, VII; S. Spiegel, "On Medieval Hebrew Poetry," *The Jews*, I, 547 f.

22 Cf. Baron, *SRH*, VI, 244 f., VII, 32 f.

23 VII.351, 354, 359, 377; Epilogue.127, 142 f.

24 Among the outstanding names omitted by Ibn Daud were Menahem b. Saruq, Dunash b. Labrat, Isaac ibn Ḥalfon, Joseph ibn Abitur and Judah ibn Bal'am. For a survey of the poets of the period, cf. Schirmann's study referred to in the Introduction, p. xix n.

nowhere is Samuel ibn Nagrela specifically praised as a poet, while, on the other hand, Solomon ibn Gabirol, who had been the target of all of Ibn Daud's animus in another work, is here singled out for praise.25 In all likelihood, Ibn Daud valued—in the context of *Sefer ha-Qabbalah*—not poetry as such but *consolatory* poetry, religious compositions that prayed for the messianic age, which is the theme permeating much of the liturgical compositions of the men he does list.26 Significantly, too, all of the poets mentioned in *Sefer ha-Qabbalah* were part of that extended circle that had its origins in the Ibn Falija-Ibn Nagrela houses27 and that had been responsible for the cultivation of all branches of "Greek wisdom"—science, astrology, philosophy, *belles-lettres* and rhetoric—along with traditional Jewish subjects—Bible exegesis, Talmud, liturgy. It was the circle of Maecenases, courtiers, jurists and communal leaders, whose poetry cried out not only for personal salvation but for Jewish national redemption and power.28 Ibn Daud was quite deliberate when he coupled in one sentence the virtue of doing good for Israel with that of composing hymns and poems of consolation.29

Poetry was to him but an outstanding manifestation of a whole pattern of life that had taken root in Andalus and produced outstanding fruits—men, literature, thought—and that, in turn, had helped recapture Jewish pride and hope. Consolatory and liturgical poetry, as Shalom Spiegel has shown, in-

---

12. However popular Oheb b. Meir may have been as a poet in Ibn Daud's circle, he was certainly not a major figure; nor after all was Joseph b. Zaddik, however saintly he may have been.
25. Epilogue.152.
26. Cf. Epilogue.127, 155 f. For representative specimens of the poetry of men mentioned by Ibn Daud, cf. Schirmann, *Ha-Shirah ha-Ibrit*, I; for full bibliographies, cf. *ibid.*, end of vol. II. Solomon ibn Gabirol and Moses ha-Kohen ibn Gikatilla are excellent cases in point. Although Ibn Daud found the former's philosophy unacceptable, he doubtless considered his poetry a model of consolation and religious inspiration; cf. the discussion of J.N. Simhoni, "R. Solomon ibn Gabirol" [in Hebrew], *Ha-Tequfa*, XVII (1922), 266 f.; I. Davidson in Solomon ibn Gabirol, *Selected Poems*, ed. by I. Davidson, tr. by I. Zangwill (Philadelphia, 1923), pp. xxvi f.; Spiegel, "On Medieval Hebrew Poetry," p. 550. At the very end of this chapter, I have suggested that Ibn Daud took exception to some of Moses ibn Gikatilla's biblical exegesis, at least to the unconcealed way in which his conclusions were made available to the public. Nevertheless, Ibn Daud doubtless found the traditional message reiterated in such liturgical pieces as those published by H. Brody, "Poems of Moshe Hacohen ibn Chiquitilla" [in Hebrew], *Studies of the Research Institute for Hebrew Poetry*, III (1936), 73 f., nos. 1, 2, 3, 8, 9. If our appraisal of Ibn Daud's partiality to poets and poetry is correct, it would also be fair to conclude that his tastes coincided with those of Maimonides; cf. above, n. 17.
27. Cf. VII.65; Cohen, *SFC*, pp. 118 f.
28. Cf. Introduction, pp. XVI f.
29. Epilogue.125 f.

evitably evoked an association with the Psalms of David; and no single book bespoke better the yearnings of the men of Andalus—piety, Torah, elegance, hope.[30] Ibn Daud measured men and their activity by the yardsticks of his class, and poetry was high on the list for the reasons we have set forth.

However, even a pure talmudist, Isaac al-Fasi, although not a native Spaniard, was singled out for special praise, for he had composed a work that by being a miniature Talmud matched anything that had been produced in the gaonic age.[31] Al-Fasi's work clearly demonstrated that Judaism had reached a new stage, and Spanish Jewry a new height, even as the earlier productions of Simeon Qayyara and Aḥa of Shabḥa had for the previous gaonic stage.[32] Andalus was thus now the ideal soil for the cultivation of Torah in every respect—students, rabbis, literature.

Moreover, the very structure of the Andalusian community reflected classical models and was thus an authentic replica of ancient Jewish society. As in ancient times there had been a distinct difference between the head of the academy and the nasi, or prince, so too in Andalus some leaders exercised communal powers, others merely religious authority, and a very few the combination of both.[33] Ḥisdai ibn Shaprut, Jacob ibn Jau, and Joseph Cidellus represented the first type.[34] R. Moses, R. Ḥanok and all those memorialized exclusively for their rabbinic achievements were, of course, of the second category. The third and final class numbered outstanding men like Samuel ibn Nagrela, his son Joseph, Isaac ibn Albalia, and, above all, Judah ibn Ezra.[35]

B. The Noblest of the Noble: the Courtier-Rabbi

Interestingly enough, it is in the aretalogies of the men of this third class—rabbinic courtiers—that *Sefer ha-Qabbalah* attains its climax by means of a totally different typology, which is reflected by a new and deliberately selected idiom.

With the biography of Samuel ibn Nagrela, Ibn Daud's tendentious historiography achieves a new level of subtlety, for he scrupulously avoids the open theological proemium with which he had introduced the story of the four captives.[36] Nevertheless, or rather precisely because of this, the miraculous and

30 Spiegel, *op. cit.*, pp. 533 f.
31 VII.380–391.
32 VI.19, 26.
33 Cf. above, p. 152.
34 All three held only the title of nasi; VII.73, 129; Epilogue.57. Cf. also *ibid.*, 63–64.
35 Cf. above, n. 10.
36 Compare VII.2 with 191 f.

providential quality of the Nagid's achievement is all the more dramatic. By sheer coincidence, as it were, Ibn Nagrela rose from obscurity to fame, from meager means to wealth and power. Thanks to his willingness to compose letters for a servant girl of the vizier of Granada, Ibn Nagrela was able to display his singular talents in the art of writing and thereby come to the vizier's attention. From that moment, his life consisted of one success after another, until he himself finally became vizier over the kingdom of Granada and nagid over the Jewish community. As already indicated, the story was lifted by Ibn Daud from a biography of a personality whose life was no less dramatic than the nagid's, al-Mansur ibn Abi 'Amir, and of whom, incidentally, the same story was no more true than it was of Ibn Nagrela. Ibn Daud simply appropriated a Cordovan success story and touched it up with a few literary motifs from other works.[37] The result was a tale that was thrilling but which did not test credulity by invoking the supernatural.

But if God has now been pushed into the background, a new idiom and typology have suddenly made their appearance. In Ibn Daud's presentation, Ibn Nagrela enters the stage amid a fanfare of phrases that unmistakably classify him as a latter-day manifestation of the biblical courtiers, Joseph, Daniel and Mordecai. His story, like theirs, represented a combination of wisdom with piety, which when properly blended would yield a brew of success, material and spiritual. "Skilled in wisdom . . . and one having ability to stand in the king's presence," Ibn Nagrela, like Daniel of old, ultimately attained glory by dint of his knowledge of the king's "tongue."[38] Like Joseph, the courtier prototype of Daniel, Ibn Nagrela first wallowed in the pit of poverty, until a lowly slave brought the clever Jewish lad to the attention of the court.[39] Thereupon, "he was rushed" from his dungeon of a shop to the palace of the vizier of Granada, as Joseph of old had been brought to the palace of Pharaoh,[40] and there he performed like the wise courtiers of old, Joseph, Ahitophel and Daniel, so that "the counsel which he gave was as if one consulted the oracle of God."[41] Needless to say, thanks to the presence of the Jew in his household, the vizier

37 Cf. above, p. 203.
38 Cf. VII.182 and Dan. 1.4. The beauty of Ibn Nagrela's literary style is a surrogate for the *physical* attractiveness of Daniel and his friends and of Queen Esther. The medieval exegetes may well have noticed the similarity of motifs called to attention by M. Gan, "The Book of Esther in the Light of the Story of Joseph in Egypt" [in Hebrew], *Tarbiz*, XXXI (1961–1962), 144 f.
39 Cf. VII.184, 191 f. and Gen. 39.20 f.; VII.196 f. and Gen. 41.9 f. Even the way in which the summons was issued to the vizier to return home, VII.196–197, evokes a biblical association with another (Jewish) courtier; cf. Neh. 13.6.
40 Cf. VII.202 and Gen. 41.14.
41 VII.205 and II Sam. 16.23; but cf. also Gen. 41.38–39.

who had employed him became "exceedingly great."[42] Following the latter's death, and in accordance with his good advice, given in words which Nebuchadnezzar had used with reference to the prophet Jeremiah, the Jew became a "father and priest" to King Ḥabbus, even as Joseph had been designated Abrek by Pharaoh.[43] As in the case of ancient Joseph, it was in accordance with Samuel's wishes that ultimately everyone in the realm bestowed the kiss of fealty and adoration.[44] Thus, the two lessons of the classical Joseph-Daniel-Esther cycles were artistically reasserted: the success of a Jewish courtier stems from his wisdom, his humility,[45] his loyalty to the faith of his fathers;[46] secondly, such a courtier earns his rewards by the most objective standard of measurement, for he is the medium by which his royal overlord achieves blessings and successes greater than ever before.[47] Ibn Daud cleverly puts the testimony on the manifestation of the divine approval of Ibn Nagrela in the mouth of a Muslim—"Do whatever he says," Ibn al-'Arif advises Ḥabbus, "and God will help you"—for the admission of a Gentile was here worth more than a thousand verses.[48]

If Ibn Nagrela represented the first generation of the rabbinate, he was, in Ibn Daud's view, also the father of a new type in Jewish history, the latter-day courtier. Ibn Daud, of course, knew that Ibn Nagrela was not the first Jew to enter the royal service. He makes several references to Ḥisdai ibn Shaprut, who had achieved fame and honor under 'Abd ar-Raḥman III, and whom he calls the Nasi, or prince.[49] However, he has nothing specific to say of Ḥisdai ibn Shaprut, possibly becuase he knew little, but far more probably because Ibn Shaprut was not numbered among the class sired by R. Ḥanok and Samuel the

---

42 VII.206. Cf. also Gen. 39. 3, 23.
43 VII.204, 211 and notes there. On "father and priest" cf. Jud. 17.10 and esp. Gen. 41.43 and Targum *ad loc.*
44 Cf. VII.221, 223 and cf. Gen. 41.40. Badis' ultimate success in eliminating his brother, VII.232, is worded in a way reminiscent of Solomon, I Ki. 2.46, who had also liquidated his brother.
45 Cf. Gen. 40.8; Dan. 2.27–28.
46 Cf. Gen. 39.9; Dan. 1.8 f.
47 Cf. Gen. 41.39 f.; Dan. 2.46 f.; Esther 2.21–23, 6.1 f., 8.1 f., 10.1 f.
48 VII.212. This line of salesmanship became a fairly fixed feature in Jewish courtier circles and was expressed even as late as the sixteenth century; cf. H.H. Ben-Sasson, "Exile and Redemption through the Eyes of the Spanish Exiles" [in Hebrew], *I. F. Baer Jubilee Volume*, p. 224; *idem*, "The Generation of the Spanish Exiles and its Fate" [in Hebrew], *Zion*, XXVI (1960–61), 30. That *Sefer ha-Qabbalah* represented the ideology of the Jewish courtier class has been shown by Ben-Sasson in "Li-Megamot ha-Chronografia ha-Yehudit shel Yemay ha-Baynayyim u-Be'ayoteha," *Historians and Historical Schools* (Jerusalem, 1962), pp. 36 f.
49 VI.159; VII.73; Epilogue.29, 130.

Nagid. Ibn Shaprut had been a nasi, one among many before and after,[50] but apparently not quite of the noble stock that was destined to play a special role in Spanish Jewish history, as Ibn Daud understood it. Ibn Nagrela, on the other hand, was qualitatively different, for he not only had attained much greater power, but he also embodied those classical qualities which Ibn Shaprut had apparently only stimulated and supported financially in others. In other words, Ibn Nagrela himself was a typological figure, and that typology bespoke Jewish royalty, the quality of men who wore crowns. It was a royalty shorn of much of its power, but far more patently regal than anything the Jews had enjoyed for a long, long time. Since neither Ibn Nagrela nor his descendants ever attained the full glory and function of kingship, they themselves were obviously not messiahs. But they did serve a vital function in establishing the criteria for the cultivation of a regal group that would ultimately play its teleological role.

In *Sefer ha-Qabbalah*, as in many theories of royalty, two elements occupy positions of first magnitude: a man's stock and his traits.[51] Ibn Nagrela was a Levite, in other words of sacred and exalted stock.[52] His traits were of the finest, and even his charities betrayed his royal essence.[53] So it would be in subsequent generations with all of the communal leaders whom Ibn Daud singled out for praise.

Although lesser luminaries are treated much more briefly and much less imaginatively, even in their case the typological element is clearly discernible. Isaac ibn Albalia, who was spared the fate of Joseph ibn Nagrela only by a miracle,[54] attained a post in the court of al-Mu'tamid, a matter which again is described in words reminiscent of Joseph of old.[55] That Ibn Albalia was a

---

50 Cf. above, n. 34.
51 Cf. VII.418; Epilogue.99–100.
52 VII.180. On Ibn Nagrela's own pride in his stock, cf. below.
53 Cf. S.N. to VII.245.
54 VII.321.
55 VII.330. There is something very suspicious about Ibn Daud's chronology for his grandfather. In VII.328 f., Ibn Daud makes it quite clear that Isaac ibn Albalia's rise to power in 1068–69 was connected with al-Mu'tamid's conquest of Cordova, but al-Mu'tamid did not enter Cordova until at least a year later. Ibn Daud may have connected Ibn Albalia's appointment with the conquest of Cordova in order to make the latter's rise to power over the Jewish community similar to that of Ibn Nagrela, who also became nagid over the Jews as a consequence of his political power; or, he ante-dated the event by one year in order to make Ibn Albalia's appointment occur exactly 1000 years after the destruction of the Second Temple. Since Ibn Albalia was a direct descendant of the exiles of Jerusalem, the date of the appointment was a manifestation of the divine consolation. There is one further flourish about Ibn Albalia that Ibn Daud added out of filial piety. Although other men were accorded the *laudes* that Ibn Albalia was, only he had all three placed together in one sentence; cf. above, nn. 9–10.

quasi-biblical figure is further suggested by the fact that he was a direct descendant of the "nobles of Jerusalem," who established a Jewish community in Merida.[56] That community, in turn, attained the status of a quasi-Jerusalem to all the Jewish communities in its vicinity.[57] From Isaac ibn Albalia's youth, his extraordinary character was manifest to all; even a total stranger, his French tutor R. Paregoros, is described as having consented to remain with him by a verbatim quotation from Judges 17.11.[58] Although his contemporary Isaac ibn Giat is described in rabbinic terms,[59] the story of his death is told in biblical phrases that are forced and invoked obviously only in order to lend a classical touch.[60] As noted earlier, the minor figures of that second generation of rabbis are described as "judges of Israel," thereby indicating that they played only secondary and interim roles as their prototypes, the Judges, had done in the days of the Bible.[61] The Ibn Megash family was also heir to qualities of high biblical ancestry, for not only did Joseph ibn Megash the elder succeed in "entering the service of King Ibn 'Abbad"[62]—after having been politically on the opposite side of the fence from Samuel ibn Nagrela[63]—but his son Meir ibn Megash and Isaac ibn Albalia maintained ties that re-enacted the relationship of David and Jonathan.[64] As for the great Joseph ibn Megash, who became the leading rabbinic authority of his day, Isaac ibn Albalia could testify in writing that he had been blessed with qualities that surpassed those of the outstanding men of the generation of Moses. Indeed, Ibn Daud concludes, his exemplary traits were tangible proof of the fact that he himself was of the very seed of Moses, the most humble of all men.[65]

In keeping with the biblical typology of the leading men of Andalus, the

---

56 VII.298. The word for "noble" is biblical; cf. Isa. 32.5; Job 34.19. However, Ibn Daud's use of the expression (cf. also VI.144) seems to have been influenced by *Josippon*; cf. Ben Iehuda, *Thesaurus*, XIV, 6978a, where many examples are listed. It is possible that in mentioning the occupation of his ancestor, "maker of curtains" for the arks of synagogues (VII.299), Ibn Daud intended another hint at the regal character of the family; cf. Midrash Ruth 2.2.

57 Cf. the salutation of Saadiah's letter cited in VII.304–305 with the expression in Zech. 7.7. I do not mean to imply that the salutation in the Gaon's letter was not exactly as Ibn Daud cited it. However, he obviously quoted it to show that Merida had attained that kind of recognition.

58 VII.312–313.
59 Cf. above, n. 9.
60 VII.349.
61 Cf. above, n. 11.
62 VII.398 and cf. I Chr. 26.30.
63 VII.219, 397.
64 VII.402–403.
65 VII.408–419.

entire survey of the period is strategically sprinkled with phrases which suggest that the age of the rabbinate had been foreseen by the prophets of yore. Persons and events in Spain fulfill ancient oracles, thereby demonstrating that the age and its actors, as in the days of classical history, were very much the concern of divine scrutiny. This is most palpably felt in Ibn Daud's descriptions of tragic turns of events. The assassination of Joseph ibn Nagrela and the pogrom in the community of Granada are at last understood to be the fulfillment of an unexplained fast day decreed in ancient times for the ninth of Tebet.[66] That the house of Ibn Nagrela came to an untimely end with the death of young Azariah ibn Nagrela is explicitly attributed to the will of God, against which even the efforts of the pious Isaac ibn Giat were of no avail.[67] The death of Joseph ibn Megash, seven years before the Almohade deluge, is understood as the merciful decree of the Almighty, in accordance with a principle revealed through Isaiah.[68] The terrible sufferings experienced by the Jews after 1147-48 were clearly fulfillments of the calamities predicted by Amos, Jeremiah and the Psalmist, not only for events of their own days and ages, but, as could now be seen, for latter-day Jewry as well.[69] The meager shreds of hope and comfort that were left to the survivors were obviously granted by the same hand that had willed the evil, once again in fulfillment of biblical prophecies.[70] The Christian king through whose hospitality the Jewish remnants of Andalus had found a new home had, as noted in the preceding chapter, achieved his power and success by the will of God and obviously in order that His people should find rest.[71] If we are not in a world which is the primary focus of prophecy, we are very much in the world of aggadic midrash, where prophecies, especially those of doom and calamity, were often explained as having relevance in more than one context.[72] The implication of Ibn Daud was clear, again in accordance with an old rabbinic theory, that now that the evil had been fulfilled the time was ripe for the messages of consolation to come to pass, and soon.[73]

Thus, the whole of the last section of Ibn Daud's chronicle leads to the éclat of adulation that is heaped on the last of the courtiers, Judah ibn Ezra.[74] If there is nothing marvelous about his rise to power, we must not forget that it was God who put it into the heart of the king to place him in charge of all

66 VII.258–262. For biblical phrases, cf. VII.251, 253–254.
67 VII.339–345.
68 VII.452.
69 VII.455, 460, 465; Epilogue.75, 77, 80, 84.
70 Epilogue.77, 87.
71 Cf. above, pp. 260 f.
72 Cf. above, pp. 213 n. 123, 225 n. 8.
73 Cf. *B*. Mak. 24a–b.
74 Epilogue.86 f. and notes indicating biblical allusions.

royal provisions, even as the Almighty had done with Joseph and Pharaoh, Mordecai and Ahasuerus, the four friends and the Chaldean kings. The appointment was an appropriate one, for Ibn Ezra was descended from the cream of the nobility of Judah. His ancestors were of royal blood, from the very apex of Jerusalemite society, heirs to power and high office generation after generation. All these terms are clearly designed to associate the Ibn Ezra family, and Judah in particular, with Davidic lineage and characteristics, which would make him an appropriate candidate for the messianic assignment that might befall him. An ideal Jew, who fulfilled the highest ideals of religion enunciated by Isaiah,[75] he displayed all the magnanimity one would expect of true royalty: "Although but a youth, he was exalted above the people and lorded it over a company of spearmen," as the ancient Psalmist had predicted of the anointed king.[76] While the time had obviously not yet come for him to disclose the full extent of his glory, he had already made it clear that he was the modern counterpart of the Agrippa whom the Jews of ancient times had acclaimed as a legitimate king.[77] A Joseph, David, Agrippa, rabbi, Maecenas and warrior, he was truly a balm sent of the Lord to bring healing to an ailing and afflicted house of Israel. Like Joseph he had been sent to Toledo ahead of his people "to save life" and pave the road.[78] Hence, if the messianic era was around the corner, the Jews of Spain were ready, for they had a standard-bearer and leader whose life and ways bespoke authenticity and triumph.

Are we reading too much into what, it may be contended, was nothing but a normal, indeed quite common, genre of expression to medieval Jews? They wrote in clichés and hyperboles, and to see in stock and hackneyed phrases the traces of a political plea may appear to be carrying things too far. What is more, latter-day fulfillments of prophetic visions were not confined by Ibn Daud to the age of the rabbinate. He had similarly quoted the books of Kings and Daniel to explain the ages of Bar Kokba and Judah the Prince.[79] Why, then, should he not have done so for his own age? However, this kind of reasoning overlooks the obvious fact that the very genre of writing, the style of expression, reflects a writer's basic orientation and innermost convictions. At the very least, the style must echo something of the convictions of the audience to which it is addressed and whom it hopes to influence. The fact that prophecies were fulfilled in talmudic times does not mean that they would not be fulfilled again in later, perhaps even less meritorious, days. Only one who believes in the

75 Epilogue.103; cf. above, n. 16.
76 Epilogue.108–110.
77 Epilogue.112 and cf. *M.* Sotah 7.8.
78 Epilogue.116, 118–119. Note also the allusion to Jehoshaphat in Epilogue.114.
79 III.65, 81.

revealed character of Scripture expresses himself in this way, and such a man knows that his God lives and operates in the twelfth century no less than in the first and second. What is more, whatever God chooses to do, He does only after He has revealed His intention to His servants the prophets.[80] Since the age of prophecy had long since come to an end, Jews knew that whatever of consequence did occur had already been revealed.[81] The function of the rabbi was to locate the source.[82] Such assumptions were as obvious and as axiomatic to Ibn Daud as they were to tannaim and amoraim, to Christian and Muslim.

C. The Sources of Inspiration of Ibn Daud's Typology

In the case of the aretalogies and typologies, which Ibn Daud made the climax of his message, we are able to be far more specific and affirmative about the influence that shaped his thinking. What may appear to many as vapid cliché, as empty hyperbole, in short, as mere pious flattery, was in reality the echo of a theme, nay, of a theory of destiny and obligation, that had been proclaimed and shared for two centuries by that whole class of Jewish courtiers in whose glory Ibn Daud took delight.

"In the days of R. Ḥisdai the Nasi," Ibn Daud tells us, "the bards began to twitter, and in the days of R. Samuel the Nagid they burst into song."[83] In other words, what had been faintly sensed and covertly intimated in the tenth century was consciously felt and loudly proclaimed in the eleventh and twelfth. Since it was in the Hebrew poetry of the "golden age" of Andalusian literature that these feelings were given their clearest expression, it is to Spanish Hebrew verse of that period that we must turn for a glimpse at the self-image of the elite and for a hint of their understanding of their role in history.

"I am the David of my day," the Nagid had proclaimed,[84] and his poems and the reports of others testify to the extent to which the image of grandeur obsessed him. David the warrior, the psalmist, the rabbi, the king was forever on his mind. Every victory on the field of battle, every escape from impending calamity, was proof to the Nagid of the providential fate that had been meted out to him because of the merit of his fathers, the virtue of his life, the needs of

---

80 Amos 2.7.
81 II.20; *B. Meg.* 14a.
82 Cf. above, n. 72.
83 Epilogue.150–151.
84 Samuel ibn Nagrela, *Diwan* (ed. Sassoon), p. 41, line 38; (ed. Habermann), I, part 1, p. 37; Schirmann, *Ha-Shirah ha-Ibrit*, I, 111.—The following description of Ibn Nagrela's personality is not new. However, I have gone over old and long-trodden ground to provide the context for the problem under discussion.

his people.[85] Obviously he was consumed by ambition and by insatiable passion for fame and power. However, what is most revealing is *how*, that is, the words and metaphors by which, he expressed these drives. The Nagid thought always in biblical terms, which interpreted as well as gave expression to his dreams. He lived in a land peopled by Edom, Amalek, Philistines, Ishmaelites led, on occasion by Agag, Haman, and Goliath.[86] He himself was Samuel the prophet reincarnate,[87] Levi the minister, Assaf the psalmist,[88] Mordecai the courtier.[89] His triumphs and his poems he wanted publicized and declaimed, his victories celebrated as new Purims,[90] for he was the instrument of God and to him personally had been vouchsafed the promise reserved for the age of redemption: "When thou passest through the waters, I will be with thee, and through the rivers, they shall not overflow thee."[91] He may or may not have said to Ibn Ḥazm that he was the fulfillment, or a fulfillment, of the prophecy of the redemption in Genesis 49.10, "until Shiloh come, and the homage of peoples be his."[92] It is enough that Ibn Ḥazm should have thought that he had for us to realize that the hope for the fulfillment of the messianic dream in Andalus, through the class of Jewish courtiers, was not a secret of the Jewish underground. The Jewish pride, which the Muslims construed as hybris and defiance of Islam,[93] drew its nourishment from the assumption that the age of the Bible was again come to life and that the exiles of Judea in Sefarad would soon assume their rightful station.[94]

85 Cf. *idem, Diwan* (ed. Sassoon), p. 7, no. 10; p. 20, nos. 27 and 29; pp. 26 f.; (ed. Habermann), part 1, pp. 3 f., 15, 16 f., 28 f.; Schirmann, *Ha-Shirah ha-Ibrit*, I, 85, 93, 94 f., 102 f.
86 Cf. the first poem cited in the previous note, lines 12, 102, 104, 105; the third poem, *ibid.*, lines 14, 47.
87 Cf. S.N. to VII.204–205 and the very revealing opening in the poem "Samuel, approach the One Who sits on the Cherubim," in *Diwan* (ed. Sassoon), p. 62, no. 91; (ed. Habermann), part 1, p. 59; Schirmann, *Ha-Shirah ha-Ibrit*, I, 120 f. The tone of the poem recalls the fashioning of the prophet in Jer. 1.
88 See lines 39 f. in poem referred to in n. 84.
89 Cf. the first poem referred to in n. 85, lines 105, 145.
90 *Ibid.*; cf. also *Diwan* (ed. Sassoon) pp. 27, lines 54 f., 53 lines 28 f.; (ed. Habermann), pp. 33, 43; Schirmann, *Ha-Shirah ha-Ibrit*, I, 105, 181.
91 How seriously Ibn Nagrela took this vision may be seen from the number of poems in which he made reference to it; *Diwan* (ed. Sassoon), pp. 9 line 88, 20 no. 27, 112 no. 180. Schirmann, *Ha-Shirah ha-Ibrit*, I, 78 f., 89, 93.
92 Posnanski, *Schiloh*, pp. 105 f.; Schirmann, "Samuel Hannagid, the Man, the Soldier, etc.," pp. 101 f.
93 Cf. notes to VII.254–255.
94 The messianism of the Ibn Nagrelas was noted by Bargebuhr, *op. cit.*, pp. 197 f. While I am incompetent to evaluate the iconographic thesis of his paper, and I certainly cannot subscribe to his projection of "secularism" on the two Negidim and their supporters,

Careful scrutiny of Ibn Nagrela's poetry will reveal that Ibn Daud's evaluation of Ibn Nagrela and of his disciples was basically an echo of what the Nagid had said about himself. Ibn Nagrela unabashedly confessed that he was pretty much a complete and ideal Jew. Steeped in *halakah*, he combined his knowledge of all branches of the Torah with the study of science and philosophy.[95] Master of Hebrew exegesis and Hebrew grammar—or, at least, so he liked to be thought of[96]—he wrote with equal facility and flourish in the language of his Arabic masters as he did in that of his biblical-talmudic ancestors. Orthodox in faith and practice, he was relentless in his persecution of the Karaites *ad maiorem rabbinorum dei gloriam*.[97] Possessor of wealth and cultivated in taste, he supported the needy of his own land and of those far and wide, as far as Babylonia, Sicily and Palestine. Humble before overlords, unwavering before underlings, indomitable in the face of threat or opposition, he rose, or so he said, to the heights of the moon, as he had dreamed of doing when he left Cordova.[98] Hebrew, Torah, philosophy, Arabic, and politics—these were the elements that made a full career and a whole man. Needless to add, this ideal man was magnanimous with the deserving, taking pains to see that there should be an orderly succession and unimpeded continuity in the class and ideals which had combined to mold him. The moralizing verses of Samuel to his son Joseph were not the clichés of a Polonius; for however similar the platitudes, the fact remains that Ibn Nagrela was a vizier, a ruler in fact, who had every right and duty to mirror for his prince the light he had seen.[99] Moreover, he was sensitive to young talent even outside his immediate family, as seen from the case of Isaac ibn Albalia, for whose education he displayed the concern of a father for a son.[100] Class interests could even override political differences: Isaac ibn Albalia served as the link between the Ibn Nagrelas and the Ibn Megashes, after the latter had been forced to flee from Granda and the Nagid's henchmen.[101]

While Ibn Daud accepted the Nagid's image of himself, particularly since

---

his evaluation of their overall self-image appears to me to be confirmed by Ibn Daud and the other men of the circle.

95 Cf. Ibn Nagrela, *Diwan* (ed. Sassoon), p. 63 lines 23-24; (ed. Habermann), p. 60 (end); Schirmann, *Ha-Shirah ha-Ibrit*, I, 122. On his distinction in rabbinics, cf. Margalioth, *Hilkhot Hannagid*, pp. 11 f.
96 Cf. Baron, *SRH*, VII, 45 f., 237 n. 52.
97 Cf. Introduction, p. XLVII nn. 12, 15.
98 The expression is Ibn Nagrela's; *Diwan* (ed. Sassoon), p. 15, lines 10–11 and cf. lines 14 f.; (ed. Habermann), part 3, p. 5; Schirmann, *Ha-Shirah ha-Ibrit*, I, 83.
99 Cf. Schirmann, "Samuel Hannagid," pp. 117 f.
100 VII.313 f.
101 VII.398 f.

he found this appraisal confirmed by others, he made it clear that the Nagid had not written and worked in a Jewish vacuum. He had not single-handedly revived the ancient ideals and forms of expression that came to be the hallmarks of his associates and disciples. He had merely crystallized and achieved ideals of the geonim that had been germinating in the milieu in which he was tutored.

Although we have stressed the shift in Ibn Daud's style from drab catalogue to engaging narrative and typology at the point of transition from the age of the gaonate to that of the rabbinate, the change in style had already been anticipated in his account of the last generations of the geonim. Actually, the first exemplars of the *laudes* and virtues characteristic of the nobility of Andalus were R. Saadiah Gaon and R. Hai Gaon, with whom Ibn Daud employed some of the clichés and types of *laudes* which he used for the Andalusian leadership.

R. Saadiah, a descendant of the highest nobility of the tribe of Judah and of one of the saintliest of tannaim, fought the heretics and accomplished great good for Israel.[102] R. Hai, "the last of the geonim," descended from even nobler stock and traced his ancestry to the Davidic rulers of the Jews in the first exile. His signet ring bore the seal of the kings of Judah, graphic proof of his exalted family origins.[103] His distinction was in keeping with his genealogy. As a rabbinic type par excellence, "he spread Torah abroad throughout Jewry more than all of the other geonim." "By his light walked" for forty years "those who sought the Torah from east and west," even as Jews had done in the days of Moses and Hillel. He simply had no peer among the geonim, even as Moses had had none among the prophets and Josiah among kings.[104]

Now although these superlative praises echo the eulogies of Samuel ibn Nagrela and Solomon ibn Gabirol in honor of R. Hai,[105] in the context of *Sefer ha-Qabbalah*, where such virtues were enumerated sparingly and with exactitude (and of the other geonim not at all), they inevitably gave the impression that those rabbis and courtiers of Spain who did merit these descriptions were not only the logical and legitimate successors of the geonim; they were destined to fulfill even greater accomplishments. In any event, Ibn Daud showed that the style of life and achievements of the Andalusian rabbinate were continuing and advancing patterns that had been legitimized and pursued in Babylonia.

102 VI.144–145, 151–152, 157. Note that the genealogical statement was inserted after the story of Saadiah's conflict with the exilarch, in other words as a kind of reasoned explanation of the Gaon's behavior.
103 VI.186–191.
104 VI.181–183, 186.   105 Cf. note to VI.183 and S.N. to VI.184.

In Andalus itself, Ibn Daud informs us, the first echoes of this style of life could be heard in the twitterings of Ibn Shaprut's bards, in their *laudes* to their patron.

"Lily of the valleys (Song of Songs 2.1)
Ever opened blossom (*Ibid.* 7.13)
Who shines like the gold
Of the frontlet on Aaron's brow (Ex. 28.36, 38).
Generous and firm,
When you began to shine,
The ends of the earth
Broke forth into song (Isa. 49.13)."[106]

Menahem ben Saruq, the author of this panegyric, subsequently returned to the subject of his praise, who he claimed had wronged him unjustly, in equal bitterness but in biblical imagery nonetheless.

"Hear, now, O son of man,
Art not thou a valiant man?
And who is like to thee in Israel? (I Sam. 26.13)
Is it not for you to know justice? (Mic. 3.1)"[107]

Each phrase and each simile is selected with an eye to its biblical context and to the meaning which the rabbis of the Talmud and the exegetes of Spain would read into the phrase. By the time Dunsah ben Labrat replaced Menahem as "court" poet, the genre was established; only the meter would change.

"Attired in honor and glory (Ezek. 24.17)
Clothed with divine salvation (Ps. 132.16)
. . .
Seeking the good of his people (Est. 10.3),
He caused their enemies to scatter."[108]

Ibn Shaprut was adorned with the attributes of biblical heroes, and the virtues associated with his name became the hallmarks of the class of which he was really the first.

"Friend of many
Who forgives sin (Mic. 7.18)
And speaks in quiet (Eccl. 9.17)
When he sits by the gate (as judge)."[109]

Father to the poor, he patronized the academies of Babylonia and sought out

---

106 Schirmann, *Ha-Shirah ha-Ibrit*, I, 8 lines 8–12.
107 *Ibid.*, p. 15 lines 116–118.
108 *Ibid.*, p. 38 lines 40–41; p. 39 lines 61–62.
109 *Ibid.*, lines 63–64.

the brethren of Khazaria.[110] This last point is most germane to our discussion, for whether or not the so-called Khazar correspondence is genuine, Ibn Daud and the courtier class certainly thought it was.[111] Certainly the opening of Ibn Shaprut's letter to the Khazar king, with its messianic prayer, was the work of Menahem ben Saruq and reflected the convictions of his master.[112] Even if the hope, expressed in prose in the letter itself, that the Khazar kingdom proves that "the scepter has not departed from Judah," and the question as to whether the king of the Khazars has accurate information on the date appointed for the messianic redemption[113] are judged later interpolations, they are in the spirit of the opening poem and in keeping with the sentiments of Ibn Shaprut, Menahem, Dunash and the whole of the Andalusian Jewish aristocracy.

A generation later, in the days of Ibn Nagrela, the biblical imagery turned into a clarion call, combining all the motifs that we have enumerated as characteristic of the class. In the view of Ibn Nagrela and his beneficiaries, the song of the generation of the Nagid became the song of the Levites, the psalms of Judea, the vision of the prophets.[114] Since the Jewish elite were of the nobility of Judea, the Gentiles about them were the descendants of the pagans of Bible times, the seed of Ishmael and Esau, whose destiny had been determined and foretold no less than that of Israel. In identifying themselves and the nations in biblical terms, the courtiers of Andalus took the first open step in moving towards their goal.[115]

Accordingly, all men of this class addressed each other in panegyrics that were suffused with rabbinic and biblical typology. The modern reader often shudders at the depths of flattery to which gifted poets of the golden age could descend. In reality, there were cheap imitators and meretricious parrots, who turned out poems which were little more than a patchwork of clichés. But the vituperations of these epigones, after their efforts had been rejected, and of the masters from whom they had stolen expressions and whole verses, give ample evidence that they were quickly detected and widely detested even in their own day.[116] On the other hand, the panegyrics of the great to the great, particularly in the "golden age," deserve to be taken seriously, however

---

110 *Ibid.*, lines 65 f.; pp. 6 f.
111 Epilogue.27 f.   112 Schirmann, *Ha-Shirah ha-Ibrit*, I, 6 f.
113 P.K. Kokovtzov, *Evreisko-Khazarskaya Perepiska v X vieke* (Leningrad, 1932), pp. 18 f.
114 Cf. above, nn. 86–90; below, p. 282.
115 Obviously the Andalusians were not the first to identify latter-day nations with biblical ones, but they did make the identifications of Saadiah and the early philologists part of their daily speech; cf. IV.141 f.; Epilogue.25 f.
116 Moses Ibn Ezra, *Shirat Israel*, pp. 7 f.; J. Schirmann, "The Function of the Hebrew Poet in Medieval Spain," *Jewish Social Studies*, XVI (1954), 240 f.

alien they may be to our taste. Surely they are historical documents of the first order for determining how the courtiers wanted to be understood and lauded. Men the like Ibn Nagrelas were beset on all sides with requests for favors and handouts. But they were no fools, and not likely to be taken in merely by flattery. Indeed, they would suspect an overdose as much as an insufficiency of homage. The man of taste, accordingly, dipsensed his metaphors and similes judiciously and appropriately.

The panegyric of Joseph ibn Ḥisdai to Samuel ibn Nagrela, which achieved considerable renown in Spain and was hailed as unequalled even 150 years after it had been composed, was considered a poetic masterpiece for the way in which it combined content and form.[117] To the aristocracy it bespoke sweetness and authenticity, adulation without fawning, and it therefore speaks with authority on how Ibn Nagrela wanted to be known and how his disciples agreed that he should be regarded.

> "Prince unique is R. Samuel
> Whose name has filled the earth.
> As a tower it has risen over the people of Israel,
> Established aloft as a fort for his nation.
> Through him was renewed for his sacred tribe
> A seat of honor above the starry heavens.
> This Samuel is none other than the Samuel of yore
> Who had been summoned to enter the Temple of God.
> Who knows, indeed, but that he has been magically revived
> To rise from the dead, body and soul.
> And if, indeed, that is not the case,
> In their righteousness complete, they are none but the same."[118]

When a rabbi of note, Isaac ibn Giat, mourned Samuel ibn Nagrela as "the lamp of the west," he meant, of course, the light of the Maghreb;[119] but which of his readers failed to recognize the allusion to the western lamp in the Temple of Jerusalem that was never supposed to be extinguished?[120] The death of the Nagid was thus a national calamity, the quenching of a flame that had been a spark of the redemption. The same eulogy noted that Samuel had been the Nagid "who led out and brought in" the people, a clear reference to the terms of homage with which King David had been addressed by the elders of Israel.[121]

---

117 Cf. Schirmann, *Ha-Shirah ha-Ibrit*, I, 172, II, 110; Steinschneider, *Gesammelte Schriften*, p. 137,.
118 Schirmann, *Ha-Shirah ha-Ibrit*, I, 173, lines 12–17.
119 Margalioth, *Hilkhot Hannagid*, p. 67; cf. also p. 37 n. 2.
120 *M.* Tamid 6.1.   121 II Sam. 5.2 and cf. S.N. to II.129.

The poets who lauded Ibn Nagrela as a second Samuel (the prophet), or as one "anointed for the redemption of the people of God," were re-echoing what had become quasi-official formulae of praise and apparently standard usage with reference to the Nagid.[122]

His son, Joseph ibn Nagrela, would also be acclaimed as "offspring of the lion's whelp (Judah)" and heir to "the fruitful bough." "Joseph the second, like Joseph son of Rachel," would triumph over his foe. He, too, like Ibn Daud's heroes, would be hailed in his lifetime as an "apostle of God ... sent to save life (Joseph) to a people afflicted and tossed by tempest in the land of Spain."[123]

There is no need to give here even a partial catalogue of typology in the poetry of the period. Examples aplenty can be easily located and identified in the *diwans* and collections of "secular" poetry of the great poets of the golden age—Solomon ibn Gabirol, Moses ibn Ezra, Judah ha-Levi. Each of them displays the same infatuation with the same values—Torah, philosophy, astronomy, magnanimity, powers of rhetoric, friendship, patronage, communal responsibility—and adoration in biblical and rabbinic phraseology for the men who exemplify them. Their tragedies are construed as the heavy hand of fate, their triumphs as the favor of Providence and the omnipotent hand of God. Their prayers echo the Psalms, their eulogies Lamentations, their terms of love the Song of Songs, their reflections the books of wisdom. Their heroes embody virtues chosen from the whole range of Hebrew literature, but always in accordance with the man's station, real or imaginary, as understood by the poet and, it goes without saying, the person or group to whom the poem is addressed.

What held these men together? What forged them into a distinct *class* within the Jewish community? On this last point let there be no doubt. The heroes of Ibn Daud's chronicle, the circle of courtiers, patrons, and poets were not typical of Andalusian Jewry, not even of its middle class, let alone of its lower strata. They were, like all aristocracies, a minority, a select class that was jealous of its station and prerogatives and that, accordingly, established the rules for membership and entry into that coveted sphere. The intense competition between them for fame and adulation was conducted within a unified context, which served as ground for meaningful contact in love as well as in hate. Even the

---

122 Stern, "Life of Shmuel ha-Nagid," pp. 142 line 15, 144 line 8. For Ibn Gabirol's adulation of the Nagid as a complete man—blessed with *four* virtues including that of Levitic stock (cf. above, nn. 14, 52)—cf. *Shiray Solomon ibn Gabirol* (ed. Bialik-Ravnitzky), I, 69 lines 83-84. The latter poem concludes with blessings from the Psalms. Cf. also *ibid.*, p. 61 lines 25-26 (Samuel ibn Nagrela = Samuel the prophet), p. 64 line 4 (= Elijah), p. 65 lines 11, 13, 25, 39, 61 (= royal figure), 65-66 (= Moses and Aaron, while Ibn Nagrela's opponents are like Korah, Dathan and Abiram), p. 73 line 85, p. 79 lines 143-152.

123 Habermann, "Yehosef bar Samuel," p. 47; Stern, "Life of Samuel ha-Nagid," p. 142.

most bitter clashes between them were collisions of men within a stratum, which was held together, within and quite apart from the rest of Jewish society, by a peculiar style of living, of thought, of expression.[124]

In the first place, of course, there was the nobility of stock which these families boasted. To some extent, too, wealth must have played a role, although as good first families, they esteemed the bankrupt members of old wealth far above the *nouveaux riches* of the Ibn Jau type.[125] Thirdly, they shared a common intellectual tradition, which Ibn Daud calls "Torah, Greek wisdom and poetry."[126] In other words, they were worldly orthodox Jews, who were as chic in Arab tastes as they were fastidious in their Jewish ones. Moreover, they sought to participate actively in the political affairs of their day, offering their skills and services to the kings and chamberlains of the petty Arab kingdoms in the southern half of Spain. Finally, they understood nobility and success not only as prizes but also as trusts. *Noblesse oblige*, and as nobles of their people, they were also its stewards.[127] Whatever they did, they knew full well, reflected glory or shame not only on themselves but on their people. As Jews, they were heirs to the faith in the messianic era. As *noble* Jews, they dreamed of achieving it speedily, in their day. Complete freedom, redemption and restoration— these were the longings that obsessed them in their state of power. Yet they could never forget that this power was precarious, a gift doled out at the table of others. They had attained a point just short of the goal, and together they hoped to cross that line foreseen by Amos, pictured by Isaiah, predicted by Daniel, and formalized into dogma by their masters the rabbis.

To be sure, they lived in a society that stimulated such patterns of thought. Despite the attenuation of traditional Arab tribalism and family consciousness

---

124 This point has been made succinctly and cogently by J.G. Weiss, "Tarbut Ḥasranit we-Shirah Ḥasranit," *World Congress of Jewish Studies*, I (Jerusalem, 1947), 396 f. B. Klar, *Meḥqarim we-'Iyyunim* (Tel-Aviv, 1954), pp. 103 f., has argued that poetry and belletristic tastes became quite *popular* in Andalus and were not confined to a limited circle. While this may be true—though the evidence he adduces is by no means convincing, and Moses ibn Ezra, *Shirat Israel*, p. 33, felt otherwise—the tastes of the upper classes were not distinguished by poetry alone; cf. Introduction, ch. II. The tastes and activities of the aristocracy have always been imitated, but that did not obliterate the distinction between the masses (Arabic: *jumhur*), the halakists, the philosophers, the halakic-philosophers, and, be it added, the aristocracy; cf. Maimonides, *Guide*, III.53. Ibn Daud's coterie did not include even all Jews who had risen to political power and who engaged in poetry; cf. Pérès, *op. cit.*, pp. 264 f., for courtiers of distinction, who were also poets, totally ignored by Ibn Daud.

125 Cf. VII.98 f. and Cohen, *SFC*, p. 122.

126 VII.351 and cf. note to 350–352. Cf. also the discussion in Introduction, pp. xvi f.

127 That the noble should rule over the ignoble was established by Plato, *Laws*, III, 690a.

in all classes of Muslims in Spain, the royal courts, where the poetic tastes were given their quasi-official stamp, continued to dwell on the exalted origins of the rulers. Even outside the palace, the ethnic feelings of the various sub-groups comprising "the Arabs" were strong and often sharply expressed. *'Aṣabiyya 'arabiyya* was quite distinct and antithetical to *'aṣabiyya berberiyya*.[128] Arab Andalusians, who were proud of their wealth and letters, held Slavs and Berbers of their own faith in complete contempt. Poetry and biography, diatribe, panegyric and aretalogy were characteristic forms of expression of this Arab aristocracy. And as Arab walked, Eber followed.[129] But not blindly. Pérès' judicious observations on the use of cliché within Arabic literary circles in Spain applies no less to the Jews: *"L'imitation n'exclut pas l'inspiration personelle."*[130] The fascinating feature of Arab influence on the Jews was not in the use of Arabic, in the cultivation of the sciences, or in the rise of religious skepticism. Paradoxically, the profoundest form of Arabization of the Jewish *intelligentsia* was betrayed in the flowering of Hebrew—grammar, poetry, and, above all, neo-classicism. The revival of classical Hebrew—*but only in poetry*—was accompanied by a revival of classical metaphor, classical panegyric, classical typology. The Quran gave new life to the Bible, and the children of Mecca rejuvenated the spirit of the seed of Jacob.[131] Hence, it came about that while in France the Messiah was a prayer, in Andalus he could become a program, a class, a man.

Much has been written about the peculiar cultural pattern reflected by the Jewish courtier class of Andalus, and about the panegyrics composed in its honor. The Arabic forms and stimulus, the vanity and self-indulgence, the sensuousness and fatalism, the rigid classicism and unbounded secularism—all have been the subject of study and comment. But many a study of the poetry of the "golden age of Spain" tacitly or explicitly, some with half-embarrassment, others in open shock, throw up their hands in resignation at the

---

128 Cf. Pérès, *op. cit.*, pp. 9, 90 f., 252 f.; A.R. Nykl, *Hispano-Arabic Poetry* (Baltimore, 1946), pp. 69 f.; cf. also the illuminating discussion in Abel, *op. cit.*, pp. 222 f.
129 Cf. Moses Ibn Ezra, *Shirat Israel*, p. 63; J. Schirmann, "The Function of the Hebrew Poet in Medieval Spain," pp. 235 f.; B. Klar, *Meḥqarim we-'Iyyunim*, pp. 85 f.
130 Pérès, *op. cit.*, p. 474.
131 It is fruitless to argue that the metaphors and typologies were the Hebrew counterparts of Arabic classicism. Of course, the Arabic classicism generated certain ideal images within the Muslim community; cf. the serious and saritical comparisons in Pérès, *op. cit.*, pp. 42, 435. We shall, accordingly, have to conclude that the Muslim influence on the Jews also extended to the point of typology and self-heroification. But that does not mean that the Jews did not take the matter seriously. What has been said above about the phenomenology of texts applies also to people; cf. Analysis, beginning of ch. III.

enigma of these fawning panegyrics produced by the same pens that created the most intensely religious and moving hymns that Hebrew literature has ever known since the days of the Psalmists and the compilers of the Jewish liturgy. How could an Ibn Gabirol lick the boots of some, hurl dung at others, and then in the very same idiom burst forth into songs of inspiration that have rarely been equalled in literature? The modern critic often points to the influence of the environment and turns quickly to philological analysis.

Those modern scholars who have tried to explain the paradox of the great medieval Hebrew poets have correctly pointed to two basic drives that unquestionably stimulated the literature of flattery: money and the ego.[132] To the poet the courtier was above all a patron, and as the all-powerful and assertive consumer he could set the standards, dictate the tastes, and determine the idiom by which he was eulogized. This is, of course, perfectly true. But this will not explain the particular tastes they did choose, and, above all, the typology by which they measured themselves and which they sought to purchase through their patronage. Perhaps the money they spent on self-glorification was only the other side of the coin which they dispensed only a bit less lavishly on the building of synagogues, the composition of liturgical hymns, support of rabbinic learning, the ransom of Jewish captives, the amassing of libraries, commissioning new works, the study of philosophy, and the rigid controlling of the machinery of the Jewish community.

What we are suggesting is that the courtiers did not live compartmentalized lives, rendering homage unto themselves in their gardens and unto God in His temples. Rather, we submit, they lived in a unified milieu which, however unique and out of tune with the major themes known to us from other communities and periods of Jewish history, was integrated and endowed with an inner harmony. The hymns and the prayers, the *geulahs* and the *ahabahs*, were composed in the same idiom and the same style as the idyls and the paeans, the eulogies and the barbs. And all of them were nourished by the same drives and aspirations of the same class. What modern scholars have chosen to call the secular side of this courtier class, we think it would be more accurate to call expressions of relaxation, the partaking and enjoyment of the material, the personal, the worldly. Why assume that, in enjoying this world, a religious man had to forget the source of his pleasures and his pains, of his conquests and his defeats? Who is to decide that love of wine and song, or even of women and young boys, is secular by nature and alien to the spirit of religion? Why should we judge the courtiers of Andalus by the standards of Troyes, Mainz and Cracow? Perhaps it would be fairer and more productive historically to

---

132 Cf. the studies referred to in nn. 124, 129.

understand each age and each form of expression in its own terms. This we can do by only examining the whole of its work, and not merely each of the parts artificially isolated from the others. If we see Ibn Shaprut, Ibn Nagrela, Ibn Albalia, Ibn Ezra and the others as they were—rabbis and courtiers, materialists and pietists, Arabists and Hebraists—the picture so familiar to all students of the Jewish Middle Ages may take on a somewhat different hue. The Hebrew classicism born out of the esthetic tastes which they had appropriated from the Arabs generated a biblical-rabbinic typology, which, in turn, stimulated and refurbished their hunger and their dreams for more power, more fame, more glory. Clearly, they tried to live as though Andalus could become a second Palestine or its surrogate, and Granada and Seville latter-day Jerusalems. They were not content with having the Torah go forth from Lucena and the word of the Lord from Cordova and Granada. They wanted those cities to become their inheritance, the centers of a Jewish world renewing as of old the atmosphere of Judea.[133] That was the drive behind their Hebraism and esthetics, their ambitions and vanities. Such a passion could be expressed only in ultimate terms—terms appropriate to the glories of the past and the end of days.

I do not mean to deny or even to discredit one iota of the constant and passionate prayer for a return to the Holy Land that is echoed incessantly in the poetry of Andalus. I have not the slightest doubt that many men meant these prayers literally and with all their hearts. Even Samuel ibn Nagrela, whose poetry is notoriously poor in traditional messianic prayers, prayed openly for a restoration of the Temple, where he would minister as a Levite.[134] However, the two themes were by no means mutually exclusive. The traditional messianic dream was a religious dogma that would be effected by God in His good time. In the meanwhile, a surrogate program could be translated into reality in Andalus, as it had been in previous centuries in Babylonia. Except that in Andalus, certain facts of life probably stimulated the feeling that there the Jews could go even further. After all, had their Arab overlords not conquered a land peopled by alien ethnic groups, who in many areas outnumbered their masters, and created there a second Caliphate? Could the position not be reversed, so that Christians and Muslims would be *dhimmis* and Jews the masters?

However, all this is merely skirting the issue. If Judah ha-Levi's testimony is worth anything (and the subsequent Maimunist controversy confirms his accusations), to some Jews the prayer for the messianic era had become a social form, a figure of speech for a period of Jewish bliss and national supremacy, which

---

133 Cf. above, pp. 253 f.
134 Cf. Schirmann, "Samuel Hannagid," p. 115.

they did not mean literally.[135] The sophisticated philosopher had become too much of a skeptic and a realist to look forward to the resurrection, to a day when the lion and the lamb would lie down together, or to the beating of all swords and spears into ploughshares and pruning hooks. But he could look forward to Jewish power and to the conversion of all mankind to the one true faith and form of worship. And why should he not be able to start the ball rolling in Spain? Why wait for a return to the Holy Land, the promise of which, for all one knew, might have been as much an allegory or symbol of Jewish might as some of the more fantastic prophecies?

But however the Jews of Andalus understood the messianic promise, there can be little doubt that they were obsessed by it. The belief in the messianic redemption is, of course, part of Jewish dogma. However, at no time in the history of the Jews after the second century was there such a concentration of messianic speculation and of vigorous reaffirmation of the messianic hope as there was in Andalus in the eleventh and twelfth centuries. Solomon ibn Gabirol, Abraham ibn Ezra, Judah ha-Levi, Abraham bar Ḥiyya, Judah ben Barzillai, Moses Maimonides, Moses ibn Ezra, Abraham ibn Daud—not to mention activists whom history has condemned as the "false messiahs" of the age— all combine to point to the Messiah as a major motif in their *Weltanschauung*.[137] We have ventured to call that tradition, which was cultivated and transmitted, a program. Perhaps a better description would be a curriculum; for while active messsianism was rare and sporadic, the intellectual and emotional energy concentrated on "the end" can only be appraised as an *idée fixe*. And when men did attain political power, the longing was whetted and aroused to a point that had to erupt either in hysterical action or in the kind of fantasy we have seen in the Hebrew verse of the period.

What is of no interest to us in the present context is whether the power and aspirations of most of the class had any substantive basis in reality. The appropriateness of their imagery is also not our concern, any more than is that of the imagery used to describe the medieval Christian kings whose *laudes* glorified them as second Davids, Moseses or Christs.[138] What is important to us is whether they meant what they said. Ibn Daud leads us to think that they did. This, then,

135 Cf. below, pp. 296 f.
136 Cf. Maimonides, *Guide*, II.29; *idem*, *Mishneh Torah*, Melakim, chs. 11–12.
137 Cf. Silver, *op. cit.*, pp. 64 f. The contrast of the Andalusians with the French is blatant. While the latter speculated on one or two dates, Spanish authorities were constantly devising new approaches to the same subject; cf. also above, p. 215 n. 137. For Moses ibn Ezra, cf. his *Shirat Israel*, pp. 128, 187 f. and esp. his *Collected Liturgical Poems* (ed. Bernstein), *passim*.
138 Cf. E.H. Kantorowicz, *Laudes Regiae* (Berkeley, 1958). For "Moses," cf. Schramm, *Kaiser, Rom und Renovatio*, I, 142 f.

is the soil on which the biblical imagery of Ibn Shaprut's poets, of the Nagid and his disciples, of Judah ha-Levi and Abraham ibn Daud took root and came to flower.

Sefer ha-Qabbalah is, accordingly, the summation in prose of an ideology and style of life known from the poetry of the "men of Andalus."[139] Drab and unpolished, the book nevertheless reflects in form and substance the spirit and the hopes of two centuries of men who formed a tightly knit and fairly closed circle with a singular form of expression as well as of life and achievement. However, while the poems were pointed at individual men, Ibn Daud memorialized the class as a whole. He saw it as a chain which was linked together by the vision of those who had forged it, and which shaped the character of those who were its members in 1161.

D. Ignoble Villains

A hero must have a villain, an enemy whose downfall will prove the legitimacy of the virtuous man's claim to power and spoils. More precisely, as is demonstrated in the more developed *novella*, the hero must pluck thorns from within as well as cut down monsters from without. Pretenders and interlopers will beset his way and complicate his task, but in the end they, too, one and all, will reap the fruits of their unseemly acts.

The monster, as we have indicated, is, of course, Edom, the enemy of Israel, never outspokenly identified by Ibn Daud.[140] However, within the Jewish community the courtiers and rabbis had to contend with inimical forces of varying intensity that reared their heads from time to time. At the top of the list were the Karaites, the exoteric stimulus for Ibn Daud's history. Devoid of any historic chain that would legitimize their claims, they were portrayed by Ibn Daud as a gang of traitors, who rejected their masters and set up their own laws out of the basest of motives. Both their numbers and their attributes testified to their true worth and character. Few in number and scattered, rigidly held in check by the Rabbanites, and spared their lives only because of the legal rectitude of the Jewish leaders (all this is, of course, sheer nonsense and wish-fulfillment), they silently accepted the curses and humiliations heaped upon them by the leaders of the Jewish community of the Holy Land and Spain. Their true nature was revealed in the same way that the character of the virtuous is proved—by their actions. Neither their pens nor their hands have ever produced anything to strengthen the hearts of the Jews in their exile and dispersion.

---

[139] In at least one passage, Ibn Daud virtually paraphrased verses by Judah ha-Levi; cf. S.N. to Epilogue. 83.
[140] Cf. Analysis, ch. IV.

Never a poem or word of consolation emerged from their lips. The only books they composed were easily exposed as travesties of knowledge and distortions of tradition. But, thank God, their mouths have been clamped shut, and they are no longer able to lift their heads.[141]

Within the Rabbanite community, praise be to God again, the situation has never attained such foul proportions, at least not since the days of the lawless ones of ancient times.[142] When the latter were eliminated by the Romans and the reins of Jewish government were placed in the hands of the rabbis, the heretics became so negligible an element as to be totally ignored, that is, until the days of Anan.[143] Once in a while, to be sure, vicious informers perpetrated tragedy or near-tragedy on individuals, as in the cases of R. Sherira, Hezekiah the Exilarch and Isaac al-Fasi.[144] However, by and large the community accepted its rightful leadership with affection to its own advantage.[145] The one instance when the Andalusian community failed in its duty was quickly seen to be an abysmal error, fomented by a small coterie of power-hungry, undeserving men.

The revolt began with the efforts of Joseph ibn Abitur to become head of the academy in Cordova, and was subsequently taken up by the successful drive of Jacob ibn Jau to become nasi.[146] In other words, Ibn Abitur and Ibn Jau represented a party, which, in Ibn Daud's portrayal, wished to take over the two arms of the Jewish community.[147] However, their efforts were doomed to failure. Ibn Abitur had flouted accepted authority and was condemned to exile by the Muslim caliph, who obviously wanted no trouble within the Jewish community. Moreover, even the outspoken enemies of his rival, R. Ḥanok, rejected him, for as law-abiding Jews they recognized the legitimacy of a ban imposed even by a rabbi they did not like. Finally, Ibn Abitur demonstrated to the world his unfitness for authority by his very behavior—intemperate expression coupled with faulty grammar! Such a man was hardly of the courtier class, whose models rose to power by means of the craft of tact combined with perfect style. Nevertheless, as a student of the Torah, and no mean one at that, he displayed a spark of basic authenticity by refusing to return to Spain and displace R. Ḥanok when the opportunity to do so finally came his way.

---

141 Epilogue.16–64, 119–137.
142 Cf. Introduction, p. xxxix.
143 VI.54–55.
144 IV.37; VI.196 f., 209 f.; VII.381 f.
145 Epilogue.23–46.
146 VII.69–167.
147 Cf. above, pp. 152 f.

Elsewhere we have shown that this story is a clever tapestry of fact and wish-fulfillment.[148] Ibn Abitur was indeed forced to leave Spain and to wander to the east. However, he did not quite suffer the rejection Ibn Daud would like us to believe. A stormy man, he was also one of the most gifted rabbis and poets of his generation.[149] Moreover, he was of no mean stock, having descended from the nobility of Merida, the very same community of Judean nobles from which emerged the families of Ibn Nagrela and Ibn Albalia. If Ibn Abitur is to be believed, history had played mean a trick on him, for in Merida it was not the Ibn Albalias who were the pillars of the community but his own fathers.[150] Clearly, therefore, the story of the defection and downfall of Ibn Abitur was part of the lore preserved by the Ibn Falijas, the Ibn Nagrelas and Ibn Daud's ancestors, the Ibn Albalias, in the inter-familial wars for supremacy.

The political side of that unholy coalition, Ibn Daud lets us know, also failed ignominiously. Although Jacob ibn Jau did become nasi, he remained "the merchant" he had been from youth.[151] Driven by desire for money and power, he had *bought* his way to the top and was acclaimed by his brethren in words that classified him as an impious Abimelech.[152] However, he was unable to keep his hold on his position. Having risen by money, he could only remain there through its support, and since the Jewish well was not bottomless, his coffers finally ran dry and he fell from power. Once again, Ibn Jau may have been wicked, but he did have some saving qualities. Obviously charitable and magnanimous with his favorites, a matter confirmed for us independently of Ibn Daud,[153] his passing was mourned by his enemy R. Ḥanok as a calamity to all the poor who had regularly eaten at his table. We should perhaps put it it a bit differently. A courtier and Rabbanite, Ibn Jau probably reflected the style of life and the tastes of the courtiers praised by Ibn Daud. He had one fault: he was of the other party and *ipso facto* condemned. We can almost hear Ibn Daud echoing the cry of the Maccabees: the Ibn Jaus were not of the stock chosen to deliver Israel.[154]

To a certain extent, Ibn Daud's values reflected the pragmatic ethos of biblical wisdom literature. Success and failure were the true measures of virtue or ignominy. Thus, the tragedy of Joseph ibn Nagrela, a member of the virtuous

---

148 Cf. Cohen, *SFC*, pp. 72, 118 f.
149 Cf. *ibid.*, p. 72 n. 72.
150 Cf. *ibid.*, p. 63 n. 35.
151 For the pejorative connotation, cf. VI.174–175.
152 VII.129–130. Cf. Jud. 8.22–23; 9.1 f. For Ibn Daud's feeling about such "worthless shepherds," cf. VI.128, 192–194.
153 Cf. Schirmann, "Isaac Ibn Halfon," p. 296; Dunash b. Labrat, *Shirim*, pp. 92, 162; Ashtor, *op. cit.*, p. 245.
154 I Macc. 5.62.

class, must be explained as the result of a failing in a basic Jewish virtue, which his father had had but had failed to bequeath to him.[155] But such criteria should not amaze us. They derived from the world of politics and royalty—where sin and failure, success and virtue, were all but synonymous.

This pragmatic ethos coupled with objective standards of virtue are, finally, invoked by Ibn Daud to explain why the Almighty had apparently decided to transfer the center of His favor from Babylonia to Andalus. Both of those first exemplars of the *laudes* and virtues characteristic of the nobility of Andalus, R. Saadiah Gaon and R. Hai, had to contend with types who prefigured the unworthy pretenders to power in the Spanish era. R. Saadiah suffered persecution and privation because of his impeccable honesty and fear of the Lord.[156] Despite R. Hai's exemplary qualifications, and though he and Saadiah had spread Torah and done great good for Israel, these geonim could not achieve one goal—to establish disciples who would take over their leadership. Indeed, unwittingly these geonim laid the groundwork for the next stage of Jewish history by spreading the Torah to the far corners of the earth, so that soon the people of the Maghreb would no longer have need of the academies of Babylonia. The days of Babylonia were over, and with good reason.

In Ibn Daud's survey, the gaonic age reflects the steady decline of the leadership of the Babylonian Jewish community, culminating in actual extinction. Twice within as many pages Ibn Daud informs us that the exilarchate of Babylonia could no longer lay claim to legitimacy, inasmuch as "the exilarchs were no longer men of integrity, but used to purchase their authority from the [Muslim] kings, like publicans." How else could they be described but as "worthless shepherds?"[157] Imagine an exilarch who appointed a simple weaver to lead the academy of Sura.[158] When he finally had to appoint R. Saadiah, who was worthy of the post, he expected this descendant of R. Ḥanina bar Dosa to validate a judgment secured illegitimately. Like father like son, and the latter actually threatened "to hit R. Saadiah on the head with a shoe" to obtain approval for a dishonest judgment.[159] Under such a regime, a "merchant" soon bought his way up to the leadership of the academy.[160] What should a worthy family like that of Sherira and Hai, scions of untainted nobility, do but withdraw bag and baggage from any involvement in political affairs?[161]

155   Cf. above, n. 16.
156   VI.129 f.
157   VI.128, 192 f.
158   VI.122.
159   VI.129 f. Once again, Ibn Daud embellished the story with a cliché; cf. note there.
160   VI.174–175.
161   VI.194–195.

As worthy men, they tried to save what they could and concentrated all their efforts on the propagation of Torah. However, without worthy nesiim the proper balance of the Jewish community was destroyed. Moreover, even in the field of Torah, these men were not left to perform their task in peace but had to contend with informers, who almost succeeded in eliminating them completely. The situation decayed so rapidly that no worthy successor could be found for R. Hai, and his post had to be filled with an exilarch who, though a man of good intentions, ultimately reaped the fruits sown by his grandfather:[162] informers had him clapped into prison in chains and his children were exiled to the new haven of promise, Andalus. The family of the exilarch took refuge with the Nagid, Joseph ibn Nagrela; and finally the last of them died some seven years before the writing of *Sefer ha-Qabbalah*.[163]

The burden of Ibn Daud's last message is clear. Even if anyone should be of a mind to claim that the rightful leadership of the Jewish community in Spain properly belongs in the hands of a descendant of the house of David, let him know, says Ibn Daud, that apart from the fact that that branch of rulers was shown to be unworthy, "there no longer remains in Spain a single person known to be of the house of David."[164] That statement is not a bland observation of an accepted fact, but a tendentious political claim.

Ibn Daud must have known that Spain virtually teemed with "direct descendants of the house of David." They were as arrogant and as assertive in 1492 as they were in 1162.[165] Whence, then, Ibn Daud's certainty? Obviously, Ibn Daud had rejected their claims as unsubstantiated. The days of the house of David were, therefore, declared to be over until the resurrection or "until a prophet should arise" to prove the rightful claimant. Until that time, the Davidides by blood are replaced by the Davidides in spirit, the nobles of Judea in Spain whose traits demonstrate their rightful claim to be interim leaders.[166] Their claim has been substantiated by their own behavior and by the steady rise of the Andalusian Jewish community under their leadership, which restored the rightful balance between heads of the academy and nesiim.

E. *The Unnamed Addressees of* Sefer ha-Qabbalah

What motivated Ibn Daud to make this open and passionate plea for the nobility of the men of Andalus and for their rightful claim to leadership? Polemics

---

162 VI.208 and cf. note there.
163 VI.209–218.
164 VI.218–219.
165 Posnanski, *Schiloh*, pp. 106 f., n. 2; H.H. Ben-Sasson, "The Generation of the Spanish Exiles on its Fate," pp. 23 n. 2, 28 f.
166 Cf. Epilogue.99 ("of royal blood").

of this type clearly betray the fact that someone to reckon with has questioned a basic premise which must, therefore, be defended and validated.

In the first place and most obviously, *Sefer ha-Qabbalah* proclaimed to the survivors of the Almohade upheaval that Ibn Tumart's dream of extirpating the house of Israel had not been realized. Not only was Andalusian Jewry not wiped out, but its leadership, albeit badly shaken, had been preserved intact. Indeed, the Almighty had made certain that Judah ben Ezra, like Joseph of old, would anticipate his brethren in their exile and prepare the road for them in the new Goshen of Toledo. One wonders if, indeed, Judah ben Ezra himself may not have commissioned Ibn Daud to write this history of the Jews, which would lead up to, and culminate with, the rule of the house of Ibn Ezra.[167]

In the second instance, however, Ibn Daud pleaded not only for one man but for a class, for a whole circle and its style of life. Besides arguing for the nobility of some, he was quite manifestly arguing against the claims of others. It has long been recognized that the whole tone and tendency of the last section of Ibn Daud's history represented an attempt at the legitimization of the authority of the Spanish rabbinate and of its independence of the Babylonian gaonate. Even as late as Ibn Daud's day, the Babylonian academy had not given up its efforts bring to all Jewish communities of the Mediterranean world under its wing and control. In the east, Maimonides was drawn into the thick of the conflict, inasmuch as he was doing for Egypt and other communities under his influence what "the four captives" had done for North Africa and Spain.[168] However, this explanation alone will hardly account for the very final sections of *Sefer ha-Qabbalah*. Even if the Babylonian attempts to retrieve their exclusive position in Jewry were known in Spain, it is hardly likely that in the middle of the twelfth century the Andalusians, particularly now that they were dwelling in the Christian North, would have taken the appeal and the threats of Baghdad seriously. Indeed, they could not have submitted to Babylonian authority even if they had wanted to. Ibn Daud's tendentious account points to a conflict that was much closer to home and one that had real implications for the heirs to the Andalusian legacy. Here, at last, at the very point when the issues within the Jewish community were alive from the point of view of the author, we are left without explicit clues and can only conjecture on the basis of bits and snatches of information from other sources.

The most obvious toehold available to us is the indubitable fact that Ibn Daud was not the only one of his day to evince concern with and for the style of life that had been established by the nobility of Andalus. Moses ibn Ezra, uncle of Judah the courtier and himself an object of Ibn Daud's adulation, had

---

167   *Ibid.* 86 f.
168   Cf. Cohen, *SFC*, pp. 114 f.

only some years earlier composed two works dedicated to the exposition and defense of the men and values of the Andalusian Jewish nobility. A work of his, known to us only by name and a passing reference by its author, was entitled *A Treatise on the Excellence of the Men of Culture and Nobility*.[169] Ibn Ezra indicated that in that work he had dealt at length with the various qualities which gave men distinction—science, philosophy, Torah, medicine, and rhetoric. To the art and to the great men of the last field, rhetoric and poetry, he dedicated a completely separate treatise, which has achieved renown as the outstanding medieval work on the history and technique of Hebrew prosody. Though formally merely a work on the mechanics of poetry, the book bespeaks a total dedication to the values and luminaries of Andalus, who, the author believed, had achieved the highest form of expression in all of Hebrew literature since the days of the Bible.[170] Ibn Ezra was not mechanically repeating an empty cliché when he advanced as the first reason for the literary superiority of the Jews of Andalus to all other diaspora Jewries the *fact* that they were of the nobility of Jerusalem, and not mere country bumpkins of Judea.[171] Ibn Ezra also reflected the same disdain for the tastes and pursuits of the vulgar masses that all members of the philosopher-class shared.

However, Ibn Ezra's treatises may be dismissed as irrelevant to the polemic reflected in Ibn Daud's chronicle. His work on literary criticism may be construed as being just that and nothing more, and his partisan leanings to the men and techniques of Andalus may be viewed as deriving simply from his personal ties. Moreover, his work on the nobility is little more than a name to us, and in the absence of clear evidence it is hazardous to speculate on the circumstances motivating this treatise. Far more relevant data may be gleaned from an affair with which Ibn Daud and Judah ibn Ezra were certainly familiar, if not personally and emotionally involved in it. That was the open rejection of the whole of the Spanish Jewish pattern of culture by the foremost poet of their circle, and one of its most gifted philosophical minds, R. Judah ha-Levi.

Although the life of Judah ha-Levi is well known, and the lacunae in information are rapidly being filled through sensational discoveries made in the Cairo *genizah*, a brief review is appropriate here in order to point up the probable relevance of his dramatic turn in life to the discussion before us.[172]

---

169 Cf. Moses ibn Ezra, *Shirat Israel*, pp. 76–77; Brody's introduction to Moses ibn Ezra, *Selected Poems*, p. xxxviii.
170 Moses ibn Ezra, *Shirat Israel*, pp. 62 f.
171 Cf. Epilogue.94 f.
172 Cf. the study by Schirmann and the thrilling discoveries of Goitein in the papers referred to in the Introduction, ch. II, nn. 12, 26. The summary that follows is drawn largely from the material collected by Professor Schirmann.

Although born in the northern part of Spain, probably in the then Arab city of Tudela around 1075, Abu'l-Ḥasan Judah b. Samuel ha-Levi was reared and educated in the way of life of the southern Andalusian circle described in *Sefer ha-Qabbalah*. By the time he had come to the south, early in his youth, to live in the company of the leading figures of Jewish learning, philosophy and belles-lettres in Cordova, Lucena and Granada, he had achieved considerable renown as a prodigy in the art of Hebrew verse. As was the case in many another man's rise to fame, his talents with tongue and pen gained for him the coveted entrée into the salons of the men of taste, wealth, and knowledge. Schooled in Arabic, rabbinics, medicine, philosophy and astronomy, he soon became a favorite and finally a distinguished colleague of that whole coterie that Ibn Daud described as the second and third generations of the Andalusian rabbinate.

After spending some four decades as a typical and well-adjusted Andalusian, ha-Levi dramatically turned his back on his homeland and on the style of life of his friends, wrote a scathing denunciation of the decadent intellectual universe of discourse in which he had been reared and had lived, and left for the Holy Land. There he intended to spend the remainder of his life in a way consistent with his new convictions.

By 1135, when ha-Levi's metamorphosis was beginning to become evident, the situation in Andalus had, as we have seen, changed considerably.[173] Ha-Levi's poems of that period reflect a deep disillusionment with the political situation of the Jews and extreme uncertainty about their future on the Iberian peninsula. He was almost as bitter with his fellow-Jews for their refusal to recognize the gravity of their precarious status as he was with Muslims and Christians, who on occasion had mercilessly destroyed whole Jewish communities. The conviction steadily grew in him that the happy days of the Jews in Spain were over, and that a new home, indeed a new style of living would have to be acquired, if the Jews were to live a life free of humiliation and attrition from within and without. That Andalusian Jewish culture was in a state of rapid decline was to him most evident in the widespread religious skepticism and denial that had invaded the upper classes of Jewry. The worst form of self-delusion, if not indeed of betrayal of religious conviction, consisted in the service which Jewish courtiers rendered to Gentile kings, Muslim as well as Christian, who used their Jewish courtiers only so long as it was to their advantage.[174]

The judgment of decadence, so obvious in hindsight, is in its own time often confined to the outcast elements of a society: contemporary neurotics and the

---

173 Cf. Introduction, p. xxvi.
174 Cf. Schirmann, "Life of Jehuda ha-Levi," pp. 235 f.; Baer, "The Political Situation;" *idem, History*, I, 67 f.

dispossessed. That Moses ibn Ezra should have in his later years pretended to turn his back on the "vanities of his youth"—on wine and verse, philosophy and pleasures—was understandable. After all, he had lost all—home, wealth, family and station. Even his brothers, re-established in the court and high society of Toledo, apparently shunned him and left him to wallow in the mire of want and loneliness. But that Judah ha-Levi, unanimously ackowlegded as the supreme virtuoso of both secular and religious Hebrew verse, should in the latter part of his fifth decade (ca. 1035) suddenly turn his back on society and its values, on his career and even his family, all of which were intact and unaffected by the vicissitudes that had beset less fortunate friends, was a scandal. To renounce philosophy and Spain, and to announce to all that the road to truth lay only in the Torah and in the Holy Land could not be dismissed as the symptom of one teetering on a breakdown. He was, as far as anyone could see, at the height of his creative powers and was writing continuously and with unabated vigor. Ha-Levi doubtless enjoyed the fact that his renunciation and departure from Spain achieved even in his own day a renown far beyond his profoundest dreams. It became a subject of international conversation, and ha-Levi was invited to explain and defend his actions. He did so willingly, indeed, with a gusto and eloquence that betrayed his recognition of the profound impact his action had had on his friends. And he had wanted nothing so much as precisely that.[175]

What really drove ha-Levi to renounce Andalus we will never know, if indeed he himself knew. Such decisions, now made between a man and his analyst, were in the twelfth century secrets shared by a man and his Maker. But ha-Levi as an individual was of far less significance even in his own day than ha-Levi the public figure, and his renunciation was intended and, most important, *understood* as a rejection and indictment of the whole pattern of life that had become characteristic of Andalusian high-society. As anyone who has read *Kitab al-Khazari* knows, ha-Levi renounced philosophy and all that it implied to a twelfth-century Andalusian: a cosmopolitan relativism which regarded all religious forms as essentially irrelevant to the good life. According to ha-Levi's description of this philosophy, truth and reality were equally accessible to Jew, Christian and Muslim, not by dint of and through their inherited faiths (which had not been revealed to begin with) but through reflective and dispassionate reasoning that could be undertaken anywhere, by any human being with adequate mental faculties and the proper training. Man's redemption, if one could

---

[175] For the latest discussion of ha-Levi's departure for Palestine, cf. S. Abramson, "R. Judah ha-Levi's Letter on his Emigration to the Land of Israel" [in Hebrew], *Kirjath Sepher*, XXIX (1953–54), 133 f.

even use such a term, consisted in freeing his soul and intellect from the passions which beset them and block his pursuit of the truth.[176]

Ha-Levi totally rejected this definition of truth and of the good life. Religious truth, he insisted, came to man only through revelation from God, and that revelation was incorporated in the Hebrew Scriptures. Moreover, the truth incorporated in that revelation was not accessible to all mankind, for the human race was not essentially equal. The Jews were a superior group, thanks to the divine element which was transmitted through their seed. Not all lands were equally conducive to the pursuit of the good life. Not all languages were equally suitable vehicles. Only Hebrew and only the Holy Land, only the prophets elected by God as His messengers, only the rituals commanded by God, in short, only the Torah, led to the truth, to the good life, and to redemption.[177] As for philosophy or "Greek wisdom," it was bankrupt, a form of intellectual masturbation that sowed into the wind, flowered without fruit. Philosophy was the very opposite of Torah; and, since Torah was truth, what need had Sinai of Athens?[178] Aristotle and the Jewish Messiah were thus mortal enemies.

What he first felt as a religious conviction, he soon translated into a call for action. Down with Andalus, down with its wit. Good-bye to Avicenna, Alfarabi and Ibn Bajjah, to the sophistic doubts and the interminable speculation. An end to Jewish grandeur, which was purchased with fawning to Gentile overlords and which bred but the illusion of power and security. The stars of Iberia were seductive substitutes for the cave of Machpelah and the sacred mount of Jerusalem, which, in their ruins, were more home to the Jew than Cordova in its splendor.

> "The grandeur of Islam, the glory of Greece
> Are vanity beside the Urim and Tummim.
> Zion's anointed, its Levites and princes
> Cannot be replaced, for they are unique."[179]

Professor Yitzhak Baer has cogently argued that ha-Levi's turn in life was meant and understood as a protest against, and rejection of, the whole social order in Spain in which the Jewish aristocracy had fashioned a niche.[180] However, such a message is not only a judgment on the situation in Spain general-

---

176 Judah ha-Levi, *Kitab al-Khazari*, I.1–4.
177 Cf. Guttmann, *Philosophies of Judaism*, pp. 120 f. and esp. Abramson, "R. Juda ha-Levi's Letter," pp. 140 f.
178 Ha-Levi's renowed poem, "Thy words are scented with flowing myrrh," Schirmann, *Ha-Shirah ha-Ibrit*, I, 492 f.
179 Judah ha-Levi, *Selected Poems*, ed. by H. Brody, tr. by N. Salaman (Philadelphia, 1928), p. 6, lines 57–60. The translation in the text is my own.
180 Cf. n. 174.

ly, or on the excesses of its society. Given the men who protested against his view and to whom he replied, ha-Levi's turning was also an indictment of the leadership of that society and of the distortion of its trust. The Jewish nobility, he felt, was betraying its task, settling on its lees, petty, decadent, impotent.[181] It was not secularism that ha-Levi renounced so much as the fashionable religion of his age and home, the Andalusian Hebraism and Hispano-centered eschatology, which were predicated on the synthesis of Torah and Greek wisdom, the reason of Japheth in the tents of Shem.

Virtually every aspect of ha-Levi's anti-philosophic philosophy has been studied and analyzed in modern times—his epistemology, ontology, theology, prophetology, climatology, and philosophy of history.[182] We do not need to review here subjects that have been treated by others quite competently. There is only one aspect of ha-Levi's appraisal of philosophy that concerns us, and that, strictly speaking, has little to do with the content of philosophy itself. That is the *social function* of philosophy in twelfth-century Spain. The very same circles that cultivated poetry and literature also pursued philosophy, for the latter filled the other half of the needs created by the position of the Jews as functionaries in the Muslim courts. Philosophy provided not only much of the wit and the repartee, which were as much a courtier's stock in trade as elegance of style in speech and in writing, but philosophy provided the Jew with the intellectual tools with which to transcend the profound emotional challenge presented by alien religions that had overpowered his own. Philosophy also provided the detachment and restored the inner peace of mind that had been shaken by the fact that God had obviously showered His favor on nations that the Jews claimed had a faith that had not been revealed. Philosophy thus furnished the inner stamina and the intellectual substance which the courtier needed in his confrontation with the barbs and taunts of Muslim jurists, poets and theologians. Poetry and philosophy were, accordingly, very intimately related to each other in Judah ha-Levi's world. Both were pillars of strength in the world of the Jewish courtier-class, which saw in Spain the center and object of their messianic dream. Thus, in rejecting philosophy, ha-Levi simultaneously and explicitly renounced the program of the courtier-class.[183]

To many a man, subsequent events doubtless seemed to vindicate ha-Levi. Almoravide was followed by Almohade, and the upheaval of a few communities soon turned into a general catastrophe. The Maghreb was gone, root and flower, scarcely ten years after ha-Levi had left for the east. What had been the uncertainties of some eccentrics now probably became a communal depression

---

181 Cf. Schirmann, "Life," pp. 230, 239.
182 Cf. the bibliography in Guttmann, *Philosophies of Judaism*, pp. 404 f.
183 Cf. Judah ha-Levi's poems in Schirmann, *Ha-Shirah ha-Ibrit*, I, 492–500.

that overwhelmed all but a few. In the time-worn tradition of self-examination and self-recrimination, the collapse of Jewish society in Andalus was probably attributed by many to inner decay. The way of Andalus had served to deceive, and the vision of its nobility was doubtless condemned as a mirage.

Have we begun to assume too much? Do we have such a record of the renunciation of the *paideia* of Andalus? Not until eighty-five years after the Almohade invasion, in the heat of the Maimunist controversy, did the whole Jewish curriculum of the Judeo-Arabic aristocracy come under open attack.[184] However, Ibn Daud's works may well be documentary testimony to the fact that tongues had already begun to wag against the Jewish establishment that was trying to build in Toledo a replica of Cordova. It may well be that Judah ibn Ezra, the latest exemplar of the Andalusian tradition, summoned an articulate spokesman of the old order to defend it and legitimize its heirs.

In responding to the call, Ibn Daud doubtless recognized that the attack of ha-Levi was not devoid of a substantive basis. Philosophy and skepticism, doubt and despair had made deep inroads into the Jewish community, and they had shaken some of the foundations of Jewish hope and confidence. Some Jews had lost faith in the revealed character of Jewish law and ritual and cited in support of their nondenominational deism the arguments of Ibn Gabirol.[185]

Others lost faith that vindication of the Jews would come through a messianic redemption and national restoration. Such despondent Jews also could invoke the support of learned authorities, for outstanding exegetes of Andalus like Judah ibn Bal'am and Moses ibn Gikatilla had proclaimed that an unprejudiced reading of many of the messianic prophecies of Scripture would reveal that they were meant for the time and audience to which they were addressed, and that they were in reality poetic discriptions of events that had taken place. In short, they were not prophecies for the future, but records of events that had long since come to pass.[186] While these exegetes protested that they themselves had full faith in the messianic redemption, they based their hope on rabbinic tradition rather than on Scripture.[187] However, many of their readers drew more radical conclusions. The Messiah they said, had come and gone in the

---

184 Cf. Baer, *History*, I, 100 f.; J. Sarachek, *Faith and Reason: The Conflict over the Rationalism of Maimonides* (Williamsport, Pa., 1935).
185 Cf. Introduction, p. xxix.
186 Cf. Silver, *op. cit.*, pp. 129, 209 f.; Moses Ibn Ezra, *Shirat Israel*, pp. 187 f.; Sarachek, *op. cit.*, p. 63.
187 Cf. Joseph Albo, *Sefer Ha-'Ikkarim*, 4 vols. (Philadelphia, 1930), IV, part 2, ch. 42, p. 421. Although from the context it appears that Albo knew of this view from R. Hayyim Galipapa (cf. *ibid.*, p. 418), the latter had probably appropriated Ibn Gikatilla's views. For evidence that the latter expressed formal adherence to the belief in the Messiah, cf. above, n. 26.

days of the Second Temple. Scripture had little to say to the Jew of the eleventh and twelfth century about the future. Such statements were all the more serious to Jews like ha-Levi and Ibn Daud, for the skeptics who had made them could justifiably claim that they were relying on "scientific" conclusions, on the dispassionate findings of exegetes. And the authority of the "scientist" was as superior to that of the special pleader in the twelfth century as it would be in the sixteenth, seventeenth and subsequent centuries.

Ibn Daud's attack on the anti-messianic exegesis of the "Sadducees" of his day was thus in reality a thinly veiled cloak for a rejoinder to his own confrères. Ibn Daud had probably little knowledge of, and even less concern with, the skepticism of the Karaites of Khorasan and Jibal, whom Saadiah had taken to task on similar grounds.[188] Nowhere did Ibn Daud accuse the Karaites of Spain of such skepticism. Who, then, really irritated him? Only a statement that he regarded as sabotage from within his community could have so pained him as to make him return to it repeatedly. That Ibn Bal'am's and Ibn Gikatilla's arguments had gained adherents we know from men of even later generations, who testified time again and that this skeptical exegesis was not confined to a school-house but had become public knowledge.[189]

Ibn Daud's response consisted not only of *Sefer ha-Qabbalah* but of a tetralogy which defended Judaism, as understood by the philosophically oriented rabbinate of the Cordova-Lucena school, against two extremist camps.

Against Judah ha-Levi he restated the Saadyanic thesis that while the Torah was the fulfillment of philosophy, it could not be fully comprehended without interpreting its essential doctrines in accordance with reason and science. In showing how this could and should be done, Ibn Daud explained the essence of religion in accordance with the new philosophical mode that had made its way into Spain, namely, neo-Platonic Aristotelianism. As a sign of his reaffirmation of this approach, and of his total rejection of the anti-intellectualism represented by Judah ha-Levi's *Kuzari* —the subtitle of which was "Arguments and Proofs in Behalf of the Despised Faith"—Ibn Daud produced a work with a title, which, as Bacher long ago noted, was obviously and defiantly directed at ha-Levi—*The Sublime Faith*[189a]. That the sublime version of Judaism which the men of Andalus pursued was a legitimate interpretation of Judaism, nay, *the* legitimate one, Ibn Daud demonstrated in *Sefer ha-Qabbalah*. The rabbinic courtiers, and Judah ibn Ezra above all, walked in the path that would ultimately be vindicated by the redemption of the Jewish people through the class and tradition they were continuing. Views and acts like those of Judah ha-Levi

---

188 Cf. Introduction, p. xxxvi.
189 Cf. Moses Nahmanides, "Sefer ha-Geulah", pp. 275 f.; Albo, *loc. cit.* in n. 187; Isaac Abravauel, *Mashmi'a Yeshu'ah*, Introduction. 189a Cf. above, p. xxiii n. 34.

were not only misinterpretations of the tradition as a whole. They were precipitous and pregnant with disaster.[190]

At the same time, Ibn Daud addressed the ultra-intellectuals and the skeptics. Philosophy properly understood, he indicated, confirmed the faith of the rabbinic Jew. That this faith would produce the great redemption proclaimed by ha-Levi as well as all Rabbanites, he proceeded to argue in his three books of history.

Andalusian Judaism was thus reaffirmed and updated to meet the changed conditions of 1161. God, to be sure, had willed that the center of Jewry should move northward; but nothing basic had really changed. At least, not yet. The great event was soon to come. However, it was the one foreseen by all the authentic leaders of Andalusian Jewry, and it would come to pass through the families of nobility, who had established the community in Cordova and Seville and would now revive it in Toledo and Tudela, in readiness for the day that the Lord had ordained.

The tradition of Andalus survived the upheaval and, indeed, achieved new popularity and greater dissemination than ever before, thanks to the arrival in Spain of the works of Maimonides. But the seeds of conflict between fundamentalist and "philosophic" Jewry had been sown and were germinating rapidly; for while few followed ha-Levi's course of action, his anti-intellectualism found many sympathizers. It is one of the ironies of history that Ibn Daud's *Sefer ha-Qabbalah* would soon take its place alongside ha-Levi's *Kuzari* as a bastion of orthodoxy as understood by the defenders as well as the opponents of Aristotelianism.[191]

F. The Reasons for the Esoteric Form

If our reading of Ibn Daud's works is correct, it is not difficult to point to the reasons for his having adopted the form of polemical expression that he did. As already indicated, the formal reason was the religious injunction against revealing a calculation of the messianic end. The religious inhibition must have appeared all the more valid in an age of disillusionment and widespread despair, when open discussion could only lead to greater grief, either by precipitating hysterical action on the part of messianic activists or by fomenting even greater despondency if the events did not come to pass precisely in accordance with the

---

190 Cf. above, pp. 221, 240 f.
191 Joseph b. Todros ha-Levi Abulafia, a pro-Maimunist, claimed to be a member of the same pious class described by Ibn Daud, implying, therefore, that Ibn Daud's "men of Andalus" were above reproach; cf. below, n. 193.
192 Cf. Analysis, ch. III, n. 162.

apocalyptic time-table. Over and beyond that was the desire to keep the dispute which Ibn Daud had entered within the confines of the circle of the learned, and not to expose the not always too clean linen of the Jewish leadership to public observation and ridicule. A man who was concerned with consolation and with accomplishing good for Israel would not allow such delicate matters to come up for discussion in the circles of the vulgar masses, and certainly not in communities of sectarians or Christians, who would seize upon them for their own uses.[192] Finally, in view of the specific messianic conclusions to which Ibn Daud had come, sheer prudence demanded the most covert form of revelation. A slip of the tongue could cost lives.

According to a report composed some fifty years after his death, Abraham ibn Daud died as a martyr "on behalf of the unity of God" in 1180, some nine years before the messianic date intimated in *Sefer ha-Qabbalah*.[193] Had someone informed the authorities of the subversive message in his work? Had Ibn Daud himself abandoned esotericism and begun engaging in open messianic activity, bringing down on his head the axe of the Christian authorities? We can only ask obvious questions. Perhaps some manuscript, still to be discovered, will yet reveal the answer.

---

192 Cf. Introduction, p. xiv.
193 Cf. the epistle of Joseph Abulafia in *Jeschurun* (ed. Kobak), VIII (1872-75), Hebrew section, p. 41. The earliest references to the date of 1180 are in Isaac Israeli, *op. cit.*, IV.18, f. 35c (top); Joseph b. Zaddik, *op. cit.*, p. 94. Cf. also Hebrew text of *Sefer ha-Qabbalah*, variants, p. 1, line 1. Solomon Ibn Verga, *Shebet Judah* (ed. Shohet-Baer), p. 22, accounts for the martyrdom by Ibn Daud's defiance of the king's order to convert to Christianity. If Ibn Verga's story was based on authentic data, Ibn Daud's message may have been discovered. He was presumably given an opportunity to clear himself in the only way that would signify his renunciation of faith in the Jewish Messiah.

APPENDIX

The Language of *Sefer ha-Qabbalah*

The language and style of *Sefer ha-Qabbalah* are no less enigmatic than Ibn Daud's chronology, for the work is a remarkable compound of idiomatic Hebrew—biblical as well as rabbinic—and of unmistakable Arabisms. The former requires no special treatment, for it is what we should expect in a Hebrew work. The singularities of his Hebrew phrases have been discussed in detail. Not only do they point to an author who mastered classical Hebrew sources and who could draw on them with acumen, but they seem to me clearly to establish that at least part of the work was written originally in Hebrew.

On the other hand, the work is so generously sprinkled with Arabisms that we are driven to the conclusion that when Ibn Daud did not make a conscious effort to express himself in classical clichés or stock phrases, he tended at least to think in Arabic, or at least in Hebrew terms that betray the definite stamp of Arabic usage: e.g.,

Sentence structure (References in Arabic numerals are to the Hebrew text):

1.1	זה ספר הקבלה כתבנוהו להודיע אל התלמידים
4.28	קבל משה רבינו ע״ה
6.51	נבנה בית ראשון

Masculine singular verbs with feminine or plural subjects:

3.11	לא נחשב המלכות
6.68	נמצא בין גלות דניאל לגלות צדקיהו כ״א שנה
10.118	והכרת מלכות פרס
56.167	לא חסר לו אלא אחת

Arabic-type accusative

9.109	הכעסים שהכעיסוהו פריצי ישראל
14.54	והרג בחכמים גם הוא מכה גדולה
30.95	מלך מלכות פושטת
36.12	ולא נסמך גאון
48.32–33	עד השלמת התלמידים פסיקתם
63.273	והיה לו לרב יצחק בן נבון
65.296	והגדיל בכיה

Arabisms

לאחר ש...: 42.101; 53.116; 56.103; 60.222 (cf. Rosenthal's Introduction to Ibn Khaldun, The *Muqaddimah*, I, cxii)

ובכל זאת = وكل ذلك : 28.78

ברח : 42.108 and cf. note to VI.161

ומגדולי תלמידיו : 53.117; 61.235; 63.263; cf. S.N. to VI.180

זכר = to account, tell the history: 14.57,58;15.64 f.; 57.176; 63.267

חזר = عاد : 28.75; 44.132; 57.176; 65.29

חותנו אבי אשתו : 44.138

הידוע, הנקרא = 48.44; 49.47; 53.117; 53.144 (but this is common in Hebrew sources, too).

יצא מן הכלל = خرج من الجمعيّة 31.119; 66.310

(However, by Ibn Daud's day this Arabism, based on a classical rabbinic expression, had become standard usage; cf., e.g., Abraham b. Ḥiyya, *Megillat ha-Megalleh*, pp. 3, 49; Pinsker, *Lickute Kadmoniot*, Appendix, p. 100; Lewin, *Otzar ha-Geonim*, X, Responsa No. 329, p. 133; No. 380, p. 183; and so frequently.)

יש (מי) = منهم : 53.122, 123; 70.377–378

גדלו (כבדו) ונשאו = اكرمه واجلّه : 11.5; 35.29; 60.227; 62.257

כמו = مثل : 13.33; 28.70; 34.16; 41.95; 65.302

(However, this usage is found in original Hebrew sources; cf. Samuel ibn Nagrela, *Diwan* (ed. Sassoon), p. 11, line 18; (ed. Habermann), I part 2, p. 129; Abraham b. Ḥiyya, *Megillat ha-Megalleh*, p. 95, but cf. also pp. 95, 98, 108, 138 where כגון is used in the same way).

מוסף על = زيادة على, فضلا عن : 24.7; 60.220; 61.233; 64.280; 66.309 (variants); 60.362

מלכות פושטת : 30.95 and cf. S.N. to IV.129

נאמנות לנחמות : 6.55 (but the reading is doubtful).

על יד : 57.179 and cf. S.N. to VII.270

עמד = اقلم, قام : 6.50; 7.69; 15.71; 40.63; 62.258–259

קצה המערב : 67.338

קרא לפני = قرأ على : 48.39; 65.296–297; cf. 63.273

ראש : 12.25 and cf. S.N. to II.40 and frequently in *Sefer ha-Qabbalah*.

To these should be added the obviously Arabic forms of names which are spelled differently in earlier Hebrew sources: Alexander (10.113; 11.2), Ptolemy (21.47), Trajan (cf. note to III.48; though the confusion had antecedents in ancient sources, the mistake derives from a substitution of *d* for *t* in Arabic), Diocletian (in *ZDR*; where the fantastic form is traceable to an Arabic letter that was mistread—*f* for *q*—and to misreadings of Hebrew letters that compounded the error).

Ibn Daud also gives the original Arabic forms of names and phrases which he could have translated in whole or in part, but did not; cf. 11.14; 21.47; 72.410–413. In one instance there is even a play on words that makes sense only in Arabic and Hebrew; Epilogue. 130.

However, neither individually nor collectively do these phenomena necessarily point to an Arabic original of *Sefer ha-Qabbalah*. They may reflect Ibn Daud's sources, the influence of the environment, and the general penetration of Arabisms into Hebrew usage. Even the talmudic stories which were distorted through a confusion of the antecedents of pronouns (cf. above, p. 174) cannot be cited as definitive evidence. After all, even Maimonides transmitted a story that had been distorted by a similar confusion; cf. above, p. 174 n. 89. It seems that medieval authorities occasionally relied on intermediary anthologies and adhered to them closely, thereby twisting a story somewhat.

On the other hand, there are a number of instances, which, if the MSS transmission is correct, more clearly point to an Arabic original, for Ibn Daud would not have used them in Hebrew no matter how much he thought in Arabic:

14.58   וכמו שיש עליהם ; cf. S.N. to II.86.
49.134   ונתלה בידו אחת ; cf. S.N. to VI.199.
46.8   הכנסת כלה ; cf. note to VII.13.

Moreover, if *Sefer ha-Qabbalah* was part of a tetralogy, the philosophical section of which was certainly written in Arabic, it is likely that the other parts were, too. Non-legal prose works were normally composed in Arabic in Andalus, and while Ibn Daud wrote in Christian Spain, emotionally and intellectually he and his audience were still in the South. However, none of these considerations are conclusive. The errors in translation are too few to be decisive. Ibn Daud could have written his more popular books in Hebrew to reach the widest audience possible.

The most likely solution seems to to be that he wrote *Sefer ha-Qabbalah* in Hebrew and Arabic, even as R. Nissim had done in his works (cf. above, pp. 175, 186 f.) and that the Arabic portions were translated very shortly after the publication of the book. Perhaps a more thorough study of the style of his two other works of history— based on critical editions—will yield more conclusive results.

GLOSSARY, CHRONOLOGICAL TABLE,
ABBREVIATIONS, BIBLIOGRAPHY,
INDICES

GLOSSARY OF BASIC TERMS USED BY IBN DAUD

amora — rabbinic teachers in Palestine and Babylonia who expounded the Mishna and cognate tannaitic literature.

ben — the son of.

bar — Aramaic for "ben," q.v.

beribbi — a rabbinic honorific.

gaon — lit., glory; abridged from "Rosh Yeshibat Geon Jacob," the head of the academy of the glory of Jacob (cf. Ps. 47.5). Hence, gaon came to mean "head of the academy" in Babylonia in the period following the redaction of the Talmud. Originally the prerogative of the head of the academy of Sura, the title was appropriated probably in the eighth century by the heads of Pumbeditha as well and is employed by Ibn Daud for the heads of both academies.

halakah — rabbinic law, as distinct from aggadah or homily.

ibn — Arabic for "ben, bar," q.v., often used to designate a surname rather than a patronymic.

mar — lit., sir; a title frequently employed for teachers who had not been officially accredited by a rabbinic academy with the title of Rabbi or Rab. In latter times it seems to have been used even as a proper noun.

nagid — lit., prince, ruler; a title used by Jewish communal heads of non-Davidic lineage in North Africa and Andalus beginning in the eleventh century.

nasi — lit., head, leader, prince; used in Palestine for the head or patriarch of the Sanhedrin, in Babylonia for the exilarch, and elsewhere for people of Davidic descent, especially Davidides who were recognized as heads of communities.

qabbalah — rabbinic tradition.

Rabban, Rabbenu — Our Rabbi, an honorific reserved for the nasi in Palestine.

sabora — lit., expounder, a term used to designate the rabbis of the post-amoraic and pre-gaonic periods.

tanna — authority cited in the Mishna; used by Ibn Daud to denote mishnaic authorities who flourished after the destruction of the Second Temple.

TABLE OF BASIC CHRONOLOGY IN *SEFER HA-QABBALAH*

Event	Date Anno Mundi	Sept.–Oct., C.E.
Creation	1	3761/60 B.C.E.
Flood	1656	2105/4 B.C.E.
Birth of Abraham	1948	1813/12 B.C.E.
Exodus (Theophany at Sinai)	2449	1312/11 B.C.E.
First Temple erected	2929	832/31 B.C.E.
First Temple destroyed (first exile)	3339	422/21 B.C.E.
Restoration under Cyrus	3388	373/72 B.C.E.
Second Temple erected	3409	352/51 B.C.E.
Seleucid Era begins (end of prophecy)	3449	312/11 B.C.E.
Second Temple destroyed	3829	68/69 C.E.
Mishna compiled	3949	188/89 C.E.
Rab came to Babylonia	3979	218/19 C.E.
Talmud redacted	4260	499/500 C.E.
Saboraic period ends — Gaonic period begins	4449	688/89 C.E.
Sefer ha-Qabbalah written	4921	1160/61 C.E.

ABBREVIATIONS

References to books of the Bible and tractates of the Mishna, Tosefta and Talmud have been made by the standard abbreviations.

ARN	Abot de Rabbi Nathan
b.	ben = the son of
B.	Babylonian Talmud
B.N.	Brief Notes
EH	*Encyclopaedia Hebraica*
EI	*Encyclopaedia of Islam*
EJ	*Encyclopaedia Judaica*
HUCA	*Hebrew Union College Annual*
ISG	Iggeret R. Sherira Gaon
JAOS	*Journal of the American Oriental Society*
JE	*Jewish Encyclopedia*
JQR	*Jewish Quarterly Review*
JQR, NS	*Jewish Quarterly Review*, New Series
M.	*Mishna*
MBSh	Abraham ibn Daud, *Dibray Malkay Israel be-Bayyit Sheni*
MGWJ	*Monatsschrift fuer Geschichte und Wissenschaft des Judentums*
MJC	*Medieval Jewish Chronicles* (ed. by A. Neubauer)
PAAJR	*Proceedings of the American Academy for Jewish Research*
R. (before name)	Rabbi
R. (after name of biblical book)	Rabbah = Midrash Rabbah
REJ	*Revue des Etudes Juives*
SFC	*Story of the Four Captives*
SHQ	*Sefer ha-Qabbalah*
S.N.	Supplementary Notes
SRH	*A Social and Religious History of the Jews* (by S.W. Baron)
STW	*Seder Tannaim wa-Amoraim* (ed. K. Kahan)
Tos., *Tosef.*	Tosefta
Yer.	Yerushalmi = Palestinian Talmud
ZDMG	*Zeitschrift der Deutschen Morgenlaendischen Gesellschaft*
ZDR	Abraham ibn Daud, *Zikron Dibray Romi*
ZfHB	*Zeitschrift fuer Hebraeische Bibliographie*

BIBLIOGRAPHY

Manuscript Sources

Abraham Ibn Daud, *Sefer ha-Qabbalah*. Listed and described in Hebrew Introduction.
Judah b. Kalonymos, *Sefer Yiḥusay Tannaim wa-Amoraim*. Library of the Jewish Theological Seminary of America.
Nathan Ab ha-Yeshiba, *Payrush 'al ha-Mishna*. The Library of the Jewish Theological Seminary of America.
Samuel ha-Nagid (b. Hananiah ?), *Mebo ha-Talmud* (Part II). Sassoon Library, Letchworth, England.

The Works of Abraham ibn Daud: Editions and Translations Cited

(Ibn Daud) Abraham b. David ha-Levi, *Das Buch Emunah Ramah*. Edited and translated by S. Weil. Frankfurt a. M., 1852. Facsimile edition: Berlin, 1919.
Bages Tarrida, J., tr., *Sefer Ha-Kabbalah (El Libro de la Tradicion)*. Granada, 1927.
Genebrard, G., *Hebraeorum Breve Chronicon*. Paris, 1572.
Katz, M., tr., *Abraham Ibn Dauds Sepher Hak-Kabbala*. s.l., 1907.
Muenster, Sebastian, *Kalendarium Hebraicum*. Basle, 1527.
Seder 'Olam Rabba we-Seder 'Olam Zuta u-Megillat Ta'anit we-Sepher ha-Qabbalah le-ha-RABD "zal" we-Dibray Malkay (Israel be-) Bayyit Sheni we-Zikron Dibray Romiyyim. Mantua, 1514; Amsterdam, 1710/11.

Tannaitic, Amoraic and Anonymous Rabbinic Sources

Abot de R. Nathan. Edited by S. Schechter. Vienna, 1887.
―――, *The Fathers According to Rabbi Nathan*. Translated by J. Goldin. New Haven, 1955.
Babylonische Talmud. Edited by Lazarus Goldschmidt. 9 vols. Leipzig, Berlin and The Hague, 1906–1935.
Bereschit Rabbah. Edited by J. Theodor and C. Albeck. Berlin, 1903–1931.
Higger, M., ed., *Seven Minor Treatises*. New York, 1930.
Lichtenstein, H., "Die Fastenrolle," *HUCA*. VIII–IX (1931–1932).
Masseket Semaḥot. Edited by M. Higger. New York, 1931.
Masseket Soferim. Edited by M. Higger. New York, 1937.
Mekilta de-Rabbi Ishmael. Edited by J.Z. Lauterbach. 3 vols. Philadelphia, 1933–1935.
Midrash Debarim Rabbah. Edited by S. Lieberman. Jerusalem, 1940.
Midrash Echah Rabbati. Edited by S. Buber. Vilna, 1899.
Midrash Haggadol. Genesis. Edited by M. Margulies. Jerusalem, 1947. *Exodus*. Edited by M. Margulies. Jerusalem, 1956. *Leviticus*. Edited by E.N. Rabinowitz, New York, 1932. *Numbers*. Edited by S. Fisch. 2 vols. London and Jerusalem, 1957–63.
Midrash Rabbah. 2 vols. Vilna, 1878. Facsimile edition: New York, 1952.
Midrash Samuel. Edited by S. Buber. Cracow, 1893.

Midrash Tehillim. Edited by S. Buber. Facsimile edition: New York, 1947.
Mishna. Horeb edition. Jerusalem, London and New York, 1951.
―――――. Edited by C. Albeck. 7 vols. Jerusalem, 1952–59.
The Passover Haggadah. Edited and translated by N. Glatzer. New York, 1953.
Pesiqta de R. Kahana. Edited by S. Buber. Lyck, 1868.
―――――. Edited by B. Mandelbaum. 2 vols. New York, 1962.
Seder Eliahu Rabba und Sefer Eliahu Zuta. Edited by M. Friedmann. Vienna, 1902.
Seder 'Olam. Edited by B. Ratner. Vilna, 1897.
―――――. Edited by A. Marx. Berlin, 1903.
Sifra de-Bay Rab. Edited by I.H. Weiss. Vienna, 1862. Facsimile edition: New York, 1946.
Finkelstein, L., *Sifra or Torat Kohanim According to Codex Assemani LXVI.* New York, 1956.
Siphre ad Deuteronomium. Edited by L. Finkelstein. Berlin, 1939.
Siphre ad Numeros. Edited by H.S. Horovitz. Leipzig, 1917.
Talmud Babli. Vilna, 1881. Facsimile edition: New York, 1948.
Talmud Yerushalmi. Venice, 1523. Facsimile edition: (New York), s.a.
Tosefta. Edited by M.S. Zuckermandel. Jerusalem, 1938.
―――――. Zera'im and Moed. Edited by S. Lieberman. 2 vols. New York, 1955–62.
Tractate Aboda Zara of the Babylonian Talmud. Edited by S. Abramson. New York, 1957.
Wayyikra Rabbah. Edited by M. Margulies. Jerusalem, 1953–1958.

Gaonic and Post-Gaonic and General Works: Texts and Secondary Sources

Aaron b. Elijah, *Gan Eden.* Eupatoria, 1864.
Abel, A., "Spain: Internal Division," in G.E. von Grunebaum, ed., *Unity and Variety in Muslim Civilization.* Chicago, 1955.
Abraham bar Ḥiyya, *Sefer ha-'Ibbur.* Edited by H. Filipowski. London, 1851.
―――――, *Sefer Megillat ha-Megalleh.* Edited by A. Poznanski. Berlin, 1924.
Abraham b. Isaac, *Sefer ha-Eshkol.* Edited by S. and Ch. Albeck. 2 vols. Jerusalem, 1935–38.
Abraham b. Moses Maimonides, *Payrush ha-Torah.* Edited by S.D. Sassoon. Translated by E.J. Wiesenberg. London, 1959.
Abramson, S., "From the Works of R. Nissim Gaon" [in Hebrew], *Tarbiz,* XXVI (1956–57).
―――――, "Imray Ḥokmah we-Amre Inshay," *Minḥah li-huda Mugash le-ha-R. Judah Loeb Zlotnick.* Jerusalem, 1950.
―――――, "R. Judah ha-Levi's Letter on his Emigration to the Land of Israel" [in Hebrew], *Kirjath Sepher,* XXIX (1953–54).
―――――, "R. Samuel b. Hofni's Introduction to the Talmud" [in Hebrew], *Tarbiz,* XXVI (1956–57).
Abravanel, Isaac, "Mashmi'a Yeshu'ah," *Payrush* (Commentaries on Scripture), 4 vols. Jerusalem and Tel Aviv, 1954/55–59/60.
Abu'l Fida, *Géographie.* Texte Arabe. Edited by M. Reinaud and M. de Slane. Paris, 1840.
Abulafia, Joseph b. Todros, "Iggeret," Edited by S.J. Halberstamm, *Jeschurun* (Edited by J. Kobak), VIII (1872–75).

Adler, E.N., "An Eleventh Century Introduction to the Hebrew Bible," *JQR*, IX (1897).
Aguado Bleye, P., *Manual de Historia de España*. 7th edition. 3 vols. Madrid, 1954.
Aḥa of Shabḥa, *Sheiltot de Rab Aḥai Gaon*. Edited by S. Mirsky. 3 vols. Jerusalem, 1959–63.
Ahimaaz b. Paltiel, *Megillat Ahimaaz*. Edited by B. Klar. Jerusalem, 1944.
Albeck, Ch., "Ha-Sanhedrin u-Nesi'ah," *Zion*, VIII (1942–43).
Albeck, S., "Sof ha-Hora'ah wa-Aḥaronay ha-Amoriam," *Sinai, Sefer Yobel*. Jerusalem, 1957–58.
Albeck, S. (II), "Rabbenu Tam's Attitude to the Problems of his Time" [in Hebrew], *Zion*, XIX (1953–54).
Albo, Joseph, *Sefer ha-Ikkarim*. Edited by I. Husik. 4 vols. Philadelphia, 1930.
Alfonso X el Sabio, *Primera Cronica General de España*. Edited by R. Menendez Pidal *et al*. 2 vols. Madrid, 1955.
Alon, G., *Toledot ha-Yehudim be-Ereṣ Israel bi-Tequfat ha-Mishna we-ha-Talmud*. 2 vols. Tel Aviv, 1952–1955.
Alonso, M., "Las Fuentes Literarias de Domingo Gundisalvo," *Al-Andalus*, XI (1946).
Altmann, A.A., "The Climatological Factor in Yehuda Hallevi's Theory of Prophecy" [in Hebrew], *Melilah*, I (1944).
Ankori, Z., "Elijah Bashyachi: An Inquiry into his Traditions Concerning the Beginning of Karaism in Byzantium" [in Hebrew], *Tarbiz*, XXV (1955–56).
———, *Karaites in Byzantium*. New York, 1959.
———, "Some Aspects of Karaite-Rabbanite Relations," *PAAJR*, XXIV–XXV (1955–56).
———, "Studies in the Messianic Doctrine of Yehuda Hadassi" [in Hebrew], *Tarbiz*, XXX (1960–61).
The Apocrypha and Pseudepigrapha of the Old Testament in English. Edited by R.H. Charles. 2 vols. Oxford, 1913.
Aptowitzer, V., *Introductio ad Sefer Rabiah* [in Hebrew]. Jerusalem, 1938.
———, "R. Chuschiel und Chananel," *Jahresbericht der Israelitisch-Theologischen Lehranstalt in Wien*, XXXVIII–XXXIX (1933).
Arfa, M., *Abraham ibn Daud and the Beginning of Medieval Jewish Aristotelianism*. Unpublished doctoral dissertation. Columbia University, 1954.
Aronius, J., *Regesten zur Geschichte der Juden*. Berlin, 1902.
Ashtor, E., "Prices of Books from the Geniza" [in Hebrew], *Tarbiz*, XXXIII (1963–64).
———, *Qorot ha-Yehudim bi-Sefarad ha-Muslimit*, vol. I. Jerusalem, 1960.
Asin Palacios, M., *Abenhazam de Cordoba y su Historia Critica de las Ideas Religiosas*. 5 vols. Madrid, 1927–32.
Assaf, S., "Ancient Book Lists" [in Hebrew], *Kirjath Sepher*, XVIII (1941–42).
———, *Gaonic Responsa from Genizah MSS* [in Hebrew]. Jerusalem, 1928.
———, *Gaonica* [in Hebrew]. Jerusalem, 1933.
———, "Le-Qorot ha-Rabbanut," *Reshumot*, II (1926–27).
———, "Letters of Babylonian Geonim" [in Hebrew], *Tarbiz*, XI (1939–40).
———, "Letters of R. Samuel b. Eli and His Contemporaries" [in Hebrew], *Tarbiz*, I, part 1 (October, 1929).
———, "Li-Ṣemiḥat ha-Merkazim ha-Yisraeliyyim bi-Tequfat ha-Geonim," *Haschiloah*, XXXV (1918).

———, " 'Megillath Setharim' of R. Nissim b. Jacob of Kairuwan" [in Hebrew], *Tarbiz*, XII (1940–41).
———, *Meqorot le-Toledot ha-Ḥinuk be-Israel*. 4 vols. Tel Aviv, 1925–47.
———, *Meqorot u-Meḥqarim be-Toledot Israel*. Jerusalem, 1946.
———, *Ha-'Onashim Aḥaray Ḥatimat ha-Talmud*. Jerusalem, 1921–22.
———, *Responsa Geonica* [in Hebrew]. Jerusalem, 1942.
———, *Tequfat ha-Geonim we-Sifrutah*. Edited by M. Margalioth. Jerusalem, 1955.
Atlas, S. and Perlmann, M., "Saadia on the Scroll of the Hasmoneans," *PAAJR*, XIV (1944).
Atlas of Islamic History. Edited by H.W. Hazard. 3rd edition. Princeton, 1954.
Auerbach, M., "Der Streit zwischen Saadja Gaon und dem Exilarchen David ben Sakkai," *Juedische Studien Joseph Wohlgemut... gewidmet*. Frankfurt a.M., 1928.
Augustine, *City of God*. Translated by J. Healey. 2 vols. New York, Everyman's Library, 1945.
Ausfeld, A., *Der Griechische Alexanderroman*. Leipzig, 1907.
Bacher, W., "Der Arabische Titel des religionsphilosophischen Werkes Abraham ibn Dauds," *ZDMG*, XLVI (1892).
———, *Tradition und Tradenten*. Leipzig, 1914.
Baer, F.Y., "Abner Aus Burgos," *Korrespondenzblatt des Vereins zur Gruendung und Erhaltung einer Akademie fuer die Wissenschaft des Judentums*. 1939.
———, "Eine juedische Messiasprophetie auf des Jahr 1186 und der drittle Kreuzzug," *MGWJ*, LXX (1926).
———, *A History of the Jews in Christian Spain*, I. Philadelphia, 1961.
———, "The Political Situation of the Spanish Jews in the Age of Jehuda Halevi" [in Hebrew], *Zion*, I (1935–36).
———, "Sefer Yosifon ha-'Ibri," *Sefer Dinaburg*. Jerusalem, 1949.
Bamberger, B.J., "Revelations of Torah after Sinai," *HUCA*, XVI (1941).
Baneth, D.Z., "Ta'uyot be-Shimush Leshon 'Arab," *Tesoro de los Judios Sefardies*, IV (1961).
Bargebuhr, F.B., "The Alhambra Palace of the Eleventh Century," *Journal of the Warburg and Courtauld Institutes*, XIX (1956).
Baron, S.W., "The Historical Outlook of Maimonides," *PAAJR*, VI (1935).
———, "Saadia's Communal Activities," *American Academy for Jewish Research, Saadia Anniversary Volume*. New York, 1943.
———, *A Social and Religious History of the Jews*. 8 vols. and Index vol. Philadelphia, 1952–60.
Beḥayye b. Asher, *Midrash R. Beḥayye 'al ha-Torah*. New York, 1948.
Ben Iehuda, E., *Thesaurus Totius Hebraitatis*. 17 vols. Jerusalem, 1948–59.
Ben-Menahem, N., "Aggadot 'Am 'al R. Abraham ibn Ezra," *Minḥah li-huda Mugash le-ha-R. Judah Loeb Zlotnick*. Jerusalem, 1960.
Ben-Sasson, H.H., "Exile and Redemption Through the Eyes of the Spanish Exiles" [in Hebrew], *I.F. Baer Jubilee Volume*. Jerusalem, 1960.
———, "The Generation of the Spanish Exiles and its Fate" [in Hebrew], *Zion*, XXVI (1960–61).
———, "Li-Megamot ha-Chronografia ha-Yehudit shel Yemay ha-Baynayyim u-Be'ayoteha," *Historians and Historical Schools*. Jerusalem, 1962.
Benedict (= Benedikt), B.Z., "R. Moshe b. R. Joseph of Narbonne" [in Hebrew], *Tarbiz*, XIX (1947–48).

———, "Notes on the Biography of R. Isaac Alfasi" [in Hebrew], *Kirjath Sepher*, XXVI (1950-51).
———, "On the History of the Torah-Centre in Provence" [in Hebrew], *Tarbiz*, XXII (1950-51).
Benjamin of Tudela, *Itinerary*. Translated by M.N. Adler. London, 1907.
Berman, L.V., *Ibn Bajjah and Maimonides*. Dissertation submitted to Hebrew University. Jerusalem, 1959.
Bernstein, S., *'Al Naharot Sefarad*. Tel Aviv, 1956.
———, "Seliḥot Bilti Yeduʻot le-R. Joseph ibn Abitur," *Sura*, I, (1953-54).
Bet Ab, Seder Ḥamesh Taʻaniyyot ke-Minhag Q.Q. Sefardim. Leghorn, 1877.
Bickerman, E., "A Propos d'un Passage de Chares de Mytilène," *La Parola del Passato* XCI (1963).
———, "La Chaine de la Tradition Pharisienne," *Revue Biblique*, LIX (1952).
Blumenkranz, B., *Les Auteurs Chrétiens Latins du Moyen Age sur les Juifs et le Judaisme*. Paris, 1963.
Bodenheimer, F.S., "The Biology of Abraham ben David Halevi of Toledo," *Archives Internationales d'Histoire des Sciences*, IV (1951).
Bolgar, R.R., *The Classical Heritage*. New York, 1964.
Bornstein, H.J., "Dibray Yemay ha-ʻIbbur ha-Aḥaronim," *Ha-Tequfa*, XIV-XV (1922).
———, *Maḥloqet R. Saadiah Gaon u-Ben Meir*. Warsaw, 1904.
———, "Ta'arikay Israel," *Ha-Tequfa*, VIII (1921), IX (1921-22).
Bousset, W., *The Antichrist Legend*. Translated by A.H. Keane. London, 1896.
Brockelmann, C., *History of the Islamic Peoples*. Translated by J. Carmichael and M. Perlmann. New York, 1944.
Brody, H., "Moses ibn Ezra — Incidents in His Life," *JQR*, NS, XXIV (1933-34).
———, "Poems of Moshe Hacohen ibn Chiquitilla" [in Hebrew], *Studies of the Research Institute for Hebrew Poetry*, III (1936).
Bruell, N., ed. *Jahrbuecher fuer juedische Geschichte und Literatur*. 10 vols. 1874-1890.
Bultmann, R., *Theology of the New Testament*. Translated by R. Goebel. 2 vols. New York, 1951-55.
Cantera, F. and Millas, J.M., *Las Inscripciones Hebraicas de España*. Madrid, 1956.
Carey, S., *The Medieval Alexander*. Cambridge, 1956.
Castro, A., *The Structure of Spanish History*. Princeton, 1954.
Cohen, B., *Law and Tradition in Judaism*. New York, 1959.
———, *Mishna and Tosefta*. New York, 1935.
Cohen, G.D., "The Story of the Four Captives," *PAAJR*, XXIX (1960-61).
———, "The Story of Hannah and her Seven Sons in Hebrew Literature" [in Hebrew], *Mordecai M. Kaplan Jubilee Volume*. 2 vols. New York, 1953.
Cohn, N., *The Pursuit of the Millennium*. New York, 1961.
Comparetti, D., *Vergil in the Middle Ages*. Translated by E.F.M. Benecke. New York, 1929.
Conforte, David, *Qoray ha-Dorot*. Edited by D. Cassel. Berlin, 1846.
Cowley, A.E., "Bodleian Geniza Fragments," *JQR*, XVIII (1906).
D'Alverny, M.T., "Avendauth?" *Homenaje a Millas-Vallicrosa*. 2 vols. Barcelona, 1954-56.
Daniel, N., *Islam and the West*. Edinburgh, 1960.
Daniel al-Kumissi, *Commentarius in Librum Duodecim Prophetarum*. Edited by I.D. Markon. Jerusalem, 1957.

Davidson, I., *Thesaurus of Medieval Hebrew Poetry*. 4 vols. New York, 1924–33.
Davis, G., "The Development of a National Theme in Medieval Castilian Literature," *Hispanic Review*, III (1935).
Deane, H.A., *The Political and Social Ideas of St. Augustine*. New York, 1963.
Defourneaux, M., *Les Français en Espagne au XIe et XIIe siècles*. Paris, 1949.
de Sola Pool, D., *The Kaddish*. New York, 1929.
Dinur, B.Z., *Israel ba-Gola*. 2nd edition. 5 vols. Tel Aviv, 1961–65.
Dozy, R., *Histoire des Musulmans d'Espagne*. New Edition. Edited by E. Lévi-Provençal. 3 vols. Leiden, 1932.
———, English translation of the earlier 3rd edition by G. Stokes under the title *Spanish Islam*. London, 1913.
———, *Recherches sur l'Histoire et la Littérature de l'Espagne pendant le Moyen Age*. 3rd edition. 2 vols. Leiden, 1881.
———, *Supplément aux Dictionnaires Arabes*. 2nd edition. 2 vols. Leiden and Paris, 1927.
Dunash b. Labrat, *Shirim*. Edited by N. Allony. Jerusalem, 1947.
———, *Teshubot*. Edited by H. Filipowski. London, 1855.
Dunlop, D.M., *The History of the Jewish Khazars*. Princeton, 1954.
Duran, Simeon, *Magen Abot*. Leipzig, 1855.
Efros, I., *Philosophical Terms in the Moreh Nebukim*. New York, 1924.
Elbogen, I., "Abraham ibn Daud als Geschichtsschreiber," *Festschrift zum siebzigsten Geburtstage Jakob Guttmanns*. Leipzig, 1915.
———, "Wie steht es um die zwei Rezensionen des Scherira-Briefes," *Festschrift zum 75-Jaehrigen Bestehen des Juedisch-Theologischen Seminars Fraenckel'scher Stiftung*. 2 vols. Breslau, 1929.
Epstein, A., *Kitbay R. Abraham Epstein*. Edited by A.M. Habermann. 2 vols. Jerusalem, 1949/50-56/57.
Epstein, J.N., *Mabo le-Nusaḥ ha-Mishna*. 2 vols. Jerusalem, 1948.
———, *Prolegomena ad Litteras Tannaiticas* [in Hebrew]. Edited by E.Z. Melamed. Jerusalem, 1957.
———, "Seder R. Amram," *Ṣiyyunim: Qobeṣ le-Zikrono shel I.N. Simhoni*. Berlin, 1929.
Erdmann, C., *Forschungen zur Politischen Ideenwelt des Fruehmittelalters*. Berlin, 1951.
Esser, A., *Das Antlitz der Blindheit in der Antike*. Leiden, 1961.
Estori ha-Parḥi, *Kaftor wa-Peraḥ*. Edited by A.M. Luncz. Jerusalem, 1897.
———. Edited by J. Blumenfeld. 2 vols. New York, 1958–64.
Eusebius, *Eusebi Chronicorum Libri Duo*. Edited by A. Schoene. 2 vols. Berlin, 1866–75.
———, *Eusebi Pamphili Chronici Canones*. Edited by J.K. Fotheringham. London, 1923.
———, *Ecclesiastical History*. Translated by K. Lake. 2 vols. Loeb Classical Library. Cambridge, Mass., 1953.
Even-Shmuel, J., *Midreshay Geulah*. 2nd edition. Jerusalem, 1954.
Al-Fasi, David b. Abraham, *Hebrew-Arabic Dictionary of the Bible*. Edited by S. Skoss. 2 vols. New Haven, 1936–45.
Al-Fasi, Isaac, *Responsa*. Edited by W. Leiter. New York, 1954.
Finkelstein, L., *Commentary of David Kimhi on Isaiah*. New York, 1926.
———, *Mabo le-Messektot Abot ve-Abot d'Rabbi Nathan*. New York, 1950.
———, *Ha-Pershim ve-Anshe Keneset ha-Gedolah*. New York, 1950.

———, "The Ten Martyrs," *Essays and Studies in Memory of Linda R. Miller.* New York, 1938.
Fischel, W., *Ibn Khaldun and Tamerlaine.* Berkeley, 1952.
Flusser, D., "An 'Alexander Geste' in a Parma MS" [in Hebrew], *Tarbiz,* XXVI (1956-57).
———, "The Author of the Book of Josiphon: His Personality and His Age" [in Hebrew], *Zion,* XVIII (1953).
Folz, R., *L'Idée de l'Empire en Occident.* Paris, 1953.
Frankel, Z., *Introductio in Talmud Hierosolymitanum* [in Hebrew]. Breslau, 1870.
Friemann, A., "Meschullam b. Kalonymos' Polemik gegen die Karaeer," *Judaica: Festschrift zu Hermann Cohens siebzigsten Geburtstage.* Berlin, 1912.
Friedlaender, I., "The Arabic Original of the Report of R. Nathan Habali," *JQR,* XVII (1904-1905).
———, *Die Chadhirlegende und der Alexanderroman.* Berlin, 1913.
Friedlaender, M., "Ibn Ezra in England." *Transactions of the Jewish Historical Society of England,* 1894-95.
———, *Ibn Ezra Literature, IV: Essays on the Writings of Abraham ibn Ezra.* London, s.a.
Gan, M., "The Book of Esther in the Light of the Story of Joseph in Egypt" [in Hebrew], *Tarbiz,* XXXI (1961-62).
Garcia Gomez, E., "Polemica Religiosa entre Ibn Hazm e Ibn Nagrela," *Al-Andalus,* IV (1936-39).
Gardet, L. and Anawati, M.M., *Introduction a la Théologie Musulmane.* Paris, 1948.
Gaster, M., *Studies and Texts.* 3 vols. London, 1925-28.
Geiger, A., *Divan des Castiliers Abu'l Hasan Juda ha-Levi.* Breslau, 1857.
Gibb, H.A.R. and Kramers, J.N., eds., *Shorter Encyclopedia of Islam.* Leiden, 1953.
Gibbon, E., *Decline and Fall of the Roman Empire.* Edited by J.B. Bury. 7 vols. London and New York, s.a.; 2 vols. New York. The Modern Library.
Gilson, E., *History of Christian Philosophy in the Middle Ages.* New York, 1955.
———, *The Spirit of Mediaeval Philosophy.* New York, 1940.
Ginsberg, H.L., *Studies in Daniel.* New York, 1948.
Ginzberg, L., *'Al Halakah wa-Aggadah.* Tel Aviv, 1960.
———, *A Commentary on the Palestinian Talmud* [in Hebrew]. 4 vols. New York, 1941-61.
———, *Genizah Studies* [in Hebrew]. 2 vols. New York, 1928-29.
———, *Geonica.* 2 vols. New York, 1909.
———, *The Legends of the Jews.* 7 vols. Philadelphia, 1909-38.
———, "Mabbul shel Esh," *Ha-Goren,* VIII (1914).
Goitein, S.D., "Autographs of Yehuda Hallevi" [in Hebrew], *Tarbiz,* XXV (1955-56).
———, "The Biography of Rabbi Judah ha-Levi in the Light of the Cairo Geniza Documents," *PAAJR,* XXVIII (1959).
———, "Jewish Community Organization in the Light of the Cairo Geniza Documents" [in Hebrew], *Zion,* XXVI (1960-61).
———, *Jewish Education in Muslim Countries* [in Hebrew]. Jerusalem, 1962.
———, "A Colophon to R. Hai Gaon's Commentary to Hagigah" [in Hebrew], *Kirjath Sepher,* XXXI (1955-56).
———, "The Last Phase of Rabbi Yehuda Hallevi's Life in the Light of the Geniza Papers" [in Hebrew], *Tarbiz,* XXIV (1954-55).

——, "New Sources Concerning the Nagids of Qayrawan and R. Nissim" [in Hebrew], *Zion*, XXVII (1961-62).
——, "From the Mediterranean to India," *Speculum*, XXIX (1954).
——, "Shemarya b. Elhanan," *Tarbiz*, XXXII (1962-63).
——, "Who Was the First Nagid?" [in Hebrew], *Zion*, XXVII (1961-62).
——, "R. Yehudah Hallevi in Spain in the Light of the Geniza Papers" [in Hebrew], *Tarbiz*, XXIV (1954-55).
Goldberg, P.S., *Karaite Liturgy*. Manchester, 1957.
Goldin, J., *The Living Talmud*. New York, 1957.
Goldstein, M., *Jesus in the Jewish Tradition*. New York, 1950.
Goldziher, I., "Proben muhammedanischer Polemik gegen des Talmud," *Jeschurun* (Edited by J. Kobak), VIII (1872-75).
Gonzalez Palencia, A., *Los Mozarabes de Toledo en los Siglos XII y XIII*. 4 vols. Madrid, 1926-1930.
——, "Vento por Deudas en Toledo a fino del Siglo XII," *Al-Andalus*, III (1935).
Graetz, H., *Geschichte der Juden*. 11 vols. Leipzig, 1897-1911.
Graf, A., *Roma nella Memoria e nelle Immaginazioni del Medio Evo*. Turin, 1923.
Grayzel, S., *The Church and the Jews in the XIIIth Century*. Philadelphia, 1933.
Gross, H., "Meir b. Simon und seine Schrift Milchemeth Mizwa," *MGWJ*, XXX (1881).
——, *Gallia Judaica*. Paris, 1897.
Grunebaum, G.E. von, *Medieval Islam*. 2nd edition. Chicago, 1953.
Guedemann, M., *Geschichte des Erziehungswesens und der Cultur der Juden*. 3 vols. Vienna, 1880-88.
——, *Das juedische Unterrichtswesen waehrend der spanisch-arabischen Periode*. Vienna, 1873.
Guttmann, J., *Philosophies of Judaism*. Translated by D.W. Silverman. Philadelphia, 1964.
——, *Die Religionsphilosophie des Abraham ibn Daud aus Toledo*. Goettingen, 1879.
Habermann, A.M., "Yehosef bar Samuel ha-Nagid," *Tesoro de los Judios Sefardies*, IV (1961).
Hadassi, Judah, *Eshkol ha-Kofer*. Eupatoria, 1836.
Al-Ḥakim b. 'Abdallah al-Naisaburi, *An Introduction to the Science of Tradition*. Edited and translated by J. Robson. London, 1953.
Halachoth Kezuboth Attributed to R. Yehudai Gaon. Edited by M. Margulies. Jerusalem, 1942.
Halakot Pesuqot 'ow Hilkot Re'u. Edited by L. Schlossberg. Versailles, 1885/6.
Halakot Pesuqot. Edited by S. Sassoon. Jerusalem, 1950.
Halevy, I., *Dorot Harischonim*. 4 vols. Pressburg and Frankfurt a.M., 1897-1918.
Halkin, A.S., "A Fragment of Saadyah's Introduction to the Commentary on the Pentateuch" [in Hebrew], *Louis Ginzberg Jubilee Volume*. 2 vols. New York, 1945.
——, "Judeo-Arabic Literature," *The Jews: Their History, Culture and Religion*. 2 vols. Edited by L. Finkelstein. New York, 1949.
——, "The Judeo-Islamic Age," *Great Ages and Ideas of the Jewish People*. Edited by L.W. Schwarz. New York, 1956.
——, "Le-Toledot ha-Shemad Bimay ha-al-Muwaḥiddin," *The Joshua Starr Memorial Volume*. New York, 1953.

―――, "The Medieval Jewish Attitude Toward Hebrew," *Studies and Texts*. Edited by A. Altmann. Cambridge, 1963.

―――, "Toledot Qiddush ha-Ḥodesh ba-'Adat ha-Qara'im," *Horeb*, II (1935).

al-Ḥarizi, Judah, *Taḥkemoni*. Edited by Y. Toporowsky. Tel Aviv, 1952.

Harkavy, A.A., "Le-Toledot R. Samuel ha-Nagid," *Meassef*. Edited by L. Rabinowicz. St. Petersburg, 1902.

―――, *Zikron la-Rishonim*. 6 vols. St. Petersburg and Berlin, 1879–1903.

Haskins, C.H., *The Renaissance of the Twelfth Century*. New York, 1957.

Hebrew Ethical Wills. 2 vols. Edited and translated by I. Abrahams. Philadelphia, 1926.

Heinemann, I., *The Methods of the Aggadah* [in Hebrew]. Jerusalem, 1949.

Hennecke, E., *New Testament Apocrypha*, I. English translation. Philadelphia, 1963.

Herford, R.T., *Christianity in Talmud and Midrash*. London, 1903.

Heschel, A.J., "'Al Ruaḥ ha-Qodesh bi-may ha-Baynayyim," *Alexander Marx Jubilee Volume*. 2 vols. New York, 1950.

―――, *The Quest for Certainty in Saadia's Philosophy*. New York, 1944.

Hirschberg, H.Z., "The Almohade Persecutions and the India Trade" [in Hebrew], *I.F. Baer Jubilee Volume*. Jerusalem, 1960.

―――, "The Bene Sogmar of al-Mahdiya" [in Hebrew], *Zion*, XXII (1957).

―――, "Qehillot Israel bi-Neot ha-Midbar shel Algeria," *Sinai, Sefer Yobel*. Jerusalem, 1957–58.

Hoffmann, D., "Der oberste Gerichtshof in der Stadt des Heiligthums," *Jahres-Bericht des Rabbiner Seminars fuer das orthodoxe Judenthum pro 5638*. Berlin, 1877–1878.

Horovitz, J., "Alter und Ursrung des Isnad," *Der Islam*, VIII (1917).

Horovitz, S., *Der Mikrokosmos des Josef ibn Saddik*. Breslau, 1903.

Hueffer, H., "Die leonesischen Hegemoniebestrebungen und Kaisertitel," *Spanische Forschungen der Goerresgesellschaft*. Erste Reihe, III (1931).

Huici Miranda, A., *Historia Politica Del Imperio Almohade*. Tetuan, 1956.

Ibn Aknin, Joseph b. Judah, *Divulgatio Mysteriorum Luminumque Apparentia* [in Arabic]. Edited and translated into Hebrew by A.S. Halkin. Jerusalem, 1964.

―――, *Einleitung in dem Talmud* [in Hebrew]. Edited by H. Graetz. Breslau, s.a.

Ibn Ezra, Abraham, "Abraham ibn Ezra's Shorter Commentary on Daniel," *Miscellany of Hebrew Literature*, II. Edited by H.J. Mathews. (1877).

Ibn Ezra, Moses, *Collected Liturgical Poems* [in Hebrew]. Edited by S. Bernstein, Tel Aviv, 1957.

―――, *Selected Poems*. Edited by H. Brody; translated by S. Solis-Cohen. 2nd edition. Philadelphia, 1945.

―――, *Kitab al-Muḥadarat w'al-Mudhakarat*. Translated into Hebrew under the title *Shirat Israel*, by B.Z. Halper. Leipzig, 1923–24.

―――, *Shiray ha-Ḥol*. Edited by H. Brody. 2 vols. Berlin-Jerusalem, 1935–41.

Ibn Gabirol, Solomon, *Selected Poems*. Edited by I. Davidson; translated by I. Zangwill. Philadelphia, 1923.

―――, *Shiray Solomon b. Judah Ibn Gabirol*. Edited by H.N. Bialik and I.H. Ravnitzky. 3 vols. Berlin and Tel Aviv, 1923/24–31/32.

Ibn Haukal, Muhammad, *Opus Geographicum*. Edited by J.H. Kramers. Leiden, 1938–39.

Ibn Janaḥ, Jonah Abu'l-Walid Merwan. *The Book of Hebrew Roots*. Edited by A. Neubauer. Oxford, 1875.

―――, *Sefer Hariqma*. Edited by M. Wilensky. Jerusalem, 1964.

———, *Sefer Haschoraschim*. Translated by Judah ibn Tibbon. Edited by W. Bacher. Berlin, 1896.
Ibn Khaldun, *Kitab al-'Ibar*. 7 vols. Beirut, 1956–61.
———, *The Muqaddimah*. Translated by F. Rosenthal. 3 vols. New York, 1948.
Ibn al-Khatib, Muhammad, *Histoire de l'Espagne Musulmane. Extraite du Kitab A'mal al-A'lam*. Edited by E. Lévi-Provençal. Rabat, 1934.
Ibn Nagrela, Samuel, *Diwan*. Edited by D.S. Sassoon. London, 1934.
———, Edited by A.M. Habermann and S. Abramson, 3 vols. under title: *Kol Shiray R. Samuel ha-Nagid*. Tel Aviv, 1946/47–52/53.
Ibn Shahin, Nissim b. Jacob, *Clavis Talmudica* [in Hebrew]. Edited by J. Goldenthal. Vienna, 1847.
———, *Ḥibbur Yafeh me-ha-Yeshu'ah*. Edited by H.Z. Hirschberg. Jerusalem, 1954.
Ibn Verga, Solomon, *Shebet Yehuda*. Edited by A. Shohet and Y. Baer. Jerusalem, 1946–47.
Ibn Yaḥya, Gedaliah, *Shalshelet ha-Qabbalah*. Venice, 1587.
Ibn Zabara, Joseph b. Meir, *Sefer Shaashuim*. Edited by I. Davidson. New York, 1914.
Isaac ibn Ḥalfon, *Poems* [in Hebrew]. Edited by A. Mirsky. Jerusalem, 1961.
Isidore of Seville, *Chronicon*. Edited by T. Mommsen in *Monumenta Germaniae Historica*, Auctorum Antiquissimorum, IX. Berlin, 1894.
———, "De Viribus Illustribus," Edited by J.P. Migne. *Patrologia Latina*, 83.
———, *Etymologiae*. Edited by W.M. Lindsay. 2 vols. Oxford, 1911.
———, [Ps.-Isidore], *Historia*. Edited by T. Mommsen in *Monumenta Germaniae Historica*, Auctorum Antiquissimorum, IX. Berlin, 1894.
Isidoriana. Edited by M.C. Diaz y Diaz. Leon, 1961.
———, *Miscellanea Isidoriana*. Rome, 1956.
Israeli, Isaac, *Liber Jesod Olam*. Edited by B. Goldberg and L. Rosenkranz. 2 vols. Berlin, 1846–48.
Issawi, C., *An Arab Philosophy of History*. London, 1950.
Jaeger, W., *Paideia*. 3 vols. New York, 1945.
Jawitz, Z., *Toledot Israel*. New edition. 14 vols. Tel Aviv, 1954/55–1962/63.
Jellinek, A., *Bet ha-Midrash*. 2nd edition. 6 vols. Jerusalem, 1938.
Joseph b. Zaddik, *'Olam Qatan*. Edited by A. Jellinek. Leipzig, 1854.
Josippon. Edited by J.F. Breithaupt. Gotha, 1707.
———, Edited by H. Hominer. Jerusalem, 1956.
Judah b. Barzillai al-Barceloni, *Commentar zum Sepher Jezira* [in Hebrew]. Edited by S.J. Halberstamm. Berlin, 1885.
———, *Sefer ha-'Ittim*. Edited by J. Schorr. Cracow, 1903.
———, *Sefer ha-Shetarot*. Edited by S.J. Halberstamm. Berlin, 1898.
Judah ha-Levi, *Diwan*. Edited by H. Brody. 4 vols. Berlin, 1901–30.
———, ———, Edited by I. Zamora. 3 vols. Tel Aviv, 1947/48–49/50.
———, *Kitab al-Khazari*. Translated by H. Hirschfeld. New York, 1927.
———, *Selected Poems*. Edited by H. Brody; translated by N. Salaman. Philadelphia, 1928.
Kahle, P., *The Cairo Geniza*. 2nd edition. Oxford, 1959.
Kamenetzky, A., "Deux Lettres de l'Epoque du dernier Exilarque," *REJ*, LV (1908).
Kantorowicz, E.H., *Laudes Regiae*. Berkeley, 1958.
Kasher, M.M. and Mandelbaum, J.B., *Sarei ha-Elef*. New York, 1959.
Kasher, M.M., *Torah Shlemah*. 21 vols. Jerusalem, 1926/27–1964.

Kasowski, C.J., *Thesaurus Talmudis*. 16 vols. Jerusalem, 1954–1966.
Kaufmann, D. *Geschichte der Attributenlehre in juedischen Religionsphilosophie des Mittelalters von Saadja bis Maimuni*. Gotha, 1877.
Kaufmann, Y., *Golah we-Nekar*. 2 vols. Tel Aviv, 1929–32.
Kirchheim, R., *Karmay Shomron*. Frankfurt a.M., 1851.
Klar, B., *Meḥqarim we-'Iyyunim*. Jerusalem, 1954.
Klein, M. and Molnar, E., "Ha-Rabad be-tor Ḥoqer Dibray ha-Yamim," *Hazofeh*, V (1921), VIII (1924), IX (1925).
Klibansky, R., *The Continuity of the Platonic Tradition During the Middle Ages*. London, 1950.
Koebner, R., *Empire*. Cambridge, 1961.
Kohut, A., *Aruch Completum*. 9 vols. Photographic reprint. New York, 1955.
Kokovtzov, P.K., *Evreisko-Khazarskaya Perepiska v X vieke*. Leningrad, 1932.
Krauss, S., *Antoninus und Rabbi*. Frankfurt a.M., 1910.
———, "Griechen und Roemer," *Monumenta Talmudica*, V, part I, Vienna, 1914.
———, "Ḥayyalotav shel Bar Kokba," *Alexander Marx Jubilee Volume*. 2 vols. New York, 1950.
———, "Die Hebraeischen Bennenungen der Modernen Voelker," *Jewish Studies in Memory of George A. Kohut*. New York, 1935.
———, *Das Leben Jesu nach juedischen Quellen*. Berlin, 1902.
———, *Paras we-Romi ba-Talmud u-ba-Midrashim*. Jerusalem, 1947–48.
———, *Studien zur byzantinisch-Juedischen Geschichte*. Leipzig, 1914.
Lane, E.W., *Arabic-English Lexicon*. 8 vols. London, 1863–93.
Lazarus, F., "Die Haeupter der Vertriebenen," *Jahrbuecher fuer Juedische Geschichte und Litteratur* (Herausgegeben von N. Bruell), X (1890).
Lazarus, F., "Neue Beitraege zur Geschichte des Exilarchats," *MGWJ*, LXXVIII (1934).
Le Strange, G., *The Lands of the Eastern Caliphate*. Cambridge, 1905.
Lemay, R., *Abu Ma'shar and Latin Aristotelianism in the Twelfth Century*. Beirut, 1962.
Levi della Vida, G., "La Traduzione Araba della Storie di Orosio," *Al-Andalus*, XIX (1954).
———, "The Bronze Era in 'Moslem' Spain," *JAOS*, LXIII (1943).
Lévi-Provençal, E., *La Civilisation Arabe en Espagne, Vue Générale*. 3rd edition. Paris, 1961.
———, *Histoire de l'Espagne Musulmane*. 3 vols. Paris, 1950–53.
———, edited and translated Ibn 'Abd al-Mun'im al-Himyari, *La Péninsule Ibérique au moyen-âge*. Leiden, 1938.
———, "Les 'Mémoires' de 'Abd Allah, Dernier Roi Ziride de Grenade," *Al-Andalus*, III (1935); IV (1936–39).
Levy, R., *The Social Structure of Islam*. Cambridge, 1957.
Lewin, B.M., "Le-Toledot Ner shel Shabbat," *Essays and Studies in Memory of Linda R. Miller*. New York, 1938.
———, *Meḥqarim Shonim bi-Tequfat ha-Geonim*. Haifa, 1929.
———, *Mi-Tequfat ha-Geonim: R. Sherira Gaon*. Jaffa, 1917.
———, *Otzar ha-Geonim*. 13 vols. Haifa-Jerusalem, 1928–43.
———, "Payrush R. Nissim le-Erubin." *Festschrift Dr. Jakob Freimann*. Berlin, 1937.
———, "Pirqay Peraqim mi-Milḥamot R. Saadiah Gaon, *Ginze Kedem*, VI (1944).

Lewy, H., "Josephus the Physician: A Medieval Legend of the Destruction of Jerusalem," *Journal of the Warburg Institute*, I (1937).
Lieberman, S., *Greek and Hellenism in Jewish Palestine* [in Hebrew]. Jerusalem, 1962.
———, *Greek in Jewish Palestine*. New York, 1947.
———, *Hellenism in Jewish Palestine*. 2nd edition. New York, 1962.
———, *Hayerushalmi Kiphshuto*. Jerusalem, 1934.
———, "Light on the Cave Scrolls from Rabbinic Sources," *PAAJR*, XX (1951).
———, "The Martyrs of Caesarea," *Annuaire de l'Institut de Philologie et d'Histoire Orientales et Slaves*, VII (1939–44).
———, *Shkiin*. Jerusalem, 1938.
———, *Tosefta Ki-Fshutah*. 5 vols. New York, 1955–62.
———, "Yaṣa le-'Olamo," *Ginze Kedem*, V (1934).
———, *Yemenite Midrashim* [in Hebrew]. Jerusalem, 1940.
Loeb, I., *Joseph Haccohen et les Chroniquers Juifs*. Paris, 1888.
———, "Notes sur l'Histoire des Juifs," *REJ*, XIX (1890).
———, "Polémistes Chrétiens et Juifs en France et en Espagne," *REJ*, XVIII (1889).
Loewinger, S., "Midrash Eleh Ezkerah," *Emlékköny Dr. Kiss Arnold*. Budapest, 1939.
L'Orange, H.P., *Studies on the Iconography of Cosmic Kingship in the Ancient World*. Oslo, 1953.
Lucas (El Tudense), "Chronicon Mundi," *Hispaniae Illustratae... Scriptores Varii*. Edited by A. Schottus and J. Pistorius. 4 vols. Frankfurt, 1603–8.
Luzzatto, P., *Notice sur Abou-Ioussef Hasdai ibn-Schaprout*. Paris, 1852.
Luzzatto, S.D., *Bet ha-Oṣar*. 3 vols. Lemberg, Przemysl, Cracow, 1847–49.
———, *Betulat Bat Yehuda*. Prague, 1840.
Machado, O.A., "La Historia de los Godos Segun Ibn Jaldun," *Cuadernos de Historia de España*, I–II (1955).
Madina, M.Z., *The Classical Doctrine of Consensus in Islam*. Unpublished doctoral dissertation. University of Chicago, 1957.
Mahdi, M., *Ibn Khaldun's Philosophy of History*. Chicago, 1957.
Mahler, R., *Karaites* [in Yiddish]. New York, 1947.
Maimon b. Joseph, *Iggeret ha-Neḥamah*. Translated into Hebrew by B. Klar. Jerusalem, 1944–5.
———, "The Letter of Consolation of Maimun b. Joseph," Edited and translated by L.M. Simmons, *JQR*, II (1890).
Maimonides, Moses, *Epistle to Yemen*. Edited by A.S. Halkin. New York, 1952.
———, *The Guide of the Perplexed*. Translated by S. Pines. Chicago, 1963.
———, *Hilkhoth Ha-Yerushalmi*. Edited by S. Lieberman. New York, 1947.
———, "Iggeret ha-Shemad," *Hemdah Genuzah*. Edited by H. Edelmann. Koenigsberg, 1856.
———, *Maimonides Einleitung in die Mišna*. Edited by M. Hamburger. Frankfurt a.M., 1902.
———, *Mishnah 'im Payrush R. Moses b. Maimon*. Edited and translated into Hebrew by J. Kafiḥ. Jerusalem, 1963.
———, *Mishneh Torah*. 5 vols. New York, 1947.
Malinowski, B., *Magic, Science and Religion and Other Essays*. New York, 1954.
Malter, H., *Saadia Gaon, His Life and Works*. Philadelphia, 1921.
———, "Saadiah Studies," *JQR*, NS, III (1912–13).

Mann, J., "Abraham b. Nathan (Abu Ishak Ibrahim b. 'Ata, Nagid of Kairowan)," *JQR*, NS, XI (1920–21).

———, "Anan's Liturgy and his Half-Yearly Cycle of the Reading of the Law," *Journal of Jewish Lore and Philosophy*, I (1919).

———, "An Early Theologico-Polemical Work," *HUCA*, XII–XIII (1937–38).

———, "A Fihrist of Saadya's Works," *JQR*, NS, XI (1920–21).

———, "Glanures de la Gueniza," *REJ*, LXXIV (1924).

———, *The Jews in Egypt and Palestine Under the Fatimid Caliphs*. 2 vols. Oxford, 1920–22.

———, "The Last Geonim of Sura," *JQR*, NS, XI, (1920–21).

———, "Misrat Rosh ha-Golah we-Hista'afutah be-sof Tequfat ha-Geonim," *Livre d'Hommage à la Mémoire de Dr. Samuel Poznanski*. Warsaw, 1927.

———, "The Responsa of the Babylonian Geonim as a Source of Jewish History," *JQR*, NS, VII–XI (1916–22).

———, "Seqirah Historit 'al Dinay Nefashot ba-Zeman ha-Zeh," *Hazofeh*, X (1926).

———, "Ha-Tenu'ot ha-Meshiḥiyot bi-May Mas'ay ha-Ṣelab ha-Rishonim," *Ha-Tequfa*, XXIII (1924–25), XXIV (1928).

———, *Texts and Studies in Jewish History and Literature*. 2 vols. Cincinnati and Philadelphia, 1931–35.

———, "Varia on the Gaonic Period" [in Hebrew], *Tarbiz*, V (1933–34).

Margalioth, M., *Hilkhot Hannagid*. Jerusalem, 1962.

———, "Mo'adim we-Ṣomoth be-Ereṣ Israel u-be-Babel bi-Tequfat ha-Geonim," *Aresheth*, (1943–44).

Marx, A., "Notes on JQR, XVIII, 399 ff.," *JQR*, XVIII (1906).

———, "Rab Saadia Gaon," *R. Saadia Gaon, Studies in His Honor*. Edited by L. Finkelstein. New York, 1944.

Mayer, E., *Historia de las Instituciones Sociales y Politicas de España y Portugal*. 2 vols. Madrid, 1925–26.

Mazar, B., *Beth Shearim*, I. Jerusalem, 1957.

Melamed, E.Z., *Halachic Midrashim of the Tannaim* [in Hebrew]. Jerusalem, 1943.

Menendez Pidal, R., *La España del Cid*. 5th edition. 2 vols. Madrid, 1956.

———, *El Imperio Hispanico y los Cinco Reinos*. Madrid, 1950.

Merkelbach, R., *Die Quellen des Griechischen Alexanderromans*. Munich, 1954.

Merriman, R.B., *The Rise of the Spanish Empire*. 4 vols. New York, 1918–34.

Mez, A., *The Renaissance of Islam*. Translated by Salahuddin Khuda Bakhsh and D.S. Margoliouth. Patna, 1937.

Miles, G.C., *The Coinage of the Umayyads of Spain*. New York, 1950.

Mirsky, A., "The Origins of the Forms of Liturgical Poetry" [in Hebrew], *Studies of the Research Institute for Hebrew Poetry in Jerusalem*, VII (1958).

Mishnah of R. Eliezer [in Hebrew]. Edited by H.G. Enelow. New York, 1933.

Mommsen, T.H., *Medieval and Renaissance Studies*. Edited by E.F. Rice, Jr. Ithaca 1959.

Moore, G.F., *Judaism*. 3 vols. Cambridge, 1927–30.

Morag, S., "On the Form and Etymology of Hai Gaon's Name" [in Hebrew]. *Tarbiz*, XXXI (1961–62).

Moses ha-Darshan, *Midrash Bereshit Rabbati*. Edited by Ch. Albeck. Jerusalem, 1940.

Mueller, J., *Die Responsen der Spanischen Lehrer des 10. Jahrhunderts*. Berlin, 1899.

———, *Teshubot Geonay Mizraḥ u-Ma'arab*. Berlin, 1888.

Muir, W. and T.H. Weir, *The Caliphate*. Edinburgh, 1915.
Munk, S., *Mélanges de Philosophie Juive et Arabe*. Paris, 1859.
———, *Notice sur Abou'l Walid Merwan ibn Djana'ḥ*. Paris, 1851.
———, *Notice sur Joseph Ben-Iehouda*. Paris, 1842.
Nahmanides, Moses, *Kitbay R. Moses b. Nahman*. Edited by H.D. Chavel. 2 vols. Jerusalem, 1963.
———, *Sefer ha-Geulah*. Edited by I.M. Aronson. Jerusalem, 1958.
Nemoy, L., "Anan ben David — A Reappraisal of the Historical Data," *Semitic Studies in Memory of Immanuel Loew*. Budapest, 1947.
———, *Karaite Anthology*. New Haven, 1952.
———, "Al-Qirqisani's Account of the Jewish Sects and Christianity," *HUCA*, VII (1930).
Neubauer, A., "Documents Inédits: I. Une Pseudo-Biographie de Moise Maimonide," *REJ*, IV (1882).
———, *Medieval Jewish Chronicles*. 2 vols. Oxford, 1887–95.
Neusner, J., *A Life of Rabban Yohanan ben Zakkai*. Leiden, 1962.
Neustadt, D., "Some Problems Concerning the 'Negidut' in Egypt during the Middle Ages" [in Hebrew], *Zion*, IV (1938–39).
Nicholson, R.A., *A Literary History of the Arabs*. Cambridge, 1956.
Noeldeke, Th., "Geschichte des Artaschir i Papakan," *Beitraege zur Kunde der Indogermanischen Sprachen*, IV (1878).
Nykl, A.R., *Hispano-Arabic Poetry*. Baltimore, 1946.
Obermann, J., *Studies in Islam and Judaism. The Arabic Original of Ibn Shahin's Book of Comfort*. New Haven, 1933.
Orosius, Paulus, *Pauli Orosi Historiarum adversum paganos Libri VII*. Edited by C. Zangemeister. Leipzig, 1889.
———, *Seven Books of History Against the Pagans. The Apology of Paulus Orosius*. Translated by I.W. Raymond. New York, 1936.
Otto of Freising, *Chronica, sive Historia de Duabus Civitatibus*. 2nd edition. Edited by A. Hofmeister. Hannover and Leipzig, 1912.
Panofsky, E., *Renaissance and Renascences*. Stockholm, 1960.
Pérès, H., *La Poésie Andalouse en Arabe Classique*. 2nd edition. Paris, 1953.
Perles, J., "Die Berner Handschrift des kleinen Aruch," *Jubleschrift ... H. Graetz*. Breslau, 1877.
Perlmann, M., "Eleventh Century Authors on the Jews of Granada," *PAAJR*, XVIII (1949).
———, "Ibn Hazm on the Equivalence of Proofs," *JQR*, NS, XL (1949–50).
———, "Ibn Qayyim and Samu'al al-Magribi," *Journal of Jewish Bibliography*, III (1942).
Pines, S., "A Tenth Century Philosophical Correspondence," *PAAJR*, XXIV (1955).
Pinsker, S., *Lickute Kadmoniot*. Vienna, 1860.
———, "Toledot R. Abraham ibn Daud," *Ha-Mizpah*, III (1886).
Platner, S.B. and Ashby, R., *A Topographical Dictionary of Ancient Rome*. London, 1929.
Posnanski, A., *Schiloh*. Leipzig, 1904.
Post, G., "Blessed Lady Spain — Vincentius Hispanus and Spanish National Imperialism in the Thirteenth Century," *Speculum*, XXIX (1954).
———, "Two Notes on Nationalism in the Middle Ages," *Traditio*, IX (1953).

Poznanski, S., "Anan et ses Ecrits," *REJ*, XLIV (1902), XLV (1902).
―――, *Babylonische Geonim im nachgaonaeischen Zeitalter*. Berlin, 1914.
―――, "R. Dosa be-R. Saadia Gaon," *ha-Goren*, VI (1905-1906).
―――, "Ephraim b. Schemaria de Fostat," *REJ*, XLVIII (1904).
―――, *Esquisse historique sur les Juifs de Kairouan* [in Hebrew]. Warsaw, 1909.
―――, "Jacob ben Ephraim, ein anti-karaeischer Polemiker des X. Jahrhunderts," *Gedenkbuch zur Erinnerung an David Kauffmann*. Breslau, 1900.
―――, *Karaite Literary Opponents of Saadiah Gaon in the Tenth Century*. London, 1908.
―――, "Liqqutim min Sefer Megillat Setarim le-R. Nissim b. R. Jacob mi-Qairawan," *Hazofeh*, V (1921), VI (1922).
―――, "Miscellen ueber Saadja," *MGWJ*, XXXIX (1895).
―――, "Reshit Hityashbut ha-Qaraim bi-Jerusalem," *Jerusalem*. Edited by A.M. Luncz. X (1913).
―――, *Studien zum Gaonaeischen Epoche* [in Hebrew]. Warsaw, 1909.
Puech, H.C., *Le Manichéisme: Son Fondateur, Sa Doctrine*. Paris, 1949.
al-Qirqisani, Ya'qub, *Kitab al-Anwar wal-Maraqib*. Edited by L. Nemoy. 5 vols. New York, 1936-43.
Rabbinovicz, R., *Variae Lectiones in Mischnam et in Talmud Babylonicum*. 16 vols. Munich, Mainz and Przemysl, 1867-1897.
Rankin, O.L., *Jewish Religious Polemic*. Edinburgh, 1956.
Rapoport, S.J.L., *Erech Millin*. Prague, 1831-52.
―――, *Toledot*. Warsaw, 1913.
Rassow, P., "Urkunden Kaiser Alfonso VII von Castilien 1126-1155," *Archiv fuer Urkundenforschung*, X (1928), XI (1930).
Ratner, B., *Mabo le ha-Seder 'Olam Rabbah*. Vilna, 1894.
Ratzabi, I., "The Translation of Lamentations by R. Saadya Gaon" [in Hebrew], *Tarbiz*, XIII (1941-42).
Rawlinson, G., *The Seventh Oriental Monarchy*. 2 vols. New York, s.a.
Rieger, R., "The Foundation of Rome in the Talmud," *JQR*, NS, XVI (1925-26).
Rivkin, E., "The Saadia-David ben Zakkai Controversy: A Structural Analysis," *Studies and Essays in Honor of Abraham A. Neuman*. Leiden, 1962.
Rosenthal, E.I.J., *Political Thought in Medieval Islam*. Cambridge, 1958.
Rosenthal, F., *A History of Muslim Historiography*, Leiden, 1952.
―――, *The Technique and Approach of Muslim Scholarship* (= *Analecta Orientalia*, 24). Rome, 1947.
Rosenthal, J., "From 'Sefer Alfonso'" [in Hebrew], *Studies and Essays in Honor of Abraham A. Neuman*. Leiden, 1962.
―――, "Hiwi al-Balkhi," *JQR*, NS, XXXVIII (1947-48).
―――, "The Law of Usury Relating to Non-Jews" [in Hebrew], *Talpioth*, VI (1953).
―――, "She'elot 'Atiqot ba-Tenak," *HUCA*, XXI (1948).
Ross, J.B., "A Study of the Twelfth-Century Interest in the Antiquities of Rome," *Medieval and Historiographical Essays in Honor of James Westfall Thompson*. Edited by J.L. Cate and E.N. Anderson. Chicago, 1938.
Rossi, Azariah de', *Meor Enayyim*. Edited by D. Cassel. Vilna, 1864-66.
――, ――, Edited by I. Ben Jacob. 2 vols. Vilna, 1864-65.
Roth, E., "A Gaonic Fragment Concerning the Oral Chain of Tradition" [in Hebrew], *Tarbiz*, XXVI (1956-57).

Rowley, H.H., *The Zadokite Fragments and the Dead Sea Scrolls.* Oxford, 1952.
Rushforth, S. McN., "Magister Gregorius de Mirabilibus Urbis Romae: A New Description of Rome in the Twelfth Century," *Journal of Roman Studies,* IX (1919).
Saadiah b. Joseph al-Fayyumi, *The Book of Beliefs and Opinions.* Translated by S. Rosenblatt. New Haven, 1948.
———, *The Book of Doctrines and Beliefs.* Edited and translated by A. Altmann. Oxford, 1946.
———, *Essa Meshali.* Edited by B.M. Lewin. Jerusalem, 1943.
———, *Oeuvres Complètes.* Edited by J. Derenbourg et al. 4 vols. Paris, 1893–99.
———, *Siddur R. Saadja Gaon.* Edited by I. Davidson et al. Jerusalem, 1941.
———, "Commentary on Ezra and Nehemiah by Rabbi Saadiah," Edited by H.J. Matthews. *Anecdota Oxoniensia,* Semitic Series, I, part 1. Oxford, 1882.
al-Sabi, Hilal, *Rusum dar al-Khilafah.* Edited by M. Awad. Baghdad, 1964.
Salmon b. Yeruḥim. *The Book of the Wars of the Lord* [in Hebrew]. Edited by I. Davidson. New York, 1934.
Samau'al al-Maghribi, "Ifham al-Yahud," Edited and translated by M. Perlmann, *PAAJR,* XXXII (1964).
Sanchez-Albornoz, C., *La España Musulmana.* 2nd edition. 2 vols. Buenos Aires, 1960.
Sarachek, J., *Faith and Reason: The Conflict over the Rationalism of Maimonides.* Williamsport, Pennsylvania, 1935.
Sassoon, S.D., *Ohel David.* 2 vols. Oxford, 1932.
Schacht, J., *The Origins of Muslim Jurisprudence.* Oxford, 1950.
Schechter, S., *Aspects of Rabbinic Theology.* New York, 1961.
———, *Saadyana.* Cambridge, 1903.
Scheiber, A., "Die Parabel vom Schatz des Gelehrten," *Acta Antiqua Academiae Scientarum Hungaricae,* X (1963).
Schickard, W., *Tarich, h.e. Series Regum Persiae.* Tuebingen, 1628.
Schirmann, Ch., "The Function of the Hebrew Poet in Medieval Spain," *Jewish Social Studies,* XVI (1954).
———, "Isaac ibn Halfon" [in Hebrew], *Tarbiz,* VII (1935–36).
———, "Isaac b. Mar Saul ha-Meshorer mi-Lucena," *Sefer Assaf.* Jerusalem, 1952–53.
———, "The Life of Jehuda ha-Levi" [in Hebrew], *Tarbiz,* IX (1937–38).
———, "Poets Contemporary with Moses ibn Ezra and Jehuda Hallevi" [in Hebrew], *Studies of the Research Institute for Hebrew Poetry,* II (1936), IV (1938), VI (1945).
———, "Qinot 'al ha-Gezerot be-Ereṣ Israel, Africa, Sefarad etc.," *Kobez al Jad,* III (XIII) (1939).
———, "Samuel Hannagid, The Man, The Soldier, The Politician," *Jewish Social Studies,* XIII (1951).
———, *Ha-Shirah ha-Ibrit bi-Sefarad u-bi-Provence.* 2 vols. Jerusalem and Tel Aviv, 1954–56.
———, "The Wars of Samuel Han-Nagid" [in Hebrew], *Zion,* I.
Schramm, P.E., *Kaiser, Rom und Renovatio.* 2 vols. (Leipzig and Berlin, 1929); 2nd edition of vol. I., Darmstadt, 1957.
———, "Das Kastilische Koenigtum und Kaisertum waehrend der Reconquista," *Festschrift fuer Gerhard Ritter.* Tuebingen, 1950.
Schreiner, M., *Studien ueber Jeschu'a ben Jehuda.* Berlin, 1900.

———, "Zur Geschichte der Polemik zwischen Juden und Muhammedanern," *ZDMG*, XLII (1888).
———, "Zwei Geniza-Fragmente," *ZfHB*, III (1899).
Schuerer, E., *Geschichte des Juedischen Volkes im Zeitalter Jesu Christi*. 4th edition. 3 vols. Leipzig, 1901–11.
Schwabe, M., "Zikron Bayt Romi," *REJ*, XXXV (1897).
Schwarzbaum, H., "International Folklore Motifs in Petrus Alphonsi's 'Disciplina Clericalis,'" *Sefarad*, XXII (1962).
Seder R. Amram Gaon. 2 vols. Warsaw, 1865.
Seder R. Amram ha-Shalem. Edited by L. Frumkin. 2 vols. Jerusalem, 1912.
Seder Tannaim we-Amoraim. Edited and translated into German by K. Kahan. Frankfurt a.M., 1935.
Sefer ha-Yishub, I. Edited by S. Assaf and A.L. Mayer. Jerusalem, 1944.
Shalit, A., "Two Traditions Concerning the Time of Isaiah's Prophecy on the Destruction of the Temple and the Return to Zion" [in Hebrew], *I.F. Baer Jubilee Volume*. Jerusalem, 1960.
Sherira Gaon, *Iggeret R. Scherira Gaon in franzoesichen und spanischen Version*. Edited by B.M. Lewin. Haifa, 1921.
Silver, A.H., *A History of Messianic Speculation in Israel*. New York, 1927.
Simhoni, J.N., "R. Solomon ibn Gabirol" [in Hebrew], *Ha-Tequfa*, XVII (1922).
Spargo, J.W., *Virgil the Necromancer*. Cambridge, 1934.
Spiegel, S., "On Medieval Hebrew Poetry," *The Jews, Their History, Culture and Religion*. Edited by L. Finkelstein. 2 vols. New York, 1949.
Stauffenberg, A.S. von, *Die Roemische Kaisergeschichte bei Malalas*. Stuttgart, 1931.
Steinschneider, M., *Die Arabische Literatur der Juden*. Frankfurt a.M., 1902.
———, *Catalogus Librorum Hebraeorum im Bibliotheca Bodleiana*. 3 vols. Berlin, 1852–60.
———, *Catalogus Codicum Hebraeorum Bibliothecae Academiae Lugdono-Bataviae*. Leiden, 1858.
———, *Gesammelte Schriften*. Edited by H. Malter and A. Marx. Berlin, 1925.
———, *Die Geschichtsliteratur der Juden*. Frankfurt a.M., 1905.
———, *Die Hebraeischen Uebersetzungen des Mittelalters*. Berlin, 1893.
———, "An Introduction to the Arabic Literature of the Jews," *JQR*, XI (1899).
———, *Ozrot Chajim Katalog der Michael'schen Bibliothek*. Hamburg, 1948.
———, *Polemische und Apologetische Literatur in Arabischen Sprache*. Leipzig, 1877.
Stern, S.M., "Life of Shmuel ha-Nagid" [in Hebrew], *Zion*, XV (1950).
———, "A New Fragment from the 'Sepher Ha-Galuy' of R. Saadyah Gaon" [in Hebrew], *Melilah*, V (1955).
———, "Two New Data about Hasdai b. Shaprut" [in Hebrew], *Zion*, XI (1945–46).
Strack, H., and Billerbeck, P., *Kommentar zum Neuen Testament aus Talmud und Midrasch*. 3rd edition. 4 vols. and indices. Munich, 1961.
Strauss, A., "Darkay ha-Pulmus ha-Islami," *Sefer ha-Zikaron le-Bayt ha-Midrash le-Rabbanim be-Vienna*. Jerusalem, 1946.
Strauss, L., "Farabi's Plato," *Louis Ginzberg Jubilee Volume*. 2 vols. New York, 1945.
———, "Maimonides' Statement on Political Science," *PAAJR*, XXII (1953).
Sultanski, M., *Zeker Ṣaddiqim*. Edited by S. Poznanski. Warsaw, 1920.
Swain, J.W., "The Theory of Four Monarchies," *Classical Philology*, XXV (1940).

Sweetman, J.W., *Islam and Christian Theology*. 2 parts in 3 vols. London, 1945–55.
al-Tabari, *Annales*. Edited by M.J. de Goeje *et al.* 15 vols. Leiden, 1897–1901.
———, *Chronique*. Translated by H. Zotenberg. 4 vols. Paris, 1867–74.
Tate, R.B., "Mythology in Spanish Historiography of the Middle Ages and the Renaissance," *Hispanic Review*, XXII (1954).
Taylor, C., *An Appendix to the Sayings of the Jewish Fathers*. Cambridge, 1900.
Tha'alibi, *Histoire des Rois des Perses*. Edited and translated by H. Zotenberg. Paris, 1900.
Théry, G., *Tolède, Grand Ville de la Renaissance Médiévale*. Oran, 1944.
Tobiah b. Eliezer, *Leqah Tob*. 2 vols. I. Edited by S. Buber. Vilna, 1880. II. Edited by A.M. Padua. Vilna, 1884.
Twersky, I., *Rabad of Posquières*. Cambridge, 1962.
Tyckoczynski, H., "Bustanai Rosh ha-Golah," *Debir*, I (1923).
Ullmann, W., *The Growth of Papal Government in the Middle Ages*. 2nd edition. New York, 1961.
Urbach, E.E., "Halacha and Prophecy" [in Hebrew], *Tarbiz*, XVIII (1946–47).
———, *The Tosaphists* [in Hebrew]. Jerusalem, 1955.
Vasiliev, A.A., *History of the Byzantine Empire*. 2 vols. Madison, 1958.
Walzer, R., "Arabic Transmission of Greek Thought to Medieval Europe," *Bulletin of the John Rylands Library*, XXIX (1945–46).
———, *Galen on Jews and Christians*. London, 1949.
———, *Greek Into Arabic*. Oxford, 1962.
Weiss, J.G., "Tarbut Hasranit we-Shirah Hasranit," *World Congress of Jewish Studies*, I (Jerusalem, 1947).
Weiss, P.R., "Ibn Ezra, the Karaites and the Halakah" [in Hebrew], *Melilah*, I–IV (1944–50).
Wertheimer, S.A., *Battay Midrashot*. 2 vols. Jerusalem 1950–53.
Wieder, N., "Judah ibn Shabbatai's Burnt Book" [in Hebrew], *Metsudah*, December, 1943.
———, *The Judean Scrolls and Karaism*. London, 1962.
———, "Three Terms for 'Tradition'," *JQR*, NS, XLIX (1958–59).
Williams, A.L., *Adversus Judaeos*. Cambridge, 1935.
Wolfson, H.A., "The Classification of Sciences in Medieval Jewish Philosophy," *Hebrew Union College Jubilee Volume*. Cincinnati, 1925.
———, *Philo*. 2 vols. Cambridge, 1947.
———, *The Philosophy of the Church Fathers*, I. Cambridge, 1956.
———, *Religious Philosophy*. Cambridge, 1961.
Yaari, A., "Hag ha-Sukkot bi-Jerusalem," *Sinai*, XXXVI (1955).
Yadin, Y., ed., *Scroll of the War of the Sons of Light Against the Sons of Darkness* [in Hebrew]. Jerusalem, 1955.
Yellin, D., "Ha-Shem ha-'Ibri le-Sefer ha-Galuy," *Studies in Jewish Bibliography... in Memory of A.S. Freidus*. New York, 1929.
———, and Abrahams, I., *Maimonides*. Philadelphia, 1903.
Yeivin, S., *Milhamot Bar Kokba*. Jerusalem, 1946.
Yesh'ua b. Joseph ha-Levi, *Halikot 'Olam*. Lisbon, 1490.
Zacuto, Abraham, *Liber Juchasim*. Edited by M. Filipowski. 2nd edition with an introduction by A.H. Freimann. Frankfurt a.M., 1925.
Zimmels, H.J., *Ashkenazim and Sephardim*. London, 1958.

Zucker, M., "Against Whom Did Se'adya Gaon Write the Polemical Poem *Essa Meshali*" [in Hebrew], *Tarbiz*, XXVII (1957–58).

———, "Fragments from Rav Saadya Gaon's Commentary to the Pentateuch" [in Hebrew], *Sura*, II (1955–56).

———, "Le-Pitron Ba'yat Lamed bet Middot," *PAAJR*, XXIII (1954).

———, *Rav Saadya Gaon's Translation of the Torah* [in Hebrew]. New York, 1959.

———, "Shenay Qeta'im Neged Qara'iyyim," *PAAJR*, XVIII (1949).

———, "Tegubot li-Tenuat Abaylay Zion ha-Qaraiyyim ba-Sifrut ha-Rabbanit," *Sefer ha-Yobel la-R. Ḥanok Albeck*. Jerusalem, 1960.

Zuckerman, A., *The Jewish Patriarchate in Western Europe During the Carolingian Age*. Unpublished doctoral dissertation. Columbia University, 1963.

Zulay, M., "Bayn Kotlay ha-Makon le-Ḥeqer ha-Shirah ha-Ibrit," *Alei Ayin: The Salman Schocken Jubilee Volume*. Jerusalem, 1948–52.

———, "Le-Ḥeqer ha-Siddur we-ha-Minhagim," *Sefer Assaf*. Jerusalem, 1953.

———, "Shibray Ṣelilim," *Sinai*, XXVIII (1950–51).

Zunz, L., *Ha-Derashot be-Yisrael*. Edited by Ch. Albeck. Jerusalem, 1947.

———, *Die Synagogale Poesie des Mittelalters*. 2nd edition. Edited by A. Freimann. Frankfurt a.M., 1920.

INDEX OF PERSONS AND PLACES

Except for certain well accepted names, such as Alfarabi, Almohades and several others, the definite article (Hebrew ha-, Arabic al-) has been ignored in alphabetization. Occasionally a name is followed by an abbreviation in parentheses (A = Amora, G = Gaon, S = Sabora, T = Tanna) to distinguish persons bearing the same name. A number following the letter indicates the generation of the authority within his given category. Unless the description of ha-Kohen or ha-Levi was deemed vital for identification, such terms have been omitted. Wherever it was possible to do so without confusing the reader, persons with distinguished surnames, e.g. Ibn Ezra, Ibn Megash, Ibn Nagrela, have been listed under a surname-heading rather than under their given names.

Aaron, 19, 24
Aaron b. Sarjada, 58, 131
Abaye, 34
Abba Arika; *see* Rab
Abba Siqra, 24, 117
Abbasids of Seville, xvii
'Abd Allah, king of Granada, xxi
'Abd-ar-Raḥman II, 137
'Abd-ar-Raḥman III an-Naṣir, 63, 66 f., 158, 189, 200, 271
Abdon, 6
Abijah, 7
Abimelech, 6, 291
Abraham, 5, 108, 165, 216, 218
Abraham ibn 'Ata, 136
Abraham b. Ḥiyya, 41, 220 f., 235, 238, 257, 288
Abraham b. Isaac, 89
Abraham b. Sherira, 51 f., 129, 183 f.
Abraham b. Solomon of Torrutiel, xiv
Abraham Kahana (G), 48, 127

Abramson, S., 127
Abtalion, 22
Abulafia, Joseph b. Todros, 302
Abulafia, Todros, xlix
Abu'l-Faraj Furqan ibn Asad, xlvii f., 94 f., 100 f., 144, 146, 164
Abu'l Taras, xlvi f., 94 f., 164 f.
Ada (G), 48
Adam, 5, 165, 216, 218
Afendopulo, Caleb, xiv
Africa, North, xvii, xl, 40, 96, 133 f., 157 f., 200; *see also* Ifriqiya; Maghreb
Agag, 277
Agrippa, 14, 98, 275
Aḥa of Shabḥa, 47 f., 179, 269
Aḥa b. Raba, 35
Aḥai b. Huna, 44, 126
Aḥai ha-Kohen, 52
Ahasuerus, 15, 31, 40, 125, 167
Ahaz, 7, 226
Ahaziah, 7

INDEX

Ahitophel, 270
Aḥunai (G, 3), 50
Aḥunai (G, 4), 51
al-'Ajab b. al-Khalfa, 84
Akiba b. Joseph, 27 f., 118 f., 177, 206 f., 241 f., 247, 249 f.
Alani, 252
Albo, Joseph, 300
Alexander the Great, lxii, 15 f., 37, 39 f., 112, 125, 154 f., 232 f.
Alexander Jannaeus, 19 f., 21 f., 38, 114, 173, 229
Alexandra Salome, xxxix, 22
Alexandria, 20, 64, 114, 136
Alfacar, Joseph, xlviii
Alfarabi, xxiv, 298
Alfasi; see al-Fasi
Alfonso VI, xlviii, 145, 257
Alfonso VII, xxvi, 95 f., 97 f., 144 f., 253, 258 f.
Alfonso VIII, 261 f.
Alfonso IX, xlviii
Alfonso el Batallador, xviii
Alfred of Sarashel, xxvii
'Ali ibn Abi Talib, 44 f., 232
'Ali ibn Hammud, 72
Almeria, 67
Almohades, xxvi, 83, 87 f., 96 f., 141 f., 158, 260, 262, 267, 274
Almoravides, xvii f., xxvi, 83
Amalek, 277
Amaziah, 7
Amemar, 41, 46 f.
Amirids; see Ibn Abi 'Amir
Ammi, 33
Amon, 7, 227
Amos, 274, 284
Amram (G), 52 f.
Anan (A, 1), 33
Anan b. David, the heretic, xxxviii f., xlvi, xlix, lxii, 17, 24, 48 f., 91 f., 107, 113, 117, 127 f.
Antigonus of Soko, xxxviii, 17 f., 20, 113, 174
Antioch, 40
Antiochus III, 38
Antiochus Epiphanes, 19, 38, 170
Antipus, 30
Antoninus b. Severus, 30, 39, 120, 175, 184, 230 f.
Apulia, 93
Arabia, 40, 92, 113
Aragon, xl, 263
Archelaus, 21
Ardashir, 31, 39 f., 125
Aristobulus, 22, 38, 229
Aristotle, xxiii, xxvii, xxxi, xlii, 40, 125, 298
Arius, xxxiii
Armilus, 248 f., 253, 263
Arnulf, 256
Artaxerxes, 15, 31, 111, 125, 261
Asa, 7
Ashi, lv, 35 f., 41 f., 46, 126
Ashkenaz; see Slav country
Assaf, the psalmist, 277
Assaf, S., 204
Assi, 33
Assyria, 192, 226, 236, 238
Asturia, 255
Athaliah, 7
Augustine, 217
Augustus Caesar, 21, 38 f., 124, 242 f., 246 f.
Avendahut, Johannes, 221, 253; see also Avendauth
Avendauth, xxvii f.
Avicenna, xxiv, xxviii, 298
Azariah, the companion of Daniel, 10

Azariah b. Joseph; see Ibn Nagrela, Azariah

Baanah, 9
Babylon, 12, 150, 228, 231, 235 f., 239 f.
Babylonia, 8, 22 f., 32 f., 44 f., 48, 60, 64, 66, 74, 83, 86, 133 f., 138, 157 f., 167, 181, 201 f., 204, 206, 211, 264, 279, 292, 294; see also Iraq
Bacher, W., 301
Badis, 73 f., 85, 97
Baer, Y., xlix, 253, 298
Baghdad, xix, xxvii, 61, 135
Bahram, 41
Bajjana; see Pechina
Balaam, 213, 215, 221, 249
Balkh, 56
Banu Hud, 62
Banu Sogmar, 78
Bar Kokba; see Ben Koziba; Koziba
Bar Qappara, 31
Barak, 6
Barcelona, 53, 83, 141 f., 260 f.
Bari, 64
Baruk of Merida, 79
Bashyachi, Elijah, xiv
al-Basra, 57
Bebai ha-Levi, 50 f., 129
Belshazzar, 11 f., 37
Ben Dama, 27, 119
Ben Koziba, 29, 120, 156, 174, 176, 222, 241 f., 247 f., 250, 263, 275; see also Koziba; Rufus b. Koziba; Romulus b. Rufus
Ben Meir, Aaron, 57, 92
Ben Sakri; see Isaac b. Moses
Ben Tema, 119
Benjamin, 97

Berbers, xvii f., 40, 62, 72 f., 76, 96 f., 285
Berechiah, Babylonian Nasi, 8
Berekiah (A), 213
Bethar, 28, 230
Bethel, 244
Bickerman, E., 114
Bigvai, 9
Bilshan, 9
Boethus, xxxviii, 18, 113, 155, 174
Bulgars; see Togarma
Buluggin, 73 f.
Burgos, xlviii
Bussai, 45
Bustanai, 45, 126
Byzantium, xlvi, 40, 93, 143, 159

Cairo, xxii, 64, 165
Calatrava, xviii, xxvi, 96 f., 145
Calsena, 79
Canaan, 5
Caracalla, 184
Carrion, xlviii
Castile, xlvii f., 62, 94 f., 99, 258, 262 f.
Catalonia, 142
Chaldeans, 12, 15, 37, 239
Cidellus; see Ibn Ferrizuel
Claudius, 247
Commodus, 30
Conforte, David, xiv, 180, 182, 185 f.
Constantine, xxxiii, 40
Constantinople, 93, 143
Constantius, xxxiii
Cordova, xviii f., xxi, xxvi f., xli, 63, 65 f., 69 f., 71 f., 78 f., 81 f., 84, 135 f., 140 f., 158, 200 f., 265, 270, 276, 300 f.
Cutheans, 17 f.; see also Samaritans
Cyrus, 10, 13, 15, 37, 111, 196 f., 232

d'Alverny, M.T., xxviii
Damascus, 68, 136
Dan, 244
Daniel, xxxiii, 10 f., 29 f., 108, 111, 150 f., 166, 194, 196 f., 216, 235 f., 238 f., 241 f., 247, 262, 270, 284
Darius the Mede, 12 f., 37
Darius the Persian, 10, 15, 111
David, xlvi, 7, 22 f., 28, 48, 59, 62, 85, 98, 109, 145, 248, 261, 273, 275, 282
David b. Hezekiah the exilarch, 133
David b. Zakkai, 54 f., 58, 61, 130 f.
David al-Muqammiṣ, xxxiii
al-Daylam, 92
Deborah, 6
Dedan, 92
Denia, xviii, 78, 82 f., 140 f.
Dimi, 33, 35
Domitian, 28, 241, 247 f.
Dosa b. Horkinas, 26, 117 f., 174
Dosa b. Saadiah, 56 f., 164
Dudai; see Durai
Duero, River, 69
Dunash b. Labrat, xlvii, 267, 280 f.
Dunlop, D.M., 136, 145
Durai, 50, 127

Edom (Christian Spain), xlvii, 62 f., 96, 237 f., 248 f.
Efes, 31
Egypt, xxvi, xlvi, 5, 20, 40, 54, 63 f., 74, 86, 92 f., 108, 130, 133 f., 157, 200, 238
Ehud, 6
Elagabalus, 184
Eldad ha-Dani, 251
Elders (who succeeded Joshua), 6, 9
Elead, 108
Eleazar b. Ananias, 222

Eleazar b. Arak, 26
Eleazar b. Azariah, 26 f., 118
Eleazar b. Dama, 119; see also Ben Dama
Eleazar b. Judah, 30
Eleazar b. Pedat, 33
Eleazar b. Perata, 30
Eleazar b. Shammua, 28 f., 119
Eleazar b. Simeon b. Yoḥai, 30
Eleazar Alluf, xlvi
Eleazar Ḥisma, 26
Eleazar ha-Qappar, 31
Eli, 7
Eliezer b. Hyrcanus, 26
Elijah, 51, 129
Elisha b. Abuya *aḥer*, 27
Elon, 6
Elvira, 79
Emperador; see Alfonso VII
'Ena, 44, 208
England, xxvii
Ephraim (tribe), 5, 108
Ephraim of Qalʻat Ḥammad, 78
Epstein, A., 179 f.
Esau, 238, 248, 253, 281; see also Edom
Esther, 15, 31, 270 f.
Estori ha-Parḥi, 182
Ettenberg, M., 123
Euphrates, 247
Eusebius, lix, 151
Evil-Merodach, 11f., 111, 167
Ezekiel, 214, 241
Ezra, lxii, 16 f., 26, 113

Fars, 92
al-Fasi, Isaac, xix, xli, 78, 84 f., 91, 137, 141, 269, 290
Ferdinand II, 261 f.
Fez, xxvi, xl, 67, 84

Fostat, 64; see also Cairo
France, xxvii, xli, 40, 88, 93, 115, 139, 142 f., 206

Gaius, 247
Galba, 247
Galen, xxiii, 30
Galilee, 23
Galipapa, Ḥayyim, 300
Gamaliel I, the Elder, 8, 22 f., 109, 116 f., 173, 206 f.
Gamaliel II, 8, 25 f., 116 f., 177, 179, 206 f.
Gamaliel Beribbi, 8, 31
Gans, David, xiv
Gebihah of Be-Kethil, 42, 126
Genoa, 93, 143
Gerard of Cremona, xxvii
Gerizim, Mount, xxxviii, 17 f., 113
Germany, xl
Gideon, 6
Gilead, 5, 108
Ginsberg, H.L., 192
Girgashite land; see Jurjan
Gog and Magog, 214, 249, 253
Goliath, 277
Goths, xxxiv, 252 f., 255 f., 263
Graetz, H., xiii
Granada, xvii f., xxi, 61 f., 72 f., 76, 80 f., 85, 97, 158, 276, 287, 296
Great Assembly, Men of, lv, lvii, 3, 9, 16, 112 f., 150, 205
Greece, Greek empire, Greeks, 15, 19, 23, 37 f., 40, 124, 154, 235 f., 238 f., 250
Greek sea, 63, 93
Gregory the Great, 162, 254 f.
Gregory VII, 257
Guadalquivir, River, xviii, xli
Gundisalvus, Dominicus, xxvii

Ḥabbus, 72 f., 97, 271
Hadassi, Judah, 160 f.
Hadrian, 28 f., 119, 241, 247, 250
Haggai, 9, 13, 17, 91, 217
Hai b. David, 52 f., 57 f., 129 f.
Hai b. Sherira, 58 f., 67 f., 70, 77, 83 f., 131 f., 134 f., 177, 201 f., 204, 206 f., 218, 279, 292 f.
al-Ḥakam II, 63, 66, 68, 158
Ḥalafta, 26
Halevy, I., xiii, 178 f., 186
Ḥalfon b. Nethanel, xxi f.
Halkin, A.S., 137, 138
Ḥama of Nehardea, 35
Ḥama b. Ezekiel, 32, 121 f.
Ḥama b. Gurya, 33
Haman, 277
Hamath, 40
Hamnuna, 33
Hanan of Ashiqiyya, 44
Hanan b. Phinehas, 30
Hananel b. Ḥushiel, 63 f., 77 f., 84, 91
Hananiah, the companion of Daniel, 10
Hananiah, the priest, 112
Hananiah, the father of Sherira, 58
Hananiah b. Meshullam, 8
Ḥanina (S), 44
Ḥanina b. Abbahu, 192, 212 f.
Ḥanina b. Dosa, 55, 292
Ḥanina b. Ḥama, 31, 33, 207
Ḥanina b. Mesharshia, 50
Ḥanina b. Teradion, 27 f., 119
Ḥanok, 64 f., 134 f., 137, 140, 201 f., 269, 271, 290, 292
Haran, 5, 108, 165
Harkavy, A.A., 203
Hasadiah, 8
Hasmonean, the, 18 f.

INDEX

Hasmoneans, 22 f., 38, 156, 170, 172, 193, 228
Ḥayyim b. al-'Ajab, 84
Ḥayyuj, Judah, 101 f.
Herod, 21
Herodians, lxii, 22
Hezekiah, King, 7, 36, 225 f.
Hezekiah, the exilarch, 59 f., 130 f., 137, 290
Hezekiah b. Neariah, 8, 167, 174
Hilai b. Hananiah, 53
Hilai b. Mari, 52, 54
Hilai b. Mishael, 54
Hilai b. Natronai, 54
Hilai ha-Levi, 46
Hillel, liii, 8, 22, 24, 59 f., 109, 114 f., 118, 167 f., 173 f., 177, 179, 200 f., 206 f., 265, 279
Ḥinena (S), 44, 126
Ḥinena of Nehar Peqod (G), 46
Ḥinenai b. Abraham, 50
Hippocrates, xxiii, 30 f.
Ḥisda, 33 f., 122 f.
Ḥisdai b. Isaac; see Ibn Shaprut
Hisham 69 f.
Ḥiwi al-Balkhi (Kalbi), lix, 56 f., 113
Ḥiyya of Messena, 46
Ḥiyya b. Ashi, 33
Ḥiyya Beribbi, 31, 121
Ḥiyya al-Daudi, 62, 133
Holy City; see Jerusalem
Holy Land; see Palestine
Honorius, 252
Hormizd, 41
Horovitz, J., li
Hoshaiah Beribbi, 31, 33
Hoshea, King, 227
Huna (A), 33 f., 122
Huna (S), 44, 126; see also Mar Huna

Huna b. Isaac ha-Levi, 50, 129
Huna b. Joseph, 46
Huna b. Joshua, 34 f., 187
Huna Mar, 42, 125
Ḥushiel, 64, 77
Ḥuspith, 27 f., 119
Hyrcanus I; see Johanan Hyrcanus
Hyrcanus II, 38, 229

Ibn 'Abbad, 85, 273
Ibn Abi 'Amir, xvii, 69, 72
Ibn Abitur, Joseph, 66 f., 69, 119, 136, 158, 267, 290 f.
Ibn Albalia, Baruk b. Isaac, xvi, xix, xxi f., xli, 82, 85 f., 137, 142.
Ibn Albalia, Isaac, xvii, xix, xxii, 78 f., 80, 82, 85 f., 91, 137 f., 269, 272 f., 278, 287, 291
Ibn Aqnin, Joseph, 88, 237
Ibn al-'Arif, Abu'l-Qasim, 72 f., 271
Ibn Bajjah, xxiv, 298
Ibn Bal'am, Judah, xlvii, 267, 300 f.
Ibn Danan, Saadiah, xiii
Ibn Daud, Abraham (references to himself), 3, 20, 79, 81, 86, 87, 88, 101
Ibn Ezra (family), xvii, xix, 97, 139
Ibn Ezra, Abraham, xxi f., xxxvi, xlviii, 101, 103, 142, 237 f., 253, 288
Ibn Ezra, Isaac, 98
Ibn Ezra, Joseph, 98
Ibn Ezra, Judah, xli, xlviii, 97 f., 145 f., 259 f., 269, 274 f., 294 f., 301
Ibn Ezra, Moses, xviii f., xxi f., xlviii, 98, 102 f., 283, 287 f., 294 f., 297
Ibn Falija (family), 66, 70, 137, 141, 268, 291

Ibn Ferrizuel, Joseph (Cidellus), xxii, xlviii, 95, 98, 144
Ibn Gabirol, Solomon, xxiii f., xxix, xlii, 100, 102, 126, 131, 136, 244, 279, 283, 286, 288, 290
Ibn Giat, Isaac, xix, 78, 81 f., 86, 91, 102, 273 f., 282
Ibn Giat, Judah, xxi
Ibn Gikatilla, Moses, 101 f., 268, 300 f.
Ibn Halfon, Isaac, 66, 267
Ibn Hazm, xxx, xxxiii, xlv f., 277
Ibn Hisdai, Joseph, 282
Ibn Janah, Marenos (Jonah), 101 f.
Ibn Jau, Jacob, 68 f., 136, 269, 284, 290 f.
Ibn Jau, Joseph, 68
Ibn Khaldun, 145
Ibn Laktush, 83, 141
Ibn Megash (family), xli
Ibn Megash, Joseph I, 73 f., 85
Ibn Megash, Joseph (b. Meir) II, xix, xxi, lv, 85 f., 91, 141 f., 217, 273 f., 278
Ibn Megash, Meir, 85, 87
Ibn Megash, Meir II, 87 f., 273
Ibn Megesh, Meir (nephew of Joseph II), 87, 273
Ibn Muhajir, Joseph, 84, 268; *see also* Ibn Shortmeqash.
Ibn Nagrela, Azariah, 81, 274
Ibn Nagrela, Joseph, xxi, xlviii, 58, 61 f., 75 f., 80 f., 138, 266, 269, 272, 274, 278, 283, 291, 293
Ibn Nagrela, Samuel, xiii, xxi, xxv, xxx, 63, 71 f., 77 f., 80 f., 91, 102, 132, 136 f., 158, 180 f., 187, 265, 268 f., 276 f., 281 f., 287, 289
Ibn Qayyim, xlv
Ibn Rumahis, 63 f., 66

Ibn Sahl, Joseph, xxi, 82, 103, 137
Ibn Sarjada; *see* Aaron b. Sarjada
Ibn Shahin, Jacob b. Nissim I, liii
Ibn Shahin, Jacob b. Nissim II, 77
Ibn Shahin, Nissim b. Jacob, liii f., 77 f., 84, 91, 118 f., 174 f., 186 f., 211, 219
Ibn Shaprut, Hisdai b. Isaac, 57, 67, 70, 93, 102, 164, 200, 269, 271 f., 276, 279, 281, 287, 289
Ibn Shatnash; *see* Ibn Abitur
Ibn Shortmeqash, 84; *see also* Oheb b. Meir
Ibn al-Taras; *see* Abu'l-Taras
Ibn Tibbon, Judah and Samuel, xxi
Ibn Tumart, xxvi, 88, 141
Ibn Verga, Solomon, xiv
Ibn Yahya, Gedaliah, xiv, 173
Ibn Zaddik, Joseph, of Arevalo, xiii, 268
Ibn Zaddik, Joseph, of Cordova, xxi, xlviii, 82, 103, 139 f.
Ibumai; *see* Ahunai; Isomai
Ibzan, 6
Iddo, the priest, 16, 112, 154
Idi b. Abin, 36
Ifranj; *see* France
Ifriqiya, 63 f., 74, 77 f., 92, 134
Ikumai; *see* Ahunai; Isomai
India; *see* Dedan
Iraq, xlvi, 40, 83, 92
Isaac, 5, 216
Isaac (S), 44 f., 232
Isaac b. Ashayan, 33
Isaac b. Hiyya, 52
Isaac b. Jesse, 53
Isaac b. Leon, 73 f.
Isaac b. Moses b. Sakri, 78, 82 f., 91, 132, 140

Isaac b. Reuben al-Bargeloni, 78, 83 f., 91, 140
Isaiah, 11, 274 f., 284
Isaiah b. Abba, 51, 54, 129
Isaiah b. Hasadiah, 8
Ise b. Judah, 30
Ishkafa, Nehemiah, 73 f.
Ishmael (Islam), 41, 44, 59, 233 f., 237 f., 253, 281
Ishmael (T, 2), 27, 119
Ishmael b. Elisha, 24 f.
Ishmael b. Jose, 30
Isidore of Seville, xiii, 151, 162 f., 217, 254 f., 257 f.
Isomai b. Mordecai, 53
Israeli, Isaac, of Toledo, xiii
Italy, xxvii, 93, 201

Jacob, 5, 218
Jacob (G), 54
Jacob of Kefar Ḥittaya (T), 30
Jacob of Nehar Peqod (G), 46
Jacob b. Meir Tam, 89
Jacob b. Mordecai, 53
Jacob b. Samuel, 110
Jair, 6
James son of Zebedee, 257
Jamnia, 25, 27
Jannaeus; *see* Alexander Jannaeus
Japheth, 252
Jeconiah; *see* Jehoiachin
Jehoahaz, 7 f., 195, 227
Jehoiachin, 7 f., 111, 195, 210
Jehoiakim, 6 f., 10 f., 166, 195, 227
Jehoram, 7
Jehoshaphat, 7
Jehudai, 48, 50, 91, 122, 127
Jephthah, 6
Jeroboam I, 226, 244
Jeremiah, 11 f., 88, 271, 274

Jerome, 151
Jerusalem, xxxviii, xlvii, lxii, 10, 16, 19, 20, 24, 74 f., 79, 94, 97 f., 138, 201, 273
Jeshua, 9
Jesus, xxxii f., xl, lix, 20 f., 39, 114 f., 124, 156, 171 f., 229 f., 246
Jibal, xxxvi, 301
Joash, 7
Johanan, the scribe, 23
Johanan b. Baroqa, 26
Johanan b. Napha, xxxvii, 33, 39, 122
Johanan b. Nuri, 26 f.
Johanan b. Zakkai, lv, 22, 24 f., 26 f., 91, 117 f., 174 f., 207
Johanan Hyrcanus, lxii, 19, 114, 170
John of Seville, xxvii
John Hyrcanus; *see* Johanan Hyrcanus
Jonathan, 85, 273
Jonathan b. Mattathias the Hasmonean, 19, 170
Jonathan b. Uzziel, 22
Jose the Galilean, 26
Jose b. Ḥalafta, 28 f., 212
Jose b. Joezer, 20
Jose b. Johanan, 20
Jose b. Qisma, 26
Jose ha-Kohen, 26
Joseph, 5, 87, 270 f., 275, 283
Joseph, king of the Khazars, 70, 93
Joseph (A), 33 f.
Joseph (G), 47
Joseph b. Abba, 51
Joseph b. Gorion, xxv, 222
Joseph b. Ḥiyya, 52
Joseph b. Jacob b. Mordecai, 55 f.
Joseph b. Judah, 51, 179
Joseph b. Shela, 51
Joseph b. Waqar, 145

Joseph Beribbi (G), 52
Joseph ha-Kohen, xiv
Joseph ha-Levi the Nagid; see Ibn Nagrela
Josephus, xxxiv
Joshua, xliii, 6, 9, 108, 153, 166, 209
Joshua b. Hananiah, 26 f., 118, 174 f., 179
Joshua b. Jehozadak, 17
Joshua b. Peraḥyah, 20 f., 114 f., 173
Joshua b. Qarḥa, 30
Josiah, King, 7, 59, 227
Josiah b. Ḥiyya al-Daudi, 133
Josiah b. Zakkai, 55
Jotham, 7
Judah (tribe), xlvi, 55, 59, 97
Judah (G), 46
Judah the Maccabee, 19, 170
Judah the Patriarch; see Judah the Prince I
Judah the Prince I, lv, 8, 29 f., 35, 39, 120, 175, 184 f., 206 f., 211, 230 f., 275
Judah the Prince II, 8, 150, 152, 187, 209 f.
Judah b. Baba, 27 f.
Judah b. Barzillai, xlvii, 288
Judah b. Bathyra, 27
Judah b. Ezekiel, 32 f., 121 f.
Judah b. Ilai, 28 f., 119
Judah b. Samuel, grandfather of Sherira, 51, 57
Judah b. Samuel ha-Levi, xviii f., xxi f., xxvii, xlviii, liv, 102 f., 142, 145, 152, 211, 221, 287 f., 295 f.
Judah b. Tabbai, 20, 173
Judah b. Tema, 27, 118
Judah ha-Levi; see Judah b. Samuel
Julian, xxxiii

Julius Caesar, 38, 229, 242 f., 245 f.
Jurjan, 92

Kahana I, 33
Kahana II, 34
Karaites, *passim, but see especially* xxxvi f., Introduction, ch. III, 3, 17 f., 24, 48 f., 56, 91 f., 106 f., 149 f., 155 f., 164 f., 289 f.
Khazars, 92 f., 281
Khorasan, xxxvi, 103, 301
Khosrau (Chosroes), 126
Khuzistan, 40, 92
Kimhi, David, xxxix
Kittim, 238, 252
Kohen-Ṣedeq (G), 47
Kohen-Ṣedeq b. Isomai, 53
Kohen-Ṣedeq b. Joseph, 58
Koziba, 28, 120, 247 f.

Lactantius, lix
Leander, 162, 254 f.
Leo IX, 257
Leocadia, 255
Leon (country), 255, 257, 263
Levi (tribe), 277
Levi (T), 31, 213, 226
Lewin, B.M., liii
Lieberman, S., 109
Lombardia, 93
Lucena, xvii, xix, xxi, xlvi, 77, 79, 81, 84 f., 87 f., 142, 217, 296, 301
Luciliardus, 255
Lucinianus, 255
Lydda, 26, 117

Maccabees, xxxv, xxxix, 18 f., 170 f., 288, 237, 291
Maghreb (West), xviii, 37, 63 f., 66, 70, 74, 92 f., 134 f., 141 f., 282

Magnesia, 38
al-Mahdiyya, xxvi, 78, 88, 96
Maimon, xxvi, xl
Maimonides, Moses, xxii f., xxx, xl, xlii, liv, 109, 122, 137, 152, 190, 206, 209, 218, 220, 235, 238, 266, 288, 294, 302
Malachi, 9, 12, 17, 91, 217
Malaga, xviii, xxvi, 72
Malkiah (G, 3), 50
Malkiah (G, 5), 54
Manasseh, King, 7, 227
Manasseh b. Joseph, 50
Manasseh b. Joshua, the priest, 18
Mani, 41, 113
al-Manṣur, 69 f., 270
Mar b. Ashi, 36, 123, 207
Mar Huna (S), 45
Mar Rab Mar b. Huna, 126
Mar Raba (S), 45
Mar Yanqa, 46
Marcianus, 254
Marcus Aurelius, 184
Margalioth, M., 182 f.
Mari (S), 44
Mari b. Mesharshia, 50
Mari ha-Kohen, 48
Marrakesh, xvii
Mars, 41
Martini, Raymund, xxxvi
Matha Meḥasia, 32, 46, 48, 50, 52, 54, 57, 121; *see also* Sura
Mattathias the Hasmonean, 18, 170
Mattena, 33
Mattithiah Beribbi, 52
Mauricius, 254 f.
Mebasser ha-Kohen, 58
Media, 23, 228, 230, 233, 235 f., 239
Meḥoza, 34
Meir (T), 28 f.

Meir b. Joseph, 89
Meir b. Vives, 79
Me'iri, Menahem, xiii, 175
Melchizedek, 96
Menahem, the teacher, 22, 115, 174
Menahem b. Joseph, 52
Menahem b. Saruq, xlvii, 267, 280 f.
Menendez Pidal, R., 256
Meremar, 36, 123, 207
Merida, xxxiv, 79 f., 137 f., 273
Mesharshia (A), 41
Mesharshia b. Taḥlifa, 45
Meshullam, Babylonian nasi, 8
Messena, 93
Mishael, 10
Mispar, 9
Modi'im, Mount, 19
Monobaz, 14, 98 f., 112
Moore, G.F., xiii
Mordecai, 9, 31, 270, 277
Mordecai ha-Kohen, 51
Moses, xliii f., li, liv, lviii, 8 f., 24, 59 f., 85 f., 109 f., 118 f., 152 f., 192, 209, 212, 265, 273, 279
Moses, R., the captive, 64 f., 135, 141, 158, 200 f., 265, 269
Moses b. Jacob, 53
Moses b. Joseph, 89
Moses ha-Darshan, 245
Moses de Leon, xlix
Mount of Olives, 94
al-Mu'allima, xlviii, 95, 144, 165
Mubashshir; *see* Mebasser
Muhammad, xxx, 45, 126, 141, 178, 185, 233, 254 f.
al-Mu'tadid; *see* Ibn 'Abbad
al-Mu'tamid, 81, 272

Naḥman the Prince (A), 32, 122
Naḥman b. Huna, 36

Naḥman b. Isaac, 33 f.
Naḥman b. Zadok, 54, 130
Narbonne, xxxiv, 79, 88f, 142 f.;
see also France
Naresh, 35
Nathan (T), 29
Nathan the Babylonian, 54 f., 130 f.
Nathan the Pious, 65 f.
Nathan Ab ha-Yeshiba, liv, 127
Natronai, xlvi, 48 f., 127 f.
Natronai b. Hilai, 53
Naupaktos, 143
Navarre, 260 f.
Neariah, 8, 109
Nebuchadnezzar, 10 f., 37, 108, 110 f., 152, 160, 167, 169, 195 f., 228, 230, 247, 261, 271
Nebuzaradan, 28
Nehardea, 32 f., 35, 122, 178, 182
Nehemiah, 9, 17, 232
Nehemiah (G), 58
Neḥumi, 126
Nero, 24, 222, 247
Nerva, 247
Nissim b. Jacob; see Ibn Shahin
Nittai the Arbelite, 20, 173

Obadiah, 251
Obadiah b. Isaiah, 8
Octavian, 222; see also Augustus
Oheb b. Meir, xxi, 102
Ordoño III, 256
Orosius, Paulus, xiii, 162 f.
—— Ps.-Orosius, 225
Othniel, 6
Our Saintly Master; see Judah the Prince I

Palestine, xl, xlvi, 8, 17, 23, 28, 33, 40, 48, 63, 92 f., 133 f., 136, 167, 206, 218, 289
Paregoros, 79 f., 139, 273
Paltoi, 52
Papa, 34 f., 187
Pechina, 67, 79
Pedath, 30
Pelimo, 30
Peroz-Shahpuhr, 45
Persia, Persians, xxxv, lxii, 15 f., 36 f., 39 f., 44 f., 125, 150, 154, 156 f., 162, Analysis, ch. 4 *passim*
Peter, 256
Peter the Venerable, xli
Petrus Alfonsi, xli
Pharisees, 114
Philistines, 277; see also Berbers
Phinehas b. Jair, 30
Plato, xxiii
Pompey, xxxix, 230
Portugal, xviii
Ptolemy, author of Almagest, 29
Pumbeditha, 35, 42, 44 f., 48, 50 f., 122, 163, 178, 181, 184 f.

al-Qadir, 60
al-Qaim, 61
Qairawan, liii, 64, 77, 136, 138, 265
Qal'at Ḥammad, 78, 84
Qimoi b. Aḥunai, 57
Qimoi b. Ashi, 53
al-Qirqisani, Ya'qub, xxxvi, xlix, liv, lxii, 17, 24, 107, 128, 155, 165

Rab, 31 f., 121 f., 179, 181, 211
Raba (S); see Mar Raba
Raba b. Joseph, 34
Raba b. Natronai, 46
Rabbah b. Abbuha, 32 f., 59
Rabbah b. Ammi, 52

INDEX

Rabbah b. Huna, 33
Rabbah b. Joseph, 123
Rabbah b. Naḥmani, 33 f.
Rabbah Jose, 43, 123, 126, 185, 199
Rabbah Tosefa'ah, 36, 224
Rabia, 46, 48
Rabin, 33
Rabina I, 34
Rabina II, 42 f., 125, 177
Rabina of Umṣa, 44
Rafram, 42
Rafram b. Papa, 35
Ramerupt, 89
Rami b. Ezekiel, 121 f.
Rami b. Ḥama, 32, 122
Rapoport, S.J.L., 180 f., 184, 186
Reccared, xxxiv, 252
Reelaiah, 9
Rehoboam, 7
Rehum (of Great Assembly), 9
Rehum, the commander, 10
Reḥumi, 42
Remulus; see Remus
Remus, xxxiii, 37, 226, 244
Reuben Strobili, 30
Rhone, River, 93, 144
Roderic, 139
Rome, Romans, xxviii, xxxii f., xxxix, lxii, 21, 24, 28, 30, 36 f., 38 f., 40, 103, 124 f., 156 f., 162, 172, 197, 222, Analysis, ch. 4; see also Byzantium, Constantinople
Romulus, xxxiii f., 37, 226 f., 241 f., 248 f.
Romulus b. Rufus b. Koziba, 28, 248
Rossi, Azariah de', xiv, 169
Rufus b. Koziba, 28, 241, 248 f.

Saadiah b. Joseph, xxiv f., xxix, xxxvi f., xlii, lii f., lvi, lxii, 48 f., 54 f., 60, 79, 92, 110, 130 f., 135, 146, 159 f., 164, 167 f., 176, 211, 237, 279, 281, 292, 301
Sadducees, xxxv f., xxxviii f., l, 17 f., 103, 128
Sala (Salé), 92, 142
Salmon b. Yeruḥim, xxxvi, 106
Sama b. Judah, 126
Sama b. Raba, 42
Samaria, 226
Samaritans, xxxvii f., lviii f., 16, 50, 113, 155; see also Cutheans
Samua'al al-Maghribi, xxx, xlv
Sambari, Joseph, xiv, 182
Samson, 6
Samuel, the prophet, 7, 277
Samuel (A), 31 f., 41, 121 f.
Samuel, descendant of Amemar (G), 46 f.
Samuel the Nagid; see Ibn Nagrela
Samuel ibn Abbas; see Samua'al al-Maghribi
Samuel b. Hofni, liv, 60, 182 f., 186
Samuel ibn Hananiah, 182 f., 201, 203 f.
Samuel b. Josiah, 67
Samuel b. Mar de Iqri, 127
Samuel b. Mari, 47, 127
Samuel ibn Moriel, xxi
Samuel b. Naḥman, 33
Samuel b. Raba, 44
Samuel ha-Qaton, 26
Sanballat, xxxviii, 17 f., 113, 132
Santiago de Compostela, 255 f.
Sar-Shalom b. Boaz, 53
Saragossa, xviii, 62, 72
Sardinia, 143
Saul, King, 7
Saul b. Anan, xlix, 48, 91, 113, 127
Schirmann, H., 203

Scythians, 15, 112
Sefarad (Sepharad); see Spain
Sefastin, 64
Ṣemaḥ b. Hayyim, 54, 130, 251
Ṣemaḥ b. Paltoi, 52
Sennacherib, 17
Seraiah, 9
Severinus, 115
Severus, 120
Seville, xvii f., xxvi, 79, 81, 85, 142, 255, 287
Shahpuhr, 40 f.
Shalmaneser, 226
Shalom b. Mishael, 54
Shamgar, 6
Shammai, xliv, 22, 24, 114, 207
Shealtiel, 8 f.
Shecaniah, 8
Shefaram, 28
Shela (A), 32
Shelah, son of Judah, 55
Shemaiah, Babylonian nasi, 8
Shemaiah, teacher, 22
Shemariah b. Elhanan, 64
Sherira, xlii, lii f., 46, 51, 58 f., 66, 107, 119, 131 f., 135, 177 f., 290, 292
Sheshet, 33, 122
Sheshna, 45
Shimi b. Ashi, 33
Shimshai, 10
Sicily, 74, 93
Sijilmasa, 69
Silves, xviii, xxvi, 88, 142
Sinai, 27 f., 119
Simeon the Righteous, lxii, 16 f., 154 f., 208, 232, 266
Simeon b. Azzai, 27
Simeon b. Gamaliel I, 8, 22, 24 f., 206
Simeon b. Gamaliel II, 8, 27, 29, 119, 207

Simeon b. Hillel, 173, 206
Simeon b. Johanan b. Baroqa, 30
Simeon b. Judah, 30
Simeon b. Mattathias the Hasmonean, 19, 170
Simeon b. Nethanel, 26
Simeon b. Shetaḥ, 20, 114, 173
Simeon b. Yoḥai, 28 f.
Simeon b. Zoma, 27
Simeon Beribbi, 31
Simeon Qayyara, 47, 127
Simona, 44, 208
Sisebut, 254
Slav country, 40, 93
Solomon, King, 7 f., 59, 108 f., 169, 194, 209, 226, 234, 244
Solomon b. Formash, 78
Solomon b. Ḥisdai, 47
Spain, Introduction, *passim*; 39 f., 53, 59, 61 f., 63, 65 f., 72, 74 f., 78 f., 81, 84 f., 93, 96 f., 133 f., Analysis, *passim, but see especially* 250 f., 263 f.,
Spiegel, S., 268
Strack, H.L., xiii
Suevi, xxxiv, 252
Sura, 32 f., 35 f., 42, 44 f., 121 f., 163, 178, 181 f., 184, 186; see also Matha Meḥasia
Symmachus, 30
Syria, xlvi, 136; see also Palestine

Tabarestan, 92
Tabyomi, 36, 123
Tagus, River, xli
Tahert, 92
Takurunna, 68
Talavera, xlvi
Tangiers, 96
Tarfon, 27, 119

Tarragona, 68
Tate, R.B., 254
Teḥina, 44
Theodoric, xxxiv
Theodosius, 254
Tiber, River, 38, 243, 246
Tiberius, 222, 247
Tineius Rufus, 249
Titus, xxxiv, xxxix, 12, 14, 24 f., 28, 79, 138, 152, 160, 222, 247
Tobiah the Ammonite, 132
Tobiah b. Eliezer, 159 f., 163
Togarma, 93
Tola, 6
Toledo, xvi, xxii, xxiv, xxvi f., xl, xliii, xlvi f., xlix, 72, 88, 93, 96, 98, 145, 158, 160, 162, 217, 257, 260 f., 275, 300
Toledano (Ximenez de Rada), 254, 302
Trajan, 28
Tubal b. Japheth, 252
Tudela, xviii, 296, 302
Twersky, I., 135

Ulla, 33
'Umar ibn al-Khattab, 44 f.
Umayyads, xviii, 63 f., 67, 69, 72
Usha, 28
Uz; see Goths
Uzziah, 7

Valencia, xviii
Vandals, 252

Venice, 93, 143
Vespasian, xxxix f., 12, 14, 24, 79, 112, 115, 118, 156, 222 247
Vincentius Hispanus, 259,
Visigoths; see Goths
Volga, 92

Weiss, I.H., xiii
Werejlan, 93

Yannai (A), 33
Yannai, poet, 109
Yanka; see Mar Yanqa
Yeshebab, 27 f., 119
Yeshu'ah b. Judah; see Abu'l-Faraj
Yezdegerd, 45, 126
Yom-Tob (G), 54, 130

Zacuto, A., xiii f., xxviii, 166, 169, 197
Zadok, xxxviii, 18, 113, 155, 174
al-Zahra, 67 f., 137
Zakkai b. David, 55
Zakynthos 143
Zealots, xxxix, 14, 25, 112, 132, 241
Zebid, 35
Zechariah, the prophet, xxxv, xxxvii, xl, 9, 12, 17, 91, 103, 170, 213 f., 217, 232, 241
Zedekiah, 7, 11, 13, 110 f., 169, 195, 209
Ze'era, 33
Zerubbabel, xxxvi, lv, 8 f., 25, 42, 59, 152, 166, 232, 237

INDEX OF PASSAGES FROM CLASSICAL LITERATURE CITED BY IBN DAUD

Bible	Page	Mishna	Page
Gen. 45.5	99	Ber. 1.1,2	4
Deut. 1.13, 15	85	Shab. 2.1	4
1.16, 18	9	R.H. 2.8–9	26 f.
17.9, 12	24	Hag. 2.2	22
Josh. 4.1	99	Abot 1.3	18
II Ki. 14. 26	29	1.4, 6, 8	20
Isa. 21.5	11	1.10, 12	22
56.10	100	2.8	24
57.1	87		
Jer. 6.9	96		
15.2	88	*Tosefta*	
27.7	11 f., 37		
47.3	97	Pe'ah 4.18	98
52.28, 31	11	Yoma 3.2	65
Hos. 7.1	97		
Zech. 11.4	103		
Ps. 68.23	64		
83.5	88	*Sifre*	
121.1	81		
124.1	97	Deut. § 357	22, 25
Prov. 8.21	89		
10.7	103		
Lam. 4.4	97		
Dan. 8.7	37	*Babylonian Talmud*	
9.1 f.	12 f.		
11.33	29	Ber. 27b–28a	27
11.34	30	Git. 56a–b	24
Ezra 4.8	10	Sanhed. 11b	23
4.24	10	A.Z. 10b	39
Neh. 4.17	14	Bekorot 36a	27

ACKNOWLEDGMENTS

While the bibliographical references and acknowledgments in the notes reflect my indebtedness to the many scholars on whose work and expertise I drew, it is a pleasure to single out a number of persons and institutions who were especially helpful. To my teachers and colleagues at The Jewish Theological Seminary of America and at Columbia University I am beholden for many hours of advice and consultation on various aspects of my research. To Chancellor Louis Finkelstein and Professor Saul Lieberman of the Seminary and the late Professor Arthur Jeffrey of Columbia I am grateful for their sustained interest and help on many occasions. To Professor Abraham S. Halkin, whom I consulted at virtually every step of my work, I must register my profound gratitude.

The Bodleian Library at Oxford University, the Bibliothèque Nationale in Paris, the Stadtsbibliothek in Frankfurt, the Biblioteca Mediceo-laurenziana in Florence, the Biblioteca Palatina in Parma, the Jews' College in London, Mr. D.S. Sassoon of Letchworth, England, and Baron James Rothschild provided the manuscripts and microfilms which I needed for my work. The librarians and resources at Columbia University and Union Theological Seminary were ever helpful. I am especially indebted to the Library of The Jewish Theological Seminary and its staff for manuscripts and printed materials as well as for assistance in many ways. Professor Seymour Feldman and Rabbi Alexander Goldstein checked my collations against the original manuscripts and photostats, and their sharp eyes saved me from many a blunder. The onerous task of typing the Hebrew text and critical apparatus was done with dedication and expertise by Mrs. Ada Turner.

I am grateful to the American Academy for Jewish Research for permission to reprint, in a slightly revised form, a portion of Chapter VII of the translation (pp. 63–71), which was first published in its *Proceedings,* XXIX (1960–61) under the title "The Story of the Four Captives."

Dr. Solomon Grayzel, the editor emeritus of the Jewish Publication Society, and his successor, Dr. Chaim Potok, as well as the editorial and executive staff of the Society, have been most helpful in the arduous task of seeing this book through the press.

Above all, however, I know that but for the unflagging emotional and moral support of my wife and children, this work would never have been completed.

My profound indebtedness to all of these good people and institutions should in no way be construed to detract from the exclusive responsibility which I must claim for myself for all inanities and errors of omission and commission.

G. D. C.

ממקורות ישראל
מקורות ותרגומים

*

סדרה ראשונה
כרך ג'

ספר הקבלה לר' אברהם אבן דאוד הלוי

ספר הקבלה
לר' אברהם אבן דאוד הלוי

יוצא לאור על־פי כתבי־יד עם חלופי נוסחאות
בצרוף לתרגום והערות ומבוא בשפה האנגלית

מאת
גרשון דוד כהן

פילאדלפיא
החברה היהודית להוצאת ספרים אשר באמריקה
תשכ"ז

כל הזכויות שמורות
בידי המו"ל

תוכן

מבוא . . . . ט

ספר הקבלה 1

מבוא

מבוא

א. מהדורות ספר הקבלה

ספר הקבלה (=סה"ק) לר' אברהם אבן דאוד הלוי נדפס לראשונה במנטובה בשנת רע"ד יחד עם שני חיבוריו ההסטוריוגרפיים האחרים והם "זכרון דברי רומי" ו"דברי מלכי ישראל בבית שני", בצירוף ל"סדר עולם רבא" ו"סדר עולם זוטא" ו"מגלת תענית"[1]. פרט לאחת, כל ההוצאות של סה"ק, והוא הדין בנוגע לשני החיבורים האחרים, נדפסו על-פי דפוס ראשון, אלא שבהוצאות אחדות הושמטו וסורסו שורות ומלים ספורות מחמת הצנזורה הנוצרית[2]. מהדורה חדשה על-פי כתבי-יד הוכנה על-ידי א. נויבואר בחלק א' של "סדר החכמים וקורות הימים" (אוקספורד, תרמ"ח), ע' 47—82, ומאז ועד היום שימשה מהדורתו יסוד לכל דיון בספר ובידיעות הנמסרות בו.

אעפעלפי שבמהדורתו שיפר נויבואר (=נ.) במדה גדולה את גוף הטכסט של ספר קלסי זה, ואף הועיל לחוקרים ע"י צירוף שנויי נוסחאות רבים, אין מהדורתו מספקת את תביעות המדע מכמה פנים. בראש ולראשונה, המהדיר תיקן את גוף הספר על ימין ועל שמאל ללא תשומת לב, כנראה, לטיב המקור אשר ממנו דלה את גירסתו. בדיקה מפורטת תוכיח שמהדורת ג. היא לאמיתו של דבר נוסח ה"דפוסים", המתוקן על-פי גירסאות כתבי-יד כאשר נראה התיקון בעיני המהדיר. מהדורתו אינה מאפשרת לקורא לבדוק את נוסח הטכסט, ובעיקר נוסח לקוי או תמוה, היות והמהדיר לא מסר את חילופי הגירסאות בעקביות כלשהי, ואף כשהביאם לא הודיע תדיר על מקורות. הקורא נתון איפוא כמעט לגמרי לחסדו ולשפוטו של המהדיר, ללא כל קנה מדה לשקילת גירסא אחת מול שנייה או שלישית. בכמה מקומות תיקן נ. את גוף הספר ללא כל מסמך, ואפילו לא רמז על כך לא בהקדמה לספרו ולא

1. וז"ל הקולופון שבחתימת דפו"ר: "נשלם ספר הקבלה להראב"ד פה מנטובה ד' מרחשון שנת ושב ה' אלדיך את שבותך ורחמך [=3 באוקטובר 1513 לסה"נ]..." הדברים המצורפים לצילום של סה"ק באנציקלופדיה העברית, ח"א, ע' 198 (ע' אבן דאוד) מוטעים משני פנים: הצילום שהובא שם, כדוגמא מדפו"ר, קושטא רע"ז, אינו אלא מדפוס ויניציא ש"ה—ש"ו, ולא עוד אלא שהצילום מורכב מחצי האחרון של דף כ"א וחצייו הראשון של דף כ"ז ע"ב של אותה הוצאה, ומלת המעבר "מזכירי" שבסוף דף כ"ז ע"א נמחקה. הוצאה של סה"ק מקושטא רע"ז אינה ידועה לי ממקור אחר.
2. ליתר דיוק, הדפוסים מתחלקים לשני סוגים: (א) נוסח דפו"ר מלא, שעל פיו נדפסו רוב ההוצאות, כגון דפוסי ויניציא ש"ה—ש"ו (לפי החתימה של אותו דפוס נגמרה ההדפסה בר"ח כסליו ש"ו), פריז 1572 (הוצ' גנברדוס); ברם, רק חלק מהספר נדפס באותה הוצאה, והחל מתקופת התנאים נמסר רק קיצור פרפרסטי, קארעץ תקמ"ה, לעמבערג תר"י, "אמסטרדם" [=שקלאוו? תרי"ב?] ורשה תרל"ז, ירושלים תשט"ו. בכל ההוצאות הללו, חוץ משל פריז, הופיע סה"ק כנספח ל"סדר עולם". (ב) נוסח דפו"ר מצונזר, שממנו הושמטו הפיסקאות על ישו ועל אדום, כגון דפוסי בזל ש"מ, אמסטרדם תע"א, פראג תקנ"ה; בשתי ההוצאות האחרונות הושמט גם מבואו של הראב"ד לסה"ק והספר מתחיל בפיסקא "מאדם ועד המבול וכו'". לרשימה ביבליוגרפית של הוצאות סה"ק ר' ח. ד. פרידברג, בית עקד הספרים, ע' סדר עולם.

מבוא

בהערות לסה"ק גופו³. ואם מצד אחד לא באנו לערער על חשיבות תרומתו, מאידך אין
צורך להדגיש את הסכנה שבדרך עבודה זו. יש לציין ביחוד כי ביחס לספרו של הראב"ד
העלתה עבודתה של נ. טכסט־כלאיס, ואין ספק שכמה וכמה מהבעיות שהועלו ע"י החוקרים
ביחס לסה"ק היו נפרקות ומתרצות מאליהן אילו נמסרו (לכל הפחות בהערות) עיקרי
הגירסאות שבכתבי היד.

במהדורה חדשה זו נסינו למלא את החסר שבהוצאת נ. ולשחזר עד כמה שאפשר את
מקור הספר כפי שיצא מעטו של הראב"ד. את מהדורתנו זו הכינונו על פי ששה כתבי יד
(בסיוע עוד שני כ"י) ודפוס ראשון, וציירפנו את חילופי הגירסאות עם מקורותיהם בכדי
שיוכל הקורא בעצמו לשקול את הנוסח שבררנו, ולעמוד ג"כ על השתלשלות נוסח הספר
ע"י מעשיהם של מעתיקים, מגיהים ומדפיסים.

ב. כתבי היד

כתבי היד מתחלקים לשתי מחלקות: מחלקה ש הכוללת כ"י אבהיפק, ומחלקה ת
הכוללת דפוס ראשון (ד) וכ"י למסר. לפני שנתאר את דרך עבודתנו בעריכת הטכסט,
נמסור סקירה על כה"י הללו (לפי סדר א"ב):

1. א = כת"י אדלר 2237 שבספרית ביהמ"ד לרבנים באמריקה. כ"י זה נכתב ע"י הסופר
קומפראט דוין דוויש על נייר הנושא סימן־מים דרום־צרפתי מהעשור השמיני למאה
הט"ו לסה"נ, וגם צורת הכתיבה גם תכנו של כ"י זה מעידים על מוצאו הפרובנסאלי⁴.

---

³ נציין תריסר מקומות המדגימים את דרך עבודתו של נויבואר. (המספר הראשון הוא לעמוד, והשני
לשורה בסדר החמים ח"א):
1.48 שעמדו במצרים] כך רק בדפוסים, ואילו בכל כה"י: שיצאו.
2.48 אבימלך מ'] גירסא זו היא טעות המדפיס המנטובני, ואע"פ שהטעות נתקבלה בכל הדפוסים
אין לה סעד מכה"י, והערתו של נ. מוטעית היא.
12.49 ומה שאמרנו – כי] כך רק בדפוסים.
17.50 שאז פסקה נבואה מישראל] כך רק בדפוסים.
4.51 הכעסים] חסר רק בדפוסים.
22.51 והיא שנת ג' אלפים ות"ן ליצירה] חסר בכ"י ש.
22.33 וקבלת אמת וכו'] "קבלה" זו נמסרה בצורה מסורסת, כנראה עפ"י כ"י ק.
23.53 וגרי צדק היו] חסר בכ"י ש.
18.55 ור' יהודה בן דימא] גירסא זו היא המצאתו של נ.
24.58 ורב אמי] חסר בדפו"ר ובכל כה"י חוץ מכ"י S.
16.61 תתכ"ו] לא מצאתי גירסא זו בשום מקום.
1.65 י"א שנה] לא מצאתי גירסא זו בשום מקור אחר.

ולאחרונה, עלינו להטעים כי לא מחסור כ"י־ים גרם ללקויים שבמהדורת נ., שהרי שלשת כה"י שהיו
לפנינו ושלא היו לפניו (והם כ"י ש במר) לא הוסיפו חמר חדש ביסודו.

⁴ ר' Catalogue of Hebrew Manuscripts in the Collection of Elkan Nathan Adler (Cambridge,
1921, p. 81); מ. היגער, שבע מסכתות קטנות (ניו־יורק, תר"ץ), ע' ט"ז. סה"ק נמצא בדפים ר'
ע"ב עד רל"ו ע"א. בדף רמ"ג ע"ב שבכ"י A רשם הסופר "אני הכותב יעקב ב"ר מכיר" ויתכן
כי צדקון. (עיין בהערה הבאה) ואדלר בזיהוי יעקב ב"ר מכיר זה עם הסופר של כה"י כולו שרשם
את שמו בסוף כה"י "קומפראט דוין דוויש". ואולם, איני יודע על מה קבעו את זמן
כתיבת כה"י בשנת 1271, אא"כ פירשו את ראשי התיבות "י־יהב־א" (או י"הכ־א) הבאות מיד
אחרי שם זה כתאריך ההעתקה. איך שיהיה, התאריך שבקטלוג אדלר אינו נכון, שהרי סימני המים
שהוטבע בנייר, בדפים י"א וי"ב של כה"י, זהה עם החותמת שהדפיס A. M. Briquet, Les Fili-

העתק זה של סה"ק מפורסם לרגל הקטע הארוך והחשוב על גדולי נרבונה שנוסף בתוכו ושנדפס ע"י נ.⁵ ואם דווקא לקטע הזה יש ערך מיוחד, מצד שני ערכו של נוסח סה"ק בכ"י זה אינו גדול, שהרי הוא משקף עיבוד יסודי ע"י מגיה. דבר זה מתברר לא רק מהתוספת על נרבונה שהובלעה לתוכו, ושאינה פרי עטו של הראב"ד⁶, אלא גם מהתוספת על הרמב"ם⁷ ובעיקר משינויי הסגנון, הקיצורים והתיקונים הרבים על כל צעד ושעל בספר. ואעפ"י שביסודו שייך כ"י זה לכי"י של מחלקה ש, ולענף כי" איפק שבתוך מחלקה זו, הנוסח הגלום בתוכו הוא נוסח מעובד ועצמאי⁸, ועל כן אינו יכול להחשב בגדר עדות להערכת נוסחאותיו של סה"ק. ובכל זאת, כ"י זה חשוב לנו כחוליה בשלשלת כתבי היד וכעדות מסייעת לעדויות אחרות. את גירסאותיו, איפוא, לא הבאנו בחילופי הגירסאות אלא אם כן הן תואמות או קרובות לנוסח שבכ"י אחר, ויש בהן משהו המסייע להבהרת הטכסט.

2. ב = כ"י אדלר 1737, שבספריית ביהמ"ד לרבנים באמריקה. בקטלוג אדלר רשום כ"י זה כ"קיצור ספר הקבלה"⁹, אבל כפי שמתברר מהצילום של עמודו הראשון של כה"י שנכלל באותו קטלוג¹⁰, שם זה ניתן לו ע"י בעליו לשעבר, הרב י. מ. טולידאנו. ואמנם, השם "קיצור" הולם רק את חלקו השני של כה"י, החל ממעשה ארבעת השבויים (להלן ע' 46 ואילך), ואילו חציו הראשון של כה"י הוא העתק מלולי של סה"ק. מאידך גיסא,

---

graues (2ed. 4 vols. Leipzig, 1923), IV, no. 15637. ומשם מוכח כי נייר זה לא הגיע לשוק לפני העשור השמיני למאה הט"ו לסה"נ. ואמנם תאריך מאוחר זה מתאים יותר לטיב נוסח סה"ק המופיע בכ"י זה. עיין להלן.

5. A. Neubauer, "Documents Inédits XVI. Documents sur Narbonne," *REJ*, X (1885), 99 f.
סדר החכמים, ח"א, עמ' 82 ואילך.

6. אני מקווה להרחיב את הדיבור על קטע זה במקום אחר.

7. ר' סדר החכמים ח"א, ע' 76 הערה 8, ובטעות נתיחסה תוספת זו לכ"י פ.

8. והנה כמה דוגמאות לדרכו של המעבד של נוסח כ"י א (המספרים הם לעמודים ולשורה שבהוצאתנו; ערך ראשון הוא גירסת הוצאתנו, ומשמאל לחצי־הלבנה גירסת כ"י א):

2.1. כתבנוהו] כתבנו.
4.1—5. מאנשי כנסת הגדולה] והם אנשי כנסת הגדולה.
8.1. אני] אתה.
9.3. בתמ"ט] בתמ"ח.
10.3 בתתק"ט] בתתקכ"ח (בעקביות עם הדוגמא הקודמת, אבל בניגוד לכל כה"י, והוא הדין ביחס לכי"י ת).
14.3 עבדון] פרעתוני.
26.3—27 רבינו הקדוש בנו] א ~ ושמו ר' יהודה הנשיא.
37.5. המתחדשות] אשר נתחדשו.
45.5. לנביאים] א ~ ונביאים לנביאים.
63.7. והוזכרו] והם נזכרים.
63.7—64. כי ראשי־ירמיהו] כי ירמיה לא הזכיר כי אם ראשי אבות.
7.11. והמלך צוה לעשות כן] וצוה המלך להעשות כן.
על אלה אפשר להוסיף עוד הרבה, חוץ מהפעמים הרבות אשר בהן א פשוט דילג על מלים וקיצר משפטים שלמים. ולאחרונה, כבר העיר ניבואר כי כה"י לקה מידי הצנזורה הנוצרית, כפי שנרשם בשולי הגליון (להלן ע' 14 שו' 46): "החקירה יש"ו תלש הדף מכאן אשר היה כתוב בו האמת על זמן יש"ו."

9. ר' קטלוג אדלר הנ"ל, ע' 44.

10. שם, חלק הצילומים, מס' 83.

מטיב עיבודו של החלק השני ניתן להצביע בקרוב על מוצאו של כ"י זה. לרגל הדמיון הגדול שבין הקיצור שבכה"י וסדר דורות הקבלה שבס' "יסוד עולם" לר' יצחק בן יוסף הישראלי, שיער הרב טולידאנו כי קיצור זה הוא פרי עיבודו של ר' יצחק הישראלי עצמו. היות וספרו של ר"י הישראלי עוד לא זכה למהדורה מדעית, אין בידינו להעריך את השערתו של הרב טולידאנו הערכה סופית, אבל ברור כי יש לקבל את השערתו הכללית וכי עלינו להסיק כי כה"י נבע מבית מדרשו של הרא"ש וכי כ"י זה, או אביו, נכתב או בימי חייו של הרא"ש או סמוך לפטירתו. למעלה מכל ספק הוא שנוסח כ"י זה קשור בדרך איזושהי עם הקיצור שנמסר בס' "יסוד עולם" מאמר ד' פרק י"ח כפי שיווכח משתי הפיסקאות הבאות.

כ"י אדלר 1737   יסוד עולם

ע' 15:

וה"ר ר' אברהם הלוי בן דאוד היה איש משכיל ונבון ובקי בכל מיני חכמה ובן אחותו של ר' ברוך הנזכר היה. וחבר ספרים רבים האחד מהם **הוא ספר הקבלה** (!) שסדר בו כיצד קבלו התורה דור אחר דור ממשה רבי' ע"ה ועד הרב ר' יהוסף הלוי בר' מאיר בן מגאש ור' ברוך דודו בר' יצחק בר' ברוך בן באליא. ומספרו זה האמור לקטתי רוב מה שהבאתי בפרק (!) הזה. והוא ז"ל מת על קדושת השם בעיר טוליטולה. ואחרי כן כמה צרות על ישראל...

ע' 16:

ומקודם לזה בזמן מרובה היה עוד בספרד חכמים גדולים יודעי דעת ומביני מדע ומשכילים בכל חכמה כמו ר' שלמה החכם המשורר בן גבירול ז"ל וכמו ר' יהודה הלוי המשורר בר' שמואל הלוי ז"ל. ור' אברהם החכם ן' עזרא. והמשכיל הנבון ר' משה ושלשת אחיו (!) בני עזרא ר' יצחק ור' יהודה ור' יוסף כלם בני משרה ובעלי חסד ומדות טובות ז"ל. ובזמנגנו באו לטוליטולה כמה חכמים גדולים כמו רבי' יונה מגירונדה שהרביץ בה תורה ונפטר בשנת ד' אלפים ועשרים וד'. וכמו ר' מאיר הכהן בר' יצחק מנרבונה שנפטר

(הוצ' גאלדבערג וראזענקראנץ) דף ל"ה ע"ב ובשנויים קלים בס' יוחסין (הוצ' קראקא ש"מ) דף קס"ב ע"ב:

ואח"כ היו בספרד חכמים גדולים וגם בארץ צרפת ואשכנז וארצות אדום וישמעאל מהם ר' אברהם הלוי בן דוד ז"ל איש חכם ונבון ובקי בכל חכמה ובן אחותו של ר' ברוך הנזכר היה. והוא חבר ספרים רבים האחד מהם הוא הספר שקראו ספר הקבלה סדר בו כיצד קבלו התור' דור אחר דור ממשה רבינו ע"ה עד סוף ר' יהוסף בן מיגש הלוי ור' ברוך דודו ז"ל. ומספרו זה לקטתי והעתקתי רוב מה שכתבתי בפרק הזה מיחס אנשי השם וגדולי החכמים שבכל דור ודור. ועוד חבר ספרו החשוב שחיבר בעיקרי האמונה הנקרא אל עקיד"ה אל רפיע"ה (והעתקתו בלשון עברי אמונה רמה) ועוד חבר ספרו החשוב והנכבד בחכמת התכונה וכמה ספרים אחרים עוד. והוא קדש השם ברבים ומת על יהודו ונקבר בעיר טלטולה ואח"כ באו כמה מהומות וצרות רבות ורעות על ישראל...

שם, שם, ע"ג (יוחסין דף קס"ג ע"א): ומקודם לזה עמדו בספרד כמה חכמים גדולים מבינים בכל חכמה כמו ר' שלמה

ספר הקבלה

באותו פרק. וכמו ר׳ אהרן הלוי ז״ל שעמד בה מעט וחזר לארצו. וכמו ר׳ שלמה בר׳ יוסף בן עמיאל ש״ץ שהרביץ בה תורה וכמו ר׳ דוד הכהן ש״ץ ובשנת חמשת אלפים וששים וחמש ליצירה העיר את רוח הרב ר׳ אשר בן הרב ר׳ יחיאל זצ״ל שיצא מאשכנז ארץ מולדתו ובא ובניו ובני ביתו לטוליטולה להאיר את עיניו (!) ולהשיב את נפשותינו השם יסכים על ידו...

[עד כאן כה״י אשר ממנו נשר לכל הפחות עמוד אחד (אחרון?)]

בן גבירול המשורר ז״ל שהיה בקי בכל החכמות וסדר ספרים רבים וכן החכם ר׳ אברהם בן עזרא ז״ל שפי׳ התור׳ ושאר כתבי הקודש וחבר כמו כן ספרים הרבה ונפטר בשנת ד׳ אלפי׳ תתקכ״ה למנין העולם בן ע״ה שנה וכן המשכיל והנבון משה בן עזרא ז״ל ושלשת אחיו ר׳ יצחק ור׳ יוסף ור׳ זרחיה ז״ל בני משרה ויחוס וגדולה ובעלי מדות טובות משכילי׳ בכל חכמה ומהם ר׳ זרחיה הלוי ז״ל בעל ספר המאור והרב המופל׳ ר׳ אברהם ב״ר דוד ז״ל והחכם הנבון הרב ר׳ אברהם ב״ר חייא הספרדי ז״ל שחבר ספרים הרבה וכמה חכמים אחרים עוד היו בספרד ושאר ארצות זולתי אלה זכר כולם לחיי עולם הבא. ובזמנינו באו לטוליטולה כמה חכמים גדולים ונבוני׳ מהם ר׳ יונה ז״ל מעיר גירונא ומהם ר׳ מאיר הכהן ז״ל הבא מעיר נרבונא שהרביו תורה בטוליטולה והעמידו בה תלמידים הרבה ונפטרו בחדש מרחשון משנת ה׳ אלפים וכ״ד למנין העולם. אחריהם בא לטוליטולה ר׳ אהרן הלוי ז״ל מזרע נשיאי׳ שבא מעיר ברצלוני לטליטלה בשנת ה׳ אלפי׳ ומ״ו לבריאת עולם ועמד בה ימי׳ מועטי׳ ושב לארצו. ובימים האלה היה בברצלונה החכם ר׳ שלמה בן אדרת ותלמידו היה ר׳ שלמה ש״ץ בר יוסף בן עמיאל ז״ל שהרבה תורה בטליטלה כמה שנים והעמיד תלמידי׳ רבים. וכן ר׳ דוד הכהן ז״ל. ובשנת ה׳ אלפים וששים וחמש העיר ה׳ את רוח הרב הגדול ר׳ אשר ז״ל בר יחיאל ז״ל לצאת מארץ אשכנז ארץ מולדתו ובא הוא ובניו ובני ביתו בטילטולה להאיר את עינינו ולהוציאנו מחושך הסכלות והפתיות לאור החכמה והתבונה והרביץ תורה והעמיד בה תלמידי׳. לכבודו ולמצותו חברתי הספר הזה. השם יסכים על ידו ויזכנו...

מבוא

קטעים אלה מספיקים להוכיח את הקירוב המיוחד שבין "קיצור סה"ק" ומאמרו של הישראלי ועל כן יש מקום לטעון ששניהם מיד מחבר אחד יצאו. ביחוד בולטת ההודאה מטעם מחבר הקיצור כי מסה"ק "לקטתי רוב מה שהבאתי בפרק הזה," הרי שהקיצור היווה פרק אחד בספר יותר מקיף, כגון ס' יסוד עולם,[11] או שהמקצר פשוט העתיק, בשינויי לשון קל, את דברי הישראלי. ואולם, שתי הצעות אלו אינן מתקבלות על הלב. ברור כי הקיצור שבכה"י, לכל הפחות בנוסחו המקורי, קודם לעיבודו של הישראלי, שהרי החלק הראשון של כה"י הוא העתק מילולי של סה"ק, ואילו הישראלי עיבד ושינה אף באותו חלק ראשון. עיבודו של הישראלי ניכר לא רק בפרפרזה שהכניס בכל שורה, אלא בעיקר בפרישתו ממנין בהר"ד המונח ביסוד סה"ק והמופיע גם בקיצור (שעל פיו נקבעה יציאת מצרים בשנת תמ"ט לבריאה) ובקבלת מנין וי"ד כיסוד לכרונולוגיה המסורתית (שעל פיו נקבעה יצ"מ בשנת תמ"ח לבריאה).[12] יתר על כן, אע"פ שגם המקצר השמיט שורות רבות ואף נתן הרבה מדברי הראב"ד בפרפרזה, סגנונו קרוב למקור לעיבודו של הישראלי. והנה כמה דוגמאות לכך:

יסוד עולם	כ"י אדלר 1737	סה"ק
ויצא שמו בספרד ובכל ארצות המערב ובאו לו תלמידים ללמוד ממנו מכל צד	והקול נשמע בכל ארץ ספרד וארץ המערב ובאו תלמידים לקרות. וכל שאלה ששואלין מן הישיבות ממנו שאלו	ע' 48: והקול נשמע בכל ארץ ספרד וארץ המערב ובאו התלמידים לקרות לפניו. וכל השאלות שהיו שואלים מן הישיבות ממנו שאלו
ומגדולי תלמידיו היה רב שמואל הלוי הנגיד בר יוסף הידוע בן גיקטילה מקהל קרטובה איש משכיל עד מאד ובקי בכל חכמה	ומגדולי תלמידיו היה הנגיד ר' שמואל הלוי בר' יוסף הלוי הידוע בגראנאטה וזה היה תחלתו מקהל קורטובה ת"ח מהמשכילים	ע' 53: ומגדולי תלמידיו היה רב שמואל הלוי הנגיד בר' יוסף אבן נגרילה מקהל קורטובה היה תלמיד חכם מן המשכילים הגדולים ועוד

11. המקצר גם הוסיף קטע אחד שאינו ידוע לי ממקור אשר ובודאי אינו מסה"ק המקורי. במעשה על ארבעת השבויים, מיד לאחר המלים "שאין היהודים שבמלכו תוצריכין לאנשי בבל" (להלן, ע' 48 שו' 38), הבליע המקצר סיפור על קידוש החדש בקורטובה. את התוספת הזאת נפרסם במקום אחר. ואולם, כאן עלינו לציין כי מיד אחרי התוספת הזאת השאיר הסופר רווח של שלש שורות, ורק אז המשיך "והקול נשמע בכל ארץ ספרד" (להלן, שם). בתוך אותו רווח הכניס סופר אחר את הכותרת "פרק חמישי", שאינה הולמת לא את סה"ק ולא את מבנה ס' "יסוד עולם", ולא עוד אלא ששתי מלים אלו נראות ככתובות כלאחר-יד, ונכתבו ברשלנות מפליאה, ממש כאילו השתנעשה ילד בכתב-יד וניסה להראות את כחו כסופר!

12. עובדא זו, כשלעצמה, מספקת לעורר חשד במהימנותו של נוסח פרק י"ח במאמר ד' שב"יסוד עולם" כפי שהוא לפנינו. שהרי, כידוע, קבע הישראלי עצמו כי מנין השנים לתאריך העולם צריך להחשב עפ"י מנין בהר"ד (שם, מאמר ד' פרק ג') והוא בעצמו קובע את תאריך שנה א' למנין שטרות בשנת גת"ן לתאריך העולם ומפרש "שהיא שנת אלף לצאתם מארץ מצרים" (שם, פי"ז, דף ל"א ע"ב; פי"ח דף ל"ג סע"ד), ואילו התאריכים בריש פי"ח הם כולם לפי מנין וי"ד, יציאת מצרים בתמ"ח, וחרבן בית ראשון גשל"ח "לתאריך העולם."!

ספר הקבלה

היה בקי בספרי הישמעאלים	הגדולים. ועוד היה בקי	מהיר בלשון ישמעאל
ובלשונם ומאשר כח בהם	בספרות הישמעלים (!)	ובכתביהם ובדברי חידותם
לעמוד בהיכל המלך	ובלשונם ומאשר כח בהם	
	לעמוד בהיכל המלך	

ע׳ 56: ועמד על כנו ר׳ | כמו שהוא בסה״ק בשנויים | וישב על כסאו רב יוסף
יהוסף הלוי הנגיד בנו. | קלי ערך | הנגיד בנו בחור נחמד ונעי׳
ומכל מדות טובות שהיו | | ומשכיל ולא חסר מכל מדות
באביו לא חסר לו אלא | | הטובו׳ שהיו באביו אלא
אחת שלא היה ענוותן כאביו | | שגבה לבו ברוב עשרו
מפני שגדל בעושר ולא | | וחכמתו וגדולתו והי׳ מתנשא
נשא עול בנעוריו. וגבה | | על השרים והסגנים עד
לבו עד להשחית ויקנאו בו | | שקנאו בו
סרני פלשתים

הפרפרזה שב״יסוד עולם״ מקבילה כמעט בדיוק לזו שבכה״י רק החל מהמעשה על ר׳
ברוך בן אלבאליה והליכתו אל ר״י אלפאסי ע״פ פקודות אביו (להלן, ע׳ 64).

כאמור, כל עוד לא זכינו למהדורה של ״יסוד עולם״ המבוססת על כתבי־יד שלמים,
אין בידינו להעלות מסקנה סופית על היחס שבין שני העיבודים הללו. ברם, אם עלינו
לשפוט על פי החומר שהגיע לידינו, הרי עלינו להניח לפי שעה כי הקיצור שבכ״י אדלר
הוכן ע״י עורך־מעתיק אלמוני שהתכוין להכניס את קיצורו כפרק אחד בתוך ספר מקיף
יותר. מחבר זה היה אף הוא תלמיד מבית מדרשו של הרא״ש, ויתכן אפילו שהכין את
קיצורו בשביל ספרו של ר״י הישראלי. הלה, כנראה, לא היה מרוצה לגמרי מהעבודה,
בעיקר לרגל הכרונולוגיה הספרדית הנראית חולקת על מסורות חז״ל מפורשות ותיקן
את התאריכים בהתאם לצורת המנין התלמודי שהוא מנין וי״ד[13]. באותה שעה עיבד את
כל הקיצור מחדש ואף הוסיף פה ושם תוספות שנכנסו לכתבי היד של מחלקה ת.

למרות זה שהקיצור בכ״י אדלר הכיל הרבה יותר מסה״ק מאשר הפרק ב״יסוד עולם״ —
כגון, כל הפרשה על ר׳ יוסף אבן ג׳ו. החסרה בעיבודו של הישראלי — היות ובחלק השני
של קיצורו המחבר השמיט של קיצור סה״ק שורות וחצאי שורות על ימין ועל שמאל, החל
ממעשה ארבעת השבויים נהגנו בגירסאות כ״י זה, כפי שנהגנו בגירסאות כ״י א, ולא
הבאנו את חילופיו לגירסאות סה״ק אלא אם כן יש להם סעד ממקור אחר.

כ״י ב הוגה ע״י סופר שני שהוסיף הערות כרונולוגיות בשולי הגליון ולעתים תיקן
אף בגוף הטכסט. גירסאות אלו, כשהובאו בחילופי הגירסאות, סומנו בסימנית ב[1]. במקומות
ספורים ניכרת צורת כתיבה שלישית, וכשהבאנו גירסאות מסופר שלישי זה סימנום
ב[2].

---

13. ברור כי הישראלי ידע כי שני המנינים מכוונים לשנה אחת; ר׳ ח. י. בורנשטיין, תאריכי ישראל,
התקופה כרך ח׳ (תרפ״א), ע׳ 315 ואילך, שם כרך ט׳ (תרפ״א), ע׳ 222 ואילך; ועל כן, עלינו
להסיק לפי שעה כי צורת ה״סטיה״ הספרדית בתאריכים קלסיים היא אשר לא היתה רצויה
לבעל ס׳ ״יסוד עולם״.

מבוא

3. ה = כ"י אוקספורד, Heb. e. 9, שבספריה הבודליאנית¹⁴. כ"י זה, אשר זמן כתיבתו אינו ידוע, כתוב על נייר בכתב ספרדי ברור. כה"י אינו שלם, וכנראה אבד ממנו אך עמודו האחרון, שכן החלק שנשמר מגיע עד "ר' משה גיקאטיליא הכהן ורבים חכמים אחרים שכתבו לנו ספרים" (להלן, ע' 73). כ"י זה הוא מהמשובחים שבכה"י ואת גירסאותיו הבאנו תדיר.

3א. ר' להלן מס' 10.

4. ל = כ"י בית המדרש דק"ק אשכנזים בלונדון, מס' 1528. כ"י זה הכתוב על קלף בכתב אשכנזי, נעתק אחרי 1453, ומשקף את נוסח סה"ק לאחר עיבודו עפ"י מנין וי"ד. כחברו כ"י ר (ר' להלן, מס' 9), הושלם סה"ק ע"י רשימת החכמים שלאחר אלה המנויים ע"י הראב"ד מתוך פי"ח ממאמר ד' של ס' "יסוד עולם", ועוד נוספו עליו שני חיבוריו ההיסטוריוגרפיים האחרים של הראב"ד, "זכרון דברי רומי" ו"דברי מלכי ישראל בבית שני." הגהות מספר נרשמו בשולי הגליון ע"י סופר שני ואותן הבאנו בסימנית ל¹.

5. מ = כ"י מרצבכר אשר בספריה העירונית והאוניברסיטאית בפרנקפורט ע"נ מיין. לפי תיאורו של ר' רנ"נ ראבינאוויטץ¹⁶, כ"י זה נכתב בכתב אשכנזי על קלף בתחלת האלף הששי, כלומר סמוך לשנת 1240 לסה"נ. ואולם, מכיון שנוסחו הוא נוסח מחלקה ת, מסתבר יותר לאחר את זמן כתיבתו לכל הפחות לתחלת המאה הי"ד לסה"נ, כלומר מיד לאחר עיבודו של סה"ק לפי מנין וי"ד.

חבל שכ"י זה, שהוא מהמשובחים שבמחלקה ת ואף משקף את נוסח כ"י ת בשלבם הראשון (עיין להלן), לקה בחוסר השליש האחרון של סה"ק, כלומר החל מהפרשה על חיי ר' שמואל הנגיד. שתי טעויות בכתיב נותנות מקום להשערה שהסופר כתב מפי מקריא ולא מטופס כתוב: שמו של ר' מלכיה נכתב מלקיה (להלן, ע' 38 שו' 35), ושמו של רבה תוספאה נכתב רבה טופסאה (להלן, ע' 27 שו' 61). ואעפ"י שכתיב שני שמות אלה נרשם נכונה לאחר מכאן (ר' שם שו' 63, וע' 41 שו' 80), דומה כי קליטתו הראשונה של הסופר מעידה על דרך עבודתו.

6. ס = כ"י די־רוסי 1409 שבספריה הפאלאטנית בפרמה¹⁷. כ"י זה, הכולל גם את "זכרון דברי רומי", נעתק באיטליה כנראה במאה הט"ו לסה"נ, ונוסחו כל כך קרוב לנוסח דפו"ר שלא הבאנו את גירסאותיו בחילופי הנוסחאות אלא לעתים נדירות.

7. פ = כ"י די־רוסי 1,117 שבספריה הפאלאטנית בפרמה¹⁸. כ"י זה, הכתוב בכתב ספרדי ברור, והכולל גם את דרשת הראב"ד על נבואת זכריה ואת אגרת ר' שרירא גאון ועוד, נשלם בתשרי ק"ה (ספטמבר, 1344). כ"י זה שלם הוא, ואעפ"י שלקה בכמה טעויות סופר, הרי הוא מהמעולים שבכל כה"י שהיו לפנינו, ואת גירסאותיו הבאנו תדיר. הגהות שנרשמו בכה"י ע"י סופר שני סומנו פ¹.

14. A. Neubauer and A. Cowley, *Catalogue of the Hebrew Manuscripts in the Bodleian Library* (2 vols. Oxford, 1886–1906), II, 216 no. 2800.

15. A. Neubauer, *Catalogue of the Hebrew Manuscripts in the Jews' College, London* (Oxford, 1886), p. 11 no. 12, ור' שם, בסוף ע' 9.

16. ר. נ. נ. ראבינאוויטץ, אהל אברהם, (מינכן, תרמ"ח) ע' 12 מס' 122.

17. P. Perreau, "Catalogo dei codici ebraici della Biblioteca di Parma non descritti del De-Rossi," *Cataloghi dei Codici Orientali di Alcune Biblioteche d'Italia* (Firenze, 1878–1904), p. 141 no. 32.

18. *MSS Codices Hebraici Biblioth.* I. B. De-Rossi (3 vols. Parma, 1803), I, 74 no. 117.

8. ק = כ"י אוקספורד, 162, Opp. Add. 4 to שבספריה הבודליאנית.[19] כ"י משובח זה, הקרוב לכ"י פ בגירסאותיו, נעתק, לפי דברי נויבואר, בשנת 1519 לסה"נ ע"י סופר מזרחי (ביזן?), ואף הוא כולל את דרשת הראב"ד על נבואת זכריה. כה"י לקה בחסר, שכן נקרע ממנו דף ט' שבו, ופה ושם לא ניתנו גירסאותיו לקריאה לרגל אכילת תולעים בנייר. ההגהות של סופר שני סומנו ק[1].

9. ר = כ"י רוטשילד 24, שבבית הנכות הלאומי בצלאל בירושלים,[20] דף צ"ז ע"א עד קי"ב ע"א. כ"י נהדר זה נכתב על קלף וצוייר באיטליה בסוף המאה הט"ו לסה"נ. סה"ק (שנסמן בשולי הגליון כ"סדר עולם"!) הושלם ע"י רשימת החכמים שלאחרי תקופת הראב"ד מס' "יסוד עולם". כ"י זה יקר כעדות על גירסאות כי"י מחלקה ת, וערכו גדול מכיון שכה"י שלם ומהווה מעין חוליית הבינים בין כ"י מ לכ"י ל (עיין להלן).

10. י = כ"י ר"א עפשטיין שאבד בשואה הנאצית. כ"י זה לא היה לפני, אבל חילופי גירסאותיו נרשמו בטופס סה"ק (דפוס ורשה, תרל"ז) ע"י נ. בריל ששמסרו לנויבואר, ונויבואר מסרו למורי הפרופ' ר"א מארכס ז"ל. מורי נתן לי את הטופס היקר הזה, ועתה הוא מונח בספרית ביהמ"ד לרבנים באמריקה. כ"י זה נעתק בסלוניקי בשנת 1509,[21] וגירסאותיו זהות כמעט תמיד עם גירסאות כ"י ק (אף כ"י י כולל את הדרשה על זכריה), ויתכן כי כ"י ק נעתק ממנו או ששניהם נעתקו מכ"י אחד. מכיון שלא יכלתי לבדוק את כה"י בעצמי, וגירסאותיו מיוצגות ע"י כ"י ק, לא הבאתי את גירסאות כ"י י אלא באותם המקומות שבהם כ"י ק לקה בחסר.

חוץ מכי"י אלה, היו לפני עוד כמה כי"י שבדקתי, אבל את גירסאותיהם לא הבאתי בחילופי הגירסאות.

1. כ"י פלוטיאוס 7,1 שבספרית מדיציאה-לורנציאנה שבפירנצי.[22] כ"י זה הקרוב מאד בגירסאותיו לכי"י בה, מכיל את סה"ק אך עד דור ראשון לסבוראים. היות והוא קטוע וגירסאותיו משובשות מאד לא הכללתיו בחילופי הגירסאות.

2. כ"י אוקספורד Heb. C 8 שבספריה הבודליאנית.[23] כ"י זה נעתק מדפו"ר או מטכסט הקרוב לו, וחילופי גירסאותיו אינם בני-סמכא כל עיקר.

3. כ"י מיכאל 190 שבספריה הבודליאנית באוקספורד,[24] כתוב בכתב איטלקי מאוחר, ומכיל את הטכסט אך עד דור ראשון לסבוראים.

4. כ"י ביהמ"ד דק"ק אשכנזים בלונדון, 3,494,[25] כתוב באותיות איטלקיות, ונוסחאותיו הן של מחלקה ת.

---

19. Neubauer-Cowley, *op. cit.*, I, 906 no. 2521.
20. I. Lévi, "Le manuscrit hébreu no. 24 de la bibliothèque du Baron Edmond de Rothschild à Paris," *REJ*, LXXXIX (1930), 281–292.
21. A. Marx, "Eine Sammelhandschrift im Besitze des Herren A. Epstein," *ZfHB*, V (1901), 54 f., 58 no. 9.
22. A. M. Biscioni, *Bibliotecae Mediceo-Laurentianae Catalogus*, I (Firenze, 1752), Catalogus Pluteus, I, VII, pp. 5–6 [= idem, *Bibliothecae Ebraicae Graecae Florentinae sive Bibliothecae Mediceo-Laurentianae Catalogus* (Firenze, 1757,) Bibliothecae Hebraicae Florentinae Catalogus, pp. 19–21].
23. Neubauer-Cowley, *op. cit.*, II, 215–216 no. 2799, 3.
24. Ibid., I, 198 no. 914, 2.
25. ש. ז. ח. הלברשטם, קהלת שלמה (ווינען, תר"ן), ע' 99 מס' 372.

מבוא

5. כ״י פריז שבספריה הלאומית הצרפתית[26], מכיל רק קטע קטן מסופו של סה״ק וכנראה נעתק מדפו״ר.

ג. מיון כתבי־היד (רצנזיה)

גירסאות כה״י ניתנות למיון דיאגרמטי זה:

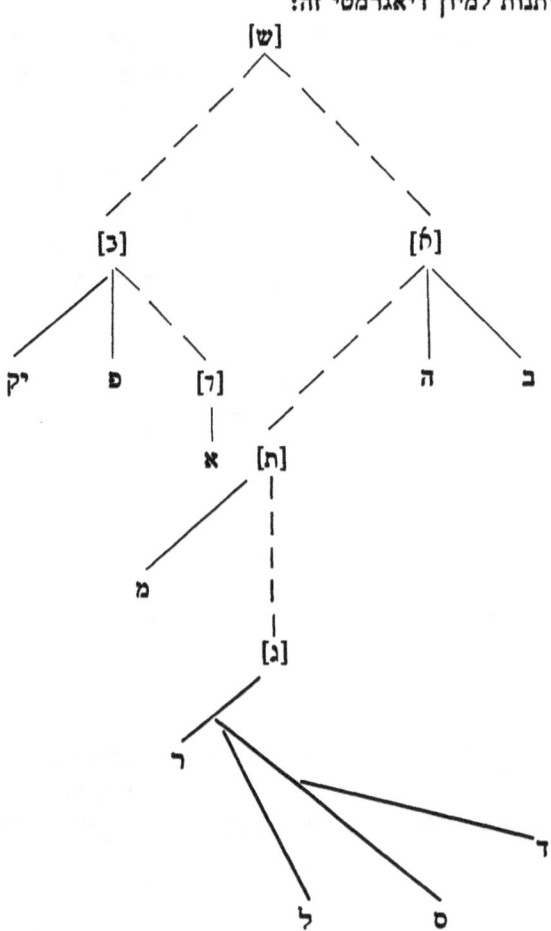

וזה פירושו של שחזור תיאוריטי זה של השתלשלות כה״י:
1. כה״י מתחלקים לשתי מחלקות־אב ש ו־ת, החלוקות בגירסאותיהן בערך 450 פעם. אעפ״י שכי״י ש חלוקים לעתים רבות אף בינם לבין עצמם, הרי גירסאות כה״י בתוך מחלקת־אב זו קרובות ביסודן אחת לרעותה ונבדלות הבדל מהותי מגירסאות כי״י ת, החלוקות לעתים אף הן חלוקה פנימית.

26. N. Zotenberg, *Catalogue des Manuscrits Hébreux et Samaritains de la Bibliothèque Impériale* (Paris, 1886), p. 62 no. 585, 6.

2. מתוך הספר גופו, וכן מעדויותיהם של ראשונים (עיין להלן), משתקפת עליונותה-קדמותה של מחלקה ש; כלומר, בסופו של דבר כל כי״י ת נובעים מכי״י של מחלקה ש.
3. מכיון שאף אחד מכה״י שלפנינו אינו העתק ישיר ושלם של סה״ק כפי שיצא מעטו של הראב״ד, נאלצנו להעמיד לפני הקורא טכסט ״אקלקטי״ אשר נוסחו נקבע לאחר השוואת הגירסאות ובירורן.[27]
4. מחלקה ש, נחלקת אף היא לשתי תולדות, או מחלקות-משניות, והן תולדה א׳ הכוללת כי״י ב ו–ה, ותולדה ב׳ הכוללת כי״י פ(י)ק. חלוקה זו מתאשרת מתוך ההבדל המהותי בגירסאות בין שתי תולדות אלו בערך 300 פעם.
5. על יסוד כי״י שאינו לפנינו, וששימש ג״כ אב-טיפוס לכי״י בה, עובד סה״ק עיבוד סגנוני-תכני ונוצר אב-טיפוס ת. השערה זו מבוססת על העובדא כי לרוב קרובה גירסת ת לגירסת בה (ובעיקר ל–ה), הרבה יותר מאשר לגירסאות אפיק. ואולם, היות ומאידך לעתים מסכימות גירסאות כי״י ת לגירסאות אפיק, בניגוד לגירסאות בה, נאלצתי לשער כי כ״י ת לא עובד מאחד מכה״י שלפנינו, אלא מכ״י שקדם ל–בה.
6. כ״י ת שינה לא רק את סגנונו של הראב״ד בהרבה מקומות, אלא גם כן תיקן את המנין ליצירה עפ״י מנין וי״ד, הוסיף כמה הוספות בהתאם למסורות התלמוד או מסורות אחרות מימי הבינים, ולפעמים תיקון כתיב של שמות שנשתקלקל או שלא היה ברור לו. כך יצא שכמה משגיאות ש תוקנו ב–ת, הן בהבאת עובדות מהמקרא וכדומה, הן בכתיב שמות מקומות. עיבוד זה נעשה כנראה בתחלת המאה הי״ד לסה״נ.
7. מחלקה ת נחלקת אף היא לשתי תולדות, והן א׳ הכוללת כי״י למר, וב׳ הכוללת דס. יתר על כן, מתוך פיסקא אחת בכ״י ת ניתן לנו לעמוד על השלבים השונים בהתפתחות נוסח ת מעיבודו הראשון ועד לצורתו הסופית ב–ד. בדור תשיעי להוראה בבית המקדש חוזר הראב״ד על דבריו כי בנו יורשו של הלל הזקן היה רבן גמליאל הזקן (להלן, ע׳ 4 שו׳ 25, וע׳ 16 שו׳ 84). כ״י ת תיקן את הפיסקא הראשונה והכניס את שמו של שמעון בן הלל לשלשלת הנשיאות שם.[28] ואילו בפיסקא השניה נשאר הטכסט בצורתו הברורה והמקורית, וכן הוא בכ״י מ. מגיה אחר עמד על הסתירה הפנימית שבין שתי הפיסקאות, והוסיף הערה שעל צורתה שמר סופר כ״י ר והעתיק את ההערה בשולי הגליון. מגיה-סופר אחר הבליע את ההערה בגוף הספר וכך היא מופיעה בכ״י לסד: ״לעיל כתב שמעון בנו וכו׳״ (להלן, ע׳ 16 בחילופי הגירסאות לשו׳ 83). הווה אומר, שכ״י מ, שבו חסרה ההערה הזאת לגמרי, משקף שלב ראשון, כ״י ר שלב שני וכי״י לסד שלב שלישי. יתר על כן, נראה כ״י ל כקודם ל–ס, והלה כקודם קצת ל–ד; ברם, מכיון שאי אפשר היה לנו להוכיח כי אחד מכי״י אלה הועתק מחברו הבאנו את גירסאות כי״י דלמר תמיד.

ד. עדותם של ראשונים

הראשון אשר שאב מסה״ק במדה ניכרת הוא מחבר החלק הכרונולוגי של ״מבוא התלמוד״ המיוחס לר׳ שמואל הנגיד, הנמצא בכ״י בספריית ר׳ דוד ששון.[29] מחבר המבוא הזה קיצר את סה״ק ושינה בסגנונו על ימין ועל שמאל, עד שתוכן כל סה״ק הובא בי״ח עמודים וחצי של כ״י. במקום אחר נסינו להוכיח כי מחבר המבוא הזה אינו ר״ש הלוי הנגיד אבן נגרילא,

---

27. להסברת השיטה שנקטנו בה, ר׳ P. Maas, *Textkritik* (2 ed. Leipzig, 1950).
28. יתכן כי מגיה כבר תיקן כך בכמה כי״י ש; ר׳ את גירסאות כ״י ק להלן, ע׳ 4 שו׳ 25, וע׳ 16 שו׳ 84.
29. ר׳ ד.ס. ששון, אהל דוד (אוקספורד, תרצ״ב), ח״ב ע׳ 1066 ואילך.

וכי מחבר קיצור זה הסתמך על סה"ק ולא להפך[30]. ואם אמנם עדיין אין זהותו של מחבר המבוא הזה ודאית, הרי תלותו בספרו של הראב"ד אינה בגדר ספק, ויש איפוא להתחשב בספר זה כעדות תנינית לגירסאות כ"י קדמון. יתר על כן, בכמה מקומות תואמות גירסאות מחבר המבוא את גירסאות המחלקה המשנית איפ̇ק, בעיקר בכתיבת שמות חכמים ומקומותיהם: כך, למשל, בדור ראשון לסבוראים כותב המקצר את שמו של רב תחינא רב חנינא", ואת שמו של רב סימונא "רב סמא", ורב חנן מאשיקיא הוא "רב חנן מאשיא" (להלן, ע' 34, והשוה גירסאות אפ̇ק שם). ואעפ"י שעדות זו עדות קדמונית היא, אין היא מספקת לפי דעתנו להכריע נגד שאר כה"י. קדם כל, ברור כי לעתים תיקן המקצר עפ"י מקורות אחרים. למשל, מנין יציאת מצרים הוא לפי מנין וי"ד, בתמ"ח גאולים, ואילו התאריך לחרבן בית ראשון ולהתחלת מנין שטרות הוא לפי מנין בהר"ד. לפעמים פשוט טעה המחבר בהעתקתו, או העתיק מכ"י משובש. מכיון שדרכו למסור לוח שמות ותאריכים כמעט ערטילאי, כלומר בהשמטת רוב הפרטים הצדדיים שהובאו בסה"ק והמגוונים את סגנונו של הראב"ד, קשה לשפוט בוודאות על תכן כה"י שעמד לפניו. ואחרון אחרון היות וזהותו של המחבר עדיין אינה למעלה מכל ספק, אין לדעת אם לפני המקצר היה מונח כ"י בן דורו של הראב"ד, שעוד לא לקה מטעויות מעתיקים ומתיקוני מגיהים ומסגננים.

ובכל זאת, חשוב לנו כ"י זה כקנה מדה להערכת טיב כ"י איפ̇ק. מכיון שגירסאות המקצר והגירסאות הספורות העולות לנו מפירורי הגניזה[31] הן בנות אותו ענף באילן כה"י, הרי ברור שלכל הפחות למצרים הגיע כ"י מסוג איפ̇ק. אופיים המצרי, וליתר דיוק הצפון־אפריקאי, של גירסאות אלו מסביר את הקירבות שבין כ"י י̇ק והעתקת ר"א זכות בס' יוחסין השלם. ברור ג"כ שגירסאות מחלקה משנית זו הן בעלות ערך מיוחד, היות ונפוצו לא רק במצרים ובצפון אפריקא ויון, אלא ג"כ בספרד ובפרובנס (כ"י א̇פ).

עדות שנייה היא הקיצור שבכ"י ב, שעליו הרחבנו את הדיבור לעיל. כאן עלינו רק להעיר שעדות זו חשובה לא רק לרגל עתיקותה, אלא מפני שהיא מייצגת מאזן נגד גירס־אותיהם של כ"י איפ̇ק.

ר' סעדיה אבן דנאן אף הוא קיצר את סה"ק במאמרו על סדר הדורות[32]. ואולם, מכיון שר' סעדיה עיבד את הדברים עיבוד יסודי — "גם סדרתי אותו על נכון והרחקתי הידיעות המפסידות" — אין ספרו יכול לשמש קנה מדה כלשהו בהערכת כתבי היד. מכתיב שמות חכמים נראה שכה"י ששימש יסוד לקיצורו היה אף הוא ממחלקת איפ̇ק.

קיצורו של ר' יוסף בן צדיק[33] נעשה מכ"י ממחלקה ש, אלא שהמחבר הבליע לתוך חיבורו הרבה פרטים ושנויי סגנון מקיצורו של ר' יצחק הישראלי.

המחבר היחידי אשר ציטט במדה גדולה את סה"ק מלה במלה ואף העתיק חלק גדול מספרו והבליעו לתוך חיבורו היה ר' אברהם זכות בס' יוחסין[34]. החל מתקופת האמוראים, ספרו של הראב"ד מובא ע"י ר"א זכות כמעט מלה במלה. הודות להעתיק זה כמעט ודאי שכה"י

---

[30]. G. D. Cohen, "The Story of the Four Captives," *PAAJR*, XXIX (1960–61), 124 f.; ור' מ. מרגליות, הלכות הנגיד (ירושלים, תשכ"ב), ע' 68 ואילך.
[31]. כ"י אדלר, 3365, 3408 שבספרית ביהמ"ד לרבנים באמריקה.
[32]. ר' חמדה גנוזה לר' צבי הירש עדעלמאן, חוברת א' (קאניגסברערג, תרט"ז), דף כ"ה ע"א ואילך.
[33]. סדר החכמים, ח"א, ע' 85 ואילך.
[34]. ס' יוחסין השלם, בהוצ' צ. פילפאווסקי (לונדון, תרי"ז; הוצ' שלישית, ירושלים, התשכ"ג).

שעמד לפני ר"א זכות היה מטיפוס כ"י א, שהרי רק בס' יוחסין ובכ"י א נמצאת טעות שלפיה נקרא חברו של רבי יהודה הנשיא ר' ישמעאל בנו של ר' יוחנן בן ברוקא[35]. יתכן כי לפני זכות היה גם כ"י א ממש או כ"י הקרוב אליו, שכן הוא מסכם בקצרה את התוספת על קהלת נרבונה בשם "קבלת החסיד"[36]. מאידך, ברור ג"כ כי תוספת זו לא היתה בגוף הספר שממנו העתיק זכות, שהרי כשהוא בא להעתיק את סדר דורות הרבנים, העתקתו מקבילה לטכסט של כ"י שבהם חסרה תוספת זו[37]. מובן שאפשר לטעון כי את טיב כה"י שהיה לפני ר"א זכות יש לשפוט מגוף ספרו שבו הוזכר סה"ק תוך כדי דיבור ולא על פי העתקה שבמאמרים ב', ג' וד' שיתכן ונעשתה ע"י סופר אחר. יתכן, אלא שאף העתק זה יעיד כי התוספת שבכ"י א לא היתה בשאר כה"י ממחלקה זו.

בסיכומו של דבר, המקצרים, המעבדים והמעתיקים הראשונים מעידים על קדמותה של מחלקה ש למחלקה ת. מצד שני, אין הציטטות שבספרים אלה מספיקות לנו לעקוב אחרי השתלשלות הטכסט של סה"ק, ולכך עלינו להזדקק לבירורו פנימי של כה"י עצמם בסיוע עדויות הראשונים.

ה. מהדורה זו

כפי שהסברנו, הטכסט הנמסר פה הוא אקלקטי. עד כמה שאפשר היה, בכרנו את גירסת כ"י ש, ולא עברנו לנוסח כ"י ת, אלא אם נראתה לנו גירסת ש כמוטעית לחלוטין. בכל אופן, מקורה של כל גירסא מתברר מתוך הסימונים שבחילופי הגירסאות. לא הבאנו חילופי גירסא של כתיב מלא וחסר, או של "מ" ו"נ" סופיות בצורת ריבוי של שמות אלא אם כן שינויים אלה נתנו מקום לפירוש אחר לטכסט. את הספר חילקנו לפרקים בהתאם לחלוקות הפנימיות שבספר גופו. מובן מאליו שמספור הפרקים הוא תוספת המהדיר ועל כן הוכנסו מספרי הפרקים בחצאי לבנה. את המספרים הללו הוספנו היות וכמה מכתבי היד העתיקו את שמות הפרקים, (שמספריהם בהוצאתנו הם ד' ה' ו') באותיות גדולות, ויתכן אפילו כי הראב"ד בעצמו סימן את הפרקים הללו כך. בכל אופן, מהספר עצמו ברור שמחברו התכוון לחלק בין פרק לפרק, היינו בין תקופה אחת לחברתה, ואנו מלאנו אחריו.

---

35. ס' יוחסין השלם, ע' 41א; להלן, ע' 22 שו' 62.
36. ס' יוחסין השלם, ע' 84ב.
37. שם, ע' 214ב.

הסימניות שבחילופי הגירסאות

א כ״י אדלר 2237
ב כ״י אדלר 1737
ד דפוס מנטובה רע״ד
ה כ״י אוקספורד Heb. e. 9
י כ״י עפשטיין
ל כ״י ביהמ״ד דק״ק אשכנזים בלונדון, 28
מ כ״י מרצבכר
ס כ״י די־רוסי 1409
פ כ״י די־רוסי 1,117
ק כ״י אוקספורד 162
ר כ״י רוטשילד 24
ש כי״י אבהיפק
ת כי״י דלמסר
> חסר
~ נוסף
[ ] מלה זו (או מלים אלו) נוספו בכה״י המסומן בלבד
( ) מלה זו (או מלים אלו) חסרות בכה״י המסומן בלבד
< > שנוי גירסא למלה האחרונה בכ״י מסויים בלבד
— — קו בין שתי מלים מורה כי חילופי הגירסא כוללים את המלים ממלה ראשונה ועד השנייה.

ספורה יחידה בצד מלה בחילופי הגירסאות מסמנת את השורה; שתי ספורות את העמוד והשורה. ספורה מלמעלה למלה מסמנת את הפעם הראשונה, שנייה או שלישית שבה מופיעה אותה מלה בשורה מסויימת.

ספר הקבלה

[ספר הקבלה]

זה ספר הקבלה כתבנוהו להודיע אל התלמידים כי כל דברי רבותינו
ז״ל חכמי המשנה והתלמוד כלם מקובלים חכם גדול וצדיק מפי
חכם גדול וצדיק ראש ישיבה וסיעתו מפי ראש ישיבה וסיעתו מאנשי
כנסת הגדולה שקבלו מן הנביאים זכר כלם לברכה. ולעולם חכמי
תלמוד וכל שכן חכמי משנה אפילו דבר קטן לא אמרו מלבם חוץ
מן התקנות שתקנו בהסכמת כלם כדי לעשות סייג לתורה. ואם לחשך
אדם שיש בו רוח מינות לומר מפני שנחלקו בכמה מקומות לפיכך אני
מסתפק בדבריהם אף אתה הקהה את שיניו והודיעהו שהוא ממרא על
פי ב״ד. ושלא נחלקו רז״ל לעולם בעיקר מצוה אלא בתולדותיה
ששמעו עיקרה מרבותם ולא שאלום על תולדותיה מפני שלא שמשו
כל צרכן. כיוצא בו לא נחלקו אם מדליקין נר שבת אם לא. על מה
נחלקו במה מדליקין ובמה אין מדליקין. וכן אם חייבין אנו לקרוא

---

1 [ספר הקבלה] ד אמר החכם תפארת הישרים רבינו אברהם הלוי בן דוד זכרונו לברכה
 ס עזרי מעם י׳ עושה שמים וארץ בהנרא] [= בעזרת ה׳ נעשה ונצליח ⟨או: נתחיל ונגמור⟩
 אמן] מ זה ספר הקבלה שחבר הראב״ד ז״ל ב זה ספר חבר אותו החסיד הגדול ר׳ אברהם
 הלוי בן דאור (!) זצ״ל המקדש את השם ברבים ומסר עצמו על יחוד השם. ונתלה
 בטוליטולה השם יתן חלקו עם עשרה הרוגי מלכו׳ ויקיים בהם קרא דכתי׳ אספו לי
 חסידי כורתי בריתי עלי זבח |
2 זה] ק ⟨ ⟩ | ספר] אב סדר | הקבלה] ה קבלה ק ~ לר׳ אברהם ן׳ דאוד ז״ל | להודיע –
 התלמידים] ה התלמידים ל התלמידים | להודיעם] להודיעם | אל⟩ | את ⟩ ד לתלמידים | רבותינו] ל רבינו |
3 בהלמ ותלמוד | מקובלים] ק ~ מפי |
4 חכם גדול וצדיק] ה ⟨ ⟩ | ישיבה] ¹/² | פק ישיבתו | מאנשי] פ של אנשי ק עד אנשי |
5 קדלר מהנביאים | זכר–לברכה] הפ ז״ל |
6 בהלמ תלמוד] אדר התלמוד פק תורה | משנה] אדר המשנה פ התלמוד |
7 ב מהתקנות |
8 אדם] אפק ~ לומר ~ | ק רוח מינות בו | רוח] הת ריח | לומר | אפק ⟩ ק שמפני |
 בכמה] מ בהרבה (בגליון: בכמה) | לפיכך] ד לכך | אני] ה יש |
9 מסתפק] ה ספק ד מסופק |
11 ל עקרו | בת מרבותיהם | ל ושלא |
12 כיוצא] ק ראיה | בו] פ בדבר ק לדבר | לא] ק שלא | אם | ה באם | פק בשבת | לא]
 אב לאו | על | אק אלא על אך ועל |
13 פק וכן] א וכן לא נחלקו ה לא נחלקו ת ולא נחלקו | חייבין אנו] א אנו חייבין למר
 חייב ד חובה | פלמד לקרות |

קריית שמע ערבית ושחרית אם לא. על מה נחלקו מאימתי קורין את
שמע בערבין ומאימתי קורין את שמע בשחרין. וכן בכל דבריהם.

14 שמע] מ ~ אם לא | אפק שחרית וערבית | אם] ד או | אם לא] במ | > | על] ק אלא
על דמ ועל | ק באימתי ל אימתי |
15 בערבין] ד בערבית ב בשחרית | ה מאימתי ק או אימתי | קורין את שמע²] ב < | את
שמע] ק | > | בשחרין] פ שחרית ק בשחרית ב בערבית | וכן] ל וכל (!) | בכל] הד לכל |

ספר הקבלה

[א]

מאדם ועד המבול אלף ותרנ"ו שנה. מן המבול ועד אברהם רצ"ב שנה. משנולד אברהם עד שיצא מחרן פעם ראשונה נ"ב שנה. ומצאתו מחרן עד מעמד בין הבתרים י"ח שנה. ושב לחרן ועמד שם ה' שנים. וחזר לארץ כנען בן ע"ה שנה. ועד שנולד יצחק כ"ה שנה. ועד שנולד יעקב ס' שנה. ועד רדת יעקב למצרים ק"ל שנה. ועד מות יעקב י"ז שנה. ועד מות יוסף נ"ג שנה. ומשמת יוסף עד שיצאו נביאי השקר מבני אפרים וגלעד והטעו את ישראל ונהרגו ק"י שנה. ועד צאתם מארץ מצרים שלשים שנה.

יצאו ממצרים בניסן שנת בתמ"ט. ועד בנין בית ראשון ת"פ שנה. נבנה הבית בשנת בתקכ"ט. ועד חרבן הבית תל"ג שנים. אבל ת"י שנה מנו לו. כי מתחלת גלות יהויקים לא נחשב המלכות. וזה פרטן: במדבר מ' שנה. יהושע כ"ח. זקנים שהאריכו ימים אחרי יהושע י"ז. עתניאל מ'. אהוד פ'. ובסוף שמגר שנה אחת. דבורה וברק מ'. גדעון מ'. אבימלך ג'. תולע כ"ג. יאיר כ"ב. יפתח ו'. אבצן ז'. אילון י'. עבדון ח'. שמשון כ'. עלי מ'.

1 ועד¹] דלר עד | אהק מן המבול] בפ ומן המבול מ ומהמבול דלר מהמבול | ועד] הת עד | רצ"ב שנה] פק קצ"ב שנה ⟨ ק שנים⟩ מצאתי בקבלה קצב והזמן ההוא רצב ה קצ שנה |
2 אם ומשנולד | ב ועד | מהרן] ל מחרון | אפק בעת צאתו ב משיצא |
3 מחרן] ל מחרון | מעמד] פ ⟨ ב שעמד | שם⟩ ה' | ש ח' |
4 יצחק] אה ⟨ |
5 יעקב¹] ה ⟨ | פ מצרים בה מצרימה | ק"ל שנה] לר ק"ל | ועד²] מ עד | אבה מות פק פטירת ת שמת | יעקב] אפק ~ במצרים ~ י"ז שנה] י"ז שנה | קלם י"ז |
6 מות] פק פטירת ד שמת | נ"ג שנה] ב נ"ג פק ~ מצאתי בקבלה כן והם נ"ד | משמת שיצאו] ד שעמדו במצרי' |
7 ק"י שנה] פ ⟨ | מארץ מצרים] אפק ממצרים |
8 מצרים] ר ⟨ |
9 יצאו] ק ויצאו ישראל | בניסן] אק ⟨ שנת] מ ⟨ | בתמ"ט] אק ⟨ את בתמ"ח | שנה] ב ⟨ | אק ונבנה |
10 הבית¹] א בית ראשון ב ~ הא ב¹ הראשון | בשנת] ת שנת | הבית²] פ ⟨ | שנים] בה ⟨ שנה] בהם ⟨ |
11 גלות] ר מלכות | יהויקים] ה יהודים | וזה פרטן] ה ⟨ | וזה] אבק וזהו |
12 כ"ח] אפק ~ שנה ~ ק וזקנים ~ ל אחר | י"ז] אב¹ פק ~ שנה | מ'] אבפק ~ שנה |
13 אהוד פ'] — וברק מ'] ה ⟨ | פ'] ק ס' אב¹ פק ~ שנה | ר ובסופר | וברק מ'] אפקמ ~ שנה | ג'] ד מ' אפק ~ שנים |
14 כ"ג] ב כ' הק ג' פק ~ שנה | כ"ב] ה כ"ו אפק ~ שנה ו'] בפק ~ שנים | ז'] פק ~ שנים | אילון] י' עבדון ח'] א פירעתוני עשר אילון י' פק עבדון י' שנים אילון י' ⟨ ק ו' ⟨ שנים | כ'] ה י' פק ~ שנים | מ'] פק ~ שנה |

3

ספר הקבלה

שמואל י״א. שאול ב׳. דוד מ׳. שלמה מ׳. ונבנה הבית בשנת ג׳ למלכותו. רחבעם י״ז. אביה ג׳. אסא מ״א. יהושפט כ״ה. יהורם ח׳. אחזיהו שנה אחת. עתליהו ו׳. יואש מ׳. אמציה כ״ט. עוזיהו נ״ב. יותם י״ו. אחז י״ו. חזקיהו כ״ט. מנשה נ״ה. אמון ב׳. יאשיהו ל״א. יהואחז ג׳ חדשים. יהויקים י״א שנה. יהויכין ג׳ חדשים. צדקיהו י״א שנה. הרי כאן תל״ג מסוף השנה השלישית לשלמה עד שחרב הבית.

יהויכין שאלתיאל בנו זרובבל בנו משולם בנו חנניה בנו ברכיה בנו חסדיהו בנו ישעיהו בנו עובדיהו בנו שכניהו בנו שמעיה בנו נעריהו בנו חזקיהו בנו. ואומרים כי אחי חזקיהו בן נעריהו היה הלל. כל אלה נשיאי ישראל בבבל. ועלה הלל מבבל והיה בארץ ישראל לנשיא מאה שנה קודם חרבן בית שני. רבן גמליאל הזקן בנו רבן שמעון בן גמליאל בנו רבן גמליאל בנו רבן שמעון בן גמליאל בנו רבינו הקדוש בנו רבן גמליאל ברבי בנו ר׳ יהודה הנשיא בנו.

קבל משה רבינו עליו השלום תורה מסיני עשרת הדברות בסיון שנת

ספר הקבלה

בתמ"ט. ושאר המצות באותן מ' יום שעמד בהר עד יום י"ז בתמוז
שירד ושבר את הלוחות ובשאר השנה הראשונה לצאתם מארץ מצרים
ובשנה השנית עד ט' באב ששבו המרגלים מתור הארץ ולא אבו לעלות.
ונגזרה גזירה על אבותינו שלא יכנסו לארץ. ומשם ואילך לא נצטוו
על שום מצוה כלל. ונפטר משה רבינו ע"ה ביום שבת בעת המנחה בז'
באדר שנת בתפ"ט.

יהושע בן נון ע"ה קבל ממנו תורה שבכתב ותורה שבעל פה. שהרי
משה רבינו ע"ה היה יושב ודן את כל ישראל מן הבקר עד הערב ואילו
תורה שבכתב אין בה אחת מני אלף מכל הקורות המתחדשות. ואחר
כך שם עליהם שרי אלפים שרי מאות שרי חמשים ושרי עשרות.
ואמר להם שמוע בין אחיכם ושפטתם צדק. והוא אומר על עצמו ואצוה
אתכם בעת ההיא את כל הדברים אשר תעשון. ואין מצוה זו אלא תורה
שבעל פה. ובעניין שחיטה והלכותיה כתיב כאשר צויתיך ואכלת.
מלמד שנצטוה בשחיטה מצות שאינן כתובות בתורה. ואי אפשר שלא
הודיע אותם ליהושע.

יהושע מסרה לזקנים ונפטר לחיי עולם בשנת בתקי"ז. זקנים שהאריכו
ימים אחרי יהושע מסרוה לנביאים דור אחר דור עד חגי זכריה

29 בתמ"ט] ק ~ ביום שבת | באותן] באותם פק בשאר אותם | מ' יום] ק הימים פ מ' ימים | יום²] הת | >
30 את] את | > | ובשאר] אפק ~ ימי |
31 מתור] בה ~ את |
32 אר ונגזר | גזירה] ת | >
33 ע"ה] פ | > | אק השבת | אה מנחה | בז' באדר] אפק באדר בשבעה בו |
34 שנת] ת בשנת ר בע' (!) | בתפ"ט] ק תפ"ט |
35 ע"ה] ב | >
36 רבינו ע"ה] מ | > | ע"ה] אב | > | היה] אה | > | את] אפק | > | כל] פ לכל | ל בקר | בקל ועד | ל ערב |
37 בה] מ בו | אחת] ת אחד | מ ואחרי |
38 כך] אבפמ כן | אבה ושרי מאות | דר שרי | ואמר] פ ויאמר ל ואומר |
39 בין] פ פ בן | צדק] פ ~ בין איש וגו' | ק ~ בין איש ובין אחיו ובין גרו | אומר] בהדר אמר | ואצוה | ל ומצוה |
40 ההיא] ה ~ לאמר | את כל הדברים — תעשון] ת וגו' |
41 ובענין] ב ובמנין ק כעין | והלכותיה] פ ולכותיה (!) | כתיב] ב ככתוב' ק דכתי' | כאשר] ד אשר | צויתיך] ת ~ תזבח | ואכלת] פק | >
42 שנצטוה] פק ~ משה | בשחיטה] פ על השחיטה |
43 הודיע] פק להודיע ה הורה מ למד | הודיע אותם] ר הודיעם |
44 בדלר ויהושע | עולם] ב העולם (!) | ה העולם את העולם הבא | שנת | ת בתקי"ז] ה תחקי"ז | אק וזקנים ה | >
45 ל אחר | לנביאים — נביאים מסרוה] ה | > | לנביאים] א ~ ונביאים לנביאים ת ~ ונביאים מסרוה | > ל מסרו | > זה לזה |

ומלאכי. נביאים מסרוה לאנשי כנסת הגדולה והם זרובבל בן שאלתיאל בן יכניה מלך יהודה והבאים עם זרובבל ישוע נחמיה שריה רעליה מרדכי בלשן מספר בגוי רחום בענה. אלה ראשי כנסת הגדולה. נבנה בית ראשון בשנת בתתקכ״ט ועמד תכ״ז שנה וחרב אחר שהיתה מלחמה ז' שנים. ועמד בית ראשון חרב שבעים שנה. אבל בשנת מ״ט לחרבנו שהיא שנת אחת לכורש מלך פרס התחילו לבנותו. וכתבו עליהם רחום בעל טעם ושמשי ספרא אגרת לכורש מלך פרס והשיב בתשובתו כען שימו טעם לבטלא גובריא אלך וקריתא דא לא תתבני עד מני טעמא יתשם והות בטלא עד שנת תרתין לדריוש מלכא.

בא וראה כמה נאמנות לנחמות של אלהינו יתברך שמו כי כעין גלותם כך היתה גאולתם. מתחלת גלותם ועד חרבן הבית וסור המלכות כ״א שנה. ומעת הוחל להבנות עד שכלו כ״א שנה. כי בשנה שמקצתה שנת שלש ליהויקים ומקצתה שנת ד' ליהויקים מלך נבוכדנצר ועלה לירושלם ונתן יי בידו את יהויקים מלך יהודה ודניאל חנניה מישאל ועזריה בשנת ג' למלכות יהויקים היא השנה הראשונה למלכות נבוכדנצר

46 אפקמ ונביאים | ל מסרוהו | ל מסרווה | פק הם
47 מלך] ק בן | זרובבל] בגליון ק ~ הדור הראשון | ישוע] פ יהושע (!) | רעליה] אק ~ נחמני
48 בלשן] ב בלשון (!) | פ בלשון | מספר] אק | בגוי] אפ < | רחום] מ ~ בעל טעם ושמשי ספרא | אקם בענא ה בענאי | אלה] דלר אלו ת ~ הם
49 אק ונבנה | ראשון] שלר שני ה¹ פ¹ ראשון ה¹ ~ ולפי חז״ל יצא בשנת בתתקכ״ז והחרבן שנת גשמ״ט | בתתקכ״ט] ב גתל״ב ה בתתק״ט | תכ״ז] ק ת״כ | שנה] ה | < | וחרב] אב ונחרב | אחר] מ עד (ובגליון מ: אחר) | שהיתה] ת ~ בו
50 ועמד] ר < | ועמד בית ראשון] ב ובית ראשון עמד | אבל] ד ומה שאמרנו שעמד בית ראשון חרב שבעים שנה כך היה כי | מ״ט] למר ~ שנה
51 שנת] אהק שנה | אבה לבנות
52 עליהם] ה עליו | ר ובעל | פ אגרא ק אגרתא
53 ל בתשובתן | אלך] ר אלין | וקריתא] ל וקמיתא | דא] בלם דך | לא] פ לך ל ולא ר הלא (?)
54 למר תרתי | פ לדרויש (!) | מלכא] בגליון ה¹ ~ שהיא שנת גתי״ח ועמד ת״י שהיא שנת גתכ״ח וכן עשר סימן (?) לחרבן שנת ע״ק... לחרבן נשלם באלף הד'
55 כמה] ב < | (ונוסף בגליון ע״י ב¹) | לנחמות] בד נחמותיו למר נחמות ה תנחומותיו יתברך] פת ית' | כי] למר < | כעין] אלר כענין
56 כך] אד כן | גאולתם] ק < | ועד] אק עד ב ועמיד ב¹ ועד | וסור] ה יסוד
57 ק שהוחל | ק ליבנות | שכלו] בהד אשר כלו ק ~ אותו | בשנה] ד השנה
58 שנת¹] ק < | שלש] למ ~ שנים | אפקלר נבוכד נצר (וכן הוא להלן בכ״י אלה)
59 לירושלם] ק בירושלים פק | יי׳] ר הש' | את] מ < | אב וחנניה
60 למלכות יהויקים] אד ליהויקים | בהד והיא | ד שנה | במר הראשונית ד ראשונה למלכות] למר למלך | ק נבוכד ראצר

מלך בבל. ולקץ ז' שנים מת יהויקים ומלך יהויכין. ועלה נבוכדנצר והגלה את יהויכין מלך יהודה ועשרת אלפים גולה ואנשי החיל ז' אלפים הרי אלו י"ז אלף. והוזכרו בספר ירמיהו ג' אלפים וכ"ג כי ראשי האבות הזכיר ירמיהו ולא הזכיר עלות נבוכדנצר על יהויקים בהגלותו את דניאל. ועוד עלה נבוכדנצר בשנה הששית למלכות צדקיהו היא שנת י"ח למלכות נבוכדנצר והגלה מישראל תתכ"ב איש. ועוד בשנת כ"ג לנבוכדנצר הגלה את צדקיהו והחריב את הבית. ומפני שנים מקוטעות שהיו ביניהם נמצא בין גלות דניאל לגלות צדקיהו כ"א שנה שלמות. ועמד הוא עוד במלכותו כ"ב שנה כי מ"ה שנה מלך. ומת ומלך אויל מדורך בנו כ"ב שנה. ובשנת מלכו נשא את ראש יהויכין מלך יהודה. ומת אויל מדורך ומלך בלשצר בנו ג' שנים וקשרו עליו שריו והכוהו וימת בבית משתהו. וזהו שנתנבא ישעיהו ערוך השלחן צפה הצפית אכול שתה קומו השרים משחו מגן. ונתקיים לנבוכדנצר ועבדו אותו כל הגוים ואת בנו ואת בן בנו. הרי כאן מ"ה לנבוכדנצר וכ"ב לאויל מדורך וג' לבלשצר. הרי למלכות בבל ע' שנה.

ומפני שלא נגאלו בשנת אחת לדריוש בן אחשורוש מזרע מדי אשר המלך על מלכות כשדים תמה דניאל עליו השלום. וזהו שכתוב בשנת אחת למלכו אני דניאל בינותי בספרים מספר השנים אשר היה דבר יי

אל ירמיהו הנביא למלאת לחרבות ירושלם שבעים שנה עד שבועים
שבעים נחתך על עמך ועל עיר קדשך לכלא הפשע ולהתם חטאת
ולכפר עון ולהביא צדק עולמים ולחתום חזון ונביא ולמשוח קדש
קדשים. הודיעהו ימי הגלות וימי הגאולה. שבועים שבעים הם ת"ץ
שנה שבעים שעמד חרב ות"כ ימי בית שני עד עלות אספסינוס וטיטוס.
לכלא הפשע ולהתם חטאת ולכפר עון זה בנין בית המקדש. ולהביא
צדק עולמים זה שחזרו ישראל למוטב ולא עבדו אלהים אחרים ולא
הושיבו נשים נכריות ולא הלעיגו על המצות והתקינו שיהו קורין בתורה
בשני ובחמישי ובשבת. ולחתום חזון ונביא פטירת חגי זכריה ומלאכי.
ולמשוח קדש קדשים בנין בית המקדש וההיכל ולפני לפנים. ותדע
ותשכיל ממוצא דבר להשיב ולבנות ירושלם עד משיח נגיד שבועים
שבעה. זהו שהתחילו לבנות ירושלם בשנה השנית לתפילת דניאל בשנת
אחת לכורש מלך פרס. ונקרא משיח שכך כתוב כה אמר יי למשיחו
לכורש אשר החזקתי בימינו. והודיע המלאך לדניאל כי ממוצא דבר
כלומר מעת שדבר ירמיהו דבר זה שהוא מגלות צדקיהו עד משיח
נגיד והוא כורש שבועים שבעה שהם מ"ט שנה. וכי אין החשבון מגלות
דניאל אלא מגלות צדקיהו. וזהו פרטן: נבוכדנצר אחר החרבן כ"ב
שנה אויל מדורך כ"ב בלשצר ג' דריוש א' ושנה ראשונה לכורש הרי

79 במד ירמיה | עד] ק ועוד |
80 שבעים] אב שבעה | עיר] ד בית | לכלא הפשע – צדק עולמים] ת וגו' | בפק לכלה |
82 מ והודיעוהו ר הודיעוהו ד הודיעו | שבועים] ת ושבועים | שבעים] פ ⟨ אר שבעה ב¹ פי' שבעים שבועי שנים |
83 שבעים] הפ ~ שנה | עד עלות] ב ⟨ ⟨ונוסף בין השיטין ע"י ב¹⟩ | עלות] ה גלות מ עלה |
84 ה לכלא] אבפקת לכלה | זה] ב ⟨ |
85 זה] ה עד ל ~ מי | ישראל] ת ⟨ | אלהים אחרים] ד ע"ז | אלהים] ק אלים |
86 אדלר שיהיו |
87 ונביא] אפק ~ זה | ומלאכי] ה מלאכי ד ~ שאז פסקה נבואה מישראל |
88 בנין] אפק זה בנין ד בבנין | וההיכל] פק ואת ההיכל | אפק ולפני לפנים] ב ⟨ לפני לפנים ה לפנים ת לפני ולפנים |
89 ב מן מוצא |
90 בשנת] אפ בשנה |
91 שכך] ר כי כך דל שכן | כתוב] פ כתי' בדלמ ~ כי |
92 בימינו] פ ~ וכו' ק ~ וגו' | ל והודיעו |
93 מעת] אק ⟨ | דל ירמיה |
94 והוא כורש] ב ⟨ ⟨ונתלה בין השיטין ע"י ב¹⟩ |
95 אלא] ב ⟨ ⟨ונתלה בין השיטין ע"י ב¹⟩ | בה וזה | פרטן] ה ⟨ | ק חורבן | כ"ב שנה] ק ⟨ |
96 שנה] בת ⟨ | מדורך] ⟨ | בה ⟨ מ מרודך ⟨ כ"ב] ק נ"ב אפק ~ שנה ~ ג'| פ ~ שנים א' | אפק שנה אחת | אבת הראשונה |

כאן מ"ט והם שבועים ז'. כלומר עוד נשארו כ"א שנה לאחר שהתחילו לבנותו ברשיון כורש. צא משבועים שבעים שבעה נשארו שבועים ס"ג. צא מהן שבועים ס"ב והם ת"כ שנה שעמדה המלכות נשאר שבוע אחד שהיו במלחמת אספסינוס וטיטוס חורגו הנקרא בנו. ועל ת"כ שני הישוב הוא אומר ושבועים ששים ושנים תשוב ונבנתה רחוב וחרוץ. וזה שאמר ובצוק העתים כי בצער גדול נבנתה החומה ככתוב ואין אני ואחי ונערי ואנשי המשמר אשר אחרי אין אנחנו פושטים בגדינו איש שלחו המים ושאר הענין. ואחר ת"כ שנה הוא אומר ואחרי השבועים ששים ושנים יכרת משיח ואין לו זה אגריפס המלך ומונבז בנו שהשכם אספסינוס וימיתם שלש שנים ומחצה קודם לחרבן הבית. ועלה אספסינוס וטיטוס והגביר ברית לרבים בשבוע האחרון. אבל בחצי השבוע כפר בבריתו והשבית זבח ומנחה ועל כנף שקוצים משומם מפני הכעסים שהכעיסוהו פריצי ישראל. וזהו והעיר והקדש ישחית עם נגיד הבא.

וכן היתה גאולתם של ישראל. נהרג בלשצר והמלך על מלכות כשדים דריוש בן אחשורוש מזרע מדי ומלך שנה אחת ומת. ומלך כורש ג' שנים. ובשנת אחת למלכו העיר יי את רוחו לבנות בית המקדש ואחר כך בטלו.

97 מ"ט] הפד ~ שנה | והם שבועים — כ"א שנה] ה | > | כלומר] דלר > | כ"א] ק כ"ח | שהתחילו] ל שיתחילו ק ~ אותו |
98 ה לבנות וברשיון | שבועים שבעה] פק שבעה | ב ונשארו |
99 שבועים ס"ג] בפ ס"ג | מ"ב] > פ שבעים ושנים (ומלת "שבעים" תוקנה ל"ששים" ע"י פ¹) | שנה] אפ > | נשאר] פק ושאר |
100 שבוע] ל שבועי' | שהיו] ד שהיה | למ במלחמה | אספסינוס] ב אפסינוס | וטיטוס] ה וטיטוט | חורגו] מ בנו (ובגליון: חרגו) |
101 דלר שבועים | למד תשובו | רחוב] ב טוב |
102 אבקר וזהו | כי] ק > | ככתוב] ק | ה כ"ב שנה (!) | ת כדכתיב |
103 הק משמר | אשר אחרי אין אנחנו] פק > | ה אנו |
104 איש שלחו המים] א איש שנה תמימה ב איש ששלחו (ובגליון הוסיף ב¹ המים) ה איש המימה פק וגו' | ת"כ] ד ת"ק | אה ואחר |
105 זה] פק > ~ היה | המלך] מ > |
106 פ אספסאינוס | ומחצה] ק וחצי | ת חרבן | לחרבן הבית] ב לקרבן (!) |
107 פ אספסאינוס | והגביר] פ > (ונוסף ע"י פ¹ בין השיטין) אק והפר | בשבוע] ל בשבועה האחרון] ב < | בחצי] בה בשני פ > (ונוסף בין השיטין ע"י פ¹) | בחצי השבוע] א בשבוע חציו |
108 השבוע] פ בשבוע ל השבועה | כפר] ק הפר | ועל] א על | ב ועד ה על |
109 הכעסים] ד > | בהק אשר הכעיסוהו | דלר הפריצים מישראל | ל העיר | ר הקדש |
110 עם] ה > |
111 וכן] ב וכך | נהרג] ה והרג | והמלך] אק והוא מלך פדר והומלך |
112 ומלך] ²ק מלך |
113 יי] בקמר השם פ > | בית] דלר > |

ומלך הוא ג' שנים והרגתהו מלכת שטים מפני שהרג הוא את שני בניה ומלכים גדולים היו. ומלך אחריו אחשורוש י"ו שנה ומת. ומלך בנו אשר ילדה לו אסתר הוא דריוש והוא ארתחשסתא. ובשנת שתים למלכו נבנה הבית. בן ז' שנים היה במלכו ול"ב שנה מלך. ועלה עליו אלסכנדרוס מוקדון ויכהו וימיתהו בשנת ל' לבנין הבית. והכרת מלכות פרס והתחילה מלכות יון.

---

114 ג'] פק חמש | שנים] אה ~ | ונהרג ב ~ | ומת ונהרג | בפ והרגתהו | ה כי הרגתהו א הרגותהו (!) | ק ונהרג על [ק¹ ~ ידי] ת והרגתו | מלכת] ל מלכות | שטים] ק¹ ~ (בין השיטין) היא תלמידה (!) | שהרג] ב שֶנָהרג (!) | הוא] ק | את] ת | >

116 אשר ילדה לו] ת שילדה | אסתר] ר ~ המלכה | ארתחשסתא] ל ארתחסתא | ובשנת] ד בשנת |

117 ול"ב — מלך] ת ומלך ל"ב שנה | שנה] ב י' | ועלה עליו] פמ ועליו עלה | עליו] ק אליו |

118 פ אלסכנדרוס] ה אלסכנדרון אבד אלכסנדרון ל אלכסדרוס מ אלכסונדרוס ר אלכסנדרוס בהד מקדון | ויכהו] לר והכהו | וימיתהו] ב ויכהו בי' וימיתהו | הק והכרת] אב ונכרת פ והכרית (?) ת ותכרת |

119 ה והתחלה ל והתחילו |

ספר הקבלה

[ב]

הדור השני מאנשי כנסת הגדולה שמעון הצדיק ושמו עדו בן יהושע בן
יהוצדק הכהן הגדול. בימיו נשמדה מלכות פרס על יד אלסכנדרוס
מלך יון. ובא אלסכנדרוס זה אל ירושלם לאחר שהשמיד את מלכות
פרס ובקש להחריב את ירושלם ולהגלותה פעם שניה בשנת מ' לבנין
בית המקדש. ויצא שמעון הצדיק אל המלך וכשראהו המלך גדלו
5 ונשאו ונתן לו שאלתו. ושאל שמעון הצדיק ממנו שלא להחריב את
הבית ושלא להגלות את העיר. והמלך צוה להעשות כן. ותמהו שריו
ועבדיו שהיו יודעין שאמר להחריבן ולעולם לא חזר בדבורו. והוא
אמר להם דמות דיוקנו של זה מנצח לפני במלחמתי. והתנה המלך על
שמעון הצדיק שכל בן שיולד לו ולכהנים באותה שנה יקרא אלסכנדר
10 על שמו ושיתחילו ישראל מנין שטרותיהם מאותה שנה והיא שנת אלף
לצאתם ממצרים. ובאותו הזמן נפטר עזרא הכהן וחגי זכריה ומלאכי
ונסתלקה נבואה מישראל. ונעשה להם נס גדול זה על יד שמעון הצדיק
לא נעשה כן לענן ולא ללקרקסאני ראשי המינות.

---

1 ושמו] ל ~ עדה | ~ בהק עדוא ק¹ ~ (בין השיטין) והוא היה כהן משמש בבית אחר
    מות הכהן הגדול | בן יהוצדק] מ < |
2 בימיו] ק כאשר | בת ידי | אבקת אלכסנדרוס |
3 מלך יון] פקר ~ | ובא – אל המלך] פקר < | אל ירושלם] פק ועל ירושלם רצה לעלות | ה אלסכנדרוס | אבת אלכסנדרוס | זה] ל < | אל ירושלם] דלר ליושלם | את] קת < |
4 את] דלר < | ת השנית | מ' | פ הארבעים | לבנין] ה לבנותה |
5 המקדש] ה מקדש ש ~ | שני מ ~ השני | אל המלך] ת אליו | וכשראהו] לר וכשראו
6 לו] ל < | את] אד ~ |
7 ושלא] ה ולא | להגלות] ב להגלו כה (?) | להעשות] ד < |
8 שאמר] פ שהוא אומ' ק שהוא אמ' | קלמר להחריבו ה להחריב ד להחריבה | הם ומעולם
9 הל אומר | דמות] ב < | ד דקיונו | ד במלחמות מ במלחמה | על] אפק עם |
10 לו] אהת ~ | ולכהנים] ב < | ולכהנים באותה שנה] בה באותו < ב באותו > שנה לכהנים
    פל באותר | שנה] אקל שעה ק ~ | ובאותה שנה] למר שיקרא ד יקראוהו פ ~ | על שמו
    ב ~ באותה שנה (!) | בה אלסכנדר] פ אלסכנדאר אקת אלכסנדר |
11 על שמו] פ ~ | ב שיתחילו | ישראל] את > | ל מאותו | אלף] ה > |
12 בהר מארץ מצרים ת ~ | והיא שנת ג' אלפים ות"ן ליצירה | בה זמן | הכהן] את הסופר
    פ הסופר הכהן | בת וזכריה |
13 ונעשה] ה ועשה | להם] ה ק לישראל | נס גדול זה] ת זה הנס הגדול | זה] אפק > |
14 לא] אפק ולא | לענן] א לפניו ה לעני ס לעכן | ולא ללקרקסאני] ה ולקרקסאני ב
    ללקרקסאני] למר לקרקסאני ד לקרקסאני פ לקרסאסני ק ללקדס אסאני (!) | המינות
    ת המינין שרי |

ספר הקבלה

ומצא אלסכנדר המלך בארץ ישראל כותיים הרבה מימי סנחריב וראשיהם סנבלט החורוני ומקצת ישראל ומבני יהושע בן יהוצדק הכהן הגדול נתחתנו בהם. והבריחום עזרא הכהן ונחמיה התרשתא מבית יי. וכבוא המלך אלסכנדר לארץ ישראל סר אל משמעתו סנבלט החורוני וראשי הכותיים ושאלו ממנו שיבנו הכהנים חתניו וכל אשר הושיבו נשים נכריות ולא אבו לשלחן בית המקדש אחר בהר גרייזים. וצוה המלך להעשות כן ובנו את הבית. אז יחלק העם לחצי. חצי העם היה אחרי שמעון הצדיק ואנטיגנוס תלמידו וסיעתם וכפי מה שקבלו מעזרא ומן הנביאים והחצי אחרי סנבלט וחתניו. והקריבו עולות וזבחים חוץ לבית יי. וחקקו חוקים ומשפטים כאשר בדו מלבם. ובבית זה כהן מנשה בן יהושע בן יהוצדק. וצדוק וביתוס חברו היה לראש. וזאת היתה תחלת המינות.

אנטיגנוס איש סכה קבל משמעון הצדיק וסיעתו. הוא הדור השלישי. והוא היה אומר אל תהיו כעבדים המשמשין את הרב על מנת לקבל פרס אלא הוו כעבדים המשמשין את הרב על מנת שלא לקבל פרס. וצדוק וביתוס שאלוהו על דבר זה והשיב תשובה שעל פרס בעולם

15 ה אלסכנדר] ב אלסכנדרו' ‖ פ אלסכנדראר ת אלכסנדר ‖ אלסכנדר המלך] ר המלך אלכסנדר ‖ הל כותיים ‖ כותיים הרבה] מ הרבה כותיים ‖ הרבה] מ > קד ~ שהיו ‖
16 סנבלט] פ > ‹ונתלה בין השיטין ע״י פ1› ‖ ומקצת] אפק עם מקצה ל ומקצה ‖ ב מבני ‖
17 והבריחום] ת והבריחם ‖ הכהן] ה הסופר פ ~ הגדול ‖
18 קדמ וכבוא ‖ ה אלסכנדר] ב אלסכנדר ‖ פ אלסכנדראר אקת אלכסנדרא (!) ‖ א בארץ ת אל ארץ ‖ פ למשמעתו ‖
19 הדמר הכותיים ל כותים ‖ הכהנים] ה הכותיים ‖
20 ולא אבו לשלחן] ק > ‖ אבת לשלחם א ~ ‖ ובנו ב ~ ויבנו ‖ ה מקדש ק קדוש ‖ אחר] אבק אחד ‖
21 רבנו] אפק ריבנו ל ובכן (!) ובגליון ל:1 ויבנו ‖ את] אמ > ‖ ק העם] אפ ישראל בה העם ישראל ת עם ישראל ס עם ה' ‖ לחצי] ק לשני כתות ‖
22 ב ואטיגנוס ‖ תלמידו] ב > ‹ונוסף על הגליון ע״י ב1› ‖ וסיעתם] אפ עם סיעתם ק עם ישיבותם דל וסיעתו ‖ ר כפי ‖ ב שקבל ‖
23 פק מן עזרא ‖ אמ ומהנביאים דל > ‖ פ אחר ‖
24 וחקקו] ל וחזקו ‖ כאשר] ה אשר ‖ אבק בדאו ‖ מ הזה ‖ ת כיהן ק היה כהן ‖
25 וצדק] ל וצדיק ‖ ב גם ביתוס ה וגם ביתוס ת עם ביתוס ‖ חברו] אפק וחביריו ל חיברו (!) ‖ היה] אפק היו ת זאת ‖
27 אנטיגנוס] אפק הדור השליטי אנטיגנוס ‹ א אנטיוכוס (!) › ‹וכן גם לעיל בשורה 22 בכ״י א› ‖ בה סכה] פ סכה ק שוכו את סרכו ‖ הוא הדור השלישי] אפק > ‖
28 אק הוא ‖ והוא היה] ב והיה ‹ב1 מוסיף "הוא" בין השיטין› ‖ ב שמשמשין ‖ על מנת שלא לקבל פרס] פ > ‹ונוסף על הגליון›‖
29 אלא הוו — שלא לקבל פרס] ת > ‖ ב היו פרס] ב ~ ‖ ויהא מורא שמים עליכם ‖
30 והשיב] ת ~ להם ‖ שעל] אפק מנת לקבל ‖ בעולם] ד עולם ב באלזם (!) ב1 בעולם ‖

הזה אינו בטוח אלא על העולם הבא. והם כפרו בדבריו ואמרו מימינו
לא שמענו על העולם הבא. והם היו תלמידיו וחלקו עליו והלכו למקדש
הר גריזים והיו שם לראשים. ועמד בית זה ביד הכותים והמינים כמו
מאתים שנה.

שבשנת רי"ב לבנין בית שני שהיא שנת גתרכ"א מרד מתתיהו בן יוחנן
כ"ג והוא הנקרא חשמונאי באנטיוכוס מלך יון. ועמד הוא ובניו על
משנה מלך יון המולך בירושלים והרגוהו ואת כל חילו. ומלך חשמונאי
שנה אחת ומת. ואחריו יהודה בנו הגבור הגדול מלך ו' שנים ומת. ואחריו
יונתן אחיו בן חשמונאי מלך ו' שנים ומת. ואחריו שמעון אחיו בן מתתיהו
מלך י"ח שנה ומת. ואחריו יוחנן בן שמעון בן חשמונאי והוא הנקרא
הורקנוס הראשון. הוא עלה והחריב בית מקדש הכותיים והרג את
המינים. ובשובו בשלום עשה משתה לחכמים. וטוב לב זקן אחד מן
החכמים אמר לו רב לך כתר מלכות הנח כתר כהונה לזרעו של אהרן.
שאם המלך שבויה היתה נשבית בהר המודיעים. שהצרו הגוים שמעון
אביו בהר וברח ונלכדו נשיו ואחרי כן שבו לידו. מפני כן היו לוחשים

31 הזה] ד זה לר | והם כפרו — העולם הבא] פ > | עליו] ה > | אפק אל מקדש |
33 ביד] ת בית ל | ונוסף על הגליון | אב כותיים פ הכותיים והמינים] ר > | כמו] בה > |
34 מאתים] ק ת' |
35 רי"ב] ל מ"ב (?) | שנת] פ אחת ומת (!) | גתרכ"א] כל כה"י משובשים והגהתי עפ"י
מבוא התלמוד לר"ש הנגיד, ר' יוסף נ' צדיק ור"א זכות, ב גתרב"א (!) פקת גתרפ"א ה
גתקכ"א (וכנראה נתקן מתרכ"א. ובגליון ה¹ גתר"ל). אפקת מתתיה | בן יוחנן כ"ג] ב > |
36 והוא] ב > ד הוא | מ חשמוני | בהלם באנטיוכס | באנטיוכוס — ומלך חשמונאי] פ > |
מלך יון] ה המלך של שריון (!) |
37 כל] ב > | מ חשמוני |
38 ומת] א | ואחריו] א | ומלך אחריו פק ~ מלך | הגדול] מ > ת ~ מבניו | אפק ומלך
ואחריו] פ ~ באנטיוכוס מלך יון ועמד הוא ובניו על משנה מלך יון המולך בירושלים
והרגוהו ואת כל חילו ומלך חשמונאי שנה אחת ואחריו (ומלמעלה למלת "באנטיוכוס"
ציין סופר פ שפיסקא זו שייכת לעיל) |
39 פק יהונתן | במ חשמוני פ חושמנואי | מלך] ק > | ו'] ק שתי | ואחריו] פקמ ~ מלך
ואחריו שמעון — ומת] ב > | אחיו] ק > | בן מתתיהו] ת > |
40 מלך] פקמ > א ומלך | בן חשמונאי] ה > מ בן חשמוני ק מ בן מתתיהו | הוא] פ הוא
41 הוא עלה] מ ועלה | והחריב] ל וחריב | בית] קת > | ה המקדש של | הדמר הכותיים
ק כותיים | את] ת > |
42 המ לשלום | לב] ק לבם | זקן] ה > | מן החכמים] פל > | דמר מהחכמים |
43 אמר] ל אומר | לו] פק למלך דלר | רב] ת די | כתר] ה > | ת והנח |
44 בה שאם המלך—נשבית] פק > לפי שנשבית אמו של המלך א לפי שאמו של המלך שבויה
היתה שנשבית ת שאמך שבויה היתה ונשבית | שבויה היתה] ב > היתה שבויה | בהר
המודיעים] פ במודיעים לר בהר המודיעית דה בהר המודיעית א בהר של מודיעות (!) |
שהצרו] ק שצרו | ת גוים | בה לשמעון |
45 אביו] דלר מס אביך (!) | בהר] אמ > | וברחו] פ > | ל נשין | ד ואחר כך ל ואחר
כן | שבו] ב שבא | שבר לידו] ק ילדו אותו | כן]² ר זה |

שהמלך חלל היה. וכשמוע המלך דבר זה כעס מאד. ואמר להרוג את כל החכמים. והמלך זקן מאד ולאחר ששמש בכהונה גדולה מ' שנה נעשה צדוקי.

ומת המלך יוחנן ומלך תחתיו אלסכנדר בנו. והוא הנקרא ינאי מלכא. והיה שונא את החכמים. והיה מנהג ישראל באותו זמן לשמוח ביום ערבה והיו מכין זה את זה במורביטות של ערבה. ויום ערבה אחד עשו כן והמלך אלסכנדר עמד על המזבח להקטיר ורגמו אחד מן התלמידים באתרוג על מצחו. וירם ימינו מעל המזבח ויאמר חרב. והרג בחכמים גם הוא מכה גדולה חוץ משמעון בן שטח שהיה אחי אשתו. וברח יהושע בן פרחיה חברו לאלסכנדריא של מצרים עד שבקש עליו שמעון בן שטח רחמים מן המלך והחזירו.

ואין אנו רוצין להפסיק סדר הקבלה בזכרון מלכי בית שני. וכשנשלים סדר הקבלה נזכור את כלם וכמו שיש עליהם מדברי נביאים ז"ל שיש בכך נחמות גדולות.

יוסי בן יועזר איש צרידה ויוסף בן יוחנן איש ירושלם קבלו מאנטיגנוס איש סוכו. והם וסיעתם הדור הרביעי.

יהודה בן טבאי ונתאי הארבלי קבלו מהם. והם וסיעתם הדור החמישי.

46 ת היה חלל | ואמר להרוג — ופ' תלמידים היו לו (שו' 81) א ‹ › (ועיין במבוא) | ואמר ת רצוה |
47 את] דלר ‹ › | כל] הק ‹ › |
48 גדולה] ב ‹ › | מ' שנה] פל ‹ ק שמונים שנה |
49 פק יוחנן המלך | ומלך] ה וימלוך | הק אלסכנדר] פ אלסכנדאר בת אלכסנדר | פ הוא הנקרא] ב נקרא |
50 באותו זמן] ה ‹ › | ל הזמן | ה לשמח | הת הערבה |
51 והיו] ל והיה | ת וביום | ערבה אחד] ק אחד של ערבה | אחד] במ אחת |
52 ה אלסכנדר] פ אלסכנדאר בקת אלכסנדר | דלר עומד | ה מהתלמידי' |
53 באתרוג] ה ~ אחד | מצחו] ב ~ ומֹת (!) | מעל] ק על | חרב] ק חרבו הרג בחכמים והרג — הוא] ק וגם הוא הרג ת והרג גם הוא בחכמים |
54 הוא] ה ~ בחכמים (!) פ ~ הרג | גדולה] מ רבה |
55 חברו] ל ‹ › ה ובא | דר לאלסכנדריא ל לאלכסנדריאה מ לאכסנדריא | עד] ב על |
56 עליו] ק ~ רחמים | ב משמעון | רחמים] פקת ‹ › | ב והחזירוהו |
57 ואין — גדולות (59)] בפ ‹ › | אנו רוצין] ת רצוני | ה קבלה (וכן בשו' 58) | מלכי] ה מלכות |
58 הק וכמו] ת ורמז | ק הנביאים | ז"ל] ת ‹ › |
60 יוסי] הפמ יוסף | ויוסף] קדלר ויוסי |
61 איש סוכו] ב ‹ › (ונתלה בין השיטין ע"י ב') | סוכו] ה שכה | פק הם | ב וסייעתם הרביעי] ק החמישי |
62 ל הארבאילי | ב וסיעתם | פק הם | וסיעתם] ב החמשי] ה החמשי (!) ק הששי | החמישי — הששי] ל ‹ › (ונוסף בגליון) |

ספר הקבלה

יהושע בן פרחיה ושמעון בן שטח קבלו מהם. והם וסיעתם הדור הששי. וכתבי זכרונות בישראל אומרין שיהושע בן פרחיה זהו רבו של ישו
65 הנצרי. ואם כן הוא בימי ינאי המלך היה. וכתבי זכרונות באומות העולם אומרין כי בימי הורודוס נולד ובימי ארקילוס בנו נתלה. ומחלוקת גדולה היא שהפרש גדול יש ביניהם יותר מק״י שנים. ומזכירי האומות העולם מסיימין דבריהם בכמה סיומין ואומרים שבשנת ג׳ מאות וי״ב למנין שטרות נולד ולאחר ל״ג שנה נתלה. ושהיה מולדו בשנת ל״ח
70 למלכות אגוסטוס מלך רומי בימי הורודוס ונתלה בימי ארקילוס בנו. והם טוענים כל כך לאמר שלא עמד הבית ומלכות ישראל אחר תלייתו אלא מעט. ומסורת אמת בידינו מן המשנה והתלמוד שלא החליפו שום דבר כי ר׳ יהושע בן פרחיה ברח למצרים בימי אלכסנדר והוא ינאי ועמו ברח ישו הנצרי. וקבלת אמת בידינו כי בשנת ד׳ לאלכסנדר המלך
75 נולד והוא שנת רס״ג לבנין הבית ושנת נ״א למלכות בני חשמונאי. ובשנת

63 בן¹] פ 〉 〈ונוסף בגליון ע״י פ¹〉 | פרחיה] פק ~ זהו רבו של ישו 〈 ק ישׁוּ 〉 הנצרי | פק הם | ב וסייעתם | הדור הששי] ק | 〉
64 וכתבי] קד כותבי מר וכותבי ל וכותבין | זכרונות] פ זרונות | אומרין] ל אומר | זהו] פ זה ק הוא מ היה דלר 〉 | ישו ק יש״ו ר י״ש | ישו הנצרי] ה פלוני |
65 לר הנצרי | הוא] פק היה ינאי] ב 〉 | למר המלך ינאי | היה] פק 〉 | וכתבי ~ מעט (72)] ה 〉 | וכתבי] קת וכותבי
66 אומרין] ב 〉 〈ונתלה בין השיטין ע״י ב¹〉 ל אמ׳ | הורודוס] פ הודורוס ל הורדוס ב ~ הוא | ארקילוס] ב 〉 ב¹ אֶירַקְלֵס (!) |
67 היא] בת ~ זו | גדול] בת 〉 | יש] ב 〉 | יותר] פת יתר | שנים] ת ~ ונראין הדברים שהיה בימי הלל ושמאי יהושע 〉 ל יהושועה 〉 בן פרחיה חכם אחר 〉 ד אחד 〉 שהלך ג״כ לאלכסנדריא 〉 מ לאלכסנדריא 〉 של מצרים וישׁ עמו ומשש 〉 ד משם 〉 נחלקו שהרי | ת מזכירי
68 מסיימין] מ מזכירין 〈ובגליון: מסיימין〉 בדלר ~ את | ת ג׳ | ת ג׳ מאות וי״ב] בפ שתים עשרה ושלש 〉 ב ושש (!) | מאות ק נ״ב (!) |
69 שנה] ר 〉 | מולדו] ק זה ל״ח | מ ~ שנים |
70 למלכות] ד למלך ל 〈 〉 | אגוסטוס] ב אגוסורוס (!) | פ אגוסטרוס מ אגוסטוס | הורודוס] פ הורקיוס ק הורקנוס | ארקילוס] ב 〉 ב¹ אֶירַקְלִיס (!) |
71 והם] ת ואפשר שהם | ב לומר | ת תלותו |
72 מעט] פ ~ מועד (?) | אמת] ל אחת 〈ובגליון ל: אמת〉 פק ~ יש ד ~ הוא | בת מהמשנה | ב ותלמוד פק ומן התלמוד | הפ לשום |
73 ר׳] בק 〉 | ברח] ה ירד ר 〉 〈ונוסף בגליון ר〉 | אלכסנדר] פ אלכסנדאר ק אליסכנדר ב אלכסדר ת אלכסנדר בה ~ המלך | ה וינאי ק ~ המלך |
74 ישו ק יש״ו | ישו הנצרי] ה אותו הפלו׳ ר יש״ה | קל הנצרי | אמת] פ ~ היא כי בשנת] ת שבשנת | ד׳ לאלכסנדר — ושנת נ״א] ד 〉 | ל לאלכסנדרי מר לאלכסנדר לאלכסנדר המלך] ק למלך אליסכנדר זה | המלך] בפ 〉 〈ונתלה בין השיטין ע״י ב²〉 |
75 הפ והוא] במ והיא לר 〉 | והוא שנת — חשמונאי] ק 〉 | הבית] למר בית שני ב ~ נתפש (!) | ושנת] פ 〉 | בני] ה 〉 ת בת הבית | בה חשמונים מ חשמונוני |

ספר הקבלה

רצ"ט לבנין הבית נתפש והוא בן ל"ו שנה בשנת שלש למלכות ארסטובלוס בן ינאי.

שמעיה ואבטליון קבלו מהם. והוא הדור השביעי.

הלל ושמאי קבלו מהם. והוא הדור השמיני. הלל עלה מבבל והוא בן
מ' שנה ולמד מ' שנה ולימד מ' שנה וק"כ שנה היו ימי חייו. ומבית דוד
היה ומזרע המלוכה. ופ' תלמידים היו לו גדול שבכלם יונתן בן עוזיאל.
וקטון שבכלם רבן יוחנן בן זכאי. והיה חברו מנחם ומת בימיו ולא
נחלקו. יצא מנחם ונכנס שמאי.

ובנו היה ר"ג הזקן. ובן בנו רשב"ג הראשון. שלשה אלה נהגו נשיאותם
בבית המקדש ק' שנה במלכות בני הורודוס שכן היה המנהג בבית שני
שהמלך מבני חשמונאי או מעבדיהם בני הורודוס היה המוציא והמביא
למלחמה ולכל דברי מלכותו. אבל כל דברי תורה וחוקים ומשפטים
על פי הנשיא מבית דוד היו נעשים ועל פי הכהן הגדול והסנהדרין.
וכן אתה מוצא במסכת סנהדרין: מעשה בר"ג הזקן שהיה יושב על גב
מעלה בהר הבית ויוחנן סופר הלז יושב לפניו ושלש אגרות חתוכות

76 רצ"ט] ה רס"ט ק רס"ג | פר נתפס
77 ה ארסטובלוס] קד אריסטובלוס פלמר ארסתבבלוס ב ארסתכבלוס
78 שמעיה] ק הדור השביעי שמעיה | מהם] ת ~ וגרי צדק היו | והוא הדור השביעי]
ק > | והוא] ת והם | ל דור |
79 הלל] ק הדור השמיני הלל | והוא הדור השמיני] ק > | והוא] ת והם | ל דור | והוא
בן מ' שנה] פק > |
80 ולמד מ' שנה] פ > | ולימד מ' שנה] דלר > | שנה)3] מ > | וק"כ] ת כי ק"כ ה והוא
בן ק"כ | שנה] מ > | היו ימי חייו] מ כשמת |
81 בהד מזרע המלוכה] פק ~ היה | תלמידים] ק ~ לו] ק ~ והעשרים היותר קטנים
שבכלם] ק שבהן |
82 בק וקטון ת קטן | ל קטון > | שבכלם] ק שבהן |
83 בת ריצא | שמאי | דל וגליון ר ~ לעיל כתב | ל כתי' > שמעון בנו ר"ג [דל הזקן] בנו
רשב"ג [ד בנו] וכן אית' בגמ' הלל ושמעון גמליאל ושמעון נהגו נשיאותם ק' שנה
לפני חרבן הבית | ר החורבן > וכו' |
84 ר"ג הזקן] ק רבן שמעון | ובן בנו] ק ~ היה רבן גמליאל הזקן ובן בן בנו | שלשה]
ת > | אלה] ב לא (!) ה אלו | נהגו] ב נהגו |
85 בנו] אפ > | בני הורודוס] ק > | פ הודורוס ל הורדוס
86 מ חשמוני | מעבדיהם בני הורודוס] ב מבני הורודוס עבדיהם | בני] אפק מבני | אפ
הודורוס ל הורדוס
87 למלחמה] ק > | דלר במלחמה | ולכל] אפק לכל דר ובכל ל וכל | מלכותו] ת המלכות |
את חוקים |
88 נעשים] ב נעושין (!) | הכהן הגדול] הכהן הגדול | ב הכהן הגדול (! והתיקון ע"י ב1) ה הכהן והגדול
ת כהן גדול ק ~ היו |
89 אתה] ה את | הזקן] דלר > | אף גבי |
90 סופר] ה שוער פ כהן | ד ולפניו שלש |

בידו. ואמר לו טול אגרתא חדא וכו' עד וטול אגרתא חדא וכתוב
לאחנא בני גלותא דבבל ולאחנא בני גלותא דמדי ולאחנא בני גלותא
דיון ולשאר כל גלותהון דישראל שלמכון יסגא. מהודענא לכון דאמריא
דעדקין וגוזליא רכיכין וירחא דאביבא לא מטא ושפרת מילתא באנפאי
ובאנפי חבראי ואוסיפית על שתא דא ירחא חדא. הרי ידענו שר"ג זה
95 ראש ישיבה ונשיא ומעשיו מקובלים בכל ארץ ישראל ובכל גליות
ישראל ולא מיחה המלך ולא אדם בעולם. ואלו ללקרקסאני לא היו
נשמעין כן ולא לענן. והב"ה אמר ובאת אל הכהנים הלוים ואל השופט
וגו' והאיש אשר יעשה בזדון לבלתי שמוע אל הכהן וגו' או אל השופט
100 ומת האיש ההוא. בא וראה אם היה זה שופט ישראל אם לא.
והלל וסיעתו הם הדור התשיעי.
רבן יוחנן בן זכאי קבל מהלל ומשמאי. בימיו עלה אספסינוס על
ירושלים והיה בירושלים אבא סקרא ראש הלסטים והוא בן אחותו של
ריב"ז. הוא יצא בלט אל המלך אספסינוס ושאל ממנו שיצא אליו
105 ריב"ז. ועשה המלך בקשתו ויצא ריב"ז אל אספסינוס. וידע המלך את

91 פק בידו] א לפניו בידו בהת | >
ואמר] פ ואומ' ל והיה ב שהיה יושב על גב מעלה בהר הבית (!) | וכו' עד] ב טול
אגרתא חדא | וכו' — חדא²] את | חדא²] פ > | וכתוב] אפק ~ עלה |
92 אבפק לאחונא | ולאחנא בני גלותא דמדי] ה > | ולאחנא²] בר ולאחנא ד לאחנא |
ולאחנא³] בפ ולאחונא |
93 שלמכון] ל > | יסגא] אק ~ לעלם פ ~ לעולם | ת מהודעני |
94 וגוזליא] ה וגמליא | רכיכין] פ דכיכין | וירחא] אפק רזמן ירחא | דאביבא] ק ~ עדיין
מילתא] ק ~ דא | הת באנפי |
95 בהר חבראי] פק חבריא ל חברייי מ חברי | ואסיפית מ והוסיפית | פק חדא] בהת חד |
שר"ג] ל שר"ש ב"ג |
96 ונשיא] אפק ~ היה | המ גלות | ישראל] דלר > |
97 ואלו] בה ולא א¹ ראלו | פדלר לקרקסאני ק ללקרקסני מ קרקסני | ללקרקסאני — ולא
לענן] א כהנים ולוים לא היו כשמעון כן ולא לשום ענין (!) | לא היו — ולא לענן] ת
וענן | > ר ולענן | שר"י] שר"י לא היו נשמעין כן | דל כאן | >
98 כן] פ כך | לענן] ה לעון פ לענין | והב"ה אמר] ב כמו שאמ' הקב"ה ת והקב"ה אמר
| ל אומ' > | השופט] פ ~ אשר יהיה |
99 וגו'] אק אשר יהיה בימים ההם פק ~ ואומר | לבלתי שמוע אל הכהן] אבת | > הכהן]
ק הכהנים | אל] ל על | השופט] ב ~ אשר (!) |
100 זה] פ > | ישראל] ישראל] פק ישר ר ישר' | אם] פק או | אבה לאו |
101 והלל — התשיעי] ה > | והלל] פק הלל מ > | ב וסיעתו |
102 מהלל] פ ממנו | ומשמאי] ה ושמאי הוא וסיעתו הדור הט' | אספסינוס] ב אפסיינוס |
103 והיה בירושלים] ב > | (ונוסף בגליון ע"י ב¹) | סקרא] ב שקרא הת סיקרא | הלסטים]
ב הלסתים | והוא] ת והיה |
104 הוא יצא] ב > | ויצא | פק אל המלך אספסינוס בלט |
105 ריב"ז אל אספסינוס] ת אליו | אל אספסינוס] פ המלך ק אל המלך אספסינוס | פ ידע
את] אק | >

רוב חכמתו וכבדו ונשאו והוא היה צר על ירושלם. ומת נרון מלך רומי ונמנו יועצי רומי להמליך את אספסינוס. ונסע לרומי והשאיר טיטוס בנו לצור על ירושלם וצוהו לכבד את ריב"ז מאד. וחרב בית המקדש בשנת גתתכ"ט ונהרג ר' ישמעאל בן אלישע כ"ג ורשב"ג הזקן והוא היה נשיא. ורצה טיטוס להרוג את ר"ג בנו ופייסו רבן יוחנן בן זכאי ונתפייס. נמצאו עשרה דורות מזרובבל והבאים עמו עד רבן יוחנן בן זכאי. גם הוא חיה ק"כ שנה. ארבעים שנה נתעסק בפרקמטיא וארבעים שנה למד תורה וכל חכמה שהיתה בדורו וארבעים שנה לימד ושפט את ישראל. ולאחר חרבן הבית עלה ליבנה ושם שפט את ישראל ותקן תקנות וסייגות לתורה עד שנפטר ביבנה.

ספר הקבלה

[ג]

רבן גמליאל בן רשב״ג הנהרג בשמד הוא היה ראש ישיבה ונשיא אחר
פטירת ריב״ז. ובעל אחותו היה ר' אליעזר בן הורקנוס. וחברו ר'
יהושע בן חניה חכם גדול ואב ב״ד אבל פחמי היה. ור' יוסי הגלילי
כהן ור' שמעון בן נתנאל ור' אלעזר בן ערך ור' יוחנן בן נורי ור' יוחנן
5 בן ברוקא ושמואל הקטן ור' אלעזר חסמא. ור' אלעזר בן עזריה כהן
עשירי לעזרא ועשיר גדול היה. ור' חלפתא ור' יוסי בן קיסמא. כל
אלה דור אחד הן.

ונחלקו רבן גמליאל ור' יהושע על עדות החדש. שבאו עדים בלוד
ואמרו ראינוהו שחרית במזרח וערבית במערב. אמר ר' יהושע עדי
10 שקר הן. היאך מעידין על האשה שילדה והרי כריסה בין שיניה. וכשבאו
ליבנה קבלן ר״ג. שלח לו רבן גמליאל לר' יהושע גוזרני עליך שתבא
אצלי במקלך ובמעותיך ביום הכפורים שחל להיות בחשבונך. ועשה
ר' יהושע כדברי ר״ג. ועוד נחלקו על תפלת ערבית אם היא רשות
או חובה. ועוד נחלקו על בכור שנפרטה שפתו אם בעל מום הוא אם
15 לאו. ובכלן כפה רבן גמליאל לר' יהושע. וזעפו שבעים זקנים חביריו

1 בן] אפק בנו של | הוא] מ > | בה לראש | ונשיא] בין השיטין ק ~ שם ביבנה |
2 ובעל] ב ובא על (!) | וחברו] ת והברייו |
3 אבל פחמי] קת ופהמז | הגלילי כהן] בה הכהן הגלילי ק הגלילי ר' יוסי כהן ת
   הכהן הגלילי |
4 בן נתנאל — נורי ור' יוחנן בן (5) פ > |
5 אלעזר1] פ ~ בן ערך ור' יוחנן בן נורי ור' אלעזר | אפדר בן חסמא ל
   ב הכהן |
6 לעזרא] ב ~ | וכהן גדול (!) | היה] דלר > | קיסמא] בגליון ל ~ ל (?) ר' עקיבא חסר
   כאן |
7 מ אלו | אלה דור] ה > |
8 קת ונחלק | פ ללוד |
9 פק ראינוה ל ראינהו |
10 היאך] פק מפני שהיאך הם | ת האשה | שילדה | ב > | והרי] פ והיא ת ולמחר |
11 קבלן] ה ~ ליבנה (!) | יהושע] מ יהודה | גוזרני] פ גזרתי |
12 אצלי] אב אלי ב¹ אצלי | ובמעותיך] ל ובמעותך מ ומעותיך | להיות] ר > |
13 ת דברי | נחלקו] ק > | היא] אב > | בת רשות היא |
14 או] בהם אם | או חובה] ק > | שנפרטה] א שנטרפה ת שנפרמה | ה הוא בעל מום
   הוא אק | אם²] ל או |
15 לאו] פדמר לא | לר'] אק את ר' | לר' יהושע — והוסר רבן גמליאל] פ > | שבעים]
   ק על זה | זקנים חביריו] ב חביריו הזקנים ק זקנים חביריו |

ונמנו והוסר רבן גמליאל מהיות ראש ישיבה והוקם ר' אלעזר בן עזריה
והיה לראש. ואחר כך נתפייסו זקנים לרבן גמליאל והחזירוהו ולא
הוסר ר' אלעזר בן עזריה אלא היה רבן גמליאל דורש ב' שבתות ור'
אלעזר בן עזריה שבת אחת. ונפטר רבן גמליאל בימי ר' יהושע ועמד
20 ר' יהושע לסתור את דבריו וכעס ר' יוחנן בן נורי. והעלו את רבן
שמעון בן גמליאל לראש בנשיאות. הרי זה דור אחד אחר החרבן.

ר' עקיבא היה ראש ישיבה אחר רבן גמליאל. והיו חביריו שמעון
בן עזאי ושמעון בן זומא ואלישע אחר ור' טרפון ור' ישמעאל ור'
יהודה בן בבא ור' יהודה בן תימא ונקרא בן דמא ור' חנינא בן תרדיון
25 ור' ישבב הסופר ור' סימאי ור' חוצפית התורגמן. כל אלה דור שני
אחר החרבן. והיה בבבל בימיהם ר' יהודה בן בתירא ומחביריו של
ריב"ז היה אלא שהאריך ימים הרבה.

ובימי אלו עמד אדם אחד שהיה שמו כוזיבא וטען שהוא משיח בן דוד.
ושלח יד במלך דמשטיאן מלך רומי והרג את משנהו אשר היה בא"י.
30 ודמשטיאן מלך רומי עודנו נער ולא התחזק לפניו. ומלך כוזיבא זה
בביתר שנת נ"ב לחרבן הבית ומת במלכותו. ומלך בנו ושמו רופוש

16 ונמנון] ב > ‹ונתלה בין השיטין ע"י ב› | מהיות] ק > | ישיבה] פק בית דין | אלעזר]
ב אליעזר (!) פ אלעיזר |
17 והיה לראש] ב > ‹ונוסף על הגליון ע"י ב› | לראש] פק ~ ישיבה |
כך] ד כן | ת הזקנים | ק ולרבן | ק החזירוהו אפק ~ לנשיאותו ‹ ק אל נשיאותו ›
ולראש ישיבה |
18 אלעזר] פ אליעזר | בן עזריה] מ > | אק ~ מהכל פ ~ לגמרי | אלא היה] ה והיה
היה ר"ג] פק רבן גמליאל היה |
19 רבן] ל ר' |
20 את¹] הדמר > | וכעס] ב ונמס ב¹ וכעס | ד והעלה |
21 פ בנשיאותו | אחד] אבק > |
22 בהל עקיבה | והיו חביריו] ק והיה |
23 אחר] פ ארור | ל ישמאעל | ב בר' יהודה בן בבא |
24 ונקרא בן דמא] ה > | בלמר דמא] א דמה פקד זומא | חנינא] אבפל חנניה |
25 חוצפית] ב חוספית | אבה אלו |
26 והיה] ד והיו | והיה־בימיהם] אפק ובימיהם היה בבבל > ‹ פ בבל (!) › | ומחביריו] ק
וחביריו (?) |
27 היה] פק > |
28 ב ובימים אלה | אדם] ד > | אחד] ב > | שהיה שמו] דלר ששמו | כוזיבא] ה בן כוזיבא
ב בן בוזי בא ב¹ כוזיבא | ה וטוען | שהוא] ת שהיה |
29 למד דמשטיאן] א דמשטיאן ה דמשטין פ דמשיטין ק דומשטיין ד דמסטיאון דמשטיאן
מלך] ב > | רומי] ק רואי | והרג – רומי (30)] פק > | את] ת > | אשר היה] א אשר ת
שהיה |
30 א וזה דומשטיאון ד ודמסטיאון מ ודמסטיאן ב > | ומלך] ק נתחזק ל אתחזק | כוזבא] ה
31 שנת נ"ב] ק נ"ב שנה | רופוש] אפק פיירוש מ רופוס |

ופירוש רופוש אדמוני. ומת גם הוא ומלך בנו ושמו רומלוש. ונקבצו אל
כוזיבא ואל בניו עם רב מאד מישראל ששבו מכל מקומותיהם. ובימי
רומלוש בן רופוש בן כוזיבא התחזק אדריאנוס ועלה אל ארץ ישראל
35 ולכד ביתר בתשעה באב שנת ע"ג לחרבן הבית והרג את רומלוש והכה
בישראל מכה גדולה שלא נראתה ולא נשמעה לא בימי נבוזראדן ולא
בימי טיטוס. ונשרף ר' חנינא בן תרדיון וספר תורה עמו. ונהרג ר' ישבב
הסופר ור' סימאי ור' חוצפית התורגמן. ור' יהודה בן בבא הוא
נהרג על שגזר מלך רומי שמד שכל הנסמך יהרג והסומך יהרג ועיר
40 שסומכין בה תחרב. והלך הוא וישב בין שתי עיירות גדולות בין אושא
לשפרעם וסמך ה' זקנים ר' מאיר ור' יהודה ור' יוסי ור' שמעון ור'
אלעזר בן שמוע ובאו עליו אויבים ועשו את כל גופו ככברה. ונהרג
ר' אלעזר בן שמוע. וקודם לכן סרקו את בשרו של ר' עקיבא בן יוסף
במסרקות של ברזל. כל זה בא להם בפולמוס של אדריאנוס ומפני כעסו
45 של בן כוזיבא. ונתקיים להם מה שכתוב על ידי דניאל ומשכילי עם
יבינו לרבים ונכשלו בחרב ובלהבה ובשבי ובבזה ימים.
ובימי אלו היה בטלמיוס ונכתב ספר אלמגסטי.

ספר הקבלה

רבן שמעון בן גמליאל השני הוא היה לראש אחרי מות ר' עקיבא. וחביריו היו ר' מאיר ראש כלם ור' יהודה ור' יוסי ור' אלעזר בן שמוע ור' נתן ור' שמעון בן יוחאי. והסכימה דעת ר' מאיר ור' נתן לביישו ברבים שהיו חכמים ממנו. ונגלה לו הדבר ומשם ואילך לא הוזכרו ר' מאיר ור' נתן בשמותיהם אלא לר' מאיר קראו אחרים ולר' נתן יש אומרים. הרי זה דור שלישי אחר החרבן.

רבינו הקדוש הוא ר' יהודה הנשיא וראש ישיבה בן רבן שמעון בן גמליאל כי ראה יי את עני ישראל מורה מאד וקיים להם מה שכתוב ע"י דניאל ובהכשלם יעזרו עזר מעט. ומת אדרינוס ומלך ברומי אנטונינוס בן אסוירוס. והיה אוהב את רבינו הקדוש כנפשו ואומרים שגיירו בסתר. והיו ימי רבינו הקדוש כלם ימים טובים לישראל. והאריך ימים ובימיו מת אנטונינוס ומלך אנטיפוס. ואחר מות אנטיפוס קומדוס וכלם כבדו ונשאו לרבינו הקדוש כל ימיו.

ור' יהודה הנשיא זה קבל מר' אלעזר בן שמוע ומר' יוסי. והיו חביריו ר' ישמעאל בר' יוסי ור' שמעון בנו של ר' יוחנן בן ברוקא ור' אלעזר בר' שמעון בן יוחאי ור' אלעזר ור' שמעון בני ר' יהודה ור' יהושע בן

ספר הקבלה

קרחה וסמכוס ופלימו ואיסי בן יהודה ור' ראובן אצטרובלי וחנן בן
פנחס ור' פדת ור' אלעזר בן פרטא ור' יעקב איש כפר חטיא ור' פנחס
בן יאיר. וחבר את המשנה בשנת גתתקמ"ט שהיא שנת ת"ק למנין שטרות
ושנת ק"כ לחרבן. זה דור רביעי לחרבן.

ובימי רבינו הקדוש נכתבו דברי ספרי רפואות שבימיו היה גאלינוס.
אבל ספרי אבוקראט הרופא בימי מרדכי ואסתר כתבם שבאותו הדור
היה.

ר' חנינא בר חמא היה ראש ישיבה לאחר פטירת רבינו הקדוש שכן
צוה רבינו הקדוש. והיו חביריו ד' בני רבינו הקדוש ר' אושעיא ור'
שמעון ורבן גמליאל ור' אלעזר הקפר ור' חייא ובר קפרא ולוי ור'
אפס ואבוה דשמואל ורב שהוא בן אחי ר' חייא ובן אחותו. בר קפרא
כתב תוספתא. ר' חייא ור' אושעיא ברבי ור' שמעון ברבי כתבו
ברייתות ומכילתות. ואלו הן סוף התנאין. הרי אלו ה' דורות של
תנאין.

---

64 אפק קרחא | אקמר וסומכוס | ופלימו] ופלימוס | ב ופלימוס ור' ראובן] אחת ~ בן ~ א אצטרבולאי
ב אצטרוביל י פ אצטרבולי ק האיצטרובולי מ אצטרובולי | וחנן] ב ~ יוחנן ק ויוחנן |
65 ל פרטה | כפר] ~ עיר | חטיא] בהד חנניה |
66 וחבר] אפק ועה רבנו הקדוש חבר | את] פדלר > | בשנת] ת שנת | גתתקמ"ט] ה ג'
תתק"ט |
67 ק"כ] אה ק"ן | לחרבן] פק ~ הבית א למנין חורבן הבית | זה] א וזהר ק וזה ל מר
זהר | דור רביעי] אהפ הדור < | דור > הרביעי | לחרבן] ת ~ הבית |
68 ובימי רבינו – היה ‒ (70)] ב < | אפק ועוד בימי | נכתבו] ד נעשר לר > | אפ דברי]
ק ~ הת רוב | פ ספר ק ספרים | ברפואה | ק ברפואה | גאלינוס] אלמר גאלינוס ה ג'ילינו (!) פ גליונוס
ק גאליינוס ד גליאנגוס |
69 ספרי] פק ספרו של | ה אבקרט מ אבוקרט | הרופא] פק ~ היה א ~ היו | כתבם]
אפק > | פק ובאותו |
70 היה] פ כתבו ק כתבם ה הזה |
71 בר חמא] אבת > | אפק היה ראש ישיבה] בהת < | פק פטירתו של | הקדוש] ה ~
היה בראש ב ~ ישב ר' חניננא בן חמא ת ~ ישב בראש והוא < | ד הוא > | ר' חנינא
בר חמא |
72 ד'] פקד > | בה נתלה בין השיטין; גליון ל-... הקדוש. צריך... אם ב' בנים; גליון ר
טער' כאן שלא היו לר' רק ב' בני' רבן שמעון ור"ג | בני רבינו] ד בניו מרבינו
הקדוש] ק ~ שמעון ורבן גמליאל | פ ר' הושעיה ק ור' הושעיא | ור' שמעון ורבן
גמליאל] ק ור' חייא ברבי אפ ~ ור' חייא ברבי |
73 ורבן] אמ ור' | ובר] אה בר | ת ור' לוי |
75 ת התוספתא | ר' חייא] ק > ד ור' חייא | פק הושעיא | ברבי] ק > | שמעון] ה שמואל |
76 ת הברייתות | פ ומכליתות (?) ת והמכילתות | קד אלו | סוף התנאין – של תנאין] ק >
ה'] ל הן | של תנאין] ק ~ והן חמשה דורות |

ספר הקבלה

[ד]

סדר אמוראים

הדור הראשון רב ושמואל. רב ירד לבבל בסוף ימי רבינו הקדוש בשנת
גתתקע"ט. ומצא בבבל ר' שילא והיה רב ענו מאד ולא רצה להמנות
ראש ישיבה כל ימי ר' שילא עד שנפטר. ועוד לא רצה להיות לראש
בנהרדעא במקומו של שמואל והלך לסורא והיא מתא מחסיא והיה
שם לראש עד שנפטר בשנת ד"ג. ובאו בני ישיבתו לשמואל ונפטר
שמואל בשנת ד"י. והיה חכם גדול בכל חכמה יונית מוסף על תורתו.
ואלו תלמידיהם. רב יהודה ורמי בר חמא ורב חמא בני יחזקאל ורב
נחמן הנשיא ורבה בר אבוה ורב ששת וסגי נהור היה ורב ענן ורב מתנה
ורב שימי בר אשי ורב חייא בר אשי ורב יצחק בר אשיין ורב חמא בר
גוריא ורב כהנא הראשון.

ובימיהם היה ראש ישיבה בארץ ישראל ר' יוחנן שקבל מר' אושעיא
ברבי והאריך ימים כי פ' שנה היה ראש ישיבה. ואלו תלמידיו ר' אמי
ור' אסי ור' אלעזר בן פדת ור' ינאי ועולא ורבין ורב דימי ור' שמואל
בר נחמני.

2 רב¹] ק ר' שמעון ורב | התּ ירד רב | ימי רבינו] ל ימים רבים |
3 ומצא] ב ימצא | ה השילא | רב] ב רוב (!) | ב ענותן | להמנות] א להיות נמנה פ להיות
ראש נמנה (!) ק נמנה |
4 ראש] פ לראש | עד שנפטר] ב < | לראש] פק ראש |
4—5 ה בנהרדעא לראש |
5 לסורא] בד לסוריא | והיא] המ והוא ד היא | מתא] פ מתה |
7 ד"י] פ ד' | מוסף] ה תוספת |
8 ואלו ~ ת] הם ~ פק תלמידיו | יהודה] א ~ בר יחזקאל ק ~ ור' אמי בני יחזקאל |
בר חמא] ה בר' חמא מ ~ דלר בר יחזקאל | ורב חמא] בה < | ורב חמא בני יחזקאל]
ר < | בפם בני] הדל בר | בני יחזקאל] אק < |
9 נחמן] מ נחמיה א ~ חתן | ורבה] מ ורבא | אפק והיה סגי נהור | ענן] מ עינן | מתנה]
ב מותנא פק מתתיה |
10 ורב שימי בר אשי] ה < | חייא] פ ~ היא | יצחק] פק נחמן | בר²] ה בן ב ~ אבא |
פדמר אשיאן א אשיא ל אשיאון | ורב חמא] ה ור' חמא |
12 ישיבה] דלר < | ישראל] ב < | (ונתלה בין השיטין ע"י ב¹) | פ הושעיה |
13 ימים] ה ימיהם ל < | ישיבה] ת ~ | והוא חבר תלמוד ירושלמי לה' סדרים כי אין
מסדר טהרות < ל טהרות > רק מסכת נדה. וחובר הירושלמי בקרוב ממאתים <ר שנה>
אחר החרבן. ב¹ (בגליון) וחבר התלמוד הי'רו'שלמי ובקרב (?) לשנת דק"ק (?) |
ואלו ~ ת] הם ~ תלמידיו] פק ~ של ר' יוחנן |
14 ור' ינאי — ורב דימי] ת < | ורב דימי] אפ בר רב דימי | בה ורב שמואל |

ספר הקבלה

הדור השני רב יהודה ורב הונא. אחרי מות שמואל בשנת ד"י היה לראש רב יהודה בר יחזקאל בנהרדעא ורב הונא בסורא. ורב יהודה היה גדול מרב הונא בחכמה אבל רב הונא היה קרוב לנשיא ולפיכך גברה ישיבת סורא. ונפטר רב יהודה וחזרו שתי הישיבות לרב הונא. ועוד נפטר בימיו ר' יוחנן ראש ישיבת ארץ ישראל בשנת דל"ט והיה לראש ישיבה בארץ ישראל ר' אמי. ונפטר רב הונא שנת ד"נ לאחר שהיה ראש ישיבה מ' שנה. ואלו תלמידיהם רב חסדא ורבה בר נחמני ורב יוסף ורב נחמן בר יצחק ור' זירא ורבה בר רב הונא ורב המנונא.

הדור השלישי רב חסדא ורבה ורב יוסף. רב חסדא היה תלמיד חבר לרב הונא וד' שנים קודם פטירת רב הונא בנה בית המדרש לעצמו. ואחר כך נפטר רב הונא והיה רב חסדא ראש ישיבה עשר שנים עד שנת ד"ס. והוקם רבה בר נחמני והיה ראש ישיבה כ"ב שנים. וברח לאגם מפני מלשינות ומת באגם בשנת דפ"ב. וישב על כסאו רב יוסף שנתים וחצי ומת בשנת דפ"ה. ורב יוסף היה נקרא סיני ורבה עוקר הרים. ותלמידיהם אביי ורבא בר יוסף בר חמא בר יחזקאל ורבינא הראשון ורב כהנא השני ואחרים רבים כי י"ב אלף תלמידים היו לו לרבה.

הדור הרביעי אביי ורבא. אביי היה לראש ישיבה בשנת מות רב יוסף

---

16 מות] פק פטירת | ד"י] פ ד' | היה] אפק והיה |
17 לראש] פק ~ ישיבה |
18 גברה] במ גברא |
19 שתי] פ < |
20 ארץ ישראל] בה ~ נפטר | לראש] ת ראש |
21 ל ישיבת א"י | שנת ד"נ] מ ש"ן (!) ד"נ פ ד' ק ד' אלף |
22 ישיבה] ל ישיבת א"י | אק תלמידיו | ורבה] ל ורבוה מ ורבא |
23 בר יצחק] מ < | רב הונא] ב הונא |
24 ב דור שלישי] רב חסדא² פ ורב חסדא | היה] פק < |
25 לרב הונא] ק דרב הונא | דלמ מדרש ר המדרש (ואות "ה" נמחקה) |
26 מ ואחרי] כך] דמ כן | עד] ד < |
27 כ"ב שנים] ת ~ והוא חבר בראשית רבה ושאר הרבות |
28 ל מלשינים | ומת] ד ~ שם | דפ"ב] פ ד' כ פ"ב (!) ק ד' אלף ופ"ד |
29 ד שתי שנים | ומת] פק ונפטר | פק והיה נקרא רב יוסף א והיה רב יוסף נקרא |
30 אביי — כהנא השני (31)] ק < | בר יוסף] א ורבה בר רב יוסף המ בר' יוסף פר בר רב יוסף | בר חמא] ב ברחמא דק בר' חמא ר רב חמ' אפ ורמי |
31 ואחרים רבים] פ ותלמידיהם רבים אחרים ק רבים אחרים | לו] מ < |
32 לרבה] ב לרבא |
33 ב דור רביעי | אמ ראש | ישיבה] הת / | מות] ל < (ונוסף בגליון) |

ספר הקבלה

י"ד שנה ונפטר בשנת דצ"ט. ואחריו היה לראש במחוזא רבא בר יוסף י"ד שנה אחרות ונפטר בשנת דקי"ג.

הדור החמישי רב נחמן בר יצחק ורב פפא ורב הונא בריה דרב יהושע. לאחר מות רבא בשנת דקי"ג היה לראש ישיבה בפום בדיתא רב נחמן בר יצחק ומחביריו של רב חסדא היה אבל האריך ימים והיה ראש ישיבה ד' שנים ומת בשנת דקי"ז. ובתחלת היותו לראש ישיבה נחלקו הישיבות פעם שנייה. והיה לראש ישיבה בנרש עיר שקרובה לסורא רב פפא וחיה רב פפא י"ט שנה והוא ראש ישיבה ומת בשנת דקל"ב. ואחר שנפטר רב נחמן בר יצחק היה ראש ישיבה בנהרדעא רב חמא מנהרדעא. ומת בשנת דקל"ב גם הוא וט"ו שנה היתה גדולתו. ולא הוזכר רב הונא בריה דרב יהושע בראשי ישיבות.

הדור הששי רב אשי וראשי הישיבות שהיו בימיו. ומימות ר' ועד רב אשי לא מצאו תורה וגדולה במקום אחד. בימי רב פפא בשנת דקכ"ז היה רב אשי ראש ישיבה בסורא ס' שנה. ובשנת ה' לגדולתו נפטרו רב פפא ורב חמא והיה רב זביד לראש ישיבה בפום בדיתא ח' שנים ומת בשנת דק"מ. ואחריו רב דימי ג' שנים ומת בשנת דקמ"ג. ואחריו רפרם

34 י"ד] ק ד' | ד' צ"ט — ונפטר בשנת (35) ה | < | דצ"ט] ב דפ"ט
35 שנה] למר | ונפטר] ת ומת | פ שנת
36 ב דור חמישי | בר יצחק] ה בר' יוסף
37 בה לאחר] א אחרי פק אחר ת ולאחר | מות] פק פטירת | בשנת | ישיבה] ד | < | אדר בפומבדיתא
38 היה] פק | <
39 אבה ראש] פקות לראש | ד' שנים | ה מ' שנה | ומת] פק ונפטר | ד' קי"ז] פ ד' ק"א ק ד' וקי"ח | ישיבה] בה | <
40 אם ראש | אבה שקרובה] פק הקרובה ת קרובה
41 ה לסורייא (?) | וחיה] א והיה בפ וחייא ל וחי | וחיה רב פפא] ק ורב אדא בר פפא | רב פפא] פ בר פפא | והוא] ה והיה | ההוא ראש ישיבה] את | < | ומת] פק ופנטר
42 דקל"ב] ב דקל"ג | שנפטר] ת פק מות
43 רב חמא מנהרדעא] הדלר | < | מנהרדעא] אם | < | ומת] פק ונפטר | הק וגם | בהק ט"ו היתה גדולתו] ק | <
44 בריה דרב] ק ורב
45 ב דור ששי | וראשי — בימיו] ד | < | הלמד ישיבות | שהיו בימיו] לר | < | בימיו] ב | < | (ונוסף ע"י ב3) | אהת ומימות] ב מימות פק ומימי | ר'] את רבינו הקדוש פ רב את עד | רב] ה | <
46 ב נמצא | תורה] ת ~ וחסידות וענוה | במקום אחד] ק | < | בשנת] בת שנת | בת דקכ"ז אק דק"ו ה דקנ"ז פ דתק"ז
47 ה בסורי' | ס'] ק פ' (?) | נפטרו] ת מתו
48 את ראש | דמר בפומבדיתא א לפומבדיתא ל בפומדיתא | ומת] פק ונפטר
49 דק"מ — ומת בשנת (49)] ק | < | ומת2] פ ונפטר

בר פפא ומת באותה שנה. ואחריו רב כהנא השני כ"ה שנה ומת בשנת
דקע"א. ואחריו רב אחאי בריה דרבא ב' שנים ומת בשנת דקע"ג. כי
רב פפא ושֵשת ראשי ישיבות אלו כלם בימי רב אשי נפטרו. ונפטר רב
אשי בשנת דקפ"ז והיא שנת תשל"ח למנין שטרות. והוא החל לכתוב
את התלמוד.

הדור השביעי מרימר ומר בר רב אשי וחביריהם. אחר פטירת רב
אשי היה לראש ישיבה במקומו בסורא מרימר ה' שנים ומת בשנת
דקצ"ב. ואחריו רב אידי בר אבין כ' שנה ומת בשנת דרי"ב. ואחריו
רב נחמן בר הונא ג' שנים ומת בשנת דרט"ו. ואחרי אלו ישב מר בר רב
אשי על כסא אביו י"ג שנה וימים טובים היו ימיו לפיכך קראוהו רב
טביומי ומת בשנת דרכ"ח והיא שנת תשע"ט לשטרות. ואחריו רבה
תוספאה ו' שנים ומת בשנת דרל"ד. חמשה אלו תלמידי רב אשי ויש
מהן חבר כמרימר ורב אידי בר אבין והשאר תלמידים.
ובשנת מות רבה תוספאה גזרה מלכות פרס שמדות גדולות על ישראל

50 ומת] פק ונפטר | ל באותו | ומת² פק ונפטר | בשנת] פ שנת |
51 דקע"א] ב ד' קפ"א (ותוקן ל־דקע"א) ק ד' וקע"ז | ואחריו רב אחאי – ד' קפ"ז (53)]
ק > | אבי¹ פ אחאי] בה אחי ת אחא | ומת] פ ונפטר |
52 ה ושֵשת] ת ושֵשה אבפ ורב שֵשת | פ נפטרו בימי רב אשי |
53 אשי] פ > | בשנת] ב שנת | והיא] ד היא |
54 את] מ > | התלמוד] ת ~ ולא הספיק לסיימו ב¹ (בגליון) ~ ורע"ג שנה אחר מותו
נחתם שהיא שנת דר"ס |
55 ב דור שביעי | וחביריהם] ת ~ הם סיימו [ד את] התלמוד הבבלי ונחתם בשנת ד'רס"ה
ליצירה ונתפשט בכל ישראל וקבלו אותו > מ וקבלוהו > עליהם ולמדו אותו ברבים
חכמי כל דור ודור והסכימו עליו וכל ישראל ועליו אין להוסיף וממנו אין לגרוע.
ובימי רבה [ד רב] יוסף > בר [ד רב] יוסי > מ יוסי > שהיה ראש ישיבה מרבנן סבוראי
נחתם > ל נחתום > התלמוד. וכמו פ' שנה היה משהתחיל > ד משהתחילו > רב > ל
לרב > אשי וחבר > מ לחבר > אותו עד שנחתם ובשנת ע"ג למותו נחתם > ל נחתום > |
56 פק מרימר במקומו בסורא | ה בסוריא | ומת] פק ונפטר | בשנת] אפ שנת |
57 ד'קצ"ב] א תשע מאות ותשעים ושתים פ ד' תתקצ"א (ואותיות "תת" נמחקו) דלר
תקצ"ב | אידי (!) | ב – וְרִבִין (!) | ומת] פק ונפטר | בשנת] אפ שנת |
58 בר הונא] אפק | ג' שנים] מ > | ומת] פק ונפטר | רבי¹ פ > |
59 וימים טובים] ד וי"ט שנים ל ~ יָמיו | ב > |
60 ומת] פק ונפטר | דרכ"ח] אק (?) | ד'רכ"א | רבה] אבלר רבא |
61 תוספאה] ב תוספתאה ל תוספתא מ טופסאה | ו' שנים] פ > | (ונתלה בין השיטין)
ב ג' שנים (ונתקן לו' בין השיטין) | ומת בשנת – תוספאה (63)] פ > | (רעיין להלן
בשורה 64) | ומת] ק ונפטר | ד'רל"ד] ה דכלג (!) | ד ד' רל"ג | חמשה אלו – רב אשי]
ק וחמש תלמידים אלו לרב אשי | ה חמשת | חמשת | למד אלה |
62 בר אבין] ה > |
63 מות] ק פטירת | ב תוספתאה | ל תוספתא מ תופסאה | גדולות] אה > |

ספר הקבלה

כשקרב אידם של פרסיים לבא פעם שנייה. כי שתי פעמים מלכו
פרסיים וכן רומיים.
כי כרך גדול של רומי נבנה בימי חזקיהו מלך יהודה ובנוהו ב' אחים
מלכים גדולים שם האחד רומולוס ושם השני רמולש. ורומלוס קשר על
אחיו והרגו מהרה ומלך הוא לבדו. והחזיר את כל ארץ מערב תחת
רגלי רומיים. ומת ברומי ועשו לו רומיים כבוד גדול במותו. ועשו על
קברו בנין גדול עגול משפת עגולו אל שפתו כמו נ' אמה בקרקעיתו.
וקו מאה ועשרים אמה יסוב אותו. והצירוהו למעלה עד שעשאוהו
כמין צריף וגובה גדול מאד מאד. והוא ברומי עד היום הזה לא חרב.
וכן לאחר מות רומולוס היו רומיים בהשקט ואין אדם בעולם מושל
בם עד שבא נבוכדנצר ומשל בם כדכתיב ועבדו אותו כל הגוים. ובימי
בלשצר בן בנו נשמדה מלכות כשדים וחזרה המלכות לדריוש ואחר
כך לכורש וכן למלכים אחרים עד שקם עליהם אלסכנדרוס המוקדוני
המלך הגדול והשמיד כל מלכות פרס כדכתיב ויתמרמר אליו ויך
את האיל וגומ'. ובכל זאת רומיים תחת ידי כשדים תחלה ותחת ידי

א

64 כשקרב] אקס ~ יום | אידם] ק איתן (?) פ ~ וחמשה (!) תלמידים אלו לרב אשי
וריש מהם חבר כמרימר ורב אידי בר אבין והשאר תלמידים ובשנת פטירת רבה...
(!) | ת פעם שנייה לבא | ק מלכו פרסיים שתי פעמים |
66 כי] ל ~ כך | דם חזקיה | ק המלך | יהודה | הק | ב בנאוהו ה בניהו ב בנוהו |
67 פק גדולים מלכים | ד רומולוס | השני] ק האחר | פק רמולש | א רימאלוש בר רמולש
ה רמילש ד רימולוס ל רמלוש מ רומולוס | ד ורומולוס מ ורומלוש | קשר] ב כשר
ב¹ קשר ד ~ קשר |
68 אחיו] ד ~ רימולוס ל ~ רמלוש מ ~ רומולוש ד ~ רמולוש | אפק ויהרגהו | את]
פ | > | אבה המערב |
69 רגלי] ת | > | רומיים¹] ק הרומיים | ועשו] פק ויעשו¹ פק ויעשר רומיים | במותו² – ועשו²
פק ויעשו ב ~ לו |
70 אד עגול גדול | עגול] ב ג'עול (!) ה | > | אפק ומשפט | ק ואל |
71 פ וקו מאה ועשרים | א וקב חמשים ב וקומה חמישים ה וקו מ'ה וחמשים ק וקו מאה ד
וקו נ' למר וקו | > ל וקו | > ק"נ | ק והצרו אותו ל והצריהו | קת מלמעלה | שעשאוהו]
ב ~ למעלה (!) |
72 פק וגבוה אדם וגובהו | מאד²] אק | > | הזה] אפ | > | אפק ולא |
73 ד רומולוס | אק הרומיים ל רומיים | ואין] פק עד אין | בעולם] פק | > |
74 בם] פק עליהם אד | > | נבוכדנצר] פק ~ מלך בבל | בם] פק גם עליהם ת בהם |
75 בן] אבה | > | פ כשדיים | ק וחזר | המלכות] פק ~ לפרסיים | לדרירוש] פק ~ המדי
תחלה |
76 כך] בקמק כן | לכורש | > | הפרסי חתנו ~ פק | אחרים] ק אחריהם | את אלסכנדרוס |
אר מוקדון ב המקדוני ד מקדון ל המוקדון |
77 המלך הגדול] ד | > | הגדול] למר | > | כדכתיב] ה | > |
78 וגומ'] אב | > | הק וכו' | ב רומיים ק רומי ידי] בת יד (וכן להלן) |

פרסיים ולבסוף תחת ידי יונים. וכשגברו בני חשמונאי על אנטיוכוס ועל מלכותו גם רומיים נקהלו ועמוד על נפשם והתחזקו ופרקו עול יונים מעל צוארם ומלכו עליהם ושמום למס.

ובימי ינאי המלך של ישראל התחילו למלוך פעם שנייה והמלך הראשון הוא יוליוס. וקראוהו קיסר כי אמו מתה והוא בבטנה ובקעו את כריסה. והיה מלך גדול מאד והוא החזיר המלוכה לרומיים. וכן לא פסקו שמו מכל מלכיהם שהיו נקראים פלוני קיסר. ובמותו עשו לו הכר גדול לא נעשה לכל מלך בעולם. מגדל גבוה מאד מאד ושפודים של ברזל נעוצים בו מלמטה עד ראשו והם משתרגים ועליהם ארון גדול של נחשת עבה ובו יוליוס. והארון נראה לעינים עד היום.

ואחריו מלך אגוסטוס בן אחיו המלך הגדול. ואומרים שהוא מלך על כל העולם. ובשנת ארבע למלכו שם על כל הארץ מס של נחשת ורצף נהר טברוס שרומי יושבת על שפתו עשרים מילין רצפן בלוחות של נחשת עבות מאד. ורוחב הנהר גדול מאד. ומנין הנחשת הם מונים עד היום. וספרים רבים בידי רומיים כתובים בהם שבחיו וחכמתיו וטועניו

79 וכשגברו] אפ וכשגברה מלכות [א בית] | בני חשמונאי] אפק חשמונאי ובניו | המר חשמוני |
80 ב ועמדו ל ועומד | עול] ל ~ על (ונתקן בגליון) |
81 מעל] פק מעליהם ומעל | למס] ל ~ למס (!) |
82 המלך של] ב מלך ה המלך (!) | של ישראל] ת < |
83 הוא] אמ > | פד יוליאוס | א ונקרא ה וקראו פ ויקראוהו ל וקראהו | מתה] ל מתו (!) ובקעו] אק ויבקעו פ ויקבע (!) ת וקרעו |
84 את] פקל < | מאד] ל < | החזיר] פק ~ את | וכן] ב < וכן כן | ועל כן | וכן לא] ק ולא |
85 אפק פסק | שמו] א וישימו בם פ וישימו שם ק שם קיסר | מכל] א כל ה מן כל פ ~ מכל ק מהן בכל | שהיו נקראים] פ > ק היו קורין | פלוני] א כפלו' פ כ פלו' (!) | פלוני קיסר] ק קיסר אותם (!) |
86 הכר גדול] פ כבוד גדול והכר ק כבוד גדול והידור | הם לא] אפק שלא בדלר ולא לכל מלך] ת למלך | בעולם] ב ~ כמוהו | ב גבוהה | בת מאדי] אה > פק וגדול | נעוצים] א נפרצים (?) | בו] ה > | ועליהם] פק ועליו ד ועולים |
88 ארון גדול – והארון] זדלר > | ארון] ק כיסוי | גדול] אמ > | עבה] ה > | בו] מ ~ מאד ובו יוליוס] אב > | ובו] ה ~ | שלדו של ק ~ נקבר מ ~ היה מונח שדרו של | היום] ה ~ הזה |
89 א אלוסטוס ב אנוסטוס פ אגוסטוס מ אגושטוס | אק אחי | שהוא מלך] פק שמלך | על כל] ב ~ את כל ה בכל |
90 שם] אפק וישם | כל] אה > |
91 ד טברוס] א טיבריס בה טיבאריש פ טיברש ק טובריש לר טבריס מ טיבראס ס טיברוס שרומי] הק של רומי | ורצף] אק ורצפו פ ורצפן ר רצפו | ק עבות מאד של נחשת |
92 אבפ מאד עבות | מאד] ה > | ה ורחב | בה מאד גדול | ומנין] ה ומילין ה > | הם] מ > | הם מונים] ה הסמוכין |
93 היום] ת ~ | בשטרותיהם | וספרים] ב וסופרים | בידי] ב > | בהם] ד ~ עוד | שבחיו ל שבחייו | וחכמתיו] ק וחותמותיו וטועניו] ה ~ בהם |

ספר הקבלה

שלא היה לאומות העולם מלך כמוהו. ובשנת ל"ח למלכו נולד ישו
כי נ"ב שנה מלך מלכות פושטת בכל העולם כמו שהם אומרים.
וכן פרסיים גם הם. לאחר שנכרתה מלכותם בימי אלכסנדרוס נקהלו
אחרי מות אנטונינוס בימי ר' יוחנן ועמדו על נפשם להסיר עול רומיים
מעליהם. ומפני כן כשמת אנטונינוס אמר ר' נתפרדה חבילה. אבל
לא גברו הרבה עד מות רבינו הקדוש בימי ר' יוחנן. והמלך הראשון
אזדשיר בן באבך כתב אל כל מקהלות של פרסיים שיהיו יודעים
כי חרב ארסטוטליס החכם אוכלת בהם היום ת"ק שנה מפני שהיה
אלכסנדרוס תלמידו. וכן נתחזקו ועשו מלחמות עם רומיים. ולא נצחו
אלו ולא אלו אלא נחלקה המלכות: ארץ עילם ושנער וחמת וקצת ארץ
יון וכל ארץ ישראל ועד ארץ ערב כלה ביד פרסיים. ורומי ואשכנז
וצרפת ומקצת ארץ יון וארץ מצרים ופלשתים וספרד בידי רומיים.
והיו ישראל תחת ידי פרסיים פעם שנייה. ובתחלה היו אוהבים לישראל
בימי אזדשיר והוא אחשורוש וכן בימי שבור מלכא.
ובימיו יצא מאני לעולם והיה טוען שאלהים שנים יש לעולם. אחד

94 היה] פ היתה | לאומות] א בכל דלר באומות | לאומות העולם] פ בעולם | מלך | ב < |
ל"ח] ה ל"ט | ישו] ישו"ן בק ישו' ה ישוע (!) ר י"ש א ~ הנוצרי ק ~ הנצרי |
95 כי] מ | נ"ב] ה גם כן | מלך] ב < | מלכות פושטת] ת ומלכותו פשטה | כמו – אומרים]
ב מלך | אומרים ק חומדין |
96 וכן פרסיים] ב והפרסיים | א אלכסנדר בת אלכסנדרוס | נקהלו] ה ~ בימי ר' יוחנן |
97 אפק אחר | בימי ר' יוחנן] הת < | עול] ל כל |
98 כשמת] פ במות (?) | אמר ר'] מ < | ר'] אד רבינו הקדוש | קד החבילה |
99 והמלך הראשון — שנייה (106) | ב < |
100 פ אזדשיר | א אודשייר ה אזדאשייר ק אורשיר ת אורשיך | באבך] ק באדך | ה המקהלות
של | ל < | שיהיו] אפ שהיו מ שיהו | ה שחרב |
101 קד ארסטוטליס | אפ אריסטוטליס ה ארסטוטלוס ל אריסטטלוס מ ארסטטליס ר
ארסטוטלוס | ת אכלה | היום] המ < | שהיה] ה < |
102 הפ אלכסנדרוס | א אלכסנדור ק אלכסנדר דלמ אלכסנדרוס ר אלכסנדוס | ת ובכן
אפק וישעו | נצחו] פ ~ אלו את מר ~ לא |
103 ולא] אק אק את פ ~ אלו את ~ אלא נחלקה] ק ונתחלקה | נחלקה] ה נתחלקה | ה מלוכה |
קת חמת ושנער |
104 וכל ארץ | ת וארץ | אקדלר ביד |
105 וצרפת] ק ~ בידי רומיים | ת וקצת | ופלשתים — רומיים] ק וצפת גם כן | ופלשתים]
פ < | וספרד] מ וצרפת (ובגליון: וספרד) | בידי] ה בימי ר ביד |
106 והיו] אפק ויהיו | ת יד | ובתחלה] ב בימים האלה | ת לישראל אוהבים |
107 בימי¹ — אחשורוש] ב < | א אזדשר ק אשדשיר ת אורשיר |
108 ובימיו] ב ובימי פ אלו | אפ יצאו | מאני] מאנ"י | מינים פ מינאני ק מינות | טוען] ק ~ איש
ששמו מאני | שאלהים שנים יש] אה שיש אלוהות | ה אל"ים < ששני ק ששני אלוהות
יש | למד שאלהים] בכי אלהים פ שאלים ד שאלוהות | שניים] ל < | ב תלוי בין השיטין |
לעולם] ה < את בעולם | אחד] מ ~ מהם |

ספר הקבלה

מחיה ועושה כל הטובות. ואחד ממית ועושה כל הרעות. ובדא לאמגושים
תורה מלבו והיה לגוי גדול. והרגו שבור מלכא בחכמתו.

ועוד היה לפרסיים מלך ששמו הורמיז ומת והניח אשתו הרה. ולא
רצו פרסיים להמליך איש תחת הורמיז אלא קשרו כתר מלכות על
בטנה להמליך את אשר תלד אם זכר אם נקבה. וילדה זכר והמליכוהו
ביום לדתו וקראו שמו בהרם על שם כוכב מאדים שהיה כוכבו.

ועוד מלכים אחרים גדולים וכלם אוהבים את ישראל עד שגברה
מלכות ישמעאל והשמידום מתחת השמים. וקודם לכן הפך הב"ה לבם
לשנא עמו ותפש מלך פרס ג' מגדולי ישראל אמימר בר מר ינקא בר
מר זוטרא חבירו של רב אשי ורב משרשיא וראש גלות והונא מר שמו.
והרגם מלך פרס. ותפש נערי בני ישראל והוציאם בעל כרחם מן הכלל
בטבת שנת דרל"ד.

ובאותה שנה היה רבינא ראש ישיבה שנה אחת.

ובימי ראשי ישיבות אלו שהיו בסורא היו ראשי ישיבות בפום בדיתא
רב גביהה מבי כתיל בשנת מות רב אשי. והיה לראש שש שנים ומת
בשנת דקצ"ג. ואחריו רפרם עשר שנים ומת בשנת דר"ג. ואחריו רב

ספר הקבלה

125 רחומי י"ג שנה ומת בשנת דרי"ו. ואחריו רב סמא בריה דרבא ומת בשנת דרל"ו.

הרי ז' דורות של אמוראים וה' דורות של תנאים וט' דורות של הוראה בבית המקדש. נמצאו מימות זרובבל והעולים עמו עד סוף ימי רבינא ורב סמא בריה דרבא כ"א דור והשנים תתכ"ז שנה.

---

125 ב ריחומי אפק ניחומי | ומת¹] פק ונפטר | הפק שנת | סמא] בדלר סימא | ומת²] פק ונפטר |
126 ה שנת |
127 של אמוראים] ה לאמוראין | אפק בבית המקדש (א של) הוראה | הוראה] ב הודיה (?) |
128 פק נמצא | מימות] פק מימי |
129 סמא] בדלר סימא פ סימאי | בריה דרבא] ק | < | דרבא] פ | < | אפקד דורות | תתכ"ז] אק תתפ"ז פ תתפ"ח | שנה] פקד >

ספר הקבלה

[ה]

סדר רבנן סבוראי

הדור הראשון רבה יוסי הוא ראש רבנן סבוראי היה לראש אחר רבינא ל"ח שנה עד שנת דרע"ד. ובשנת כ"ד לגדולתו שהיא שנת דר"ס והיא שנת תתי"א למנין שטרות וקודם לחשבון ישמעאלים קכ"ג שנה נחתם
5 התלמוד. כי בימי רב אשי הוחל להכתב ובשנת ע"ג למותו נחתם. נמצא משנת כתיבת המשנה עד חתימת התלמוד שי"א שנה. ומשנת כתיבת המשנה עד שנתנו זו שהיא שנת דתתקכ"א תתקע"ב שנה. ומשנת חתימת התלמוד עד שנתנו זו תרס"א שנה. ומת רבה יוסי בשנת דרע"ד.

הדור השני מן רבנן סבוראי רב אחאי בר הונא וחבריו. רב אחאי היה
10 ראש ישיבה שנה אחת ומת בשנת דרע"ה. ואחריו רב שמואל בר רבא ג' שנים ומת בשנת דרע"ח. ואחריו רבינא מן אומצא שנה אחת ומת בשנת דרע"ט. ואחריו רב תחינה ז' שנים ומת בשנת דרפ"ו. ואחריו רב סימונא ורב עינא. רב עינא בסורא ורב סימונא בפום בדיתא. והיה רב סימונא עד שנת ד"ש. כל אלה דור אחד הן.

2 ב דור ראשון | רבה] דלד רב ק ~ בר | ק והוא | רבנן] ה | ק והיה | רבינא] ק רב סמא בריה דרבינא |
3 ובשנת] פק וביומי | כ"ד] מ ע"ד | שנת² | ד |
4 ל ישמעאלים] קכ"ג | ב קל"ג ק קנ"ג | שנה] ת | > | נחתם] ב וחתם |
5 כי] ה | > | להכתב] ה | > | ע"ג] ה | ע"ב | למותו] פק לפטירתו |
6 משנת] פק משעת | שנה] אבה | > | ומשנת כתיבת – תתקע"ב שנה (7)] פ | > | ומשנת כתיבת־התלמוד עד(8)] ב | > | (ונוסף בגליון ע"י ב1) | ומשנת] ק ומשעת |
7 שהיא] אד היא | שהיא שנת דתתקכ"א] ב¹ | > | שנת] קל | > | תתקע"ב] ב¹ תתקע"ח שנה | ה | > | ומשנת] אפ ומשעת |
8 שנה] ב | > | ומת] פק ונפטר | רבה] מ רבא | בר | בשנת דרע"ד] ק | > | דרע"ד | ב תרע"ד |
9 ב דור שני | בד מרבנן | אחאי¹ | אחאי] בת אחי ה אחא | ה היה רב אחא | רב²] ק | > | אחאי | ב אחמי (!) ק אחי |
10 ומת] פ ונפטר ק | רב | > | רבא] ק | > | רבא] ה בבא ל נחמני רבא (!) |
11 ומת] פק ונפטר | ב דמן | אחת] ב | > | ומת] פק ונפטר |
12 בשנת¹ | פ שנת | ואחריו רב תחינה – דרפ"ו] ת | > | פ אחריו | ה תחינה | אפ תחנינא ב טחינא ק תחנתא | ומת] פק ונפטר |
13 סימונא¹] אפק סמא ל סימוני | רב עינא בסורא | ה רב סימונא בסורא | ורב סימונא אפק ורב סמא ה ורב עינא ד רב סימונא | אחת בפומבדיתא | והיה | ל וחיה |
14 סימונא] אפ סמא ק | > | (ובין השיטין: "עינא") | אלה] ק אלו | הן] ב ~ וכל אלה היו סבוראי |

33

ספר הקבלה

הדור השני תלמידי רב סימונא ורב עינא ולא הוזכרו בשמותיהם. כי
הישיבות בטלו כמו נ' שנה אחרי מות רב סימונא עד שנת דשמ"ט מפני
שנאת מלכי פרס ושמדותיהם.

הדור השלישי רב חנן מאשיקיא קבל מתלמידי רב סימונא ורב עינא.
ואחריו רב מרי. ואחריו רב הונא. ואחריו רב חנינא. ואחריו רב חיננא.
כל אלה דור אחד הן. ורב חנן מאשיקיא בשנת דשמ"ט היה לראש
ואחריו ארבעה ראשי ישיבות אלו ולא הוזכר מספר שניהם.

הדור הרביעי רב יצחק. ובימיו גברה מלכות ישמעאל על מלכות
פרס ונעקרה מלכות פרס מן העולם. ובא לבבל עלי אבן אבי טאלב
מלך ישמעאל לאחר שגברו עליה ישמעאל כמה שנים. כי בימי עמר
בן אל כטאב מלך ישמעאל נעקרה מלכות פרס והלכו נשיו ובנותיו
של יזדגרד מלך פרס בשבי. ועמר מלך ישמעאל נתן בת יזדגרד לר'
בוסתנאי ראש גלות וגיירה והיתה לו לאשה. כי בשנת דשע"ד התחיל

---

15 פת הדור השני] ב > ה והדור השני אק הדור השלישי | תלמידי] ב ותלמידי | סימונא]
אפ סמא | סימונא ורב עינא] ק עינא ורב סמא ב ~ רב עינא בסורא ורב סימונא
בפום בדיתא | ולא] ב לא | הפ בשמותם | כי הישיבות] ק והישיבות |
16 כמו נ'] ה בחמשים | נ'] פ כ' ק כ"ט | הת אחר | רב] ב ר' | סימונא] אפק סמא |
18 ב הדור שלישי ק > | רב חנן] ק ורב חנן ל רב נחמן | בלמד מאשיקיא] א משיא ה
מאשיקיא פ מאשיה ק מיאשיה ד מאישיקיא | סימונא] א סמא פ סימאי ק סמאי | ורב
עינא] הדלר |
19 רב מרי] ה מרי מר | בקמ מארי | ואחריו רב חנינא] אפקמ | חנינא] גליון ל חנן |
20 ב אלו | אחד] ה אחר | הן] הקלמר > | אק חנין | למד מאשיקיא] א מאשיא בה מאשיקיא
פ מאשיה ק מיאשיה ד מאישיה | בשנת־לראש] אפק היה לראש > | א ראש ישיבה >
בשנת > | א משנת > דשמ"ט |
21 פ ארבעת ה > | ראשי ישיבות] פק > | אלו] פק > | דלר > | פקדר הוזכרו | דלר שנותיהם |
22 ב דור רביעי | ת בימיו | ל ישמאעל (וכן בכ"י ל תדיר) |
23 אפק ריבא | עלי – מלך ישמעאל (24) ל > | (ובגליון: עלי אבן אבי תאלב) | עלי] א
על פ עלאי | אבן] ב נתלה בין השיטין ה בן | בת אבי טאלב] א אביטלס ה אבטאלב
פ טלאב ק אבוטלאב |
24 דלר ואחר | ל שגברה | עליה] ב על ידי הדלר מלכות | ישמעאל] פקמ ישמעאלים א
הישמעלים (!) | דמר עמר] א עמבאר ב עומר ה עמד פ עומאר ק עומאל | עמר בן
אלכטאב] ל < |
25 בן] מ אבו | בן אל כטאב – מלכות] ק יזדיגראד מלך | דר אלכטאב] א אלכאב ב אלקטב
ה אלכטב פ אלקטאב מ אלכאבט | ה ונעקרה | והלכו] פק והרגו |
26 ר יזדגרדי] א הגדר ב יזרגרה ה יזדגרר פ יזדיגרד (?) ק יזדיגראד ד יזדגרד ל יזדרד
מ יזגרד | מר ועמר] אפק ועמר ויעמוד בהדל ועמד | הלמר נתן] אפק ויתן בד ונתן | מר
יזדרד²] א הגרד ב יזדגדה ה יזדגרר פ אזדיגרר ק אזדיגראד ד יזדיגרד ל יזדרד |
27 הפ בוסתאני | ק הגלות | פ אשה |

ספר הקבלה

מחמד מלך ישמעאל לטעון טענתו. וכשבא עלי אבן אבי טאלב לבבל יצא אליו רב יצחק ראש ישיבה וכבדו ונשאו המלך עלי בשנת דת״כ. הדור החמישי מר רבא ומר הונא. מר הונא בסורא ומר רבא בפום בדיתא. ואחריהם רב שישנא ורב בוסאי. רב שישנא היה נקרא משרשיא בר תחליפא וארבעה אלה דור אחד הן. ונפטר רב משרשיא בר תחליפא בשנת דתמ״ט והוא סוף רבנן סבוראי. נמצאו רבנן סבוראי חמשה דורות ושנותיהם קפ״ז.

28 לטעון] פ ~ את | לטעון טענתו] ק ⟩ | ב טענתו ד טענותיו | עלי] פ עלאי | עלי — טאלב] ל ⟨ (ובגליון: עלי) | אבן] אבה בן | לר אבי טאלב] א יולב ב אביטלב ה אבי טאלאב פק אבוטלאב דמ אבי טלאב |

29 ה ראש ישיבה רב יצחק | וכבדו] ב ⟩ | ונשאו — עלי] ה המלך עלי בן אבי טאלאב ונשאו המלך] ק והמליכו | המלך עלי] ב ⟩ | עלי] א על כלם ושמו עלי פ עלאי כלם ק על כולן |

30 ב דור חמישי | מר רבא¹] פ מרבא | מר²] ל ומר | הונא — בפום בדיתא] מ רבא בפומבדיתא ומר הונא בסורא | הדר בפומבדיתא ל בפומדית׳ |

31 פק ואחריו | הפ ששנא¹ | בוסאי] א ביסנאי פק בוסנאי ד כוסאי | רב²] אק ורב | אהפק ששנא² |

32 וארבעה — תחליפא] פק ⟩ | אב וארבעת | ונפטר] ת ומת | משרשיא בר תחליפא] ת שישנא |

33 ב שנת | נמצאו רבנן סבוראי] ת ⟩ |

34 ה ושנותם |

ספר הקבלה

[ו]

סדר גאונים

הדור הראשון מראשי ישיבות פום בדיתא: רב חיננא גאון מנהר פקוד היה ראש ישיבה ח' שנים עד שנת דתנ"ז. ואחריו רב הילאי הלוי היה ראש ישיבה י"ח שנה ונפטר בשנת דתע"ה.

הדור השני רב יעקב מנהר פקוד היה ראש ישיבה י"ח שנה ונפטר בשנת דתצ"ג. ואחריו רב שמואל מבני בניו של אמימר חברו של רב אשי היה לראש י"ח שנה ונפטר בשנת דתקי"א. הרי אלו בפום בדיתא. ובימי ארבעה ראשי ישיבות אלו היו ראשי ישיבות במתא מחסיא רב הונא בר יוסף שנת דתמ"ט. ואחריו רב חייא ממישן. ואחריו מר ינקא והוא רבא בר נטרונאי היה לראש בשנת דתע"ט. ואחריו רב יהודה גאון. ואחריו רב יוסף בשנת דתצ"ט. ואחריו רב שמואל בר מרי בשנת דתק"ה. ובימי רב שמואל זה היה ר' שמעון קיירא ולא נסמך גאון. וחבר הלכות גדולות בשנת אלף נ"ב לשטרות שהיא שנת דתק"א בשנה השלישית לגדולת רב שמואל בר מרי ובשנת ח' לגדולת רב שמואל

ספר הקבלה

מזרע אמימר. והזכיר שמועות משמיה דכהן צדק. ולא שמענו שהיה
בימיו גאון ששמו כהן צדק. ואפשר שכהן צדק זה שהיה רבו חכם היה
ולא נסמך. ואחר רב שמואל בר מרי היה רב אחא משבחא חכם גדול
וחבר שאלתות שלו בכל מצות האמורות בתורה והספר מצוי בידינו
עד היום הזה. וכל הבאים אחריו בדקוהו ופשפשו בו ושמענו שעד היום
לא נמצא בו שום טעות בעולם. אבל לא נסמך רב אחא זה גאון מפני
שנאת ראש גלות שבאותו הדור שהיה שונאו. וסמך שמשו של רב אחא
ושמו רב נטרונאי. וכעס רב אחא והלך לו מבבל לארץ ישראל ונפטר
שם. והיה רב נטרונאי לראש י״ג שנה עד שנת דתקכ״א. הרי ח׳ ראשי
ישיבות אלו במתא מחסיא היו בימי ד׳ ראשי ישיבות בפום בדיתא.

הדור השלישי של גאונים בפום בדיתא: אחר פטירת רב שמואל בשנת
דתקי״א היה לראש בפום בדיתא רב מרי הכהן מנהר פקוד ח׳ שנים
ונפטר בשנת דתקי״ט. ואחריו רב אדא חצי שנה ונפטר באותה שנה.
ואחריו רב יהודאי ג׳ שנים ומחצה ונפטר בשנת דתקכ״ג. והוא חבר
הלכות פסוקות ומהלכות גדולות קבצם. וסגי נהור היה.

ובימיו היה ענן ושאול בנו שר״י. וענן זה מבית דוד היה ותלמיד חכם

ספר הקבלה

היה בתחלה והכירו בו שמץ פסול ומפני כן לא נסמך גאון וגם לא סייעוהו מן השמים להיות ראש גלות. ומפני קנאה וטינא שהיתה בלבו העלה שרטון ועמד להסית ולהדיח את ישראל מעל קבלת החכמים מפי הנביאים עדים כשרים מפי עדים כשרים כמו שסדרנו בספר זה. ונעשה זקן ממרא על פי ב״ד לבלתי שמוע אל השופטים. והוא חבר ספרים והעמיד תלמידים ובדא מלבו חוקים לא טובים ומשפטים לא יחיו בהם. כי אחר חרבן הבית נתדלדלו המינין עד שעמד ענן וחזקם. ואחריו רב אחוני ה׳ שנים ונפטר בשנת דתקכ״ח. ואחריו רב מארי הלוי בר רב משרשיא ג׳ שנים ומחצה ונפטר בשנת דתקל״ב. ואחריו רב ביבי הלוי י׳ שנים ומחצה ונפטר בשנת דתקמ״ג בימי רב מנשה בר יוסף ראש ישיבת מתא מחסיא.

ובימי גאונים אלו שהיו בפום בדיתא היה במתא מחסיא רב דוראי היה לראש בשנת מות רב נטרונאי בשנת דתקכ״א ו׳ שנים ונפטר בשנת דתקכ״ז. ואחריו רב חנינא בר משרשיא ד׳ שנים ונפטר בשנת דתקל״א. ואחריו רב מלכיה ב׳ שנים ונפטר בשנת דתקל״ג. ואחריו רב חינאי בר רב אברהם עד שנת דתקמ״ב והסירו ראש גלות. ואחריו רב הונא הלוי בר רב יצחק. ואחריו רב מנשה בר יוסף עד שנת דתקמ״ח.

31 היה] אמ > | ק פיסול | דר מפני | כן] אפק זה ה כך | ד לגאון מ > (ונוסף בגליון) | וגם לא] פק ולא
32 ל סייעוהו | להיות] ה > | פק קנאה וטינא] הלמר הקנאה טינה א הקנאה והטינא ב טינא ד הטינא מ הקנאה
33 העלה] את העלאתה ב מעלת | ולהדיח] דלר > | מעל קבלת] ב מקבלת | הת חכמים
34 ר נביאי׳ | מפי עדים כשרים] ב > | זה] ה >
35 זקן] ק > | אל] ה את | השופטים] פק הכהנים והשופטים | והוא חבר] ד וחבר |
36 ובדא מלבו] ו בזה בלבו | לאי] ל > (ונוסף בגליון) | ומשפטים־בהם] ת > |
37 חרבן הבית] ד החרבן | דל נדלדלו
38 אפק אחוני] הד אחונאי בלמר אחואני | ונפטר] ת ומת | אב שנת | דתקכ״ח] אלר דתקכ״א ב דתקכ״א ה דתכ״א | מארי] ה מר ד מרי
39 רב משרשיא] פק מר משרשיא | ונפטר] ת ומת | דתקל״ב] ב דתתקל״ב
40 הלוי] פ ~ בר רב משרשיה | ונפטר] מ ומת | פק שנת
41 אפק ראשי | ישיבת] אפקל ישיבות ב > | אפק במתא
42 ובימי גאונים־במתא מחסיא] ב > | (ונוסף בגליון ע״י ב1) | אהדמר בפומבדיתא ל בפומדיתא | היה] הפק היו | דוראי] ב דודאי ד יודאי
43 היה] ר > | נטרונאי] הלמר נטרוי | ונפטר] ת ומת
44 דתקכ״ז] ה דתקכ״א | דתקכ״ז – בשנת (44)] פ > | הדר חנניא
45 מלכיה] מ מלקיה | ד חנינאי
46 רבי1] בד > | דתקמ״ב] ב תקמ״א |

ספר הקבלה

הדור הרביעי מן הגאונים שהיו בפום בדיתא: אחר רב ביבי הלוי היה לראש רב ישעיה הלוי בר אבא ב' שנים ונפטר בשנת דתקנ"ו. ואחריו רב יוסף בר רב שילא י"ט שנה ונפטר בשנת דתקע"ה. ואחריו רב מרדכי הכהן ג' שנים ונפטר בשנת ⟨דתקע"ח⟩. ואחריו רב אחוני ד' שנים ונפטר בשנת דתקפ"ב. ואחריו רב יוסף בר יהודה ב' שנים וחסיד גדול היה ומלומד בנסים. ורב יהודה אבי אביו של רב שרירא היה סופר שלו והעיד שאליהו זכור לטוב היה נראה בישיבת רב יוסף זה כמה פעמים. וב' שנים היתה גדולתו ונפטר בשנת דתקפ"ד. ואחריו רב אברהם בר רב שרירא י"ב שנה ונפטר בשנת דתקצ"ו.

הדור החמישי רב יוסף בר רב חייא היה לראש ישיבה בפום בדיתא ב' שנים ונפטר בשנת דתקפ"ו. ואחריו רב יצחק בר רב חייא ז' שנים ונפטר בשנת דתקצ"ג. ואחריו רב יוסף בר' ב' שנים ונפטר בשנת דתקצ"ה. ואחריו רב פלטוי י"ו שנה ונפטר בשנת דתרי"א. ואחריו רב אחי הכהן ו' חדשים ונפטר בשנת דתרי"א. ואחר פטירת רב אחי נחלקו חצים היו אחר רב מנחם בר רב יוסף בר רב חייא לסמכו והחצי האחר

ספר הקבלה

אחר רב מתתיהו. ועמדו במחלוקת שנה ומחצה. ומת רב מנחם והיה
לראש רב מתתיהו ברבי י' שנה ונפטר בשנת דתרכ"א. ואחריו רבה בר
אמי ב' שנים ומחצה ונפטר בשנת דתרכ"ד. ואחריו היה לראש רב צמח
גאון בר רב פלטוי גאון י"ט שנה ונפטר בשנת דתרל"ג. ואחריו רב
האיי בר רב דוד ז' שנים ומחצה ונפטר בשנת דתרמ"א.

ובימי גאונים אלו שהיו בפום בדיתא הוקם במתא מחסיא אחר רב
אברהם בר רב שרירא שהזכרנו רב הילאי בר רב מארי ט' שנים.
ואחריו רב יעקב בר רב מרדכי י"ח שנה. ואחריו רב איסומאי בר רב
מרדכי ח' שנים. ואחריו רב יצחק בר ישי י"ב שנה. ואחריו רב הילאי
בר רב חניא ג' שנים ומחצה. ואחריו רב קימוי בר רב אשי ג' שנים
ומחצה. ואחריו רב משה הכהן בר' יעקב עשר שנים ומחצה. ואחריו
לא סמכו גאון ב' שנים. ואחר כן סמכו רב כהן צדק גאון בר רב איסומאי
גאון י' שנים ומחצה. ואחריו רב שר שלום בר רב בועז י' שנים.
ואחריו רב נטרונאי גאון בר רב הילאי גאון בר רב מארי ה' שנים. ואחריו
רב עמרם בר ששנא י"ח שנה. והוא שלח סדור תפלות לספרד. ובימי

63 ב אחרי ה > | אק מתתיה | ב ושנה ומחצה עמדו במחלוקת | ועמדו־מתתיהו | מ > |
ועמדו במחלוקת] ק ועמדו המחלוקת | ומחצה] פק וחצי | רב מנחם] ב מנחם דל > | בר ~ בר
רב יוסף ר ~ בר רב מנחם יוסף (!)
64 אבק מתתיה | המד ברבי] פק בר ריבי | ושנה בר' (!) אדל > | י' | ב שש | ונפטר] ת
ומת | דתרכ"א] פ דתרכ"ד ב תרכ"ד (ונתקן ל־"תרכ"א") | ואחריו רבה — דתרכ"ד]
פ > | ואחריו] ה ואחר ב ~ היה לראש | בר] ה בר' |
65 דתרכ"ד] ב תרכ"ה (ונתקן ל־"תרכ"ד) |
66 רב פלטוי] פק פלטי | גאון] פקל > (ובנוסף בגליון ל) | בהפק י"ט שנה] את ט' שנים |
דתרל"ג] פ דתרמ"א | ואחריו רב האיי — דתרמ"א] פדלר > |
67 ונפטר] ק ומת |
68 לר אלה | הדמר בפומבדיתא ל בפומדיתא |
69 בר רב שרירא] ק > | שהזכרנו] מ > | פק ~ ואחריו | רב²] ד רבי | אפק אהילאי | רב
מארי] ב מארי הפ רב מרי |
70 ואחריו¹] ה ואחר | רב יעקב] ב רב יעקב | מרדכי] ב מארי ב¹ מרדכי שנה | ה > | ואחריו²]
ה אחר ד אחריו | אפק אסומאי |
71 ואחריו¹/² | ה ואחר | ישי] ב אישי | ואחריו] אפק אהילאי ב הלאי |
72 בהל חנינא | ג'] ה י"ג | ואחריו רב קימוי — ג' שנים ומחצה] ה > | רב קימוי] אפק מר
ד קימוי | רב אשי] ב מנשה ב¹ רב אשי פק רב אסי |
73 דר ר' משה | בר'] ה בר יעקב | קר בר יעקב | ואחריו לא] ה ואחר לא אפק ולא |
74 ב' שנים ואח"כ סמכו] ה > | ואחרי] פ ואחריו | ואחר כן] מ ואחריו (!) (ובגליון: כן) |
כן] דלר כך |
75 א אסימאי פק אסומאי | ה ואחר |
76 ואחריו¹/² | ה ואחר | ה נטרוני ר נטרואי | פק אהילאי | ה מרי |
77 ששנא] ת רב שישנא | שלח] פ שלש |

ספר הקבלה

רב האיי בר רב דוד היה. ואחריו רב נחשון בר רב צדוק ח' שנים. ואחריו הוקם רב צמח אחיו מן האם בר רב חיים ז' שנים. ואחריו רב מלכיה חדש אחד ונפטר. ואחריו רב הילאי בר רב מישאל ז' שנים. ואחריו רב יעקב י"ג שנה. ואחריו לא היה במתא מחסיא חכם וראוי לסמיכה. אבל דוד בן זכאי ראש גלות לקח אורג אחד ששמו רב יום טוב והקימו.

ואחר כך שלח אל ארץ מצרים והביא משם רב סעדיה אלפיומי והיה לראש ישיבה במתא מחסיא ב' שנים. ואחר כך היתה מריבה גדולה ומחלוקת בינו ובין דוד בן זכאי הנשיא כי ראשי גליות אלו לא היו בעלי אמת והיו קונים נשיאותם מן המלכים כמו מוכסים. והיה לדוד בן זכאי דין ונעשה לו פסק דין כרצונו ולא כהוגן ושלחו לרב סעדיה לקיימו ולא רצה. ושוב פעם שנייה שלחו ביד זכאי בנו כדי לכוף לרב סעדיה ואמר לו: אם לא תקיימהו אכה את ראשך במנעל. מיד זעפו בני הישיבה כלם וקמו כלם כאיש אחד והכו את בן הנשיא במנעליהם הרבה והלך לאביו מבוזה ונכלם. והתחזק אביו במלכות ובכת גדולה מן הקהל. ורב סעדיה בכת אחרת מן הקהל והעמידו את יאשיהו בן זכאי לראש גלות תחת דוד אחיו. ואחר כך נתחזק דוד ונתלה במלכות והסיר את אחיו ובקש להרוג את רב סעדיה. ונחבא רב סעדיה כמו ז' שנים. ובמחבואו חבר כל ספריו. ורב סעדיה משועי יהודה היה מבני

ספר הקבלה

שלה בן יהודה מזרע ר' חנינא בן דוסא. והקים דוד בן זכאי רב יוסף
בר רב יעקב בר רב מרדכי. ואחר כך עשו שלום דוד הנשיא ורב
סעדיה. ואעפ"י כן לא הוסר רב יוסף ולא שב רב סעדיה לגאונות.
ורב יוסף היה גאון י"ד שנה. ואחר כך מת דוד בן זכאי. ואחריו נפטר
רב סעדיה בשנת דתש"ב והוא כבן נ' שנה מן המרה השחורה לאחר
שחבר כמה ספרים טובים ועשה טובות גדולות לישראל. והשיב תשובות
על המינים ועל הכופרים בתורה ואחד מהם חוי אלכלבי בדא מלבו
תורה. והעיד רב סעדיה שהוא ראה מלמדי תינוקות מלמדים אותה
לתינוקות בספרים ובלוחות עד שבא רב סעדיה ונצחם. ויתר דברי
רב סעדיה והטובות אשר עשה לישראל הנם כתובים על ספר הגלוי
ועל אגרת ר' דוסא בנו שכתב לר' חסדאי הנשיא בר' יצחק מ"כ. ואחר
פטירת רב סעדיה היתה ישיבת מתא מחסיא הולכת ודלה עד שברח
רב יוסף למדינת אלבצרה ומת שם.

הדור הששי בפום בדיתא: אחר רב האיי בר רב דוד היה לראש רב
קימוי בר רב אחונאי בשנת דתר"נ ח' שנים ומחצה ונפטר בשנת דתרנ"ט.
ואחריו רב יהודה בר רב שמואל אבי אביו של רב שרירא ונפטר בשנת
דתרע"א. ואחריו הוקם רב מבשר הכהן בר רב קימוי גאון והנשיא

97 בן יהודה] ה ~ היה ~ | זכאי] פ ישי זכאי (!) ב ~ את | פק ר' יוסף |
99 דמר לגאונותו ל לגאוננו |
100 פ והיה רב יוסף | ואחריו] ב ~ ואח"כן |
101 שנה] ה < | המרה] בה המכה (וב' תוקן ל"מרה") | פ השוחורה | לאחר]'ד דלר ואחר |
102 כמה] אה ~ | ועשה] ב ~ כמה ~ לישראל] ב ~ ועשה (!) |
103 מהם] ה בא | ק חוי אלכלבי] א חוי כלבי ב חיני אל בלתי (!) ה' רב קימואל בלג פ חויאל
כלבי ד חמיאל בלכי למר חיויאל בלכי מ חיויאל כלבי | ובדה פ ברא (?) | פ בלבו |
104 והעיד] ב והשיב ב¹ והעיד פק ועדות העיד | שהוא] ב < | ("והוא" נתלה בין השיטין
ע"י ב¹) פק כי הוא | מלמדם] ק מלמד | מלמדי תינוקות] פ < | מלמדים] פק מלמד |
אותה לתינוקות] ת אותם |
105 ה ולוחות | ונצחם] ב < | ל והיתר | דברי] פ דברים |
106 רב] ב < | התשעשה | ב הספר |
107 ת לרב חסדאי | הנשיא] ק < | בר'] ל בר | מ"כ] א מנוחתו כבוד ד מנוחתו בכבוד
למר מש' בכבוד |
108 ב הישיבה במתא |
109 ל מדינות | אלבצרה] פק נצרה | ומת] פק ונפטר |
110 הפדמר בסומבדיתא ל בפומדיתא | האיי] ר היי | רב דוד] פק דוד |
111 קימוי] פק קיומי | אחונאי] א אהינאי ב אחינוי ת אחואני | קמ דתר"נ] א דת"ק ב
דתר"ג פ תר"ג דלר דתרנ"ג | ח'] דלר ה' | ח' – דתרנ"ט] ב < (ונוסף בגליון ע"י ב¹) |
ונפטר] ת ומת | דתרנ"ט] א תתרנ"ט ה דתר"נ (?) |
112 ה ואחר | פק ר' יהודה | ה ר' שרירא |
113 דתרע"א] ב תרע"ה | הוקם | ואחר | ה ואחר | בפק < (ונתלה בין השיטין ע"י ב¹) | קימוי]
אפק קיומי | גאון] ב < (ונתלה בין השיטין ע"י ב¹) | והנשיא] א ודון נשיא |

42

ספר הקבלה

דוד בן זכאי הקים רב כהן צדק בר רב יוסף לפיכך נחלקו. ונפטר רב
מבשר וחזרו כלם לרב כהן צדק בשנת תרצ"ה. והיה לראש רב חנניה
אביו של רב שרירא ה' שנים וחצי ונפטר בשנת תש"א.

הדור השביעי רב אהרן הכהן בן סרגאדה אחר פטירת רב חנניה
והיה סוחר ועשיר גדול ומפני עשרו הוקם ולא מפני שהיה ראוי לכך.
ונפטר בשנת תש"כ. ואחריו רב נחמיה ח' שנים.

ואחריו רב שרירא. והאריך ימים כי כמו ק' שנים היו ימי חייו. וכשראה
שהאריך ימים ובנו רב האיי היה ראוי להיות ראש ישיבה סלק את עצמו
וישב בנו על כסאו. והוא רב האיי גאון בר רב שרירא גאון והוא רבץ
תורה בישראל יתר מכל הגאונים ולאורו הלכו דורשי התורה ממזרח
שמש ועד מבואו. והיו ימי חייו צ"ט שנה ונפטר בערב י"ט האחרון של
פסח שנת אלף שמ"ט לשטרות שהיא שנת דתשצ"ח. וכמוהו לא היה
לפניו בגאונים והוא סוף הגאונים. ומבית דוד היה מזרע המלוכה מבני
זרובבל בן שאלתיאל והנשיאים וראשי גליות שהיו אחריו. וראיתי
חותמו החתום על גליונים שהיה שולח ואריה היה חקוק עליו כמו שהיה

114 הקים] ה הוקם | ולפיכך נחלקו] פק 〉
115 מבשר] ל ~ הכהן | תרצ"ה] ת דתרצ"ה | ב חנינא |
116 וחצי] ת ומחצה | אפק שנת | תש"א] ל דלר דתש"א מ דתש"ה ה ~ אחר פטירת רב חנניה |
117 הדור השביעי — ארבעה (46:7) א 〉 | בן] ב ן' ה בר | בסר סרגאדה] פ סריגאדה ק סרג'ארה (!) ד סרגמרה ל סראדה מ סרגיאדה | אחר — חנניה] ה 〉 |
118 גדול] ה 〉 | ואל] ה לא | מפני שהיה] פק היה ~
119 ונפטר] ת ומת | ה תש"כ] בפק תש"ב ת דתש"ב | ואחריו — ח' שנים] פק 〉 | נחמיה] מ חנניה |
120 שרירא] ק שרידא (וכן להלן) | והאריך ימים] פק 〉 | ימי] בדלר ~ שני | היה] בה 〉 | את] ב נתלה בין השיטין ת 〉 |
121 וישב] ב והושיב את | האיי] ה היי | בר] פ בי | שרירא גאון] בת ~ בר רב חניא | ל חנינא 〉 גאון] בר רב יהודה גאון | והוא] ק 〉 | ד הרביץ |
122 תורה] ב בתורה | בישראל] ב כלה (!) | יתר] פק 〉 ר יותר | מכל] פק על כל | ב והלכו לאורו ה ~ אנשי | התורה] הפ תורה |
123 ה עד | מבואו] ב ~ והוא חבר מקח וממכר | בה וימי חייו היו | צ"ט] דלר ס"ט | בערב] ב בשנת בערב (!) פק ערב | בת אחרון
124 פסח] פ ~ שהיא ק ~ שהוא | שנת] ק 〉 | שמ"ט] ת שנ"ט | ב שהוא | דתשצ"ח] ב תשפ"ח ב' תשצ"ח |
125 והוא] ת ~ היה ~ | דוד] ה יהודה | המלוכה מבני] ק 〉 | בדלר ומבני | ב הגליו' |
126 וראיתי חותמו] ב וחותמו |
127 החתום] ת חתום | על — שולח] ה שהיה שולח על גליונים | ב הגליוני] שהיה| ב שהוא | ואריה] ב אריה ל ~ היה ~ עליו] ק 〉 |

על דגל יהודה ודגלי מלכי יהודה. אבל מימי ישמעאלים לא נהגו ראשי
גליות שררה כהוגן אלא היו קונין אותה בממון הרבה מן המלכים כמו
מוכסים. והיו רועי אליל ולפיכך לא רצו הוריו להיות ראשי גליות
וחזרו לגאונות. והוא מזרע רבה בר אבוה. והלשינו פריצי ישראל ברב
שרירא ורב האיי ותפשם מלך בבל ובזו את כל אשר להם ולא השאיר
להם שום מחיה בעולם. ונתלה רב שרירא בידו אחת והוא כבן ק׳ שנה
ולא הוסרו מגאונות. ובשנת תשכ״ח היה רב שרירא לגאון ובשנת תשנ״ח
היה רב האיי לגאון. וגאונותם היתה ע׳ שנה רב שרירא ל׳ שנה ורב האיי
מ׳ שנה. ודורו דור שמיני בגאונות.

ובימיו היה ראש ישיבה במתא מחסיא חותנו אבי אשתו רב שמואל
הכהן בן חפני. גם הוא חבר ספרים הרבה. ונפטר בימי רב האיי ד׳
שנים קודם פטירת רב האיי. אבל בני ישיבת רב האיי הקימו חזקיה
ראש גלות בן בנו של דוד בן זכאי והושיבוהו על כסא רב האיי ז״ל.
ועמד שנתים והלשינו בו אל המלך מלשינים ותפסו המלך ואסרו בברזל
ובכל מיני עוניים ענהו ולא השאיר לו משתין בקיר. וברחו ב׳ בניו אל
ספרד אל רב יהוסף הלוי הנגיד בר רב שמואל הנגיד שהיה אוהב

129 דגל] ת ~ מחנה | ודגלי] פק ועל דגלי > ק דגל > | מלכי] ב מחנה (ונתקן ל ״מלכי״) |
מימי] ב בימי | ישמעאלים] ב ישמעלי׳ | לא] פ > | ראשי גליות] ה ישראל | פק שררה
ראשי גליות |
130 גליות] ב ישיבות | כהוגן] פק כגון זו | אלא] ה אבל | ל אותו | הרבה] ת רב | מן
המלכים] פק למלכים | ה כמו מוכסים מן המלכים |
131 והיו] ה > | לר רועה | אליל] פ אליאל | ולפיכך] פק ולפיכך] בה לפיכך ת < | ולא |
132 וחזרו] ק והוא חזר | ברב] ב את רב |
133 פק ותפסם | מלך בבל] ד המלך ישמעאל למד המלך | ובזזו] פק ובזזו | את] דלר > | פק
השאירו |
134 להם] ב > | ונתלה] פק ~ זה | שרירא] פ ~ לגאון ובשנת (!) | בידו] ת מידו | בידו
אחת] ה באחת יד | והוא ~ ק׳ שנה] פק ק׳ |
135 פק הוסר | תשכ״ח] ה תשנ״ח ת דתשכ״ח | ה והיה רב האיי לגאון בשנת דתשנ״ח
תשנ״ח | ת דתשנ״ח |
136 היתה] ה היה | שרירא] ק ~ לגאון | ל׳ שנה] ב ל׳ | האיי] ב ~ בנו |
137 ודורו] ב ודור ה ~ היה | ל בגאונים |
138 ב חתנו |
139 ה בר חפני | הרבה] ה > | ה רבי׳ האיי (וכן גם בשו׳ 140) פ ~ גאון |
140 ת מקודם | בני] ה > | ב חזקיהו |
141 פ והושיבהו |
142 בו] פק עליו מלשינים | אל] ל על | מלשינים] הפק > | בהל ותפשו המלך] ה < |
143 ת וענהו > | ד וענה אותו > | בכל מיני עוניים > | ענהו] ה < | השאיר] ב נשאר |
ת לספרד |
144 ה לרב | ל יוסף | הלוי] ה > | הנגיד²] דלר ~ זצ״ל מ ~ ז״ל |

ספר הקבלה

145 לחזקיהו ראש גלות וראש ישיבה והיו עמו עד שהיה השמד בגראנטה.
ונהרג הנגיד וברח האחד מבני חזקיהו לארץ סרקוסטה ונשא שם אשה
והוליד בנים. ואחר כך נכנסו בני בניו לארץ אדום. ומהם היה ר' חייא
בן אלדאודי ונפטר בארץ קשטיליא בשנת דתתקי״ד. ואחריו לא נשאר
בארץ ספרד אדם מפורסם שהוא מבית דוד. ואחר חזקיה ראש ישיבה
150 וראש גלות פסקו ישיבות וגאונים.

145 ק לחזקיה | ישיבה] ישיבה | פק ישיבתו | בהמ והיו] פקדלר והיה | בק בגראנטה] ה בגרנטה פד בגרנאטה לר בגראנטא מ בגנאטה |
146 ונהרג] ת ~ רב יהוסף ⟨ ל יוסף ⟩ | הת הנגיד] ב יהוסף פק זה בעיר | ת חזקיה ה סרקוסטה] בת סרקסטא פק סרקוסטא |
147 כך] ב כן | היה] ד ⟨ |
148 בן] ב ⟨ | אלדאודי] ב ~ ז״ל שתקן מחזור של יום הכפורים נאה וטוב מחוקק בשלשלת על אופן | ד קשטיליא] במ קשטילא הל קשטילא מר קשטילה ת ~ ונקבר בארץ ליאון | דתתקי״ד] ב תתקי״א (! ונתקן ל־תתקי״ד ע״י בג) |
149 בה ואחרי | הפ חזקיהו מ ר' חזקיה |
150 פק גולה |

ספר הקבלה

[ז]

וקודם לכן היתה סבה מאת יי שנזכרת חוקם של ישיבות שהיה הולך אליהם מספרד וארץ המערב ואפריקיא ומצרים וארץ הצבי. וכן היתה הסבה שיצא ממדינת קרטבה שליש ממונה על ציים שמו אבן רמחאץ שלחו מלך ישמעאל בספרד ושמו עבד אלרחמאן אלנאצר. והלך ממונה על ציים אדירים לכבוש ספינות אדום ועיירות הסמוכות לספר. והלכו עד חוף הים של ארץ ישראל ונסבו אל ים יון והאיים שבו ומצאו אניה ובה ארבעה חכמים גדולים היו הולכים ממדינת בארי למדינה נקראת ספסתין. וחכמים אלו להכנסת כלה היו הולכים. וכבש אבן רמחאץ האניה ואסר את החכמים. האחד ר' חושיאל אביו של רבינו חננאל. והאחד ר' משה אביו של ר' חנוך אסרו עם אשתו ועם ר' חנוך בנו ור' חנוך בנו עודנו נער. והשלישי ר' שמריה בר' אלחנן. והרביעי איני יודע שמו. ובקש השליש לכפותה לאשתו של ר' משה ולענותה שהיתה יפת מראה ביותר. והיא צעקה לר' משה אישה בלשון

ספר הקבלה

הקדש ושאלה ממנו אם הנטבעים בים חיים בתחיית המתים אם לא.
והוא השיבה אמר יי מבשן אשיב אשיב ממצולות ים. וכששמעה את
דבריו השליכה עצמה בים וטבעה ומתה. וחכמים אלו לא הגידו לאדם
בעולם מה טיבם ומה חכמתם. והשלישי מכר את ר' שמריה באלסכנדריא
של מצרים ומשם עלה למצרים והיה לראש. ומכר את ר' חושיאל
באפריקיא בחוף הים ומשם עלה למדינת אלקירואן שהיתה בימים
ההם חזקה מכל מדינות ישמעאל שבארץ המערב. ושם היה ר' חושיאל
לראש ושם הוליד את רבינו חננאל בנו.
ובא השלישי לקרטבה ומכר שם ר' משה ור' חנוך שפדאוהו אנשי
קורדובה וכמדומין היו שהוא עם הארץ. והיתה בקורטובה בית הכנסת
ששמה כנסת המדרש. והיה שם דיין ששמו ר' נתן חסיד וגדול היה אבל
לא היו אנשי ספרד בקיאין בדברי רבותינו ז"ל. ואף על פי כן באותו
מעט שהיו יודעין היו עושין מדרש ומפרשים ועולים ויורדין. ופירש ר'
נתן על כל הזאה טבילה והיא במסכת יומא ולא ידע לפרש. ור' משה
יושב לפאה אחת כמו שמש וקם אל ר' נתן ואמר לו: ר' פשו להו
טבילות. וכששמע הוא והתלמידים את דבריו תמהו זה אל זה ושאלו
ממנו לפרש להם ההלכה ופירשה כהוגן. וכל אחד ואחד שאל ממנו

ספר הקבלה

כל ספקות שהיו להם והשיב תשובות ברוב חכמתו. והיו בעלי דינין
מחוץ למדרש שלא היה להם רשות להכנס עד השלמת התלמידים
פסיקתם. ובאותו היום יצא ר' נתן הדיין והלכו אחריו בעלי דינין ואמר
להם: אני איני דיין וזה הלובש השק והאורח הוא רבי ואני תלמידו
אהיה מהיום ואתם מנוהו על קהל קורטובה דיין. וכן עשו. ועשו לו על
הקהל פסיקא גדולה וכבדוהו במלבושים יקרים ובמרכב. ורצה השליש
לחזור בו ממכירתו ולא הניחו המלך כי שמח המלך על הדבר שמחה
גדולה כששמע שאין היהודים שבמלכותו צריכין לאנשי בבל. והקול
נשמע בכל ארץ ספרד וארץ המערב ובאו התלמידים לקרות לפניו.
וכל השאלות שהיו שואלים מן הישיבות ממנו שאלו. ודבר זה בימי
רב שרירא בקרוב לשנת דתש״נ הן פחות הן יתר מעט.

ונתחתן ר' משה הרב לבני פליאג' ומשפחתם היתה גדולה מכל
משפחות קהל קורטובה ולקח מהם אשה לר' חנוך בנו. ובת ר' חנוך
היתה לאחד מבני פליאג'. ומפני כן נקראו בזה השם בבני פליאג' עד
היום.

והיו לו לר' משה תלמידים הרבה ומהם ר' יוסף בר' יצחק בן שטנאש

---

31 ק **כל ספקות**] א ספקותיהם] ה הלכות וספקות פ כל ספקותיהם בת בכל ספקות] ד הספקות] והשיב] > אפק ~ אפק | להם ~ | אפ תשובתם ק תשובה ל תשובת | אפק ברוב] בת כרוחב ה ברוחב

32 ל היו] בהפ להכנס] אקת ליכנס]

33 פסיקתם] ל בסיקתם] הדיין] אד <] והלכו אחריו — גדולה מכל (42) כ״י ק קרוע פה ובמקומו השלמתי עפ״י גירסאות כ״י י

34 דיין] ה יודע] וזה] א אלא זה יף אבל זה] והאורח] אפ והוא אורח רבי] פ ~ ומרי]

35 מהיום] א ~ והלאה יף ~ ואילך] יף הקהל של] בלמר קרטבה] דיין] איפ כי הוא נבון [פ ונבון] וגאון] וכן עשו] פ <] ועשו] אבהמ <] על] ה כל אי] >

36 פ **פסקא**] גדולה] ה >] פ ומרכב

37 בו] אהי ~] אבת במכירתו] הניח] המלך²] פ ~] יפ שמחה גדולה על הדבר]

38 ה שהיהודים שבמלכותו אין צריכין] שבמלכותו] ל >]

39 **וארץ** ~ ואנשי] יף ובאו] איף ויבאו כל] בהדל תלמידים] לקרות] א < מ ללמוד] לפניו] בת <]

40 השאלות] פ שאלות ממנו] פ <] את שאלו ממנו] שאלו] פ שאלות] יף שאלום] בימי] ל כימי]

41 שרירא] ת ~ גאון] ת קרוב] ה משנת] ת דתש״נ] אבהפ דש״נ י דש״ל (?) פ¹ דתש״נ פחות] בת ~ מעט] מ יותר]

42 ונתחתן] פ ונתחזק] א פלאייג פ פליגא מ פליג׳ת] היתה גדולה] פ >] מכל] פק ~ אותן]

43 פ המשפחות ר משפחת] קהל] אפק שהיו בקהל בר < (ובר נתלה בין השיטין) ב קרטובה ק קורדובא ד קורטובה למר קרטבה] הלמר לקח] פ לבנו ר' חנוך] ובת] איף ובתו של]

44 פליאג¹] א פלאייג פקמ פליגא] דלר מפני] כן] אפ זה ק <] נקראו בזה ק] נקראו בזה השם] ה זה השם נקרא] פליאג²] א אבן פלאייג פק אבן פלאג]

46 ה והיה] ומהם] ה ~ היה] קל בר יצחק] בן] ק אבן] פק שנטאש ל שטאנש מ שאטנש

ספר הקבלה

הידוע אבן אביתור. והוא פירש את כל התלמוד בלשון ערבי למלך
ישמעאל אלחכם. ומפני גדולתו וחכמתו בעט בר' חנוך הרב היושב
על כסא אביו. ונחלק הקהל מחלוקת גדולה אחר פטירת ר' חסדאי
הנשיא הגדול בר' יצחק שאלו בימיו אין אדם בעולם שהיה יכול לחלוק
על הרב ר' חנוך. ובכל יום היו יוצאים מקורטובה אל עיר אלזהרה
ז' מאות איש מישראל רוכבים על ז' מאות מרכבות וכלם היו לובשים
לבוש מלכות וחובשים מגבעות כדת שרי ישמעאלים וכלם עם הרב.
וכת שניה עם אבן שטנאש. עד שגברה כת של הרב ונדו את אבן שטנאש
והחרימוהו. והמלך אמר לו אלו היו הישמעאלים בועטים בי כאשר
עשו לך היהודים הייתי בורח מפניהם ואתה ברח לך. והלך מספרד
אל בגאנה ומצא שם ר' שמואל הכהן בר' יאשיהו והוא מבני קהל פאס.
וחש לנדוי הרב ר' חנוך ולא ספר עם אבן שטנאש. וכעס עליו אבן
שטנאש וכתב לו אגרת גדולה בלשון ארמי וטעה בה. ור' שמואל הכהן
השיב לו תשובה והודיעו שטעה אבל בלשון רכה ונחת רוח. ונכנס אבן
שטנאש בספינה והלך עד ישיבת רבינו האיי. וכמדומה היה שרבינו

ספר הקבלה

האיי היה מקבלו ושהיה שונא לר' חנוך מפני שארבעת חכמים שהזכרנו
כרתו חק הישיבות עד שבאו הישיבות לידי דלדול. ואעפ"כ שלח לו
רבינו האיי שלא יבא שאם יבא יחוש לנדוי הרב. והלך אבן שטנאש
לדמשק ומת שם.

וקודם לכן נתדלדלה הכת החולקת על הרב וכל חברי אבן שטנאש.
ומהם שני אחים סוחרים עושי משי יעקב בן ג' ויוסף אחיו. פעם אחת
נכנסו לחצר אחד מסריסי המלך שהיה ממונה על ארץ תאכדנא ובאו
זקני ישמעאלים מן הארץ שהיתה תחת ידו לזעוק על הפקיד שהפקיד
עליהם והביאו לו דורון אלפים זהובים געפריה. וכשהתחילו לדבר
צוה הסריס לבוזתם ולהכותם במקלות ולהוציאם לבית הסהר מבוהלים
ודחופים. ובמוצאי היכלו היו כמה עקמומיות ונפלו באחת מהן האלפים
זהובים וצעקו ואין שומע להם. ולאלתר נכנסו ב' אחים אלו יעקב בן
ג' ויוסף אחיו ומצאו הזהובים והלכו לדרכם. ונתיעצו בחצרם ואמרו:
זה הממון מצאנוהו בהיכל המלך בוא ונשבע שכלו ישוב להיכל המלך
במנחות ומתנות ואולי נסיר מעל נפשנו חרפת צורריגו ונתלה במלך.

ספר הקבלה

ועשו כן. והתחזקו במלאכת המשי ועשו בגדים יקרים ונסים שמעלים
על ראשי הדגלים יקרים לא נעשו כמותם בספרד. והעלו מנחה למלך
השאם ולמלך אלמנצור אבן אבי עמר אומנו עד שאהב המלך אלמנצור
את יעקב בן גו'. וכתב לו גליון שנשאו על כל קהלות ישראל שיש מן
סגלמאסא עד נהר דויירה שהיה קצה מלכותו. ושהוא שופט את כלם
ושהוא רשאי למנות עליהם כל מי שירצה ולקצוב כל מס וכל פרעון
שעליהם. והעמיד לפניו י״ח מסרייסיו לובשי פסים והרכיבוהו במרכבת
המשנה. ונקהלו כל בני קהל קורטובה מנער ועד זקן וכתבו לו הסכמה
בנשיאות וכתוב בה: משול בנו גם אתה גם בנך גם בן בנך. ועמד
בגדולתו. ושלח שליח אל הרב ר' חנוך שאם ידין בין שני אנשים ישים
אותו באניה מבלי משוטים וישליכהו בים.

וכל הקמים על אבן שטנאש שבו אליו וכתבו כלם אגרות לאבן שטנאש
שישוב לקורטובה ויסירו את הרב ר' חנוך וימנוהו לרב עליהם. והוא
השיב להם תשובה קשה ואמר להם על הרב מעיד אני על עצמי שמים
וארץ שאין כמוהו בספרד ראוי לישיבה.

ספר הקבלה

ולקץ שנה אחת לנשיאות אבן גו' אסרו המלך אלמנצור. שהיה כמדומה
לו שישיב לו מנחות גדולות ויקח ממון ישראל מכל הקהלות כהוגן ושלא
כהוגן ויתן לו. ומפני שלא עשה כן אסרו בבית האסורים ועמד שם כמו
שנה עד יום איד של ישמעאלים עבר המלך השאם על בית הסהר
בצאתו מהיכלו אל בית עבודתו. ועמד אבן גו' לפני המלך השאם בפתח
בית הסהר וכשראהו שאל את אומנו אלמנצור על מה עשה לו כן. והוא
השיב מפני שאינו מוביל שי מכל גדולתו. ולאלתר צוה המלך השאם
להוציאו ולהשיבו לגדולה ונעשה לו כן. אבל לא שב כמו שהיה.

ומפני כן ומפני שאבן שטנאש השיב תשובה קשה לקהל קורטובה לא
הוסיף הרב אחרי שוב אבן גו' לגדולתו עד שמת בימי הרב. והרב בחסידותו
עגמה נפשו וקשה לו שמת. כי בליל שבת מת ובא אל הרב אחד מחתניו
בני פליאג' והוא היה כמבשר בעיניו שספר לו שמת יעקב. וגעה הרב
בבכיה עד שתמה אבן פליאג ואמר לו: אני באתי לבשר אותך במות
אויבך ואתה אוהב את שונאך. אמר לו הרב אני מצר על העניים שהיו
רגילין לסמוך על שולחנו מה יעשו למחר. אם אתה מפרנס אותם אני
לא אבכה שהרי איני יכול לפרנסם. שלא היה הרב בעל ממון מפני

92 שנה אחת] ה האחד שנה | אחת] ב אחד | לנשיאות אבן גו'] ר > | ת בן | גו'] ק גי' |
שהיה] ה שיהיה | ה דומה |
93 לו] ת > | פק ~ כשמיניהו | מנחות] ה מתנות | גדולות] ק > | ממון] פק ~ של א ~ מכל
דלר ~ כל | פ כהוגן |
94 אסרו] דלר ~ המלך | ה אסורין פלר האיסורין | שם] ה > |
95 עד] ד ~ יום אחד | איד] ה אידי | של] דק הישמעאלים | השאם] ה תשאם |
96 אל] ל על | אבן] ת בן | גו'] ק גי' | השאם] ה > | ד ~ בבית הסהר | בפתח] פ > |
97 ה אומני |
98 השיב] מ > | מפני שאינו] ק > | אם שאין | מכל גדולתו] פ מגדלתו | השאם] ה תשאם |
99 הדל ולהושיבו | אדם לגדולתו לגדלה ל אל גדולתו ר על גדולתו | שב] פ ישב ל
שהיה (ובגליון: שב) |
100 ד מפני¹ מ ומפני (!) | ומפני²] ל > | ת שבן | ר שטנאש | הל שטאנש פ
שנטאש ק שאנטאס ד שטנאס מ שאנטנש | השיב] ד כתב | תשובה] ק > | קשה] ה > | ד
אק אל קהל פ של קהל | ק קורדובא ד קרטובה למר קרטבה |
101 הרב] פק > | ר' חנוך | פק אחר | שוב] ק > | ת בן | גו'] ק גי' | שמת] פק ~ אבן גו'
< ק גי' > ד ~ בן גו' |
102 וקשה] ת והוקשה | מת] ת ~ בן גו' | אלם מחותניו ר ממחותניו |
103 פק מבני ~ פליאג'] פליאג' | א אבן פלאייג פ פלאג' ק אבן פלאג' מ פליג' ר פליג' פליאג (!)
ה ~ שיספר לו | שספר] ה ד ספר | שספר ~ יעקב] ה > | יעקב] ת ~ בן גו' |
104 ת בן | פליאג'] פק פלאג' מ פליג' | ק והוא אמ' ל ואומר | לו] קת > | ת לבשרך |
105 אוהב את שונאך] ק אוהבו ובוכה על מיתתו | את] מ > | אדל שונאיך | מצר] אפק
עצב ומצר ת ~ ובוכה | על] בת ~ כל |
106 אם] ק ~ אין (!) | ר מפרנסם | פק לא אבכה אני |
107 לם לפרנס אותם | שלא] ת כי לא |

חסידותו שלא היה רוצה ליהנות מכבוד תורה לפיכך היו חייו חיי צער. ונפטר הרב ר' חנוך בשנת דתשע"ה קודם פטירת רבינו האיי ז"ל י"ג שנה. ואעפ"כ לא השיבו מנחה קהלות מערב ומזרח לישיבות מפני שחכמים אלו העמידו תלמידים הרבה ופשט התלמוד בכל הארץ. וכך היה מנהגו של הרב ר' חנוך ז"ל שהיה עולה לסיים את התורה בכל שנה ושנה ביום טוב האחרון של חג והיו עולים עמו גדולי הדור ועיני העדה. ובשנת דתשע"ה עלה כמנהגו ועלו עמו והתיבה היתה ישנה ונשברה ונפלו ונשברה מפרקתו של הרב ומת לימים מועטים לאחר שהעמיד תלמידים הרבה.

ומגדולי תלמידיו היה רב שמואל הלוי הנגיד בר' יוסף הידוע אבן נגרילה מקהל קורטובה היה תלמיד חכם מן המשכילים הגדולים. ועוד היה בקי בספרי הישמעאלים ובלשונם ומאשר כח בהם לעמוד בהיכל המלך. והיה רוכל מפרנס את עצמו בצער עד שהיו ימי חירום בספרד לאחר שנפסקה מלכות בני אבן אבי עמר וגברו סרני פלשתים. ונדלדלה מדינת קורטובה וברחו יושביה. יש מי שברח לסרקוסטה ועוד זרעם שם עד היום. ויש מי שברח לטוליטולה וזרעם ניכר שם עד היום.

ספר הקבלה

ור' שמואל הלוי זה ברח למלאקה והיה יושב בחנות והוא רוכל. והיתה חנותו סמוכה לחצר אבן אלעריף סופר המלך חבוס בן מאכס מלך פלשתים בגראנטה. והיתה שפחת הסופר מפייסת ממנו וכותב ספרים לאדוניה המשנה אבו אל קאס בן אלעריף. והיה רואה ספריו ותמה מחכמתו. ולקץ ימים נשאל משנה זה בן אלעריף ממלכו חבוס לשוב לביתו אל מלאקה ושאל את אנשי ביתו מי היה כותב לכם הספרים הבאים אלי. אמרו לו יהודי אחד סמוך לחצרך מקהל קורטובה הוא כותב לנו. מיד צוה הסופר והריצו אליו ר' שמואל הלוי. ואמר לו אין אתה ראוי לשבת בחנות אל תסור ממני ימין ושמאל. ונעשה סופרו ויועצו והוא היה יועץ המלך. וכל עצתו היתה כאשר ישאל איש בדבר האלהים. והצליח המלך חבוס בעצות שלו והגדיל למעלה. ואחר כך חלה הסופר אבן אלעריף ונטה למות ונכנס המלך חבוס לבקרו. ואמר לו מה אעשה ומי ייעצני במלחמות אשר סבבוני. והוא השיב לו: אני לא יעצתיך מלבי מעולם אלא מלב זה היהודי הסופר

124 ה ורב | הלוי] ק \> | זה] אה \> | פ למלאקה א למאליקה ב למלקא ה למלאקה ק למלקאה ד למליקה ל לקמלה (!) מ למאליקה ר למלקה | והוא] דלר והיה מ והיתה |
125 אבן] ת בן | אלעריף] אל אלעדיף ק עדיף | חבוס] ה חבוש | לר מאכס ה מארסן ה מארכן פ מאסכן ק ? ד מאחס |
126 פל בגראנטה א בגרנטה ה בגרנטא ק ? דר בגראנטה | ממנו] דר בגרנאטה | וכותב] פק והיה כותב לה |
127 לאדוניה – נשאל (128)] ל \> (ונוסף בגליון) | אבו אלקאס בן אלעריף] פק \> | אבו אלקאס] א אבן קאסם ה אבולקאסים | אלעריף] א אלעדיף ה אלעאדיף |
128 מחכמתו] ק מסתריו....(?) | ימים] פ ~ רבים | נשאל] ה שאל דל ~ מלפני | בן] ה אבן | אלעריף] אהפקל אלעדיף | חבוס] ה חבוש |
129 לשוב] אפ \> | פ אל מלאקה] ה למלאקה ק מלאקא אד מאליקה לר למאלקה | את אנשי] אהר לאנשי |
130 אלי] פק ~ מכם |
131 קדל קרטבה ר קרטובה | הוא] אפק ~ היה | אליו | ר'] ק \> | הלוי] ה ~ הנגיד זצ"ל פק ~ זה |
132 ואמר לו] ל ואומר | לשבת] ה \> ר לישב | בחנות] ה לחנות | ושמאל] פ ושמואל (!) אפק ~ וכן עשה |
133 ה והיה הוא | יועץ] אפק ~ אל | המלך] פק ~ בעצת ר' שמואל הלוי ז"ל |
134 האלהים] ת השם | חבוס] ה חבוש | בעצות שלו] ר בעצתו |
135 ואחר כך] ה וכאשר | ת בן | אלעריף] הקל אלעדיף | ונטה] ה \> | ונטה למות] ק \> (ונוסף בגליון) | חבוס] ה חבוש |
136 ואמר] מ אמ' ל ואומר | אשר] ל \> | דר שסכבוני |
136—137 ת והשיב |
137 לו] הל \> | אה לעולם | הסופר שלי] ת \> |

ספר הקבלה

שלי שים עיניך עליו ויהיה לך לאב ולכהן וכל אשר ייעצך עשה והאלי״ם יעזרך.

140 ולאחר מות הסופר לקח המלך חבוס לר׳ שמואל הלוי להיכלו והיה סופר ויועץ. ובשנת דתש״פ היה בהיכל המלך. והיו למלך ב׳ בנים הגדול באדיס ומשנהו בלקין. וכל סרני פלשתים נטו אחרי בלקין הקטן להמליכו ושאר העם אחרי באדיס. וגם היהודים ומהם ר׳ יוסף בן מגש ור׳ יצחק בן ליון ור׳ נחמיה הנקרא אשקאפה מגדולי גרנאטה שלשה
145 אלה היו אחרי בלקין. ור׳ שמואל הלוי היה אחרי באדיס. וביום מות המלך חבוס עמדו סרני פלשתים וגדוליהם בשורה להמליך בנו בלקין. מיד הלך בלקין ונשק יד אחיו הגדול באדיס והמליכו בשנת תשפ״ז. ונהפכו פני אוהביו כשולי קדרה ובעל כרחם המליכו את באדיס. ואחרי כן נתחרט בלקין אחיו והיה מתגבר על אחיו באדיס. ולא היה
150 המלך יכול לעשות שום דבר קטן או גדול אלא אחיו היה מכשילו. אחר כך חלה אחיו ודבר המלך לרופא להניח רפואתו ממנו וכן עשה הרופא.

138 אפק עינך | ת מה שייעצך | עשה] ת כן תעשה |
139 ה והא״לים] אלר והשם ד וה׳ | והאלי״ם יעזרך] פק < | ה יעזרך] א אשר יצרך לא יעזבך ת יהיה בעזרך |
140 הסופר] פק ~ החולה | חבוס] ה חבוש | א ר׳ ת את ר׳ | שמואל] אפק ~ הרב | להיכלו] אפק והביאו אל היכלו |
141 ובשנת] א והיה בשנת פק והוא היה בשנת | דתש״פ] ה תש״ף פ דתשש (ולמעלה ל״ח כתובה ״ע״. פ¹ בין השיטין: תשע״ה) | היה] אפק < | המלך] אפק ~ חבוס | בנים פק ~ שם |
142 באדיס] הפק באדים (וכן בכ״י אלה להלן) | בלקין] 1/2 א באלקיף פק באלקין | נטו] א נסו פק נאספו |
143 ושאר] פ ואשאר ת ~ כל | מגש] פ מאגש ת מיגש |
144 ליאון] ת ליאון | הנקרא אשקאפה] פק < | ה אשקאפה] א איש נאפה דר אשכאפה ל אשכפא | מגדולי – בלקין] ה < | ק גראנטא לר גראנטה | ה | ת שלשה אלה] א ושלשתם פק שלשתם |
145 ת בלקין] א בלאקיף (!) פק באלקין | הלוי] א < | פק זה הרב | היה] אה < | מות] ה מת |
146 חבוס] ה חבוש | בשורה] פק בשחר | בנו] ה את ק < | בלקין] פק באלקין (וכן בשו׳ 147) |
147 מיד הלך] ה והלך | ונשק] ה ~ את | הגדול] פקל < | ד והמליכוהו | אה תשפ״ז] פק תש״פ ת דתשפ״ז |
148 ה לשולי | פק ועל | כרחם] אפק ~ שלא בטובתם | ת לבאדיס |
149 ואחרי כן־באדיס] פ < | אה ואחר כך | בלקין] א באלקיף ק ~ ת ~ שהמליך | אחיו] ק במה שעשה א ~ במה שעשה | ולא היה – ביד באדיס (152)] ה < |
150 דבר] פ נתלה בין השיטין ופ ~ ואחר כך נתחרט במה שעשה והיה מתגבר על אחיו קטן – אלא אחיו] פ < | היה] ק < | א ואחרי ת ואחר |
151 כך] ק כן | אחיו] א אחי המלך פק ~ באלקין | ת וידבר | המלך לרופא] פק < | רפואתו ממנו] א לו ממונו פק לו הכל | וכן עשה הרופא] פק ונעשה כן |

ספר הקבלה

ומת בלקין והממלכה נכונה ביד באדיס. וברחו שלשת היהודים גדולי
העיר שהזכרנו למדינת אשביליה.

ונסמך רב שמואל לנגיד בשנת תשפ״ז. ועשה טובות לישראל בספרד
ובארץ המערב ואפריקיה וארץ מצרים ואיסקליה ועד ישיבת בבל
ועד עיר הקדש. כל בני תורה בארצות האלה היה מהנה מנכסיו. וקנה
ספרים הרבה מכתבי הקדש והמשנה והתלמוד שגם הם מכתבי הקדש.
וכל מי שהיה רוצה להיות תורתו אומנותו בכל ארץ ספרד ובארצות
שהזכרנו הוא היה מוציא עליהם ממונו. וסופרים היו לו כותבים משנה
ותלמוד ונותן במתנה לתלמידים שלא היו יכולין לקנות משלהם בין
בישיבות ספרד בין בארצות שהזכרנו. עם שמן זית שהיה מספיק לבתי
כנסיות שבירושלם בכל שנה ושנה מביתו היה יוצא. ורבץ תורה הרבה
ומת בשיבה טובה זקן לאחר שזכה לד׳ כתרים. כתר תורה וכתר
גדולה וכתר לויה וכתר שם טוב עולה על גביהן ומעשים טובים על
שלשתן. ובשנת דתתט״ו נפטר.

ועמד על כנו ר׳ יהוסף הלוי הנגיד בנו. ומכל מדות טובות שהיו באביו
לא חסר לו אלא אחת שלא היה ענותן כאביו מפני שגדל בעושר ולא

152 אפק רימת] בלקין> א המלך בלאקיף פק באלקין | ל והמלוכה | וברחו] פק והלכו וברחו |
אה שלשה היהודים] ת היהודים השלשה | היהודים] פק <
153 העיר] ק ~ היהודים | שהזכרנו] ת הנזכרים למעלה | א שביליה פ אשבליאה ק
אישביליא ד אשקיליה |
154 שמואל] ת ~ הלוי | ה הנגיד ז״ל | ת דתשפ״ז
155 ב ואפריקיא] את ובאפריקיה ה ואפריקיה פ ואפרקיאה ק ואפריקיאה | וארץ] את ובארץ
א ואסקליה ב וציקיליא פ ואסקליאה ת ובאיסקליה |
156 הקדש] ה המקדש | אק וכל | בת האלו ה אשר באו אליו | ק מנכסיו מהנה |
157 הרבה מכתבי הקדש] פק מכתבי הקדש הרבה | מכתבי] ה מספרי | והמשנה־הקדש²
בל | < | דר שגם הם] א שנכתבו פק שבסתם | שגם הם מכתבי הקדש] ה > |
158 להיות] פק שתהא | תורתו] ק < | בכל ארץ] פק בארץ
159 ל שהוזכרנו | פק אליהם | אפ מממונו | דר והיה לו סופרים ל והיו לו סופרים |
160 במתנה] פ < |
161 פק שזכרנו | פק עם] ה עד את ועוד ק ~ שהיה מספיק | שמן־מספיק | ת [לר הוא] היה
מספיק | ר מספק | שמן זית | ה מספק |
162 שבירושלם] פ שבישרלם (ובגליון: ... שלים) | ושנה־יוצאא] ת | > | ה מביתו היה יוצא | א
היה מוציא מביתו | היה יוצא] פק | ד והרביץ |
163 כתר גדולה־לויה] פק וכתר לויה > ק לוי > וכתר גדולה <פ גדלה>
164 עולה על גביהן] הת | ק שעולה | בהת ומעשים | אפק במעשים | בה על שלשתן | א >
פק על כל אלו ת על גביהם
165 ת ונפטר בשנת דתתט״ו <ל דתנט״ו> | תתט״ו] א תתכ״ז ב ? | נפטר] פ נפתר (ובגליון:
נפטר) |
166 בה רב | ת בנו הנגיד | פ מכל |
167 לו] פק > | אחת] ת > |

ספר הקבלה

נשא עול בנעוריו. וגבה לבו עד להשחית. ויקנאו בו סרני פלשתים עד
שנהרג ביום שבת בט' בטבת שנת תתכ"ז הוא וקהל גרנאטה וכל הבאים
מארצות רחוקות לראות תורתו וגדולתו. ואבלו הלך בכל מדינה
ומדינה ובכל עיר ועיר. ועוד מימי רבותינו הקדמונים שכתבו מגלת
תענית תעניות שגזרו תענית בט' בטבת ולא ידעו על מה הוא. מכאן ידענו שכוונו
ברוח הקדש ליום זה. ולאחר פטירתו נתפזרו ספריו ומחמדיו ופשטו
בכל העולם. וכן תלמידים שהעמיד הם היו רבי ספרד ומנהיגי הדור
אחר פטירתו.

ונחזור להזכיר דברי ארץ אפריקיה. אחר פטירת רב חושיאל נסמכו
במדינת אלקירואן בנו ותלמידו רב חננאל ורב נסים בר' יעקב בן
שאהון שקבלו מר' חושיאל. וקבל רבינו נסים הרבה מרבינו האיי שהיה
אוהבו מאד ושולח לו ספרים בתשובות כל ספיקותיו על יד. ורב
שמואל הנגיד על יד רב נסים היה שותה מימיו של רבינו האיי. והיה
מהנה לרב נסים מנכסיו מאד שלא היה בעל ממון. ולאחר כן נתחתן
בו ושלח בתו לרב יהוסף הנגיד לאשה. ולא מצאה חן בעיניו מפני
שהיתה גנסת. אבל היתה בעלת תורה ויראת שמים. וכשנהרג אישה
הנגיד ברחה למדינת אליסאנה ופרנסוה קהל אליסאנה בכבוד גדול
עד יום מותה.

ספר הקבלה

ורב חננאל עשיר גדול היה שהיו בקירואן סוחרים הרבה מטילים
מלאי לכיסו. והיו לו ט׳ בנות. ועשרת אלפים זהובים הניח אחר מותו.
וכן רב נסים לא היה לו בן. ונפטרו שניהם ופסק התלמוד מארץ
אפריקיה. ונשאר מעט מזער במדינת אלמהדיה בידי בני זוגמאר
ובמדינת קלעה חמאד ביד מר שלמה הדיין בן פרמש אבל לא נסמכו 190
ברבנות ולא יצא טבעם בעולם. ודורם של שלשה אלה רב חננאל
ורב נסים ורב שמואל הלוי הנגיד הוא הדור הראשון ברבנות.

וחזר כח התלמוד בארץ ספרד והיו שם ה׳ רבנים ושמות כלם יצחק.
שנים ספרדים. ושלישי קרוב להם. ושנים באו מארץ אחרת. שנים
הספרדים אלו הן: רב יצחק בר׳ ברוך ורב יצחק בר׳ יהודה. 195

רב יצחק בר׳ ברוך בר׳ יצחק בר׳ יעקב בר׳ ברוך בן אלבאליה
מקהל קורטובה. וקודם לכן מקהל מראדה היו אבותיו. וכשגבר טיטוס
על ירושלם פייס ממנו שלישו שהיו לו על ספרד שישלח לו משועי
ירושלם. ושלח לו מקצתם והיה בהם עושה פרכות ויודע מלאכת משי
ושמו ברוך. ועמדו במראדא והולידו שם. וקהל גדול היו במראדא. 200

---

186 היה] פק > | שהיו] פק > | שהויא (!) ר שהיה | הק בקירואן] א בקיראן פ בקירואן | פ סחרים |
187 ת והניח עשרת אלפים זהובים | מותו] פק פטירתו |
188 פקר רב] אהדל ר׳ | לא] ה > | היה] ה > | היו] ל > | פק ונפסק | ת אפריקיה] ה אפריקיא פק אפריקיאה |
189 מזער] דל מצער | פק אלמהדיאה | ביד] פ > | זוגמאר] א זוג מאד ה זוגמיור פ זוגאמר | ובמדינת] פ ובמנדינת |
190 חמאד] פ חמאר | מר] ד מ״ר | פק בן פרמש הדיין | א פרמאש דר פורמש ל פוראש |
191 אפק ודורותיהם | ה ור׳ נסים |
192 הלוי] אפק > | הנגיד] ה ~ ז״ל | הדור] ק > |
193 כח] ה > | בארץ ספרד] ת בספרד | ת ושמות | א שם ה > | ושמות] ק > | רשמות־שנים] פ > |
194 פק ספרדיים | שנים²] אפק > |
195 ה ספרדים ה הספרדייי׳ | ב״ר¹] דל בר | בר׳ יהודה] הר בר יהודה ק ~ מגאיית ת ~ בן גיאת ‹ל גיאות› |
196 רב יצחק] פק ורב יצחק | בר׳ ברוך¹] ל בר ברוך | בר׳ יצחק־ברוך] ק > | ‹וכנראה נוסף בגליון› | ב״ר יצחק] א רב יצחק ד ור׳ יצחק ל בר יצחק | בר׳ יעקב בר׳ ברוך] ל בר יעקב בר ברוך | ת אלבאליה] אפ אלכאליה ה אלביליא ק אלבליא |
197 מקהל¹ – לכן] פק > | אה קורטובה] ד קרטובה לר קרטבה | את היו אבותיו מקהל מארדה ‹א מריאנה› | הפ מראדה] ק מרידא | אבותיו] פ אבותינו ‹ותוקן ל"אבותיו"› |
198 שהיה] ל שהיו | שהיו לו] ה ~ ממונה | ה לשלח | לו²] אק אליו |
199 ירושלם] ה המלך | אלר והיו | ה ׳עושה בהם (!) | את עושי | אהק פרוכת | אק המשי |
200 פק ועמד | ה במראדא | א במאריכה פ במרדה ק במרידא ת במארדה | והולידו – במראדא] ת > | ק והוליד | שם] א בנים ק ~ בנים | אק היה פ ~ שם | במראדא] א לשם |

ספר הקבלה

ושח לי ר' מאיר בן ביבש שראה גליון של רב סעדיה גאון ז"ל וכתוב
עליו: לקהל קורטובה ואלבירה ואליסאנה ובגאנה וקלסאנה ואשביליה
ומראדה העיר הגדולה וכל ערי ישראל אשר סביבותיה. ומפני מלחמות
חרבה מראדה. וגלו אבותיו של ר' יצחק זה הרב בן אלבאליה ושכנו
בקורטובה והיו מגדולי העיר. ונולד ר' יצחק זה באייר שנת דתשצ"ה 205
והיה אוהב חכמה ודורש תורה מימיו. ובא למדינת קורטובה חכם
גדול מצרפת שמו ר' פרייגורס ועשה לו ר' יצחק זה טובה הרבה וספק
לו כל צרכו ויואל לשבת את האיש ולמד ממנו. ור' שמואל הלוי הנגיד
היה אוהב אותו והוא עודנו נער והיה משגר לו ספרים ומתנות ומצוהו
להשתדל ולקרות. ונפטר ר' שמואל הלוי הנגיד בשנת דתתט"ו. וכתב 210
ר' יצחק זה מחברת עבור וכל סודו לרב יהוסף הלוי הנגיד בנו. ונשא
אותו רב יהוסף הלוי הנגיד בממון והלך אליו לגרנאטה. והיה הולך
ושב לקורטובה מגרנאטה ובגרנאטה היה ביום השמד ונעשה לו נס
ונצל. ואחר כך קנה ספרים הרבה מאד כי עשיר גדול היה ומספרי

201 **ושח**] ק ושלח ת וסח | לי] ק לו | ק ביבאש | גאון ז"ל] ק < ז"ל] ה > | עליו] פ להם |
202 ד קרטובה לר קרטבה | דר ואלקרטבה | א ואלימנייה ה ואוליאסינא פ ואליסאנאה ק ואוליאסנא ל < | פדר ובגאנה] א < ה > ובאגינא ק ובגבזנה (?) ל וברגונה | דר וקלסאנה] א < ה וקלאסינא פ וקאל אסאנה ק וקהל אסאנה ל וקלסנה | א ואשביילייאה פ ואבליא ק ואישביליא (?) |
203 ומראדה] א > ומאדידה ק ומרידה ת ומארדה | ה סביבתיה |
204 מראדה] א מאדידה ק מאד ת מארדה | ר'] ת רב | זה] אה > | בן] ל של | א אלבאליה] ה אלביליא פק אלבליא דר באליה ל במליה | ושכנו] ל ושבט (?) |
205 ד בקרטובה ל קרטובה ר בקרטבה | פל והיה | ר'] ת רב | זה] פ ~ בָּאָרֶץ (!) ק ~ הרב | ק בשנת | דתשצ"ה] א דתשנ"ה |
206 והיה] פ והיא | ק אוהב] ק דורש | חכמה] ת תורה | ודורש] ק ואוהב | תורה] ת חכמה | ק בימיו | ד קרטובה לר קרטבה |
207 אפק ושמו | פרייגורס] א פדי גורס ה פרייגוס פ פרייגוראס | זה] ה > | וספק] פק ופסק |
208 את צרכיו | הלוי] הק > |
209 היה] א ~ ר' שמואל אביו פק ~ אביו | משגר] ה שולח | ומצוהו] ה מצוהו | ומצותו |
210 הלוי] את | ק הנגיד הלוי | דתתט"ו] אה ת תתט"ו |
211 ר'] ת רב | ק זה ה"ר יצחק | לרב] פק לר' | הנגיד בנו] ת בן הנגיד | ונשא אותו] ק וכשראה |
212 הלוי] ל < | הנגיד] ל < | ז"ל] ק ~ ת < | בממון] ל < | גדול] ל ~ אליו] אפק < | אפ לגרנאטה] הקדר לגרנאטה ל לגראטה |
213 א מקורטובה ד מקרטובה לר מקרטבה | פ מגרנאטה] א לגראנטה ה > | ק מגראנטא ת לגראנטה | אר ובגרנאטה] דל ובגראנטה ה ומגראנטה פק | ובגראנטה פ < | והוא היה לגרנאטה] ה > | היה] ק והיה | הפ וביום | הפ נעשה |
214 ונצל] אדל ונצול ר ונוצל | מאד – מאד (215)] ה > | היה] פ > | (ונתלה בין השיטין ע"י פ19) |

ספר הקבלה

הנגיד שנתפזרו בכל הארצות קנה הרבה מאד. והוא חבר ספר גדול
וקרא שמו קופת הרוכלים. ופירש בו מהלכות קשות שבתלמוד הרבה
מאד. אבל לא השלימו ונפטר והוא עודנו לא נשלם. והיה חכם בחכמה
יונית. ובן ל״ד שנה היה כשיצא טבעו בעולם ונסמך ברבנות ובנשיאות
בשנת דתתכ״ט. כי מלך ישמעאל הנקרא אלמעתמד שמו לשר בביתו
ובהיכלו שהיה שומע לו בחכמת אצטגנינות שהיה יודע מוסף על תורתו.
ועמד בגדולתו כמו עשרים שנה ונפטר במדינת גרנאטה בניסן בשנת
דתתנ״ד לאחר שרבץ תורה והעמיד תלמידים ועשה טובות גדולות
לישראל. ונ״ט שנה היו ימי חייו. והוא זקננו אבי אמנו.

ורב יצחק בר' יהודה בן גיאת מגדולי מדינת אליסאנה גם הוא היה
אוהב חכמה ודורש תורה מימיו. והנגידים השנים רב שמואל ורב יהוסף
בנו מכבדים ומנשאים אותו. וכשנגזרה הגזרה על רב יהוסף הנגיד ברח
עזריה בנו לר' יצחק זה הרב. וזכר חסד אבותיו שעשו לו וכבדו ונשאו.
ורצה להקימו לראש על קהל אליסאנה ושאר קהלות ספרד והוא
עודנו נער. אבל אם יי לא יבנה בית שוא עמלו בוניו בו. ונפטר ר' עזריה
הלוי. ונסמך ר' יצחק בר' יהודה ברבנות עד שנת דתתמ״ט. וחלה מאד
והביאוהו עבדיו לקורטובה להתרפא ונפטר שם ביום שבת. והוציאוהו

ספר הקבלה

עבדיו מת מקורטובה וילכו כל הלילה ויאר להם באליסאנה ויקבר
שם עם אבותיו. ומוסף על חכמתו ותורתו היה פייטן גדול ויודע בחכמה
יונית ורבץ תורה הרבה והעמיד תלמידים הרבה.

ומגדולי תלמידיו היה ר' יוסף הדיין בר' יעקב בן סהל חכם גדול
ופייטן גדול וירא שמים נסמך בדיינות במדינת קורטובה בשבט שנת
דתתע״ג ונפטר בניסן שנת דתתפ״ד ושפט את ישראל י״א שנה.

ומתלמידי ר' יצחק בר' ברוך היה ר' ברוך בנו שנזכיר. ור' יוסף
בר' צדוק בן צדיק חכם בן חכם ופייטן וירא שמים. ונסמך בדיינות
קורטובה בסיון שנת דתתצ״ח ונפטר בשנת דתתק״ט ושפט את ישראל
י״א שנה.

והנקרא חבר לר' יצחק בר' ברוך ור' יצחק בר' יהודה וכך היה
מכונה אלחבר ר' יצחק בר' משה הידוע בן סכרי מן קהל דאניה.
פעמים נקרא רב ופעמים נקרא חבר. ולא היה חבר לאלו ולא עצר
כח בימיהם. והלך מדאניה לארץ מזרח ונסמך שם גאון וישב על כסא
רבינו האיי ז״ל. ולפי דרכנו למדנו שלא נשאר שם ושאר לתלמוד בכל
ארץ שנער.

ספר הקבלה

ורביעי רב יצחק בר׳ ראובן אלברגלוני שבא מברגלונא עד מדינת
דאניה. והיא בישובה היתה חזקה בים והיתה בה קהלה קדושה וגדולה
בעושר ומעשים טובים. וכבדו ר׳ יצחק זה ונשאוהו ונתחתן לאבן
לכתוש מגדולי דאניה. וישב שם ושפט את ישראל עד יום מותו.
ופייטן היה וחבר אזהרות וחבר פירוש לפרקים ממסכת כתובות
ופירוש ממסכת עירובין המעידים על חכמתו ותבונתו.

ועוד גדול מכלם רב יצחק בר׳ יעקב בן אלפאסי מקלעה חמאד
ותלמידו של ר׳ נסים בר׳ יעקב ותלמידו של ר׳ חננאל. הלשינו בו
בארצו אלעגאב בן אלכלפא וחיים בנו עד שברח ונכנס בספרד בשנת
דתתמ״ח. וכבדו ונשאו ר׳ יוסף הנשיא בר׳ מאיר בן מהאגיר. ונכנס
למדינת קורטובה ועמד שם מעט. ואחר כך הלך למדינת אליסאנה
ועמד שם עד יום מותו. ונפטר בניסן שנת דתתס״ג והוא כבן צ׳ שנה.
והעמיד תלמידים הרבה ויצא טבעו בכל העולם. וחבר הלכות כמו
תלמוד קטן. ומימות רב האיי לא נמצא כמוהו בחכמה.

ספר הקבלה

ובחמשה אלה הם הדור השני.
ומגדולי תלמידיו של רב יצחק בר׳ יעקב היו רב יוסף בר׳ מאיר הלוי ור׳ ברוך בר רב יצחק. ורב יוסף הלוי בר׳ מאיר אבן מאגש נולד באדר ראשון שנת דתתל״ז. והיה ר׳ מאיר אביו תלמיד חכם ונשוא פנים. ור׳ יוסף הורו הוא היה הבורח ממדינת גרנאטה מלפני המלך באדיס כמו שזכרנו למעלה. והיה עובד עבודת המלך אבן עבאד. ומנערותו של רב יוסף הלוי היה מכיר בו ר׳ יצחק בר׳ ברוך שאדם גדול היה בחכמה. והיה משתדל לר׳ מאיר ללמדו ביום ובלילה שהיו שניהם אוהבים זה את זה כנפשותם ר׳ יצחק בר׳ ברוך ור׳ מאיר הלוי אבן מיגאש. וכשנכנס רב יצחק בן אלפאסי לספרד ונתיישב באליסאנה הלך ר׳ יוסף הלוי אליו ממדינת אשביליא והוא כבן י״ב שנה ועמד לפניו כי״ד שנה לקרוא יומם ולילה והיה לו לרב יצחק בן נבון והגדילו בחכמה וסמכו קודם פטירתו. וכתב לו ספר שאפילו בדורו של משה לא אשתכח כותיה. דאלו בדורו של משה כתיב הבו לכם אנשים חכמים ונבונים וידועים וכתיב בתריה ואקח את ראשי שבטיכם אנשים חכמים וידועים ואלו נבונים לא כתיב בהו והוא חכם ונבון. ולאחר פטירת

ספר הקבלה

רב יצחק ישב רב יוסף הלוי על כסאו מחדש סיון שנת דתתס"ג עד
אייר שנת דתתק"א ל"ח שנה. ובכלם היתה תורתו אומנותו וטבעו יוצא
מספרד עד מצרים ועד בבל ובכל הארצות. ומוסף על חכמתו הגדולה
היו מדותיו מעידות בו שהוא מזרע משה רבינו ע"ה שהיה ענו מכל
האדם. ונתן לו הקב"ה רוחב לב ועובר על מדותיו ועובר על פשע.
הקב"ה יגמלהו כל הטובה שעשה לישראל.

ורב ברוך בן רב יצחק בן אלבאליה גם הוא נולד באדר ראשון שנת
דתתל"ז ששניהם בשבת אחד נולדו. וקבל מאביו רב יצחק. וקודם
פטירת רב יצחק אביו היתה מחלוקת בינו ובין רב יצחק אלפאסי.
וכן היתה מחלוקת גדולה בין רב יצחק בר' יהודה אבן גיאת ובין ר'
יצחק אלפאסי. וכשנפטר ר' יצחק בר' ברוך ר' ברוך בנו היה כבן י"ז
שנה. והוא סח לי שבשעת פטירת אביו קרא אותו ולחש באזנו שלא היה
יכול לדבר דברים נשמעים ואמר לו: לך לרב יצחק אלפאסי ואמור
לו שהריני יוצא מן העולם הזה ונכנס לעולם הבא. והרי אני מחלתי

---

278 יצחק] ה ~ אלפסי ז"ל פ ~ אלפאסי | הלוי] ה ~ ן' מיגאש פ ~ אבן מאגש | מחדש
סיון] ת מסיוון אה ~ של | ת דתתס"ג] אפק תתס"ג | דתתס"ג – אייר שנת] ה < |
279 דתתק"א] ה ד' אלפים תשע מאות פ תתקל"א | ל"ח] ה ל"א | היתה] ת < | ל אומנתו |
אהק יוצא] ת יצא פ עד אייר (!) |
280 עד] פ ועד | ועד בבל] ת | ובבבל] ד וכל |
281 שהיה] פ שהיאה (!) | שהיה ענו] ת שענו מאד היה |
282 ר אדם | פק הב"ה | רוחב] פ רחבת | ועובר על מדותיו] את < | על¹] ק ~ כל |
ועובר²] ת והיה עובר |
283 ה הב"ה ק והב"ה | יגמלהו – לישראל] ק גמלהו | ימחול עוונתיו] פק כל] א על ת
ככל | פלד שעשה] אקד אשר עשה | לישראל] ד ~ אמן |
284 ורב] קור' | בן¹] את בר | רב] ק ~ לר אלבאליה] פ אלביליא ה אלביליאה ק אלבליא
ד אלכאליה | ת נולד גם הוא | ר הראשון | פ בשנת |
285 בשבת] ד בשנה ר בשנת (?) | אהק אחד] פת אחת | הפ מרב יצחק אביו |
286 אפק אביו רב יצחק | הפ מחלוקת ה ~ גדולה | רב יצחק²] ה הרב ר' יצחק לר ~ בן
הק אלפסי
287 וכן] הפ וכך | הפ מחלקת | בר'] אקד בר לר בן | הק אבן] אפת בן | גיאת] ק גאיית
ר'] את רב הפ הרב ר' |
288 יצחק] את ~ בן ~ | הק אלפסי הפ ~ ז"ל ~ ר' יצחק²] את רב יצחק | בר'] דל בר
ברוך] פק ~ בנו ~ | ה ר' ברוך בנו היה] א היה רב ברוך בנו פ ר' ברוך היה ק היה ת
היה רב ברוך | כבן] ק בן
289 סח] ה דבר פ שח | לי] ה < | שבשעת] ד שבעת | א פטירתו' (!) הפ פטירתו |
ת קראו | ולחש] הפ ~ לו | פק לאזנר |
290 יכול] פ < | ל דברי | לו] ק לי | אפק לר' | יצחק] ת ~ בן | פלד אלפאסי] אבהק
אלפסי ד אלפיסי
291 הק שהריני] אר שאני ב כי אני פ שחירצי (!) ד שהרי אני ל אני | מהעולם] והרי
אני] בת וכבר |

לו כל דברים קשים שדבר לי בין בכתב בין בעל פה. וכן אני מפייס
ממנו שיעשה כך. ועמוד לפניו. ויודע אני שיעשה לך טובה הרבה וילמד
אותך בכל לבו. ואחר שקברתי את אבא מרי הלכתי אליו לאליסאנה
295 ודברתי לו כל דבריו אשר שלחני. ובכה רב יצחק בן אלפאסי
והגדיל בכיה וחזר לנחמני ולדבר על לבי ואמר לי: אם מת אביך
ז"ל אני אהיה לך לאב ואתה תהיה לי לבן. ועמדתי בביתו עד שקראתי
לפניו כל התלמוד. וכשמת רב יצחק בן אלפאסי ז"ל טבעם של זוג
אלו של רב יוסף הלוי ורב ברוך בר רב יצחק היה פושט ויוצא בכל
300 הארץ. והיה רב ברוך זה יודע בחכמה יונית מוסף על תורתו וחכמתו
והעמיד תלמידים הרבה ואני קטן שבכלם. ונפטר בסוף אלול שנת
דתתפ"ו. והאריך ימים אחריו רב יוסף הלוי ז"ל כמו ט"ו שנה ואין לו
שני בדורו ודורו הוא הדור השלישי.

ולאחר פטירת רב יוסף הלוי ז"ל שמם העולם מן הישיבות של חכמה
305 ודורו הוא הדור השלישי ברבנות. ואע"פ שר' מאיר בנו ור' מאיר בן
אחיו הם תלמידיו ובעלי קבלתו והם חכמים גדולים אבל מפני הרעה
נאסף הצדיק. ואחר פטירת רב יוסף היו שני חירום וגזרות ושמדות על
ישראל ויצאו בגלות ממקומותם אשר למות למות ואשר לחרב לחרב

292 לו] בת ~ על | דברים] ל דברי | קשים שדבר לי] ה שדבר בי קשים | ד בכתבים |
ד על פה ל בבעל פה |
293 כך] ק כן ת ~ | וילמד ⟨ ד וילמוד | אותך ⟩ ק כי יודע | הרבה | ד ~ מאד |אד וילמוד |
294 בל קברו דר קברי | ב אביו ל אביו אבא (!) | מרי] ה מיד ל מורי | אליו] ת ⟨ | הפלר
לאליסאנה] א לאלייסנה ב לאליוסאנה ל לאוליסנא ק לאליסנה ד לאליסנה |
295 אשר שלחני] ת שציוני | רב] ד ר' | בן] אהל ⟨ | לר אלפאסי] אהקד אלפסי פ ⟨ |
296 ת בבכי | ולדבר] ק ודבר |
297 ז"ל] אהפ ⟨ | ה לאב לך | לבן] ה ~ ואמ' לי אתה תהיה על ביתי | שקראתי] ת שלמדתי |
298 התלמוד] פק ~ כלו | ה הרב | בן] ה ⟨ | אהק אלפסי | אפ זצ"ל | זוג] ק הפד ⟨ |
299 אלו] אפק זה | הפק של] את ⟨ | ק ור' ברוך | בר רב] ד בר ר בר' | יצחק] ק ~ בן
גאיית | ל ריצא
300 אפק בחכמה] ה בכל חכמה דל חכמה ר חכמת |
301 הרבה] ל ⟨ | פ קטון דר הקטן ל הקטון | אפק והוא נפטר |
302 דתתפ"ו] א דתתס"ר ב תשצ"ג ל תשע"ו (! ובגליון: תתער") ק דתתקכ"ט | בה יהוסף | אקד ז"ל |
בפ ⟨ ה אבן מיגאש לר זצ"ל |
303 בדורו] את בכל העולם | השלישי] קת ~ ברבנות |
304 רב] ה ⟨ | אפלר זצ"ל |
305 ודורו – ברבנות] ת ⟨ |
306 הם] א ~ היו ה היו |
307 פ פטירתו | ה יהוסף ד ~ הלוי ז"ל | שני] ל ⟨ | ה שנים | חירום] אה ⟩ | פק וגזרות] א
גזירות גדולות ה גזרות ת ⟨ | פ שמדות |
308 ה ממקומותיהם ק במקומותם | למות] ק ⟩ | לחרב¹ – לשבי²] פ ואשר לשבי לשבי
ואשר לחרב לחרב ואשר לרעב לרעב ק ואשר לשבי לשבי ואשר לחרב ואשר לרעב |

ואשר לרעב לרעב ואשר לשבי לשבי. ועוד נוסף על נבואת ירמיה
ואשר לצאת מן הכלל מפני חרב אבן תומרת שיצא לעולם בשנת תתע״ג. 310
שגזר להוציא ישראל מן הכלל ואמר לכו ונכחידם מגוי ולא יזכר שם
ישראל עוד. וכן לא השאיר להם בכל מלכותו שם ושאר ממדינת שלב
בקצה העולם עד מדינת אלמהדיה. ומפני כן לא יכלו בניו של רב
יוסף להושיב ישיבות אלא גלו בראש גולים למדינת טוליטולה. והם
משתדלים להעמיד תלמידים כפי יכלתם והקב״ה הסכים על ידם 315
והם סוף חכמי התלמוד בזמן הזה.

ושמענו שיש בארץ צרפת חכמים גדולים וגאונים וכל אחד ואחד רב
ממלא מקום התורה להנחילה. והנחילוה על מה שנא׳ להנחיל אוהבי
יש ואוצרותיהם אמלא. כל אחד ואחד היה במקומו הרב הגאון ר׳ משה
בר׳ יוסף ז״ל והרב הגאון ר׳ אברהם בר׳ יצחק ז״ל והרב הגאון ר׳ 320
מאיר בר׳ יוסף ז״ל בנרבונה שהאירו את התורה בחומש במקרא
במשנה בתלמוד בירושלמי על לומדיהם. ואחר במדינת רומרו שמו
ר׳ יעקב. הקב״ה ישמור על לומדיהם ונוחליהם ויחיים ויזכם ללמוד
וללמד ולהרביץ תורה בישראל.

309 את מוסף | נבואת] פ גזרת ונבואת | אפר ירמיהו |
310 ואשר] ה \ | הכלל] לר ~ לצאת מן הכלל | ומפני] ל ומפני | מפני — תומרת] ה מרוב הצרות |
ת בן | לר תומרות| א תומרות פ הזמרת ק הזמרת הממזרת (!) | ד תמורת | ה תמורת | פ תתע״ג |
א תתע״ב ד ד׳ אלפים שמונה מאות ושבעים ושלש ק תתפ״ג דל דתתק״ב ר דתתקנ״ב |
311 שגזר — הכלל] ה \ | אפק שגזר] ד גזר לר עזר | להוציא — הכלל] ק על ישראל שיצאו
מן הכלל | הק ואמרו | ולא יזכר — עוד] ה \ פ וגו׳ |
312 ישראל] ל \ | ק מלכות | ד במדינות ל ממדינות | שלב] ה צלא
313 בקצה] ה שהוא בסוף ק מקצה | עד] ל אל | את אלמהדיה] ה אלמריאה פק אלמהדיאה |
314 אפק טוליטולה] הלר טליטלה ד טוליטלה | והם] ת ויהיו |
315 תלמידים] ק ישיבות | תלמידים — יכלתם] הפ הפ כפי יכלתם תלמידים | יכלתם] ת כחם
הק והב״ה | ה מסכים פ יסכים |
316 ל תלמוד | דר בזה הזמן | הזה. ושמענו] ק אשר שמענו |
317 אפ שישי] ה \ ק ריש | שיש — צרפת] ת שבארץ צרפת היה | חכמים — לאחר (322)] ת
חכם גדול ורב מובהק | גדולים] ה \ | ואחד] ה \ | רב] ה \ |
318 להנחילה — שנא׳] ה \ | ק אוהביו |
319 ואחד] ה מהם | הרב] ק ~ הגדול | הרב הגאון] ה רב וגאון |
320 ז״ל] פ זצ״ל | ז״ל²] ה \ | הגאון] ק ~ הגדול |
321 בר׳] ק בר | בנרבונה] פ בנרבוה (!) | את] ק \ |
322 ה ירושלמי | לומדיהם] ד שמריהם (?) ק ~ ונוחליהם] פ רומרו] ה רומנו ק רומדו ת
דומרוג | שמו] ק \ |
323 ק הב״ה דל השם | ישמור — ונוחליהם] ת ישמרהו | על] ק ידיו | לומדיהם] פ ~ ואחר
במדינת | ונחליהם] ה \ | ת ויחייהו ויזכהו | ללמוד־בישראל] ה לחיי עד אמן |
324 ולהרביץ] לר ולרבוץ | פד בישראל | ק ברבים לר \ | פק ~ למען יהיו שפתותיהם [ק
של אלו הגאונים] דובבות בקברים לקיים מה שנ׳ דובב שפתי <פ שפתו (!) \> ישנים |

הרי אלו עשרה דורות מן הנביאים חגי זכריה ומלאכי עד ריב"ז וה' 325
דורות של תנאים וז' דורות של אמוראין הרי אלו כ"ב דורות עד סוף
האמוראין. ורבנן סבוראי ה' דורות וח' בגאונות וג' דורות ברבנות
דורו של רב נסים ורב חננאל ורב שמואל הנגיד. ודורן של ה' רבנים
ושמם יצחק ודורו של רב יוסף הלוי ורב ברוך בן רב יצחק. הרי אלו
י"ו דורות מחתימת התלמוד עד פטירת רב יוסף הלוי ז"ל. סך הכל 330
ל"ח דורות מחגי זכריה ומלאכי עד רב יוסף הלוי ז"ל. כלם עדים
נאמנים מפי עדים נאמנים. לא נפסקה הקבלה ושלשלת הקדושה שלהם.
ואלו במינין אי אתה מוצא כן. שהרי ענן הרשע ושאל בנו שר"י תלמידיו
של רב יהודאי היו וחלקו עליו ועל קבלתו בלא שום טענה בעולם אלא
מפני קנאה שהיה להם. ואינם יכולים לומר כך מקובלים אנו מפי פלוני 335
ופלוני מן הנביאים אלא שהם בודים מלבם.

ועוד שהם בטלים במיעוטם. שאתה מוצא קהלות ישראל שהיו
פושטות ממדינת סלא בקצה המערב אל תאהרת בראש המערב וקצה
אפריקיה ומצרים וארץ הצבי וארץ ערב וארץ שנער וארץ עילם וארץ
פרס וארץ דדן וארץ הגרגשי ונקראת גרגאן וטברסטאן וואלדילאס 340

325 אלו] ת < | ה מהנביאי' | אר מלאכי |
326 דורות2] ד < | של[2] פ | הרי אלו–האמוראין] ה < | דורות3] ר דור |
327 ק אמוראים | וח'] ת ~ דורות | דל בגאונים ר בגיאני' | דורות2] ה < |
328 דורו של רב נסים — ורב ברוך בן רב יצחק] הפ < (329) | ורב חננאל] א ושל ר"ב (!) חננאל ת ורבינו חננאל | ורב חננאל–הנגיד] ק ורב שמואל הנגיד ורב חננאל | קר ודורן] א ודורות דל ודורו |
329 ושמם[ם] א כלם דל שמות כלם ר ששם כלם | יצחק1] א רבינו יצחק ת רב יצחק ר ודורם | ודורו של רב] א ורב | ברוך] ל < | בן רב] דל בר רב ר בר' |
330 פ י"ו] אקדר י"ד הל י"ג | עד] ל < | אחר] ז"ל| אפ זצ"ל ה < |
331 ל"ח] ד ל"ו | ז"ל] אפ זצ"ל ה < |
332 ד פסקה | ת שלשלת | הקדושה] הקדולה | ה הגדולה | הקדושה — בנו שר"י] ל < | הפ שלהם] א שבהם ק < ת שלה |
333 במנינין] ה במגין | דל אין | ענן] ק עכן | פ שאול | שר"י] אה ~ פ י"ש |
334 רב] ה < | יהודאי] ד ~ זצוק"ל לר זצק"ל | אלא] ק ק |
335 ק הקנאה | שהיה להם] א שהיתה בהם ת < | את אנו מקובלים | ה אנחנו |
336 ופלוני] קדל ומפי פלוני | מן] א ומן ת ומפי | שהם בודים] ת < | מלבם] א ~ נשמתם בגיהנם ישחקו עצמותים ק ~ נשמתם ישחקו עצמותיהם לאבדון |
337 במיעוטם] ת < | ישראל] הפ הקדש |
338 הת סלא] א צלא פ סליא ק טיליא | אל] ת עד | תאהרת] א תאהרת ה תהרת ק תהרת |
339 את אפריקיה] הק אפריקא פ אפריקאה ת ~ וכל ארץ אפריקיה | וארץ ערב] א < ה ומערב (!) | אפק וארץ שנער] ה ~ ת ושנער | וארץ עילם | וארץ עילם] ת ועילם |
340 ה ונקרא ק שנקראת | ת גרגאון | ה ג'ירגראץ אק < | פ גארן | וטברסטאן] א טרבטסטא ה וטברסאלן (!) פ וטבר?סתארון ק גארגושתאן | ואלדילאס] א ואלדלה ה ואלדיאלם פ ואלדילס דר ואלדילאן ל ואל דיאן |

ספר הקבלה

עד נהר אתל. שהיו שם גוי כוזרים שנתגיירו ויוסף מלכם שלח ספר
לר' חסדאי הנשיא בר' יצחק בן שפרוט והודיעו שעל דעת רבנות
משתדל הוא ועמו. וראינו בטוליטולה מבני בניהם תלמידי חכמים
והודיעונו ששאלתם על דעת רבנות. וכן בכל האיים שבים יון מארץ
345 נבקרי וגנגת עד קסטנטינה ורומי הגדולה וכל ארץ אשכנז ותוגרמה
וצרפת וכל ארץ פוליא ומגינסיא ואיסקיליאה וארץ לונברדיאה עד
נהר דוראנו עד ארץ ספרד בקצה המערב. כלם המקום ישיב שבותם
ויקבץ גליותיהם שהם על דעת חכמי המשנה והתלמוד. חוץ ממדינה
אחת במערב במדבר שמה ורגלאן ומעט מהם במצרים ומעט מהם
350 בארץ הצבי.

וכשהיו ישראל חוגגים חג הסוכות בהר הזתים היו חונים בהר מחנות
מחנות אוהבים אלו את אלו ומברכין אלו את אלו. והמינין חונים כנגדם
כב' חשיפי עזים. והרבנין היו מוציאין ספר תורה ומחרימים שמות המינים
בפניהם והם שותקים כמו כלבים אלמים.

341 **אתל**] אפק ה טילי ת אובל (גליון ל: ס״א אֹהֵל (!)) | פ גוי] ה גירי ק הרבה ת גוים | ת כזריים | **ויוסף**] ה ~ בן אהרן הכזרי ל ואסף |
342 **לר'**] ת לרב | **חסדאי**] ה ~ בן יצחק | **את בר'**] ה על יד פק ור' | ק **והודיעו**] שעל־הוא] ת (ל שהוא) על דעת רבנות |
343 **הוא**] ל והוא | **וכל עמו**—**רבנות** (314)] ר < | אק בטוליטולה] הדל בטלטלה פ בטוליטליה | מבני בניהם] ה מבניהם | **בניהם**] ק בניו |
344 ה **והודיעו** | אה ששאלנו | **ששאלתם**] פ שאלתם ק < | ד ששאריתם ל אשר שאריתם | **על דעת רבנות**] ה < | **בכל**] ק כל | שבים] ל שבין | שבים יון] א שביסמן פ שביסיון | יון] ק < | ק מן ארץ |
345 פ **נבקרי**] א נבקר ה נבקארי ק נבקארי ת נבקדי | **וגגנת**] ת וגננת] א גיא גאות ה ג'א ג'ואנת פ וגנאבת ק וגנאת | ת קסטנטינה | א קונסטטינה ה קסטוטינה פ קרטוסיאה (?) ק **ארץ קושטנטינה** | ה ורומה | **ותוגרמה**] אפ ותורגמה |
346 פק וצרפתה | **וכל ארץ**] ת וארץ | א פולייאה ה פוליאה הק ומגינסיא | פ ומג'נסיא ה ומננסיא | ק ואיסקיליאה] ה ואי סקליא פ ואסקילאה ת וארץ סקליא | **אהל לונברדיאה**] פק לומברדיאה ד לונברדיא ר לוברדיא |
347 **הפק דוראנו**] אדר רודנו ל רודונו | **המקום**] ק < |
348 **ויקבץ**] פ < | **ויקבץ גליותיהם**] ה < | ל משנה ותלמוד |
349 **במדבר**] אפ ~ | ק שמה במדבר | **ורגלאן**] ה ונבלאץ | **ומעט²**] ת ~ | **היה**] ל מהם² | ק ~ היה |
351 **חוגגים**] אקר ~ | **את** ~ את |
352 **אלו¹/³**] ק נתלה בין השיטין | **את נגדם** |
353 **כב'**] ה בשני ר כבני | **עזים־שותקים**] ל < (ונוסף בגליון) | ת **והיו הרבנים** | פ ספרי |
354 **בפניהם**] ה < | **אלמים**] קת ~ | לא יוכלו לנבוח |

ומאלה שהיו בארץ הצבי היה אלשיך אבו אלפראג עצמותיו בגיהנם. 355
והלך לשם כסיל אחד מקשטילה סיד אבו אלטראס וראה את הרשע
אלשיך אבו אלפראג. והוא הסיתו והדיחו וכתב זה אבו אלאטראס
ספר מן אלשיך אבו אלפראג הוא הספר המסית והמדיח והכניסו
לקשטילה והטעה הרבה מהם. ומת אבו אלטראס לגיהנם ונשארה אשתו
הארורה והיו קורין אותה אלמעלמה וסומכין עליה בקבלתן והיו 360
שואלין זה לזה איך היתה עושה אלמעלמה ועושין כמוה. עד שנתחזק
ר' יוסף הנשיא בן פרולבצל הנקרא מבצירל והשפילם מוסף על
שפלותם. ויגרש אותם מכל מבצרי קשטילה חוץ ממבצר אחד קטן
שנתן להם מפני שלא רצה להרגם. שאין דנין דיני נפשות בזמן הזה.
ואחר פטירתו העלתה טינתם של מינים שרטון. עד שמלך המלך דון 365
אלפונשו בן ריימונד מלך מלכים הוא האנפרדור. והיו בממשלתו נשיאים
ממלאים מקום אבותם והשפילום. וזה הדבר אשר השפיל את המינים בארץ

ספר הקבלה

קשטילא. כי זה המלך דון אלפונשו בן רימונד מלך מלכים היה ומלך צדק היה וגברה ידו על כל הישמעאלים הנמצאים בארץ ספרד וישימם למס עובד. ועצמה מלכותו ויי הניח לו מכל אויביו מסביב. והימים אשר מלך על אדום ל"ח שנה. ולפי שחזקה הממלכה בידו לקח מיד הישמעאלים גבע רבה אשר על אם הדרך מארץ ישמעאל לארץ אדום. והמורדים במלכות פלשתים עברו מעבר לים אל ארץ ספרד אחר אשר לא השאירו פליטה לישראל מן טנגאה עד אלמהדיה. השב ידך כבוצר על סלסלות. ובקשו לעשות כן בכל מדינות מלכות ישמעאל בארץ ספרד לולי יי שהיה לנו יאמר נא ישראל. כי שמעו קול היהודים שבאו עליהם המורדים להדיחם מעל יי אלהי ישראל הירא את דבר יי נס על נפשו וכמעט לא הפנו אבות על בנים מרפיון ידים. יש נכבשים בידי אדום ונמכרים להם להניסם מארץ ישמעאל. ויש מהם נסים רגלים ערומים ויחפים התגנפו רגליהם על הרי נשף. ועוללים שאלו לחם פורש אין להם.

אבל המקדים רפואה למכה יתעלה שמו שכן כתי' כרפאי לישראל ונגלה עון אפרים והקדים ונתן בלב המלך אלפונשו האנפרדור להפקיד

368 ה קשטילא] פ קשטיליא ק קאשטילא ד בקשטיליאה ל בקשטילא ר בקשתילה | ק דון אלפונשו] ה דון אנפוש פ דונפוש ד אל ריאלפונש לר אל ריפונש | פלר רימונד] ה דיימרונאד ק דיימונד ד ריימונדו ד רימרנדו | הקד ומלך] פלר ומלכי |
369 צדק] אק אם צדיק | היה] ה ~ | וגברה] דר וכבדה ד וכבדה אק ~ וכבדה | כל] > את | ספרד] ה ~ ואחר (!) שלא השאירו פלטה לישראל מן טנגאה עד אלו (!) | פ וישמם ת רשמם כל |
370 ק והניח לו יי ת והניח יי לו | מכל אויביו] ר מעבריו (!) | אויביו] קל עבדיו ד עבריו | מסביב] ל מסביר |
371 ל"ח] ד מ"ח | ולפי] ת וכי | קת חזקה | ת המלוכה | אק בידו] הפ > ת על ידו |
372 רבה] א רבע ת רבה | אק ישמעאלים |
373 במלכות] ת בארץ | את אחרי |
374 הפ שלא | ת פליט | ה מן טנגאה] א מן טרטאנה פק מן סאנגגה ת מתנגגה | פ ועד ת אלמהריה] ה אלמהריאה פק אלמהדיאה | ידך] ה ידם פ ידים |
375 ובקשו] ה ~ בן (!) | מלכות] ק > |
376 יי] ר הש' | יאמר נא ישראל] אהפ > | שמעו] א כשמוע ק שמע ד כאשר שמעו לר כששמעו | קול] > את |
377 ת כי באו | דבר] ד > |
378 על[2] פד אל | יש] את ~ מהם |
379 בידי] אה את בארץ | הפ רגלים] אק > ת רוגלים |
380 הפ יחפים | רגליהם] ל > |
382 ת מקדים | יתעלה] ה הק יתברך | שמו] א ~ ויתעלה מלכותו פק ~ וית' זכרו ומלכותו ד ~ אמן | את כתוב | ר ברפאי |
383 אפרים] ק ~ | וכו'] ~ | את הקדים | ק אלפונשו] א אנפוש ה דון אנפוש פ אל דונפוש ד ריאלפונסו לר אל ריפונש | האנפרדור] פ האנפראדור | א האינפרדור ה האנפיראדור ק האינפיראדור ת | >

ספר הקבלה

על גבע רבה על כל מנת המלך מרנא ורבנא רב יהודה הנשיא בן עזרא.
היו אבותיו מגדולי גראנטה ויורשי עצר ומשרה בכל דור ודור במלכות
באדיס בן חבוס מלך פלשתים ומלכות המלך חבוס אביו. ומסורת בידי
קהל גרנאטה שהם מיושבי ירושלם עיר הקדש מבני יהודה ובנימין
ולא מן הכפרים וערי הפרזי. אבל ר' יהודה הנשיא זה ואביו ודודיו
ארבעה שרים ר' יצחק הגדול ומשנהו ר' משה והשלישי ר' יהודה
והרביעי ר' יוסף כלם מדותיהם מעידות עליהם שהם מזרע המלוכה ומן
הפרתמים. וכאשר הופקד הנשיא הגדול ר' יהודה זה על גבע רבה
עיר מקלט הגולה על ידו עברה הגולה והוא הוציא אסירים בכושרות
ושלח רצוצים חפשים ושבר עול ונתק מוסרות. ובביתו ועל שלחנו
מצאו בני הגולה מנוח והשביע רעבים והשקה צמאים והלביש ערומים.
ונהגם בבהמות לכל כושל עד אשר הגיעו למדינת טוליטולה בכבוד
מפני מוראו וכבודו שהיה על אדום המביאים אותם. ועודנו בחור היה
מורם מעם וגער חית קנה וכסף לא חשב וזהב לא חפץ בו. ולא גנז
לעצמו מכל חלקו מעבודת המלך. וכל מעשיו כמו בן אגריפס שאמר
אם אבי גנז אוצרותיו למטה אני אהיה גונז אוצרות למעלה. ומלאכה

384 רבה] א נבח ד רקח ל רכח ר ראבח | על²] אה ועל | מרנא ורבנא] ת > | רב] אק ר'
הנשיא] את ~ בן ⟨א בר⟩ רב יוסף הנשיא | ה אבן |
385 היו] ת | מגדולי] לר ~ מדינת | אר גרנאטה ה גרנטא | ויורשי] ק ויושיע | במלכות־
אביו] ק > | במלכות] ל במלכוס (!) |
386 הר באדיס] א באריס פ באדים דל באדס | ומלכות] ת ומלך | במסורת | אהר ביד |
387 אר גרנאטה] ה גרנטא פקל גראנאטה ד גראנאטה | עיר הקדש] ד > לר ע"ה |
388 פ הפרזים ל הפריזי | ר'] ה הרב | ואביו] ל < | ודודיו] ה והוריו ד דודיו |
389 יצחק] ק צדוק | את ומשנהו ר' משה] הפ ור' משה ק > | ד השלישי | והשלישי ר'
יהודה] הפ ור' יהודה |
390 והרביעי ר' יוסף] ה ור' יהוסף פ ור' יוסף | הפ מדותיהם] את מדותיו ק מדותיו | ומן
הפרתמים] לר והפרתמים |
391 אל הפקיד ק ~ עליהם | הגדול] ת | ר'] ד | ה הרב | ר' יהודה זה] ק > | יהודה] פ > |
הפ רבה] א נבח ד רקח ל רכח ר ראבח |
392 עיר] ד | ועל לר על | עברה הגולה] פ עצרה הגלות |
393 עול] ק עולם | ק מוסרתם | שלחנו] ק > |
394 מנוח] ת מנוחה |
395 ד שהגיעו ק אשר הרגיעו | אק טוליטולה] הת טליטולה פ טוליטולה |
396 ה ומפני | שהיה] ת ~ | לו | אדום] הפ > | ת והוא עודנו | היה מורם מעם] ת |
397 מעם] ה > | חית קנה] ה חיה | קנה] ק השדה | בו] ד > | גנז] ה גס (!) |
398 וכל מעשיו—למעלה] ת > | כמו] א כמונבז ה ~ מונבז המלך | אגריפס] א ~ המלך
399 אם אבי—למעלה] ק אבותי גנזו אוצרות למטה ואני גונז למעלה

ספר הקבלה

גדולה היתה לו. שאלו לא עשה כי אם צדקות אלו דיו כי למחיה שלחו 400
יי לפני הגולה.

ויהי כאשר תמו כל הגוי לעבור על ידו שלח המלך בשבילו ויקחהו
וישימהו אדון לביתו ומושל בכל אשר לו. והוא בקש מאת המלך לבלתי
תת למינין פתחון פה בכל ארץ קשטילה ויאמר המלך להעשות כן.
ויכנעו המינין ולא יספו לשאת ראשם והם מתמעטים והולכים. 405

ועוד סימן שלישי יהא בידך. כי לעולם המינין לא עשו שום טובה
לישראל ולא ספר שיש בו חזוק תורה או דבר חכמה ואפילו שירה אחת
או פיוט אחד ונחמה אחת. כי כלם כלבים אלמים לא יוכלו לנבוח.
וכאשר נמצא בהם אחד שחבר ספר אחד חרף וגדף והטיח דברים כלפי
מעלה כאשר עשה זקן אשמאי אלשיך אבו אלפראג שתחלת ספרו 410
פי אוול טלאם בכל סדר בראשית דבר בו על אלהים תועבות גדולות
מעידות על סכלותו וחסרון דעתו. ובסדר אלה מסעי בדה מלבו דיני
ממונות ודיני נחלות ובלא שום טענה ולא שום קבלה ולא שום ראיה
אלא שהוא אומר אלעקל יקתצי כדא. ואני כתבתי תשובות ספרו
והראיתי לתלמידים סכלותו. 415

ואלו ברבנים אתה מוצא שלשלת הקדושה שכתבנו. וחוצה לה אלף

ספר הקבלה

אלפים חכמים קדושים כי לא הזכרנו כי אם בעלי ישיבות בלבד. ועוד מחברי ספרים בכתבי הקדש כגון ר' יהודה בר' דוד אלפאסי ז"ל הנקרא חיוג שהעמיד לשון הקדש על בוריו אחר שנשכח בכל הגולה. ור' מרינוס בן גנאח הוא השלים כל אשר התחיל ר' יהודה בר' דוד זה. ועוד ר' משה הכהן בן גיקאטיליא ורבים חכמים אחרים שכתבו לנו ספרים ומחזורות ושירות ותושבחות ליוצרנו ית' שמו ונחמות לישראל לחזק את לבם בארץ גלותם. בימי ר' חסדאי הנשיא התחילו לצפצף ובימי ר' שמואל הנגיד נתנו קול מהם ר' שלמה בר' יהודה בן גבירול חכם גדול ומשורר והרב ר' יצחק בר' יהודה בן גיאת ור' אוהב הנשיא בר' מאיר הנשיא אבן שרתמיקש. ור' משה בר' יעקב בן עזרא מזרע המשרה וחכם גדול בתורה ובחכמה יונית ובעל שירות ותושבחות ואשר בזה את העולם הזה והבטיח על העולם הבא וכל השומע אותם ירך לבבו וימלא יראת יוצרו. ור' יוסף הדיין בר' יצחק בן סאהל ור' יוסף הדיין בר' צדוק בן צדיק ור' יהודה הלוי בר' שמואל הלוי ור' אברהם בן עזרא. כלם חכמים גדולים וקדושים ומחזיקים את ישראל

417 הפ וקדושים] ל הוזכרנו] כי אם] ת אלא] בלבד] ה לבד ק] >
418 בר'] קדל בר פ ~ יהודה] (!) | פ אלפאסי] א אלפיסי הק אלפסי ת פאסי !
419 ז"ל] את | בוריו] ה עמדו | אפק אשר נשכח |
420 מרינוס] ה יונה ז"ל | בן] ק אבן | ה גאנאח פ גאנח | אשר] ד מה לר < | ת שהתחיל ר' יהודה] א זה ר' יהודה ה ~ זה |
421 בר'] קדל בר | פק זה] הלר | א ז"ל ד זכר צדיק לברכה | ד כהן | הכהן בן גיקאטיליא] ה גיקאטיליא הכהן | א גיקוטילה פלר גקטיליה ד קטליא | חכמים אחרים] ת אחרים וחכמים |
422 ספרים] עד כאן נשמר כ"י ה | ומחזורות] פק ~ ושירים | ליוצרנו] פ לשם | ית'] א יתברך ד יתעלה | שמו] פ < | ית ~ אק > | וית' <א ויתעלה> זכרו ותפארתו במלכותו ד ~ אמן |
423 בארץ גלותם] ד בגלות |
424 פ ומהם | בר'] ד בן ל בר | בר' יהודה] ק | > | גבירול] ק ג'אבירול ל גביאל |
425 פק והרב ר' יצחק] את ור' יצחק הרב | ק בר יהודה | בן] פ < | גיאת] א גאית ק גאיית אוהב] א משה ק יהודה |
426 בר'] ד בר | בר' מאיר הנשיא] ל < | אק אבן | פת בן | ד שרטמיקאש | אפ בר'] ק בן ת בר | לר עזרה |
427 יונית] ר ~ היה | פ ותושבחותיו א ~ וליוצרם יתעלה שמו של הקב"ה מפייט בשירותיו ובתושבחותיו ק ~ אצל הב"ה ומפייט בשירים ותושבחות |
428 ואשר בזה – העולם הבא] ת < | ק העולם הבא | פ שומע |
429 ק יראת] את מיראת פ את | יוצרו] ל אצרו | ת בר יצחק | פק סאהל] א סבאל ת סהל |
430 ק בר' צדוק] פדל בר צדיק בר' צדיק | בן צדיק] ל < | דל בר שמואל | הלוי²] לר < |
431 ור' אברהם] את | בר' <דל בר> מאיר | לר עזרה | אד ומחזיקים פ מחזיקים | את] אד | את ~ ידי |

ספר הקבלה

בשירותם ובנחמותם. על אלה נאמר זכר צדיק לברכה. ועל אותם המינין נאמר שם רשעים ירקב.

וכשהשלמנו סדר הקבלה נזכיר זכרון מלכי ישראל בבית שני להוציא מלבם של צדוקים שאומרים כי כל הנחמות הנאמרות בנביאים כבר קבלום ישראל בבית שני. ונכחש ונפרש כי לא כן הדבר. ונפרש נבואת זכריהו שאמר לו הקב"ה רעה את צאן ההרגה ונבאר את כל הנבואה. ועוד זכרון דברי רומי להודיע לאחר כמה שנים נכתבו גליונות שלהם. והב"ה יסכים על ידינו ללמוד וללמד לשמור ולעשות אמן סלה.

435

432 ת בשירות ונחמות | קד אלו | צדיק] פ > (ונוסף בגליון ע"י פ1) | אותם] את > |
433 המינין] ק רשעים | את ושם | ירקב] ק ~ ד ~ והמשכילים יזהירו כזוהר הרקיע ומצדיקי הרבים ככוכבים לעולם ועד ל ~ תם ונשלם ד ~ תם ונשלם תהלה למלך עולם |
434 וכשהשלמנו] מכאן ואילך רק עפ"י אפק | א השלמנו | הקבלה] פ קבלת | נזכיר] א פ מ' (!) | זכרון] פ ~ דברי ק (בין השיטין) ~ דברי |
435 כי] א > | הנאמרות] א הכתובות |
436 פ ונכחש] ק > | ונכחש ונפרש2] א ועוד עתידים אנו להכחיש ולפרש |
437 ק הב"ה
438 נכתבו גליונות] ק גליות | א והקב"ה | יסכים] פ יספיק |
439 ולעשות] א ~ את כל דברי התורה הכתובה על ידי משה נביאנו אדון כל הנביאים פ ~ כן | סלה] א ~ חזק... נשלם סדר הקבלה בעוז אשר לו השבח והגדולה | פק מוסיפים כאן את דרשת הראב"ד על נבואת זכריהו "רעה את צאן ההרגה", ובפ מסתיימת הדרשה במלים אלו: נשלם ספר הקבלה בסיעתא דשמיא. |

הוספות ותקונים

צ"ל	במקום	שורה	עמוד
י	בראש העמוד		י
אחר	אשר	1	יד, הערה 11
שבמלכותו צריכין	שבמלכו תוצריכין	2	יד' הערה 11
יעקב אבן ג' ו	יוסף אבן ג' ו	8 מלמטה	טו
נוספה (נוספו)	נוספו	8 מלמטה	כב
חסרה (חסרות)	חסרות	7 מלמטה	כב
—	— —	5 מלמטה	כב
למלה	למלה למלה	2 מלמטה	כב
לתלמידים להודיעם	לתלמידים | להודיע	2	1 בח"נ לשורה
עתניאל מ'	עתניאלמ'	12	3
ה >	ה >	44	5 בח"נ לסוף שורה
א	א	2	12 בח"נ לשורה 27, ריש שו'
ישו] ק יש"ו	ישו ק יש"ו]	64	15 בח"נ לשורה
ק אנטיפרס פק ~ מלך	ק אנטיפרס	3	22 בח"נ לשורה 59, בריש שו'

CORRIGENDUM

P. 306 lines 6-7 from the bottom should begin: ראש: 12. 25 etc.

www.ingramcontent.com/pod-product-compliance
Lightning Source LLC
Chambersburg PA
CBHW030329240426
43661CB00052B/1579